Knight's Modern Seamanship

EIGHTEENTH EDITION

Knight's Modern Seamanship

EIGHTEENTH EDITION

EDITED BY
JOHN V. NOEL, JR., CAPTAIN, U.S. NAVY (RET.)

ASSOCIATE EDITORS
Cmdr. Frank E. Bassett, U.S. Navy (Ret.)
Dr. Carvel Blair
Prof. Dee Fitch

VAN NOSTRAND REINHOLD
New York

Library of Congress Catalog Card Number 88-4582

ISBN 0-442-26983-8

Van Nostrand Reinhold
115 Fifth Avenue
New York, New York 10003

Chapman & Hall
2-6 Boundary Row
London SE1 8HN, England

Thomas Nelson Australia
102 Dodds Street
South Melbourne, Victoria 3205, Australia

Nelson Canada
1120 Birchmount Road
Scarborough, Ontario M1K 5G4, Canada

16 15 14 13 12 11 10 9 8 7 6 5 4 3

Library of Congress Cataloging-in-Publication Data

Knight, Arthur Melvin, 1854-1927.
    [Modern seamanship]
    Knight's modern seamanship.—18th ed. / revised by John V. Noel,
Jr.; associate editors, Frank E. Bassett, Carvel Blair, Dee Fitch.
        p.   cm.
    Includes bibliographical references and index.
    ISBN 0-442-26983-8 :
    1. Seamanship. I. Noel, John Vavasour, 1912–   II. Title.
III. Title: Modern seamanship.
VK541.K55   1988
623.88—dc19   88-4582

Preface to the Eighteenth Edition

This 18th edition of Knight's *Modern Seamanship* presents most of the basic knowledge that sea-going people need. For 83 years it has provided, on many subjects such as ship construction or ship handling, merely the basics or introduction to the subjects. On others, such as weather, much more technical detail is included, enough to assist those hoping to avoid a typhoon, for example. In other important areas, such as the Rules of the Road, the information is presented accurately and in detail for these are matters of law and of safety at sea.

Knight's appeals to the small boater with limited space, who at times may need a refresher course in some aspects of seamanship or who needs a ready reference. He will also have, in Appendix 4, the full text of the Inland Navigation Rules of 1980 which he is required by law to carry if his boat is over 12 meters in length. Merchant marine and naval students will find in Knight's a firm foundation for that lore of the sea that they will eventually acquire.

While a moderate amount of obsolete material has been deleted, there has been considerable new information and guidance added. This is especially true in the chapters on ships and boats, oceanography, communications, towing and salvage, boat and ship handling, and the new chapter on channel marking.

An experienced and learned team has produced this work. Dr. Carvel Blair, a well-known oceanographer, has overhauled the chapters on ships and boats, revised the chapter on oceanography and ocean pollution, and provided useful advice on the book as a whole. Cdr. Frank Bassett, USN (ret.), a prominent authority on the Rules of the Road, has contributed Part IV, including a significant new chapter on the Maritime Buoyage System, as well as a strong new chapter on communications. Professor Dee Fitch of the New York State Maritime College has been responsible for the revised chapters on ships and their characteristics.

Other contributors are: Prof. Robert Zubaly—Ship Structure, Stability and Maintenance; Prof. Jose Feminia—Propulsion and Steering; Prof. Dee Fitch—Ground Tackle; Captain Edward Wilmot—Cargo Handling and Underway Replenishment; Lt. Lee Price, USN and Lt. Kenneth Rome, USN—Navigation; Captain George Reid—Towing and Salvage; Prof. George Munkenbeck—Boat Handling and Helicopter Operations, as well as Ice Seamanship; Ernest Sauve—Part III, Weather; and BMCS Michael P. Holland—Appendices 1, 2, and 3, Rope and Cordage, Knotting and Splicing, and Mechanical Weight-Lifting Appliances.

John V. Noel, Jr.
Captain, USN (ret.)

Preface to the First Edition

An attempt is made, in the following pages, to cover a wider field than that covered by most of the existing works on Seamanship.

The admirable treatises of Luce, Nares, and Alston, originating in the days when Seamanship was almost wholly concerned with the fitting and handling of vessels under sail, have preserved through later editions the general characteristics which they naturally assumed in the beginning. These treatises will never be out of date until the time, still far in the future, when sails shall have been entirely driven out by steam. It will hardly be denied, however, that the Steamer has long since established its claim to consideration in Seamanship, and that there is room for a work in which this claim shall be more fully recognized than in the treatises above referred to. The excellent work of Captains Todd and Whall, *Practical Seamanship for the Merchant Service,* deals more fully than either of its predecessors with the handling of steamers; but its point of view is, as its name implies, primarily and almost exclusively that of the Merchant Service.

Shortly after the present work was begun, a circular letter was addressed to officers of the Merchant Service and extensively circulated through the Branch Hydrographic Offices at New York, Philadelphia, Baltimore and Norfolk, requesting the views of the officers addressed.

The answers received to these questions were unexpectedly numerous and complete. More than forty prominent officers of the Merchant Service replied, many of them writing out their views and describing their experiences with a fullness of detail far beyond anything that could have been anticipated.

The thanks of the author are due particularly to the following for letters or for personal interviews covering the above points: Capt. W. H. Thompson, *S.S. Belgenland;* Capt. T. Evans, *S.S. Runo;* Capt. J. Dann, *S.S. Southwark;* 1st Officer T. Anfindsen, *S.S. Southwark;* Capt. J. C. Jameson, *S.S. St. Paul;* Capt. H. E. Nickels, *S.S. Friesland;* Capt. G. J. Loveridge, *S.S. Buffalo;* Capt. F. M. Howes, *S.S. Kershaw;* Capt. T. J. Thorkildsen, *S.S. Trojan;* Capt. Otto Nielsen, *S.S. Pennland;* Capt. H. Doxrud, *S.S. Noordland;* Capt. C. O. Rockwell, Clyde S. S. Co.; Capt. S. W. Watkins, *S.S. Montana;* Capt. Anders Beer, *S.S. Nordkyn;* Capt. J. M. Johnston, *S.S. Sardinian;* Capt. A. R. Mills, *S.S. Westernland;* Capt. J. S. Garvin, *S.S. Cherokee;* Capt. Robt. B. Quick, *S.S. El Cid;* Capt. Wm. J. Roberts, *S.S. New York;* Capt. T. Richardson, *S.S. Noranmore;* Capt. E. O. Marshall, *S.S. Maryland;* 1st Officer H. S. Lane, *S.S. Maryland;* Capt. W. F. Bingham, *S.S. Marengo;* Capt. R. Gowing, *S.S. Greatham;* Capt. H. J. Byrne, *U.S.A.T. McPherson;* Capt. Paul Grosch, *S.S. Stuttgart;* Capt. Geo. Schrotter, *S.S. Belgravia;* Capt. F. C. Saunders, *S.S. English King;* Capt. Chas. Cabot, *S.S. Venango;* Capt. Chas. Pinkham, *S.S. Queen Wilhelmina;* Capt. A. Traue, *S.S. München;* Capt. W. Thomas, *S.S. Quernmore;* Capt. H. O. Nickerson, Fall River Line; Capt. Geo. Lane, Baltimore Steam Packet Co.

Important assistance was received from Naval Constructor W. J. Baxter, U.S. Navy, who prepared Chapters I and XVIII; and from Lieutenant E. E. Hayden, U.S. Navy, who contributed several Charts and much valuable information upon Meteorology, for Chapter XIX.

Chapter V was suggested by a paper, "Mechanical Appliances on Board Ship," by Captain Thomas Mackenzie, issued by the London Shipmasters' Society as No. 29 of their valuable series of publications.

It would be impossible to mention all the naval officers who have assisted the author with criticism and suggestions; but acknowledgment is especially due to Lieut.-Commander A. W. Grant, Lieut. John Hood, Lieut. W. R. M. Field, Lieut. John Gow, Lieut.-Commander W. F. Worthington, Commander J. E. Pillsbury, Lieut. V. S. Nelson, Lieut. Ridgely Hunt, and Chief Boatswain W. L. Hull, all of the United States Navy.

Above all, acknowledgment is due to Chief Boatswain C. F. Pierce, U.S. Navy, who not only assisted in the preparation of many parts of the text, but prepared sketches for fully one-half the illustrations of the volume.

Austin M. Knight

United States Naval Academy
April 1, 1901

Contents

PART III / WEATHER, OCEANOGRAPHY, AND OCEAN POLLUTION

PART IV / RULES OF THE ROAD

APPENDICES

Knight's

Modern
Seamanship

EIGHTEENTH EDITION

Ships and Boats

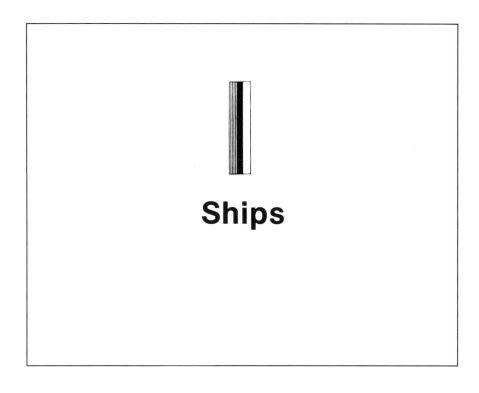

Ships

Ships can be classified in several ways. One is by *hull material* (steel, aluminum, ferro-cement, glass-reinforced plastic, wood); another is by *propulsion* (steam, diesel, nuclear reactor, gas turbine, sail). They can also be grouped by *ownership* (government, private) or by *use* (warship, fishing craft, merchantman). The first part of this chapter describes warships and other government vessels; the second, merchantmen. In the former category, major emphasis is on U.S. Naval vessels since the U.S. Navy includes ships of most important types. A separate section describes foreign warships that lack a counterpart in today's U.S. fleet. The final sections of Chapter 1 are devoted to merchant ships. Chapter 2 discusses boats and other small craft.

1.1 Tonnage and Dimensions The size of ships is normally given in terms of length, beam, draft, and tonnage. *Length* is given as either *overall* (LOA), which is the horizontal distance from farthest forward structure to farthest aft, or *waterline* (LWL or LBP), which is the fore-and-aft distance along the load waterline. *Beam* is the transverse measurement at the widest part. *Draft* is the vertical distance from keel to waterline. (See Chapter 3, Fig. 3.3.) Tonnage for warships is a measure of the ship's weight as determined by its displacement, which is the number of tons of seawater displaced by the ship's hull. Merchant ships' tonnage is a measure of volume, as explained in Sections 3.18 and 3.19.

U.S. Naval Vessels

The Chief of Naval Operations has established four ship categories: combatant ships, combatant craft, auxiliary ships, and service craft. Combatant ships include aircraft carriers, battleships, cruisers, destroyers, frigates, submarines, amphibious warfare ships, and mine warfare ships. Combatant craft are smaller vessels whose mission is patrol, amphibious landing, mine countermeasures, or riverine warfare. Auxiliary ships are oceangoing vessels whose task is to support the combatants; service craft are smaller vessels, usually of limited range and not necessarily self-propelled, with a similar support mission.

1.2   Names and Hull Numbers   Each ship type is assigned an abbreviated designation (for example, BB for battleship) together with a hull number (BB 62 is the U.S.S. *New Jersey*). If the ship is nuclear powered, the designation ends in N (CVN 70 is the nuclear-powered carrier *Carl Vinson*). The letter G indicates that the ship is armed with guided missiles. (CGN 40 is the nuclear-powered missile cruiser *Mississippi*.) An auxiliary ship's designation begins with A (ASR 21 is the submarine rescue ship *Pigeon*).

Except for a few service craft, every ship has a name. Systems of nomenclature, and the rigor with which they are followed, vary over the years. Destroyer tenders, for example, bear the names of rivers (*Shenandoah*), national parks (*Yosemite*), and labor leaders (*Samuel Gompers*). Submarines in World War I had only numbers; in World War II they were named for fish and other sea creatures (*Trout* and *Sea Wolf*). Today submarine names include those of cities (*Omaha*), states (*Florida*), humorists (*Will Rogers*), and congressmen (*L. Mendel Rivers*). Today, although subject to change because of public relations and politics, ship names are chosen according to the following rules:

States: battleships, cruisers, Trident-missile submarines.
Cities: attack submarines, amphibious transports (dock), auxiliaries
Counties: tank landing ships
Distinguished naval officers and officials: cruisers, destroyers, frigates
Battles: aircraft carriers, assault ships, cruisers
Famous warships: aircraft carriers
Fish: attack submarines
Indian tribes: fleet tugs

Volcanoes: ammunition ships

Politicians: important ships of any type.

Combatant Ships

1.3 Aircraft Carriers Carriers have angled, armored flight decks with an island superstructure on the starboard side (Fig. 1.1). Catapults are fitted for launching aircraft, arresting gear for recovering them. Below the flight deck is the hangar deck, where the planes are stored and maintained. Several elevators transfer aircraft between decks. Displacing nearly 100,000 tons, the newest carriers are over 1000 feet long and draw over 35 feet,

Fig. 1.1 The nuclear-propelled carrier USS *Nimitz* (CVN 68) with a deckload of aircraft. The angled flight deck and steam catapults are clearly visible. Nuclear reactors drive the ship without the need of refueling, but the air wing's jet fuel supply requires periodic underway replenishment. (*U.S. Naval Institute photograph*)

with a flight deck 250 feet wide. The attached air wing includes nearly 100 aircraft. Ship's company plus air personnel total over 6000. Two nuclear reactors and four geared steam turbines can drive the ship at over 30 knots.

1.4 Battleships The world's last battleships were constructed during World War II, and most were laid up when hostilities ended. The U.S. Navy, however, has from time to time brought the *Iowa* class ships back into service. In 1982, the *New Jersey* was recommissioned for the fourth time, to be joined over the next five years by her three sister ships (Fig. 1.2). Completely overhauled and modernized, they retain their 16 in. guns, primarily for shore bombardment, and have been fitted with new aviation facilities and armament. Tomahawk and Harpoon missiles plus new electronic and communications equipment permit each of these veteran 45,000 ton, 900-foot warships to form the nucleus of a powerful battle group.

1.5 Cruisers Several different classes, some propelled by nuclear reactors and some by conventional gas and steam turbines, make up the cruiser force (Fig. 1.3). High-speed, long-range vessels with limited armor, their main task is antiair warfare (AAW). They are also armed with guns and antisubmarine weapons including sonar, rockets, helicopters, and torpedoes. Their size varies from 15,000 tons with a length of 700 feet down to that of large destroyers (6,000 tons, 500 feet).

Fig. 1.2 The battleship USS *New Jersey* (BB 62), originally commissioned in 1943, returned to active duty for the fourth time in 1982. Missiles have replaced part of the secondary gun battery, the electronics have been modernized, and the air detachment consists of helicopters rather than seaplanes. (*U.S. Naval Institute photograph*)

Fig. 1.3 The guided-missile cruiser USS *Ticonderoga* (CG 47) features the AEGIS Weapons Control System. Its electronically-scanned radar, with nonrotating antenna, provides surveillance, detection, and tracking of antiship missiles and high-performance aircraft. (*U.S. Naval Institute photograph*)

1.6 Destroyers DDG's are primarily designed for antiaircraft warfare (AAW), DD's for antisubmarine warfare (ASW). Fast and versatile, their missions can also include action against surface ships, shore bombardment, patrol, or search and rescue (Fig. 1.4). Their helo facilities allow them to handle helicopters. Some large destroyers have been slightly modified and then rated as cruisers.

1.7 Frigates Replacing the destroyer escort (DE), the frigate is built along destroyer lines but is smaller (about 3,000 tons, 450 feet) and slower (Fig. 1.5). All can handle helicopters, and some (FFG's) carry surface-to-air missiles. The smallest oceangoing multipurpose combatant, frigates are the most numerous type in the fleet.

1.8 Submarines As soon as the *U.S.S. Nautilus* proved the feasibility of the nuclear-powered submarine, the U.S. Navy began a conversion from

Fig. 1.4 The guided-missile destroyer USS *Kidd* (DDG 993). Fitted with both antiair warfare (AAW) and antisubmarine warfare (ASW) systems, general-purpose destroyers act as escorts to battle groups built around a carrier or a battleship. (*Official U.S. Navy photograph*)

Fig. 1.5 The guided-missile frigate USS *Fahrion* (FFG 22). With a top speed of 29 knots, these versatile ships can escort either warships or merchant convoys against air or submarine threat. About one third of the fleet's frigates are rated as DDG's; the others serve primarily in the ASW role. (*Official U.S. Navy photograph*)

diesel to nuclear propulsion. Freed from the necessity of surfacing or snorkelling to supply air to engines and crew, the nuclear submarine has unlimited submerged endurance. At almost the same time, the development of underwater-launched ballistic missiles made possible the SSBN—the fleet ballistic missile submarine. Because of these two innovations, the U.S. submarine force of today bears little resemblance to that of World War II.

SSN's (attack submarines) have the primary mission of destroying enemy submarines and surface ships. Operational details are highly classified, and there is constant progress in weaponry, sonar, depth capability, and quietness. A new class, the SSN 21 *Seawolf,* will incorporate the newest advances.

SSBN's were first commissioned in the 1960s to fire the Polaris missile. This was replaced by the more potent Poseidon, and then by the Trident missile. The latter are carried by the *Ohio* class, a huge ship displacing nearly 19,000 tons submerged and nearly as long (560 feet) as a cruiser (Fig. 1.6). These SSBN's carry 24 missiles in vertical tubes, together with torpedoes in four bow tubes.

1.9 Other Warships With its emphasis on high-seas warfare, the U.S. Navy today has only limited coastal and riverine forces. If necessary, these smaller vessels could be mass-produced following the design of successful

Fig. 1.6 The nuclear-powered strategic-missile submarine USS *Ohio* (SSBN 726) carries 24 Trident ballistic missiles. Attack submarines (SSN's), smaller but more versatile, carry torpedoes as well as antisubmarine and cruise missiles. (*Official U.S. Navy photograph*)

prototypes now operational. A new design for the U.S. is the hydrofoil patrol gunboat, officially designated as PHM or Patrol Combatant Missile (Hydrofoil). A gas turbine drives the PHM at 48 knots when foilborne. It carries a 76 mm gun and Harpoon antisurface ship missiles.

1.10 Amphibious Warfare Ships These include the tank landing ship (LST), the transport dock (LPD), and the assault ship (LPH and LHA). The latter are large vessels (nearly 40,000 tons, LOA 820 feet) with a flight deck for helicopters or VSTOL Harrier aircraft and a floodable docking well for landing craft (Fig. 1.7).

1.11 Mine Warfare Vessels The fleet no longer includes minelayers; mines are deployed by submarines or aircraft. Mine warfare ships include ocean minesweepers (MSO) and mine countermeasure vessels (MCM). They feature special mine detection equipment and nonmagnetic hulls. Minesweeping is also conducted by specially equipped Sea Stallion helicopters.

Combatant Craft

The vessels known as *Naval craft* are smaller than ships, more restricted in range, and limited in crew facilities. Thus, they are usually dependent on tenders (or mother ships) or on shore facilities.

Riverine craft include fast patrol craft, river patrol boats, and monitors. Minesweeping boats work in areas too shallow for the MSO's. Among the landing craft that operate between amphibious ships and landing beaches are the LCM (landing craft mechanized), LCU (landing craft utility), and LCVP (landing craft vehicle and personnel).

Auxiliary Ships

There are many different types of auxiliaries. One important mission is underway replenishment: transferring ammunition, stores, and fuel to the combatants. Other auxiliary ships (tenders and repair ships) maintain the rest of the fleet (Fig. 1.8). These floating navy yards can operate either in U.S. home ports or in remote anchorages overseas. Tugs and salvage ships go to the aid of damaged or sunken ships. Other auxiliaries have scientific missions such as hydrography or oceanographic research.

Service Craft

These vessels are based in major naval ports and in shipyards. Floating drydocks can handle ships as large as aircraft carriers. They can be towed

Fig. 1.7 The amphibious assault ship USS *Saipan* (LHA 2). With a top speed of 24 knots, *Saipan* can carry a reinforced battalion of Marines, together with their weapons, landing craft, and helicopter or VSTOL air support. (*Official U.S. Navy photograph*)

Fig. 1.8 The submarine tender USS *McKee* (AS 41). Designed specifically to support nuclear submarines, this auxiliary ship can provide services to four SSN's alongside. Destroyer tenders (AD's) fill a similar role for surface combatants. (*Official U.S. Navy photograph*)

across an ocean and paired with tenders or repair ships to make up an advanced base. Other service craft perform duties ranging from pile driving to collecting the fleet's garbage.

MSC Ships

1.12 Military Sealift Command The Military Sealift Command (MSC) controls a large fleet of ships whose mission is support of the active fleet and of other components of the Department of Defense. Between one and two hundred ships make up the command, about two-thirds of these owned by the government, and one-third on short-term charter. Except for communication detachments on a few ships, all are manned by civilians. In peacetime none is armed.

MSC missions include petroleum and dry cargo transport, scientific support, overseas prepositioning of supplies for the Rapid Deployment Joint Task Force, and underway replenishment. The latter task is performed by the Naval Fleet Auxiliary Force, whose ships sail under the direct operational control of fleet commanders. In the MSC fleet are roll on/roll off (RO/RO) vehicle carriers, heavy lift ships, cable layers, ocean tugs, and lighter-aboard-ship (LASH) cargo carriers (Fig. 1.9). Brief descriptions of most of these merchant-type vessels appear in the last section of Chapter 1.

Hull numbers carry the prefix T and follow the standard system for auxiliaries. MSC vessels are designated U.S. Naval ships. U.S.N.S. *Stalwart* (T-AGOS 1), for example, is lead ship of a class of Ocean Surveillance Ships. Most MSC ships are painted gray with distinguishing blue and yellow stripes around the stack. Replenishment oilers carry their numbers painted on the bow to distinguish them from transport tankers.

U.S. Coast Guard Ships and Craft

To carry out its varied missions—which extends from search and rescue to drug interdiction to ASW—the Coast Guard includes both general purpose cutters and specialized vessels. Most Coast Guard ships and boats are painted all white with an international orange slash on either bow. Buoy tenders and tugs have black hulls with the characteristic orange slash; icebreakers have red hulls (with white stripe) for better visibility in the ice.

1.13 Cutters The name *cutter,* inherited from the Revenue Cutter Service established in 1790, is applied to ships ranging from destroyer size down to those of about 200 feet LOA with a displacement of about 100 tons. Their names are preceded by the abbreviation U.S.C.G.C.

High-endurance cutters (WHEC) can stay at sea for extended periods for patrol, weather and oceanographic data collection, or search and res-

Fig. 1.9 The LASH ship *Austral Lightning.* This lighter-aboard-ship barge carrier has been a part of the chartered "Near-Term Prepositioned Force." The NTPF and its successor, the "Marine Prepositioning Ship Force" (MPSF) are chartered and operated by the U.S. Navy's Military Sealift Command (MSC).

cue. They can be propelled by either diesels (with a range of 14,000 miles at 11 knots) or gas turbines (2,400 miles at 29 knots). They can handle helicopters and carry guns, torpedoes, and sonar for wartime service with the Navy (Fig. 1.10).

Medium-endurance cutters (WMEC) operate nearer the coasts. The newest *Bear* class are 270 feet overall and displace 1,800 tons. Diesel propelled, they can steam at 20 knots. Cruising range at 13.5 knots is 6,800 miles. For their wartime ASW mission they use a towed array with weapons launched by helicopter (Fig. 1.11).

1.14 Patrol Craft Intended primarily for law enforcement, search, and rescue, these boats include three classes. The newest, the *Sea Bird* class, are air-cushion vehicles with catamaran hulls, .50 caliber machine guns, and top speed of over 30 knots. More numerous are the 95-foot *Cape* class (bearing the names of capes) and the 83-foot *Point* class.

1.15 Icebreakers The USCG has been assigned the national icebreaking mission, and its largest icebreakers—the *Polar Star* and the *Polar Sea*—are among the most advanced in the world (Fig. 1.12). They are 399 ft long with a beam of 86 ft and displacement of 12,087 tons. They are propelled

Fig. 1.10 The high-endurance cutter USCGC *Jarvis* (WHEC-725) has a bow propulsion unit to aid in maneuvers, a closed-circuit television system, and a helicopter flight deck.

by diesel engines or gas turbines with a maximum of 60,000 hp. The Coast Guard also operates a fleet of smaller domestic icebreaking tugs. Used primarily in the Great Lakes and in North Atlantic ports, these 140-footers with 37-ft beams have displacements of 662 tons, and their diesel-electric plants provide 2500 hp.

1.16 **Designations** The Coast Guard uses a system similar to the Navy's plus an initial W. Patrol craft hull numbers begin with two digits corre-

Fig. 1.11 The medium endurance cutter USCGC *Bear* (WMEC 901) is lead ship of a class replacing a number of much older cutters. The orange slash identifies *Bear* as a Coast Guard vessel. In time of war she would be painted gray for operations with the Navy. (*U.S. Naval Institute photograph*)

Fig. 1.12 The USCGC *Polar Star* (WAGB-10) can break 6-ft thick ice at a continuous speed of 3 knots.

sponding to the length overall. The 95-footer *Cape Henlopen*, for example, has hull number 95328 painted on the bow.

Type	Designation
High-endurance cutters	WHEC
Icebreakers	WAGB
Medium-endurance cutters	WMEC
Patrol craft, large	WPB
Harbor tugs, small	WYTL
Patrol craft, surface effect ship	WSES
Oceanographic cutters	WAGO
Buoy tenders, seagoing	WLB
Buoy tenders, coastal	WLM
Buoy tenders, inland	WLI
Training cutters (the *Eagle,* Fig. 1.13)	WIX
Icebreaking tug	WTGB

Fig. 1.13 The *Eagle,* the Coast Guard's famous bark for training cadets.

1.17 Other U.S. Government Ships Besides the Navy and the Coast Guard, several other government agencies operate ships and craft. The Army Corps of Engineers formerly owned a fleet of dredges, but most dredging work is now contracted out to civilian firms. The Army Transportation Corps operates tugs, lighters, utility landing craft, and air-cushion vehicles. The U.S. Geological Survey conducts research and surveys from three oceangoing vessels. The National Ocean Survey, a component of the National Atmospheric and Oceanic Administration, maintains a fleet of over 20 ships, although the number on active service varies with the NOAA appropriation. The crews are civilian with uniformed officers of the NOAA corps, the seventh uniformed service. Their ships are grouped in six classes. The largest, Class I, are 303 ft in length, 52 ft in beam, with a range of over 12,000 miles; they can stay at sea over a month. The smallest, Class VI, are 65 ft in length with a range of over 1,000 miles; they can stay at sea a week. The *Surveyor*, NOAA ˢ132, is fitted with swath sonar (wide-beam) and a helicopter deck and can berth 20 scientists in addition to its 12 NOAA officers and crew of 64 mariners. (See Fig. 1.14.)

1.18 Foreign Naval Ships For a variety of reasons, some other navies include modern ships of types not found in the U.S. fleet. Sometimes the

Fig. 1.14 The NOAA ship *Surveyor* (S132). Operated by the National Ocean Survey, this ship and others like her conduct marine, geodedic, geophysical, and oceanographic surveys. Their officers are uniformed members of the NOAA commissioned officer corps.

reason is economics, sometimes a difference in naval missions, sometimes varying opinions on strategy and tactics. Details on these, and in fact all the world's warships, both foreign and U.S., are available in *Jane's Fighting Ships* and other standard references. (See list at end of chapter.) A few of the most important types are briefly discussed in this section.

Diesel-electric submarines have an inherent advantage in the quietness of battery/slow speed motor propulsion. In addition, construction and training costs are much lower than for nuclear-powered craft. For some navies these advantages are persuasive enough to build conventional submarines despite their dependence on air for crew and engines. China, France, West Germany, Japan, Norway, Sweden, U.S.S.R., and the U.K. all have significant numbers of modern diesel-electric boats, in some cases as their only type and in others to supplement their nuclear fleets. Several more navies include smaller numbers of modern conventional submarines, often purchased from yards in the major naval countries.

There are no other aircraft carriers equal to those of the U.S. Navy, but several of the larger fleets include light carriers. The U.S.S.R. and the U.K. have also built modern ships specially designed for both helicopter and vertical/short take off (VSTOL) aircraft.

Patrol craft and inshore/coastal minesweepers are more important components in most of the world's fleets than in that of the U.S. Even a small vessel can carry a very powerful missile. Small, fast, and lethal, combatant craft have gained an importance in naval tactics far greater than their size suggests.

Merchant Ships

Merchant ships fall into five broad categories: freighters, container ships, bulk carriers, passenger ships, and coastal vessels. Steam turbines and diesel engines are the most numerous propulsion systems. Other power plants in past or present use include steam reciprocating, diesel-electric, gas turbines, nuclear, and sail. Cargoes vary widely: some are dry, some liquid; some are of low unit value (coal, oil), some high (autos, electronics); some are handled in bulk (grain), some in containers. A few merchant ships are built to carry a wide variety of cargoes, but more and more frequently, designs have been specialized for a particular commodity. The most important types are briefly described in the following sections.

1.19   Terminology   As with warships, special names and abbreviations have evolved to identify or describe merchant vessels and their cargoes. The meaning of some of these is obvious; others need translation. The following list includes some of the most common.

ASPHALT	Asphalt tanker
BULK CAR	Bulk carrier
CHEM TKR	Chemical tanker
COLLIER	Coal carrier
COMBO P&C	Combination passenger and cargo
COMBO/REF	Combination passenger and cargo refrigerated
CONTSHIP	Container ship
CONT BARGE	Container barge
CONT CAR	Container/car carrier
CONT RAIL	Container/rail carrier
L.N.G.	Liquified natural gas carrier
L.P.G.	Liquified petroleum gas carrier
LU	Laid-up in National Defense Reserve Fleet
MS	Motor ship
MV	Motor vessel
OBO	Ore/bulk/oil
PART CONT	Partial container ship
POL	Petroleum, oil, and lubricants
R/V	Research vessel
REFRIG	Refrigerated
RO/RO	Roll on/roll off ship
SS	Steamship
T/B–BLK	Integrated tug/barge–bulk
T/B–TNK	Integrated tug/barge–tank
TEU	Twenty-foot equivalent unit (volume of container 8 × 8 × 20 ft)
ULCC	Ultra large crude (oil) carrier

1.20 Freighters These ships carry *break-bulk cargo:* items that are loaded one by one into the holds or on deck. Most freighters are fitted with booms, winches, and cranes that allow the ship to bring cargo aboard and unload it without the need of shore cranes (Fig. 1.15). Individual loads are handled by pallets, barrel slings, and cargo nets. A representative ship is the *S.S. American Ranger* with a length of 507½ ft, a beam of 75 ft, a draft of 32 ft, and a deadweight of 13,264 tons. It has a steam turbine drive and is rated at 20 knots.

1.21 Container Ships In contrast to the freighter's open cargo, the container ship carries cargo already stowed in *containers.* These are large wood

Fig. 1.15 Four freighters handling break-bulk cargo. Each ship uses its own booms to load and unload cargo on railroad cars and trailer trucks. Cargo moves slowly, but such uncomplicated shore-side facilities can be found at almost any port in the world. (*Photo courtesy of Virginia International Terminals, Inc.*)

or metal boxes of standard size, usually 8 × 8 × 20 ft or 8 × 8 × 40 ft. Special locking devices in each corner allow containers to be stacked either on deck or below. Many containers hold items that are light in weight. Thus an apparently top-heavy fully loaded container ship can actually be completely stable. (Fig. 6.12)

The advantages of containers are freedom from pilferage and weather damage, together with speed of loading, offloading, and intermodal transfer to truck, rail, or barge. Emphasis throughout the container trade is on speed. The ships are larger and faster than freighters. The *Hawaiian Enterprise* class, for example, transports over 1000 containers between San Francisco and Hawaii in three and one half days. The Evergreen Line's 16 G-type ships carry 2700 TEU's (see Section 1.19) on a "round-the-world" route, circling the globe in 80 days.

In the terminal, containers are staged and loaded by computer-generated plan to ensure ship trim, stability, and access for rapid unloading at subsequent ports. Turnaround time in harbor is often less than a single eight-hour shift. Speed is achieved, however, at the cost of flexibility. Rapid loading and unloading require special cranes and shore transfer equipment in a large terminal area for temporary storage of containers. As a result, terminals are not located on downtown urban waterfronts, but in the outskirts where large acreage of land is available (Fig. 1.16).

1.22   Barge Carriers   A special type of container is the *LASH* or Lighter-Aboard-SHip. Barges measuring about 60 × 30 × 8 ft are filled with cargo, often at shallow-water piers inaccessible to an oceangoing vessel. They are towed to the LASH ship and then taken on board by one of several novel methods. Ships like *Austral Lightning* (Fig. 1.9) carry large gantry cranes spanning the entire width of the ship. The crane moves all the way aft on tracks extending past the counter, so that the gantry is directly over the lighter. After lifting it to deck level, the crane rolls forward to spot the lighter on deck or in a stack. Another class, the Japanese-built *Mammoth Oaks,* resembles a Landing Ship Dock. By flooding ballast tanks to submerge the cargo deck, the ship can float on board up to 18 LASH barges. Ballast is then pumped to raise the cargo deck above the waterline. One hundred eight TEU's can be stowed on deck also. Other LASH ships use a semisub-

Fig. 1.16   The container ship *American Lynx*, of the U.S. Lines, loading at Norfolk, Virginia. Note the standard-size containers, the special crane, and the extensive cargo marshalling area. Container ships need remain in port for only a few hours at a modern container terminal, but such terminals are large, expensive, and relatively few in number. (*Photo courtesy of Virginia International Terminals, Inc.*)

mersible stern elevator to load the barges, or else carry them between twin catamaran-style hulls.

1.23 Roll On/Roll Off Ships Also known as RO/RO carriers, these vessels load and offload vehicles on their own wheels rather than lifting them by crane—a sort of seamobile parking garage. Some are configured solely for passenger car delivery; others handle tractor-trailers carrying containers. Vehicles drive on and off over side or stern ramps. Then, through a system of internal ramps, they are spotted in position for the ocean crossing. Both ships and barges are used in the RO/RO mode. They are adapted both to commercial routes and military supply (Fig. 1.17).

1.24 Dry Bulk Carriers These ships carry grain, ore, coal, and other materials that can be loaded, stored, and offloaded loose. *Colliers,* or coal carriers, particularly important in times of oil shortage, have been built with very large capacities and very deep draft. They are unable to enter some harbors and must be loaded from lighters in deep water offshore (Fig. 1.18). A few bulk carriers (*self-loaders*) can fill or empty their own holds, but most depend on elaborate shore facilities to handle their cargoes.

Fig. 1.17 The Roll On/Roll Off ship *Barber Perseas.* Vehicles are loaded and offloaded on their own wheels across the ramp of this Barber Blue Sea Line RO/RO ship. A limited number of containers are carried on deck. (*Photo by Backus Aerial Photography, Inc.*)

Fig. 1.18 The Italian collier *Centauro*. Dry bulk carriers like these require special shore terminals to load and unload their cargoes of coal. Together with the tanker fleet, colliers are responsible for meeting the world's energy needs.

1.25 Tankers Carriers of wet bulk cargo, most *tankers* transport crude oil or other POL products. Others are specially configured for a variety of liquids: ammonia, orange juice, wine, refrigerated butane, and propane under high pressure. *Oilers* are tankers equipped to transfer fuel to warships while underway at sea.

As the value of crude oil has risen, so has the size of tankers (Fig. 1.19). One of the world's largest is the Ultralarge Crude Carrier (ULCC) *Esso Atlantic*. Built in Japan and registered in Liberia, she is larger than an aircraft carrier. A 45,000 HP steam turbine drives this 500,000 deadweight ton, 1,334 ft supertanker at 16 knots on the Middle East–Europe route. Her full load draft of 82 ft requires special offshore terminals.

1.26 Passenger Ships Compared to cargo ships, passenger ships are few in number, thanks to rapid air transport. The largest of the passenger ships, or *ocean liners* as they are sometimes called, also carry cargo. In contrast is a type of passenger ship that also stresses cargo: the passenger-combination ship. As a general rule, these accommodate between 12 and 40 passengers. Some characteristics of passenger ships are their larger size, higher speeds, hotel-like accommodations, special safety features, numerous lifeboats, and moderate capacity for baggage, mail, and special cargo. Today, many are used as cruise ships (Fig. 1.20).

1.27 Combination Cargo Carriers Although most merchant ships are built for a particular cargo and sometimes for a particular trade route, oth-

Fig. 1.19 An ultralarge crude carrier, the U.S.T. *Atlantic*. At nearly 400,000 deadweight tons, this supertanker is one of the largest ships ever built in the United States.

ers are designed with the flexibility to carry mixtures of cargo. Oil/ore carriers, for example, have a number of holds that can store either wet or dry commodities, according to the need of shippers. An unusually versatile ship is the Danish MS *Skandeborg*. Special configuration and equipment allow her to handle container, RO/RO, heavy lift, and break-bulk cargo on Atlantic routes.

1.28 Towboats and Tugs These specialized commercial craft pull or push other vessels, providing the propulsion and direction to move them to their destinations. Some are designed to push long strings of barges ahead of them. Harbor tugs move lighters and railroad car floats from place to place and help to dock large ships. Seagoing tugs often tow strings of barges along the coasts. Some tugs measure 100 ft in length and can handle transoceanic tows. Salvage tugs are built to render aid to the largest of ships, even under the most arduous conditions. A first-rate tug of this kind will exceed 280 ft in length and have a 17,500-hp drive. Her 25-man crew handles elaborate navigation and fire-fighting equipment, large pumps, and automatic-tension towing winches.

1.1.29 Integrated Tug/Barges (ITB) Two different types of vessels have been defined as ITBs by the USCG Bureau of Marine Inspection: (1) The

Fig. 1.20 The *Cunard Adventurer* can carry 700 passengers on luxury cruises in tropical waters. The 15,000 ton liner was built in Holland for the British Cunard Line.

pushing-mode ITB, which consists of a propelling unit rigidly connected to a barge and is designed to remain so for the duration of the voyage. Some units with an articulated connecting system are also included in this category, and (2) the *dual-mode ITB,* which consists of a tug capable of operating in either pushing or towing mode, and a barge fitted out to accommodate either mode of propulsion.

The tugs of the push-mode ITB type may be of either conventional monohull or catamaran configuration. The monohull tugs are secured firmly in a notch at the stern of the barges by mechanical devices. The tugs may be affixed rigidly to the barges, although in the case of the *articulated ITBs* the tugs can pitch, but due to the make-up of the connecting devices and fender systems cannot roll. The catamaran tugs are rigidly connected to the barges and sit astride an extension of their sterns that fits between the two hulls and supports the structural elements that connect them.

The dual-mode ITBs are sometimes referred to as Deep-Notch Tug/Barge Units. This subject is discussed in greater detail in Chapter 11.

The barges of both push-mode and dual-mode ITBs may be constructed to carry liquid, bulk, and containerized cargoes.

1.30   Merchant Marine Support Projects   Three projects that the U.S. Navy is vitally concerned with are Arapaho, Sea Shed, and the Rapid Deployment Force. All three projects utilize merchant cargo vessels for logistic support.

The Sea Shed is essentially a large open-topped container which can function as a portable 'tween deck. This would enable container vessels to carry tanks and other odd or oversize vehicles in the event of war.

The Arapaho project is a plan to utilize merchant vessels to carry helicopters and Harrier jets for use in ASW operations and close air support for the Marine Corps.

The Rapid Deployment Force involves the speedy transport of troops and supplies to crisis areas in various parts of the world. One of the central components of the force is the TAKR Fast Sealift ship, formerly the SL-7's owned by Sealand. Each vessel can carry tanks, helicopters, and wheeled support for an armored division. The former containerships now have RO/RO capacity and heavy- and medium-life capability, which enable them to work cargo independent of port facilities. These vessels are stationed about the country in a four-day ready-for-sea status.

1.31   Coastal Vessels   In the United States, most domestic freight moves by truck or over rails. Elsewhere in the world, coastal vessels carry many short-haul cargoes. For this purpose, there are small versions of most of the oceangoing types: freighters, container ships, bulk carriers, and passenger liners. Particularly in the Third World, water transportation is often the cheapest, if not the only, link between coastal towns and cities. Harbors, rivers, and coastal waters of Europe, South America, Asia, and Africa are filled with an interesting and varied collection of small merchantmen rarely seen in North America.

References

Couhat, Jean L. *Combat Fleets of the World, 1986/7.* Annapolis, MD: U.S. Naval Institute, 1986.

LaDage, John H. *Modern Ships,* 2nd ed. Centreville, MD: Cornell Maritime Press, 1965.

Moore, John, ed. *Jane's Fighting Ships,* 1984–85. London: Jane's Pub. Co. Ltd., 1985 (biennial).

Munro-Smith, R. *Merchant Ships & Shipping.* Cranbury, NJ: A. S. Barnes, 1970.

Munro-Smith, R. *Merchant Ship Types.* London: Marine Media Management Ltd., 1975.

Schonknecht, Rolf et al., *Ships & Shipping of Tomorrow,* Centreville, MD: Cornell Maritime Press, 1983.

Ships & Aircraft of the U.S. Fleet, 13th ed. Annapolis, MD: U.S. Naval Institute, 1985.

Talbot-Booth, E. C. *Merchant Ships,* Vol I–III. New York: Nichols. Pub. Co., 1978–9.

Warship. London: Conway Marine Press; distributed in USA by Ships Book Press, New York, NY 10022 (quarterly journal).

Warships International. Toledo: International Naval Research Organization (quarterly journal).

2

Boats

Seamen apply the term *boat* to a variety of craft, but in general a boat is relatively small, usually intended for inland or coastal operation, and sometimes designed for hoisting on board ship. Although most boats measure no more than fifty feet in length and displace only a few tons, distant-ground fishing boats are in reality small ships, and well-found cruising yachts can and do cross the oceans. In the absence of a universally recognized classification scheme, this chapter discusses boats under five broad groups: Navy and Coast Guard boats, lifeboats, fishing vessels, pleasure craft, and nonconventional designs. Preceeding these is a general discussion of construction, maintenance, and safety. Boat handling is covered in Chapter 12.

2.1 Construction Boats are made of many different materials ranging from fabric to steel. These include canvas, rubber, fiberglass reinforced plastic (FRP), wood, aluminum, ferro-cement, and steel. For smaller boats, FRP is probably the most commonly used material, while larger boats are usually built of wood or steel.

Wooden boats have traditionally utilized fore-and-aft planks fastened to transverse frames (Fig. 2.1). A more modern design is molded plywood.

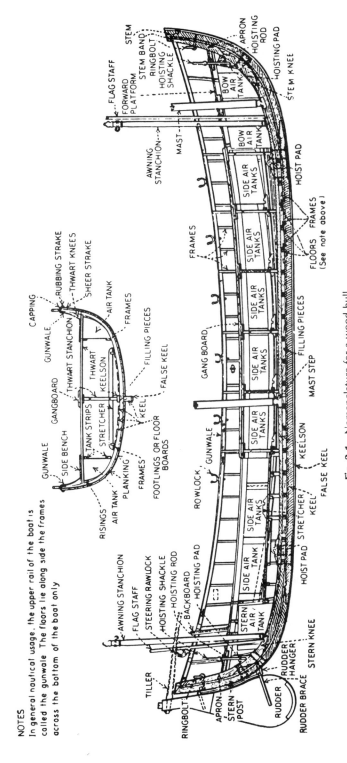

NOTES

In general nautical usage, the upper rail of the boat is called the gunwale. The floors lie along side the frames across the bottom of the boat only

Fig. 2.1 Nomenclature for a wood hull.

Thin strips, impregnated with glue, are diagonally bent over a mold to the shape of the hull desired, building up a skin of several layers thickness. The structure is then placed in an autoclave, where, at increased temperatures, the strips are curved and formed into a one-piece hull that is light, strong, seamless, and as with all wood hulls, inherently buoyant.

Metal hulls consist of a steel or aluminum shell riveted or welded to the frames. *Fiberglass reinforced plastic* boats are built of layers of glass cloth laid in or over a mold of the desired shape for the final hull form. Each layer of cloth is impregnated with either epoxy or polyester resin, and the completed hull is permitted to dry before being removed from the mold. Plastic boats do not have seams. Those less than 26 feet in length ordinarily use bulkheads for athwartship stiffness rather than frames. Longitudinal strength is provided by plastic members built up inside the shell.

The hulls of *ferro-cement* boats are built in two steps. First a framework of iron or steel rods is welded together and a layer of wire mesh (like chicken wire or hardware cloth) fastened to it in the shape of the finished boat. The builder then covers the mesh with concrete, either sprayed or trowelled in place. Although this technique has been successfully used for boats as small as canoes and as big as river assault craft, ferro-cement has never truly caught the fancy of boat builders and operators, and such craft are uncommon in the western world.

2.2 Buoyancy Unless made of wood, a flooded boat tends to sink. As a safety precaution, therefore, many boats are given added buoyancy in the form of air tanks or plastic foam inserts. Lifeboats and personnel boats are always designed with sufficient buoyancy to float when completely flooded. Styrofoam and cellular cellulose acetate (CCA) are the most popular forms of buoyant material used in wood or metal boats. This material, in "plank" form, is customarily installed as near the sheer level as possible. In plastic boats, normal practice to use liquid foam rather than built-in planks. Poured or sprayed into buoyancy chambers, the foam sets up as a low-density solid to provide emergency flotation.

In self-bailing boats, a watertight deck runs the length of the boat slightly above the load waterline. The space below thus becomes a watertight compartment. Water from this deck runs overboard through freeing ports or *scuppers* in the side of the boat. Water that leaks into the compartments below the deck is pumped out by a *bilge pump*. Many sailboat cockpits are similarly designed to be self-bailing.

If the buoyancy of a boat can be carried high, above the waterline, the boat will tend to right itself should it capsize. Self-righting boats are built in such a shape as to permit carrying the bow air tanks and stern air tanks high; they are also fitted with a heavy keel. Self-bailing and self-righting features are sometimes combined, as in the larger motor lifeboats used by the Coast Guard.

2.3   Maintenance   Although written primarily with large ships in mind, the appropriate sections of Chapters 3, 4, and 5 are also useful reading for the boat owner and operator. This section contains additional material specially applicable to small craft.

Wooden boats require special attention to ventilation, drainage, and leakage. To this end, all ventilation terminals should be kept open. The lazaret, stern, and bilge areas should be provided with a reliable means of ventilation. Standing fresh water, even in small amounts, is particularly harmful as it may cause dry rot.

Deck seams, in the plank sheer area especially, must be carefully caulked and maintained. Decks must be sanded with care to retain the proper camber to allow water runoff and to prevent low areas where fresh water would tend to stand. During fair weather, hatches and deck plates should be opened to increase air circulation. Wet dunnage, rope, and life jackets in lockers and forepeak spaces should be removed and aired out.

For removing salt accumulations from varnished surfaces, chrome and brass fittings, and windows, the use of fresh water is recommended. Wooden boats should not be washed down with fresh water if there is a chance of water penetration into the wood. Salt water, which has some preservative value, should be used instead. Since salt does attract moisture from the air, however, its exclusive use for the washdown of wooden boats is no cure-all for rot—which is caused by retention of dampness in timber.

Boat crews must be alert for any leaks beneath the covering board or the deckhouse. Since moisture is trapped by thick coats of paint, overpainting must be avoided. On some wooden boats the stem, stern, and bilge areas are purposely left unpainted. In such areas, wood preservative solutions rather than paints are used.

Metal boats call for added care in the matter of corrosion prevention. Proper upkeep of paint and other coatings in all interior and exterior surfaces is a necessity. Zincs must be installed on steel hulls to prevent electrolytic corrosion.

Plastic hulls avoid both rot and corrosion, but like others must be protected against fouling. Since sandblasting and heavy scraping can damage the hull, it is especially important to scrub off marine growth immediately after the boat is hauled, while still wet. Grass and barnacles are much harder to remove after they have dried.

Propeller shaft alignment should be checked regularly. Crankcase oil should be changed after every 100 hours or so of running time. Boats alongside one another should be separated by boat fenders. When the boat is lifted from the water, the struts, propeller, sea suctions, and shaft bearings must be checked. Worn propellers or worn shaft bearings bring on heavy vibrations, eventually damaging hull and engine. Gear housings, steering mechanisms, and other moving parts must be kept well lubricated.

It is not possible to paint or caulk oil-soaked bottom planking in wooden boats. An oil-soaked bilge is a fire hazard in any boat. When draining or filling fuel tanks or engine crankcases, avoid spillage. Gasoline fumes in bilges are especially dangerous, since a spark from static electricity or ignition of the engine can set off an explosion.

Ashore and aboard ship, wooden blocking and wedges should support a stowed boat's overhang both fore and aft. Chocks should be located opposite frames or bulkheads. In order to spread the stress, the loads imposed by gripe pads should be distributed as widely as possible. Take-up devices on the gripes should be marked at the limit of the tightening required.

2.4 Capacity Most boats are fitted with a plate giving the capacity both in personnel and in weight. If this information is not shown, it can be estimated by the following rules of thumb:

$N = LB/15$, where

N = maximum number of persons (round off to nearest whole number)
L = length overall in feet
B = maximum beam in feet

$W = 7.5 LBD$, where

W = capacity, including personnel, in pounds
D = minimum effective deepness in feet (vertical distance from keel to lowest point where water can enter the boat, often the motor cutout in the transom.

When people are carried by boat, the designated carrying capacity should not be exceeded; in carrying stores, the load in pounds (of both men and stores) should not exceed the maximum allowable cargo load. Passengers, stores, and baggage should not be carried topside on motorboats. If stores and baggage are carried in motorboats, the number of passengers should be reduced. The man in charge of the boat, either the coxswain or the senior officer embarked, must make this judgment carefully, as several catastrophic accidents will attest. The factors of weather and sea conditions must not be ignored, despite inconveniences caused by reduced loads.

2.5 Safety   Entire volumes have been written on safety in small craft, and this section can touch only a few of the most common hazards. The reader should refer to the references listed at the end of the chapter. The Coast Guard pamphlets and Henderson (1972) are particularly valuable. The Coast Guard will, on request, conduct a Courtesy Motorboat Examination—an extremely useful check on a boat's condition and safety equipment. A few hints are listed below.

Weather. Pay attention to weather forecasts, both before getting underway and while on the water. Be alert for changes and do not delay in battening down or returning to port until it is too late. (See Chapters 14–18)

Fire. Be careful of open flames on board, especially in the galley. Follow all safety precautions while fueling. Keep fire extinguishers charged and accessible.

Overloading. Don't carry excess people and stores. Reduce load in heavy weather.

Drugs and alcohol. Drugs have no place on board, and drinking is best delayed until safely at anchor or mooring.

Rules of the Road. Know and follow them. Small craft should keep out of the way of ships and fishing vessels.

Equipment. Keep all gear in good operating condition and securely stowed in its designated location. After use, put it back where it belongs.

Navy and Coast Guard Boats

2.6 Navy and Coast Guard Craft   Many of these are carried on board ships for use as workboats, picket boats, or personnel and cargo transport at anchorage. Others are operated by shore-based boat pools. The Coast Guard has developed and employs an additional class of boats for patrol, security, search, and rescue. Some common types are listed below.

Inflatable rubber boats (like Captain Cousteau's Zodiacs) are both portable and versatile. They are used by swimmers and scuba divers and for other special operations.

Personnel boats resemble cabin cruisers and carry officers and crew between ship and shore. They have largely replaced the traditional officers motorboat. The captain's boat is called a *gig;* the admiral's a *barge* (Fig. 2.2).

Utility boats in the Navy carry both personnel and cargo. They are taking the place of the conventional ship's motor launch. Coast Guard utility boats are general-purpose twin-screwed craft used for rescue, security, and law enforcement.

Amphibious craft and Riverine Warfare Boats. See Fig. 2.28.

Motor Lifeboats, in the Coast Guard, have the mission of rescue work in all weather. The 26-foot MLB is carried on board oceangoing cutters.

Fig. 2.2 An admiral's barge under way.

The 44- and 52-footers work from shore bases. The latter is a twin-screw double-ender with a steel hull and aluminum superstructure. She carries a 500 gal/min fire and salvage pump and a power windlass. The 44-footer is designed to run through the surf to reach a ship in distress (Fig. 2.3). Her speed is 16 knots and her radius 150 miles. The crew is only three, but loaded with survivors the 44-foot MLB can carry a total of 40.

Ports and waterways boats (PWB) are 32-foot Coast Guard craft outfitted for harbor patrol, port security, and firefighting. (See Section 1.16 for USCG numbering system.)

Lifeboats

2.7 Lifeboats Tradition and law require that ships carry their own lifeboats to save crew and passengers in case of disaster. Unlike the Coast Guard MLB's ships' lifeboats are designed primarily for survival rather than for speed and power of propulsion. Ships of the U.S. Merchant Marine are subject to the construction and safety standards administered by the Coast Guard in conformity with an international agreement among the world's maritime nations. Under this agreement, all large oceangoing cargo ships and tankers must provide a lifeboat capacity of 200 percent for all persons aboard. In contrast, the lifeboat capacity of an oceangoing passenger ship is reduced to 100 percent, because the ship's hull is built to higher standards of internal subdivision.

Fig. 2.3 The 44-ft U.S. Coast Guard steel motor life boat can roll over in high waves and keep on operating.

The most recently built lifeboats in this country are of steel, aluminum, or fiberglass construction, with internal blocks of plastic foam to provide extra buoyancy. Each lifeboat is required to be equipped with a considerable inventory of survival equipment, including food, drinking water, and pyrotechnic signals. Diesel-propelled and hand-propelled lifeboats are also in use. The hand-propelled mechanism consists of a propeller that is driven by a flywheel, that in turn is rotated by a hand lever-and-crank system operated by the occupants seated in the lifeboat.

Covered lifeboats and escape capsules have been developed that provide protection against fire, chemicals, and weather for escapees from a ship or oil rig. See Chapter 12. Information on davits and on launching and recovering lifeboats is also included in Chapter 12.

Inflatable life rafts supplement the lifeboats carried by passenger vessels in the merchant marine. These rafts are also the primary lifeboats on board Navy and Coast Guard vessels. A naval vessel such as a large carrier could not possibly carry sufficient boats to act as lifeboats in case the ship must be abandoned. The answer is the inflatable life raft. Large aircraft carriers sometimes carry over two hundred of these rafts. Life rafts in the deflated condition are very compact and easy to stow. They can usually be launched by one or two men or by hydrostatic action (Fig. 2.4). Carbon dioxide bottles contained in the raft inflate it automatically after a tug on the seapainter.

Fig. 2.4 Inflatable raft being launched from the side of a ship. (*Courtesy of the Switlik Parachute Co., the manufacturer*)

Modern rafts are extremely seaworthy and provide excellent protection for the occupants from the elements (Fig. 2.5). Rafts are available in sizes ranging from a small four-man raft suitable for small boats or yachts up to rafts of 25-man capacity. The most up-to-date rafts are shipped and stowed in cylindrical fiberglass containers that keep them from exposure to the elements and damage from the sun and stack sediment burns. The container permits the raft to be sealed so that it will be safe from pilferage of raft supplies.

Recent improvements in lifesaving equipment include rafts and capsules that will not capsize in extremely rough weather. Examples are the Givens stablized inflatable raft and the Brucker capsule. Some inflatable rafts are now being launched by davits. Inflatable slides, as long as 70 ft, are also being used, notably by ferries in Alaska.

Fig. 2.5 Inflatable raft fully inflated in the water. (*Courtesy of the Switlik Parachute Co., the manufacturer*)

Rafts for use on board merchant vessels, U.S. Coast Guard vessels, and private yachts must meet the construction requirements of the Coast Guard. Such rafts must also be reinspected by an authorized test facility at specified intervals.

Fishing Craft and Equipment

Commercial fisheries are of two general types: *pelagic* and *demersal*. Pelagic species are those that live at or near the surface of the sea; demersal species inhabit the sea bottom. Distinct craft and gear have evolved for catching each of these types of fish.

2.8 Craft for Pelagic Fishing Pelagic fish include mackerel, herring, tuna, and shark. They habitually travel in schools that move rapidly through the upper layers of the ocean. The captain in quest of pelagic fish selects his fishing ground through past experience or sometimes from interpretation of sea temperature and other oceanographic data. He pinpoints his quarry by eye or by underwater sound. For visual search, pelagic fishing craft are equipped with a crow's nest and high-power optics. A helicopter or light airplane may be employed to extend search range. Fish-finding sound gear ranges from simple flasher-type depth indicators and echo sounders to scanning-type "fish scopes." High sonic frequencies give sharp resolution that shows echoes from schools or even from single fish as well as from the sea floor.

Once located, pelagic fish are taken by purse seines, drift nets, harpoon, or hook and line. *Purse seines* take much of the world pelagic catch. A purse seine is a long deep net of small mesh. The seiner, usually with the aid of one or more workboats, lays the net in a circle around a school of fish and joins the ends. The bottom is then closed by a purse line strung through eyes along the lower edge of the net. When hauled in, the purse line acts as a draw string, gathering together the bottom of the seine and preventing the escape of the fish. (See Fig. 2.6.) The net is then brought on deck—by hand in smaller or older boats, by power block in larger and more modern craft—until the catch is concentrated in a small pocket of water. The fish are then taken aboard by dip nets or by fish pumps.

A typical New England mackerel seine measures 1500 ft along the cork line (upper edge) by 30 ft deep. Heavy and expensive, it includes nearly 3000 corks, 2000 leads, 30 6-in. purse rings, and 350 fathoms of steel, ny-

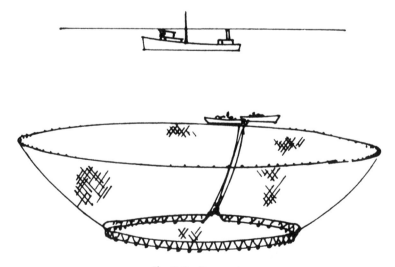

Fig. 2.6 Purse seine.

lon, or manila purse line. Other seines are even larger; a typical West Coast tuna seine is about twice as long and ten times deeper. The cost may range into hundreds of thousands of dollars.

Figure 2.7 shows an Alaskan *salmon seiner.* The net is stowed on the low, wide fantail on top of a rotating turntable. A power-operated roller and a heavy boom are used to handle the seine. The high bow and bridge give excellent sea-keeping qualities, and the crow's nest gives the lookout good visibility. The skiff is stowed atop the seine. *Tuna seiners* are larger, faster, and longer-legged. The newest ships are 200 ft or more in overall length and are capable of 16 knots, with a long high seas endurance. They can fish the most distant grounds. Seiners based in California work grounds in the South Pacific and eastern tropical Atlantic.

Another pelagic fishing craft, the *tuna clipper,* uses a pole and line technique (Fig. 2.8). Like the tuna seiner, it originated in the Pacific, but now fishes off the Atlantic coast of Africa as well. In both oceans it ranges far beyond the continental shelf in search of skipjack and other large tuna.

After a school is located, the crew attract them alongside by throwing overboard bait fish. When the tuna reach a feeding frenzy, the crew take station on the fishing platform around the stern. The tuna strike large feathered, barbless jig hooks, with one or two poles and lines attached to each jig. The polemen swing the catch on deck where other hands shake them off the hook and strike them below in refrigerated holds.

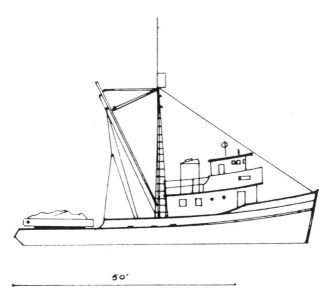

50'

Fig. 2.7 Alaskan salmon seiner.

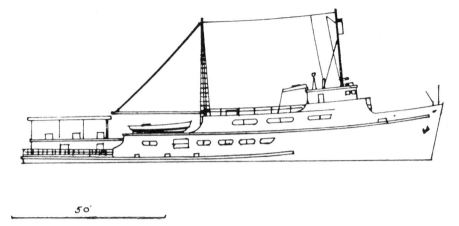

50'

Fig. 2.8 Tuna clipper.

The tuna clipper, like the purse seiner, is built for long voyages on the high seas. It has a high crow's nest for good visibility and a low stern with outboard "racks" or stages for the pole handlers. A tank aft holds the live bait, and there are facilities to trim down aft so that the racks are nearly at sea level. Cold-storage capacity may be as great as 1,000 tons. Clippers carry *lampara nets* to catch bait and sometimes purse seines for taking the smaller varieties of tuna.

The *drifter* is another common type of pelagic fisherman. As illustrated by Fig. 2.9, drifting gear consists of long "fleets" of *gill nets*. Each net is about ten fathoms long by several fathoms deep. The mesh is larger than that of a purse seine, wide enough so that fish can pass only part way through. They are then entangled in the mesh until brought on board and

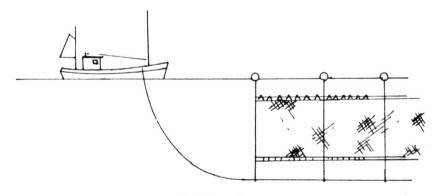

Fig. 2.9 Drift net.

pulled free by the fishermen. The drifter "shoots" up to 100 nets in a continuous line that is suspended near the surface by wooden or plastic floats. Nets are laid at dusk so that the fish cannot see the mesh. Moored to the leeward end, the boat drifts until dawn—whence the name "drifter"—and then the nets are hauled and the catch recovered. Sometimes they are hauled by hand, but now, to an increasing extent, by a powerful winch or reel.

The drifter is particularly important in European pelagic fisheries. A typical *North Sea drifter* is shown in Fig. 2.10. Designed to work grounds close to port, the drifter brings in its catch fresh. Slow and rugged, it has limited accommodations and few comforts. The foremast mounts a long boom for handling the catch. The mast is often mounted in a tabernacle so that it can be lowered to increase stability. The short mainmast carries a steadying sail to reduce rolling and keep the boat headed into the wind. Drifters vary in size from small 20-footers to modern craft of over 100 ft.

In many parts of the world, pelagic fish are taken by *trolling.* The Bay of Biscay tunny fishery was worked for many years by sailing craft called *thoniers.* These ruggedly built yawls and ketches, now replaced by power boats, streamed their baits from long lines attached to *tagnons,* or poles. The salmon fishery in the U.S. Pacific Northwest is also worked by trolling. A typical troller is shown in Fig. 2.11. Diesel powered, it is flush decked with mast and deckhouse forward. Six or eight lines can be handled, and a power winch, or *gurdy,* is fitted to pull in the hooked fish.

Jigging is a hook-and-line method in which a lure is pulled vertically up and down to attract the fish. Originally a hand operation, jigging can now

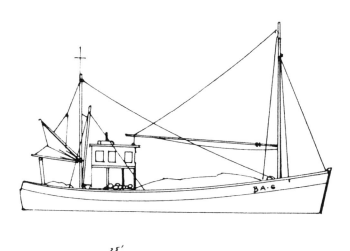

Fig. 2.10 North Sea motor drifter.

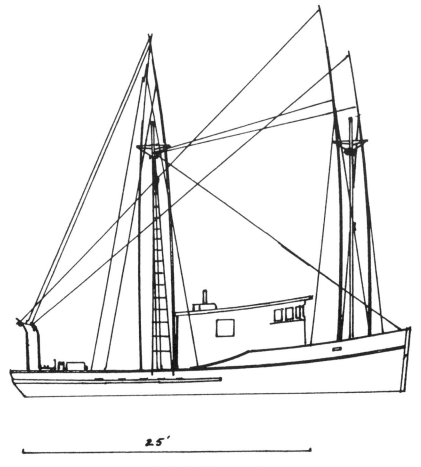

25′

Fig. 2.11 Salmon troller.

be accomplished by power-driven machines that not only jig the lure but also haul in the catch. This gear is fitted on Norwegian cod and saithe boats and on squid fishermen in the Western Pacific.

Whales, although mammals, comprise a pelagic fishery. Over-exploitation has reduced populations severely, and the catch is now regulated by international agreement. Most countries have abandoned whaling, and there is strong pressure for complete protection of all marine mammals. Acting through the International Whaling Commission Japan and Russia have opposed the ban, and the future is difficult to predict. Both countries have perfected the technology of whaling. Highly organized Russian and Japanese flotillas include store ships, tankers, factory ships, whale catchers, carcass towers, and aircraft. The grounds are in the North Pacific and Ant-

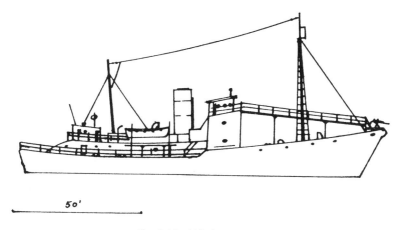

Fig. 2.12 Whale catcher.

arctic waters. A whale catcher (Fig. 2.12) is a fast, maneuverable craft mounting a harpoon gun. Its job is to pursue the whale, harpoon it, buoy the carcass, and set off after another whale. The carcass is towed to the factory ship where it is hauled aboard and processed.

2.9 Demersal Fishing Gear Cod, flounder, pollack, and shellfish are among the most important demersal fish. They are usually taken by *trawling*. The term *trawler*, commonly applied to many types of fishermen, should properly be reserved for vessels that use trawls. An *otter trawl* is sketched in Fig. 2.13. A cone-shaped net bag, its forward end is spread

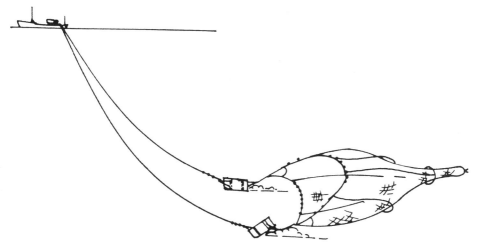

Fig. 2.13 Otter trawl.

open either by a beam, in the smaller sizes, or by a pair of otter boards or "doors." Weights in the form of steel bobbins or chains hold the lower edge of the mouth on the sea bottom, while steel or aluminum floats on a head rope support the upper edge. Otter boards are heavy, flat structures of steel or steel-reinforced wood. Rigged to tow at an angle like underwater kites, they can extend a trawl mouth 100 ft wide and 15 ft high. Long warps allow the trawl to be dragged along the bottom in water as deep as 200 fathoms. The rugged construction of a large trawl permits catches of 25,000 pounds or more. The midwater trawl, a recent development, is towed at an intermediate depth between bottom and surface. Fish-finder sonar, either with a tilting hull mount or a towed transducer, tells the skipper the depth and direction of the school so that he can tow the trawl through it.

To stream his gear, the trawler lies to across the wind. He then lowers the trawl over the side and begins to circle around it. As he approaches the trawling course, he lowers the otter boards. The warps are paid out as the trawl doors set properly. In 200 fathoms of water, about 450 to 600 fathoms of warp are used. The warps are led to a special hookup or towing block on the inboard quarter, and the vessel steadies on course at 2 or 3 knots. After a run which may last several hours, the trawl is winched back on board. The cod end is opened to dump the catch on deck. If the ground is especially good, it may be marked with a buoy for future reference.

2.10   Craft for Demersal Fishing   Trawlers vary widely in size. Among the smallest are the *New England draggers*. With good fishing grounds close by on the continental shelf, short and frequent cruises are feasible. The design that has developed is shown in Fig. 2.14. Normally of 100 ft or less, the typical dragger is diesel-propelled and mounts two masts with a steadying sail aft. Sturdy and seaworthy, they operate year-round in the stormy North Atlantic. In the North Sea, whose shallow waters support an ancient and important demersal fishery, the trawler fleet is composed of craft generally similar to the New England draggers.

Distant ground trawlers are operated by most of the European countries and by Japan. Built for long trips and large catches, they are strong ships with heavy gear, complete freezing or processing equipment, and modern electronics. They range in size to over 200 ft and 500 tons. British trawlers work the Barents Sea; French craft operate on the Grand Banks; Russian distant water boats fish off the East Coast of the United States; and Japanese trawl in the Barents Sea. (See Fig. 2.15.)

An important fishery in the Gulf of Mexico and off the southeastern United States is shrimping. The *double trawl rig* developed there has spread to other shrimp grounds throughout the world from the Gulf of Alaska to the Indian Ocean. A typical *shrimper* is shown in Fig. 2.16. It streams two otter trawls, rigging the warps through blocks mounted at the ends of the

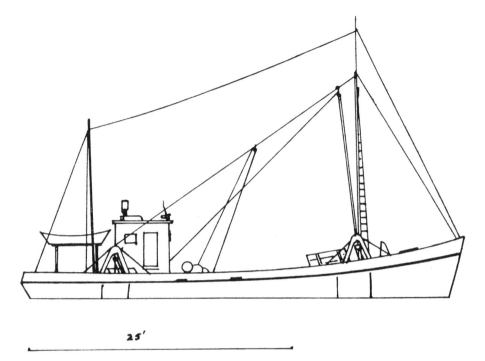

Fig. 2.14 New England dragger.

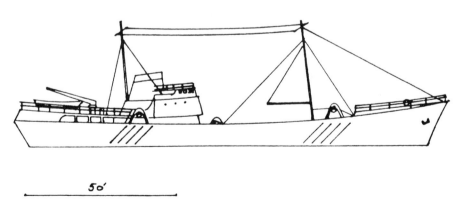

Fig. 2.15 European trawler.

port and starboard outriggers. Sometimes they tow a third trawl directly over the stern. Motor-driven, Gulf Coast shrimpers usually work shallow coastal waters but sometimes cross the Gulf of Mexico to fish the fertile Campeche Bank.

A newer and safer type of boat is the *stern trawler*. Net handling over

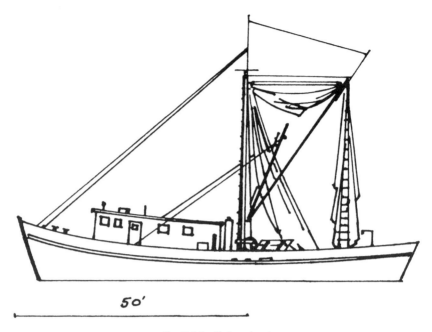

Fig. 2.16 Shrimp boat.

the side of a conventional side trawler is a slow procedure, hazardous in heavy weather. Damage to gear and catch is possible, and automation of the operation is infeasible. By shifting the trawl to the stern and installing a sloping ramp, it has become possible to reduce manhandling and to locate the men in a safer position. The warps on a stern trawl are run through blocks on the quarters, slung either from gallows or from an inverted U-shaped gantry. A winch amidships hauls in the warps and sometimes coils the trawl on a drum. The blocks, winches, rigging, and deck fittings are designed for remote operation, often by a single man. Some ships are fitted with an hydraulically operated door that can close the after end of the slip-way for added safety. Reduction of personnel and increased efficiency are important economic factors that have led to an increase of the number of stern trawlers in most fishing fleets. A Soviet bloc stern trawler and fish factory is sketched in Fig. 2.17. This class has a long slipway and a novel stack arrangement with twin funnels located port and starboard of the fish deck.

Another technique of demersal fishing is *pair trawling*. In this system, two craft steam on parallel courses, towing between them a trawl that may be as wide as 300 ft. Since each boat supplies only half of the total towing force, pair trawlers tend to be of small to medium size. They are fitted with

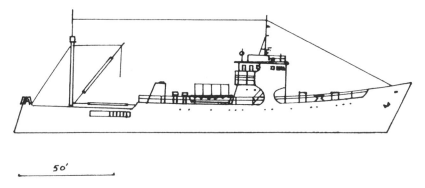

Fig. 2.17 Stern trawler (Soviet bloc).

winches but do not require gallows. Pair trawling is common in the Yellow and China Seas.

Offshore trap fisheries take various species of shellfish, including king crabs in the North Pacific and lobsters on the Continental Shelf of the eastern United States. A "West Coast Combination design" has evolved and is numerous in the Alaskan crab fleet based in Kodiak. A raised forward deck with the pilothouse forward gives a long open main deck aft for handling pots or, when rigged for trawling, for working the trawl and sorting fish. The hull has pronounced sheer to keep bow and stern clear while allowing a low waist for easy gear handling. Figure 2.18 shows a modern boat of this type. A somewhat similar although smaller craft has come into use in the New England offshore lobster fishery (Fig. 2.19). Both boats have high bow and low stern with cabin well forward in contrast to the typical houseaft dragger and drifter. New England offshore lobstermen range from 45 to 65 ft overall, half again as large as the older inshore boat. A 200- to 300-hp diesel gives a speed of about 10 knots with a full load of 50 or more traps on the after deck. A crew of two or three set the pots, 10 to 20 to a string, in waters up to 50 fathoms. Individual pots are separated by 10 or more fathoms to reduce the load on the pot hauler. A modern boat has extensive electronics, including radar, loran, and VHF and Citizen's Band radiotelephone.

2.11 Long Line Fishing The *long line* is used for demersal fishing the world over and in some fisheries for pelagic fishing. Baited hooks are secured every 2 or 3 fathoms to a heavy hemp, nylon monofilament, or wire line (see Fig. 2.20). After one end is buoyed and anchored, the boat pays out the line along a chosen track. For bottom fish, the line lies on the bottom; for billfish and tuna, it is buoyed every 50 fathoms to remain about

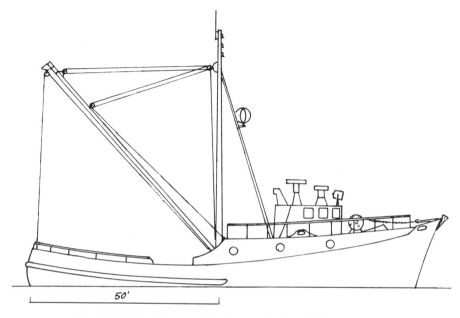

Fig. 2.18 West Coast combination vessel rigged for king crabbing.

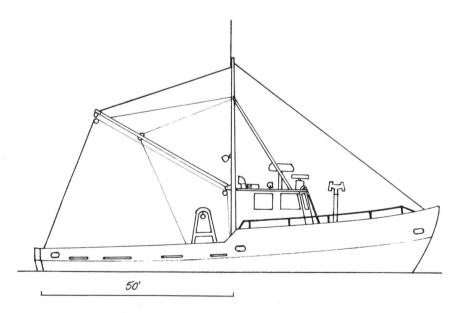

Fig. 2.19 New England offshore lobster boat

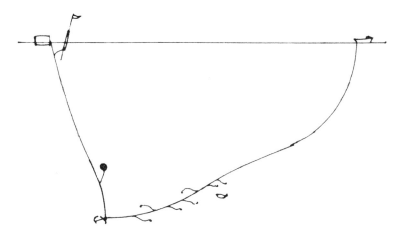

Fig. 2.20 Long line (bottom)

100 ft below the surface. When the entire line is set, the far end is buoyed and anchored, and the boat works its way along the line, removing the catch and rebaiting the hooks. Lines of 100 fathoms are handled by one or two men in an open boat. Farther seaward, medium-sized vessels run lines up to 50 miles in length. They are fitted with power winches to bring the line on board. Distant water longliners sometimes handle lines and catch themselves or, in the case of *dorymen,* from fleets of pulling boats. Similar in hull shape to long-range trawlers, they carry nests of dories on deck. Among the last modern sailing fishermen are Spanish and Portuguese dorymen that work the Grand Banks. Utilizing their diesels for the long voyages to and from the banks, they conserve fuel by using sail while on station.

2.12 Fishery Trends and Problems There are many variations of the craft and gear described above, and many have local names. Fishery research continues to produce new types, and the quest for new profitable fisheries continues worldwide. Midwater trawls, fished at a controllable depth above the bottom to take fish located by sonar, have entered the pelagic fishing picture. A trend continues towards combining several capabilities in a single hull for increased flexibility and greater profit. Rising fuel costs have caused fishermen and marine architects to consider alternative power plants to replace the ubiquitous diesel. A few sailing fisheries survive; among the largest is a fleet of *scow sloops* that fish with seines in Mexico's Laguna Madre on the Gulf. (See Fig. 2.21.) Some power boats are now using sail to supplement their engines on the grounds or in transit.

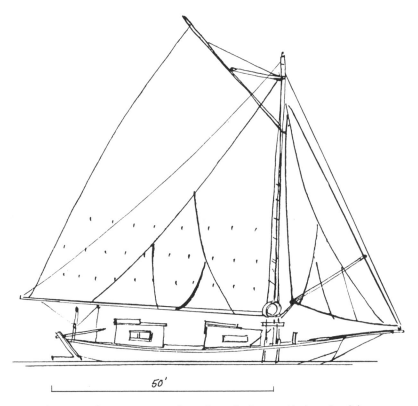

Fig. 2.21 *Campo,* or scow sloop, from the Laguna Madre seine fishery.

Steam is being reconsidered, using either coal or a wood derivative, such as compressed sawdust pellets, for fuel.

Fishing vessels at work are often hampered in their movements. The Rules of the Road recognize the problem and prescribe special lights and day marks (see Part IV).

Unfortunately, there is no consensus on the right to fish off foreign coasts. The facts of geography and biology make for international disagreement. Small, densely-populated countries want to catch fish not only along their own shores but also worldwide, wherever they can obtain this valuable source of protein. Such nations prefer minimum restrictions on their fishing fleets. At the other extreme are states whose chief resource is the fisheries of their adjoining high seas. Those governments favor laws banning foreign boats from wide areas of the ocean for the benefit of their own fishermen. Even within the United States opinions have differed. The San Pedro tuna captain would prefer narrow limits so that he can set his seine close to the west coast of South America; the Gloucester dragger would prefer a 200-mile limit to keep Russian vessels off the New England banks.

A series of United Nations conferences on the Law of the Sea has failed to produce a treaty acceptable to all countries. During these long-term negotiations, the United States took unilateral action by enacting the Fishery Conservation and Management Act of 1976. The Act established a 200-nautical-mile-wide fishery conservation zone within which the United States exercises "exclusive fishery management authority." A number of existing bilateral treaties were renegotiated, and responsibility for enforcement was assigned to the Coast Guard. Foreign fishing is allowed only with U.S. permission, and American inspectors may be placed on board the foreign craft. Joint ventures have become numerous; these are arrangements whereby foreign vessels process fish caught by U.S. boats. Quarrels over fishery regulation, however, remain a continuing international irritant, an incomplete chapter in the Law of the Sea.

Pleasure Boats

The two broad classes of pleasure craft are power and sail. Built and operated in many countries, they are less plentiful in the Third World where leisure time is scarce. Most are found in coastal and inland waters, although ocean-cruising yachts regularly sail around the world and occasionally past Cape Horn.

Powerful and reliable outboard motors drive sturdy inflatable boats, cabin cruisers, houseboats, and dozens of different models of small craft that can be carried on trailers behind motor vehicles. Some are hauled out in the winter and often stored in large multilevel sheds. Mooring space in marinas is often scarce and expensive.

Most large pleasure boats are driven by inboard or inboard/outboard motors, either gasoline or diesel. The latter is safer and more economical to run, but gasoline engines are cheaper. Although hobbyists and a few custom builders still use wood for hull construction, most modern pleasure craft are made of fiberglass. This construction prevents rot, is not inflammable, and provides greater hull space per foot of length because less internal bracing is required. Steel and aluminum masts and synthetic fiber for cordage and sails reduce upkeep and improve reliability. Electrically powered anchor winches and even powered mainsail furling are available, as well as roller reefing on foresails, to reduce the need for extra hands on larger yachts. Modern electronics have produced navigation aids compact and inexpensive enough for boat owners of modest means. Radar, autopilots, radiotelephone, depth finders, loran, speed and distance logs, wind velocity and direction meters, and satellite navigators can be found in most marinas.

Fig. 2.22 A typical cabin cruiser. (*Courtesy of the Bayliner Marine Corp., Seattle*)

2.13 Power boats Small outboard-powered boats, often transported by trailers, are used for fishing, waterskiing, cruising in sheltered waters, and commuting. Larger powered boats, *cabin cruisers* (Fig. 2.22), usually have inboard engines and are used for pleasure cruising, commuting, and fishing. Special *sport fishermen*, 25 to 50 ft, have hulls that can be driven at high speed (30 knots) by large engines in order to travel long distances in search of fish.

Houseboats for use on rivers, canals, lakes, and sheltered waters have become increasingly popular. Some are fast enough to pull waterskiers and seaworthy enough to go to sea in calm weather. They are all comfortable and spacious as compared to conventional cabin cruisers and much less expensive.

2.14 Sailboats Working sail has almost disappeared; a recent worldwide survey declared them an endangered species threatened with extermination by small, reliable engines. Sailing yachts, by contrast, are more numerous than ever before. *Daysailers* are small open boats, without accommodations, intended for daytime sailing. *Cruising boats* (Fig. 2.23) can sleep two or more crew members and are fitted with galleys and heads to allow longer trips, ranging from overnight to months-long ocean passages. *Racing*

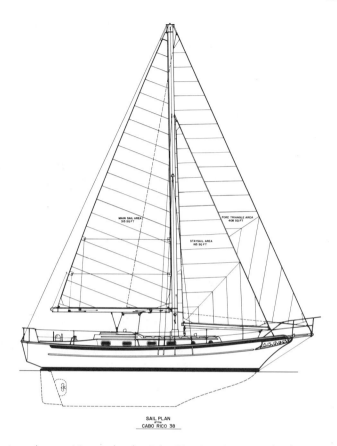

Fig. 2.23 A modern cruising yacht, the Cabo Rico 38. (*Courtesy of Cabo Rico USA, Inc.*)

yachts (Fig. 2.24) are built with primary emphasis on speed and often little regard for comfort. A successful ocean racer, for example, has a specially designed hull, a fairly large crew, special sail-handling winches, and a large set of expensive sails. Perhaps the ultimate in racers, the 12-meter boats, are true products of high technology and cost millions of dollars. Cruising yachtsmen who want to race as well are able to do so through special measurement or rating systems that handicap boats of different design.

Many major colleges and universities, as well as the U.S. Naval Academy, U.S. Coast Guard Academy, U.S. Merchant Marine Academy, and all of the state maritime academies, carry on a vigorous intercollegiate program of sail racing. In these races, standard designs of dinghies and larger sailing boats are used, such as the well-known "Shields Class" sloops. (Fig. 2.25) Organizations such as the International Ocean Racing Committee and the North American Yacht Racing Union determine yacht racing rules.

Fig. 2.24   A large sloop-rigged ocean racing yacht. (*Official U.S. Navy photograph*)

2.15   New Sailboat Designs   At the small end of the size range are *sailboards*—a single-sailed adaptation of the surfboard. The mast is stepped in a socket and held in place by the single-person crew, who trims the sail by holding the boom while balancing on the long, narrow hull. Best suited for warm waters because of frequent capsizes, sailboards and wet-suited sailors are to be seen even in frostbite conditions. They have become accepted as a standard racing class.

Multihulls, adapted from the Polynesian outrigger canoe, have been modernized in the form of racing and cruising craft. Catamarans and trimarans have achieved considerable acceptance as racing and cruising boats in recent years. Catamarans have twin hulls and trimarans have a main hull with two smaller hulls, one on each side. Multihulls are shallow draft, roomy, very fast if not overloaded, and considerably cheaper than single hulls. The latter must be built very heavy and strong, with a keel to provide stability. They move *through* the water, whereas a multihull moves for the most part *over* the water, depending on the wide separation of its hulls for stability.

Fig. 2.25 Typical intercollegiate racing dinghies. (*Official U.S. Navy photograph*)

Under very extreme and heavy storm conditions, when exposed to the occasional large freak wave with a vertical face, a multihull like any other vessel can capsize, but unlike a single hull cannot easily be righted. Multihulls, however, have been successful in ocean racing and are quite safe even in bad weather. They do not usually sail to windward as fast as a single hull but can easily reach superior speeds off the wind. Small catamarans have become popular for day sailing, racing, and surfing. Large multihulls often have small auxiliary engines, although the sensitivity of a multihull under sail to very light breezes makes auxiliary power less important.

In 1980, Captain Jacques Cousteau began to develop *Moulin à Vent*, a wind-driven craft without sails. The 65-foot catamaran was propelled by aerodynamic force on an orientable, aspirated cylinder. A hollow aluminum structure 44 ft high and 5 ft in diameter, the cylinder has two perforated vents running from top to bottom. A "shutter-flap" positioned by a computer closes one of the vents while a 12-hp fan draws air into the cylinder through the open vent. The resulting lift force drives the hull through

Fig. 2.26 *Alcyone*, Captain Cousteau's two-masted windship, under way in company with *Calypso*. (*Photo from The Cousteau Society, a member-supported, nonprofit environmental organization*)

the water. By 1983, she had completed Mediterranean sea trials and started a trans-Atlantic passage. Near the end of the crossing the cylinder failed in heavy weather, but the principle had been proved. The "*Windmill's*" successor, *Alcyone* ("*Kingfisher*") is larger and carries two cylinders (Fig. 2.26). In 1986, she crossed the Atlantic, entered the Pacific, and in 1987 was making her way around the world.

Despite initial difficulties, this novel system has proven highly efficient in extracting propulsive energy from the wind. Its designers have calculated that a set of cylinders mounted on a commercial vessel can save 30 to 40% in fuel costs.

Nonconventional Boats

Conventional boats rely on buoyancy to support their hulls, but nondisplacement craft (*hovercraft* and *hydrofoils*) utilize aerodynamic or hydrodynamic lift for that purpose. The *SWATH* (Small Waterplane Area Twin Hull) boat has both above-water and underwater hulls, a design yielding remarkable stability in a seaway.

2.16 Hydrofoil Boats The *hydrofoil* uses underwater foils to obtain lift just as wings lift an airplane in air. With the hull partially above water, resistance is greatly reduced and speed increased. Fixed foils, the most common, are used for ferries up to several hundred feet in length, particularly in Russia on rivers and lakes. The Supermar PT series, made by Rodriguez in Italy, are used mainly in Europe in sheltered and semisheltered waters. Boats with movable foils, controlled by a wave sensor and a computer, are more seaworthy because they allow the boat to rise and fall in response to the waves it passes over. A combatant hydrofoil (Fig. 2.27) of this type has been developed by the United States, West Germany, and Italy. Powered by a gas turbine water jet, this design is intended as a standard NATO unit.

2.17 Hovercraft Air cushion vehicles (ACVs) or *hovercraft* (Fig. 2.28) ride over waves, land, or marsh on a cushion of air. A skirt contains the air bubble, which is maintained by gas-turbine driven compressors. Hovercraft ferries cross the English Channel. Other designs are used for military craft and for exploration. A water-only craft, driven by diesels and underwater propellors, serves as a ferry on the French Mediterranean coast.

2.18 SWATH Boats Named for her *Small Waterplane Area Twin Hull* design, the SWATH has three main structural sections: a wide shallow above-

Fig. 2.27 The guided-missile patrol combatant *Taurus* (PHM 3).

Fig. 2.28   An amphibious, air-cushioned assault landing craft. (*Official U.S. Navy photograph*)

water upper hull, a pair of submerged lower hulls mounted catamaran-style port and starboard, and the vertical struts connecting lower hulls to the upper hull. The two submerged hulls, shaped like torpedoes with propellors at the after ends, are large enough to provide buoyancy to keep the upper hull out of water. Only the struts pierce the water surface. The waterplane area is thus small, and the center of buoyancy remains almost fixed even as the boat passes through large waves. It is the change in location of the center of buoyancy that causes conventional hulls to roll and pitch; by preventing the center of buoyancy from moving the SWATH boat rides as steadily as ships three times as long.

To date only a few SWATH craft are in operation. These include an 88-foot U.S. Navy test craft, *Kaimalino* (Hawaiian for "calm sea" (Fig. 2.29), an 80-foot scalloper, and a 50-foot sport fisherman. Other and larger craft are under consideration for applications requiring stability in heavy seas such as hydrographic survey boats, rescue craft, acoustic surveillance vessels, and oceanographic research ships. Greater than normal draft and beam together with an inherently low cargo capacity will prevent universal adoption of the SWATH concept, but its stability may give it a unique place among rough-water craft.

References

Blair, Carvel Hall. *Seamanship: A Handbook for Oceanographers.* Centreville, MD: Cornell Maritime Press, 1977.

Fig. 2.29 The nonconventional Navy boat *Kaimalino*. Her Small Waterplane Area Twin Hull (SWATH) design gives unusually high stability in a seaway. (Photo from U.S. Naval Institute)

Chapman, W. *Piloting, Seamanship and Small Boat Handling*. New York: American Book-Stratford Press, 1984.

Henderson, Richard. *Sail and Power*, 3rd Edition. Annapolis, MD: U.S. Naval Institute Press, 1979.

Henderson, Richard. *Sea Sense*. Camden, ME: International Marine Publishing Co., 1972.

Noel, John V. *Boating Dictionary: Sail and Power*. New York: Van Nostrand Reinhold, 1981.

Rickey, Michael and Street, Donald M. The Sailing Encyclopedia. New York: Harper and Row, 1980.

Rousmaniere, John. *The Annapolis Book of Seamanship*. New York: Simon and Schuster, 1983.

U.S. Coast Guard. Motorboat Examination (aux 204). Washington, D.C.: Government Printing Office, 1986.

U.S. Coast Guard. Official Recreational Boating Guide (CG 340). Washington, D.C.: Government Printing Office, 1971.

Ship Structure, Stability, and Maintenance

Hull Structure

The main body of a ship exclusive of masts, superstructure, and the like, is called the *hull*. For a steel ship it is made up of plates covering a framework that in many ways is similar to the framework of a building or bridge. The hulls of various types and classes of vessels are basically similar despite the modifications that must be made to suit the particular mission of each. The sizes and arrangement of the hull plating and framing members must be chosen so that the ship can withstand the forces or loads imposed on it by the weight of cargo or other burden carried, by its own buoyancy, and by the conflicting dynamic forces caused by waves, wind, machinery vibrations, and ship motions.

Taken together, the hull structural members comprise a "box girder" of stiffened plating that must limit the tendency of the ship to bend longitudinally and thus prevent it from breaking in two in even the most severe seas. In addition, the structure must withstand the water pressure and local loads caused by heavy equipment, water shipped on deck, and drydocking loads, to name only a few.

3.1   Framing Systems   There are two major framing systems used in the construction of ships: the transverse and the longitudinal. In reality, most ships are built employing a combination of the two; however, one of the two systems will usually predominate. Both systems make use of transverse watertight bulkheads—from innerbottom to main deck—for watertight subdivision.

The transverse framing system employs closely spaced floors, side frames, and deck beams at right angles to the keel, with widely spaced longitudinal stiffeners. This system offers volumetric advantages for breakbulk cargo in that hold areas are relatively uncluttered by hull structure. Fore and aft strength is provided mainly by shell plating and decks, with some contribution being made by longitudinal deck girders in a typical "normal mixing" of transverse framing with limited longitudinal framing. Many merchant dry cargo ships and most naval auxiliary-type ships employ this mixed, but predominantly transverse, framing system. (See Fig. 3.1.)

The longitudinal framing system consists of longitudinally placed strength members on the shell plating and decks, supported by widely spaced, deep transverse web frames. Such longitudinal strength members, effectively continuous through most of the length of the ship, add appreciably to the longitudinal strength of the hull as a structural girder. Merchant tankers and bulk carriers can successfully utilize this framing system; conventional break-bulk dry cargo ships, however, suffer loss of cargo volume because of the protrusion of the deep webs into the cargo space. (See Fig. 3.2.)

The structural advantages of the longitudinal framing system are so significant in reducing structural weight while maintaining adequate strength that most modern ship designs employ this system as much as possible.

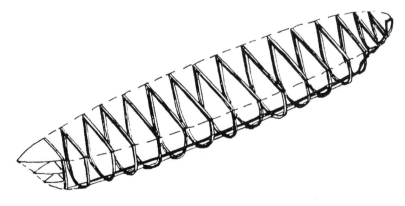

Fig. 3.1 Transverse framing system.

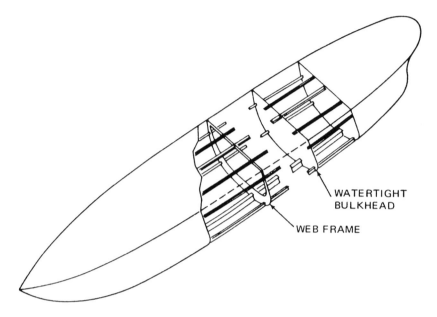

Fig. 3.2 Longitudinal framing system.

Thus the traditional transverse framing system in its "pure" form has given way to various combined systems. Dry cargo ships today usually have longitudinal stiffeners in decks and bottom structure, while retaining transverse framing in their sides. Special-purpose ships such as container ships, barge carriers, and roll-on/roll-off (RO/RO) ships employ predominantly longitudinal framing that has been adapted to their required arrangement of spaces. Naval warship construction uses a basically longitudinal framing system, with some combination of the two systems to achieve the greatest strength and least weight consistent with other design parameters.

3.2 Bottom Structure A very important part of the framing of any vessel is the bottom centerline longitudinal, known as the *keel*. This assembly is normally made up of vertical and horizontal members—the vertical member being called the *center vertical keel*; the bottom horizontal member, the *flat keel*; and the upper horizontal member, the *keel rider plate*. These three members form a deep girder type of structure of longitudinal continuity and strength that will withstand the various severe loadings to which the ship may be subjected, as when it is drydocked or inadvertently grounded. This girder is often referred to as the backbone of the ship. It is continuous from the forward end, where it joins the stem, to the after end, where it joins the stern post or the stern assembly. Merchant ships, except tankers, usually have double bottoms in order to protect holds from flooding after bottom damage so long as the second inner bottom remains intact. The double bottom spaces are used as fuel or ballast tanks.

3.3 Decks Decks are used primarily to provide structural strength, shelter, cargo stowage, working spaces, and living quarters. In transversely framed ships, the decks are supported by deep fore-and-aft members called *deck girders* and by athwartship members called *deck beams.* Deck girders are in turn supported by *stanchions,* or pillars, to provide the decks with support additional to that afforded by the bulkheads. In longitudinally framed ships, the decks are supported by longitudinal members that in turn are supported by transverse bulkheads and by deep athwartship beams. The uppermost deck extending from stem to stern is called the *main deck.* A partial deck above the main deck at the bow is called the *forecastle deck;* at the stern, *poop deck;* amidships, *upper deck* or *bridge deck.* A complete deck below the main deck is called the *second deck.* Two or more complete decks below the main deck are called the *second deck, third deck, fourth deck,* etc. Within *deckhouses,* decks above the upper deck are named according to their principal use (*boat deck, navigating deck,* etc.)

3.4 Bulkheads Transverse watertight *bulkheads* subdivide the ship into independent compartments to limit the extent of flooding in case the hull is open to the sea by collision, enemy action, or accidental causes. They also help maintain the shape of the hull against transverse deformation. Other bulkheads are fitted as necessary to provide separate spaces for cargo, tanks, engines, living and navigation needs, etc. Bulkheads are stiffened plated structures similar to those of the side shell.

Hull Shapes

The power required to achieve the design speed of a ship depends to a great extent on the shape of her hull below the waterline, that is, the *underwater body.* The maximum width of the hull, called the *beam,* is near the halfway point between the bow and stern, and the hull in this vicinity is called the *middle-body section.* The *parallel middle body* refers to that portion of the hull through which the section shape remains unchanged. From the middle-body section, the lines of the hull slope smoothly to the bow and stern. The narrowing part of the underwater body forward of the middle-body section is called the *entrance.* The corresponding part aft is called the *run.* A ship that has a long and tapering entrance and run and a proportionally short middle-body section is said to have *fine lines,* or a *fine form,* as may be found, say, in a fast naval vessel. A ship with a long parallel middle body combined with a relatively short entrance and run—such as a large, slow bulk carrier—is said to have a *full form.* Her boxlike middle body is comparatively long to give her greater carrying capacity.

3.5 Lines The hull form can be completely defined in a three-view line drawing, in which the detailed shapes of various cross sections (*stations*), horizontal sections (*waterlines*), and longitudinal vertical sections (*buttocks*) are shown. There are many variations in underwater shape to suit each vessel to its particular speed, size, and mission. For example, a cigar-shaped bulb may be fitted at the lower part of the stem. This shape is known as a *bulbous bow* and enables a vessel so fitted to attain greater speeds at or near full power than a vessel not so equipped. Terms defining the shape of ship sections are defined in Fig. 3.3.

There are a wide variety of shapes for bows in addition to the bulbous bow. Most common on modern ships is the *raked bow*. Illustrations of several types of bow shapes are shown in Fig. 3.4.

Stern shapes vary depending on whether a ship is single- or multiple-screw, on ship speed, and on an analysis of the flow patterns around the stern that are needed to optimize propeller performance. Typical stern shapes are shown in Fig. 3.5.

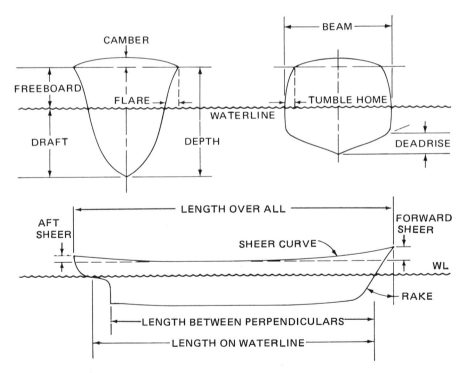

Fig. 3.3 Definition of hull form terms.

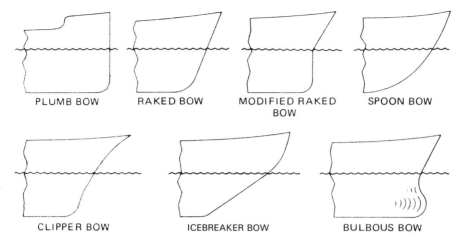

Fig. 3.4 Common bow shapes.

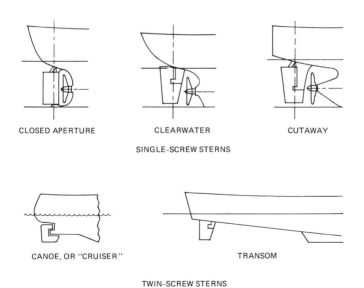

Fig. 3.5 Common stern shapes.

Stability

The static stability of a ship is the measure of her tendency to return to the upright after being inclined by external forces such as wind or waves. A ship's stability is influenced by her underwater form, or shape, and by the amount and position of the weights or loading placed aboard the ship. Determining the dimensions, proportions, and shape of the hull for adequate stability in a properly loaded ship is the business of the ship designer. It is the ship's operating personnel, however, who have control over her loading. Hence they must understand the basic principles of stability so as to avoid loading conditions that will produce too little or too much stability.

3.6 Weight and Buoyancy A ship when afloat is acted on by two principal forces—its weight and its buoyancy—that are equal to each other but act in opposite directions. (See Fig. 3.6.) The weight acts downward through a point called the *center of gravity, G.* The buoyancy acts upward through the *center of buoyancy, B.*

The *weight* force is the sum of the weights of the *light ship* (fully equipped but unladen) plus its *deadweight* (total weight carried, including cargo, fuel, fresh water, stores, passengers, crew, baggage, etc.). The location of G depends on the amount and location of each deadweight item, and it must be calculated (as described later) for each voyage of the ship. Weights are normally loaded in such a way that G lies on the centerline plane of the ship, otherwise the ship would have a permanent list.

The *buoyancy force* is the sum of the vertical components of the hydrostatic pressure on the underwater body. It is also equal to the weight of the water displaced by the underwater body. (This weight displaced by a ship, called her *displacement,* is normally expressed in long tons. A *long ton* equals 2240 lb and is equivalent to the weight of 35 cubic feet of sea water or 35.9 cubic feet of fresh water. The *metric ton* used by many nations equals 1000 kg, or 2205 lb.) In order for the ship to remain afloat, the buoyant force must equal the weight, and both are called the displacement, Δ. The force of buoyancy thus keeps the ship afloat, but it may be overcome and the ship sunk if too much weight is introduced, as would be the case when too many holds or compartments are flooded. The center of buoyancy, B, represents that point through which the resultant of all upward forces is considered to act; it lies in the geometric center of the underwater form of the vessel. When the ship is upright, B is in the vertical-longitudinal centerline plane, and the upward force of buoyancy is directly under the point G, where all the weight of the vessel is considered concentrated. It is thus seen that B depends on the ship's geometry, whereas G depends on the ship's loading.

The condition just described, illustrated by Fig. 3.6(a), is called an *equi-*

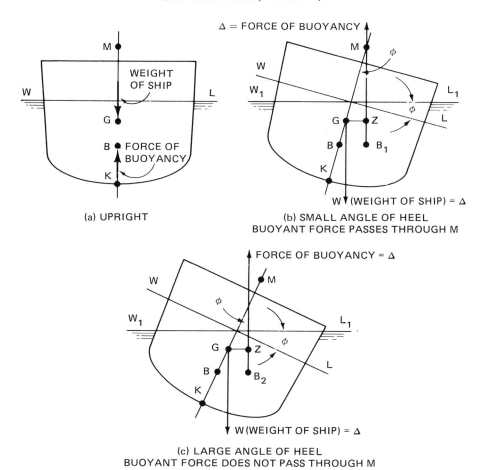

Fig. 3.6 Forces acting on a hull.

librium ("state of balance") condition of the floating ship. The question of a ship's stability when upright depends on whether the upright equilibrium condition is a *stable* or *unstable* equilibrium. If it is stable, the ship will return to upright after a slight inclination. If unstable, the ship will incline further after the force causing inclination is removed. At best, an unstable ship assumes a small angle of *loll* (heel, or list, caused by instability), at which stable equilibrium is regained. At worst, a very unstable ship may capsize because stability cannot be achieved except in an inverted condition.

3.7 Righting Moments When an external force heels the ship to an angle of ϕ degrees away from upright, the center of buoyancy moves toward the lower side of the ship, as shown in Fig. 3.6(b). The underwater shape under waterline W_1L_1 (as distinct from the waterline of equilibrium, WL) is then not symmetrical about the ship's centerline, and the buoyant force shifts from B to B_1. The ship is no longer in equilibrium (B is not below G), and the weight and buoyancy forces comprise a *couple* (parallel instead of in-line equal opposites), this couple being measured by the product of the displacement, Δ, times the distance between the weight and buoyancy forces. That distance, GZ, is called the *righting arm* whenever, as in the case shown in Fig. 3.6(b), the resulting couple will produce a rotation sufficient to reright the ship. The product $\Delta \times GZ$ is called the *righting moment*.

When the *angle of heel,* ϕ, is small (up to about 10 degrees), the vertical through B_1 intersects the ship centerline at point M, called the *transverse metacenter.* The location of M depends on the hull form and is largely influenced by the beam of the ship. On a broad ship, B_1 will move far from the centerline, but on a narrow one, not nearly so much. Thus, M is, in general, higher in the broader ship, making it more stable.

What causes a ship to be unstable? In Fig. 3.6(b), depicting a small angle of heel, it can be seen that since G is below M, a righting moment exists, but if G had been above M, the couple would rotate the ship so as to increase the angle of heel rather than to right the ship. The moment would then be a *heeling moment* instead of a righting moment, and the ship would be said to be unstable.

3.8   KG and GM Calculations   The height of M above the keel (point K) varies only with the *draft* of the ship (that is, the depth of water it draws) and with the hull shape, and is not under the control of the ship operator. The location of the center of gravity, on the other hand, is very much under his control, since it depends on the distribution of the deadweight items carried. For each loading condition, the height of the center of gravity above the keel, KG, is calculated as follows.

$$KG = \frac{W_L KG_L + W_1 Kg_1 + W_2 Kg_2 + \ldots + W_n Kg_n}{W_L + W_1 + W_2 + \ldots + W_n}$$

$$= \frac{\text{Sum of moments about keel}}{\text{Loaded weight, or displacement}}$$

where

$$
\begin{aligned}
KG &= \text{height of } G \text{ above keel in loaded condition} \\
W_L &= \text{light ship displacement (weight)} \\
KG_L &= \text{height of } G \text{ above keel in light ship condition} \\
W_1 \ldots W_n &= \text{weights of all items loaded} \\
Kg_1 \ldots Kg_n &= \text{heights of loaded items above keel}
\end{aligned}
$$

This calculation is performed for each voyage by entering into a loading calculation form, provided on the ship, the weights loaded into each compartment on the ship (holds, tanks, etc.). The loading form includes the Kg values for each space. Thus, the ship's officer can plan his loading in advance so that the fingal KG will provide adequate stability.

Adequate stability involves calculating the *metacentric height, GM,* which is the distance of the center of gravity below the transverse metacenter. This calculation is as follows:

$$GM = KM - KG$$

where

GM = metacentric height
KM = height of M above keel (recorded in stability booklet for any draft)
KG = height of G above keel (as calculated using the loading form)

The minimum GM required for safe operation differs from ship to ship and is provided in each ship's stability booklet. It is based on predictions of the loss of stability the ship would sustain if various spaces were flooded.

3.9   Free Surface   In light of the foregoing, special precautions must be exercised in the distribution of liquids in the ship's fuel, water, liquid cargo, and ballast tanks. If any liquids do not completely fill their tanks, they are said to be *slack* and to have a *free surface.* As the ship heels, such liquids shift to the low side, thus causing the ship's center of gravity to shift as well and the angle of heel to increase. The effect of free surface is to reduce the metacentric height by an amount that depends not only on the number, size, and proportions of the tanks that are slack but also on the density of the liquids carried. Care must be taken to limit free surface by minimizing the number of tanks left slack at any one time.

The *Trim and Stability Booklet* furnished on every ship contains tables and calculation procedures that enable the ship's officer to calculate the reduction in stability caused by free surface for any combination of slack tanks.

3.10   Overall Stability   Metacentric height is a measure of the stability of a ship when it is upright or within a few degrees of upright. When the ship heels to larger angles, the buoyant force does not pass through the metacenter, as it does for the small angle shown in Fig. 3.6(b). For large angles of heel, the buoyant force may be that shown through point B_2 in Fig. 3.6(c). Assessing the ship's stability then requires the direct calculation of the righting arm, GZ. This is a complex task performed by the naval architects who designed the ship, but a few general observations on stability at large angles of heel are useful for shipboard personnel to know.

As the ship heels to ever-larger angles, the righting arm increases until it reaches a maximum approximately when the main deck edge is first awash. Further heeling starts to decrease the arm until it becomes zero, and the vessel can no longer right itself. The angle of heel at which the righting arm becomes zero is called the *angle of vanishing stability,* and it defines the limit of the *range of stability.* Heeling or rolling beyond this angle will capsize the ship. Fortunately, for undamaged ships of normal form, the range of stability is quite large, often more than 90 degrees. Because the righting arm increases until the deck edge immerses, a ship with *high freeboard* (a passenger ship, for example, its freeboard deck being especially high above the waterline) tends to have a large range of stability and can thus tolerate a relatively small *GM.* The reverse is the case for a low-freeboard tanker, which reaches maximum *GZ* at a smaller angle of heel and hence requires a larger *GM* to develop adequate righting arms at large angles of heel.

Some *Trim and Stability Booklets* contain the information needed to calculate the righting arms at any angle of heel and condition of loading. With this information, the ship's officer can determine and plot a statical stability curve for each voyage. This curve shows the trend of *GZ* against angle of heel through the angles of deck-edge immersion, maximum stability, and vanishing stability.

3.11 Stability Summary   Several aspects of a ship's stability are important for the safety of the ship, as follows:

1. Its *initial* and *overall stability.* Initial stability is the resistance of a ship to initial heeling when upright. Overall stability is the resistance of a ship to heeling caused by static forces throughout its range of stability.
2. Its *range of stability.* Range of stability is the total angle through which the righting arm is positive. It is the angle of heel either to port or to starboard through which a vessel tends to return to an upright position.
3. Its *dynamic stability.* Dynamic stability is the righting energy available to resist heeling through an angle not greater than the angle of vanishing stability.

Initial stability is measured by the transverse metacentric height in feet, which is the distance from the center of gravity up to the metacenter. The center of gravity and the *KM* remain fixed for any particular condition of loading. Both may change for different loadings, with a resulting change in the metacentric height (*GM*). Any change in this can be quickly estimated by the formula:

$$GM = \left(\frac{0.44B}{T}\right)^2$$

where

   GM = approximate transverse metacentric height, in feet
     B = ship's beam, in feet
     T = time, in seconds, of a complete roll (e.g., port to starbord to port)
  0.44 = a constant representing an average for various hull forms

Thus, if flooding has caused the period of the roll to be doubled, the *GM* has been quartered, and in all probability the ship is in danger. The decision to abandon a ship or to attempt to save her is based greatly on this newly calculated *GM*.

A dangerously low *GM* can be increased by lowering the center of gravity by completely flooding some of the lowest tanks and by casting overboard heavy topside weights. Another tack would be to remove any free surfaces by completely flooding, or pumping out, fresh-water or fuel-oil tanks, especially if those tanks run athwartship, and to remove water from the bilges.

A ship with a long, easy roll makes a good platform and a good passenger ship, but the very fact that she has an easy roll is a sign of a low metacentric height. A ship with a too-large *GM* will have a quick, jerky roll that is uncomfortable and potentially dangerous. It can cause cargo to break loose in heavy seas.

The relationship of freeboard-to-beam is an important factor in stability. A ship with a large beam has very large initial stability (small heel angle), whereas a ship with a large freeboard tends to develop large righting arms at large angles of heel because the deck edge does not immerse at small angles. Thus there is a trade-off between freeboard and beam. Ships with a large freeboard-to-beam ratio achieve a large range of stability even though they have a low *GM*. On the other hand, ships in which this ratio is small must have a large *GM* to achieve such stability.

The work utilized in the inclining of a ship is the meaure of its dynamic stability. If the force of the sea acting on a ship becomes great enough to heel her over until the righting arm becomes zero, the ship will not be able to right itself. The apparent force of the sea is greatest when the period of the ship and that of the waves are in synchronism, thereby building up a much deeper roll. This force can be controlled by the ship's changing course or speed or both, for these actions alter the apparent period of the waves relative to the ship.

3.12 Stability of Submarines The principles presented above for surface ships apply equally to *surfaced* submarines. However, the rapidly increasing righting arm at moderate angles of inclination exhibited by surface ships, up to the point of deck edge immersion, is not experienced in submarines. This is true principally because, with their nearly circular cross-section, the waterline breadth does not change appreciably when inclined. Because the center of gravity is normally very low in a submarine, it enjoys relatively good stability both on the surface and when fully submerged. During the transitional period of submerging, a submarine possesses the least transverse stability, primarily as a result of the free-surface effect of water being flooded into the main ballast tanks. This free-surface effect does not exist when the submarine is on the surface, except what may be caused by a small quantity of residual water in the tanks, and it does not exist when the sub is fully submerged, as the main ballast tanks are then completely filled.

3.13 Anti-rolling Devices Certain artificial methods are sometimes used to reduce a ship's roll. *Bilge keels* are plated structures attached outside the hull and extending from the turn of the bilge. These keels have the function of damping the roll of the ship. Since their introduction in the late 1800s, bilge keels have been installed on nearly all ocean-going ships, both commercial and military. Some large warships built during this period were not fitted with bilge keels, their sheer bulk being presumed to provide enough resistance to roll; these ships were almost invariably fitted with bilge keels after service showed them to be heavy rollers.

Other anti-roll devices have been designed and installed on limited numbers of ships. These include anti-roll tanks, gyroscopic stabilizers, and anti-roll fins. The first two share with bilge keels the advantage that they do not depend on ship speed for their effectiveness. All active-fin stabilizing systems are designed to take advantage of the hydrodynamic lift forces created by the fin, which is at an angle to the water flow created by the ship's speed. Fin stabilization is ineffective when the ship is stopped or at anchor.

Although both anti-roll tanks and stabilizing fins—and gyroscopic stabilizers to a lesser degree—have proven very successful in reducing roll, their disadvantages in cost, weight and space required, and power consumption (if required) have restricted their use. Bilge keels—of slight weight and cost, completely passive, requiring no power, and, since installed on the exterior, requiring no internal space, will undoubtedly remain the predominant form of anti-roll device.

Hull Damage Control

The stability principles considered in this chapter are useful to the seaman to the extent that they explain in general why the undamaged, properly loaded ship remains upright in heavy weather. They also reveal the range and type of response that may be expected from the undamaged ship. If damage occurs, it is necessary to apply these principles quickly to save the ship. In the application of these principles it is important to realize how damage may reduce margins of buoyancy and stability. Damage sustained by vessels in peacetime accidents is often similar to the effect of wartime enemy action; a peacetime collision with possible attendant fires and explosions may be just as serious as an enemy hit.

After serious damage or in heavy weather, the captain must be guided by three factors if he is to save his ship: He must maintain *power*, buoyancy, and *stability*. The damaged ship sometimes may be able to survive in calm waters by maintaining only buoyancy and stability, but it may often be impossible to do this without power. Flooded engineering compartments or water that reaches main switchboards (through flooding or through ventilators) are important causes of power loss.

3.14 Shipboard Fire Uncontrolled fire aboard ship is the single greatest catastrophe that can occur to a ship that remains afloat. Although modern construction techniques and materials have reduced the danger of shipboard fire, consumable supplies, such as paint stores and dry and liquid cargo, pose an ever-present threat. Once started, shipboard fires are difficult and sometimes impossible to extinguish. Several classic examples of relatively small initial fires, that eventually completely destroyed ships are the *S.S. Normandie,* which capsized at her berth as a result of added water used for fire fighting, the *U.S.S. Lexington,* and the *U.S.S. Franklin.* The *Lexington* was lost as a direct result of uncontrolled fire resulting from battle damage; and the *Franklin,* although saved from fire damage, cost about 2000 casualties. Small fires may disrupt essential circuits, causing a loss in power and communications. Except for carbon dioxide systems, all fire extinguishing systems add free-surface water and a resultant loss in stability during the course of fire-fighting.

3.15 Overall Consequences of Hull Damage War experience has shown that whenever a ship suffers damage involving serious flooding, either the damage is so extensive that the vessel never stops listing or settling in the water and goes down within a few minutes, or the vessel stops heeling, changing trim, and settling in the water shortly after initial damage.

Experience has also shown that in most cases in which a vessel did survive for several hours after damage, but then sank, she might have been saved by controlling secondary flooding. To do so requires proper training of the crew. The flooding usually comes about in the following manner:

As a result of a hit or collision, a large hole is opened in the side. Several bulkheads and decks may be carried away just inside this hole. Immediate flooding occurs through these added large holes, giving the ship her initial list, trim, and reduced stability.

In addition to the large holes, there may be a certain amount of subsidiary damage, with riddled or warped bulkheads and decks, leaking doors and hatches, etc. These permit slow leakage and progressive flooding past the boundaries of the damage. The slow flooding is aggravated if personnel escaping from the damaged area leave doors or scuttles open behind them.

3.16   Action Before and After Damage   Precautions before any damage is sustained will often determine whether or not efforts to save the ship afterward can be successful. As a rule, warships are better able to cope with damage. They are usually more fully compartmented than merchant ships and have more men and equipment to rally against the damage. There has been an increasing tendency both to design and to operate merchant ships with a higher capacity to resist damage. Moreover, on both naval and merchant ships there has been a growing understanding that the captain or master has a vital primary role in ensuring precautions against damage at sea. These consist generally of the following:

1. Utilization of designed hull safety features at all times when at sea (such as ensuring that watertight boundaries are faithfully maintained)
2. Ensuring that the ship is not overloaded
3. Ensuring that deck loads are not exceeded
4. Ensuring proper amount and distribution of liquid and other cargo and ballast
5. Ensuring that crew members are trained to localize damage insofar as facilities of the ship permit

The loss of the *Andrea Doria* is well known by mariners as an example of how improper liquid loading can doom a ship to sinking. When one of her huge, off-center, empty fuel tanks ruptured and filled, the *Andrea Doria* suddenly increased her list nearly 20 degrees.

There exists, in any situation where the vessel does not sink immediately, an excellent chance of saving her if slow leaks can be patched and plugged. Bulkheads that have not collapsed under the blast and onrush of water from the hit are not likely to collapse under hydrostatic pressure.

Immediately after serious damage, *two important decisions* must be made: (1) whether all hands should remain aboard, whether all but the salvage party should be evacuated, or whether all hands should abandon ship; and (2) what corrective measures will improve the situation instead of making it worse. The first of these decisions is made by the captain, but his conclusions must be based on information that he receives from the engineer. The second decision is frequently the problem of the engineer, unless it involves ship handling or loss of military efficiency (as through jettisoning ammunition).

3.17 The Enemies of Stability If a ship's tank or void is only partially full, the liquid contents may "slosh" back and forth with the motion of the ship (previously defined as *free surface*). A similar effect is noted if a compartment is partially flooded.

If the hull is ruptured so that one or more compartments are open to the sea, *free communication with the sea* results.

Free surface and free communication with the sea are, when combined, the deadly enemies of stability.

There is little excuse for excess free surface; the captain who takes his ship into heavy weather with excessive or avoidable free surface in his tanks is foolhardy. The ship with initial free surface space that is so damaged that it also acquires loose water and free communication with the sea will almost surely be in danger. Free surface should be avoided, since it always causes a reduction in *GM* and overall stability, as described earlier. Free communication with the sea not only reduces *GM, but GZ as well*. Thus, not only is some initial stability lost, but since *GZ* decreases, there will be a decrease in the ship's righting moment.

Tonnage and Load Lines

3.18 Measurement—Gross and Net Tonnages Under the current U.S. regulations for existing ships, *gross tonnage* is a volume measure of the total enclosed space of a ship (with certain space exemptions) expressed in tons of 100 cubic feet each. This unit of volume was originally used in the "Moorsom system," and this system, with some annoying variations in application, has been adopted by most maritime nations.

Net tonnage, which was intended to relate to the earning power of a ship, is derived from gross tonnage by deducting spaces that may have no earning capacity. Spaces such as engine and boiler rooms, shaft alleys, bunkers, and crew accommodations are generally considered deductible. Laws of the various maritime nations vary in the extent to which deductions are permitted.

A 1961 survey of the Inter-Governmental Maritime Consultative Organization (IMCO) of the United Nations (now called the International Maritime Organization, IMO) determined that, among the 25 major maritime nations responding, there was considerable disparity in the ways that gross and net tonnage were used for charges, fees, and statutory purposes. Because of the differences, the International Convention on Tonnage Measurement of Ships (1969) developed a universal system subject to acceptance by member states of the United Nations. This Convention came into force in July 1982 for new vessels. Existing ships may be exempt from the new convention for up to 12 years.

3.19 Tonnage Log Functions   Under the 1969 Convention, the gross tonnage is a logarithmic function of the total enclosed volume of the ship (in cubic meters) without exemptions, whereas the net tonnage is a logarithmic function of the total cargo volume with adjustment for high-freeboard ships and an additional function for the number of passengers when these number more than 12. One effect of the 1969 Convention is that the tonnages are no longer measures of "tons" of 100 cubic feet each. In fact, the volumes must be measured in cubic meters, the ratio of cubic meters to tonnage is no longer constant, and the word "tons" no longer appears.

This adjustment was necessary in order to maintain numerical values of tonnage as reasonably close as possible to those determined under various national systems for existing vessels.

3.20 Load Line Markings   In accordance with the International Load Line Convention (1966), which became effective in July 1968, load lines were established for all new vessels 79 feet or more in length and for all existing vessels of 150 gross tons or over if they engage in foreign voyages or international voyages by sea (other than solely on Great Lakes voyages) and fly the flag of a country adhering to the convention. (Exceptions to this rule are the following: ships of war, fishing vessels, pleasure craft (yachts) not used or engaged in trade or commerce, new vessels less than 79 feet in length and existing vessels of less than 150 gross tons.)

Special load lines for vessels engaged in voyages on the Great Lakes and in coastwise voyages by sea must conform to the Coastwise Load Line Act of 1935 (as amended).

3.21 Meaning of the Markings   Load line markings indicate the drafts at which, for various conditions and types or classes of vessels, there will still be left a sufficient percentage of reserve buoyancy to ensure the vessel's safety. On it are indicated the maximum safe drafts for salt and fresh water, for winter and summer, and for various geographical regions defined by the Convention.

3.22   American Bureau of Shipping Responsibility   As provided in the Load Line Act, the American Bureau of Shipping assigns load lines and issues load-line certificates. Corresponding classification societies in other nations serve the same purpose. The authority by whom the load lines are assigned may be indicated by letters marked alongside the disk and above the centerline (Fig. 3.7).

3.23   U.S. Navy Markings   Although excepted from the International Load Line regulations, U.S. Navy warships display a draft limit marking, in addition to draft numerals. The mark, shown in Fig. 3.8, may be located either near the draft numerals or amidship.

3.24   Draft in Fresh Water   The draft of a ship will be greater in fresh water than in sea water because fresh water is less dense. Hence, as shown in Fig. 3.7, the fresh water load line ''F'' allows a deeper draft loading than that allowed by the summer load line ''S,'' or the center of the marker disk, which is the limiting load draft in sea water, unless in tropical waters. The fresh water draft mark permits loading to a point exceeding the sea water mark in a fresh water port, river, or lake, and then proceeding out to sea without immersing the sea water mark.

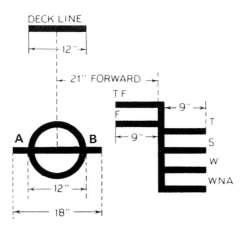

Fig. 3.7 Explanation of symbols of the load line mark for cargo ships and tankers:
TF—Tropical fresh water load line   S—Summer load line
F—Fresh water load line   W—Winter load line
T—Tropical load line   WNA—Winter North Atlantic load line

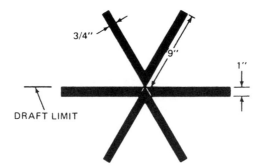

Fig. 3.8 U.S. Navy load line marking.

Hull Maintenance

Without proper care, both wood and metal hulls deteriorate rapidly to the point of being unsafe and unusable. Wooden hulls are subject not only to rot and deterioration when not properly protected from the atmosphere but also to damage from marine animals and marine growths that attack the underwater body. Metal hulls must be protected from fouling, corrosion, and erosion in order to maintain their seaworthiness.

3.25 Fouling Marine animals and marine growths that damage the hull of a ship or retard its speed are natives of salt water and, in general, are more common and damaging in tropical waters than in colder climates. The underwater pest that causes the most trouble on steel hulls is the barnacle, although mussels and marine grasses of various sorts are also found attached to the underwater body. Barnacles and other marine growths apparently do little damage to a steel hull, except to destroy the protective paint and allow seawater to promote corrosion, but they may reduce the speed of a ship as much as several knots by increasing skin friction between the water and the hull. Modern anti-fouling paints have been developed that are effective in preventing or retarding fouling.

3.26 Corrosion The greatest problem in the care and preservation of metals is corrosion. Corrosion is the gradual disintegration of a metal caused by chemical or electrochemical attack by atmosphere, moisture, or other agents. There are many different types of corrosion. A technical discussion of the various types may be found in any standard reference work on the subject.

Although a ship does not encounter any corrosion problems that may not be found anywhere else, it does encounter virtually all types of corrosion. A bronze propeller secured to a steel shaft and turning in an electrolyte (sea water) introduces the possibility of electrochemical attack on the shaft and the ship's hull. The propeller itself may suffer from cavitation and corrosion-erosion attack. Pumps handling seawater are subject to similar conditions. Propeller and pump shafts are also subject to corrosion fatigue.

The hull and superstructure of a vessel are usually made of plain carbon steel, and any seaman knows the amount of chipping and painting necessary to combat the severe rust caused by a marine atmosphere. Some superstructures have been built of aluminum alloys that resist atmospheric corrosion and save topside weight. Aluminum, however, is not fire-resistant.

The various means for preventing or minimizing corrosion may be classified under four headings:

1. *Use of Alloys That Resist Attack by Particular Environments*   The resistance to atmospheric attack of such materials as the copper-base alloys, stainless steels, and Monel metal is well known, but there is no single alloy that is immune to all corroding media. However, the addition of alloying elements in even small amounts may greatly improve the resistance of a particular material to a given environment. About 0.25 percent copper added to a carbon steel will double its resistance to atmosphere corrosion. Copper-nickel is an excellent material for condenser tubes, but its resistance to seawater is greatly improved by the addition of 0.2 to 0.6 percent iron. Depending on environment, the corrosion resistance of stainless steels may be improved by small additions of manganese, silicon, columbium, titanium, molybdenum, or nitrogen.

2. *Use of Galvanic Protection*   The electrochemical mechanism may be utilized for protecting a structural metal in contact with an electrolyte. This *galvanic protection* (also called *cathodic protection*) consists of attaching to the structure a metal that is anodic to the one to be protected, thus sacrificing the added metal and protecting the structure. Zinc is commonly used to protect steel, cast iron, brass, and bronze. The zinc must be in good electrical contact with the metal to be protected and with the electrolyte. Galvanic protection is used for propeller shafts, rudders, and hull plates by attaching zinc plates near the propellers.

3. *Control of Environment*   Metals have very low corrosion rates in dry gases and in pure water free from air. An outstanding example of control of environment is the dehumidification practiced in the mothballing program carried out by the armed forces since the end of World War II. The sealed interiors of ships were kept dry with air-conditioning machines; guns, tanks, planes, etc., were completely sealed in moistureproof covers and provided with moisture-absorbing agents.

4. *Use of Protective Coatings*   These may be divided into four classes: (a) chemical coatings, (b) organic coatings, (c) inorganic coatings, and (d) metallic coatings.

Chemical coatings are those formed by chemical reaction between a metal surface and an appropriate solution. The application of phosphate coatings to the ferrous metals is representative of this group. The part to be protected is dipped in or sprayed with a solution of phosphates, and the coating that forms not only is resistant to atmospheric corrosion but serves as an excellent base for paints. Some magnesium and aluminum alloys are similarly protected with chromate coatings. Oxide and silicate coatings may also be chemically produced on certain metals.

Organic coatings include paint, varnish, plastics, natural and synthetic rubbers, and bituminous and petroleum products. In general, these materials form a mechanical film to exclude air and moisture from the metal surface. Their effectiveness depends on the initial cleanliness of the metal and on the film thickness. All of them may be satisfactory for prolonged periods of time, depending on the environment and whether or not the protected surface is subjected to abrasion.

Inorganic coatings consist of inorganic zinc silicates. Depending on the composition, some adhere to the surface by a mechanical bond, whereas some adhere by a combination of mechanical and chemical bonding.

Metallic coatings serve to cover a corrodible metal with a thin layer of another metal that is more resistant to attack. Sometimes the coating also provides galvanic protection, as is the case with zinc or cadmium coatings on the ferrous metals. Metallic coatings may be applied by electroplating, hot dipping, or metallizing, as follows:

Electroplating consists of making the clean base metal the cathode in an electrolytic cell containing a water solution of some salt of the metal being deposited. Close control of the process is essential to good non-porous plating. Copper, nickel, chromium, cadmium, and zinc are electrodeposited on iron and steel as corrosion preventives.

Hot dipping consists of immersing the cleaned base metal in a molten bath of the coating metal. The process is suitable for those metals that will wet each other. Zinc and tin coatings are commonly applied by hot dipping.

Metallizing is a metal-spraying process in which a wire or powder of the coating metal is melted by an oxyacetylene flame in the presence of an air jet that atomizes the metal and sprays it onto the base metal.

The base metal must have a roughened surface since the bonding is purely mechanical. Virtually all metals can be sprayed, and the process is used to build up worn parts and provide hard surfaces as well as for corrosion resistance.

No protective coating that will last indefinitely under water has been devised. Damage to underwater fittings may occur that will remain undetected as long as the fittings remain submerged. The only practical method for preserving the underwater hull is to remove it from the water at intervals, make needed repairs, and give it the best protective coating available before refloating. This routine is generally known as *drydocking.*

Drydocking

3.27 Schedules and Routine Merchant ships classed with the American Bureau of Shipping are drydocked for special periodic surveys. The outer shell, stem, and stern frames, as well as the keel, are cleaned and inspected. Tanks are tested under pressure. The rudder and its supports are checked for unusual wear and rebushed if necessary. The anchor chain is ranged and inspected and usually repainted. Every third year a merchant ship's tail shaft is drawn and inspected.

3.28 Types of Drydock For the ordinary steel vessel, the usual methods of drydocking are by the use of marine railways, floating drydocks, and graving docks.

A *marine railway* is an inclined shipway having a cradle on wheels that runs on rails. It is moved by means of a windlass and endless chain. Few marine railways will handle a ship larger than a moderate-sized destroyer.

The typical *floating drydock* (see Figs. 3.9 and 3.10) is made up of rectangular, open-ended sections that can be fastened firmly together. Tanks are flooded with water to sink the dock far enough for a ship to enter the cradle and then are pumped out so as to raise the ship and the inner part of the dock clear of the water. By using enough sections of suitable dimensions, all except the very largest ships can be accommodated. Sections of the dock also can be used to dock one another. One of the great advantages of floating drydocks is that they can be towed to the localities where they are most needed. The mobility of floating drydocks has been increased greatly as a result of the types of construction developed by the U.S. Navy in the past few years. Floating drydocks for smaller vessels are built in one piece with the usual ship-type bow and are equipped with a steering mechanism. For ease in towing, a section with a ship-type bow may also be provided for larger sectional drydocks. Most floating drydock sections are self-contained. They have pumps for emptying their ballast tanks and power

Fig. 3.9 The floating drydock U.S.S. ARD 30 set up for its next ship. All blocks are precut to fit ships individually. (*Official U.S. Navy photograph*)

Fig. 3.10 A medium auxiliary floating drydock (AFDM 6) moves into its mooring facilities. (*Official U.S. Navy photograph*)

plants and other facilities for the storage and distribution of such services as oil, compressed air, steam, and electric current; they may also be equipped with machine shops and with quarters for their crews.

A *graving dock* (Fig. 3.11) is a permanent installation in a shipyard. It is a basin with walls and a floor, usually built of reinforced concrete, into which vessels may be floated and from which the water may be pumped out, leaving the vessels dry and supported on blocks. It is used not only for

Fig. 3.11 Flooding begins in drydock at the Long Beach Naval Shipyard prior to the entry of a ship. (*Official U.S. Navy photograph*)

repairing and cleaning the underwater hulls of ships but in some cases for building ships.

Graving docks are built at the shore line, with one end left open to navigable water in order to allow the entrance of ships. This open end is usually closed by a caisson or gate, either floating or sliding. In some docks, a double swinging gate is used. The most usual type, the *floating caisson*, is a self-pumping hollow gate that is floated and towed clear when the dock is flooded. After a ship enters the dock, the caisson is moved into place and flooded with water, which causes its ends to sink into wedge-shaped grooves cut in the walls of the dock while its base fits against and is supported by a sill that extends across the entrance of the dock and is raised somewhat above its floor. The depth of water over the sill at high tide determines the greatest draft of any ship that can be docked. In a naval shipyard dock especially, it is desirable that this depth be greater than the ordinary draft of any ship that it is expected to accommodate so as to allow for any increased draft occasioned by battle damage.

Power capstans and fixed bollards are installed to control the lines used in hauling the ship in and out of the dock. Blocks are heavy wooden structures used to build up the cradle in which the ship rests while in dock. The *keel blocks,* upon which the ship's keel is supported, are large cube-shaped, semi-fixed structures built up of concrete, hardwood, and soft pine caps. Other blocks, called *bilge blocks* or *side blocks,* are prepositioned in accordance with the individual ship's docking plan. Should bilge blocks not be available and a ship have insufficient flat bottom for the installation of enough keel blocks to keep her upright, *wale shores* may be used. These are spars extending from the ship's side to the side of the dock and wedged in place as she settles upon the keel blocks. If several small vessels are to be docked at once, blocks may be set up for them on appropriate sections of the dock floor.

3.29 Preparations for Docking   In preparing a dock to receive a vessel, the dockmaster or docking officer first refers to the ship's docking plan. This furnishes necessary information concerning the underwater hull for docking purposes. To place the blocks accurately and to build them up to the proper height and angle, the docking plan must provide the following information:

1. Full extent of keel, with flat and rising portions accurately delineated
2. Peculiarities of stern post and rudder
3. Sections—amidships and elsewhere—to show proper height and angle of bilge blocks, if these are necessary.
4. Shape and location of keels, docking keels, struts, propellers, underwater fittings, projections of all kinds, and all openings in the hull (drains, etc.)

Furthermore, since it is often necessary to provide more blocks than usual under heavy weights, the docking plan should show:

5. Location of boilers, engines, and other unusual weights.

To assist in locating sighting battens, the plan should also show:

6. The length on the load waterline

Finally, in order to enable the dockmaster to determine whether or not the dock can take a ship, or can place her accurately in the dock, the plan must show:

7. The length overall, the beam, and all projections, such as blisters, that might increase the normal beam.

3.30 Docking The dockmaster of any particular dock, knowing the ship's draft, the maximum depth over the sill, and the current and tidal variations in the vicinity, decides on the time the ship should enter the dock and so informs the commanding officer. The commanding officer makes the necessary arrangements to ensure that, at the time specified, the ship is without any list to either side and presents trim, if any, as specified by the dockmaster or docking officer.

The dock being already prepared, water is admitted, the caisson is floated and removed, and the ship is brought to the dock entrance, usually with the assistance of tugs. When the bow of the ship has safely crossed the sill of the dock, the responsibility for her safety rests upon the dockmaster, who hauls her into the dock, replaces and sinks the caisson, centers the ship, starts dock pumps, and proceeds with the docking until the ship is safely landed on the blocks; the dock is then pumped dry.

Should any extraordinary conditions exist, such as those caused by an accident or battle damage to the ship, the special precautions taken in docking her must depend upon the judgment of the dockmaster.

During the period when the ship is in dock, no change of any kind in her weights should be made without the knowledge and consent of the dockmaster. Improper changes in weights may cause the ship to do serious damage to herself or the dock when she is floated, as a result of sudden changes in list or trim.

3.31 Routine Work in Drydock The following routine drydock work is done in addition to any special underwater repairs or alterations:

1. Clean bottom, including scaling or wirebrushing of badly corroded parts.
2. Overhaul underwater valves.
3. Repack underwater stuffing boxes.
4. Renew zinc and mild steel anodes as necessary.
5. Take propeller shaft clearances and replace stern and strut bearings as necessary.
6. Check pitch of propellers and clean and polish them.
7. Examine rudder pintles and gudgeons and rudder shaft packing; take rudder bearing clearances.

8. Paint bottom and also draft marks and boot-topping.
9. Inspect and repair bilge keels.
10. Clear all sea strainers.

3.32   Undocking   After all underwater repairs are completed and the bottom is painted, a time for flooding the dock is agreed upon between the commanding officer of the ship and the dockmaster. The former stations men at the outboard valves, and elsewhere as he deems necessary, to ensure that water does not enter the ship. The latter stations men at the various shores and lines to prevent as far as possible any injury to the ship or dock from a change of weights or any unexpected alteration in tide or wind.

Water is admitted to the dock under the dockmaster's control. When all sea-valve openings are covered, flooding is usually stopped until their watertightness can be reported. When the water has risen to a sufficient height, the ship lifts from the keel blocks. Once the ship is safely afloat, flooding is continued until the water level within the dock is the same as that outside. The caisson is floated as quickly as possible, then removed, and the ship is hauled out of drydock.

3.33   Elevator Drydocks   The newest drydocks, especially for relatively small vessels, are *marine elevators* that feature a rail transfer system. This permits movement of the vessels from the elevator platform to remote areas of the shipyard where repairs or building can be done while leaving the elevator platform free to dock other vessels. The platform is lowered vertically and stopped at a predetermined depth. The vessel to be dry-docked is floated over the submerged platform, which is then raised until the vessel and platform are completely above the water level. (See Fig. 3.12.)

The platform that supports the vessel during the drydocking operation is raised and lowered by electrically controlled hoists with wire rope cables. The hoists are supported by fixed structures on both sides of the platform and are normally supported by standard marine piling of concrete or steel. The number of hoists, capacity of each hoist, and their spacing is varied to provide the required drydocking capacity. Each hoist consists of an electric motor, a reduction gear system, a wire rope cable drum, and a double brake arrangement. The electric motor is a specially designed alternating-current synchronous induction motor. It has operating characteristics necessary for the wide range of loads required in drydocking. The motors are designed to operate at a fixed rate of speed regardless of the load variations imposed by the ship's weight distribution. All electric motors are interconnected and controlled at one central control point. In effect, the motors act as though they were connected mechanically, and no variation in speed

Fig. 3.12 Aerial view of Syncrolift platform, transfer system, and workberths at Fisheries Development Corporation, Walvis Bay, South Africa. Platform is 260 ft long by 50 ft wide, operated by twenty-two 180-ton hoists. Rated capacity is 2310 long tons. (*Courtesy of Syncrolift Pearlson Engineering Company*)

from one motor to the other is possible. This assures constant lifting speed at all hoists, which in turn keeps the elevator platform level.

The platform construction consists of steel structural members and wood planks for decking. Platforms using only four hoists have their steel members welded together to form a single structure. Platforms using eight or more hoists have an articulated platform that consists of a series of main transverse lifting beams supported by a hoist at each end. They do not have to be connected to each other because the constant speed of each hoist assures that all beams will remain at the same level.

Fittings

3.34 Fittings Fittings are various structures and appliances attached to the hull to assist in handling the ship or performing the ship's work, to provide for the safety and comfort of the crew, or merely for ornamental purposes. (See Fig. 3.13.) They may be affixed solidly to the hull or may be capable of a limited amount of motion. They may be operated by hand or by power. They may be found in any part of the ship, including the underwater body, although the commonest and most useful fittings are generally encountered around the weather decks.

Chocks are some of the most numerous and useful fittings found aboard ship. They generally take the form of castings, weldments, or forgings welded to the hull near the side along weather decks; they are used for the purpose of leading guiding lines aboard. The most common form is the *open chock,* which has an opening on top through which the line is

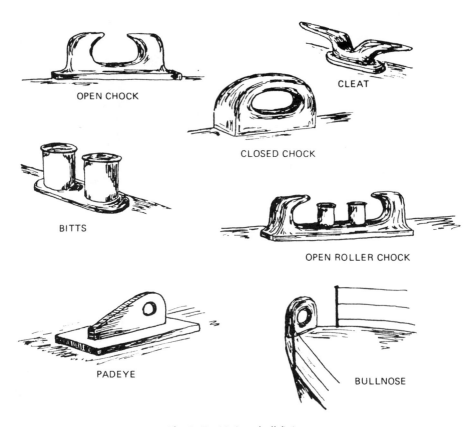

Fig. 3.13 Various hull fittings.

dropped and two curved parts called *horns* to hold it in. If the horns meet and the line must be led through the opening, it is called a *closed chock*. The heavy closed chock built at the extreme bow of destroyers and other light vessels for guiding a towline is commonly known as the *bullnose*. The inner surfaces of chocks are smoothed and rounded to avoid chafing the lines. Some have rollers fitted on each side for the same purpose, in which case they are known as *roller chocks*.

Bitts are usually found in the neighborhood of chocks and somewhat inboard of them. They are heavy vertical cylinders, usually cast in pairs; they are often used for making fast lines that have been led through the chocks. The upper end of a bitt is either larger than the lower end or is fitted with a lip to keep lines from slipping off accidentally. As bitts are often required to take very heavy loads, extra frames are worked into their foundations to distribute the strain. Bitts are sometimes built and installed ruggedly enough so that the ship may tow or be towed by them. When built in pairs, each bitt is sometimes called a *horn*.

Another common fitting is the *davit*. Davits are set in sockets that allow them to rotate. They are made of heavy pipe or plates and are angled so that their upper end or head will plumb some space below them at a distance from their base. A tackle is rigged at the davit head so that weights can be lifted and swung as the davit is rotated. The most common use for davits is to carry lifeboats, but they are sometimes rigged to lift or lower weights over the side or out of trunks and holds. (See Section 12.1.)

There are numerous smaller but very useful fittings found about the weather decks. A plate with an eye attached, riveted to the deck to distribute the strain over a large area and to which a block can be hooked or shackled, is called a *pad* or *padeye*. An *eyebolt* serves the same purpose and may be attached to the deck or to a bulkhead or a frame overhead. If the eyebolt carries a permanent ring, it is called a *ringbolt*. *Cleats* are light, double-ended horns on which lines are made fast. *Awning stanchions* and *lifeline stanchions* are found at the ship's side on weather decks and are used to rig awnings and lifelines. Some of these are either hinged or set in sockets so that they can be cleared away as necessary. Sockets are often set in the deck for special purposes, such as setting the king post for a boom and topping-lift.

Ports are fixed or hinged, framed, heavy glass plates set in the ship's side or superstructure.

Winches and cranes are the most common and most useful power fittings found aboard ship. A *winch* consists of a heavy frame fastened solidly to the deck and an engine or motor that turns a horizontal shaft mounted in the frame, usually with a drum fastened to each end of the shaft. If the line is revolved around the drum for several turns and is tended carefully, it will withstand a heavy strain and can be accurately controlled. Blocks rigged to padeyes or eyebolts are commonly used to give lines a fair lead to the winch drums. In case a line has a limited and repeated travel—as when cargo is being handled in and out of a hold, and for heavy loads— the line is attached permanently to a winch drum and handled by winding and unwinding it on the drum according to the direction of the shaft's rotation. Winches take the place of an enormous amount of manpower and are invaluable in speeding up operations even when sufficient manpower is available. A winch that is used primarily to handle the anchor cables, but that usually has horizontal drums or a vertical capstan in addition, is called an *anchor windlass.*

Cranes may be regarded as large, power-driven davits. A crane may be built up as a solid structure or rigged with a boom that can be raised and lowered so as to plumb different distances from its base. The hauling part of a permanently rigged wire rope tackle for lifting weights is made fast to a drum. Motors or engines lift or lower weights by rotating the drum, rotate the crane, and lift or lower the boom. The crane is used primarily for hoisting and lowering heavy weights, such as boats or airplanes, over the side, but it can be used for many other purposes within its radius.

Hull Piping Systems

Piping built into the hull that carries a liquid or a gas is known as a *hull piping system.* The principal hull piping systems are as follows:

Firemain	Fresh water
Sprinkling	Drainage
Sanitary	Compressed air
Damage control flooding	Fuel-oil
Ballasting	Aircraft fuel

3.35 Firemain System The firemain system in large ships forms a loop throughout the greater portion of the ship. Cross-connections are installed between mains in most of the principal transverse watertight subdivisions. The loop may be arranged in a horizontal or vertical plane. In aircraft carriers, a bypass main is installed below the uppermost service mains, thus incorporating the features of both the horizontal and vertical loop.

In small ships, such as ocean escort types, a single main is provided on the damage control deck.

In combatant ships, the firemain can be segregated into smaller independent sections so as to minimize loss of pumping capacity in event of localized system damage.

3.36 Sprinkling System The magazines of a warship are divided into groups, according to location. Each group is supplied by a separate sprinkling system connection leading from the firemain at a convenient location and controlled by a group control valve. The group control valves are operated from remote control stations, either hydraulically or mechanically. Sprinklers may also be actuated automatically by a thermostat whenever there is a temperature rise in the magazine.

3.37 Ship Sanitary Piping Separate sanitary piping systems are installed because current regulations prohibit discharge of raw sewage overboard. Holding tanks and/or sewage treatment plants are therefore installed.

3.38 Flushing System For sanitary spaces, flushing water is supplied at pressures around 30 psi. Present practice is to provide branches from the firemain, via stop valves and reducing valves, wherever flushing services are required.

3.39 Damage Control Flooding (Naval Vessels Only) In aircraft carriers, remote-operated, hydraulically controlled flood valves are installed in counterfloodable voids. The latest practice provides a single flood valve to service several such voids in order to minimize the number of openings in the hull. These valves permit rapid counterflooding even when power is temporarily lost.

3.40 Fresh-Water System Fresh or drinkable water, called *potable water,* is usually stored aboard ship in special tanks, low in the ship. From these tanks, it is delivered to necessary outlets, such as scuttlebutts, lavatories, galley sinks, and the like, through the fresh-water system. This consists of a pump and pressure tank or continuously operating centrifugal pumps that maintain pressure in the system. Pumps are usually located near the freshwater tanks, and frequently in engineering spaces.

3.41 Drainage System Each ship has some means provided for removing water from within its hull. Systems of piping, with or without pumping facilities installed for this purpose, are termed *drainage systems.*

Drainage systems are divided, on most ships, as follows:

1. Main drainage system
2. Secondary drainage systems
3. Plumbing and deck drains
4. Weather-deck drains
5. Feed drains in machinery spaces

In addition to the above systems, the following portable pumps are used to drain flooded areas not provided with drainage facilities:

1. Electric submersible pumps
2. "P-250-type" pump
3. Jet pumps (eductors)

The main drainage system runs throughout the main machinery compartments. However, on some ships it extends well into the bow and stern. On smaller ships the main drain consists of a single pipe running fore and aft, usually amidships. On larger ships it is a loop system, extending along both sides of the engineering compartments and joined at the ends. Main drainage systems may be used on many later types of ships to drain "floodable" voids used in counterflooding after such voids have been flooded, and to empty fuel-oil tanks that have been ballasted with seawater. Eductors, actuated from the firemain, are used to provide suction lift.

Secondary drainage systems serve to drain spaces forward and aft of the main machinery compartments. The piping is smaller in size than that used in main drainage systems. It may be a continuation of the main drainage system, but they are often not connected.

Plumbing and deck drains are provided for draining fixtures and compartments within the ship by gravity. Gravity drainage piping is installed most extensively in compartments above the waterline. On large ships, some compartments near or below the waterline may be drained to compartments lower in the ship, where the water can be pumped overboard. These lower compartments may be bilges and bilge wells, shaft-alley sumps, drain tanks, or sanitary drain tanks.

3.42 Compressed Air System Ships rely on compressed air for many tasks and services. Examples of tasks include starting of emergency diesel generators, launching torpedoes, and operating valves and controls. Examples of services include operating of pneumatic tools, servicing vehicles, and charging divers' tanks.

On the submarine the compressed air system is of major importance. This is because compressed air is used in blowing ballast tanks for maintaining the proper buoyancy. Other uses include the operation of control systems, torpedo ejection, and emergency breathing.

Compressed air is provided, normally, by shipboard compressors and stored in receivers or flasks for use as required.

3.43 Fuel-Oil System The fuel-oil pumping system in large ships consists of a loop serving all fuel-oil tanks and permitting transfer of fuel from storage tanks to service tanks and thence to fuel-oil service pumps. The latter pump the fuel oil to the fuel-oil heaters and thence to the burners in the boilers. Included in the system are topside fuel-oil filling connections, which lead down to the loop.

This system is also used for transfer of liquid for correction of list and trim, or improvement of stability or reserve buoyancy after damage, but furnishes a possible avenue for progressive flooding.

3.44 Aircraft Fuel Systems   Ships carrying or tending gas-turbine-engine-type aircraft store and handle gas-turbine-engine fuel (JP-5). This fuel has a high flash point and is considered safe for storage aboard ships in unprotected tanks similar to those for diesel oil tanks. The use of a high-flashpoint fuel also allows elimination or reduction in the safety requirements associated with gasoline systems, such as explosion-proof equipment and special firefighting and ventilation requirements. However, because of gas-turbine fuel's affinity for water, special system installation requirements are necessary for quality control of the fuel, such as two-stage filtration.

The gas-turbine fuel is stored in regular ship's tanks. The fuel is transferred via transfer pumps and purifiers or filter/separators to gas-turbine-fuel service tanks. Delivery of gas-turbine fuel to aircraft fueling stations, such as hangar and flight deck stations on an aircraft carrier, is via service pumps and filter/separators. Gas-turbine aircraft fueling stations are distributed along the hangar and flight deck areas to serve any aircraft parked in these areas.

References

The Society of Naval Architects and Marine Engineers publishes two comprehensive and authoritative reference books on the theory and practice of naval architecture, written by a group of acknowledged experts in their respective specialties:

Comstock, John P., ed., *Principles of Naval Architecture.* New York: Society of Naval Architects and Marine Engineers, 1969.
Taggart, Robert, ed., *Ship Design and Construction.* New York: Society of Naval Architects and Marine Engineers, 1980.

Somewhat less comprehensive treatments, written especially for seamen and officers in the Merchant Marine and emphasizing ship operation, are the following:

Derrett, D. R. *Ship Stability for Masters and Mates.* London: Stanford Maritime Limited, 1973.

LaDage, M. and Van Gemert, N. *Stability and Trim for the Ship's Officer* (Edited by W. E. George). Centreville, MD: Cornell Maritime Press, 1983.
Munro-Smith, R. *Ships and Naval Architecture*. London: The Institute of Marine Engineers, 1973.

An introduction to the special nature of Naval vessels, but including the basic physical theories of ship statics, dynamics, and propulsion, is the following:

Gillmer, T., and Johnson, B., *Introduction to Naval Architecture*. Annapolis: Naval Institute Press, 1982.

4

Propulsion and Steering

Seamanship involves an understanding of the means available to maneuver a ship: the power plant and the steering mechanism. A ship's captain or deck officer must know the minimum and maximum responses of his ship to backing, accelerating, and rudder angle. The expert shiphandler will always avoid putting his ship into such a situation that judicious use of his engine and rudder cannot extricate him. Regardless of its apparent complexity, any propulsion device is based on the fundamental principles of energy conversion. The energy available in a fuel—whether conventional fuel such as oil or coal, or nuclear fuel—is converted to mechanical energy, which is then used to give the ship its energy of motion.

Due to the inherent high efficiency of modern diesel engines, most of the world's merchant ships are diesel powered. Only the U.S. merchant marine has a significant number of steam turbine-driven vessels, and the majority of these were built before 1980.

4.1 Internal-Combustion Engines The fuel for an internal-combustion engine is burned within the engine itself, and the products of combustion pass directly through the engine. The transformation of heat to mechanical energy is thus accomplished completely within the engine. There are basic

95

differences in the methods used to initiate combustion in various internal-combustion engines—by spark ignition in gasoline engines and by compression ignition in diesel engines.

In *gasoline engines* (spark ignition), fuel and air are mixed in the carburetor and admitted to the combustion chamber by the inlet valve. This mixture is compressed and then ignited by an electrical spark. The burning fuel expands and converts heat energy to mechanical energy by driving a piston down. The products of combustion are then removed through the now opened exhaust valve. The gasoline engine is seldom used today in commercial marine applications because of the hazards present in its highly flammable fuel. The operation of a four-stroke cycle (four-cycle) gasoline engine is shown in Fig. 4.1. Some spark-ignition engines, such as the common outboard engine, use a two-stroke cycle (two-cycle) with loop or crossflow scavenging, as shown in Fig. 4.2. Most gasoline engines are connected to the propeller shaft via a reversing transmission. Where high efficiency is desired, the reversing transmission incorporates a reduction gear to allow for a better matching of desired engine and propeller speeds.

4.2 Diesel Engines The large diesel engines (compression-ignition) used for marine application may employ either two-stroke cycle or four-stroke cycle principles. Regardless of the mechanical cycle, all diesel engines utilize the heat of compression to ignite the fuel. In this type of engine, the combustion air in the cylinder is compressed to a pressure high enough to

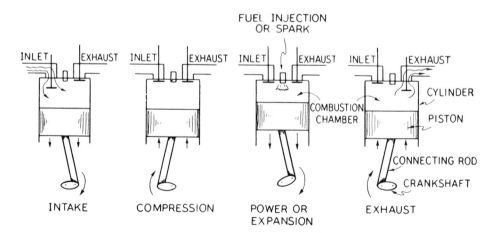

Fig. 4.1 One cylinder of a spark-ignition engine (four-stroke cycle) showing the four phases in one complete firing cycle.

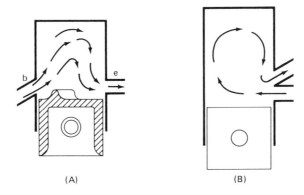

Fig. 4.2 Scavenging: (a) direct, or cross-flow; and (b) return, or loop.

raise the temperature of the air above the auto-ignition temperature of the fuel. The fuel then injected into the cylinder is ignited by the high-temperature air. This burning fuel-air mixture expands, driving the piston down and thus converting heat energy to mechanical energy. When the piston is at the bottom of the cylinder, the products of combustion are swept out by a scavenging process (two-stroke cycle) or by an exhaust stroke (four-stroke cycle).

Two-stroke cycle engines can use a variety of scavenging systems to sweep out the combustion products from the cylinder and recharge the cylinder with fresh air such as crossflow, loop, or uniflow scavenging. Figure 4.3 shows the very fuel-efficient, two-stroke, uniflow cycle.

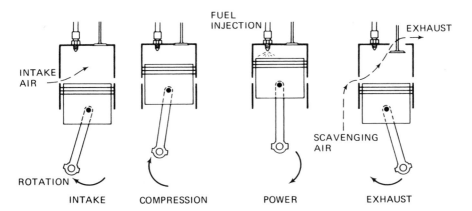

Fig. 4.3 Two-cycle diesel engine, uniflow scavenged.

Propulsion marine diesel engines are classified according to speed (based on rpm and piston speed) and fall, in general, into three categories:

Slow Speed	Less than 200 rpm
	Up to 5000 BHP per cylinder
	Approximately 80 lb/hp
Medium Speed	400 to 600
	Normally in the range of 500–1000 BHP per cylinder
	Approximately 30 lb/hp
High Speed	Above 1000 rpm
	Available in low powers
	Approximately 10 lb/hp

As a general rule, slow-speed engines are two-stroke cycle engines directly connected to the propeller shaft. Medium-speed and high-speed engines are available as both two- and four-stroke cycle engines that are normally connected to the propeller shaft via a reduction gear. In general, the slow- and medium-speed diesels can be obtained as nonreversing (unidirectional rotation) or direct-reversing engines, the choice depending on the transmission system and/or the type of propeller—fixed pitch or controllable pitch. Another generality is that slow- and medium-speed engines can operate on heavy fuels, whereas high-speed engines must operate on the lighter distillates. Although high-speed engines are normally started by a starting motor (electric, hydraulic, or pneumatic), medium- and slow-speed engines are direct air-starting, that is, compressed starting air is directed into the cylinders to crank the engine over.

The principal advantage of the diesel engine is its efficiency. Large-bore slow-speed diesel engines are available with thermal efficiencies greater than 50%, which result in fuel consumption of less than 120 gr/bhp-hr. High-speed engines of several hundred horse-power have fuel rates of about 180 gr/bhp-hr. These fuel rates are specific and must be corrected for transmission system losses and, in some cases, for ship electrical loads.

To achieve high engine thermal efficiency and reasonable specific weights (lb/hp), most marine diesel engines are fitted with turbochargers (exhaust gas driven superchargers).

For greater thermal efficiency, many marine engineers use various waste-heat reclaiming devices such as exhaust gas boilers, cooling-water-motivated distilling plants, and power-augmenting exhaust gas turbines. Many modern vessels fitted with waste-heat boilers use the generated steam to power electrical generators and thus provide the ship's electricity without running auxiliary diesel generators. Some diesel vessels use shaft-driven or main-engine-driven generators in order to use the most efficient prime mover to power electrical generators.

4.3 Use of Diesels Because of the inherent fuel efficiency of diesel engines, they have become the principal prime mover for merchant ship propulsion. Most modern seagoing merchant vessels use directly connected, air-starting, reversing, slow-speed diesel engines capable of burning heavy fuel oil. (Fig. 4.4). Medium-speed engines are used whenever engine room volume or weight is a matter of concern or when multiple engines per shaft are desired. In addition to using reversing reduction gears or controllable pitch propellers, nonreversing medium-speed and high-speed engines can also use electric drive to obtain necessary reversing capabilities and speed reduction.

Diesel propulsion systems are capable of providing full backing power for indefinite periods of time. Deck officers must remember, however, that when a vessel is fitted with direct-reversing diesel engines, there is a limit to the number of engine stop-starts and reverses that can be called for in a short period of time. Classification societies call for the starting air receivers on vessels with direct-reversing diesels to have a capacity for at least 12

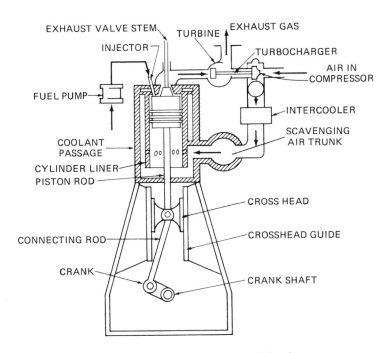

Fig. 4.4 Elements of a typical slow-speed diesel engine.

engine starts (including reversals). For normal maneuvering, the combination of starting air receiver capacity and starting air compressor replenishment capability will ensure sufficient starting air, but it should not be wasted.

In addition, deck officers must know that diesel power plants with extensive efficiency-enhancing devices should not be taken off steady steaming without notifying the engineers.

4.4 Steam Power Plants   Steam power plants operate in a closed vapor cycle in which the working fluid—water—undergoes a series of processes: boiling in a steam generator, expanding in a turbine (or reciprocating engine), condensing in a condenser, and then repressurized by a pump. These processes eventually return the working fluid back to its original state. Although all closed cycle steam plants (Fig. 4.5) must have the four essential components (boiler, turbine, condenser, and feed pump), practical shipboard plants are fitted with numerous devices to improve overall plant efficiency and the longevity of the system (Fig. 4.6).

The most noteworthy of these devices are the *feed water heaters*. The primary purpose of feed water heaters is to improve overall efficiency by using bleed steam (partially expanded steam bled or extracted from the turbine before reaching the condenser) to preheat the feed water prior to its entering the boiler. Power plants using feed water heaters are said to operate on a *regenerative cycle*.

Of such importance are these cycles that merchant vessel steam plants are now characterized by the number of feed heaters used. Many steam-powered vessels built before the energy crisis of 1973 had "two heater" cycles. Most steam vessels built after 1973 have more sophisticated "four heater" or "five heater" cycles. In general, the more feed water heaters used in the cycle, the more efficient the steam plant, but at the same time,

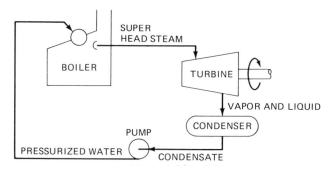

Fig 4.5   Basic steam power plant (closed vapor cycle).

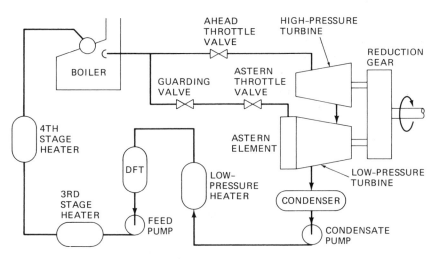

Fig. 4.6 Four-heater regenerative cycle with a cross-compounded reversing-geared turbine in ahead mode.

the more care it takes to operate and maintain the power plant. One of the feed water heaters, the deaerating feed water heater, *DFT* (commonly called the *direct contact*, or *D.C. heater*), has an additional function to that of heating the feed water. It is designed to "deaerate" the water (that is, to remove the oxygen from the feed water before it enters the boiler, thereby minimizing corrosion).

Cycle conditions—in particular, the pressure and temperature of the steam leaving the boiler and entering the turbine—have a profound effect on the efficiency of the power plant. The higher the pressure and temperature of the steam, the more efficient the cycle. All modern marine plants use superheated steam.

The most sophisticated steam plants aboard merchant vessels use a regenerative reheat steam cycle. In reheat cycles, the high-pressure steam is partially expanded in the turbine and then sent back to the boiler to flow through the reheater tubes, thereby having its temperature raised back to its initial value prior to entering the turbine. After reheating, the steam re-enters the turbine and continues to expand. Since reheat plants are fitted with feed water heaters, their true classification is as regenerative reheat plants. The main reason for using a regenerative reheat cycle is its ability to handle very high-pressure steam without adversely affecting the turbine and thereby to achieve high overall thermal efficiency. Deck officers on vessels with reheat power plants must familiarize themselves with possible restrictions when calling for astern power.

Boilers Marine boilers supplying steam for propulsion are usually water tube boilers of the express (small tube) type. In this type of boiler, the water flows inside the tubes. The products of combustion change the water to steam by transfer of heat through the tube walls. The smallness of the tubes provides the greatest possible heat transfer surface in a given space, thereby allowing for compact boilers.

Pressures as high as 1500 psi are used in merchant vessels.

Most marine boilers are fired with residual fuel oil. Recently, some merchant vessels have been converted or even built to use coal as the principal boiler fuel. Deck officers should be aware of the fact that coal-fired boilers are less responsive to load changes than oil-fired boilers. This is especially important when a rapid increase in power, ahead or astern, is required.

The use of "dirty" fuels, such as residual oil or coal, results in rapid fouling of the firesides of the boiler. Frequent fireside cleaning is necessary to ensure good boiler efficiency and safe operation. Some deck officers seem to feel that the engineer's only reason for blowing tubes is to spread fine carbon dust over a clean topside, and consequently they refuse to allow tubes to be blown on their watch. The reasons for doing so, however, are cogent. When oil is burned in a boiler, a layer of soot is deposited on the outside of the small water tubes. This soot layer is undesirable for the following reasons: (1) The soot acts as an insulator and slows heat transfer to the water within the tubes, thereby reducing boiler efficiency. (2) If the soot is left in a boiler when fires are secured, it absorbs moisture from the air; the moisture activates the sulfuric acid in the soot, and this acid attacks the metal of the tubes and the boiler drum. (3) If allowed to remain in the boiler too long, the soot packs into a solid mass that can be removed only by tedious hand cleaning. (4) Excessive soot deposits can cause economizer fires, especially when up-powering after prolonged periods of low-power operation. To maintain maximum boiler efficiency, tubes should be blown once every four-hour watch while under way and at least twice a day when in port. As a practical matter on merchant ships under way, tubes are blown two or three times a day instead of once every four hours. Blowing tubes requires that any steam used by the soot blowers be replaced by an equal amount of water from the make-up system. This water must be replaced by the distilling plant.

When tubes are blown, high-pressure steam is admitted to the soot blowers (perforated tubes), which are permanently installed in the boiler. Steam that exits the soot blower element holes impinges on the tubes and dislodges the soot. The soot blowers have steam admitted to them in a specific order designed to sweep the soot out the stack.

Steam Turbines Steam enters a turbine through nozzles that direct it onto moving blades attached to on a rotor. The rotor is enclosed in a casing and supported on bearings at each end of the casing. When the steam has passed through the first row of moving blades, making them spin, it enters a row of stationary blades or nozzles attached to the casing; these in turn direct the steam against a second row of moving blades attached to the same revolving rotor. Alternate rows of fixed and moving blades are located along the length of the turbine. The steam flows through the turbine because of the pressure difference between the point of entry and the point of exit. As it passes through each set of fixed and moving blades (known as *turbine stages)*, the steam pressure and temperature drop since some of the energy is extracted to make the turbine rotor revolve. Theoretically, the stages necessary to extract all the energy available between the entering and final steam pressures could be housed in one casing, but the length of such a turbine would be too great for a ship. As a result, the stages are divided between two turbines known as the *high-pressure* and *low-pressure turbines.* To provide backing power, yet another turbine is required to turn the shaft in the reverse direction. This backing turbine could be housed in a separate casing, but because of its relatively short operating periods, its efficiency is sacrificed in order to keep it small and take advantage of more economical mounting in the existing casing of the low-pressure turbine. Normally, astern turbines contain only a few stages and are capable of producing approximately 40 percent of ahead power.

Turbines are most efficient when running at high speeds (3000 to 6000 rpm), whereas most propellers (discussed in a later section of this chapter) are most efficient at slow speeds (up to about 150 rpm). To allow both to run at their most efficient speed, a reduction gear is normally used between the turbine and the propeller shaft. The reduction ratio varies but is in the neighborhood of 40 to 1 for large ships. On merchant ships with single-screw propulsion, propeller rpm may vary from 80 or less on large, slow tankers and bulkers to 120 or more on higher-speed container ships. In these cases, double-reduction gears are used.

When the mate on watch gives permission to the engineers to start warming up the main plant, he should know that the engines are slowly turned by the jacking gear. The jacking gear consists of an electric motor and a hand-operated gear clutch connected to the reduction gear. Once the clutch is connected and the electric motor started, the turbines turn over slowly and the propellers even more slowly (about one revolution in 10 minutes). Although no way is put on the ship by this action, the mate should make sure that nothing can foul the propellers in their slow rotation before he grants permission to warm up. During this time, the condenser vacuum is raised to approximately 24 inches of mercury.

Approximately 1 hour before the time set for getting under way, the engineering officer of the watch will request permission to "roll the engine" with steam. Upon receiving permission, the engineer will disengage the jacking gear and commence rolling the engine. The procedure consists of admitting a quick "shot" of steam to the ahead turbine via the ahead throttle valve and bringing the propeller speed up quickly to about 5 rpm. The ahead throttle valve is then closed, and the astern valve is quickly opened to bring the shaft to a stop and to accelerate to about 5 rpm astern. The astern valve is then closed, and ahead steam is admitted to stop the shaft. If done quickly and decisively, rolling the engine should not put way on the vessel. The procedure is repeated every 3 to 5 minutes to prevent uneven heating of the turbine rotor with the resultant possibility of its warping the rotor. Because of the close fit of the rotor in the turbine casing, a slight sag would cause the blades to scrape on the casing and possibly snap off. During the roll-over period, the vacuum is raised to 28 1/2 inches of mercury.

After warming up and reaching full vacuum, the engine can be placed on stand-by. Whenever the engines are stopped, they should be spun every 5 minutes. When the word is given, FWE (finished with engines), the ahead and astern throttle valves and the guarding valve are secured, and the jacking gear is again engaged. The turbines are jacked over until cooled.

On some of the latest ships, the turbine can be placed under bridge control and monitored by audible and visible alarms. On such vessels, rolling of the engine can be accomplished automatically on a predetermined time cycle whenever the bridge throttle is in the STOP position.

4.5   Steam Plant Operating Characteristics of Interest to Deck Officers
Modern marine steam plants are inherently quite reliable but have certain operating characteristics that are important to deck officers. These characteristics generally fall into three areas: power plant efficiency, plant dynamics and response time, and astern power availability.

Power Plant Efficiency   Steam plant efficiency is dependent on specific operating parameters such as operating power level, setting of throttle and/or nozzles, steam condition, bleed valve settings, the attitude of engineers, etc. Close communication with the ship's engineers is of utmost importance if economical operation of the power plant is to be maintained.

Power Plant Dynamics and Response Time   It is important to note that many components of the system are interconnected and interrelated. An action involving one component may have severe consequences on other components. An example is the rapid opening of a main turbine throttle valve, which will not only cause the propeller to speed up, but may also cause the boiler water level to carry over; the latter, in turn may cause serious damage to the main turbine as well as to the turbogenerators. Prudent engineers and proper control systems will moderate the rate of change of the power plant in order to ensure its safe and stable operation. Very rapid changes in power (many bells in quick succession) can cause havoc, even a complete loss of power! All mates should know the response times of the plant and the engineers who operate the plant.

Astern Power Availability   The astern elements of most marine steam turbines are capable of delivering only about 40 percent power. Even at this relatively low power, the required steam flow from the boiler is quite high and may cause serious boiler water-level problems. Another characteristic problem of operating a steam turbine plant astern is that the ahead turbine (which takes up the major portion of the turbine casing) will overheat if astern power is maintained for long periods of time (15 to 30 minutes). If long periods of astern power operation are anticipated, it is vital to check with the Chief Engineer.

4.6   Nuclear Power Plants   On nuclear-powered ships, the heat to generate steam for propulsion turbines, turbogenerators, and auxiliaries comes from a nuclear reactor instead of a boiler. The reactor serves the same function as the furnace of a boiler in that it provides the heat to convert water to steam. The heat is supplied by expending a unique fuel capable of nuclear fission and is controlled by moving a neutron absorber (the control rods) in or out of the fuel area. This heat is used to heat water maintained under high pressure. The water, known as the *coolant* because it removes heat from the reactor, provides this heat to a heat exchanger, which functions as the steam generator. First-generation nuclear-power plants, such as the one shown in Fig. 4.7, consist of a primary and a secondary system.

Primary or Main Coolant System   The reactor gives up heat to the main coolant—highly pressurized water—which in turn gives up this heat to the steam generator to form steam. The coolant is then returned to the reactor, where it is again heated and the process repeated. The coolant is kept under high pressure to ensure that it will not boil in the reactor vessel, an action that might cause the reactor to fail.

Secondary or Main Steam System   The secondary system is the main steam system. The coolant from the reactor gives up heat to the feed water of the secondary system in the steam generator. The steam formed by this process goes to the engine room where it is used in the same manner as in an oil-fueled ship. The secondary system is completely isolated from the primary system in this type of nuclear plant and does not penetrate the reactor vessel.

Newer nuclear systems are now available in which the secondary system (main steam) penetrates the reactor vessel and the heat transfer from

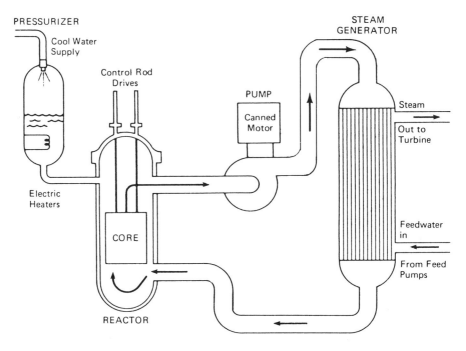

Fig. 4.7 First-generation marine nuclear plant, in which steam, once generated, is treated just like that produced from an oil-fired burner.

the coolant to the main steam system takes place within the reactor vessel. The two systems are still isolated completely from one another within the reactor vessel in this type of plant.

4.7 Gas Turbines The gas turbine is a lightweight, compact plant that can be warmed up and loaded in a matter of minutes. Figure 4.8 shows a schematic diagram of a simple-cycle gas turbine plant. The engine is started by an electric motor or other device used to rotate the compressor section, thereby forcing air into the combustion chamber.

When the gas turbine is running, air enters the compressor where its pressure is increased from about 2 to 20 (depending on the size and type of the engine) times atmospheric pressure. This air then goes to the combustion chamber where it is mixed with the fuel and burned. Starting the engine requires an external spark as a source of ignition. Once the engine has been started, combustion is continuous and self-sustaining. The combustion chamber, while a simple-appearing device, must be carefully constructed to ensure proper mixing of fuel and air, sufficient cooling, and freedom from flame "blow-out." The products of combustion enter the

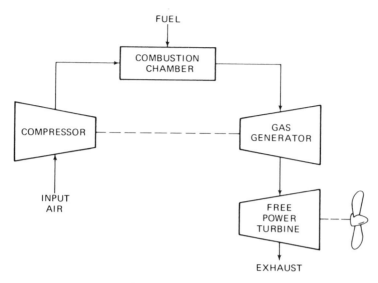

Fig. 4.8 Gas turbine plant.

compressor turbine, which usually consists of four to six simple turbine stages. The compressor turbine provides the power to drive the compressor. As soon as the compressor turbine is generating sufficient power, the starting device is disconnected and the engine becomes self-sustaining. The exhaust from the gas generator goes to the free power turbine, which drives the propeller through reduction gears. This split-shaft arrangement allows the gas generator to be operated at its most efficient speed while the free power turbine speed is varied as required.

A simpler form of gas turbine does not utilize the free power turbine but takes its output from the gas generator shaft. This single-shaft system is not as efficient for variable speed operation but is useful whenever a fixed speed is required (such as for a generator).

Since the gas turbine is a unidirectional engine, a means must be provided for backing down. This can take the form of reversing gear, an electric drive, or, as is more common, a controllable pitch propeller.

Gas turbine propulsion has not been widely accepted by merchant ship operators because of its need for a high-quality distillate fuel. Many modern naval vessels are powered by gas turbines because of the simplicity of their power plants and their weight and space advantage.

4.8 Electric Drive Any of the propulsion engines mentioned so far could be used with an electric drive for the purpose of propelling a vessel. The prime mover(s) is used to drive a generator (s), which in turn can supply electricity to electric propulsion motors that will drive the propeller either directly or through a reduction gear. Reversing the propellers can be accomplished by electric switches that reverse the driving motors. In addition to ease of reversing the rotation of the propulsion motors, electrical propulsion has the advantage of very accurate speed control over the entire range of shaft speed. Another advantage of electrical propulsion is the ability to use multiple generators in parallel to supply power to the propulsion motors. This allows the operators to use certain generators, leaving others idle for maintenance. Ships using diesel-electric propulsion include tugs, icebreakers, and passenger liners.

4.9 Bridge Control of Propulsion Plant   Newer ships are being fitted out with automated propulsion plants, and their bridges provided with propulsion control consoles that enable the bridge officer to personally regulate the speed and direction of the propeller(s) by controlling the propulsion prime mover or the pitch of the propeller. Bridge control enhances the maneuvering response time of the ship by eliminating the time lag occasioned by having to transmit speed changes from the bridge to the engine room by an engine-order telegraph. It also results in marked personnel economies.

The bridge officer may move the throttle control in any manner (swiftly or slowly) because automatic mechanisms are provided in the propulsion system to ensure its safe operation under all operating conditions. Deck officers must take note of the fact that they can move the throttle lever much faster than the plant can respond and that it is therefore very important to monitor the RPM indicator.

Since ship response is faster with bridge than with conventional control, the deck officer must familiarize himself with throttle control operation, with the response times required for maneuvering speed changes, and with the response of the ship when executing emergency crash-astern maneuvers. Normally, specific instructions for bridge console operation are posted on the console as a guide for the operator.

4.10 Propellers   After the energy of a fuel has been converted to heat and the heat in turn converted to mechanical energy, a way must be found to use this mechanical energy to drive the ship. The *propeller* is the device used to drive all large modern ships. A propeller operating in a fluid, such as a marine propeller, is a device to obtain a reactive thrust by increasing the velocity of the fluid through its disk. It thus changes the momentum of a mass and provides a propulsive force, or reactive thrust.

One method of describing a propeller is by the number of blades it possesses. The choice of the number of blades is dictated by factors such as vibration, cavitation, backing power, and mechanical efficiency. Other factors being equal, the use of fewer but wider blades fosters greater propeller efficiency. More blades normally reduce propeller-induced hull vibration. The use of skewed propellers is helpful in reducing this vibration. The blades of a propeller may be fastened to the hub (the central part of the mechanism) with bolts or may be cast with the hub in one piece.

Another method of describing a propeller is by the direction it turns when driving the ship ahead. By convention, a *right-handed propeller* is defined as a propeller that turns in a clockwise direction, viewed from astern, when driving the ship ahead. Similarly, a *left-handed propeller* turns counterclockwise, viewed from astern, when driving the ship ahead. Ships having one propeller are designated as *single-screw ships;* ships having two propellers are called *twin-screw ships; multi-screw ships* may have three or four propellers. It is unusual for modern merchant ships to be equipped with two, three, or four screws. Because of the higher propulsion efficiency of a single propeller, most merchant vessels are so fitted.

One type of propeller that can reverse the direction of a ship without requiring a change of direction of the shaft is the *controllable pitch propeller.* The hub of a controllable pitch propeller contains a mechanism that can change the pitch of the propeller as shown in Fig. 4.9. This change in pitch allows the vessel to be maneuvered without reversing the rotation of the engines. The primary advantages of the controllable pitch propeller are its reversibility and its ability to maintain a constant engine rpm under varying power conditions or to match rpm to load condition. This latter feature allows the main propulsion plant to be run at its greatest efficiency, an im-

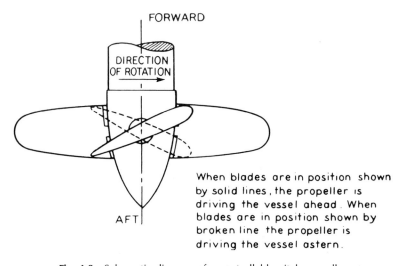

Fig. 4.9 Schematic diagram of a controllable pitch propeller.

Fig. 4.10 A conventional bladed propeller as it revolves. Note the turbulence, or cavitation, which limits its speed and efficiency. (*Official U.S. Navy photograph*)

portant feature when using diesels. Deck officers should note that vessels with reversible pitch propellers will back differently than vessels with fixed pitch propellers.

Another type of propeller, the *supercavitating propeller,* has a special application for very high speed ships such as hydrofoils. Developed by the U.S. Navy, it reduces the effect of cavitation, if not the cavitation itself. Cavitation, or water turbulence induced by vacuums (Fig. 4.10), is caused by the lower pressure on the rear face of the propeller. This lower pressure, resulting from the air-foil like shape of the blade, causes some of the fluid in the low-pressure region to vaporize. The vapor pockets thus formed both consume energy and cause erosion of the blades upon imploding. The supercavitating propeller operates at high speed, thus eliminating reduction gears in some installations, and creates a vapor cavity along the trailing edge of its new type blade that results in a minimum of power loss and erosion.

4.11 New Forms of Propulsors. Some new propulsion concepts now in use are the shrouded propeller, the cycloidal propeller, and the Grimm vane wheel. The *shrouded propeller* (Fig. 4.11) is a propeller set into a nozzle. This arrangement can provide greater efficiency at speeds up to about 15 knots. Above these speeds, the increased drag caused by the shroud overcomes the increase in efficiency and the result is a loss in total efficiency. Another disadvantage of the shroud is its reduction of backing

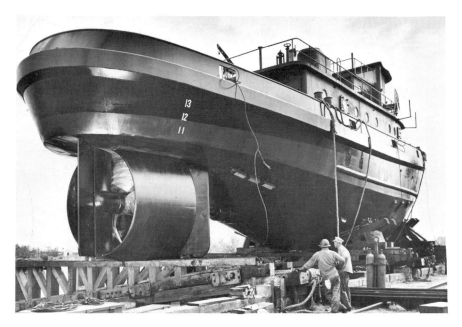

Fig. 4.11 The Dravo *Pioneer,* a tug fitted with a Kort nozzle, or shrouded propeller.

power, a reduction caused by the fact that a nozzle is basically a one-way device installed to improve ahead propulsion.

The *cyclodial propeller* provides great maneuverability but with a reduction in efficiency. In this type of propeller, the blades change pitch as the system rotates to provide equal thrust in any desired direction. One example of successful use of cycloidal propellers is on tugs where maneuverability and equal power in any direction are prime attributes.

The *Grimm vane wheel* (Fig. 4.12) is a multi-bladed free-turning turbine wheel placed abaft the propeller to convert the rotation of the propeller discharge current into usable thrust.

4.12 Steering Steering implies the ability to change and to hold a course, and for this there must be an adequate combination of fixed and movable stern control surfaces (*skegs* and *rudders,* respectively). For turning, the rudder is of major importance although it depends on some complex interaction with skegs or other fixed structure.

The usual method of changing the heading of a ship under way is by putting the rudder over to one side or the other. The action of the water on the rudder forces the stern of the vessel sideways, and the vessel changes course. Until saturation of rudder area is reached, the larger the

Fig. 4.12 Grimm vane wheel—invention to increase propulsive efficiency.

rudder, the tighter the ship will turn, because there is a larger area on which the water can act.

Besides the area of the rudder, the speed of the water past the rudder also effects the response of a ship to putting the rudder over; the faster the water is traveling, the better the response. Because the water is traveling faster directly astern of the propellers, rudders directly abaft the propellers permit getting rudder forces at low speeds. We can see then that if a ship is to be very maneuverable and have a small turning circle, the rudder should be as large as possible, or two rudders should be provided, preferably abaft the propellers in a twin-screw vessel.

Rudders are of three general types: balanced, semi-balanced, and un-balanced, as show in Fig. 4.13. When part of the rudder area is located forward of the rudder stock, the rudder is easier to turn because the action of the water on that part tends to help the rudder turn. The unbalanced rudder is the hardest to turn. The choice of rudder is determined by the shape of a vessel's stern, the number of propellers, and the speed the vessel must develop. To turn the rudder a steering gear is required.

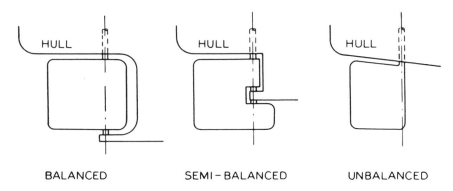

BALANCED   SEMI – BALANCED   UNBALANCED

Fig. 4.13 Common types of rudders.

4.13 The Steering Engines The electrohydraulic type of steering gear (Fig. 4.14) is used on all modern ships. The hydraulic power is furnished by a variable-stroke hydraulic pump driven by a continuously running constant-speed electric motor (M). There are many variations of the number and arrangement of the hydraulic rams, pumps, and driving motors, and of the method of transmitting the motion of the rams to the rudder cross-head, but the schematic drawing shown in Fig. 4.14 illustrates the essential principles of this type of steering gear. As shown in this plan, movement of the control mechanism *E* in one direction causes the pump *S* to take suction from one pipe leading to it and to discharge to the other. Movement of the control mechanism in the opposite direction causes the direction of pumping to be reversed. When the control mechanism is in the neutral position, a hydraulic lock is placed on the rams, and no fluid is pumped. The rate of pumping in either direction depends on the amount of movement of the control mechanism, which is constructed so that small movement will produce the maximum available rate. The pistons, P and P′, move the rudder; they are moved by fluid pressure in cylinders A, B, C, and D. Rotary steering devices are used instead of hydraulic rams on some

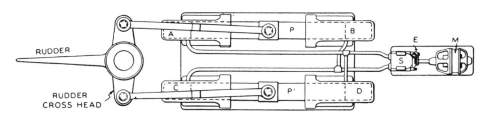

Fig. 4.14 Diagrammatic plan of electrohydraulic steering engine.

modern vessels by replacing the rams with a limited-rotation hydraulic vane-type actuator.

The electrical self-synchronous type of control is used by most modern ships. Briefly, the system consists of a synchro transmitter controlled by the motion of the steering wheel, suitable electric leads, and a synchro receiver connected to the control mechanism at the steering gear. Synchro transmitters and receivers are alternating-current electric motors designed so that the rotor of the receiver follows, in speed and amount of angular displacement, the motion of the transmitter rotor. Motion of the steering wheel, which is carried on an extension of the shaft of the synchro transmitter rotor, is therefore transmitted directly to the control mechanism, which acts to cause the steering gear to produce the desired rudder angle. Some vessels, also use a hydraulic telemotor system to transmit the steering signal from the bridge to the steering gear.

Modern vessels are normally equipped with automatic steering systems that allow them to steer a set course without the constant attention of a helmsman. Automatic steering systems on large vessels receive the heading from the gyro compass and transmit it electrically to the steering engine.

Whatever the type of steering gear control, provision is made on all naval ships and on most other ships for quickly shifting control from station to station. The practice of making this shift of steering control part of the daily routine offers valuable training for handling an emergency.

4.14 Recent Steering Devices New devices for steering now being used are a variety of rudder and propeller mechanisms that give certain ships improved handling qualities. Some ships have an active rudder that has a small propeller with its own power source installed as an integral unit. Ships fitted with Kort nozzles or shrouded propellers may have a steering rudder abaft the propeller and a pair of flanking rudders forward of the propeller. The steering rudder is used in the usual manner for ahead operation. The flanking rudders are for operation astern.

Another common device is the *bow-thruster unit*. This can be a propeller in a fixed transverse tunnel at the bow; a retractable, swiveling propeller unit; or a cycloidal unit. Bow thrusters are primarily used as assistant maneuvering devices in low-speed operation. A few vessels have been fitted with stern thrusters in addition to bow thrusters. These devices help ships dock without using tugs.

References

Femenia, J. "Economic Comparison of Various Marine Power Plants." *Transactions of The Society of Naval Architects and Marine Engineers,* 1973.

Harrington, R. L. *Marine Engineering.* New York: Society of Naval Architects and Marine Engineers, 1971.

Woodward, J. B., III, *Marine Engineering—an Introduction.* Ann Arbor: University of Michigan, 1978.

"Design of a Coal-Fired steam power plant for a Containership, Shipboard Energy Conservation '80," Marine Engineering Class of 1980, S.U.N.Y. Maritime College. Society of Naval Architects and Marine Engineers, 1980.

5

Ground Tackle

Throughout history, the seafarer has always regarded his anchor as a reliable shipmate ready to protect him when fortune has driven his ship into danger or to provide a secure mooring in a safe harbor. As such, the anchor has often been used as a symbol of hope. Regardless of how bad things may appear, if an anchor can be firmly embedded and made to take hold, there is always hope that all is not lost. However, there is more to safely securing the ship than just the anchor alone. In order to insure that a vessel is properly made fast to the bottom, the entire spectrum of ground tackle comes into consideration.

Ground tackle is the collective term applied to all equipment used in anchoring. It includes the anchors, their cables and connecting fittings, the anchor hoisting machinery, and all ancillary devices used in anchoring, mooring with anchors, or securing anchors in their hawse pipes.

5.1 Ground Tackle Elements In a normal shipboard arrangement (Fig. 5.1), the anchor cable is led through the *hawse pipes* located near the stem of the vessel. The hawse pipes are used not only for a lead for the chain but also to provide a storage place for the anchor, assuming it to be the stockless type. Coming up through the hawse pipes, the anchor cable

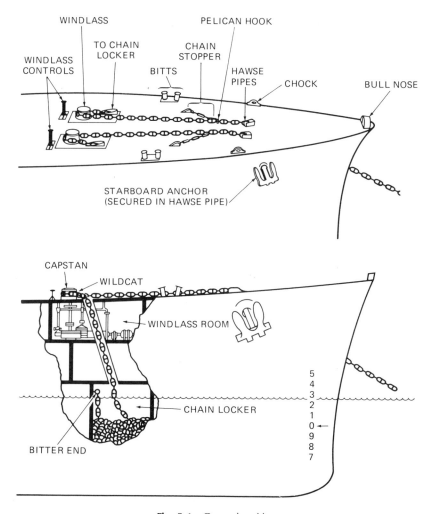

Fig. 5.1 Ground tackle.

passes through *riding chocks;* these chocks are fitted with heavy pawls or stoppers of various designs to take the stress off the *windlass* when the ship is riding at anchor in heavy weather. The chain then passes over a sprocket wheel on the windlass, known as the *wildcat.* This wheel engages the chain, link by link, and serves to apply to it the power of the windlass when the anchor is being heaved in. When the anchor is being let go, the wildcat is disconnected from the windlass and revolves freely, except for the control exerted by a friction brake band that is operated by a lever or a screw and wheel. After passing over the wildcat, the chain drops directly down the chain pipe into the chain locker below, in which it is stowed.

In many respects, ground tackle is one of the most vital parts of a ship's equipment. The vessel's safety frequently depends upon the proper design and sound construction of this gear, and suitable ground tackle has saved many ships and lives. Correspondingly, deficient ground tackle or ground tackle improperly employed has often been the cause of disaster. The seaman must know his ground tackle, understand its use and limitations, and take into account the many elements that affect its operating efficiency.

Anchors

The first anchors were undoubtedly heavy stones secured to some form of braided fiber rope that could be lowered over the side of a prehistoric floating craft. Such stones held the vessel to the bottom solely by their weight. Anchors designed to hold by virtue of their shape rather than sheer mass were developed about 2000 B.C. by East Indian seafarers. These seamen fashioned king-sized fishhooks with a single prong. By 600 B.C., the Greeks had added a second prong, or *fluke,* plus a crosspiece at the top to help position the flukes for grabbing the bottom. This was the type of anchor that moored the ships of Ulysses and subsequently those of Columbus, John Paul Jones, and many a present-day mariner.

5.2   Anchor Elements   Although anchors come in a variety of shapes, weights, and capabilities, most share a number of common structural elements (Fig. 5.2). Every anchor has one or more flukes, also called *palms,* that grab onto the bottom. All have a *shank* (or vertical bar) that joins the

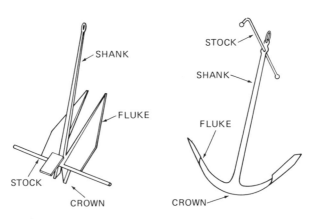

Fig. 5.2   Parts of anchors.

crown (or rounded lower section) with the ring or hole at the top where the anchor cable is attached. The tip of the fluke is called the *bill* or *pea*. Many anchors also incorporate a crosspiece, called the *stock,* which helps position the anchor properly so that the flukes can sink home into the bottom.

5.3   Grounding of Anchors   All anchors are designed to get a grip as quickly as possible after they hit the bottom. They take hold in one of two basic ways—either by hooking into the ground with one or both of their sharp flukes or by burying themselves completely, flukes, shank, and all. As an example, when an old-fashioned anchor is let go in fairly deep water, it strikes the bottom crown first and immediately falls over until it rests on one end of the stock. (See Sec. 5.4.) From this position, any drag on the chain to one side "cants" or capsizes the anchor, pulling the stock down so that it rests horizontally on the bottom and pointing one of the flukes fair for biting. As the drag continues, the fluke is forced into the bottom. If the anchor is well designed and the proper scope of chain is used, the heavier the drag, the deeper the fluke will dig in. To obtain this effect, it is imperative that the scope of chain be long enough for the pull on the anchor to be approximately parallel to the bottom. Use of too short a scope will lift the shank of the anchor and "break out" the fluke in a series of jumps. The stockless anchor works in a slightly different manner. When this type of anchor is dragged along the bottom, one fluke penetrates the sea bed. When this happens, the anchor rolls over, its "head" tumbles the other way and both flukes dig into the bottom, gaining a firm hold. (See Section 5.5.)

Anchor Types

Anchors in general use today may be classified into four basic types: old-fashioned, or *stock anchors;* patent, or *stockless anchors; lightweight* or *stock-in-crown anchors;* and *mushroom anchors* (see Fig. 5.3).

5.4   Stock Anchors   Old-fashioned, or stock, anchors have practically been abandoned by large merchant and Navy ships because they are extremely cumbersome to manipulate and difficult to stow. The anchor consists of a shank or vertical bar to which a rounded crown is attached at the bottom and a ring at the top. Arms extend from either side of the crown, to which flukes or palms are attached. These broad shield-shaped pieces located at the top of each arm provide the holding or biting surface (bill) of the anchor. The stock is located just below the ring and runs through the shank at right angles to the lower section of the anchor. Because of this angular placement, it is able to position the flukes properly for digging

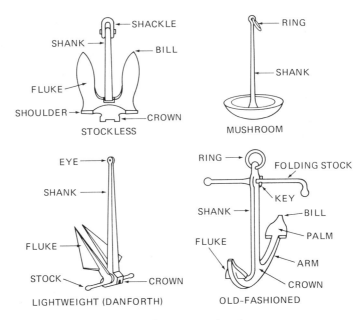

Fig. 5.3 Some types of anchors.

deeper into the seabed and thus resist breaking loose and dragging. Because of this superior holding power, stock anchors are still very much employed on many boats and by yachtsmen for small craft. (See Fig. 5.4.)

5.5 Stockless Anchors There are a number of different designs of modern stockless anchors, but all share the same distinguishing features—they are stockless. This feature provides enormous advantages, not only in ease of handling and stowing, but also in allowing the anchor to be hoisted directly into the hawse pipe and secured, ready for letting go. Although the anchors do not have the holding power of the old-fashioned anchor, they have been adopted almost exclusively on most seagoing vessels.

The stockless anchor consists of a heavy head in which the crown, arms, and flukes are forged in one piece. (See Figs. 5.5 and 5.6.) This unit is pivoted on the shank so that it can swing from 30 to 40 degrees either side of the shank. The flukes are large and long, and projecting shoulders or tripping palms are cast at the base of the flukes to make them bite. As the force of the drag exerts itself, the shoulders catch on the bottom and force the anchor to take hold by pushing the flukes downward into the bottom.

Because an upward pull on the ring of a stockless anchor has a tendency to break out the flukes, a longer scope of chain must be used than

Fig. 5.4 Large old-fashioned anchor displayed on the campus of SUNY Maritime College.

that normally required with a stock anchor. With too short a scope, or even under a steady pull with a long scope, a stockless anchor may still disengage its flukes as a result of gradually turning over and rolling them out. It also has a tendency to clog or ball on a muddy bottom, causing it to break loose from the bottom. The arms may then pivot to an angle that makes it

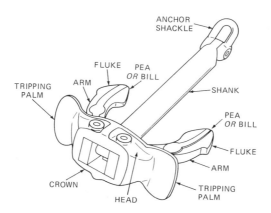

Fig. 5.5 Stockless or patent anchor.

Fig. 5.6 Large, stockless, 40,000-lb Navy bower anchor.

impossible for the flukes to bite, and the anchor can offer no resistance to dragging except by its weight.

5.6 Lightweight Anchors These anchors are constructed of comparatively light metal and are strong in tension. They gain their holding power by digging deep into the bottom rather than lying as dead weights. Lightweight anchors come in a wide variety of styles, shapes, and weights. An excellent example is the "stock-stabilized, pivoting-fluke" anchor (Fig. 5.7) developed by R. S. Danforth in 1939 and now commonly referred to as the "Danforth anchor." The main characteristic of this anchor is its placement of large flukes at such an angle that they drive deep into the bottom to ensure good holding power. The crown is designed to lift the rear of the flukes and force their points downward into the bottom. Good stability is

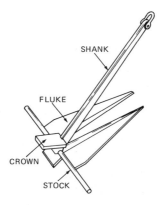

SHANK

FLUKE

CROWN

STOCK

Fig. 5.7 Lightweight anchor.

also obtained by placing the flukes close to the shank, thereby allowing a good length of stock, or antirolling rod, to be located in the crown. This rod is designed to fold parallel to the shank for easy stowage as well as to position the anchor on the bottom so that one or the other of the flukes is ready to dig.

These anchors are extremely useful in any situation where lightweight but good holding power are essential. They are carried on aircraft that land on water and have even been cast up to 3000 lb for use as stern anchors on LSTs. For recreational and commercial small craft, standard Danforth anchors are made in approximate weights from 2½ to 180 lb.

5.7 Mushroom Anchors Mushroom anchors are heavy metal weights, shaped like a mushroom with a long narrow stem serving as a shank. Because of their excellent holding ability they are used for permanent moorings and as anchors for channel buoys and other navigational aids. The rounded part, or crown, strikes the bottom first, and the upper surface of the mushroom is cupped to provide a biting surface. As the anchor shifts back and forth under strain, it digs itself deeper into the bottom, thereby increasing its holding power. Consequently, it takes a firm hold and remains fixed under the most adverse conditions. Because it has no projecting stock or flukes to foul its rode, the moored object can swing freely around a mushroom anchor without dislodging it.

5.8 Anchor Identification Marks Every anchor purchased for Navy use except small boat anchors and lightweight anchors 100 lb or less in weight has cast or cut in its crown a serial number. This number should not be confused with the weight number that also appears on the anchor. It is the practice on stock, or old-fashioned, anchors for one side of the crown to be marked with the initials of the inspector, the name of the manufacturer or commercial name of the anchor, and the serial number of the anchor. On the opposite side of the crown, the weight of the anchor, in pounds, the year of fabrication, and "U.S. Navy" are cast, stamped, or cut by the manufacturer. The same practice is adhered to in regard to stockless anchors except that all markings appear on both sides of the flat of the crown. (In the case of lightweight anchors, this legend may appear on the shank.)

The classification society for American Flag Merchant ships—American Bureau of Shipping (A.B.S.)—has also set rigid standards for the manufacturing and testing of anchors. Once an anchor has satisfactorily passed the A.B.S. requirements, the anchor is stamped by the manufacturer on one of the flukes and shank indicating the type of test, date, weight of the anchor, surveyor's initials, and so forth.

The Rode

All gear between the ship and the anchor is considered to be the *rode*. The rode usually consists of the anchor cable or chain, connecting shackles, bending shackles, and swivel pieces.

5.9 Anchor Chain Modern anchor chain is made up of die-lock or high-strength welded-steel links. Cast steel may also be used to form the links. The size of the link is designated by its diameter, called *wire diameter,* which is measured at the end, a little above the center line of the link. The length of a standard link is six times its wire diameter and the width is 3.6 times its diameter. All links are studded, that is, a solid piece is either forged or welded in the center of the link. The studs, which preclude the chain from kinking, are estimated to increase the strength o the chain by as much as 15 percent.

Under usual service conditions, the links of these types of chain do not stretch or become deformed, and the chain will operate smoothly over the wildcat during the period of its entire useful life. Cast-steel chain can be distinguished by the fact that the studs are solid and an integral part of the links, and each common link in the shot is identical. Certain types of high-strength welded-steel chain are constructed with alternating solid-forged links having integral studs. Every other link has the stud welded in place. In one type of high-strength welded-steel chain constructed of alternating solid-forged and welded links, every welded link is reforged after welding, and the entire chain has the appearance of being made of solid-forged (or cast-steel) links with integral studs throughout. The studs of the die-lock chain, although an integral part of the link, are split through the middle. The fact that the studs of cast-steel, die-lock, and high-strength welded-steel chain cannot be dislodged is a great advantage because it eliminates the danger of chain kinking and the pounding of links on adjacent links.

Die-lock links are made of two forged pieces, both roughly U-shaped. The two stems of one piece contain a series of paralleled indentations, giving them the appearance of screws. The socket piece has holes at each end of the U. In joining the two pieces to form a link, the pierced socket section is heated and the stems of the other section then thrust into the holes. The socket section is then pounded with a drop hammer, forcing its material around the stem indentations.

5.10 Standard Shots and Chain Identification Marks Lengths of chain called *shots* are connected to make up a ship's anchor cable. A standard shot is 15 fathoms in length. Each shot of the chain usually bears a serial number that is stamped, cut, or cast on the inner side of its end links at the time of manufacture. In the case of cast-steel chain, this number is preceded by the letters. "C.S." If an end link is lost or removed from a shot, the same number should be cut or stamped on the side of the new end link of the altered shot. Cast-steel, and some types of high-strength welded-steel, chain have these markings on the studs of alternate links only.

Each shot of die-lock chain has a serial number and date of manufacture stamped on the inner side of the end links. The studs of such chains are marked "U.S.N." on one side; the wire diameter of the chain appears on the other.

The American Bureau of Shipping requires that that all chain be subjected to a series of tests to determine its strength and freedom from defects and deformation. Once these tests have been satisfactorily completed, each 15-fathom shot of continuous chain must be clearly stamped by the manufacture in the manner indicated in Fig. 5.8.

5.11 Anchor Chain Marking Anchor chain is marked so that personnel tending the anchor will know exactly how much chain has already run out.

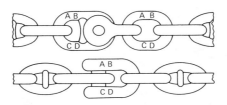

Fig. 5.8 A.B.S. shot markings: A—Number of the Certificate (furnished by surveyor); B—indication that chain has been satisfactorily tested to Bureau requirements and the grade as applicable; C—Nominal chain diameter in mm or in. (may be omitted if manufacturer embosses the diameter for permanency by forging, casting or the like); D—Classification Society stamp.

This is an extremely important matter since it is the only way of readily determining the length of the scope. The marking consists of turns of wire and stripes of white paint on varying numbers of links that are adjacent to the *detachable link* (see Sec. 5.12). Over the years, the merchant service and Navy have adopted similar anchor chain marking, which is shown in the following table:

Shot Number	Number of Adjacent Links Painted White	Turns of Wire on Last White Link	Color of Detachable Link (Navy Only)
1 (15 fathoms)	1	1	Red
2 (30 fathoms)	2	2	White
3 (45 fathoms)	3	3	Blue
4 (60 fathoms)	4	4	Red
5 (75 fathoms)	5	5	White
6 (90 fathoms)	6	6	Blue

In the Navy, all links of the next-to-last shot are painted yellow, and all links of the last shot are painted red. Painting the last two shots gives warning of the approach of the *bitter end* of the cable.

5.12   Detachable Links   A standard detachable link has been adopted for joining shots of anchor chain on almost all seagoing vessels. Its shape is similar to that of the other links in the same anchor cable to allow all links in the entire assembly to move freely over the wildcat of the anchor windlass.

The detachable link consists of a C-shaped link with two coupling plates, or lugs, that form one side of the link and a tapered forelock pin that holds the parts together and is locked in place at the large end by a lead plug, or pellet. (See Fig. 5.9)

When assembling detachable links, care should be taken to ensure that the parts are correctly matched since they are not interchangeable; matching numbers are stamped on the C-link and on each coupling plate to ensure correct assembly.

Detachable links should be disassembled one at a time to prevent the intermixing of the parts of different links. Before assembly, the parts should be cleaned and slushed with a mixture, by volume, of 40-percent white lead and 60-percent tallow. This slush serves as both lubricant and preservative.

5.13   Bending Shackles   Bending shackles are used for attaching the anchor to the chain cable. (See Fig. 5.10) A newer and often more simple method is to use a detachable anchor-joining link. This serves as a transitional member from the large-wire diameter of the anchor shackle to the smaller-wire diameter of the chain or swivel. Anchor-joining links are tested

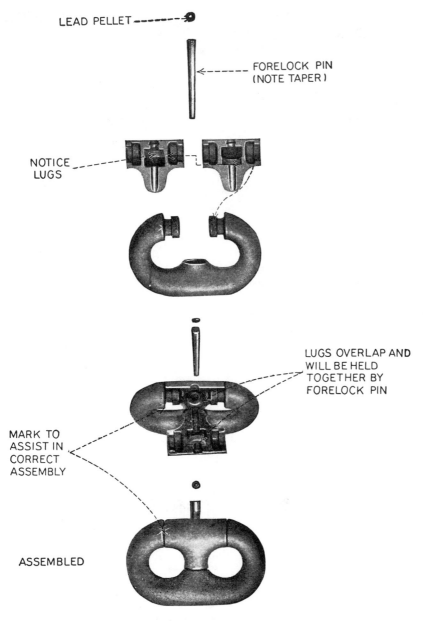

LEAD PELLET

FORELOCK PIN
(NOTE TAPER)

NOTICE
LUGS

LUGS OVERLAP AND
WILL BE HELD
TOGETHER BY
FORELOCK PIN

MARK TO
ASSIST IN
CORRECT
ASSEMBLY

ASSEMBLED

Fig. 5.9 Detachable link.

Figure 5.10 Large-sized bending shackle for 3½-in. heavy-duty die-lock chain. (*Official U.S. Navy photograph*)

and certified in accordance with the load requirements of the chain. Their ease of assembly and disassembly is superior to that of back-to-back shackles or a combination of chain-connecting links.

5.14 Swivels To eliminate the twisting and fouling of chain and anchor as a ship swings at anchor, a *chain swivel* is attached to the link that adjoins the anchor-joining link or bending shackle. The swivel is made up of two parts, a box and an eye joined with a threaded nut. The eye, or threaded portion, fits into the box and is secured with the nut. (See Fig. 5.11.) This nut is held in place with a pin. A bronze washer may be installed between the eye and the box to minimize friction within the swivel during use. *Mooring swivels* (Fig. 5.12) are large forged-steel swivels with two detach-

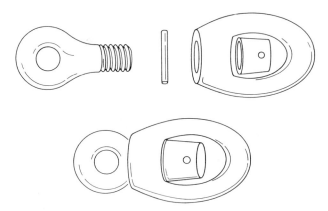

Fig. 5.11 Chain Swivel.

Fig. 5.12 Mooring swivel, large size. (*Official U.S. Navy photograph*)

able links attached at each end. They are normally used when two anchors or mooring buoys are attached to a single chain, thereby allowing the ship to swing freely without putting turns or twists in her cable.

5.15 Outboard Swivel Shots Standard *outboard swivel shots,* also termed *bending shots,* consist of detachable links, regular chain links, a swivel, an end link, and a bending shackle or anchor-joining link. (See Fig. 5.13.) They are fitted on most vessels to attach the anchor cable to the anchor. The use of an outboard swivel makes it possible to stop off the anchor (make fast the anchor chain) and break the chain between the anchor and the windlass when the ship is mooring to a buoy or mooring with

Fig. 5.13 Large swivel-shot chain with 3½-in. heavy-duty die-lock. (*Official U.S. Navy photograph*)

more than one anchor. Outboard swivel shots vary in length but usually do not exceed 5 fathoms.

5.16 Chain Stoppers Chain stoppers, which assist and supplement the operation of the anchor windlass, are a major part of the anchor hardware on deck. They are used for the following:

1. To ride to when at anchor, in conjunction with the brake band on the windlass
2. To let go the anchor more quickly than the brake band can
3. As an emergency fitting in case the brake band of the windlass should become inoperative
4. To hold a chain from running out while it is being taken off the wildcat in order to permit another chain to be put in service for heaving in
5. To hold anchors taut in the hawse pipes when housed
6. To hold an anchor chain that has been disconnected for the purpose of attaching a mooring swivel

The stopper consists of a turnbuckle inserted in a short section of chain, with a *pelican hook* or a *devil's claw* attached to one end of the chain and a shackle to the other (See Fig. 5.14.) The stopper is secured by the shackle to a permanent padeye on the vessel's deck. On naval vessels, a pelican hook is normally employed to hold the chain since it can be released under tension. The hook grips the anchor cable by straddling a link with its tongue

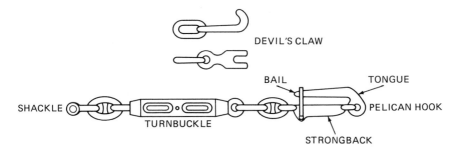

Fig. 5.14   Devil's claw and pelican hook.

and strongback. A bail is then held in place over the tongue by a pin in-serted through a hole in the latter. To release the cable from the pelican hook when under tension, the pin is pulled from the tongue and the bail knocked off with a maul, allowing the chain to run free.

On merchant vessels, a devil's claw is normally employed as a stopper because it is lighter in weight and requires less personnel to attend it than a pelican hook. The devil's claw is shaped like a two-fingered hand that grasps one link of the chain with its two fingers. Since the devil's claw can-not be released under tension, the anchor must be held by the brake of the windlass and the tension removed from the stopper by loosening the turnbuckle.

Stoppers should not be relied upon for holding anchors without taking other measures. Upon anchoring, first the wildcat brake band should be set up tight, and then the stoppers should be secured. The wildcat should be left disconnected from the engine. When riding to anchor with more than one stopper on the chain, the strain must be equalized between the stoppers by adjusting the turnbuckles.

5.17   Securing the Chain in the Chain Locker   In earlier times, the in-board end of the anchor rode was secured to bitts in the bow of the vessel. This led to the term *bitter end* for that end of the rode that is secured to the ship. Methods by which the bitter end is secured will vary greatly from ship to ship. In some cases, it has not been secured at all, presumably by accident, and the entire anchor rode has disappeared out through the hawse pipe.

The most common method of securing the chain in the chain locker is to shackle it to a ring in the deck. On some vessels, an opening has been cut in the bulkhead between the chain lockers and the bitter ends of the two chains shackled together. This is not considered prudent practice as it could lead to complications should it become necessary to slip the anchor cable. Another method which allows for quick slipping of the chain, should the need arise, is to pass the chain through a ring secured to the deck and brought up to and made fast to another ring in the overhead. A manhole on deck allows quick and easy access to the shackle or link securing the chain to the overhead ring.

For a number of years, it was believed that the bitter end of the anchor chain was supposed to be secured in the chain locker by a weakened link or shackle. Various means were devised to carry out this incorrect requirement—even to securing the bitter end with sail twine. In actual fact, the *Naval Ship's Technical Manual* requires the breaking strength of the shackle to approximate the weight of 300 fathoms of chain and the breaking strength of the padeye to be 1.75 times that of the shackle.

5.18 Care to Prevent Bending Chain Anchor chain should not be subjected to short bends in use. In fact, whenever possible, care should be taken to ensure that anchor chain is never subjected to bending, such as might occur when the cable is lying across a vessel's stem; when a vessel is riding to a single anchor in a strong wind or current and is "horsing," or tacking back and forth; or when the cable is rove (passed) through a buoy ring or passed over a bolster of small radius. Chain becomes less strong when subjected to such transverse bending, especially if constructed of die-lock detachable links; extra precaution should therefore be taken to prevent subjecting links of this kind to transverse bending.

Anchor Windlass

The anchor windlass is a machine used to raise the anchor (Fig. 5.15). It consists primarily of an engine, normally powered by electricity; a wildcat, which is the gear used to grip the chain; suitable controls for connecting the wildcat to the engine; and brakes for controlling the wildcat when it is not engaged with the engine. *Gypsyheads,* when fitted to a windlass, are used in handling lines and are driven by the same engine; they are usually fitted with controls so that they may be operated independently.

5.19 Wildcat A wildcat is a sprocketed wheel in the windlass that is fitted with ridges, called *whelps,* to engage the links of the chain and prevent it from slipping. The wildcat can be disengaged from the shaft of the windlass so that it may turn freely when the anchors are dropped. It is fitted with a brake to stop the chain at the desired length of scope.

5.20 Friction Brake This is a brake band that bears on a flywheel. By tightening the band with either a bar or handwheel, the speed of the wildcat can be controlled and even stopped. With the brake off and the windlass unlocked, the wildcat can rotate independently of the shaft, and vice versa.

Fig. 5.15 Anchor windlass of the attack transport U.S.S. *Cambria* (LPA 36.) (*Official U.S. Navy photograph*)

5.21 Locking Ring A locking ring is a device with pigeonholes into which a bar is placed to lock the wildcat to the shaft of the windlass engine. The wheel is usually turned forward to disengage the wildcat and turned aft to engage it. When the windlass is locked, starting the engine will either heave in or walk out the chain.

5.22 Capstan Heads or Gypsyheads These are large drums fitted to the windlass. An integral part of the shaft, they are used to handle the forward mooring lines and can usually be run independently once the wildcat has been disengaged.

Letting Go and Heaving In (Also see the Anchoring Section of Chapter 10 in Part II/Shiphandling).

5.23 Letting Go To let go an anchor, the wildcat is unlocked and the brake applied to hold the wildcat rigid with respect to the frame. The stoppers are then released, and the chain is ready for letting go. The anchor is let fall by releasing the pressure on the brake band, thereby allowing the wildcat to revolve and the chain to run out. This method for letting go provides good control over the run of the chain, which can be arrested with the brake as soon as the anchor strikes bottom. As the vessel rides away from her anchor, the scope of the chain can then be payed out as necessary.

An alternative method, in which the anchor is released directly from its pelican hook stopper, is normally employed by the Navy. In this case, a little extra chain is usually roused out (hauled out by hand) forward of the windlass so that the anchor will have a sufficient running start, when the stopper is released, to overcome the inertia of the chain between the windlass and the chain locker.

The brake is then set up (put on) slightly to keep the chain from taking charge and dragging the roused-out slack back into the locker. This tension on the brake must be released the instant that the anchor starts from the hawse pipe. The windlass is unlocked. One man with a heavy maul is needed to stand by the remaining stopper, and another to pull out the locking pin from the pelican hook. At the word, "Let go!," the pin is pulled out and the locking ring is knocked away. Both men must jump clear at once. The chain will go rattling out with a roar and will continue to do so until a sudden slackening speed indicates that the anchor has hit bottom. At this instant, the man at the windlass should start braking in order to keep the chain from piling up on the anchor. As the ship gradually drops downstream, the chain is veered by slackening the brake until the desired scope has been reached. Then the brake is set up, and the riding stoppers are put on.

5.24 Heaving In To heave in, the wildcat is locked to the axle or shaft of the windlass, the brake band is released, and the stoppers are removed. As power is applied to the windlass, the chain is drawn up through the hawse pipe and down into the chain locker. When the shank of the anchor is two-blocked (all the way up) in the hawse pipe, the housing stoppers are put on, the brake is set up tight, and the windlass is unlocked from the shaft.

Care, Inspection, and Painting of Ground Tackle

Modern stockless anchors are extremely rugged both in design and construction and, therefore, require little care under normal conditions. The flukes should be examined frequently to insure thay are free to move throughout their full arc on the shank. The crown socket or pivot bar should be kept free of mud, rocks, etc. Shackle pins should be examined frequently for stress cracks or elongation. This is due to the shackle pin receiving the greatest amount of strain and abrasion both when the anchor is housed in the hawse pipe and also when in actual use during an anchoring situation.

Whenever possible, anchors should be used alternately. This distributes the wear evenly between the anchors and their respective chain cables. Such practice also lengthens the life span of the chain, as chain which lies idle in the chain locker for an extended period may become brittle, with an accompanying reduction in strength.

Anchors, chains, and appendages should be kept in good condition by the ship's force. The chain cables should be overhauled whenever necessary and precautions taken to see that the various shots are properly marked and in good order. As the chain comes in when getting under way, each link should be examined for cracks and for other defects.

Once each quarter and more often if necessary, all anchor cables in sizes up to and including 1 1/2 in. should be ranged on deck and examined throughout their entire length. If necessary, they should be scaled and cleaned of rust and other foreign matter. Detachable links should be disassembled and examined for excess wear or corrosion, and where conditions warrant, the links should be replaced by new ones. Before reassembly, the links should be white-leaded. The detachable link located in the outboard swivel shot is fitted with a corrosion-resisting steel locking wire to hold the taper pin in position. Disassembly of this link requires the removal and probable destruction of the locking wire, and the availability of replacement wire of the same type should be established prior to this removal for inspection.

Shackle bolts, locking pins, and swivels should be carefully examined and put in order, and such parts as require it should be coated with the special black chain paint furnished vessels for this purpose. In cold weather, it is desirable to apply some heat to counteract the natural thickening of this paint. This may be done by an immersion electric heater or a steam coil. Experience has also shown that, when left standing for a considerable period, a turpentine substitute may evaporate to a considerable extent, with a resultant thickening of the paint. Vessels receiving anchor chain coated with green paint from stores should leave this coating intact and cover it with black chain paint.

Chain of sizes in excess of 1 1/2-inch wire diameter should be overhauled, wirebrushed, and placed in a good state of preservation as often as is necessary. At least once each 18 months, all anchor chain cable, regardless of size, including shackles, shackle pins, and detachable links, should be examined, overhauled, and placed in a good state of preservation. Shackles, shackle pins, and detachable links should be refitted and greased or white-leaded, and identification marks should be restored if necessary.

To distribute wear uniformly throughout the entire length of cable, the shots should be shifted to a new position as necessary. In the case of vessels having cable whose shots are connected with detachable links, 40- or 45-

fathom shots may be shifted to any position in the cable that in the commanding officer's opinion, will tend to distribute the wear evenly throughout the cable. In the case of vessels whose cable shots are connected with U-shaped shackles, the 40-fathom shot should remain the first shot inboard of the outboard swivel shot regardless of wear. If serious defects are discovered during this overhaul of the anchor cables, the defective shots should be shifted to the bitter end of the cable until replacement can be accomplished.

Ground Tackle for Boats

Boat anchors are similar in design to ship anchors but are, of course, much lighter and smaller. Scientific design to provide good holding power has taken the place of sheer weight for most all boat anchors. Some of the more popularly used boat anchors are shown in Fig. 5.16.

5.25   The Navy Stockless   The Navy stockless anchor, although designed primarily for large ships, has gained popularity with yachtsmen. This is due to the absence of a stock, which allows the anchor shank to be drawn into the hawsepipe by its own rode, thus easing the stowage and securing problem. The flukes and shank are designed so that when properly stowed, the shank will be securely stationed in the hawsepipe and the flukes nestled snugly against the hull of the vessel. This is not a particularly light-weight anchor, and part of its holding power and ability to dig into the bottom is the anchor's weight. Because of its weight, it can be backbreaking to handle on small vessels. Large commercial and Navy ships possess sufficient mechanical power to handle the Navy stockless anchor, but on small pleasure craft the situation is entirely different. Although this anchor has less holding power than the old-fashioned anchor, it does possess the advantage of no stock or fluke projecting above the ocean bottom to foul the rode. Because of its weight, it is less sensitive to sea bed conditions and can dig into most bottoms with the exception of hard sand. Sand bottoms present a problem due to the blunt flukes of the Navy stockless. In penetrable sand, its holding power is about seven times its weight and about three times its weight in soft mud. In a mud bottom, this anchor does have the tendency to roll out of a set due to its lack of a stock. In spite of its weight and reduced holding power, there are a number of Navy stockless variations which have become highly regarded.

5.26   Old-Fashioned or Stock Anchors   These anchors are of the hooking type and are also known as the fisherman, yachtsman, and Herreshoff. The main advantage of this type of anchor is its superior holding power and its ability to dig into hard bottoms and bury itself up the shank. The main

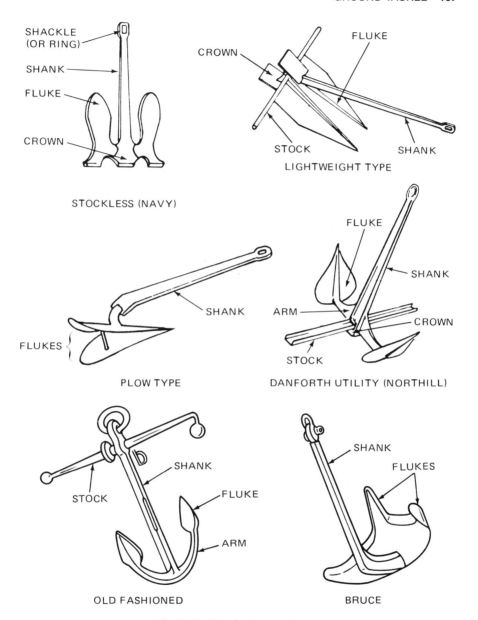

SHACKLE
(OR RING)

SHANK

FLUKE

CROWN

STOCKLESS (NAVY)

FLUKE

CROWN

STOCK

SHANK

LIGHTWEIGHT TYPE

SHANK

FLUKES

PLOW TYPE

FLUKE

SHANK

ARM

CROWN

STOCK

DANFORTH UTILITY (NORTHILL)

SHANK

STOCK

FLUKE

ARM

OLD FASHIONED

SHANK

FLUKES

BRUCE

Fig. 5.16   Popular boat anchors.

disadvantage is that the lazy fluke points upward from the bottom, which can easily foul the anchor rode. Additionally, the small size of the flukes provides little holding power in soft sea beds. These anchors are also difficult to stow due to the stock being ninety degrees from the flukes. Many are designed to be dismantled or folded, which eases the storage problem to some degree. These anchors will set with a relatively small scope of rode and can be relied upon to hook and hold in most conditions. Because of the shape of the anchor, they are difficult to handle over the side without marring the hull. Many of the newer designs are provided with features such as wide flukes for better holding power, sharp points for easier burying capability and a well-faired back edge of the fluke to reduce the tendency of the rode to foul.

5.27 Lightweight or Danforth The lightweight anchor developed by Danforth is probably the most commonly used boat anchor in America. It is composed of four basic parts—a pair of flukes, a stock, a crown assembly, and a shank. These parts are made of steel and usually hot-dipped galvanized. The long sharp flukes are designed so that a heavy strain will bury the anchor completely. It is an excellent anchor for hard sand because of the large fluke area in relationship to its weight and because its flukes are set at angles of thirty two degrees to the shank, providing an optimum burying angle. This limits, however, the amount of allowed vertical pull, so that a longer scope of rode is usually required. This type of anchor tends to break out if the strain direction changes from that at which originally set. It is also subject to fouling as the rode may get wrapped around the crown. The flukes may also become jammed by a stone or ball of mud, causing the anchor to not take a set but to merely skip along the bottom.

5.28 Northill The Northill is a very sophisticated anchor designed for lightness and ease of stowage. The arms of the Northill are set at right angles to both shank and stock and the flukes are set at an angle carefully determined to bite quickly, and with good penetration, into the sea bed. The bills of the flukes are sharp, also providing for a quick deep bite. The broadness of the fluke provides good gripping power once the anchor is set. To facilitate compact stowage, the stock of the Northill is arranged to fold up against the shank and some versions have hinged arms on stainless steel bolts so that they may also fold into an even more compact space. The Northill provides excellent holding power in most bottoms and comes in a variety of sizes to fit most boatman's needs. One drawback is that the anchor is difficult to haul aboard without scratching the topsides. Also, it has one lazy fluke that can tend to foul an anchor rode.

5.29 The Plow or CQR This is an excellent anchor for all types of sand, mud, and clay bottoms but may tend to skip across the seabed when heavy weeds prevail. The Plow or CQR is a stockless anchor whose twin flukes are shaped like a pair of plow shares back-to-back. It has a high effective fluke area and excellent holding power. The anchor lies on its side when lowered to the bottom and tips upright when a horizontal pull is applied. This action also causes the bill to dig into the seabed, providing good penetration. It is nonfouling and provides excellent holding power even when the direction of strain changes. The shank of the anchor is hinged, allowing 75° of sideways motion. As the strain changes, the sideways motion of the shank tends to keep the flukes dug in, and causes them to rotate until the anchor resets itself aligned with the new direction of pull. The CQR has been estimated to provide holding power up to 300 times its own weight.

5.30 The Bruce This is a new anchor to the yachting scene, being first introduced in the 1970s, but one that has become relatively popular in a short time. It has good holding power in sand and mud and requires a relatively short scope of rode. It is a one-piece anchor possessing no moving parts made in the shape of a three-palmed scoop. When first coming in contact with the sea bed, it lies on its side with one palm making contact with the bottom. As a horizontal strain develops, the palm touching the bottom begins to dig in, causing the anchor to swing into a more upright position. This causes the center palm to also make contact with the bottom rotating the entire anchor until finally the outer palm begins to dig in. When all three flukes are dug in, it possesses great holding power due to the large fluke area. It will not foul the rode and also possesses the ability to retain its holding power even though the direction of strain changes dramatically. The Bruce is easy to handle and stow on a bow roller but is difficult to stow on deck or below due to its odd shape.

The Anchor Rode

The anchor rode serves the same purpose on small boats as it does for large ships—to connect the anchor to ship or boat. As such, it must possess the same qualities for small craft as it does for large oceangoing vessels. These are: strength to hold the boat against the wind and waves up to the full holding power of the anchor, elasticity to absorb shock loads caused by the surging of the boat, resistance to the marine environment in which it must function and a good ability to withstand abrasion from both the sea bottom and from short chafe points on the boat or deck gear. Ease of handling by the crew without the use of special equipment is also a highly desirable attribute.

Most small pleasure craft use dacron or nylon as an anchor rode as it is easy to handle and stow without any special equipment. These materials also possess sufficient elasticity to allow the boat to surge in a seaway. This ability to stretch and absorb the shock relieves the strain on the anchor and the bitts or cleats to which the rode is secured.

Nylon is usually the preferred choice because of its greater strength in relation to its size and also because of its elasticity (stretching a third or more with safety). It possesses two or three times the strength of manila. As a consequence, a smaller diameter line may be used. In addition to its lighter weight, nylon also resists rot, decay, and mildew. It can be stowed wet, but continuous exposure to moisture, heat, chemicals, and sunlight should be avoided.

5.31 The Chain Lead A very important part of a line-type rode is the chain lead. The chain is inserted between the anchor and line rode to absorb the abrasion of ocean bottoms, help set the anchor, and allow for a smaller anchor lead angle.

The chain must equal or exceed the breaking strength of the rode and should also weigh as much as the anchor it is used with.

References

Rate Training Manual, Boatswains Mate 3 & 2. Naval Training Command, NAVTRA 10121–E.

Rate Training Manual, Boatswains Mate 1 & C. Naval Training Command, NAVTRA 10122–D.

Seamanship. Washington, D.C.: United States Government Printing Office, Navpers 16118–B.

Bamford, Don. *Anchoring All Techniques For All Bottoms.* Newport, Rhode Island: Seven Seas Press, Inc.

Bearden, Bill. *The Blue Jackets Manual.* 20th ed. Annapolis: United States Naval Institute.

Brown, Charles H. *Seamanship and Nautical Knowledge.* Glasgow: Brown, Son and Ferguson, Ltd.

Chapman, W. *Piloting, Seamanship and Small Boat Handling.* New York: American Book-Stratford Press, 1979.

Griffiths, Garth. *Boating in Canada, Practical Piloting and Seamanship.* Toronto: University of Toronto Press.

Hayler, William B. *American Merchant Seaman's Manual.* 6th ed. Centreville, MD: Cornell Maritime Press, 1980.

Hinz, Earl. *The Complete Book of Anchoring and Mooring.* Centreville, MD: Cornell Maritime Press, 1986.

Seamanship. Editors of Time-Life. New York: Time-Life Books, 1975.

Cargo Handling and Underway Replenishment

6.1 Winches Winches are the primary power source for cargo handling. They are used for topping and swinging booms, for controlling cargo whips, and for replenishment at sea rigs. On most modern vessels, steam winches have been replaced by electric-powered winches, due to ease of operation and less maintenance (Fig. 6.1).

Electric winches may be installed two ways. On older vessels and retrofitted vessels, the winch, motor, and motor brake are generally on deck, separate from the resistors and control panel, which are located in the masthouse. On newer vessels and new construction, the winch is constructed as one unit with the winch, brake, and resistors in a single housing.

Electromagnetic brakes as well as conventional brake bands are fitted in most winches. Loss of power automatically causes the electomagnetic brake to engage, suspending the load until such time as power is regained. An additional safety device on electric winches is an overload limit switch which causes a circuit breaker to cut off power to the winch when the operator attempts to lift a load in excess of the winch's capacity.

Hydraulic cargo winches have gained some popularity in recent years. This winch affords the operator precise speed control and, in general, has a greater rated capacity than electric winches. Hydraulic winches need to

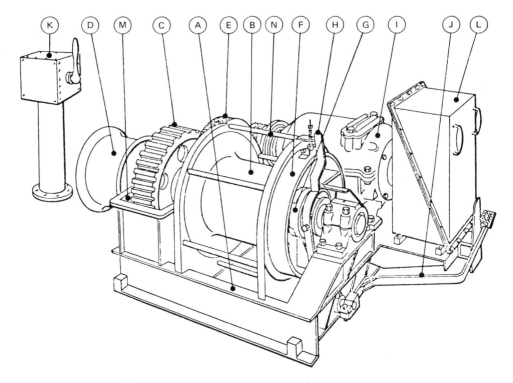

Fig. 6.1 A typical winch:

A Bedplate	F Drum Brake	K Speed Control
B Drum	G Drum Clutch	L Electric Brake
C Drum Gear	H Clutch Lever	M Oil Bath
D Gypsy Head	I Drive Motor	N Rope Guard
E Reduction Gearing	J Drum Brake Lever	

be warmed up for about thirty minutes prior to use, particularly in cold weather. Due to the hydraulic piping required, these winches require more maintenance than electric winches and are more subject to failure with repeated use.

Whatever the type of winch, it's necessary to become familiar with the operating instructions and the winch controls before operating the winch.

Excessive strains on runners and guys can be caused by an inexperienced operator accelerating or decelerating too rapidly with a heavy load. Just as dangerous is operating with an empty cargo hook. If the runner is slacked off too rapidly, loops will form on the winch and may become fouled.

6.2 Booms Navy and merchant ship booms, although built to lift the same amount, are tested differently. A tested merchant ship boom is overloaded 125 percent. For replenishment-at-sea operations requiring booms, a Navy-rated 10-ton boom is the minimum acceptable. Boom ratings are generally 3, 5, 8, 10, 15, 20, 30, etc., tons. Booms of 15 tons to 60 tons were formerly called *jumbo booms.* Today, "jumbo boom" usually refers to the largest boom on a ship. Its length is usually 60 ft, the criterion for this length being the ability to reach far enough over the side to spot cargo when the boom is topped to its most efficient angle. In Navy ships, this works out to a 25-ft outreach when topped to an angle of 60 degrees.

A heavy-lift boom is one of 50- or 60- to 150- or 200-ton capacity, and even more. Representative heavy-lift booms are the two 60-tonners found on the *U.S.S. Paul Revere* class of attack transports. As a case in point, the range of boom sizes in this class shows the variety of booms that may be found on a single ship. The *U.S.S. Paul Revere* has two 3-ton or 5-ton booms, two 8-ton, three or four 10-ton, one or two 30-ton, and a pair of 60-ton booms. Two Military Sealift Command cargo ships have a special "heavy lift" designation, each carrying a pair of 150-ton booms. A few U.S. Merchant ships and new Navy LKAs also have a heavy-lift capability. Usually, these are configured with a Steulchen or similar rig, described later in this chapter.

There are several methods of raising and lowering booms. (See Fig. 6.2 for cargo handling gear nomenclature.)

Most ships have special topping-lift winches installed on the masts and king posts. These winches offer greater speed in raising and lowering booms. Additionally, newer designs have powered guys as well. An example of this is the Ebel mechanical guy rig, devised by F. G. Ebel, Senior Naval Architect of the Maritime Administration. As can be seen in Figs. 6.3 and 6.4, there are no hand lines to tend; everything is under power. Preventers are not present. The topping-lift attachment point to the king post is offset inboard of the gooseneck, thus giving the topping lift an additional function as an inboard guy or vang. This rig has two main advantages; first, reduced time in respotting the gear, and second, the ability to use the gear in swinging boom operations. This second advantage has allowed ships fitted with Ebel gear to lift and position containers with remarkable speed in locations without shoreside facilities for the loading and discharging of containers.

6.3 Yard-and-Stay Method In the yard-and-stay method of cargo handling, two booms are used. (See Fig. 6.5.) One of these booms plumbs the hatch and is called the *hatch boom.* The other, called the *yard boom,* is rigged out over the side so that it plumbs the dock or pier.

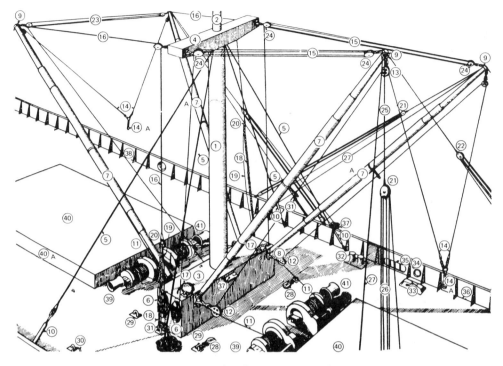

Fig. 6.2 Cargo handling gear nomenclature:

1. Mast	14A. Cargo hook	29. Padeye
2. Topmast	15. Topping lift (multiple)	30. Padeye and ringbolt
3. Mast table	16. Topping lift (single)	31. Shackle
4. Crosstree	17. Stopper chain	32. Bitts
5. Shroud	18. Bull chain	33. Open chock
6. Topping lift cleat	19. Bull line	34. Closed chock
7. Hatch boom	20. Bale	35. Freezing port
7A. Yard boom	21. Outboard guy	36. Scupper
8. Gooseneck	22. Inboard guy	37. Cleat
9. Linkband	23. Midship guy	38. Bulwark
10. Turnbuckle	24. Topping lift block	39. Hatch winch
11. Cargo whip	25. Guy pendant	40. Hatch
12. Heel block	26. Guy tackle	40A. Hatch coaming
13. Head block	27. Preventer	41. Yard winch
14. Cargo whips	28. Snatch block	

The cargo whips coming from the hatch and the yard winches are rove through their respective heel and head blocks and are shackled to the same cargo hook.

If the whip has a thimble spliced in the end in the usual manner, it may be impossible to reeve the whip through the block, making it necessary to

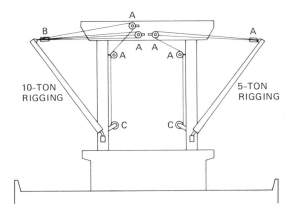

Fig. 6.3 Schematic representation of the topping lifts on the Ebel rig. All blocks are single *(A),* except the boom topping lift block on the 10-ton rig *(B);* have 14-in. sheaves; and are rove off with ¾-in., 6 by 19 improved plow steel wire rope. The hauling part is led to a topping lift winch *(C),* which is controlled from the position where the winches are operated.

remove the whip from the winch drum so that the winch end may be rove through.

Another method is often used by Navy ships on which cargo operations are not the rule and cargo-working gear is struck below until needed. A large eye is formed by turning back the end of the whip upon itself and securing, with wire rope clips, the eye thus formed. It is thus an easy matter

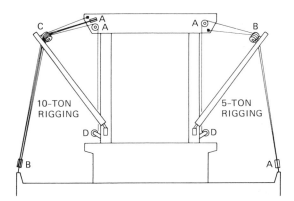

Fig. 6.4 Schematic representation of the mechanical guys on the Ebel rig. All blocks marked with an *A* are single, *B* indicates a double block, and *C* is a quadruple block. All bocks have 14-in. sheaves and are rove off with ⅝-in., 6 by 19 improved plow steel wire rope. *D* marks a guy winch that is controlled from the position where the winches are operated. Note that the standing parts are secured to the crosstrees.

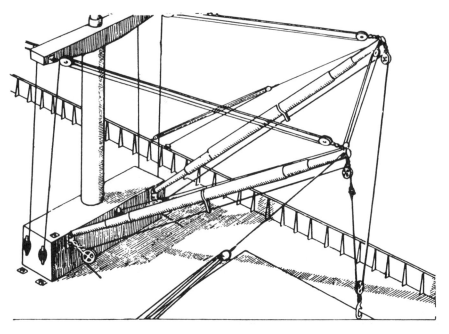

Fig. 6.5   Yard-and-stay with midship guy (block-in-bight).

to remove the clips, reeve the whip through the blocks, and replace the clips.

Booms are spotted in a working position by hauling on the guys. The yard boom is positioned over the pier, clear of the ship's side. The hatch boom is spotted slightly past the centerline of the hatch.

The booms are set up on outboard guys and preventers. Guys should be slightly more taut than preventers. The inboard or midships guys are set as taut as possible by hand. The cargo whips coming from the hatch and yard winches are rove through their respective heel and head blocks and are shackled to the same cargo hook. If the whip has a thimble spliced in the end in the usual manner, it may be impossible to reeve the whip through the block, making it necessary to remove the whip from the winch drum so that the winch end may be rove through. Cargo whips are shackled to the cargo hook, and a load is picked. The load is raised until the angle formed by the whips is about 120 degrees. Now the outboard guys and preventers are equalized by easing off the guy tackles. As outboard guys and preventers are being equalized, all slack is taken in on the inboard or midships guys. It is a good practice, when originally spotting the booms, to swing them slightly wider than desired. When guys and preventers are equalized, the booms will move inboard into position.

The winch controls for the yard-and-stay are usually so located that one man can operate both winches and have an unrestricted view of the hold. A load is moved from hold to pier in the following manner: The yard whip is kept slack as the hatch whip hoists the load from the hold and clear of the hatch coaming. Then, by heaving around on the yard whip and paying out on the hatch whip, the load is moved across the deck and over the side. When the load is plumbed under the yard boom, the hatch whip is slacked off and the yard whip lowers the load to the pier.

Most yard-and-stay rigs use ¾-inch wire; therefore, a block with at least a 12-in. sheave must be used for a runner block. Larger whips, of course, will require larger runner blocks (⅞-in. wire requires a 14-in. block).

6.4 Yard-and-Stay Double Purchase Nearly all methods of rigging yard-and-stay cargo handling gear for heavy lifts require that the cargo whip be doubled up and a block used. Doubling up the whip accomplishes two things: It doubles the load that may be lifted by the whip, and it reduces the load on the winch by half. The only difference between this rig and the ordinary yard-and-stay is that both cargo whips are doubled up and the runner blocks shackled to the cargo hook.

The end of the whip may be secured in several ways. The best method is to shackle the eye of the whip to the upper end of the boom. This tends to keep the bight of the whip from turning on itself and becoming wrapped up. It has the advantage of steadying the swing of the load in a fore-and-aft direction.

The chief advantage of the yard-and-stay double purchase is that lifts as heavy as the safe working load of the cargo booms can be handled at nearly the same rate as ordinary 1-ton or 1½-ton drafts. Light filler cargo can be handled with scarcely any loss of time.

6.5 Single Swinging Boom with Double Purchase The single swinging boom with double purchase is considered one of the best methods of rigging for handling loads beyond the capacity of a single whip up to the capacity of a single boom. It is quickly and easily rigged and has the added advantage of flexibility. Loads may be placed at any point in the square of the hatch or on the deck.

Since the yard boom will be the one to be rigged, the hatch boom is topped up and secured out of the way. (See Fig. 6.6.) The procedure is as follows:

1. The hatch whip is stripped from its drum and replaced with the yard boom's topping-lift wire, making sure that the topping lift wire has a fairlead. This can be done only with a boom having a multiple topping lift.

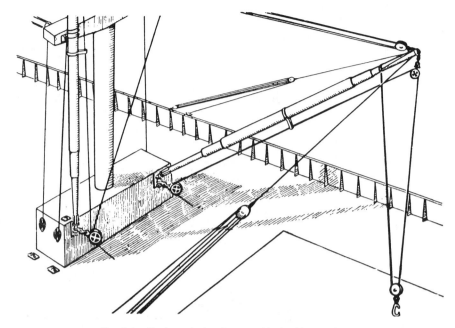

Fig. 6.6 Single swinging boom with double purchase.

2. The yard whip must be checked for sufficient length to permit doubling up (250 to 300 feet).
3. The whip is then doubled up.
4. The preventers are removed from the yard boom and the guys led to the proper fittings.
5. The boom is topped up and swung into position by hauling on the guy tackles. The hauling part of the guys may be fair-led to winches at adjacent hatches, or men may be assigned to haul on the guys when swinging a load.

6.6 Two Swinging Booms A load greater than the capacity of a single boom may be handled by using two booms working together as a single swinging boom. In this case, the whip of the two booms should be fastened to opposite ends of a lifting bar or strongback. As illustrated in Fig. 6.7, the lifting bar serves to equalize any difference in winch operation.

To move a load from the hold to the pier, it is first hoisted clear of the coaming. Then by using the guys, both booms are swung in unison until the load is over the pier. The load is then lowered to the pier. Swinging the load is a difficult operation, and it may be necessary to set the load on deck

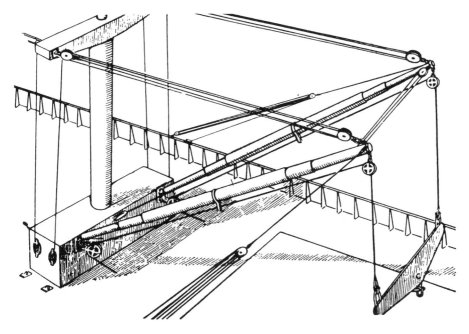

Fig. 6.7 Two swinging booms.

to change the position of the booms. Because this rig is cumbersome and difficult to handle, it should be used with great caution.

6.7 Block-in-Bight Method of Rigging a Double-Ganged Hatch Many ships have doubled-ganged hatches, that is, they are equipped with two pairs of ordinary cargo booms. Handling heavy lifts at a hatch in this manner is facilitated by rigging all four booms, as illustrated in Fig. 6.8.

The rigging procedure is as follows:

1. The forward hatch whip is rove through a runner block and its eye shackled to the eye of the after hatch whip. The forward yard whip is rove through a runner block and shackled to the after yard whip.
2. The shackles joining the two sets of whips are run to within a few feet of the head blocks of the after booms.
3. The two runner blocks are shackled to the cargo hook.
4. Heavy lifts that are slightly less than the sum of the safe working load of two parts of the cargo whips may now be loaded or discharged by the usual yard-and-stay method.

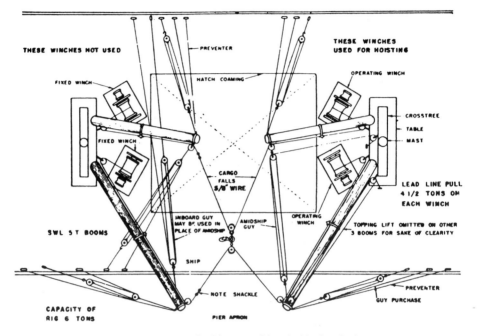

Fig. 6.8   Rigging a double-ganged hatch (block-in-bight).

This rig has the advantage of being rigged quickly without having to lower the booms, and only two winches are required for its operation. In addition, the gear may be readily singled up for ordinary light loads.

6.8   Rigging for Heavy Lift   Heavy-lift booms are normally carried in an upright position, collared to the mast, and fully rigged with topping lift, load purchase, and guy tackles already secured. The first step in rigging a heavy lift is to lead all purchases to power, four souces of power being required. Load-purchase and topping-lift wire are led through heel blocks to the winches at the hatch to be worked. Guy tackles are led to proper fittings, and the hauling parts of the guys are led to adjacent power sources. Although it is preferable to use the anchor windlass or the after warping winch, the winches at the next hatch may be substituted, depending on the boom's location. If the hatch equipped with the boom is double-ganged, the additional two winches can be used for the guys.

Freeing the boom requires release of the collar that secures it to the mast. On some ships, the weight of the boom may be taken off the collar by heaving around on the topping lift wire. On others, it is necessary to use a tackle or a special breasting-up line. This line is hitched to the boom, clapped in a snatch block on the mast, and led to the gypsy. A strain is taken on it until the collar can be released, and then the line is slacked off until the weight of the boom is on the topping lift.

Prior to making a hoist with a heavy boom, all gear should be checked to ensure that all blocks are running free and that none of the lines are chafing. Wire on the winch drums should lay tight and even. Guy tackles should be free of twists; hauling parts of guys fair-led to power sources; and hasps and hooks of snatch blocks moused securely with seizing wire. Stays, shrouds, and preventers must be checked and, if necessary, tightened.

The other cargo booms at the hatch must be swung clear of the working area. Ordinarily, it is sufficient to swing these other booms outboard against the shrouds and secure them with guys. In working deck cargo, it may be necessary to top them very high to clear the deck space.

6.9 Operation of Heavy-Lift Boom The head of the boom is positioned directly over the load, with the slings carefully slung and shackled to the lower purchase block. The load is first hoisted a few inches off the deck to check for any indication of undue strain and then hoisted carefully until it is clear of the hatch coaming. By heaving around on the guy tackles, the boom is swung over the ship's side, and the load is ready to be lowered away.

In working a heavy-lift boom, the handling of the guys requires special attention. When the boom is topped, the guys must be slacked off; when it is lowered, they must be taken in. Swinging the boom calls for heaving in on one guy and paying out on the other. This requires good coordination by the winchman. One guy serves as a hauling guy, the other serves as the following guy. The following guy gives more difficulty. Be sure to ease off on the following guy smartly otherwise it could part, causing much damage. It is good seamanship to allow a small amount of slack in the following guy but not enough slack to permit the boom to slap about.

A heavy-lift boom suspended outboard with its load could cause the ship to develop a considerable list, placing undue strain on the guys. The natural tendency is for the boom to swing outboard in the direction of the list. Smart handling of guys to maintain control of the swinging boom is absolutely essential.

6.10 Precautions during Heavy Lift All that has been said about safety awareness and common sense precautions applies doubly when working with heavy lifts. Here are a few rules with special application to heavy lifts:

1. *Do not overload.* Be sure that the rig will make the lift safely. Rig carefully, checking each piece of gear as it is rigged. Check stays and shrouds. Before picking up the load, check each part of the rig.

Hoist the load a few inches off the deck, and then check for indications of undue strain.

2. *Hoist, swing, and lower the load slowly and smoothly.* Jerking places undue strain on the rig. Hoist loads only high enough to clear the coaming and bulwarks.

3. *When a load is being moved, keep every part of the rig under observation.* Be alert for any change in sound. Normally, a wire or natural fiber rope will hum under strain, but if it starts to squeak, squeal, or smoke, it means danger. Faulty blocks can also give warning by squeaking or groaning.

6.11 Steulchen Rigs Many merchant ships and a few Navy ships now have the Steulchen rig, or a variation of it. It consists of two supporting masts (usually inclined outboard at their tops) and a heavy-lift boom. The topping tackle is fastened to swivel heads at the tops of the masts and to pivots at the boom head to prevent twisting of the tackle. Four winches are provided: two for hoisting the load and two for each of the topping tackles. The boom is raised by hauling on both topping winches. The boom is swung by hauling in on one topping winch and paying out on the other.

Among the advantages of the Steulchen rig are its greater lifting capacity, less deck gear, and the increase in speed of the cargo hook. Its main advantage and chief characteristic is that the boom head, when fully raised, can be flopped forward (or aft) between the support mastheads, thereby allowing the boom to work the adjacent hatch. (See Fig. 6.9.)

6.12 Cranes Cranes are enjoying ever increasing popularity over conventional mast-and-boom systems. They take up less deck space and are easier and quicker to spot over a desired location than the old mast-and-boom combination. (See Fig. 6.10.) The present trend is to position one crane between two hatches, thereby reducing considerably the amount of cargo-handling equipment that a vessel must carry.

Cranes are designed to handle light loads and heavy lifts. Figure 6.11 shows two different crane arrangements: a single 12.5-ton type and a twin 40-ton type. The twin crane can operate with each crane acting independently or in a twin mode for heavy lifts. In a twin-crane design, two single cranes with their own rotating mounts are mounted on a single rotating mount. When a heavy-lift capability with horizontal movement is required, the single rotating mount upon which both cranes are mounted rotates. When topping up or down is required, the two cranes top up or down together. The two cargo falls are mated with a lifting beam and operate together.

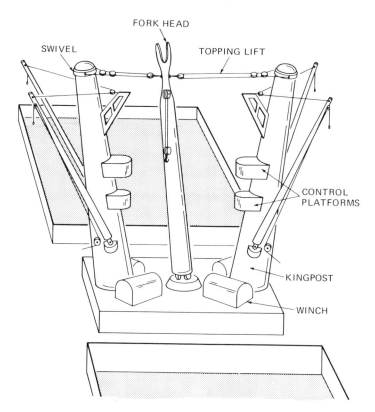

FORK HEAD

SWIVEL

TOPPING LIFT

CONTROL
PLATFORMS

KINGPOST

WINCH

Fig. 6.9 The Steulchen jumbo boom, which can swing between kingposts to work either of the two holds.

6.13 Unitized Cargo Handling Unitized cargo handling is a mode of cargo transport in which a cargo container of a particular design becomes the method of transport rather than the carrying vehicle (ship, train, etc.). Irrespective of the type of vehicle in which the container is carried and regardless of how many times the container is transferred from one conveyance to another, the cargo knows only one mode of transport: the container into which it was loaded at its point of origin and from which it will be discharged at its point of destination.

Containers are essentially large boxes of standardized dimensions that are capable of continued reuse. The container must be capable of being transferred from one mode to another and being secured quickly and easily.

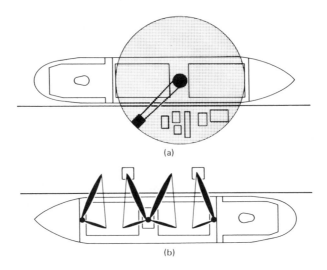

(a)

(b)

Fig. 6.10   The spotting ability of the crane is graphically compared to that of conventional gear in this sketch. (a) The spotting area of the crane is that covered by the shaded section. The shaded area of the sketch *(b)* shows the spotting areas of the conventional gear. Note that this indicates the possibility of one crane doing the work of four sets of gear provided the hook can keep up with the men in the hold. Although this would not ordinarily be possible, it is conceivable that two cranes could take the place of four sets of gear. *(Courtesy of Colby Steel & Manufacturing, Inc.)*

Container dimensions are standardized by the International Standards Organization (ISO). Common dimensions are lengths of either 20 or 40 ft, a width of 8 ft, and heights of 8, 8½, and 9 ft.

A typical container ship is shown in Fig. 6.12. It carries cargo on deck as well as below deck.

There are at present two popular methods employed for the securing of containers on deck: *lashing* and a *buttress-and-frame* system. Lashing is more popular, for varied reasons: Its mechanics are familiar to most seamen, it has a low initial cost (as opposed to the buttress-and-frame system), and it is flexible. Figure 6.13 shows a typical lashing system.

Figure 6.14 shows various appliances used to secure containers on deck in a lashing system. The object is to transform structurally a multitude of containers into one unit. *Stackers* have the function of locking corners together—single stackers, vertically; double stackers, vertically and horizontally. *Bridges* lock corners together at the top of the stow. *Lashing pendants* secure the stow to the deck to prevent it from toppling as the ship rolls.

Lashing has disadvantages. First, a weakness in any part of the system endangers the whole stow on that particular hatchtop. A weak or poorly

Fig. 6.11 Twin 40-ton and single 12½ ton electric deck cranes loading cargo. *(Courtesy of Clarke Chapman Engineering, Ltd.)*

secured pendant or a container that fails under the strain of compression during a steep roll may create a domino-effect failure in the rest of the stow. Also, lashing does not prevent racking stresses that tend to distort a container into a parallelogram from a rectangular structure whenever the containership heels over. This effect occurs because the lashing pendants stretch under load.

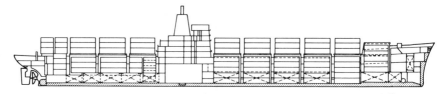

Fig. 6.12 Combination 20-ft and 40-ft containership with midship superstructure. *(Courtesy of American Mail Line)*

The buttress-and-frame system is different. (See Fig. 6.15.) All of the across-the-deck and fore-and-aft forces imposed on the containers pass through the frames and buttresses to the ship's structure itself. Racking stresses are eliminated by the rigidity of the framing structure. The only thing the containers offer is vertical support.

As containers are loaded by shoreside crane, frames are put in place and secured to the buttresses. The disadvantage of this arrangement is that all stowage positions must be filled by a container, thus precluding flexibility of stowage arrangement. Another disadvantage is the high initial cost of investment.

Below deck, containers are secured by *cell guides* that extend from the forward and aft bulkheads to hold the containers in rigid, nontoppling columns. No securing devices are required, and racking stresses are eliminated because of the rigidity of the cell guides. The shoreside simply lowers

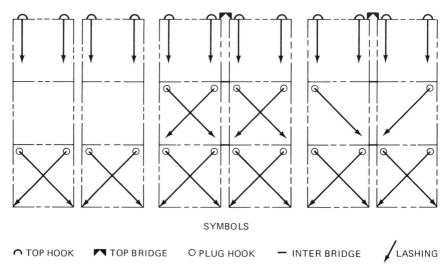

SYMBOLS

∩ TOP HOOK   ◤ TOP BRIDGE   O PLUG HOOK   — INTER BRIDGE   ╱ LASHING

Fig. 6.13 Typical lashing systems for securing containers on deck.

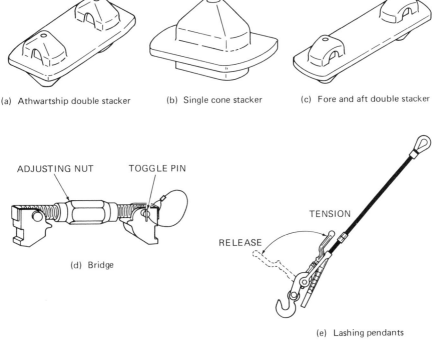

(a) Athwartship double stacker

(b) Single cone stacker

(c) Fore and aft double stacker

(d) Bridge

(e) Lashing pendants

Fig. 6.14 Lashing system securing devices.

a container into place and proceeds to latch onto another container for stacking on the first container.

Container ships are almost always loaded and discharged by means of a shoreside crane. Loading and discharge rates are figured by the number of lifts per hour rather than tons per hour. The average rate is 20 lifts per hour per crane. If 20-ft boxes were being loaded at an average gross weight of 20 tons each, the loading rate would be 400 tons per hour.

Replenishment at Sea

The United States Navy has, over the years, developed techniques and procedures of transferring consumables from logistic support ships to combatant ships while these are under way at sea. Since World War II, the U.S. Sixth Fleet operating in the Mediterranean and the U.S. Seventh Fleet operating in the Pacific have resupplied themselves by utilizing underway replenishment (UNREP) techniques. The British, French, and Canadian Navies have adopted replenishment-at-sea techniques that are similar to those used by United States Fleet units. Underway replenishment has proved use-

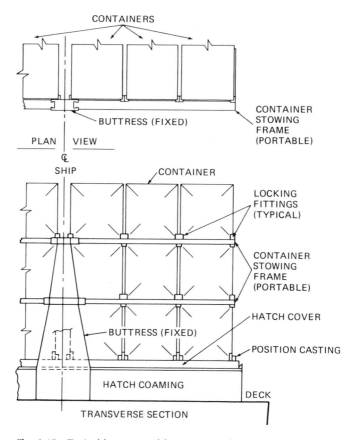

Fig. 6.15 Typical buttress-and-frame system for securing containers.

ful to Naval forces and may well have economic impact in commercial practice as ship size and operational costs warrant. The first significant replenishment operation at sea in the U.S. Navy was in 1899, when the collier *U.S.S. Marcellus,* while being towed, transferred coal to a warship, the *U.S.S. Massachusetts.* Since that time, many methods have been tried and abandoned. Those described in this chapter have been adopted as the most feasible and are currently used in the fleet. Although the reference here is to booms, most modern UNREP ships rig their replenishment stations directly from fixed king posts and sliding blocks. Otherwise, the rigging is identical.

6.14   General Discussion   The cargo of the UNREP ship is determined by one of the following considerations: (1) requisitions prior to loading, (2) anticipation of fleet requirements, or (3) need for issuing provisions and stores in standard units. A package or kit that contains a specified grouping of items in fixed quantities, usually pallet loaded, is considered a standard unit.

There are four general principles for the loading of UNREP ships to ensure maximum efficiency in unloading:

1. Lots of homogeneous cargo should be stowed, if possible, in several holds so that they may be off-loaded at as many transfer stations as possible.
2. Provision must be made for adequate passageways and working areas in and around the cargo to permit quick segregation of lots, checking, and separate handling of heterogeneous types of supplies. Loading must be planned so that the remaining cargo can be readily reshored at the completion of replenishment to reduce the danger from shifting cargo.
3. Bulky and heavy items must be placed near loading areas and in holds that can accommodate their transfer most readily. The hatch opening, the height of the hold, and the fact that certain types of receiving ships can receive bulky items only at certain stations must all be considered.
4. Replenishment must be accomplished at the highest possible tonnage rate per hour and in the shortest practicable time consistent with safety.

There are several methods that can be used to transfer cargo at sea. The tabulation shown provides the load capacities of these methods under normal operating conditions. These figures must be reduced when transferring in rough or heavy seas.

Method	Maximum Capacity per Load (lb)
Burton	6000
Housefall	2500
Double housefall	2500
Modified housefall	3500
Wire highline	3500/800*
Manila highline (5 in.)	600
Manila highline (3 in.)	300
STREAM	6000 plus†
Double burton	up to 12,000

* Load capacity with manila outhaul.
† Load capacity of STREAM depends upon preset tension in the highline wire.

6.15 Ship Formation for Underway Replenishment Normally, the receiving ship maneuvers to take station alongside the delivering ship and adjusts course and speed as necessary to maintain station during the process. Except for the gear that is rigged aboard the receiving ship, such as fairlead blocks and riding lines, the delivering ship normally provides all the equipment for the operation. Large combatants usually take station to port of the delivery ship; small combatants, to starboard. Formation course is selected on the basis of wind and sea conditions as well as tactical situations affecting the naval units. During UNREP, a "lifeguard" ship take station astern of the delivery ship should a "man overboard" occur. Course changes by ships connected alongside can be accomplished by skilled personnel. Care must be exercised not to change the speed of the delivery ship, unless a speed change is ordered. A speed of 10 to 15 knots is advisable during UNREP operations. A combination distance-phone line is rigged between ships operating alongside. This line enables rapid bridge-to-bridge communication and indicates closing or opening of the distance between ships.

6.16 Burton Method While there are various ways of rigging the delivering ship, it is usual practice for the boom on the side adjacent to the receiving ship to be used for the transfer, and the boom on the opposide side to be used to hoist the loads from the hatch. The following method is the most efficient way of burtoning carge when only one set of booms and winches is available at the active hatch. Normally, each ship furnishes its own burton whip, one whip from each ship being led to the swivel fitting above the cargo hook. In some cases, the delivery ship supplies both whips, one fairled to a high point on the receiving ship that approximately plumbs the load landing area of the receiving ship. The burton whip sizes range from ¾ to 1-in. 6 × 37 or 6 × 31 high-grade plow steel (IWRC) between 600 and 800 ft in length.

Setting Up The procedure for rigging a burton station on the delivering ship, using the port boom for transfer (burtoning) and using the starboard boom as the hatch boom (hoisting cargo out of the hold) is as follows (See Fig. 6.16):

1. Secure the thimble eye of the burton whip (running from port boom) to the triple swivel and hook. Reeve the bitter end of this wire through to the boom head and heel blocks and lead it to the winch. Secure the bitter end of the whip to the winch drum and spool the whip onto the drum.
2. Fashion a lizard of 3-in. manila with a large shackle at the bitter end (optional). Place the shackle over the whip outboard of the head block.

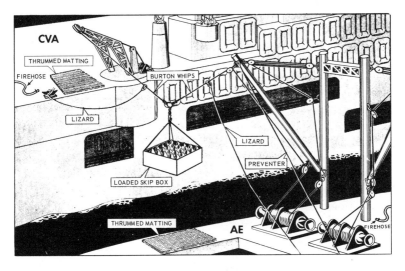

Fig. 6.16 Burton rig.

3. Secure a heavy preventer of suitable length and strength to the inboard side of the boom head.
4. Secure shackle pins with seizing wire.
5. Top up the boom in such a manner that the whip plumbs the desired loading point on the port side of the main deck.
6. Set up and belay the guys.
7. Lead the preventer to the starboard side of the ship at an angle as close to 90 degrees from the boom as possible, or to the fixed position provided. Take a strain and belay the preventer.
8. Rig the starboard boom (hatch boom) so that its whip plumbs the center of the hatch. Attach a 3–in. manila lizard to the whip. This done, the starboard boom is then ready for hoisting loads from the hold to the loading point on the main deck's port side.

The Receiving Ship Burtoning stations are rigged in accordance with ship plans and specifications that designate specific fittings for this application. The burton whip block is secured to the burton fitting. The burton whip bitter end is rove through the whip block and led to the drum or gypsy head. A 3-in. manila lizard may be shackled around the whip (optional).

The thimble eye of the burton whip whould be on deck ready for passing when the burton whip messenger with attached snap hook is received on board from the delivering ship.

Operation When the ships are steaming alongside, the delivery ship passes a messenger to the receiving ship. The receiving ship bends its burton whip to the messenger, allowing the delivery ship to haul in the burton whip. The rig is ready for use when the ship is attached to the triple swivel. the actual transfer takes place as follows:

Beckets or the sling of the load are placed into the cargo hook. The delivering ship heaves in on the burton whip and hoists the load clear of the deck and rail. The receiving ship takes a strain on its burton whip, and as the delivery ship slacks away on her burton whip, the load is thus worked across. When the load is hanging from the receiving ship's burton point, the delivery ship slacks her whip and the receiving ship lowers the load to the deck. Successful burtoning requires teamwork between winchmen on both ships.

Stress in rigging may be reduced to a minimum by keeping the load as low as possible (consistent with sea conditions) and hoisting it just high enough to clear the rails of the two ships. As the load crosses between ships, it should be kept as low as possible, yet be maintained at a sufficient height to prevent immersion. Upon completion of transfer, the rig is disconnected in reverse order of connection.

6.17 Housefall Method While burton methods require power sources on both ships and teamwork between the ship's winchmen, housefall methods utilize the power sources of the delivering ship only. Rigging for housefall transfers can be done in several ways, making use of one or two booms. The housefall boom and whip can be plumbed over the center of the hold, thus serving the twofold purpose of lifting cargo to the deck and then transfering it to the receiving ship. This method, however, reduces the rate of transfer because of the longer distance the hook travels. Rigging procedure requires two booms, as shown in Fig. 6.17.

Setting Up Rigging the normal housefall as described below requires the use of two booms of the delivering ship, one boom located at the active hold and one boom at the hold forward of the active hold:

1. Secure the thimble eye of the cargo whip to the triple swivel and hook, reeve the bitter end of this wire through the head and heel blocks of the boom at No. 2 hold and spool it onto the winch drum. The position of the boom, the guys, and the preventer are the same as for burtoning.
2. Secure temporarily the housefall block (a runner block of about 20 in.) to the bulwark with a short piece of 2-in. manila line outboard, opposite the center of the hold.
3. Secure the thimble eye of the transfer whip to the triple swivel and hook. Reeve the bitter end of the whip through the housefall block

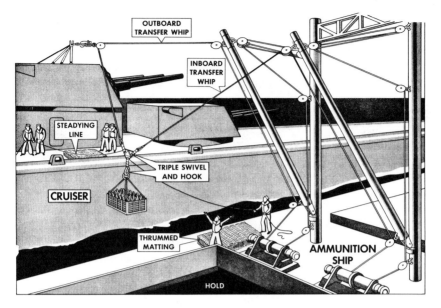

Fig. 6.17 Housefall rig.

(outboard of all projections and rigging), walk it forward, reeve it through the head and heel blocks of the boom at No. 1 hold, and then spool it onto the winch drum.

4. Secure galvanized preventer wire (at least 1½-in.) to the inboard side of each boom head. Top up the booms so that the whip clears all standing rigging projections when making transfers to the receiving ship.

5. The remaining steps in rigging the delivering ship are the same as for burtoning.

Operation The receiving ship secures a gin block to the suspension point (as for burtoning). A wire pendant with a thimble eye is run up through this block. The thimble eye remains on deck for attachment to the pelican hook of the housefall block.

During receiving, the hook is secured to the thimble of the housefall block eye. A strain is applied to the wire pendant until the housefall block is two-blocked, and the hauling part is then secured.

The housefall block messenger is detached from the bridle and used to haul the housefall block over as the delivering ship pays out on the housefall transfer whip. The block is then secured to the wire pendant and made ready for cargo transfer.

On the delivering ship, the load is hoisted clear of the rail with the housefall cargo whip. The strain is taken on the housefall transfer whip, and the load is worked over to the receiving ship.

On completion of the transfer operation, the lines are passed back to the delivering ship in the usual manner. This type of rig proves advantageous when the receiving ship cannot keep good fore-and-aft position.

When loads must be kept higher above the water than is normally possible in housefalling, the housefall rig can be modified by the addition of a trolley block on the transfer whip. This trolley rides on the outboard transfer whip. Rigging is the same as for the basic housefall except attachment points must be close together, one over the other, so that the trolley will ride in an upright manner.

6.18 Double Housefall Method   The double housefall method speeds transfer of cargo to ships that do not have sufficient suspension points to handle more than one rig. However, double housefalling is somewhat slower than housefalling to two separate receiving stations.

In a double housefall operation, the delivering ship uses two adjacent housefall rigs. Both housefall blocks are passed over the receiving ship simultaneously. In operation, one housefall rig alternately passes a loaded net to the receiving ship while the other returns an empty net to the delivering ship. The two housefall rigs on the delivering ship must have a minimum separation of 25 ft to prevent the outboard whips from fouling.

6.19 Wire Highline Method   In the wire highline method, a wire is suspended between the ships on which a trolley can ride. The load, attached to the trolley, travels along the highline. The loaded trolley is pulled to the receiving ship by an outhaul line and is pulled back to the delivery ship by an inhaul line.

Setting Up   To use the wire highline, the receiving ship must have a high attachment point. This is usually a padeye welded to the ship's structure. There is also an additional padeye of 1-in. diameter located about 12 to 18 in. below the first padeye. The block used to fairlead the inhaul line is attached to this second padeye. Sufficient deck space must be provided in the vicinity of the padeyes to handle the cargo being received.

The highline passes from a winch on the delivering ship through a block on a boom head and then across to a padeye on the receiving ship (Fig. 6.18). A trolley rides the highline and is moved toward the receiving ship by an inhaul line (manually handled) and brought back to the delivering ship by an outhaul line (winch-operated).

A boom is normally used to provide a satisfactory lead for the wire highline. However, any other point of suspension on the ship's structure

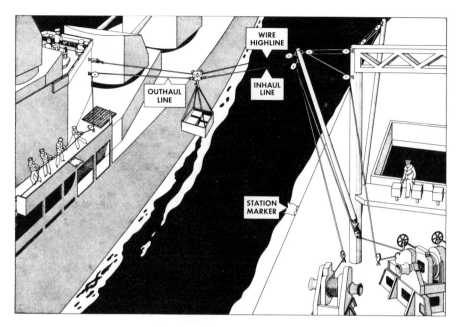

Fig. 6.18 Wire highline rig.

will serve if it is sufficiently high and strong. The highline is normally 600 ft of ¾-in. wire (high-grade plow steel) with a thimble eye on its outboard end. A highline is boom rigged as follows:

1. Reeve the inboard end of the wire through a trolley block, through the head and heel blocks of the boom, and then spool it onto a winch drum.
2. Attach a pelican hook to the thimble eye with a ⅞-in. shackle.
3. Shackle the manila outhaul line (2½-in.) to the inboard end of the trolley block and then run it through an 8-in. wooden block and a swivel attached to a becket on the underside of the head block. The outhaul line is finally taken through a fairlead to the gypsy head of a winch.
4. Equip the manila inhaul line (2½-inch) with a snap hook attached to bridle. Fake down the center section of the line on the deck clear for running and shackle the standing end to the outboard side of the trolley block.

Little preparation is required on board the receiving ship for the high-line method. Below the highline padeye, an 8-in. snatch block is secured to take the manila inhaul line. Additional snatch blocks are rigged to fair-lead the inhaul line clear of the landing area.

Operation   When the inhaul line comes on board the receiving ship, it is detached from the birdle and led into the blocks provided for it. The pelican hook or shackle is secured to the highline padeye, establishing the highline connection.

The load is now hooked to the trolley block, and a strain is taken on the highline, thus lifting the load clear of the deck and rail. The load is hauled across to the receiving ship by slackening the outhaul line and taking up the inhaul line. When the load is suspended over the landing area, the delivering ship slacks off on both the highline and outhaul line, setting the load on the receiving ship's deck.

It is important always to keep a good catenary in the highline to avoid unnecessary strain when a load is suspended.

6.20   Manila Highline Method   The manila highline can be used in transferring provisions, personnel, and light freight. Preparation for rigging is essentially the same as for a wire highline, and a 12-in. snatch block attached to a padeye at the delivering station is sufficient. It is kept taut during transfers either by manpower or by a capstan. The entire rig is relatively easy to set up and is the safest method now available for transferring personnel.

To transfer personnel singly or in pairs, the only safe rig is the manila highline with all lines tended by hand. Heaving in lines by hand, with a sufficient number of men standing by for emergency, is the best insurance against the highline's parting from sudden strains caused by rolling ships.

6.21   Vertical Replenishment (VERTREP)   Vertical replenishment utilizes helicopters to transfer goods between ships. This method does not often replace conventional methods; it merely augments them and reduces the time required to replenish ships in a dispersed formation.

6.22   STREAM   Underway replenishment techniques continue to advance with the introduction of systems and equipment of recent design. STREAM incorporates these advances into a standard, highly effective transfer system. The STREAM transfer rig utilizes a wire highline connected between ships. A trolley rides the highline. Inhaul and outhaul whips originating in and tended from the delivery ship haul the trolley, or a wire whip or manila outhaul tended on the receiving ship can be used. The fundamental difference between STREAM and the conventional methods described previously is the preset and controlled tension in the highline wire that allows STREAM to handle loads up to 9000 lb. A brief description of the major STREAM equipment follows.

Ram Tensioner   The ram tensioner maintains the present tension in the highline wire. It consists of a very large hydraulic cylinder, the piston of which acts as the ram; an air compressor; an accumulator; and air flasks. The highline is rove through a movable block on the piston and a fixed block on the cylinder and then passed to the highline winch. Air from nearby flasks keeps pressure on a piston in the accumulator cylinder, from which the pressure is transmitted to the ram. As tension on the highline or span wire is relaxed, pressure in the system causes the ram (piston) to extend, taking up the slack. (See Fig. 6.19.)

Sliding Block   The sliding block is an elevator that travels vertically on a king post of the delivery ship. The sliding block lifts the transfer load

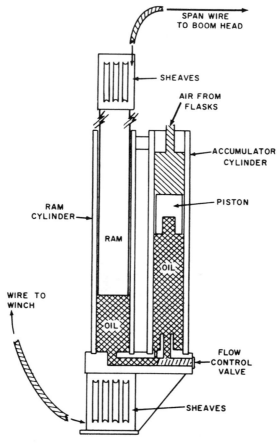

Fig. 6.19   Ram tensioner.

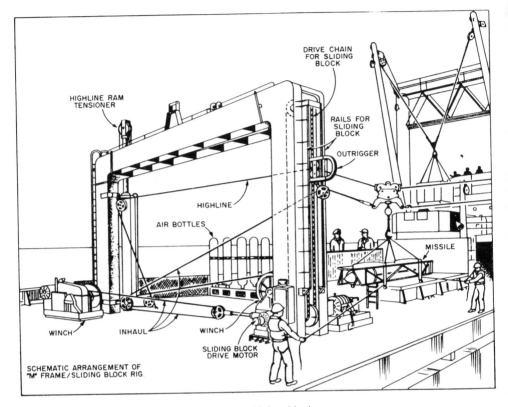

DRIVE CHAIN
FOR SLIDING
BLOCK

HIGHLINE RAM
TENSIONER

RAILS FOR
SLIDING
BLOCK

OUTRIGGER

HIGHLINE

AIR BOTTLES

MISSILE

WINCH

INHAUL

WINCH

SLIDING BLOCK
DRIVE MOTOR

SCHEMATIC ARRANGEMENT OF
"M" FRAME / SLIDING BLOCK RIG.

Fig. 6.20 Sliding block.

above bulwark obstructions before transfer. The highline is rove through the sliding block. (See Fig. 6.20.)

Sliding Padeye The sliding padeye is an elevator traveling vertically on a king post on the receiving ship. The highline bitter end is fixed in the sliding elevator. Its function is to lower loads to the deck of the receiving ship. Other devices are available with STREAM that can perform a similar function.

Various items of specialized equipment have been designed for the STREAM system. These are used to handle missiles and other large or delicate ordnance. STREAM equipment in this category includes Terrier/Tartar receivers, Talos receivers, missile strongbacks, and specialized wire rope fittings.

6.23 Fueling at Sea Fueling at sea is normally accomplished by using either of two accepted rigs, span wire, or the close-in. The method is determined by the kind of ship delivering the fuel and the conditions under which the delivery must be made. The main difference between the rigs lies in the method of extending the hose to the receiving ship. Of the two, the span wire is preferred and requires the more elaborate rig. Ships not equipped to transfer by span wire must do so by the close-in method.

6.24 Close-in Method—Setting Up for Delivery The hose in the close-in rig is supported by boom whips and bight lines leading from saddles (at least three) on the hose to booms or other high projections on one or both ships. A description of equipment and arrangements that may be used as a guide in making up the hose and lines for close-in fueling follows. (See Fig. 6.21.)

The span of hose usually consists of seven 35-ft lengths of lightweight, collapsible hose 6 or 7 in. in diameter (4-in. hose for destroyers) and flow-through saddles. To the outboard length of the hose are attached:

1. A flow-through riding line fitting
2. A 4-ft length of hose
3. Another riding line fitting
4. A 9-ft length of hose
5. End fittings for the hose

The saddle whips attach to the flow-through saddles. Three saddle whips are used. The first consists of 300 ft of ¾-in. wire rope or 5-in. manila,

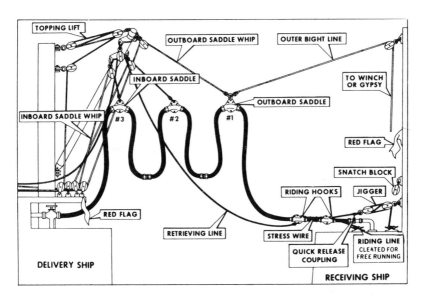

Fig. 6.21 Close-in rig.

fitted with a thimble eye and ⅝-in. shackle at one end. The whip is shackled to the outboard saddle, rove through the appropriate-size block shackled to a padeye below the head block, and then passed through a fairlead to a winch. Saddle whips 2 and 3 consist of 240 ft of ½-in. or ¾-in. wire rope or 5-in. manila, fitted at one end with a thimble eye and ⅝-in. shackle. Shackled to saddles 2 and 3 respectively, these whips are rove through blocks on the king post or boom and then through fairleads to winches.

An outer bight line is used only when fueling vessels that are larger than destroyer types. It is a 5-in. manila 50 fathoms long, with a thimble eye and a 1-in. shackle at one end. To the other end is taper-spliced a 15-fathom length of 2½-in. manila, then 15 fathoms of 21-thread manila, and to that 30 fathoms of 6-thread or 9-thread manila. The thimble eye of the outer bight line is shackled to the outboard end of the outboard saddle whip.

The retrieving line consists of 50 fathoms of 3½-in. manila, with a thimble eye and a ¾-in. shackle at one end. The thimble eye is shackled to the inboard riding line fitting, and the line is rove through a 12-in. or 14-in. snatch block on the forward side of the boom head and then through a fairlead to a gypsy head. This gypsy head may be used alternately for both the retrieving line and the inboard saddle whip.

The hose messenger is a 3½-in. manila line 40 fathoms long, with a thimble eye and a ¾-in. shackle at one end. To the other end is taper-spliced a 15-fathom length of 21-thread sisal. The thimble eye of the messenger is shackled to the outboard riding line fitting. The messenger is seized to the outboard end of the hose at 3-ft intervals with two turns of 21-thread.

The fueling boom is positioned at 90 degrees to ship centerline and in such a way that the head of the boom is just outboard of the ship's rail. In rigging, the hose should be topped up inboard-to-outboard as follows:

1. The inboard saddle is two-blocked.
2. Saddles 1 and 2 are hoisted to a point just below the inboard saddle.
3. With the retrieving line, the inboard riding line fitting is hoisted to a point just below the outboard riding line fitting that is just outboard of saddle 1.
4. The hose messenger is led to the superstructure deck and then faked down athwartships.

Receiving Ship—Setting Up A 12-in. snatch block, through which the hose line messenger is led, is provided at each fueling station. This block is placed inboard of the ship's side about 6 ft above deck. To expedite hauling in the hose, a line with a snap hook on the end should be led through the snatch block, ready to attach to the hose messenger. In some ships, additional blocks are necessary to fairlead the messenger.

On ships larger than destroyers, a 14-in. snatch block is secured at the highest convenient point above the spot where the hose will be taken aboard. This is used to fairlead the outer bight line, which helps support the outboard hose saddle.

A riding line about 3½ to 7 fathoms long, made of 4-in. or 5-in. manila, is provided at each fueling station. One end of this line is eye-spliced and secured to the hook or shackle of a jigger tackle. The other end is left free until the hose is aboard, when it will be secured to a cleat.

Operation As the receiving ship completes her approach and steadies alongside, bolos—or line-throwing gunlines—are sent over from each station on the delivering ship to corresponding stations on the receiving ship. Using these lines, the telephone cable, distance line messenger, hose line messengers, and outer bight lines are started over.

If the delivering ship has difficulty getting her gunlines across, the receiving ship may use her own line-throwing guns if so requested by the delivering ship. In all cases, gunlines must be passed back at the earliest convenience to the ship furnishing them. As soon as telephone jackboxes reach the deck of the other ship, connections must be made and communications established. Tending of the distance line and the telephone cable seized to it is undertaken at the same time.

The delivering ship pays out the hose messenger by hand. On the receiving ship, the hose messenger is either led to the snatch block provided about 6 ft above the deck and then to a winch or it is fair-led on deck for heaving in by hand. The delivery ship pays out on the retrieving line and saddle whips, allowing the hose to be hauled across by the messenger. Assistance can be rendered by men heaving on the outer bight line, if such a line is used. As the end of the hose comes on board, the stops securing it to the messenger are cut, one by one, until the bight of the riding line is slipped over the riding hook, and the riding line is set taut. The hose end is now ready to be coupled to the receiving ship's hose or to be lashed in the fueling trunk. After this is done, the messenger is restopped to the hose and removed from the snatch block, and the bitter end is returned to the delivery ship.

When an outer bight line is used, as is normal when the receiving ship is larger than a destroyer, the receiving ship takes it to the 14-in. snatch block provided at some convenient high point and tends it carefully. This line is important. As the ships roll, the hose bight may dip in and out of the water unless the outer bight line is used to raise and lower the outboard hose saddle. When the ships roll in opposite directions, the hose rises suddenly, and the bight line as well as the delivery ship's saddle whip, which is also helping to support the saddle, stretch out horizontally. If these lines are not slackened immediately, they will break under the tension.

The outer bight line, tended by the receiving ship, and the outboard saddle whip, tended by the delivery ship, need constant handling by alert, intelligent men. High-speed winches must be used. The winchmen on both ships must work together, keeping their eyes on the outboard saddle and should try to maintain the two lines in the form of an upright V.

When the outer bight line is not used, the outer hose bight is controlled by the outboard saddle whip alone.

When fueling is completed, the engineer force on the receiving ship gives the "Stop Pumping" signal, disconnects the hose after a back suction has been taken or the hose blown clear, and closes the necessary valves or replaces the end flanges or hose caps. The hose is eased out on the bight of the riding line, and as the outer bight line is being eased out, the delivery ship heaves in and two-blocks the inboard and outboard saddles. The delivery ship stops off the inboard saddle whip, removes it from the gypsy head, and belays it to a cleat. The retrieving line is placed on the same gypsy, and with it the hose is hauled aboard. Finally, the receiving ship returns the outer bight line, the telephone lines, and the messengers. The delivery ship returns the distance lines.

6.25 Span Wire Rig This method permits ships to open out to between 140 and 180 ft and, when ram-tensioned, to 240 ft. The hose is extended by use of a single-span wire stretching between the two ships, the hose hanging from trolley blocks that ride along the wire. The greater separation is safer and more conducive to easy maneuvering and better station-keeping. The span wire rig not only allows commanders a wider latitude in choosing a fueling course but also facilitates the use of antiaircraft and antimissile weapons should the need for them arise. Its higher suspension also affords protection for the hose in rough weather. (See Fig. 6.22.)

Setting Up for Delivery The hose and end fittings are coupled together as specified for the close-in rig, except that a ¾-in. galvanized stress wire is shackled between the inboard riding line fitting and the outboard saddle.

The saddle whip is made up and rigged as in the close-in method, except that wire is normally used instead of manila and the whip controls both the inboard and center saddles (3 and 2). The whip is shackled to saddle 2 and rove through a block on the forward side of the boom, through a runner block secured to saddle 3 through yet another block on the boom, and finally fair-led to a winch.

The runner is an antitoppling block, part of an antitoppling device that keeps the runner from toppling when waves hit the hose. A 70-ft, ¾-in.

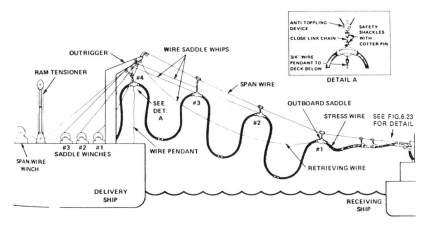

Fig. 6.22 Tensioned span-wire rig.

wire pendant running from a fitting on deck to the bottom of the saddle prevents the saddle from being two-blocked.

The retrieving line is ½-in. or ¾-in. wire, 450 to 800 ft long, fitted with a thimble eye at one end. This end is shackled to the outboard saddle and is rove through a block on the after side of the boom head and then fairled to a winch.

The hose messenger is 3½-in. or 4-in. manila line 35 fathoms long, fitted on one end with a thimble eye and a ⅞-in. shackle. Taper-spliced in succession to the other end are 15 fathoms of 2-in. manila, 10 fathoms of 21-thread, and 20 fathoms of 6- or 9-thread. The messenger is secured to the outboard end of the hose by shackling the eye to the outboard riding line fitting and seizing the line to the hose at 3-ft intervals.

The span wire of ¾- or ⅞-in. wire rope is a minimum of 600 ft long (800 ft for tensioned span wire). The hose is suspended from the span wire by trolley blocks shackled to the center and outboard saddles and to the two riding line fittings. Two free trolleys are attached by sisal stops to the outboard end of the hose. A pelican hook is secured to the outboard end of the span wire. To facilitate securing the span wire to the messenger, padeyes are welded to two wire clamps that are bolted to the wire approximately 2 and 4 ft from the shackle. About 200 ft from the end of the messenger (which is secured to the hose), two heavy-duty snap hooks are seized about 2 ft apart. These hooks are snapped into the padeyes on the wire clips. This method prevents the wire from sliding down the messenger, as it might if stopped off with small stuff. A single turn of small stuff, run through the bale, supports the pelican hook. Some span wires and highlines are tensioned to give better control of the rig and permit wider ship separation. Such span wires may be up to 800 ft long. The boom is topped and the hose hoisted as they are in the close-in method.

Receiving Ship—Setting Up   On the receiving ship, the 12-in. snatch block, riding line, and fairlead blocks are rigged as for close-in fueling. The 14-in. snatch block is not rigged because there is no necessity for the outer bight line. A length of small stuff for hauling in the messenger is rove through the fairlead and snatch blocks.

Operation   The delivery ship pays out the messenger by hand. When the end of the messenger comes across, the receiving ship attaches it to the line rove through the snatch and fairlead blocks. When the span wire comes aboard, the stop holding the pelican hook is cut, and the hook is attached to the long link in the padeye provided. Then the two snap hooks are unfastened, and hauling is recommenced. The delivery ship starts tending the span wire and positions the saddles so that the span wire carries the weight and the hose is kept from the water as it is hauled across.

When the hose end comes within reach, the trolley supporting the end is cut loose, permitting the hose to be hauled farther inboard. As soon as possible, a bight of the riding line is slipped over the riding line hook, and the riding line is set taut and secured.

When the delivery ship is a fleet oiler, the hose messenger is detached and returned to the oiler, using the hose messenger retrieving line provided. When the delivery ship is a carrier, however, the hose messenger is left shackled to the riding line fitting, and only the bitter end is returned. The receiving ship retains a bight of the messenger.

Upon completion of pumping and blowdown, the receiving ship disconnects the hose and secures the valve in the closed position (or replaces the hose cap or end flange). If the delivery ship is a carrier and the receiving ship has retained a bight of the messenger, it is restopped to the hose in at least two places.

The receiving ship slacks the riding line, easing the hose over the side, while the delivery ship heaves in on the saddle whips and hose retrieving line.

When the hose has been retrieved, the span wire is slackened, and upon signal from the delivery ship, the pelican hook is tripped and the wire eased over the side by an easing-out line. NOTE: In any tensioned rig, tension must be taken off the highline or span wire prior to tripping the pelican hook.

6.26 Astern Fueling Method   Normally, the U.S. Navy does not use this method. Agreements between NATO nations, however, call for all escort-type ships to be able to receive fuel from designated merchant tankers by alongside and by astern methods.

The rig for the astern method consists of a towed marker buoy, twenty 30-ft sections and a 15-ft section of 6-in. buoyant fuel hose. The receiving ship takes position off the quarter of the delivering ship. A shot line and hose messenger are passed to the receiving ship. The delivering ship pays out fuel hose, and the receiving ship drops back until her bridge is opposite the marker buoy. She then hauls aboard the discharge end of the hose.

6.27 Special Hose Fittings   A key part of any underway fueling rig is that section at or near the receiving ship's fueling trunk. Improved devices that bring together the end of the hose and the fueling trunk can speed the process considerably. One such device is the *breakable-spool, quick-release coupling.* Another is a combined *quick-release coupling and valve.*

Perhaps the best of these devices is the *probe fueling unit.* This assembly has two main parts: a male probe attached to the end of the delivering ship's hose and a receiver (which leads to the fueling trunk) supported by a swivel fitting on the receiving ship. (See Fig. 6.23.) A pelican hook for securing the span wire is an integral part of the swivel fitting. The key to the whole device is a sliding-sleeve valve that opens when the probe is engaged properly but that automatically closes when disengaged. Mounted on either side of the receiver are indicators showing when the probe is seated. As the probe mates, indicators rise to the vertical and then drop

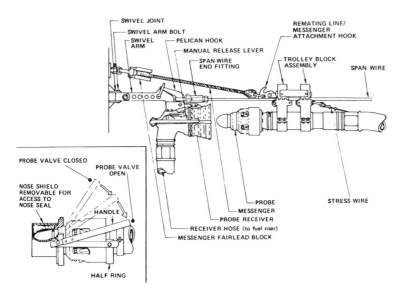

Fig. 6.23   Single-probe fueling rig.

back to a position about 30 degrees above the horizontal. When the probe is properly engaged, a latch mechanism prevents its being withdrawn under normal pull and strain, unless it is disengaged by means of a pull on a lever on the receiver. It will also be disengaged by a pull of about 2500 lb of the inhaul.

Passing the Probe Fueling Unit The probe fueling system employs a span wire that is passed in the same manner as the span wire rig discussed previously. After the span wire has been connected, and with a ship separation not greater than 140 ft, the fueling hose with probe is eased down the span wire until the probe is within reach of personnel on the receiving ship. A remating line is then attached to the hook on the outboard end of the probe trolley by the receiving ship, and the probe is hauled in to engage the receiver. A pull of from 300 to 500 lb on the remating line will seat the probe.

When ships are more than 140 ft apart, and at all times when carriers are being fueled, an outhaul must be used to haul the probe across to the receiving ship. From five to eight men, depending on the fairlead arrangement, are required for the outhaul or remating line.

6.28 Additional Reference Sources Not all methods of underway replenishment have been discussed here. For greater coverage, the reader is referred to *Boatswain's Mate 3 and 2,* NavPers 10121 series, and *Boatswain's Mate 1 and C,* NavPers 10122 series. *Naval Warfare Publication (NWP) 38* has information on methods and techniques followed when only U.S. Navy ships are involved. *Allied Tactical Publication (ATP) 16* describes procedures to be followed when ships of NATO nations are involved in underway replenishment. Also see the references at the end of this chapter.

6.29 General Safety Precautions for Transfer and Fueling

1. Personnel assigned to transfer stations must be adequately trained in all phases of safety procedures and precautions. They should wear safety helmets and clothing of the prescribed color.
2. Because transfer stations on receiving and delivering ships are in exposed locations, personnel working close to ships' sides where solid bulwarks are not installed must wear kapok-type life jackets. If it is necessary to use inflatable-type life jackets, they must be inflated.
3. During heavy weather, personnel working on weather decks should wear life jackets.
4. Personnel must be cautioned to keep clear of suspended loads whenever possible.

5. Ample provision must be made to prevent the shifting of cargo because of its risk to both personnel and material.
6. Wire highline may not be used to transfer personnel. When manila highlines are used to transfer personnel, a capstan may not be employed to haul the line; it must be tended by manpower.
7. In handling ammunition, it must be remembered that carelessness and haste, in addition to causing accidents, often result in rendering it unserviceable even when it is in containers.
8. In the transfer of personnel where water temperatures are low, "immersion suits" should be worn.
9. Whenever practicable, a rescue ship or helicopter should be stationed astern of ships replenishing at sea for the purpose of rescuing overboard personnel.
10. During night replenishment, flashlights (life-jacket type) should be pinned to the left breast of each life jacket in use. They are not to be lighted unless the order is given to do so.
11. Plastic police whistles should be issued to each man wearing a life jacket during night replenishments. They are worn on a lanyard around the neck, with the whistle tucked inside the life jacket to prevent fouling in lines or gear.
12. A lifebuoy watch should be stationed in the after part of the ship with a buoy fitted with an automatic float light.

References

Immer, John. *Cargo Handling,* San Francisco, CA: Work Saving Int'l., 1984.

Saverbier, Charles and Muern, Robert. *Marine Cargo Operations.* New York: John Wiley and Sons, 1985.

Roth, Eric. *Container Systems.* New York: John Wiley and Sons, 1973.

Guide Lines for Deck Stowage of Containers. Prepared for the U.S. Department of Commerce.

Schonknocht, W. Lusch, R., Schelzel, S. and Obenaus, N. *Ships and Shipping of Tomorrow.* Hartford, CT: MacGregor Publications, 1983.

7

Ship Communications

Communications comprises the act of exchanging information, the ways and means of doing so, and the information so given. Shipboard communications are of two types: internal and external. The latter is meant to imply rapid and reliable communications at a distance—for example, visually, by signal flags, or electronically, by radio. A ship also has internal or interior systems of communications, such as public address, telephone, engine-order telegraph, and dial or sound-powered telephone systems.

7.1 Interior Communications Equipment used for a ship's interior communications (IC) is normally less complicated than that used for exterior communications. IC equipment is essential for the orderly performance of both emergency and routine shipboard functions. IC systems are generally classed as either an *indicating* or a *sound system.*

7.2 Interior Indicating Systems There are usually one or more sound systems to provide alternative or backup communications for the indicating systems between vital locations, such as between the bridge and main engine control. IC systems normally employ a synchronous-motor system to transmit information or orders.

178

Engine-order telegraphs (annunciators) provide the conning officer a rapid and reliable means of ordering (and receiving acknowledgment of) changes in engine speed or direction. They consist of two sections. The engine-order section controls the speed range ("standard," "full," etc.); the propeller order section controls speed within a range. On most small vessels and on modern medium-sized vessels, the engines are remotely controlled directly from the bridge area. Critical systems of this type, however, are usually backed up by another system, such as a sound circuit.

Rudder-angle indicators, which show the actual position of the rudder, are a valuable aid in maneuvering the ship.

Course-to-steer indicators provide the conning officer and helmsman the course to steer, as directed by navigational or weapons-control devices. Gyrocompass repeaters, the pitometer log, and the wind direction and force indicators are also forms of interior indicating systems.

7.3   Interior Sound Systems   Whereas indicating systems communicate only raw facts or orders, sound systems can amplify and make recommendations on the information that has been transmitted by the indicating systems. Since the voice is used, the scope of information is almost infinite.

Multichannel and Public Address Systems   Multichannel systems use electronic amplifiers and push-button selector switches that allow one or more stations to communicate directly. Public address systems are announcing systems only.

Telephones   On larger ships, the standard telephone is used. Normally, it serves routine administrative purposes; however, in emergencies, it serves as an alternative system for operational purposes. Unlike the sound-powered phone system, the number of stations that can communicate directly is determined by the type of equipment.

Voice Tubes   One of the oldest IC methods, voice tubes are still found in the most modern ships. This system of metal tubes connecting various stations is the least susceptible to battle damage.

Sound-powered phone systems constitute the mainstay of internal communications in Navy ships. These phones require no external power. Speaking into the mouthpiece generates an electrical signal that is reproduced as sound on other phones on that circuit. Circuits may be (1) direct— a line connecting one or more outlets in the ship; (2) switched—lines passing through a switchboard, which allows one or more circuits to be connected together; or (3) phone type—lines between points with both a selector switch to select the desired station and a hand-crank growler or push-button buzzer to alert the station being called. Some systems pass through an amplifier to increase the volume. An automatic cutout will by-pass the amplifier should the latter fail.

7.4 Closed-Circuit Television Television facilitates the rapid display of a fast-changing or complex picture. Examples of use aboard Navy ships include the briefing of pilots and plane crews, using the tactical displays from the combat information center. Some ships mount a TV camera on the pierside bow to facilitate docking. Television also facilitates training aboard ship and assists communications between captain and crew. Closed-circuit TV (CCTV) transmits over wires the picture signal from the camera to the picture tube. In contrast, the commercial (or home) TV system transmits the signal through the air.

One such CCTV system is the Ship's Information, Training, and Education (SITE) system. Installed on most of our modern warships, it consists of a television studio similar to commercial studios. The system is equipped with cameras, tape recorders, projectors, microphones, and all the other equipment necessary for TV collection and distribution. The video is distributed through cables to television receivers at various locations in the vessel. Some of its uses are the showing of training films, discussions of various topics by key personnel, and presentation of entertainment films.

7.5 External Communications In sharp contrast to the internal systems are those that provide rapid and reliable external communications. They break down into three major classes: sound, electronic, and visual. The latter two are further broken down as follows:

Electronic Communications	Visual Communications
1. Radiotelegraph	1. Flaghoist
2. Teletypewriter	2. Flashing light
3. Radioteletypewriter	3. Semaphore
4. Radiotelephone	4. Pyrotechnics
5. Computer/Digital	5. Colored lights
6. Satellite	
7. Facsimile	
8. Television	

7.6 Sound Signaling Rules of the Road call for the use of a ship's whistle for sound signaling (employing Morse code). Navigational aids such as lighthouses and whistle, bell, gong, or horn buoys emit noises—another form of sound signaling. The procedure for sound signaling is described in the *International Code of Signals* (Pub. No. 102). It is normally limited to

Table 7.1 Single-Letter Signals

A I have a diver down; keep well clear at slow speed.

*B I am taking in, or discharging, or carrying dangerous goods.

*C Yes (affirmative, or "The significance of the previous group should be read in the affirmative").

*D Keep clear of me; I am maneuvering with difficulty.

*E I am altering my course to starboard.

F I am disabled; communicate with me.

G I require a pilot. (When made by fishing vessels operating in close proximity on the fishing grounds, it means: "I am hauling nets.")

*H I have a pilot on board.

*I I am altering my course to port.

J I am on fire and have dangerous cargo on board: keep well clear of me.

K I wish to communicate with you.

L You should stop your vessel instantly.

M My vessel is stopped and making no way through the water.

N No (negative, or "The significance of the previous group should be read in the negative"). This signal may be given only visually or by sound. For voice or radio transmission, the signal should be "NO."

O Man overboard.

P *In harbor:* All persons should report on board as the vessel is about to proceed to sea.

At sea: this signal may be used by fishing vessels to mean: "My nets have come fast upon an obstruction."

Q My vessel is "healthy," and I request free pratique.

*S I am operating astern propulsion.

*T Keep clear of me; I am engaged in pair trawling.

U You are running into danger.

V I require assistance.

W I require medical assistance.

X Stop carrying out your intentions, and watch for my signals.

Y I am dragging my anchor.

Z I require a tug. (When made by fishing vessels operating in close proximity on the fishing grounds, it means: "I am shooting nets.")

Notes:

1. Signals of letters marked by an asterisk (*), when made by sound, may only be made in compliance with the requirements of the International Regulations for Preventing Collisions at Sea.

2. Signals "K" and "S" have special meanings as landing signals for small boats with crews or persons in distress. (International Convention for the Safety of Life at Sea, 1974 Chapter V, Regulation 16.)

one-letter signals—signals that have an urgent or important meaning or that are in very common use. (See Table 7.1.)

7.7 Electronic Communications The vast majority of ship communications is conducted by electronic means. The advance of technology and the refinement of equipment have produced rapid advancement in all areas of electronic communications systems. On board U.S. Navy ships, the complexity, versatility, and the highly classified nature of communications systems prohibits a detailed presentation here. However, general categories are discussed below.

Radiotelegraph Often called CW (continuous wave), the radio tele-graph is the old steady system for transmitting Morse Code over the airways that has been in use by the Navy and other marine operators since just after the turn of the century. Its use in the complex communications systems of today is very limited and has been relegated to a backup or emergency function. Although reliable, it is much too slow to compete with the high-speed systems in use today, such as radioteletype.

Radioteletype Teletype provides a long-range, high-speed communi-cations system for ships. The sending machine is a transmitting teletype-writer which replaces the manual key of the radiotelegraph. It does not transmit in Morse Code but detects the letter or character selected by the operator, converts this information into coded electrical impulses of another kind, and transmits the impulses to the receiving machine, where the process is reversed and the information visually printed. Today, radiotel-etype is the primary method of communications used by ships, both for outgoing and incoming messages.

Traffic-handling capacities of radioteletype are further increased by the use of multichannel teletype systems. These circuits are designed to provide a large capacity for circuits between stations by the use of multiplex equip-ment. Signals from several typewriters are multiplexed into one signal for transmission. This signal is then broken down at the receiving station and distributed to the various teletypewriters as appropriate. The Fleet Multi-channel Broadcast (MULCAST) is the primary method of delivering shore-to-ship teletype communications.

The MULCAST system consists of several area networks providing max-imum coverage to all ocean areas of the world. Currently there are two types of communications being used: satellite and hf (high frequency) com-munications. Satellite communications are covered in a following section. The hf system is the backup system and consists of transmitters, tape read-ers, multiplex units, receivers, demultiplexers, and security equipment.

Radiotelephone Radiotelephone, commonly known as voice radio, is a rapid, effective, and convenient method of naval communications. It is used extensively for ship-to-ship tactical communication, for convoy work, for control of aircraft, and for countless tasks requiring rapid, short- or long-range communications. It is effective for exercising command and control since information can be exchanged directly and instantaneously between the personnel concerned. The advent of single side band (SSB) has greatly enhanced long-range voice communications, providing real-time commu-nication between an on-scene commander and a higher headquarters. The majority of voice circuits are controlled by key personnel from remote sta-tions, such as the bridge, the pilot house, or the combat information center.

With the advantages of radiotelephone go some disadvantages. Transmissions may be indecipherable because of static, enemy interference, or a high local noise level. Additionally, wave propagation characteristics of radiotelephone frequencies are sometimes erratic, allowing transmissions to be heard at great distances but not by the intended nearby addressee. Whereas nearly all teletypewriter circuits, except for routine broadcasts, are protected by security, or cryptographic, devices that make their signals unintelligible to all but authorized recipients, many long-range voice circuits do not provide secure transmissions. Consequently, in order to maintain privacy, or security of information, radiotelephone communications must be severely restricted to unclassified information unless the circuit is known to be secure. This restriction applies to both short- and long-range communications. It should be added, however, that short-range tactical circuits are now, for the most part, secure.

Computer, or Digital, Communications   These are in use aboard many ships. Several kinds of information can be translated into digital data, but this data must be recorded and processed to become useful. Several types of terminals can be connected to the control unit of a data terminal, including magnetic tape, teletypewriter, and computer terminals. These terminals are used to extract and transmit information to the data terminals. Supply requisitions and formatted routine reports, such as Defense Energy Information System (DEIS) reports, are examples of information transmitted through digital communications.

Satellite Communications   A satellite communications system is one that uses earth-orbiting satellites to relay radio transmissions between two terminals, such as a ship and shore station. There are two types of communications satellites: active and passive. The former merely reflects radio signals back to earth while the latter acts as a repeater. It amplifies received signals and retransmits them back to earth. A typical operational link involves an active satellite and two earth terminals. One station transmits an up-link signal which the satellite amplifies and transmits as a down-link signal to a receiving station, such as a ship. Figure 7.1 illustrates a typical satellite communications system with several terminals.

Facsimile (FAX)   FAX gives a receiving station a printed display of transmitted information; it is especially useful for transmitting such matter as photographs and charts. The image to be sent is scanned by a photoelectric cell and transmitted by a radio wave. The transmitted picture is simultaneously reproduced on a recorder at the receiving activity. Facsimile requires several minutes to complete the transmission of a picture twice the size of

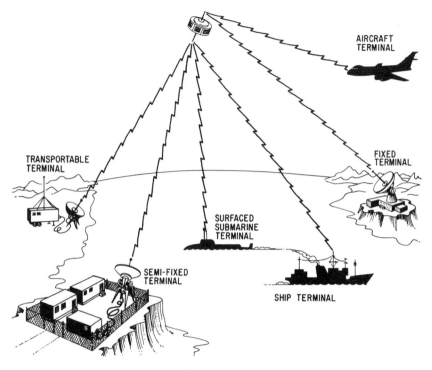

Fig. 7.1 Satellite communications system.

this page. One extensive use made of FAX is the transmission of weather maps.

Broadcast Television TV has found a number of uses to date, some of them being the following:

1. Remote guidance of missiles
2. Reception of reconnaissance data from aircraft
3. Simultaneous briefing of many commanding officers or aviators of a task force when a tactical situation is too urgent to permit duplication of weather data, charts, or other pictorial information.

7.8 Shipboard Communications Facilities As it pertains to personnel on the ship's bridge, communications mainly takes the form of visual signaling. Navy ships are provided with the following basic publications: the *Allied Maritime Tactical Signal Book;* the *International Code of Signals;* and the *Allied Guide to Mariners.* U.S. merchant ships carry the *International Code* under all conditions and are provided with the *Allied Guide* by the Navy under wartime conditions.

The *International Code of Signals* is the basic signaling publication and serves most methods of communications—whether visual, electrical, or sound. First published in 1857, it is used today by ships of all nations. The U.S. edition is further identified as Pub. No. 102, Defense Mapping Agency Hydrographic Center. This one volume contains instructions for use and one-, two-, and three-letter codes and their meanings, allowing for thousands of combinations of information units.

Language barriers are overcome by the code by virtue of its multilanguage printings. Thus, as a simple example, the signal NF—"You are running into danger"—conveys that meaning regardless of the language used. In addition to the English-language version (of which Pub. 102, is one form), the *International Code* is also published in French, Italian, German, Japanese, Spanish, Norwegian, Russian, and Greek.

By their nature, Navy ships and merchant ships have considerable differences in their requirements. These differences, in turn, are reflected in the relatively large number of Navymen with shipboard communications duties and by the variety of equipment on a Navy ship. For rapid exterior communications, Navy ships normally have two main stations where messages and signals are sent, received, and processed. These stations are known as the *radio station* and the *visual station*. Coordination of both stations in large warships takes place in the *communications center* under the supervision of the *communications watch officer* (CWO). The communications center is usually located in the vicinity of the main radio room, or *radio central.*

At the visual station, there are semaphore flags, portable signal lights, and a loud hailer ("bull horn" or electric megaphone). Signal flaghoists and flags are in the vicinity. The ship's whistle is nearby. Running lights and other navigational and anchor light fixtures are located on the masts, superstructure, and above the main deck; controls are near the visual station—usually in the pilothouse. Signal searchlights are in the superstructure in the vicinity of the visual station; blinker lights are installed on the yardarms with keying controls at the visual station. Pyrotechnic devices are located near the signal bridge.

The radio station facilities are concentrated mainly at radio central, but radio antennas are located throughout the superstructure. Radio transmitters and receivers are found not only in radio central but in special transmitter rooms and separate radio rooms. Portable and emergency radio equipment is located in a number of places. Remote-operated radiotelephone units—send/receive facilities—are found on the bridge, in the pilothouses, in CIC, and in radio spaces. Radioteletype and radiotelegraph facilities are normally operated at the main radio station.

A number of interior communications systems are employed to link the bridge and pilothouse with the key shipboard communication facilities, including regular telephones, sound-powered telephones, voice tubes, and, on some ships, pneumatic tubes. Amplifier-type announcing systems (often referred to as *squawk boxes* or *intercom units*) are also widely employed.

The communications system needs of vessels vary widely from the massive installations aboard the larger Navy ships to more modest installations aboard merchantmen and finally to the single transceiver found aboard very small craft. The needs of Navy ships are determined by senior authorities, and the installation and future revisions are carried out by highly trained technicians. Very much the same holds true for merchantmen.

7.9 Communications on Private Craft There are no requirements for private operators to carry a radio. However, each operator must determine on his own whether he needs or simply desires a communications capability on his craft. Certainly, those who operate in the open ocean or long distances from home would be well-advised to carry a radio, if only for emergency purposes.

There are three types of radios used aboard boats; VHF, single side band (SSB), and the citizens band (CB). Boats that operate inshore may need only a simple CB; those which operate within the 30-or-so mile range of the VHF radio may find that this set will suffice. For long-distance communications, an SSB radio is required.

VHF Communications VHF, or very high frequency, marine radios are the first choice for most operators for reliable and effective communications requirements for up to about 30 miles. There are many different VHF radios on the market today, varying in cost depending on the extra features desired such as push-button entry, auto-scan, programmable memory, and auto-revert to the emergency channel. However, the most important aspects to consider in a marine radio are not the extra gadgets, but its frequency stability, sensitivity, and reliability. Examples of modern marine VHF-FM radiotelephones can be seen in Fig. 7.2.

The frequency of a radio wave is the number of times per second that it goes through its cycle and, along with the power output, is one of the determining factors of the maximum range of a radio. One way of superimposing speech on a radio wave is by frequency modulation (FM) which is done by varying the basic, or carrier, frequency. Discrete frequencies determine the various channels used and there are up to 88 different channels which can be used in the VHF band for marine use. These channels are preset and can be selected by dialing or by push button controls. Some of the channels are for special purpose or commercial use only. Some are used for linkup with shoreside telephone systems. Two important channels

Fig. 7.2 Marine VHF-FM radiotelephones.

for use in small boats are channel 6 for safety communications between ships, and channel 16, the emergency and calling channel. Some channels are assigned for international uses. Some channels are restricted for use in certain areas such as the Great Lakes and parts of the Mississippi River. Local listings should be checked prior to indiscriminate use of channels in any area. Table 7.2 lists some of the primary VHF channels available in the U.S. and their uses.

Radio Procedures   The important thing to remember is that channel 16 is a calling and distress channel only. It is not to be used for convenience traffic or routine conversations. Such traffic should be shifted to one of the other authorized channels. Improper use of a radiotelephone is a criminal offense. The use of obscene, indecent, or profane language during a transmission is punishable by a $10,000 fine, imprisonment for two years, or both. Other penalties exist for misuse of the radio such as improper use of the calling and distress channel or violations of the Bridge-to-Bridge Radiotelephone Act.

There are certain basic rules to be followed when operating a marine radio. First, as has been mentioned, monitor channel 16 and use it for call-ups, first making sure it is not already being used. Switch to a mutually agreed upon and approved channel to transmit essential traffic. Make calls as short as possible and as few calls as possible consistent with the urgency of the message, limiting repeat call-ups to not more than two or three every

Table 7.2 VHF Channels for Marine Use.

Channel Number	Use
16	Calling, safety, and distress channel. This is the most important channel, as it is the primary call-up and listening channel, as well as that used for distress. Monitoring of this channel is mandatory except for recreational boats.
6	Intership safety. Used for ship to ship safety and search and rescue.
7,8,9,10,18,19, 68,69,70,71,72,78,79,80	These are all working channels used for commercial and recreational ship to ship and ship to shore messages. Specific channels are used for traffic between marinas, commercial docks, and yacht clubs for vessel-related traffic. Many boat operators use channels 9, 68, 70 and 72 for direct calls.
12	Traffic advisory channel for port operations.
13	Used for bridge-to-bridge communications for vessel approach situations in accordance with the Vessel Bridge-to-Bridge Radiotelephone Regulations. Only for the specified navigational purpose, using power of one watt or less.
14	Port operations channel. Used for communications with bridge and lock tenders.
20,65,66,73,74	Other port operations channels. Used for ship movements in and around ports, bridges and inland waterways.
22	Used for liaison with Coast Guard vessels and shore stations and for listening to Coast Guard marine information broadcasts. Contact should be made on channel 16 first.
83	Coast Guard Auxiliary.
24,25,26,27,28, 84,85,86,87,88	Marine operator for telephone calls. Channel assignment varies by areas.
WX-1 to WX-7	Weather channels.

few minutes. To contact another vessel, speaking slowly and distinctly, with channel 16 selected, press the mike button, holding two inches from the mouth and say: ''(Name of boat to be called) this is (name and call sign of boat calling), over.'' Say each name two or three times if necessary but wait a minute or two between calls if no reply is heard. After contact is made, switch to an agreed upon inter-ship channel and transmit the message. Once the conversation has been completed, say: ''This is (name and call sign of boat), out.'' Radio checks may be used to verify the radio is working, but not to the Coast Guard, by saying, "Any station, this is (name and call sign of boat), radio check, switch and answer channel ( ), over." Do not crowd the airways by making continuous radio checks.

When calling a shore station, the same procedures are used except that it is best to use the appropriate working channel. Refer to the receiving station by name, such as: "(Location) Marine Operator, this is (name and call sign), over." To receive a call, keep your receiver tuned to channel 16 and/or to a specific working channel if you are expecting a call on that channel. Many radio sets permit two channels to be monitored while being able to transmit on only one of those channels. Upon hearing your boat's name or call sign respond by saying: "This is (name and call sign), over." Switch to a designated channel if requested.

Single Side Band (SSB) For radio communications over a longer distance than can be handled by VHF, a SSB marine radio can be used. Most recreational boaters do not have a requirement for this capability. Boats operating with 80 to 100 watts of output power can have a range of over 100 miles, but much longer distances are possible, depending on many factors including weather conditions. Each SSB radio band has a range or group of frequencies within that band which can be selected to transmit or receive a message. In order to make a call, switch first to a band, then select a frequency (channel). Sending and receiving procedures are the same as for VHF radios. The distress frequency is 2182 kHz. The Coast Guard monitors several other channels and telephone calls can be made by contacting the nearest marine operator designated for that area.

Citizens Band (CB) CB radios are often used in place of, or as an adjunct to, VHF radios for informal, short-distance communications. They provide a reliable maximum working range of 10–15 miles. The distance can be made greater with a large antenna and some suitably equipped shore stations can transmit and receive at a much longer distance. A special marine antenna is needed as a car CB antenna will not work on a boat. The Coast Guard does not monitor a CB channel for emergency traffic although channel 9 is used for general calling and distress and it might be monitored by another vessel or by a local club. Also, CB has no ship-to-shore telephone hookup capability.

Licensing Requirements The Federal Communications Commission (FCC) has established certain requirements for the establishment and operation of marine VHF and SSB radio stations. Specific regulations can be ascertained at the time of purchase or from the local Coast Guard station, but in general, all vessels with VHF and SSB radios need a ship's station license. In addition, to operate a SSB radio, a restricted operators permit is

required. A radio station license is normally obtained at the time of purchase by forwarding a form 506 to the FCC in the name of the owner and
the vessel. This permits legal use of the radio and provides a temporary call
sign based on the boat's registration number. Such a license is not transfer-
rable and the FCC must be advised of a change in ownership of the boat
or radio. No operator's license is needed for VHF or CB radios on recreational boats, but vessels for hire and commercial boats have more stringent
licensing requirements. For example, commercial vessels which carry more
than six passengers require a Third Class Radiotelephone Operator Permit
for the radio operator.

Installation and Maintenance   Once needs are determined and equipment is selected, the system must be installed properly to perform satisfactorily. Although a VHF radio is fairly easy to install and connect to an antenna, the private operator might be well-advised to seek the assistance of
a marine communications professional before installing, and even selecting, his radio system. The best radio improperly installed with cheap or
poorly run coaxial cable or carelessly installed connectors will be considerably less effective than a less expensive model installed correctly. If installed
by the private operator, before the set is operated it should be checked
out by a qualified person holding the proper license to make sure the set
installation conforms to FCC rules. Radio installations on gasoline-powered
boats usually require ignition suppression shielding. If one unit of a system
can be singled out as requiring the most careful considerations, it is the
antenna. Without a suitable antenna correctly installed and properly maintained, even the best of radios cannot perform at peak levels. Most heavy-
duty stainless whip antennas mounted at the masthead or the highest point
will do the job. VHF radios require very little maintenance but a yearly
frequency check and retuning is recommended.

7.10 Visual Telecommunications   Visual communications systems have
been in use since men first sailed the seas and are often the best means for
communicating at short range.

The most important visual systems are flaghoist, flashing light, and semaphore. Pyrotechnics and colored lights have important wartime and emergency use.

Flaghoist   This is a method whereby various combinations of brightly
colored flags and pennants are hoisted to send messages. It is the primary
means for transmitting brief tactical and informational signals to other ships
nearby. Signals are repeated by addressees, thus providing a sure check on
the accuracy of reception. Texts of messages that may be sent are limited
to those found in signal books. (See References.)

Directional Flashing Light   This is a visual telegraphic system in which an operator opens and closes the shutter of a searchlight to form the dashes and dots of the Morse code. The light is pointed and trained to be seen only from the viewpoint of the receiver.

Nondirectional Flashing Light   This is sent out from a lamp on a yardarm. Dots and dashes are made by switching the lamp on and off. Since the light is visible in every direction, this method is well suited for messages for several addresses.

Semaphore   This is a communication method in which an operator signals with two hand flags, moving his arms through various positions to represent letters, numbers, and special signs. It is especially suitable for long administrative messages because of its speed. It is not readable much farther than two miles, even on a clear day.

Pyrotechnics   These have a wide variety of uses. Examples are identification of one's ship or attracting attention when in distress, where they can literally make the difference between life and death. Coastal lifesaving stations also use pyrotechnic flares to signal to vessels in distress.

7.11 Semaphore Facilities   Semaphore requires little equipment—two hand flags attached to staffs are all that is needed (Fig. 7.3). The standard semaphore flags are usually 15 or 18 in. square, and each staff is long enough to enable the sender to grasp it firmly. The flags are similar to the *oscar* alphabet flag (the International alphabet flag O). The *papa* flag (the International alphabet flag P) is sometimes substituted. Most semaphore flags issued to the fleet today are fluorescent and made of sharkskin cloth. Figure 7.4 illustrates the semaphore alphabet and numerical code.

7.12 Searchlights   Light sources for searchlights are incandescent or mercury-xenon lamp, xenon-arc, or carbon-arc. Control of the light is by means of a shutter. (See Fig. 7.5.) The front and rear doors are hinged to the searchlight case to permit access to the interior for relamping and cleaning. There is usually a handle on the rear of the case to elevate and depress the light or turn it in azimuth.

7.13 Nancy Facilities   Nancy is a system of visual communications using infrared light, which is visible only with the aid of equipment designed for this purpose.

7.14 Flaghoist Signaling   The flags of a hoist are always read from the top down. When a signal is too long to fit on one halyard—when, in other

Fig. 7.3 Signalman sending semaphore for the letter "M." (*Official U.S. Navy photograph*)

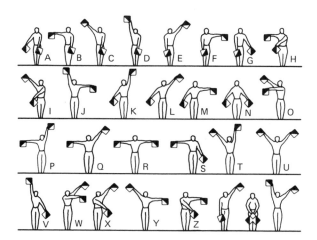

Fig. 7.4 Semaphore alphabet and numerical code. The three signals following the letter "Z" represent: (1) error, (2) end of word, and (3) shift from letters to numerals. The signals for the numerals 1 through 0 are the same as those for the letters "A" through "J."

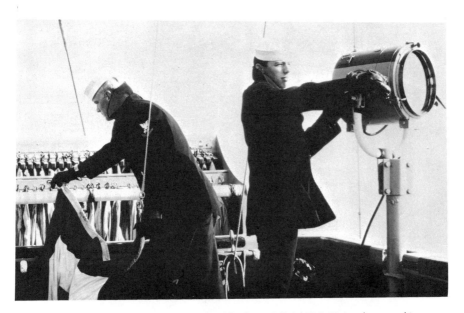

Fig. 7.5 Signalmen man the signal bridge. *(Official U.S. Navy photograph)*

words, more flags are required than can be made in a single hoist—the signal must be continued on another halyard and read outboard to inboard. When a signal is broken into two or more hoists, it must be divided at points where there can be a natural space without affecting the meaning of the signal.

Flags are stored in flagbags to permit rapid makeup of the hoist. The signal is hoisted as soon as each flag is attached.

Flags used on board ship are shown in color in the signal books. More flags are used on Naval men-of-war than on merchant ships: 40 flags on merchant ships, 68 flags on men-of-war (See Fig. 7.6).

7.15 Other Signal Light Facilities Men-of-war carry a number of lights that are used to signal not only the status of the vessel according to the requirements of the Rules of the Road but for other purposes as well:

Not Under Command Lights These are mounted on brackets extending abaft, and offset from, the mast or structure to permit all-around visibility insofar as is practicable. To facilitate pulsating these lights as a "man-overboard" signal, the rotary snap switch in the signal light switch box that controls them is fitted with a crank handle.

Fig. 7.6 Signalman aboard dock landing ship *USS Alamo* (LSD 33) runs signal flags up hoist in South China Sea. *(Official U.S. Navy photograph)*

Aircraft Warning Lights One red light is installed on the truck of every mast that extends more than 25 ft above the highest point in the superstructure. If it is impossible to locate this light so that it is visible from any location throughout 360 degrees of azimuth, two lights are installed.

Blinker Lights These lights are installed only on the signal yardarm outboard, one port and one starboard. On ships with more than one mast, they are located only on the forward yardarm. Screens are fitted at the base of these lights so that their glare or reflections will not interfere with the navigation of the ship. Lights are operable from signal keys located on the bridge; their intensity may be varied by energizing the upper bank, lower bank, or both banks.

Speed Light   This light is installed in ships of frigate (FF) size and larger to indicate the ship's speed. It is located at the truck of the mast. If it is impracticable to locate this light so that it is visible throughout 360 degrees of azimuth, two lights are provided.

Station-Keeping Lights   Two lights are installed on all minesweepers required to give sweep information at night. They are located in a vertical plane perpendicular to the keel so that accurate observations may be taken. These light are mounted to be visible from 20 degrees forward or 20 degrees abaft the beam on each side of the ship. If it is impossible to locate the lower light so that it can be seen on both sides of the ship, two lights are used, one on each side.

Towing Lights   Minesweepers, tugs, and other ships normally engaged in towing operations have permanently installed towing lights. Other ships have two portable towing lights, each of which is equipped with sufficient cable and a plug connector to permit energizing them from the nearest lighting receptacle connector.

Task Lights   These lights are installed on all ships and are displayed whenever a ship is restricted in its ability to maneuver. They consist of three all-around lights in a vertical line one over the other and not less than 6 ft apart. The highest and lowest of these lights are red, and the middle light is white.

Aircraft carriers have a complex arrangement of night-flight operations lights. These consist of such lights as deck edge lights, homing lights, parking lights, and takeoff lights.

7.16   Special Merchant Ship Considerations   Few vessels of any size go to sea without some radiotelegraph or radiotelephone capability. Coast Guard and Federal Communication Commission requirements are quite specific on that point. For vessels less than 300 gross tons, no radio equipment is required; for those from 300 to 1600 gross tons, radiotelephone equipment and a qualified operator are required; for those 1600 gross tons and over, radiotelegraph and a qualified operator(s) are required.

If the ship is a passenger type (more than 12 passengers), a 24-hr radio watch is required. The great majority of merchant ships normally have only one radio operator—the radio officer. He is on watch 8 hr out of 24. An automatic alarm system is required when a 24-hr watch is not maintained. (This is the alarm that responds to another ship's radiotelegraph signal on a frequency of 500 kHz.) If the alarm system goes out of order, it gives a signal that is audible in the radio room, in the operator's cabin, and on the bridge.

Deck officers—the watch officers of the merchant marine—must have proficiency in visual signaling as there is no one else on the bridge to handle this job. They must be able to read signal flags and to have a general competence in other visual signaling methods, including the ability to read and transmit flashing light at 8 words per minute. Usually there are but two men on a merchant ship's bridge: the watch officer and the helmsman. (The lookout is stationed at the bow.) With other duties to perform, the watch officer is often unable to respond immediately to another ship's call-up for an exchange of visual signals.

7.17   Distress Signal   A ship in distress can indicate its problem in many ways. Visual and sound distress signals are covered in Section 22.17. However, sending out a distress signal by radio is one of the most effective ways to initiate rescue. The radiotelegraph signal "SOS," which is transmitted in Morse code (· · · - - - · · ·), or the radiotelephone signal, MAYDAY, transmitted by voice, both reveal that the sending vessel is threatened by grave and imminent danger and requests immediate assistance.

Recreational boaters, as well as other mariners, should use the following radiotelephone distress signal procedures when rescue or immediate assistance is required:

   a. Activate the EPIRB (see below) if not already activated or other radio alarm signal, if so equipped.
   b. Call out the distress signal MAYDAY on channel 16 three times.
   c. Give the boat's name and/or call sign.
   d. Give the boat's position, either latitude or longitude or range and bearing from a known geographical position.
   e. Briefly state the nature of the distress, what assistance is needed, the number of persons aboard and any other information that would facilitate the rescue, such as weather conditions and the presence of any injured personnel.

A merchant ship in distress may use the radiotelegraph alarm signal to secure attention to distress calls and messages. This alarm signal is designed to actuate the radiotelegraph alarms of other ships so fitted. The emission consists of a series of 12 dashes sent in 1 min, the duration of each dash being 4 sec, the duration of interval between dashes being 1 sec.

MAYDAY is only one of the three radiotelephone safety messages, the other two being PAN and SECURITE (pronounced "saycuritay"). PAN (for urgency) indicates that the sender has an urgent message to transmit concerning the safety of a ship, aircraft, other vehicle, or a person. SECURITE (for safety) indicates that the sender is about to transmit a message concerning the safety of navigation or giving important meterological warnings.

A ship receiving a distress signal (SOS or MAYDAY) from a nearby ship acknowledges receipt, but only after ascertaining that this acknowledgment will not interfere with messages from ships in a better position to render assistance.

7.18   Emergency Position Indicating Radio Beacon (EPIRB)   The EPIRB is a light, compact, self-contained, battery-powered emergency signaling device. Once activated, it emits alert and locate signals for up to 48 hours and more on Channels 15 and 16. These channels are constantly monitored by the Coast Guard, commercial and military aircraft and can even be picked up by fellow boaters in the area. There are currently three basic types of EPIRB's:

Class A—Open ocean. Automatic. Will float free from the vessel in the event it sinks. Effective range about 200 miles. Signal duration of more than 48 hours.

Class B—Same effective range and duration of signal as the Class A, but is manually operated and not as rugged in construction.

Class C—Manually operated. Effective range of about 20 miles. Signal duration abut 24 hours.

Regardless of the class, the EPIRB is an effective way to signal an emergency. It is portable, reliable, and relatively maintenance- and trouble-free, but it should be tested periodically. Once it is turned on in an emergency situation, it should be left on so that the distress signal is continuously transmitted and the position can be determined accurately.

References

Chapman, W. *Piloting, Seamanship, and Small Boat Handling.* New York: American Book—Stratford Press, 1979.

Fundamentals of Naval Science. Annapolis: Naval Institute Press, 1984.

Naval Science for the Merchant Marine Officer. NAVTRA 10795. Washington D.C.: Government Printing Office, 1981.

Allied Maritime Tactical Signal Book, vol. II. ATP1(B) Washington, D.C.: Government Printing Office, 1983.

International Code of Signals. Pub. No. 102. Washington, D.C.: Government Printing Office, 1980.

Navigation

Navigation is the process of directing a craft from one place to another, both safely, and, in the modern world of high-cost fuels and limited time, economically. It is both an art and a science, in that today's navigator must be comfortable not only with manual techniques and instruments but with the highly sophisticated electronic methods and equipment that promise to revolutionize the routine practice of navigation during this decade.

Marine navigation is concerned with two types of situations or environments in which the navigator might find himself: *inshore* and *at-sea*. Inshore navigation can be thought of primarily as that performed when operating in close visual proximity to land, such as when transiting coastlines, sailing in bays, or motorboating in rivers or harbors; this kind of navigation is referred to as *piloting*. At-sea navigation comes into play once the navigator's craft has surpassed the distance within which he may use piloting techniques or when fog or other circumstances preclude the use of visual piloting in the larger inland bodies of water. Navigation at sea is performed primarily by *celestial navigation,* in which celestial bodies are used for position-finding, but also by *electronic navigation* through the use of electronic equipment.

Until recent times, the complexity of the mathematical and plotting techniques and of the first-generation electronic aids required made navigation a skill that only a few could master. Such is no longer the case. Today's mass-produced and frequently updated charts and reference publications, coupled with the advances in sophistication and capability of miniaturized electronic equipment, have made it possible for almost anyone with basic reading and mathematical skills and a reasonable degree of manual dexterity to become an effective navigator. As with any other discipline, of course, confidence and proficiency come only with practice and experience.

Fundamentals

Navigation is primarily concerned with position, direction, distance, depth, speed, and time, and the use of all these in the fundamental technique of navigation upon which all others depend, dead reckoning. Each of these will now be described.

8.1   Position   Perhaps the most fundamental of all concepts to the navigator, *terrestrial position* is normally expressed in the two coordinates, latitude and longitude. *Latitude* is defined as the vertical angle between a location of interest and the equator of the earth, as measured at the earth's center; *longitude* is the horizontal angle between that location and the reference meridian, or *prime meridian,* passing through Greenwich, England, as measured at the earth's center. In marine navigation, both coordinates are expressed in degrees, minutes, and tenths of a minute, with the suffixes "N" or "S" placed after the latitude to indicate whether the position is north or south of the equator (i.e., in the *northern* or *southern hemispheres*), and the suffixes "E" or "W" placed after the longitude to indicate whether it is from 0 to 180 degrees east of Greenwich or west of it (that is, in the *eastern* or *western hemispheres*).

During piloting, position is sometimes stated in reference to some land or sea mark of known location, like a prominent cliff, light tower, or buoy. Such positions are related in terms of direction and distance from the object, as in "three miles bearing 320 degrees true from Hunter's Point," or, alternatively, in terms of relative position, such as "abeam Wolf Trap Light," or "between buoys 8 and 9." Through the use of a nautical chart, these positions can be easily translated to latitude and longitude if desired.

In both piloting and navigation at sea, a position determined with the highest degree of certainty—based on at least two or more separate, simultaneously obtained, and reliable pieces of data—is referred to as a *fix*. A related position of lesser certainty—based upon nonsimultaneous yet reliable data—is termed a *running fix*. A position of low certainty—based upon incomplete data of lesser reliability but taking into account all significant sources of possible error—is called an *estimated position. Dead reckoning (DR) positions* are those developed between fixes or estimated positions; they are based solely on the vessel's steered course and ordered speed and disregard any external variables that may have affected the vessel's progress through the water. These various types of positions will be discussed more thoroughly in Sections 8.7 and 8.17.

8.2 Direction The concept of direction is of fundamental importance to navigation, as it is the means by which the vessel's course is specified. A number of different directions are involved in marine navigation. The horizontal direction of one terrestrial point from another, expressed as a three-digit angle clockwise from 000 to 360 degrees, is termed a *bearing.* If the 000-degree reference is *true north*—such as in the cases of a chart longitude line, a gyrocompass with zero gyro error, or a magnetic compass corrected for any compass error—the angle is termed a *true bearing* or *true direction.* If the 000-degree reference is the vessel's head, or her longitudinal axis, the angle is called a *relative bearing.* Finally, if *magnetic north* is the reference—as in the case of a magnetic compass corrected for any deviation—the angle is a *magnetic bearing* or *magnetic direction.* Directions in relatively unstable small boats, whose compasses are normally graduated in only 5-degree increments—are usually approximated to the nearest 5 degrees or the intermediate 2½ degrees. The stability afforded by larger vessels makes it possible to specify direction in them to the nearest whole degree, and often to the nearest half-degree. To eliminate any possible confusion about the reference for the direction specified, the abbreviation ''T'' is often placed after true bearings or directions, ''R'' after relative bearings, and ''M'' or sometimes ''p stg c'' (per steering compass) after magnetic bearings. If a three-digit angle is unlabeled, it is always assumed to be a true direction.

The vessel's *heading* is a special name for the direction in which she is pointing. The term is used to indicate both the *instantaneous direction,* which can change from moment to moment, and the *average direction* over time. It may be expressed as either a true or magnetic direction, usually in the latter case called the *ship's head magnetic.*

The vessel's course or *course line* is the intended heading over some future period of time, anywhere from the next several seconds to hours or even days. The *course made good* is the true direction from some point of departure to some point of arrival, regardless of the actual path or courses steered by the vessel in between.

The *track* is the intended path to be followed by a vessel between two points, and after the fact, the actual path taken between them. The track is normally specified in terms of true direction of the various segments, or *legs.*

An *azimuth* is the true direction of a celestial body from some reference location; the term is often used incorrectly by inexperienced mariners as a synonym for true bearing.

A special type of bearing, usually expressed in degrees true, is the *danger bearing* used by the navigator to mark the safe limits of navigable water on either side of a vessel's intended track on a chart. Hatching is often applied to the hazardous side, and the bearing is labeled NLT (not less than) or NMT (not more than) the indicated bearing.

8.3 Distance The measurement of distance is important in navigation in such applications as determining required or actual speeds, approximating the time required to travel between two points at a given speed or speeds, fixing the position of a vessel relative to a given land or sea mark or another vessel, estimating the expected time of a landfall or arrival at a navigation check-point, and a host of other important computations.

Distance is usually expressed to the nearest tenth of a nautical mile when the measure exceeds about 20 miles, and in meters (m), yards (yd), or feet (ft) for shorter measures. A nautical mile is exactly 1852 m, or a little more than 6076 ft. An approximation of 2,000 yd per nautical mile is often used for many applications involving distances under 20 miles.

Most large-scale charts of small areas such as coastal approaches, harbors, bays, and rivers—in which projection distortions are minimal—have handy distance bar scales printed on them that are graduated in feet, yards, meters, and statute and nautical miles. On smaller-scale Mercator charts depicting larger areas, bar scales are not practical because of the distortion associated with this projection as distances from the equator increase. The vertical latitude scale on these charts opposite the area of interest may be conveniently applied as a distance scale, however, by making use of the fact that 1 degree of latitude as measured along a great-circle longitude line approximates 60 nautical miles everywhere on earth; 1 minute of latitude therefore approximates 1 nautical mile. Other types of projections such as the *gnomonic* and the *Lambert* conformal have various distance scales printed on them that are effective for the chart's area of coverage.

8.4 Depth A prime concern of the navigator, especially in piloting waters, is the water depth in which his vessel is operating. Of all causes of damage or loss of marine vessels, grounding is consistently among the more prevalent.

At one time, depth of water was almost always expressed in feet and *fathoms* (1 fathom equaling 6 ft). Heights of objects and land were expressed in feet. In recent years, however, with the move toward universal adoption of the International metric system (SI), both depths and heights of navigational aids and land features are now expressed in *meters,* 1 m being approximately 3.28 ft. On large-scale charts, fractional depths are normally shown to the nearest tenth of a meter by use of a subscript after the integral meter depth, as for example 11_8, which indicates a sounding of 11.8 m. On older charts showing soundings in fathoms, the subscript indicates the number of feet, as for example, 6_3, indicating 6 fathoms, 3 ft.

A quick glance at the area near the title block on nautical charts will quickly tell the navigator which sounding units are used on the chart. Awareness of the units in use is particularly important for the small boatman operating in shallow water, as a meter is approximately one-half a fathom; mistaking soundings in meters for fathoms could therefore result in a false conclusion that the water depth was twice the actual depth, if the navigator was in fact using a chart with soundings in meters instead of fathoms.

8.5 Speed The speed of a vessel is defined as the distance covered per unit of time. Usually in marine navigation the rate of speed is expressed in *knots,* 1 knot being 1 nautical mile per hour. Sometimes during piloting, however, yards-per-minute is a convenient measure, and when docking large vessels, even their speed in feet-per-second is a critical variable.

Speed is related to distance and time by the fundamental equation,

$$S = D/T$$

where D is distance, S is speed, and T is the unit time. The navigator makes frequent use of this relationship to determine the vessel's "true" speed, or speed relative to the earth (often called *speed over the ground,* or *SOG*).

To determine distance, note that the equation becomes

$$D = S \times T$$

Two handy rules based on this formula that expedite the solution for distance, given speed, are the *three-minute* and *six-minute rules,* stated as follows:

Distance traveled in yards in 3 min = speed in knots × 100
Distance traveled in nautical miles in 6 min = speed in knots × 1/10

Both these rules are used extensively during piloting, especially when maneuvering in channels or other restricted waters.

The speed over the ground between two fixes, often called the *speed made good,* is fairly easily determined with the basic formula by measuring the distance traveled in nautical miles between the two fixes, and dividing this figure by the elapsed time in hours or fractions thereof. Once determined, the SOG in knots can then be employed with either the three- or six-minute rules to make an accurate estimate of the distance the vessel will travel during the next 3- or 6-min interval.

The other type of speed of prime importance to the navigator is *speed through the water,* which is the quantity indicated by the vessel's speed instruments, such as the *impeller* or *pit log.* Speed through the water differs from SOG by a number of factors, all of which are generally lumped together under the term *current,* which in this context includes not only any differences caused by water movement but also those caused by wind and steering errors. Obviously, speed through the water is easily and continually available from the vessel's instruments, whereas speed over the ground is a quantity that must usually be calculated. For short distances of a few hundred yards or less, the two speeds can be used almost interchangeably, but because of the cumulative and potentially great effect of current with increasing time, the navigator must always remember to use the SOG, *not* the indicated speed through the water, for all calculations involving any degree of precision, especially when in constricted waters.

8.6   Time   Almost every navigational calculation involves time in one form or another. In its simplest and earliest form, time was reckoned on the travel of the apparent sun across the sky relative to an observer's position. This *apparent solar time,* as it is called, served the ancients and later centuries well for many purposes but proved unsatisfactory for general timekeeping after the advent of relatively rapid modes of transportation such as the steamboat and the railroad. To provide a more adaptable system, *mean time* was introduced, which makes use of the average westerly travel of the sun about the earth's equator, known as the *mean sun,* at the standard rate of 15 degrees of longitude per hour, or 1 degree every 4 min. Time reckoned according to the passage of the mean sun relative to the local meridian (longitude) of an observer is called *local mean time (LMT)*; reckoned relative to the meridian passing through Greenwich, England, it is called *Greenwich mean time (GMT)*; and reckoned relative to the central meridian of each of twenty-four standard time zones, each 15 degrees wide, it is called *zone time (ZT).* (See Fig. 8.1.) Because they are all reckoned according to the passage of the mean sun, differences between any two of these foregoing mean times can be thought of as being equivalent to the difference of longitude between their reference meridians converted to units of time. Thus, GMT differs from zone time by the longitude of the standard meridian of the zone converted to units of time, and zone time differs from local mean time by the *arc-time difference* corresponding to the difference in longitude between the standard meridian of the zone and the meridian of the observer.

In recent years, a revolutionary new basis of timekeeping has emerged, required by the exacting needs of many modern industrial, scientific, and navigational applications. This is *Universal Coordinated Time (UTC)*, which is based on the frequency of vibrations of a radioactive element, usually cesium. Because UTC is based on an unchanging atomic time standard,

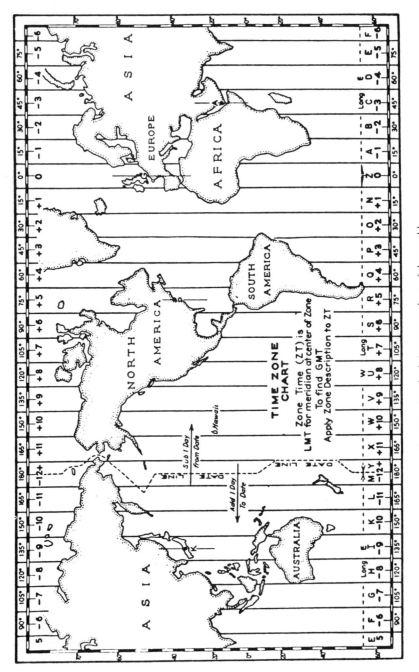

Fig. 8.1   Standard time zone chart of the world.

and GMT can be affected by variations in the rate of rotation and revolution of the earth, there can be as much as a 0.9-sec difference between the two at times. Normally, however, the difference is so small that it can be disregarded for most marine navigational purposes, and GMT and UTC can be used interchangeably.

Greenwich mean time is of prime importance to the navigator because it continues to be the reference time by which most marine navigational almanac data is tabulated, this data being used extensively in the practice of celestial navigation. The zone time of the standard time zone in which a region is located is normally kept by all those in it—both on land and at sea—except during summer, when it is a common practice to keep the time of the next adjacent zone to the east (*daylight savings time*).

In addition to keeping his vessel's clocks set to the proper standard time, the navigator is also concerned with zone time because this is the time by which tide and current phenomena are tabulated in the NOS *Tide* and *Tidal Current Table* publications covering his area of operations.

Local mean time comes into play in navigation mainly when it becomes necessary to precompute either the time of a sun- or moon-related rising or setting phenomenon or the local zone time when the apparent sun will be directly over the observer's meridian (called *local apparent noon,* or *LAN*).

UTC is of navigational importance because almost all *radio time signals* transmitted by the various maritime nations—by which the navigator checks his chronometers and sets his comparing or stop watch for celestial navigation—are now broadcast using UTC, rather than GMT, as a basis. Transit navigational satellite broadcasts, increasingly being used by small craft for navigation at sea, as well as by many larger vessels, are also timed according to UTC.

In navigation, time of day is generally written in the military four-digit format, starting with 0000 at midnight and ending with 2400. When seconds are used, as is routinely the case during celestial navigation, the time is recorded in six digits, with a dash between the hours, minutes, and seconds—for example, 18–24–07, meaning 18 hr, 24 min, and 7 sec.

8.7 Dead Reckoning All the foregoing concepts of position, direction, depth, speed, and time come together succinctly in the most fundamental procedure common to all types of marine navigation, *dead reckoning.* Essentially, dead reckoning is nothing more than a visual representation of a vessel's intended steered course and speed through the water, drawn to scale on a chart, originated at a known position, and ended at the time a new position is to be obtained and plotted. A new *dead reckoning plot* (*DR plot*), as it is called, is originated each time a new position is plotted and is then extended until the anticipated or actual time of the next subsequent position. In piloting, this interval may be 3, 6, or perhaps as many as 15 minutes, whereas at sea it may be several hours or even days.

Starting at a known fix position, indicated by a ⅛-in. circle labeled with the corresponding time (expressed in four digits), a DR course-and-speed line is drawn in the direction of the steered true course; the line is labeled as shown in Fig. 8.2, the course being written above it and the anticipated speed (in knots) below. Intermediate *DR positions* are plotted and new course-and-speed lines originated according to a set of rules that have been established and standardized through long usage and custom. These *Six Rules of DR* are as follows:

1. A DR position is plotted every hour on the hour.
2. A DR position is plotted at the time of every course change.
3. A DR position is plotted at the time of every speed change.
4. A DR position is plotted for the time at which a fix or running fix is obtained.
5. A DR position is plotted for the time at which a single line of position is obtained.
6. A new course line is plotted from each fix or running fix as soon as it is plotted on the chart.

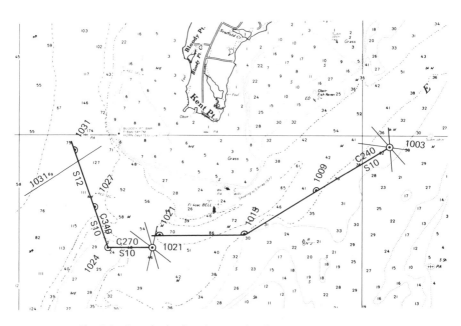

Fig. 8.2 Sample dead reckoning plot drawn on a nautical chart.

Note that intermediate DR positions are labeled with a half circle and that their time is placed at a slant or angle to distinguish these positions from a fix or a running fix, which are marked with a full circle and a horizontal time number.

Each line segment between DR positions is scaled according to the distance scale of the chart, the length representing the distance that the vessel would travel at the designated speed and during the time that this speed was effective. The various course-and-speed lines and DR positions, then, represent the vessel's best calculated path, *ignoring any effects of current*. Using this calculated path based on a known course and speed through the water permits the navigator to perceive the effects of any current. He can find an *estimated position* at any time by drawing a scaled current vector from the DR position plotted for a selected time, as shown by the broken arrow and box in Fig. 8.3.

Any difference at the end of the DR plot between the DR position on the old course-and-speed line and the new fix is assumed to be caused by the current.

If a vector is drawn between the old DR position and the new fix position, its direction represents the direction, or *set*, of the actual current that acted on the vessel, and its length indicates the velocity, or *drift*, of the actual current over the time period covered by the DR plot from its originating position. The actual current thus determined can then be used as an estimated current over the next part of the DR plot, assuming there is no reason to expect a radical change in the current.

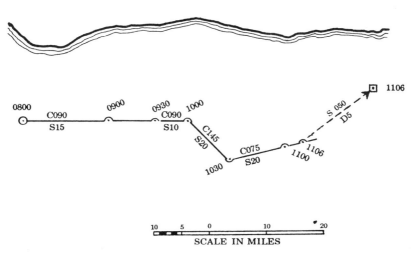

Fig. 8.3   Estimated position based on a DR plot and estimated current.

During piloting for intervals less than about 15 min, the effects of current can usually be disregarded, and DR positions projected every 3 or 6 min can be used as the anticipated future positions of the vessel at these particular times when planning course and speed changes to conform to a desired track or channel.

The DR plot as just described should also be kept whenever the vessel is at sea, the only difference between plots for piloting and open waters being the interval between fix positions and the methods by which the fixes are established (see the section on the Practice of Navigation at the end of this chapter). If properly maintained, the DR plot can always be used with confidence by the navigator as a known basis from which to judge his probable or estimated position, taking estimated current into account.

In celestial navigation, the DR position for the time of a celestial observation serves as the basis for the choice of an assumed position that will be used as an intermediate step in calculating the celestial fix. In certain types of electronic navigation such as Omega, moreover, the DR plot serves as a valuable aid for resolving any positioning ambiguities. Hence, in a very real sense, the proper maintenance of a good dead reckoning plot is the essence of marine navigation.

Tides and Current

Water movement phenomena are of obviously major importance to the navigator. Tide is of particular interest in any restricted piloting environment, especially in locations that experience a large daily rise and fall in tide level. Certain bays and river mouths in the Carolina Banks and in New England, for example, are navigable with little difficulty at times of high tide but are little more than mud flats at low tides, particularly near *spring tide* times (the times around new and full moons). Inshore currents caused by the rise and fall of tide, called *tidal currents,* are also of great concern because of the effect they can have on the course and speed of a vessel attempting to conform to a channel through confined waters. *Ocean currents* can have a major effect on vessels at sea, particularly upon their economy of operation on longer voyages.

8.8 Tide *Tide* is the vertical rise and fall of the surface of a body of water; it is caused primarily by the interaction of the gravitational forces of the moon and to a lesser extent the sun upon the rotating and revolving earth. Most of the shores on earth experience two high and two intervening low tides at a little over 6-hr intervals—the *tidal day* comprised of these four tides being about 24 hr and 50 min long because the moon revolves about the earth in the same direction as the earth rotates about its own axis.

Tide predictions for some 5000 locations throughout the world can be found in the four-volume *Tide Tables* published by National Oceanographic Survey (NOS). Each volume contains daily tide predictions for each of several principal reference ports, and height and time differences for all the subordinate stations located within the area of the volume. Volume 2 covers the Atlantic and Gulf coasts of the United States, and Volume 3, the Pacific coast and Hawaii.

8.9 Tidal Currents Current is strictly defined as a horizontal movement of water caused in large measure by tide but also by differences in the temperature and density, wind patterns, and heights of the world's oceans. Since currents in coastal waters and in confined intracoastal waters are usually the result of changing tide levels for the most part, they are referred to as *tidal currents*. A tidal current that flows inland as the result of the approach of a high tide is called a *flood current;* that which flows seaward because of a low tide is called an *ebb current.* The true direction in which a current flows is called its *set,* and its velocity is called its *drift.* In between each flood and ebb current is a time when no horizontal water movement takes place as the current changes direction; this state is referred to as *slack water.* Times of maximum flood and ebb currents will usually be somewhat different from times of high and low tide in any given vicinity because of the attenuating influence of the land and restricted openings to inland harbors, bays, and rivers.

Tidal current predictions for U.S. waters are chiefly found in the two volume *Tidal Current Tables* published by National Oceanographic Survey (NOS). Like the *Tide Tables,* each volume contains daily tidal current predictions for each of several principal reference stations as well as current strength and time differences to be applied to these data for a number of subordinate locations. Volume 1 covers the U.S. Atlantic and Gulf coasts; Volume 2, the Pacific coast. Also available from NOS is a series of graphic tidal current chartlets of the more important bays, harbors, and sounds of the United States called *Tidal Current Charts* and *Tidal Current Diagrams.* For each body of water covered, they depict by current arrows and numbers the set and drift of the tidal current for every hour after high and low tide.

Tidal current predictions for foreign waters can be found in similar tables, charts, and diagrams published by hydrographic agencies of the various maritime countries.

8.10 Ocean Currents Ocean currents are caused primarily by imbalances in temperature, density and salinity, the effect of prevailing winds, and differences in the height of the various ocean basins. Once set in motion, the flow of water in the oceans is affected by the Coriolis force associated with the earth's rotation; as a result, they form various giant patterns called *gyres*. In the United States, the Gulf Stream off the East Coast is probably the best known. At its strongest off Florida and South Carolina, its drift averages 3 to 5 knots, it is some 40 miles wide, 2000 feet deep, and 5 to 10 degrees warmer than the surrounding waters.

Ocean current predictions for various times of the year are published by DMAHTC in a series of color-coded graphic charts of various ocean basins called *pilot charts*. Pilot charts of the North Atlantic and Pacific are published for each month in quarterly editions, and in annual atlas form for certain years for several of the other principal ocean basins. For an introduction to the fundamentals of oceanography, see Chapter 19.

Equipment

Marine navigation is associated with specialized equipment that enables the navigator to carry out safe and efficient navigation. This equipment ranges in cost and complexity from the fairly inexpensive simple lead pencil, plotting aids, and basic charts and reference publications; to more costly and permanently installed equipment such as speed logs and depth finders; to very expensive electronic equipment such as radar and various electronic navigation sets. The particular equipment needed varies greatly and depends upon both the size of the vessel and the intended area of operations. In U.S. territorial waters, certain devices are required by various local and U.S. Coast Guard regulations, with their amount and complexity generally increasing in direct proportion to the size and gross tonnage of the vessel. Prospective vessel operators and buyers are always well advised to check with the local Coast Guard district headquarters to determine their requirements and recommendations.

Regardless of the exact requirements, all navigation equipment can be loosely classified into the following categories: charts, reference publications, basic instruments, and more complicated, permanently installed equipment.

8.11 Charts Because navigation is primarily concerned with going from one place to another, the navigator's *chart*—a type of map depicting water areas and intended primarily for navigation—is perhaps his most basic tool. There are a number of different kinds of chart projections, but there are only two of wide use among marine navigators—the *Mercator* and the *gnomonic*—with the former the most common.

The Mercator is a projection of the spherical earth onto a cylinder tangent to it either at the equator, along a meridian, or at some angle between the two, with the equatorial tangent being the most common. In the latter, distortion is at a minimum near the equator but increases dramatically in higher latitudes both north and south, as a projected point on the earth's surface approaches parallelism with the cylinder. Thus, most equatorial Mercator projections are cut off beyond about 80 degrees north and south latitudes, as indicated in Fig. 8.4.

Position, distance, and direction can all be determined on this chart because of its *conformality,* or true presentation of shape and angles, and because its *rhumb lines*—such as a DR course line or intended track that make constant angles with all meridians—plot as straight lines.

The gnomonic is a projection wherein the surface of the spherical earth is projected outward onto a plane tangent to the surface at some selected point. Its chief advantage to navigation is that it permits a *great circle*—the shortest distance between two points on a sphere—to plot as a straight line, whereas a rhumb line will appear curved. Thus, small-scale gnomonic charts of large ocean basins are ideal for laying down the optimum shortest track between the place of departure and desired destination, as for example the great circle route from Norfolk to Gibraltar shown on the gnomonic chart tangent to the earth at the mid North Atlantic in Fig. 8.5.

After the great-circle track has been plotted on the gnomonic projection, the rhumb line approximation to it for actual navigation can be obtained by transferring selected positions at regular intervals, such as those shown in Fig. 8.5, to a Mercator chart depicting the same area. Rhumb lines drawn between the various points picked off and plotted on the Mercator then represent a rhumb-line equivalent to the optimum great-circle route.

To do his navigating and maintain his master DR plot, the navigator uses the largest-scale (that is, covering the smallest area) Mercator chart

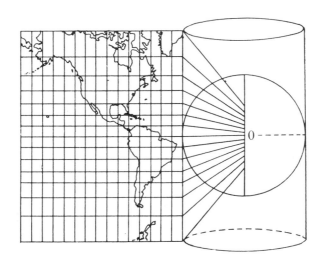

Fig. 8.4 The Mercator conformal projection.

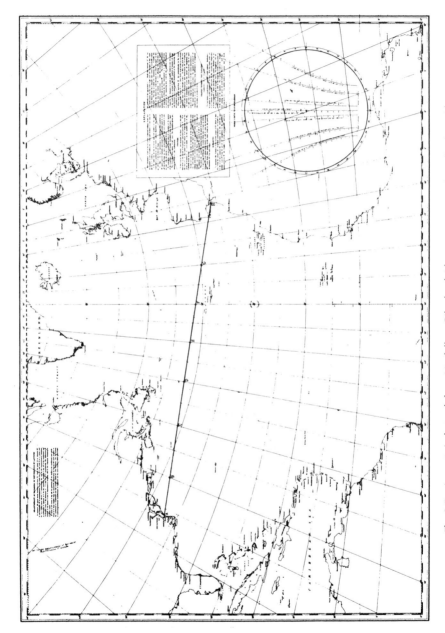

Fig. 8.5 A great circle track from Norfolk to Gibralter laid out on a gnomonic projection with point of tangency in the North Atlantic.

212

available for his area of operations. The amount of navigational information about the area that is found on such a chart—in the form of standardized symbols and abbreviations—is amazing, including among other data the nature and features of coastlines and adjoining land, descriptions of aids to navigation such as lights, buoys, and beacons, dangers to navigation of all types, depth contours and soundings, quality of the bottom, tides and currents and magnetic compass variation. Full descriptions of all standard symbols and abbreviations used on a contemporary charts produced in this country are contained in a pamphlet entitled *Chart No. 1*, published jointly by the two largest producers of American nautical charts, the *National Ocean Survey* (NOS) of the National Oceanic and Atmospheric Administration (primarily responsible for charts of U.S. waters) and the *Defense Mapping Agency Hydrographic/Topographic Center (DMAHTC)*, primarily responsible for charts of the navigable waters of the world beyond U.S. jurisdiction.

In addition to the symbolic information, many charts, especially those depicting ocean areas, are overprinted with electronic-navigation lattice lines, such as Loran-C and Omega. These charts enable the navigator to plot Loran-C or Omega lines of position directly on the chart itself without reference to any supporting publications. There are also a number of other specialized series of charts designed for various specific needs, such as a general bathymetric series for bottom contour navigation. Only navigators of deep draft merchant and naval vessels will need to make use of the latter.

The charts of both NOS and DMAHTC are available through nautical suppliers, ship chandlers, and other agents located in almost every maritime community.

The navigator must not only have on hand the latest editions of the various charts he needs but must keep them up to date. To do so, he should consult the following publications: The weekly *Notice to Mariners*, published in booklet form each week by the DMAHTC, covers charts and reference publications relating to oceanic and coastal areas worldwide. The *Local Notices to Mariners*, issued periodically by each of twelve U.S. Coast Guard districts, disseminates corrections to charts of U.S. inland waters within each district.

8.12   Reference Publications   Publications for the navigator are available from NOS, DMAHTC, the U.S. Coast Guard, other governmental agencies, and private maritime publishers. Probably no navigator would need to have them all, but all prudent navigators should have the important ones. The more important reference publications are as follows:

NOS *Nautical Chart Catalog*
DMAHTC *Catalog of Nautical Charts*

NOS *Coast Pilot* (for U.S. waters)
DMAHTC *Sailing Directions* (for foreign waters)
U.S. Coast Guard *Light List* (for U.S. waters)
DMAHTC *List of Lights* (for foreign waters)
NOS *Tide Tables*
NOS *Tidal Current Tables* and *Tidal Current Charts*
DMAHTC *Radio Navigation Aids, Pub. No. 117A* or *117B*
DMAHTC pilot charts

In addition to these, the ocean-going navigator will require various publications supporting celestial and electronic navigation, including the following:

The *Nautical* or *Air Almanac* (published by the U.S. Naval Observatory)
DMAHTC *Sight Reduction Tables No. 229* and *No. 249*
DMAHTC *Loran-C Lattice Tables* (as applicable)
DMAHTC *Omega Propagation Correction Tables* (as applicable)
DMAHTC *Omega Lattice Tables* (as applicable)

Almost all the DMAHTC and NOS reference publications and the Coast Guard *Light List* are kept up to date by means of the weekly DMAHTC *Notice to Mariners.*

8.13 Basic Instruments   The basic instruments of the navigator are those hand-held implements and tools required for elementary position-finding and plotting. The basic instruments that will usually be aboard are described in the following paragraphs.

Pencils and Gum Erasers   Perhaps the most basic of all instruments is a set of sharpened No. 2 lead pencils and a few gum erasers.

Plotters   Plotters range in complexity from a simple plastic straightedge or parallel ruler, to specially designed transparent instruments incorporating distance scales and protractors, to permanently installed drafting machines. These are usually available at marine supply shops and ship chandleries and range in price from under $10 for parallel rulers and the less complex plotters to over $200 for a precision drafting table with a universal drafting arm.

Plotting Instruments   A pair of *dividers* and a *drawing compass* are required to maintain the DR plot. Dividers, which are designed for picking off positions and measuring distances on the chart, are shaped like an inverted "V," with spreadable arms and metal points in both tips. A drawing compass is similar but has one leaded point; it is designed to allow the drawing of scaled-distance arcs on the chart. Both are available in various sizes for around $15 at most marine suppliers and ship chandleries.

Mechanical and Electronic Calculators   Several mechanical calculators have been designed for rapid solution of the speed-time-distance formula for any one quantity given the other two. Probably the best known of these is the *nautical slide rule* pictured in Fig. 8.6, available at most nautical supply stores for under $10. The hand-held *electronic calculator* is becoming common as well. Although almost any calculator with basic arithmetic capabilities will solve the speed-time-distance formula, those equipped with

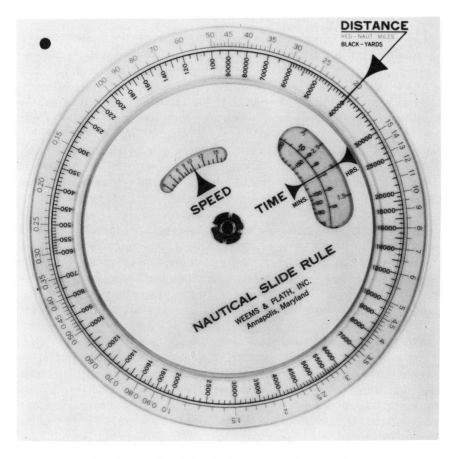

Fig. 8.6   The nautical slide rule. (*Courtesy of Weems, & Plath, Inc.*)

trigonometric functions are required for celestial observations. Many manufacturers of programmable models now include "navigation packages" as part of the optional programming, and there are even a few models built expressly for marine navigation. These range in price from under $10 for the former to several hundred dollars for the latter.

Stadimeters The *stadimeter* is a hand-held instrument designed to supply the distance to an object of known height when the latter is sighted visually through the instrument's optics. There are two general types: One, like a sextant, uses a system of reflecting mirrors that in effect determines the angle subtended by the object and converts this directly to distance; the other, like a camera, uses a lens focal effect. The latter are usually called *visual range-finders*. They are available from most larger marine supply shops for around $50.

Clocks Many different clocks are available for use in marine timekeeping, ranging from the traditional spring-powered wall models to battery-powered quartz chronometers. In general, prices vary from under $50 for the less accurate mechanically powered clocks to $250 or more for chronometers with electronic movements. Great accuracy in time is especially important in celestial navigation, where an error of as much as one mile in position can result from each second of error in time. For this reason, celestial navigators are well advised to have on board at least one and preferably two clocks of chronometer quality, since such timepieces are capable of maintaining a constant and therefore predictable and compensatable rate of error.

Sextants The navigator's sextant is designed for measurement of angles from 0 to 120 degrees or more to the nearest tenth of a minute of arc. As is the case with clocks, a variety of models are available, ranging in price from under $30 for light-duty, plastic "practice" models to $1,500 or more for highly precise metal models of professional quality. Sextants will be more fully described in the celestial navigation section of this chapter.

Magnetic Compasses and Gyrocompasses Although almost every vessel comes equipped with an installed magnetic compass or gyrocompass (or both) for steering purposes, only larger yachts and ships normally have magnetic compasses or gyrocompass repeaters (devices, similar to a magnetic compass in appearance, that display or "repeat" the main gyrocompass card's orientation) installed in positions suitable for observing visual bearings. On vessels not so equipped, in order to perform any but rudimentary piloting inshore and to determine compass error at sea, a *hand-bearing compass* such as that shown in Fig. 8.7 is required. Most models of this

Fig. 8.7 A hand-bearing compass. (*Courtesy of Weems, & Plath, Inc.*)

type, available in marine supply shops for around $100, furnish magnetic bearings of good accuracy after a little practice. Refer to Section 8.14 for further discussion of the magnetic compass and the gyrocompass.

8.14 Installed Equipment Installed navigational equipment on vessels ranges from simple, mechanically driven speed logs and magnetic steering compasses on very small craft to depth finders, gyrocompasses, radar, and various kinds of radio and electronic navigation gear in larger boats and ships. The exact equipment on any given vessel will vary according to her size, type of operations usually engaged in, and applicable local and Coast Guard regulations.

Speed Logs Equipment designed for direct measurement of vessel speed through the water is called a *speed log.* *Impeller logs* consist of a small propeller or paddlewheel actuated by the flow of water alongside the hull where they are mounted. *Pitometer logs* incorporate a hull-mounted pitot tube as the measuring device. Sophisticated *doppler sonar logs* sense speed by means of small frequency shifts in two or more transmitted sonar beams. Almost all small craft and most smaller ships are fitted with logs of one of the former two types.

Magnetic Compasses. Marine magnetic compasses are equipped with a means of adjustment for *deviation,* the difference between the magnetic meridian and the north axis of the compass caused by the influence of metal and electrical wiring. Although deviation can never be completely eliminated, its effects can be minimized by proper compass adjustment. A consistent deviation table of the type shown in Fig. 8.8 can be made up that will furnish the amount of deviation for any given heading of the vessel.

DIRECT-READING DEVIATION CARD

Mag	Dev	Com	Mag	Dev	Com
003-007°	3°E	000-004°	171-180°	2°W	172-182°
008-013°	4°E	005-009°	181-201°	3°W	183-204°
014-019°	5°E	010-104°	202-211°	4°W	205-215°
020-032°	6°E	015-026°	212-246°	5°W	216-251°
033-075°	7°E	027-068°	247-320°	6°W	252-326°
076-083°	6°E	069-077°	321-327°	5°W	327-332°
084-104°	5°E	078-100°	328-335°	4°W	333-339°
105-116°	4°E	101-112°	336-341°	3°W	340-344°
117-134°	3°E	113-131°	342-347°	2°W	345-349°
135-147°	2°E	132-145°	348-351°	1°W	350-352°
148-156°	1°E	146-155°	352-354°	0°	353-354°
157-164°	0°	156-164°	355-357°	1°E	355-356°
165-170°	1°W	165-171°	358-002°	2°E	357-359°

Fig. 8.8 A typical small craft deviation table (adapted from *Piloting* by F. Graves. Camden, Maine: International Marine Publishing Company, 1981).

Because of their relative instability, most small craft are fitted with smaller magnetic steering compasses graduated in 5-degree increments; larger ships often have 6- or 7-in. diameter compasses graduated in 1-degree increments.

Since true course lines and true bearings are normally plotted on a chart in dead reckoning, the navigator must remember to take the magnetic *compass error* into account when using this instrument either for steering or for observing bearing lines of position. The compass error, which varies with the vessel's heading, is the algebraic sum of the compass deviation on that heading plus the *local variation,* the difference between true and magnetic north, obtainable from the chart of the area.

Gyrocompasses   A gyrocompass is essentially a north-seeking gyroscope that is encased in a housing with electronic components to keep its axis aligned with terrestrial meridians. Because they are expensive, coupled with the fact that few small craft are stable enough to take advantage of their precision, they are normally found only on board larger boats and ships. The advantage of a gyrocompass is that it is always aligned with true north, normally with little or no gyrocompass error, thus eliminating the necessity for the continual conversions from true to magnetic and magnetic to true associated with the magnetic compass. On smaller vessels fitted with a gyrocompass, the main unit containing the gyro is usually located in close proximity to the steering station, with one or more remote gyrocompass repeaters located where best suited for observing bearings for navigation or maneuvering. Larger ships may be fitted with more than one gyrocompass, and all are usually located in the interior of the ship where their exposure to extreme ship motions is minimized.

Radar   The basic function of radar is to determine the range to an object by the measurement of the time it takes for a pulse of radio-frequency energy to travel from the transmitter to the target and return as a reflected echo. Although radar is required by Coast Guard regulations only for commercial vessels of 1600 tons or more, prudent operators of most larger power boats that spend more than a minimal time under way will almost always have at least a short-range navigational radar installed. By means of radar it is possible to obtain range LOPs (lines of position) in fog, at night, or when beyond visual range of land or various charted aids to navigation. Radar is also a prime means of avoiding collisions with other vessels when under way.

Radio Direction Finders   Beside radar, probably the other most commonly found electronic navigation aid found on most small craft, especially on sailboats not having a power supply sufficient to operate a radar set, is the *radio direction finder.* Almost all the more heavily traveled coastal waterways in the United States and its possessions, as well as those of most foreign countries, have navigational aids fitted with radio transmitters installed at key piloting points. These aids, called *radiobeacons,* transmit for the most part at frequencies from 250 to 400 kHz and are receivable at ranges varying from about 20 to over 100 miles in some cases. Under favorable conditions of radio signal propagation, a radio direction finder tuned to the proper frequency can determine the true bearing from the receiver to the transmitting aid to within ±2 degrees, thereby allowing the navigator to obtain one or more bearing lines of position under almost any visibility conditions and often at ranges exceeding those of most navigational radars and navigational lights. For small boatmen not having an RDF aboard, certain types of small portable marine radios can often be used to obtain very rough relative bearings to commercial radio station transmitters operating in coastal areas.

The DMAHTC publications, *Radio Navigation Aids, Nos. 117A* and *117B,* contain complete descriptive information on radiobeacons located worldwide, with volume *A* covering the Atlantic coasts of North America and Europe, and volume *B* covering areas adjoining the Pacific and Indian Oceans and Bearing Sea.

Electronic Navigation Gear   See Section 8.19.

Visual Navigation Aids

In order to assist navigation in coastal areas, various types of man-made aids to navigation have long been used. Primitive lighthouses with wood fires were established in Egypt and other Mediterranean seafaring nations as early as 700 B.C., and logs and empty kegs were in common use as buoys in the Delaware River by the time of the American Revolution.

8.15 Modern Visual Aids to Navigation   These include both permanent structures attached to the shore or bottom—such as light towers and automated light structures and beacons—and floating aids—such as buoys. Before a visual aid can be used, it must first be positively identified. Once it has been, the navigator can then correlate its position on the nautical chart and use it to determine or verify his vessel's position. Chart symbols for visual navigation aids are explained in the publication *Chart No. 1,* published jointly by NOS and DMAHTC.

By day, the general location, shape, color scheme, auxiliary features, and markings can all assist in the identification of visual aids. By night, the navigator must rely upon the type of illumination offered by lighted aids to identify them. The five-volume *Light List* series published by the U.S. Coast Guard contains full information on both lighted and unlighted aids located in U.S. coastal and intracoastal waters, whereas a similar seven-volume series published by DMAHTC contains similar information on lighted aids in foreign waters. Light characteristics and heights are also shown on large-scale nautical charts adjacent to the symbol for the aid, with italics ordinarily used for floating aids and roman type for light structures and lighted beacons.

Identifying a Navigation Light   To identify a navigation light at night, the navigator must take three of its attributes into account: its *phase characteristic,* or pattern of flashes; its *color*—normally white, green, red, and in some foreign lights, yellow; and its *period,* the time required for the light to progress through one complete cycle of changes. Of these three, the period is normally the most conclusive, especially for structural lights.

Buoys and Beacons   See Chapter 27.

Piloting

Safe navigation of a vessel within sight of land or in constricted inshore waters such as bays, harbors, and rivers is referred to as *piloting.* Positioning methods during piloting differs from those at sea in that they are determined to a large degree by lines of position derived from either visual or electronic observations of land or sea marks. It it critically important in piloting to know where you are and where you are heading, *not* where you have been.

8.16   Line of Position   A *line of position (LOP)* is defined as a locus of points along which the vessel must lie. An *observed line of bearing* to a natural or man-made landmark, a visual observation of two known objects in line one behind the other (a *visual range*), a *stadimeter distance* to an object of known height, a *radar distance* to a shore line or light platform, or an *RDF line of bearing* to a radiobeacon, all constitute different types of lines of position obtainable in the piloting environment.

Bearing lines of position are represented on a chart by a line segment drawn to the symbolized observed object, as in Figs. 8.9A and 8.9B. *Distance lines of position* are represented by circular arcs centered on the object or landmark observed, their radii equal to the observed distance per the chart distance scale, as shown in Figure 8.9C. Single lines of position are always labeled with the time of observation above the line, as indicated in the figure.

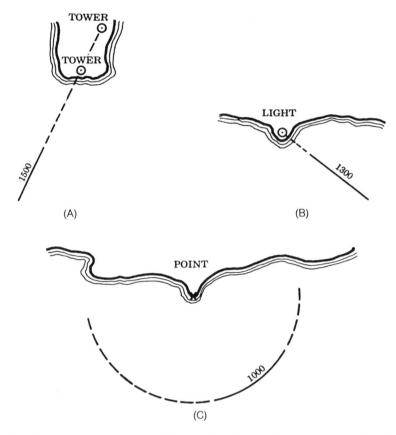

Fig. 8.9 Various types of lines of position used in piloting: (A) a visual range, (B) a line of bearing, and (C) a distance arc. Note that a single LOP is always labeled with the time of its observation above the line.

8.17 The Fix, Running Fix, and Estimated Position The intersection of two or more simultaneously obtained LOPs fixes the place along each line where the vessel must have been located at the time of the observation. Such a well-defined position is called a *fix*. A fix can be obtained by crossing any type of LOP with any other, the only restriction being that the various LOPs must have been obtained at the same time. Although the intersection of two LOPs is sufficient to define a fix, in practice a third simultaneous LOP is usually obtained and plotted to guard against the possibility of error in one of the others. If all were correctly done, the three LOPs should meet at a common point, or very nearly so, as in Fig. 8.10A. If a large triangle results as in Fig. 8.10B, one or more of the LOPs is in error. Note the labeling conventions for a fix: a ⅛-in. circle with the time printed horizontally

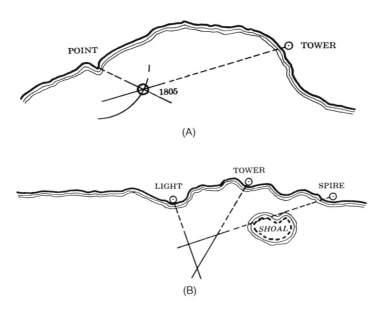

Fig. 8.10 (A) A fix plotted from three simultaneous LOPs with no error present, and (B) an attempted fix plotted with one or more of the LOPs in error.

adjacent to it. The LOPs constituting a fix need not be individually labeled if they were all obtained simultaneously.

Once the fix is plotted, as discussed in the section on the dead reckoning plot, a DR course and speed line is immediately extended from it. It is labeled with the vessel's course and speed and extended until the expected time of the next fix, for which time a DR position is plotted on the line.

Sometimes during piloting—when there is reduced visibility caused by fog or other adverse weather conditions, say, or when transiting a coastline—it is not possible to obtain more than one LOP at a time. At such times, a position of lesser reliability called a *running fix* may be plotted by advancing one or more LOPs obtained earlier to the time of the subsequent LOP by using the DR plot. The running fix is formed by the position at which the advanced and subsequent LOPs cross, these LOPs being labeled as shown in Fig. 8.11. Because the running fix thus plotted ignores the effects of current, its possible error increases with increasing elapsed time. The standardized rule of thumb in piloting, therefore, is never to advance an LOP more than 30 min to form a running fix.

If the elapsed time between LOPs exceeds 30 min during piloting, a position of lower confidence called an *estimated position* can be formed either by extending from a DR position a scaled vector drawn to represent the estimated current over the elapsed time (see Fig. 8.3), or alternatively,

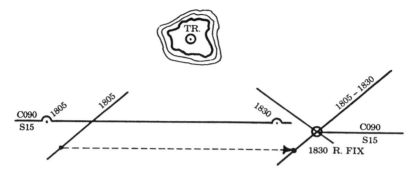

Fig. 8.11 A running fix.

a perpendicular can be dropped to a single LOP from the DR position plotted for its time of observation, as shown in Fig. 8.12.

When piloting in very restricted waters, the prudent navigator will refrain from placing undue confidence in either a running fix or estimated position. Although new DR course and speed lines may be originated from either, it is good practice to maintain the "master" DR plot from the last fix, using the running-fix/estimated-position plot as a better approximation of the actual vessel track. Of course, the optimum action when in serious doubt in restricted waters is to anchor, if water depths and traffic allow, until conditions for position-finding improve.

Celestial Navigation

Once his vessel has proceeded far enough to sea so that visual, radar, or RDF lines of position cannot be obtained, the navigator must rely upon alternative means of fixing his position to update his DR plot. Celestial navigation based on the determination of LOPs from observations of celestial

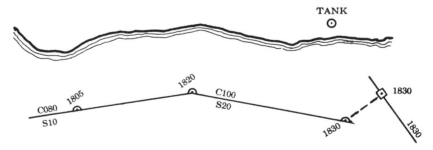

Fig. 8.12 An estimated position formed by dropping a perpendicular to a LOP from the DR position plotted for the time of observation.

bodies has long been the least expensive and most reliable method of position finding at sea.

8.18 Principles of Celestial Navigation In essence, in order to determine a celestial LOP, the *observed altitude* of the body, denoted H_o, is compared with a *computed altitude, H_c,* that the body should have from an *assumed position* (AP) of the observer at the time of the observation, to determine a so-called *intercept distance* (a), expressed as the number of minutes of difference in arc between H_o and H_c. Then, using the relationship that each minute of arc is equal to a mile upon the surface of the earth, the intercept distance a is laid off from the AP along the *true azimuth (Zn)* of the point on the earth's surface directly beneath the body (its *geographic position*, or *GP*), either toward the GP if H_o is greater than H_c, or away from the GP if H_o is less than H_c. These relationships are illustrated in Fig. 8.13.

To complete the plot of the celestial LOP, a straight-line segment is drawn at the end of the laid-off intercept distance perpendicular to the true azimuth line to the GP. This line is called the *celestial LOP;* it represents a

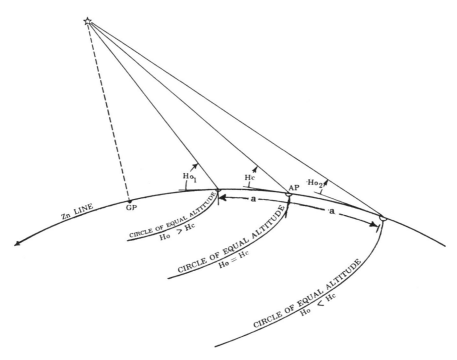

Fig. 8.13 The intercept distance a is laid off along the true azimuth line ZN toward the GP of the body if $H_o > H_c$, or away from the GP of the body if $H_o < H_c$.

portion of a so-called *circle of equal altitude* centered on the GP of the body, any point on the circumference of which the observed altitude H_o would be obtained. The celestial LOP is labeled with the name of the body above the line and the time of the observation below it, as shown in Fig. 8.14.

The intersection of two such celestial LOPs derived from simultaneous observations of two celestial bodies would constitute a *celestial fix*. (In normal practice, three or more observations are made to guard against error.) Since celestial observations are usually not simultaneous, however, care must be taken to obtain an accurate sextant altitude for each body observed. A complete round of celestial sightings of five or six bodies may take 15 to 20 min. Therefore, earlier celestial LOPs are customarily advanced to the time of the latest observation to obtain the celestial fix, exactly as is done in forming a piloting running fix.

The altitude of the body as observed using the sextant—called the *sextant altitude, h_s*—must be compensated for by several factors to arrive at the correct observed altitude H_o. Among these factors are the dip of the sea horizon resulting from the height of the observer's eye; any error in the optics of the sextant; atmospheric refraction; the radius of the disc of the sun, moon, and the planets Venus and Mars whenever the latter are observed while opposite from earth in their orbits around the sun; and the radius of the earth when the sun and moon are observed. Corrections for all these factors except instrument optical error are obtained from publications

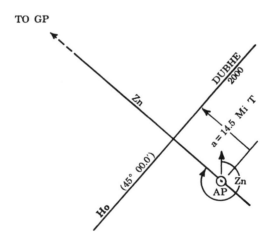

Fig. 8.14 A celestial LOP plotted for the star Dubhe observed at 2000 with an H_o of 45°00.0′ an H_c for the AP shown of 44°45.5′, and a resulting intercept distance a of 14.5′ (equivalent to 14.5 miles) toward the GP. The true azimuth is about 315°T.

called *almanacs,* which, as explained below, also contain extensive tabulations of other data of prime importance in celestial computations.

In order to compute the theoretical altitude, H_c, of the body from the assumed position at the time of the observation, it is necessary first to determine its precise GP at that time, and then to use this information to solve a so-called *navigational triangle* whose vertices are the AP, the GP, and the terrestrial pole nearest the AP. The process of transforming a sextant observation to a celestial LOP in this way is called *sight reduction.* The coordinates of the GP of the sun, moon, planets, and the 57 brightest navigational stars are obtained from one of the almanacs mentioned earlier, with the *Nautical Almanac* and the *Air Almanac* published by the Navel Observatory being the most popular in the United States.

Once the location of the body is established by an almanac, one of two sets of sight reduction tables published by DMAHTC is used to obtain H_c and the true azimuth, *Zn;* one set, called the *Sight Reduction Tables for Marine Navigation, No. 229,* is published in six volumes; the other, intended primarily for air navigation (though also used extensively for surface navigation) is the *Sight Reduction Tables for Air Navigation, No. 249,* published in three volumes. The tables of both are in essence a set of precomputed values of H_c and *Zn* for given values of the GP and AP. Various standardized *sight reduction forms* are normally used to perform manual sight reductions of this nature.

Electronic calculators with trigonometric-function capabilities are also being increasingly used for sight reduction, as are more advanced models designed specifically for electronic sight reduction. Some of the latter even eliminate the need for an almanac, as they are preprogrammed to generate almanac data for all bodies normally observed. In the late 1970s, the Naval Observatory began publication of an almanac designed expressely for electronic sight reduction, the *Almanac for Computers.* It contains formulas for the computation of all corrections to h_s to obtain H_o, as well as for the determination of the coordinates of all celestial bodies of navigational interest at any time.

In addition to the celestial fix, several other kinds of valuable navigational information is obtainable using celestial methods. Among these are the determination of the latitude line by observations of the star Polaris or of the sun at local apparent noon; the determination of compass and gyro error by azimuth observations; and the prediction of the times of twilight, sunrise and sunset and of moonrise and moonset. Progressive celestial running fixes based on periodic observations of the sun are a favorite method of monitoring the progress of a vessel by day at sea, especially on sailboats lacking electronic navigation gear. Any single celestial LOP, moreover, may be used to form an estimated position by dropping a perpendicular to it from the DR position for the time of observation, as in piloting.

Just as in piloting, the importance of maintaining an accurate DR plot between celestial fixes cannot be overstressed. Not only does the DR plot determine the selection of an appropriate AP, it may also be the only navigational information available in overcast weather when celestial observations are unobtainable.

Electronic Navigation

The rapid advances in electronics technology that have occurred since World War II have resulted in enormous gains in sophistication and capability of electronic navigation equipment in recent years. Electronic calculators designed to automate the celestial sight reduction process have already been alluded to in the previous section. Advanced electronic navigation systems and equipment now being developed could well revolutionize the practice of navigation at sea during the decade of the eighties. For the first time in history, celestial navigation may be displaced as the prime method of such navigation.

8.19 Hyperbolic Navigation Systems The most popular of the land-based electronic navigation systems at present are Loran-C, Decca, and Omega. All of these are called *hyperbolic systems* because the LOPs they provide are segments of a hyperbolic pattern generated by station pairs within each system, as shown in Fig. 8.15.

Loran-C In Loran-C, each hyperbolic line represents a locus of points along which an identical time difference reading is obtained between the arrival of an electronic pulse transmitted by one of the stations in a pair, called the *master station,* and the arrival of a sequentially transmitted pulse from the other, *secondary station.* Each Loran-C master station is grouped with a number of different secondary stations to form several different pairs,

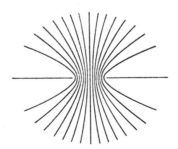

Fig. 8.15 A typical pattern generated by a hyperbolic navigation system such as Loran-C, Omega, or Decca.

collectively referred to as a Loran-C chain. Currently there are thirteen Loran-C chains, which together provide theoretical coverage over most of the littoral areas of the northern hemisphere (including the Great Lakes) with the exception of the Indian Ocean and parts of the South Atlantic and South Pacific.

All stations in the system transmit on a common carrier frequency of 100 kHz, with a bandwidth extending to 10 kHz to either side; each chain transmits on a slightly different base frequency within this band. Once set for a given chain, most modern receivers are able to track and display time-difference readings for two or more station pairs simultaneously, and some even come equipped with optional circuitry that converts the received readings into continuously displayed latitude and longitude. The primary signals from each Loran-C pair, called *ground waves,* are receivable within roughly circular areas of about 1500-mile diameter, centered on the base line connecting the pair. Reflected signals from the ionosphere called *sky waves* can be received to about 2300 miles at night.

The DMAHTC produces several series of nautical charts on which various color-coded Loran-C hyperbolic patterns are overprinted, allowing easy plotting of the Loran-C LOP once the time-difference reading has been obtained. DMAHTC also makes available a series of *Loran-C Lattice Tables* for most station pairs; these enable Loran-C LOPs to be plotted on charts and plotting sheets not having the overprinted hyperbolas. Two or more intersecting LOPs corresponding to two or more simultaneously recorded time differences constitute a *Loran-C fix.* The accuracy of such a fix determined under good conditions varies from about ±700 ft near the base line to ±2000 ft near the limits of ground wave coverage for a particular master-secondary station pair.

Decca　Decca is a British system somewhat similar to Loran-C in concept, except that the hyperbolic patterns established in a Decca chain are produced by the phase comparison of simultaneously transmitted continuous wave signals rather than the sequenced pulsed signals of Loran. Each Decca chain normally consists of one master and three associated slave stations, the latter arranged in a star pattern centered on the master station, with angles of about 120 degrees between each master-slave base line. Each master-slave pair within a chain is designated by a color—purple, red, or green. All stations in a chain transmit their signals simultaneously, on frequencies between 70 and 130 kHz. The hyperbolic pattern thus generated by each color-coded master-slave pair looks similar to that in Fig. 8.16. Whereas the different hyperbolas in Loran represent loci of constant time differences between the receipt of two pulses, in Decca a *lane* between the two adjacent hyperbolas of each master-slave pair's continuous wave signals is established by progressive phase-difference measurements from 0 to

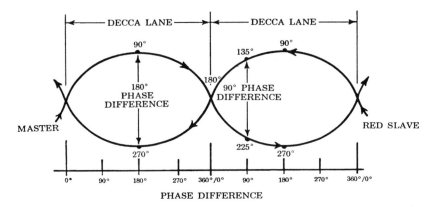

Fig. 8.16 Two Decca lanes are established by the phase differences measured between the master signal and one of its color-coded slaves. Within each lane, the measured phase difference progresses from 0 to 360 degrees, thus making continuous precision position determination within each lane possible.

360 degrees, as indicated in Fig. 8.16. The exact position within each lane can be established by precise determination of the phase difference of each signal, resulting in the Decca LOP. The intersecting LOPs generated simultaneously by the superimposed purple, red, and green hyperbolic patterns provide a continuous Decca fix of high precision, with maximum error of only 150 yd by day within the 250-mile area of coverage of a typical chain.

The lane positions within all three color-coded hyperbolic patterns constituting a given chain are continuously displayed by the Decca receiver. This information is used to plot segments of the three LOPs on a chart overprinted with the color-coded Decca hyperbolic patterns (in the same fashion as in Loran) to form the Decca fix.

Unfortunately, Decca is not deployed very extensively. Its coverage is limited at present mainly to the littoral regions of eastern Canada, northern Europe, Japan, and South Africa. Within these areas, however, its ease of use, reliability, and precision make it a favorite of mariners in all types of vessels from small craft to oil tankers.

Omega   The most recently operational and largest in scope of all terrestrial hyperbolic radio-navigation systems is Omega. Because the signals of this system are transmitted at very low frequencies (10–14 kHz), Omega is able to achieve worldwide coverage with only eight stations located some 6000 miles apart, the last of which, in Australia, was brought on line in 1981. Like Decca, the signals of Omega are continuous waves that establish a pattern of hyperbolic lanes on the phase-comparison principle, with phase differences within each lane progressing from 0 degrees at one boundary to 360 degrees at the other. Unlike Decca, however, all eight stations in the Omega system transmit on the same four frequencies, being able to do so because of a repeating 10-sec time-sharing plan in which each frequency is transmitted by only one station at a time. In effect, the Omega receiver briefly stores each transmission for comparison with other later transmissions during each 10-sec cycle. The eight stations are differentiated by the location of their transmission sequence within the overall 10-sec schedule.

Each of the eight stations in the Omega system is assigned a letter identifier from A through H. A unique feature of the system is that any two stations receivable at a given location can be used as a station pair to yield an Omega LOP that is based on a phase-difference comparison of their two signals. Because the long range of the Omega signals makes at least three stations receivable almost everywhere on earth, a three-LOP Omega fix is essentially obtainable worldwide through successive comparisons of the three possible combinations of resulting signals. Moreover, the small divergence of the Omega hyperbolic patterns results in fix accuracies, under most conditions, of about ± 1 mile by day and ± 2 miles at night.

Each Omega station is periodically taken out of operation for routine maintenance to the respective transmitting facility. Information on inoperative stations will be made available via *Notice to Mariners*.

Most Omega receivers are able to maintain and display lane-positioning data for at least two station pairs simultaneously, and some come equipped with lat/long conversion features and speed determination displays. As with Loran-C, DMAHTC produces a series of Omega charts intended for use as plotting sheets on which the color-coded hyperbolic patterns generated by selected station pairs can be overprinted. The DMAHTC also publishes a series of *Omega Lattice Tables* similar in form to those for Loran-C; use of their data permits the Omega LOPs corresponding with designated station pairs to be plotted on standard nautical charts and on plotting sheets not overprinted with Omega lines.

8.20 Satellite Navigation The precision navigation requirements of American ballistic-missile submarines led to the development of the first operational satellite navigation system, called the *Transit* or *Navy Satellite System (NavSat)*, in the nineteen-sixties. The system was made available for commercial use in 1967 with the production of the first receivers designed for such use. The *Transit System,* as it is usually referred to today, consists of some seven operational satellites in polar orbits about 600 nautical miles high. Each satellite broadcasts sequential 2-min transmissions consisting of ephemeris data (assigned places of celestial bodies at regular intervals), satellite positioning parameters, and certain other system information.

In order to obtain a fix using the Transit System, the shipboard satellite receiver determines from doppler-shift measurements its precise position relative to the satellite, as the latter passes above the radio horizon within the prescribed elevation limits of 10 degrees minimum and 70 degrees maximum. Receipt of at least four and preferably seven sequential satellite broadcasts are required to accomplish this position determination. The transmitted satellite positioning parameters must then be taken into account to establish the receiver's fix position on earth.

With at least five of the seven system satellites operational, the average time between fix opportunities as the satellites pass overhead ranges from about 35 to 100 min worldwide. Under optimal conditions, fix accuracy afforded by the system is about ±35 meters for a stationary vessel; for a moving vessel, an additional 0.2-mile longitude error is introduced for each knot of north-south speed error and a 0.05-mile latitude error for every knot of east-west speed error.

Although the Transit System was originally used only be large commercial vessels and Navy ships during the sixties and early seventies, progressive decreases in the cost and complexity of receivers have greatly extended its use in the civil sector today to the point that even larger power-driven pleasure craft can be so equipped. One such fully automatic receiver, shown in Fig. 8.17, features a continuous readout of DR latitude and longitude between fixes.

Fig. 8.17 The NCS Meridian navigation satellite receiver draws 6 watts at 12 V d-c (available for under $4000).

The follow-on navigational satellite system to Transit is the *Global Positioning System (GPS)*, previously scheduled to become fully operational in the late nineteen-eighties, is not likely to be useful until the late nineteen-nineties due to national space program difficulties. Ultimately, it will consist of a constellation of 21 satellites (18 operating satellites plus 3 active spares) spread among six orbits 10,800 miles high. Currently (January 1987), there are 10 GPS satellites in orbit, 7 of which are operational. Together, these satellites will be able to provide continuous latitude, longitude, and altitude positioning information to ships, aircraft, and ground vehicles worldwide at any time and under any weather conditions. Because the system receiver will be able to make fix determinations, based on ranging techniques, to at least three and usually four satellites *simultaneously,* extreme positioning accuracy on the order of ±10 meters should be routinely attainable. At first, receiver prices, which will be in excess of $16,000 because of the complexity of the circuitry required, will limit system use to the military and large commercial users, but eventually prices should fall to a level at which the system can be afforded by ordinary boatmen.

8.21 Combination Receivers Combination NAVSAT, Omega, Loran-C, and Decca receivers provide the navigator with an exceptional electronic navigation capability, without sacrificing a great amount of space for equipment. The price of these receivers, ranging from $16,000 to $30,000, will again limit their widespread use, however, they are readily available through electronic supply houses.

8.22 Inertial and Doppler Navigation *Inertial Navigation* This is the process of monitoring the movements of a vessel by means of special instruments that sense accelerations in the prime spatial directions, electronically integrate these accelerations to determine true speed, and from this, determine position at any time. The basic instruments used are gyros, accelerometers, and an electronic computer. Inertial navigation presently finds most widespread use in aircraft, submarines, and some larger surface ships; with continuing research and development, miniaturization of equipment, and reductions in cost, its use may one day spread to smaller vessels.

Doppler Sonar This is a fairly new type of navigational equipment that has been installed in increasing numbers of deep-draft ships in recent years. In its simplest form, the system consists of a sonar transducer and supporting equipment that transmits pulsed sonar beams fore and aft at an angle of about 30 degrees from the vertical. More complicated systems transmit additional beams to both sides. The advantage of the doppler sonar system is that very accurate speeds over the ground can be not only continually determined from the doppler shifts of the sonar beam pattern but also continually displayed, a particular advantage when the vessel is operating in relatively shallow water and the pulses are being reflected back from the bottom. In deeper water, echos are returned from the water mass itself, resulting in some degradation in the precision of the velocity determination. The ship's speed over the ground so obtained is fed into automated dead reckoning plotters and other shipboard navigational systems, thus permitting great accuracy in the computation of the ship's probable position at any time. The maximum error of currently installed equipment is about 0.17 percent of the distance run, that is, about 1.7 miles of error for each 1,000 miles covered.

The system can also be used to great advantage by large ships for precise determination of athwartship speed during docking, an extremely critical variable since serious damage to the hull and the dock can result if speeds exceed about 0.02 ft/sec. Like inertial navigation systems, doppler sonar equipment is presently prohibitively expensive for all but large commercial ships, but with passage of time and reductions in cost it may begin to appear in increasing numbers of smaller vessels.

The Practice of Navigation

The prudent navigator will make certain that he keeps himself well informed on established as well as newer techniques of navigation. He must continually study to learn more of his subject and make a habit of analyzing his performance and results to improve his technique. Not only must he understand the principles of operation of his various items of equipment, he must check them frequently to be sure all is in good working order, giving prompt attention to any need for repair or servicing.

8.23 Navigation Practice before the Voyage   Well before the start of any voyage, the prudent navigator makes a careful check of all charts, publications, and equipment, correcting any deficiencies and making certain that all updating corrections have been made. He studies the charts and sailing directions, noting all hazards and unusual conditions. He makes notes on his chart, or in another conspicuous place, of any scrap of information that may prove useful. In appropriate areas on his chart, he may add shading to shoal water and plot danger bearings. He studies light lists so that he can compute and plot visibility limits from eye level for each important navigational light to be encountered. He studies tide and tidal current tables to be thoroughly familiar with conditions his vessel will meet. He organizes his navigation team, if others are available to assist, to be certain that each person understands his responsibility and is competent to carry it out.

All these details must be taken care of in advance. Once the vessel is under way, he will be fully occupied with navigating the vessel. The time for preparation will have passed.

Several hours before the vessel gets under way, the gyrocompass is started, if it has been turned off previously, and given sufficient time to settle on the meridian. Other equipment needing warm-up is turned on in plenty of time to insure reliable operation when needed.

8.24 Navigation Practice during Piloting Once his vessel is under way, the navigator maintains a continuous dead-reckoning plot and ensures that a log is kept of all rounds of bearing and distance measurements. While proceeding out of the harbor, he notes each buoy and landmark as it is sighted and passed, and he makes sure that fixes are obtained and plotted at the proper intervals.

As the vessel leaves pilot waters, a last position is carefully determined and thoroughly checked as a point of departure for the deepwater portion of the voyage. The equipment used in piloting is then secured for sea, and the more leisurely routine of navigation away from land is set.

8.25 Navigation Practice at Sea During this portion of the voyage, electronic fixes are obtained and plotted at regular intervals if the vessel is so equipped and the sailing rules allow (certain ocean racing rules prohibit use of electronic fix information during races); if available, celestial positioning information is obtained and plotted.

Each time a fix is obtained by any method, the set and drift of the current must be determined as a guide to the future, as well as an indication of a possible major error in the navigation or of the existence of an unusual condition. Inconsistent results should be accounted for, if possible.

If celestial navigation is used, the daily routine, called the "day's work in navigation," usually consists of the following steps:

1. Morning twilight observations and sight reduction for a fix
2. Winding the chronometers and determination of chronometer error
3. Morning sun line as a check on longitude, with an azimuth observation to check the accuracy of the compass
4. Noon sight of the sun for a check on the latitude, with either a running fix by advancement of the morning sun line or a fix with a line of position from an observation of the moon or Venus
5. An afternoon sun line as a check on the longitude, with an azimuth observation to check the accuracy of the compass
6. Computation of the time of sunset and the approximate altitudes and azimuths of celestial bodies available for observation during evening twilight
7. Evening twilight observations and sight reduction for a fix
8. Computation of the times of sunrise and the beginning of morning twilight and the approximate altitudes and azimuths of celestial bodies available for observation during morning twilight

9. Computation of the times of moonrise and moonset on the following day

Variations of this routine are dictated by the weather and the availability of electronic aids to navigation.

8.26 Navigation Practice at Landfall As the expected time of landfall approaches, the navigator must use extra care in determining the vessel's position. He turns on his navigational radar and radio direction finder, if his vessel is so equipped, and readies the other equipment for piloting to prepare for this form of navigation. After landfall, he is careful to identify accurately the landmarks and aids to navigation sighted. He further verifies his position by soundings. During the passage to the pier or anchorage, he uses all the care exercised at the start of the voyage, leaving nothing to chance.

The prudent navigator is at all times throughout a voyage alert to the uncertainty of position of his vessel and to all opportunities to ensure its safe navigation. He frequently compares the magnetic compass and gyro-compass, perhaps half-hourly. He uses the radar, if available, in clear weather so as to develop an understanding of its limitations as well as its usefulness; he will then be able to interpret results with confidence when other means of checking are not available. Similarly, he uses all means available to acquire experience with each piece of equipment.

Navigation is far from a mechanical process. A reliable navigator is one who has developed good judgment through experience and constant analysis of results. The good navigator invariably asks himself, "Are the results reasonable; are they consistent with other data?" The real test of a navigator comes when the safety of his vessel is at stake and inconsistent data are being obtained. It is then that his ingenuity and judgment are tested to the limit, and the long hours of comparison, analysis, and study to understand his equipment and its limitations pays off. As stated in the report of the Court of Inquiry investigation of the Point Honda disaster off the California coast in 1923, "The price of good navigation is constant vigilance."

References

Graves, F. *Piloting*. Camden, ME: International Marine Publishing Company, 1981.

Hobbs, R. R. *Marine Navigation 1: Piloting*. 2nd ed. Annapolis: Naval Institute Press, 1981.

Hobbs, R. R. *Marine Navigation 2: Celestial and Electronic*. 2nd ed. Annapolis: Naval Institute Press, 1981.

Maloney, E. S. *Duttons Navigation and Piloting*. 13th ed. Annapolis: Naval Institute Press, 1985.

Shufeldt, H. H., and Newcomer, Kenneth, *Calculator Afloat*. Annapolis: Naval Institute Press, 1980.

Shufeldt, H. H., and Dunlap, G. D. *Piloting and Dead Reckoning.* 2nd ed. Annapolis: Naval Institute Press, 1981.

Toghill, Jeff. *Coastal Navigation for Beginners.* Sydney, Australia: A. H. & A. W. Reed Pty Ltd., 1976.

Wylie, F. J. *The Use of Radar at Sea.* 5th ed. Annapolis: Naval Institute Press, 1978.

American Practical Navigator. Washington, D.C.: Defense Mapping Agency Hydrographic Center, 1984.

Except as otherwise noted, the line sketches in this chapter are adapted from *Marine Navigation 1 and 2,* 2nd ed., by Richard Hobbs, with the permission of the publisher, the U.S. Naval Institute Press, Annapolis, Md.

PART III

Shiphandling

9

General Principles of Ship Control

Many naval and merchant ships are twin- or multiple-screw, and some have twin rudders. The ability to handle these ships can be improved by a thorough understanding of the forces set up in a single-screw ship when the propeller revolves, the rudder is "put over" (moved), and the ship proceeds through the water. We shall discuss, first, the propeller and rudder forces in a single-screw ship and then go on to consider these forces in a twin-screw ship.

9.1 Forces that Affect Maneuvering in a Single-Screw Ship* The action of a propeller in a single-screw ship brings into play many unsymmetrical forces. In order to understand these, it is necessary to have some idea of the manner in which a propeller generates forces. As a ship moves through the water, she experiences skin friction caused by the viscosity of the water and tends to drag some of the water with her. If we measure the velocity of this water relative to that of the ship at increasing distances from the hull, we find that close to the hull the relative velocity is small because the water

---

*Based, in part, on *Propeller Action in a Single Screw Ship.* (Courtesy of the Director, David Taylor Model Basin.)

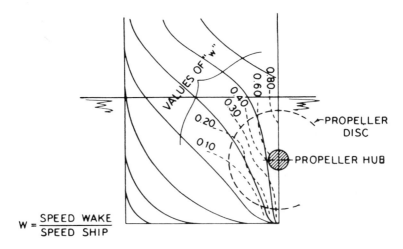

$$W = \frac{SPEED\ WAKE}{SPEED\ SHIP}$$

Fig. 9.1 Wake distribution for single-scew ship.

clings to the ship. The relative velocity increases as the distance from the hull increases until a point is reached where the water has no motion with respect to the surrounding sea. The *boundary layer* includes the water from the hull to the point where the relative velocity equals that of the ship. The width of this layer varies in some cases from zero at the bow to several feet near the stern. The net effect is that the boundary layer, a body of water, is given a forward motion by the passage of the ship.

Owing to this frictional drag upon the surrounding water, there is found aft, in the vicinity of the ship, a following current or wake called the *frictional wake*. The frictional wake is, in most cases, greatest at the surface in the vertical plane through the keel and abaft the ship. It decreases downward and outward on each side, as shown in Fig. 9.1. Streamline and wave patterns affect the velocity of the wake, but their effect is small.

The propeller revolves in this wake. Since the wake water is moving forward relative to the sea, the propeller, in effect, is advancing into a moving body of water. Its speed is less than that of the ship. Thus, if a ship is moving at 15 knots and dragging a wake with it at 3 knots, the propeller is only advancing at 12 knots *relative to the wake*. The ratio of the wake speed to the ship's speed is called the *wake fraction, w;* in this case, $w = 3/15 = 0.20$.

The speed of the advance of the propeller through the wake, V_A, is given by the formula,

$$V_A = V(1 - w)$$

where V = the ship's speed in knots. In the preceding case,

$$V_A = 15(1 - 0.20) = 15 \times 0.8 = 12 \text{ knots}$$

The wake speed of 3 knots is only an average speed and actually varies from place to place. Behind shaft struts, skeg, or rudder, the wake speed may equal that of the ship. It is this variation in wake pattern that causes the unsymmetrical propeller forces.

The wake pattern has been measured on many models. A typical wake distribution appears in Fig. 9.1. The curves on the right side are similar to those on the left. The figure shows by contours of w values the distribution of the wake velocity (the fore-and-aft components) over the propeller disc. Along the broken line, $w = 0.60$, the speed of advance of the propeller through the wake is only 40 percent of the ship's speed.

In addition to the fore-and-aft motion, the water moving aft alongside the ship has an upward and inward flow under the counter caused by the general rise of the water as the stern moves forward.

Analysis of Propeller Action   The maximum thrust is developed at about 0.7 percent of the radius from the centerline of the shaft. We shall consider the forces generated at this point. The velocity of the blade section relative to the water is the resultant of two component velocities:

1. A forward motion through the water at velocity V_A, or ship speed minus wake velocity
2. A rotational motion of the propeller given by $2\pi rN$, where r is the radius under consideration (0.7) and N is revolutions in a unit of time

The resultant velocity of the water, V_o, is a combination of the forward and rotational motions. (See Fig. 9.2.) The effect of V_o striking at the angle of attack, α, is to develop lift and drag just like the forces on an airplane wing. The direction of V_o to the face of the blade section at the angle of attack produces forces that can be resolved into two components: a fore and an aft force, the thrust T and a torque Q. The former, T, propels the ship and the latter, Q, *generates a reaction or transverse force through the shafting that tends to force the stern to port or starboard.* If we look at Fig. 9.2 in another way, we could consider V_o as one of the forces, all acting in the direction of the arrow and on the after surface of the blade. In fact, the forces act on both sides of the blade. If angle of attack a between V_o and the surface of the blade is small, the component forces T and Q will be small. If α is large—that is, if wV, the forward wake speed, is great—the force V_o will strike the surface of the blade at a more effective angle, and T and Q will be large. The wake speed, wV, varies as shown in Fig. 9.1, which explains the unsymmetrical forces acting on the hull. The amount of work done by each blade of the propeller will vary with its position in the disc.

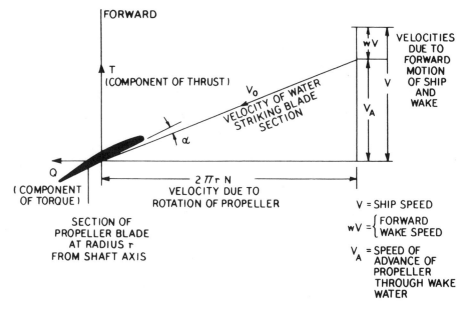

Fig. 9.2 Simplified velocity diagram for propeller blade section.

There are four regions where the maximum change in force occurs:

1. As blade A (Fig. 9.3) approaches the vertical point, Fig. 9.1 shows that it will pass through a region of relatively high wake speed and therefore low values of V_A. (Fig. 9.2 shows that a will increase as V_A drops in value; that V_o will act on the blade at a larger, more effective angle of attack; and that T and Q will increase.) The increase of torque Q *reacts* through the shafting on the stern of the ship, forcing it to port with a right-hand propeller. If we revert to our explanation of V_o above, it is clear the V_o is acting from starboard to port against the rear side of blade A. Because a right-handed propeller is being considered V_o will have two components: T, the thrust propelling the ship through the water, and Q, which generates a transverse or athwartship *force* now directing the stern to port.

2. Blade C will pass through an area opposite to that of blade A, and a transverse force to starboard will be exerted. (Since the wake speed in the lower part of the disc is much less than in the upper, however, the angle of attack will be smaller than on blade A, and the force to starboard will not be as great as that to port. The resultant force of these two forces will therefore be to port.)

3. Blade B will move downward against the upward flow of water un-

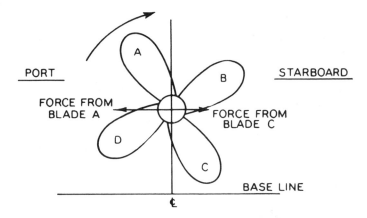

Fig. 9.3 View from astern showing force on shaft axis.

der the counter. This flow is equivalent to an increase in N in the formula $2\pi rN$. The angle of attack, velocity, thrust, and torque will increase.

4. Blade D moves up with the flow and experiences a decrease in the above factors.

It is clear that B overbalances D and that the ship's head tends to fall off to port. When going astern, the propeller turns in the reverse direction. The forces then act in the opposite direction from that when going ahead, and the ship's head will fall off to starboard.

There are two more factors that affect the steering of the ship:

1. The propeller imparts a helical motion to its slipstream that impinges on the rudder even when the rudder is amidships. That part of the helical slipstream above the axis of the propeller tends to move the stern to starboard, and the part below the axis tends to move the stern to port. The resultant force depends on the area of the rudder above and below the centerline of the shaft and on the uniformity of the slipstream.

2. The next factor is the submergence of the propeller. If the ship is in ballast or at light displacement or plunging in heavy seas, the propeller may break surface, causing a decrease in the transverse effect of blade A. When the ship has little or no speed, Blade A, which is near the surface, may draw air and again decrease the transverse force.

The ship is therefore subject to several opposing and variable forces. Her actual behavior will depend on the magnitude of these forces. General experience shows that many single-screw ships with a right-hand propeller turning ahead tend to fall off to port. There are exceptions, and no hard and fast rule can be laid down. Observe your own ship.

9.2 Getting Under Way With the ship stationary or just starting to move, the wake does not exist or is negligible. Top blade A may break the surface and thus lose some of its usual transverse force to port. If it does not break the surface, air may be drawn down with the same effect. The lower blade still acts to force the stern to starboard. The rudder, even when amidships, receives the helical slipstream at an effective angle high up on the port side. If the rudder has a larger area above the axis of the propeller than below, that force tends to move the stern to starboard. The result of these forces may be that the stern will move to starboard.

When the ship is backing, the forces caused by blades A and C are reversed. Blade A may break the surface, but in any case, blade C, acting to port, will predominate. Since no helical slipstream is thrown against the rudder and most of the water that passes through the propeller disc comes from the free surface, the rudder can exert no steering force until the ship gains sternway. The upper part of the discharge flow from the propeller strikes the starboard underwater body of the ship at a good angle; the lower part strikes the keel on the port side at a poor angle. It is probable that the force caused by the upper part predominates; at any rate, the result of these forces tends to push the stern to port.

9.3 Handling Ships with Controllable Reversible-Pitch Propellers Most of the new surface combatants being built by the U.S. Navy today have controllable reversible-pitch (CRP) propellers. The *Ticonderoga* class cruisers, *Spruance* class destroyers, *Kidd* class guided missile destroyers, and the *Oliver Hazard Perry* class guided missile frigates all have CRP. Additionally, many small ships—such as LSTs, tugs, and the Navy's nonmagnetic ocean minesweepers (MSO)—have controllable-pitch propellers (CPP). In the CRP system, the blades of the propellers are rotated by a hydraulic mechanism in a plane parallel to that of the propeller shaft. Thus the blades can be adjusted to take more or less bite or can be reversed in pitch. It is particularly this latter feature that adds maneuverability. The 10,000 ton *Ticonderoga* class, for example, can be stopped in less than two ship lengths when going ahead full power.

The forces acting on the controllable-pitch propeller are the same as those described above for conventional propellers. The shiphandler uses his rudder and engines in the conventional way except that, instead of speeding up, slowing, or reversing his engines, he adjusts or reverses the pitch of his blades by a control mechanism on the bridge. Since the response to change in propeller blade pitch is instantaneous, the shiphandler must become accustomed to this disappearance of dead time when backing. Another novelty of controllable-pitch propellers to the seaman trained to handle conventional ships will be his ability to move the ship quickly with high power. This comes about by keeping the shaft revolutions high and the propeller pitch low. An increase in propeller blade pitch then applies power to the ship very suddenly. A good rule of thumb, especially with gas turbine-powered ships, is that power will be applied to the shaft/propeller at roughly the same time as the engine whine becomes audible, i.e., within a matter of seconds. It is worth noting that, at some point, 100 percent pitch is applied. To increase speed beyond that point, more revolutions are added to the shaft. Conning orders to the engines, therefore, include a requirement for both pitch (in percent) and revolutions (rpms).

Mention should be made of one characteristic of CPPs—they do not "deadstick" very well, as the constantly turning propeller disrupts the waterflow to the rudder. Steerage ahead generally requires that the wheel carry some pitch. Line handling aft must be done very carefully, since the constantly turning propellers can easily foul a poorly tended mooring line being heaved in or slacked.

9.4 Steering a Twin-Screw Ship, Single Rudder A twin-screw ship has two propellers, one on either side of the centerline. As a rule, they are out-turning, that is, the starboard one is right-handed and the port one left-handed. They turn in opposite directions to balance the propeller forces and enable the ship to steer a straight course with no rudder.

A multiple-screw ship normally has four propellers, two on a side, out-turning, and so controlled that those on a side go ahead or astern as a unit. As the action of a multiple-screw ship is similar to that of a twin-screw ship, only the latter will be discussed.

The steering of a twin-screw ship is considerably simpler than that of a single-screw ship. The strong tendency of the single-screw ship to back stern to port does not hold with the twin-screw, and the latter backs with equal facility in either direction, barring the effect of wind, waves, and currents.

The various forces affecting the action of the single-screw ship are still present to a degree in the case of a twin-screw. Often they are considerably less because the forces emanating from one screw are balanced by similar but opposite forces from the other screw. In addition, there is a new force caused by the movement of the screws around the centerline. It will readily be seen that with one screw going ahead and the other astern, a turning moment results that tends to throw the bow to the side of the backing screw.

One powerful force should not be overlooked. It is the momentum of the ship, ahead or astern, acting through the center of gravity. If a twin-screw ship is going ahead and one screw is backed, two opposing forces are set in motion, namely: the force of the backing screw acting in one direction at a certain distance from the centerline and the weight of the ship acting in the opposite direction. These are in addition to the forces caused by the action of the wake on the rudder if the latter is "put over."

The steering of the single-rudder, twin-screw ship will be considered under the following conditions (no wind or sea):

1. Ship and screws going ahead
2. Ship going ahead, screws backing
3. Ship going astern, screws backing
4. Ship going astern, screws going ahead
5. One screw going ahead, other screw backing

9.5   Ship and Both Screws Going Ahead (Single Rudder)   In this case, if the rudder is amidships, the ship will steer a steady course. The transverse forces of the two propellers are equal and opposite in direction. As the shafts are offset equally, no turning moment is felt.

When the rudder is put over, it will receive some of the discharge flow from the propeller on that side but not as much as in a single-screw ship. The principal force that turns the ship is that set up by the wake against the forward side of the rudder.

If one screw is stopped with the rudder amidships, the turning moment of the revolving screw will take charge, and the ship will turn toward the side of the stopped screw. The discharge flow of the revolving screws does not strike the rudder.

9.6   Ship Going Ahead, Both Screws Backing (Single Rudder)   The steering effect of the rudder is the only force turning the ship from a straight course. All other forces are equalized. The effect of the rudder is reduced as the headway is lost until there is no steering control when the ship is stationary.

If only one screw is backing and the other is stopped with headway on, the turning moment of the backing screw added to the momentum of the ship going ahead will swing the stern away from the backing screw.

9.7   Ship Going Astern, Both Screws Backing (Single Rudder)   If the rudder is amidships, the various forces are equalized, and a straight course can be steered. If the rudder is put over, the pressure of the water that the ship is backing into against the back side of the rudder will enable a course to be steered. However, most of the water that passes through the screws comes from the free surface and thus has little effect on the rudder.

If one screw is stopped, the turning moment of the backing screw is added to the effect of the rudder when it is put over away from the revolving screw. The swing may be slowed or stopped if the rudder is put over toward the screw. The effect of the rudder is to counteract the effect of the screw, and how effective it is will depend on the size of the rudder and speed of the engine.

9.8 Ship Going Astern, Both Screws Going Ahead (Single Rudder) The ship will respond to the rudder, that is, a left rudder will throw the stern to port unless excessive sternway is on. The transverse forces of the screws will be equalized. The steering effect of the rudder when going astern will be reduced gradually as the ship loses headway, until all steering control is lost before the ship has lost sternway. This loss of control occurs because the discharge flow from the propellers will interefere with the flow of water against the back of the rudder.

9.9 Ship Stationary, One Screw Going Ahead, Other Screw Backing (Single Rudder) The rudder will have little effect until head or sternway has been gained. The turning moments of the two screws will be additive, but the sum may not be large when the shafts are close together. If the ship has no deadwood, she may turn easily. In narrow waters the two screws should be operated at such speeds that the ship does not gain headway or sternway when going ahead or backing at one-third or two-thirds speed. This balancing of forces will enable the captain to move the ship ahead or astern as desired by varying the speed of the backing or ahead engine. As a general rule, with the speed of engine ahead the same as that of engine astern, the ship will slowly make headway. The rudder may be used to increase the swing when some steerageway has been gained.

9.10 Twin Rudders on Twin-Screw and Multiple-Screw Ships Twin rudders, which vary in position, shape, and size, are installed on many vessels, large and small. Their installation considerably improves the maneuverability of ships, particularly of destroyers.

Rudders on destroyers receive most of the upper half of the discharge flow of the propellers when going ahead; the lower half passes under the rudder. The general rule when handling twin-screw destroyers with one rudder has been to order the proper rudder after the ship has gained headway or sternway. The installation of twin rudders has changed this rule, and the shiphandler must now order right or left rudder before the engines are moved. The rudder should be put over to take advantage of the discharge flow from the ahead propeller. This flow acts against the forward side of its rudder and thus creates a powerful force to turn the ship.

The improved turning characteristics of destroyers are best appreciated in narrow channels or when going alongside a nest or tender requiring large angles of approach. The maneuvers to shove off from a nest, tender, or pier under awkward conditions of wind and tide are also greatly facilitated.

The key to all these ordinarily difficult maneuvers is the decisive effect of the discharge flow from the ahead propeller on the rudder astern of it. If the other propeller must be operated astern, it may do so without affecting the turn adversely because the water passing through its disc comes from the free surface and does not impinge on the rudder to any great extent. Hence, the ship can be turned to port from dead in the water, for instance, by ordering ''left full rudder, ahead two-thirds'' on the starboard engine and ''back, two-thirds'' on the port engine. The speed of the port engine can be varied thereafter to allow the ship to gain steerageway as, and if, desired. The rudder and the starboard engine need not be changed until the turn is completed.

9.11 Turning Characteristics The standard method of finding any ship's turning characteristics is to turn her in a number of complete circles under varying conditions and to record the results for each turn. The variables used are (1) right or left rudder of various degrees, (2) steady speeds of different value, and (3) differences in draft and trim. When turning data is taken, the effects of wind and sea must be noted and allowed for. Most navigational turns, of course, are not as much as 360 degrees, but by studying the complete turning circle, the ship's behavior for turns of any extent can be predicted. In considering the track actually followed by a ship during a turn, certain terms must be defined. These terms may be understood more easily by a comparative study of Figs. 9.4 and 9.5. Figure 9.4 shows actual turning circles of the *U.S.S. New Mexico.* One is the circle made at 21 knots with 35 degrees right rudder; the other, the circle made at 10 knots with 10 degrees left rudder. Figure 9.5 illustrates some differences in the turning curves made by ships of different lengths and characteristics.

9.12 Definitions Some of the more common terms used to define turning characteristics are as follows:

Turning Circle The path followed by the *pivoting point* of a ship in making a turn of 360 degrees or more. For the ordinary ship, the bow will be inside, and the stern outside, this circle.

Pivot Point That spot (a vertical axis) about which the ship rotates during a turn. In general, with the ship going ahead, it is about one-third of the way aft from the bow. It can shift, however, in accordance with the various forces that affect a ship, laterally and astern.

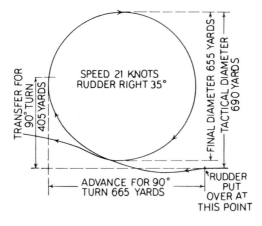

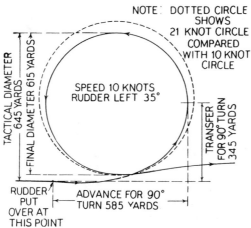

Fig. 9.4 Turning circles.

Advance The distance gained in the direction of the original course. The advance will be a maximum when the ship has turned through 90 degrees.

Transfer The distance gained at right angles to the original course when the ship has turned through 90 degrees.

Tactical Diameter The distance gained to the right or left of the original course when a turn of 180 degrees has been completed.

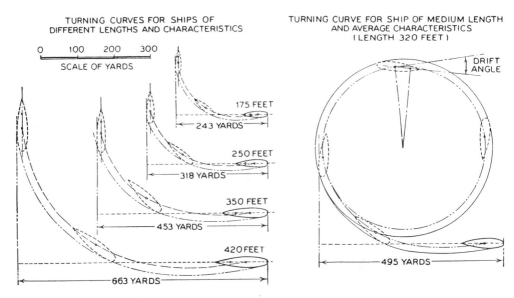

Fig. 9.5 Turning curves.

Final Diameter The distance perpendicular to the original course between tangents drawn at the points where 180 and 360 degrees of the turn have been completed. Should the ship continue turning indefinitely with the same speed and rudder angle, she will keep on turning in a circle of this diameter, which will always be less than the tactical diameter.

Kick The distance the ship moves sidewise from the original course away from the direction of the turn after the rudder is first put over. The term is also applied to the swirl of water toward the inside of the turn when the rudder is put over to begin the turn.

Drift Angle The angle at any point of the turning circle between the tangent to the turning circle at that point and the keel line of the vessel.

The turning circle is the path followed by the pivoting point during the turn. The pivoting point is in the horizontal centerline of the ship, and its position on that line depends on the shape of the underwater hull and especially on how much the after deadwood is cut away. The pivoting point moves forward if the ship is trimmed down by the head and moves aft if it is trimmed down by the stern.

This characteristic is well illustratred by the standard motor launch. When light, it pivots well aft on account of the weight of its engine, and when heavily laden, it pivots well forward. The pivoting point may also move aft along the keel line to some extent if the ship is deep in the water and forward if she is light. It is normally in the forward one-third length of the ship. When its position is once determined, it does not vary enough in the ordinary ship under different conditions of load and trim to cause any difficulty in shiphandling.

9.13   Other Forces Affecting Turning   Every seaman knows that the wind affects turning. The freeboard and superstructure act as a sail area whose effect must be considered, especially at low speeds. As the pivot point is well forward when a ship is moving ahead, the pressure acting on the greater exposed area abaft this point tends to turn the ship into the wind. Ships with high freeboard, such as a carrier, tend to turn into a wind much more rapidly and turn out of a wind much more slowly than under zero wind conditions. When going astern, the pivot point moves aft, and there is a marked tendency for the stern to seek the wind. The stronger the wind, the stronger the tendency to back into the wind. This tendency can be used to facilitate a turn when maneuvering in restricted waters. In the case where the sail area of a ship's superstructure and free-board (high bow, low stern) is concentrated forward, the effect of the wind on the ship going slowly ahead is lessened. A ship with these latter characteristics, however, will back into the wind even more rapidly.

The condition and relative direction of the sea affect both the progress and the steering of the ship by their effect on the underwater body. Any sea forward of the beam will retard the motion of the ship over the ground to a greater or less extent, whereas any sea from abaft the beam will accelerate it. The general affect of the sea on steering is to cause a ship to seek the trough. If the sea is on the bow or quarter, it may be necessary to carry a definite amount of either right or left rudder in order to maintain the course.

Current affects the underwater body of the ship. It is especially important because its existence may not always be realized. Known ocean currents may be shifted, accelerated, diminished, or even reversed by winds steadily in one direction over a long period of time. Currents in harbors, straits, and bays are caused by the action of the tides. The currents at the entrances to certain harbors (the Golden Gate, for example) are strong at times and run at an angle with the entrance course. The current may be reduced or reversed by the tide. The direction and probable force of currents in ports and along coasts may be determined approximately by study of tide tables and current charts, but every effort should be made to verify the data found in these publications because the effects of wind and weather may make them inaccurate. Observation of the shape of the shore line and of the direction in which buoys and other anchored navigational aids are leaning will give a good check on the force and direction of the current running at any given time.

The general effect of a current on the underwater body of a ship is to move her bodily in the same direction in which the current is running. When turning in a current, the ship, at the completion of the turn, may be well down in the direction of the current from her position when the turn was started. When held at any point, as by an anchor, the ship usually assumes the position where the current has the least underwater area on which to act. For this reason, an anchored ship heads into the current unless the wind or sea is strong enough to overcome its effect. For the same reason, a ship at anchor will swing with the change of the tidal current. By means of spring lines, current can be used to cant a ship or to move her toward a dock. Steering is always easier when heading into a current than when going with it, except in narrow channels.

Shallow water will modify the normal action of screws and rudder in steering or turning a ship. She may be sluggish in answering her rudder, or she may take a sudden sheer to one side. High speeds can be made in shallow water by the use of excessive power, but large waves will be formed that may cause destruction to shipping and waterfront facilities. The best seamanship in harbors and rivers is constant watchfulness, foresight, slow but steady speed, having an anchor ready for letting go, and some consideration for other craft.

When maneuvering at slow speed or turning at rest in a confined space in shallow water, the effects expected from the rudder and propellers may not occur. Since water cannot flow easily from one side of the ship to the other, the sideways force from the propellers may in fact be neutralized. Eddies may build up that will counteract the propeller forces and the expected action of the rudder. If the attempt to turn at rest in shallow water with ahead revolutions on one shaft and astern on the other fails, or if the turn is very sluggish, the situation will almost certainly become worse if the revolutions are increased. Stopping the engines to allow the eddies to subside, and then starting again with reduced revolutions, is more likely to be successful. Many harbors with an extremely small clearance between keel and bottom make such a situation not unlikely.

9.14 Casting in a Narrow Channel The expression *to cast* means to turn a ship to a particular heading in her own water. Ships turn in this manner when getting under way together in a crowded anchorage and also when headed in the wrong direction. Single vessels in restricted anchorages often have to turn in their own water too because of nearby anchored vessels or a restricted maneuvering space.

The problem of turning twin-screw ships with a single rudder is not a difficult one. Go ahead on one engine and back on the other, using the rudder when head or sternway has been gained. If the ship is fitted with twin rudders directly behind the propellers, order "hard over" or "full" rudder before going ahead on one engine. Back the other engine at the speed necessary to prevent headway or sternway being gained.

In light winds, single-screw ships can be turned quite easily in restricted waters. Take advantage of the tendency of most ships to back to port. The first move is to go ahead full with hard right rudder but reverse the engines before much headway is made. Shift the rudder after headway has been lost, back down a short distance, and then go ahead full. The rudder should be ordered right full before the engines ahead begin to turn over. In stronger winds, it is advisable to turn so that the tendency to back into the wind can be used to increase the turn. (See Fig. 9.6.)

Most seaman know that an anchor can be used to facilitate and expedite a turn in a restricted space. High-powered vessels normally use their twin screws and powerful engines to turn in places where a single-screw, low-powered steamer would use an anchor. See Section 10.18.

9.15 Navigating in a Narrow Channel A ship will be "set off" (pushed away from) the nearer bank when proceeding along a straight, narrow channel, especially if the draft of the ship is nearly equal to the depth of the water. This effect, particularly noticeable in narrow reaches with steep banks (such as certain sections of the Panama Canal), is called *bank cushion*. In the new *Clipper* class of inland waters cruise ships, bank cushion is used deliberately at times to enable the ship to follow the bank thus keeping the ship in the deepest part of the channel. This is done by applying a little constant rudder towards the bank. As the ship moves ahead, the wedge of water between the bow and the nearer bank builds up higher than that on the other side, and the bow is forced out sharply. The suction of the screw, especially on a twin-screw ship, and the unbalanced pressure of water on the quarter will lower the level of the water between the quarter and the near bank and force the stern toward the bank. This is called *bank suction*. The combined effect of bank cushion and bank suction may cause the ship to take a sudden and decided sheer toward the opposite bank. If a single-screw steamer traveling at very low speed with her starboard side near the right bank takes such a sheer, she may be brought under control by going ahead full with right full rudder. The added steering effect may overcome the bank suction. A twin-screw ship under similar conditions has a fair chance to recover from such a sheer by going ahead full on the port engine, stopping or backing the starboard screw, and putting the rudder full right. Should the sheer carry the ship across mid-channel, the starboard anchor should be dropped and snubbed if necessary. All engines should be reversed as the first anchor is dropped.

(1) NO WIND

(1) Go ahead, right full rudder
(2) Stop, left full rudder, back engine
(3) Stop, go ahead, right full rudder
(4) Stop, rudder amidships

(2) STRONG WIND — CORRECT METHOD

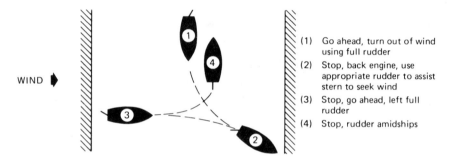

WIND ▶

(1) Go ahead, turn out of wind using full rudder
(2) Stop, back engine, use appropriate rudder to assist stern to seek wind
(3) Stop, go ahead, left full rudder
(4) Stop, rudder amidships

(3) STRONG WIND — INCORRECT METHOD

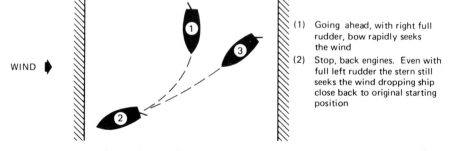

WIND ▶

(1) Going ahead, with right full rudder, bow rapidly seeks the wind
(2) Stop, back engines. Even with full left rudder the stern still seeks the wind dropping ship close back to original starting position

Fig. 9.6 Casting a single-propeller ship (right-handed propeller) in a restricted space.

9.16 Turning in a Bend There are several factors that affect a ship trying to turn in a sharp bend in a narrow channel. Two of these have been described, bank suction and bank cushion. Both are strong when the bank of the channel is steep; they are weakest when the edge of the channel shoals gradually and extends into a large shallow area. The tendency of the ship to continue along her original course when the rudder is put over will be felt in the shoaling case. If the bank of the channel is abrupt and the ship deeply laden, a bank cushion will act against the tendency to continue on her course. River or canal currents are strongest *in the bend,* and there may be eddies or counter currents on the lee side of the *point.* Turning in a bend requires a knowledge of how these forces act. The favorable forces should be used; the opposed forces avoided.

A *head current* is the safest because a ship can be stopped very quickly, but a *following current* enables the ship to proceed at a good rate with very little speed on the engines. Bank suction increases with engine speed; bank cushion, with the ship's speed. Since the force of the current against the quarter can be used to turn the ship, it is advantageous to proceed with the current.

If the current is ahead, the best position to start the turn is from the middle of the channel. The eddy under the point and the increased current in the bend are then both avoided. Proceed at a very slow speed over the ground so that the ship can be stopped quickly by the engines and the current, and by using perhaps an anchor or two.

There are three choices in making a sharp bend with a following current (see Fig. 9.7):

1. Hugging the point.
2. Staying in the bend.
3. Taking the bend side of the channel middle.

Hugging the Point If the ship hugs the point (Fig. 9.7A), the helmsman will require a small amount of rudder toward the bank to steer a straight course. Less rudder will be necessary as the channel begins to bend and the ship moves away from the bank. The signal, "less rudder," is a great help in determining when to begin to turn in clear as well as in foggy weather. However, any slack water or eddies that may be encountered around the turn may make it very difficult to prevent a sheer toward the near bank, particularly in shallow water with a laden ship. The stern may feel the current under the quarter and thus increase the sheer.

Staying in the Bend If the master decides to make the turn in the bend, that is, away from the point (Fig. 9.7B), the question arises when to turn. If he starts too late, the ship may ground on the bank in the bend. If he starts

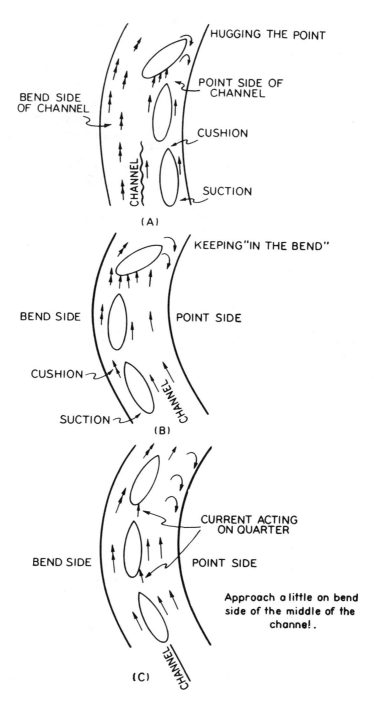

Fig. 9.7 Making a sharp bend with a following current.

too early, there is a danger that the bank suction on one quarter added to the force of the current on the other may give the ship a rank sheer. The bank cushion under the bow well increase this sheer. If the bow should enter the eddies under the point, the ship may pivot and eventually ground on both sides of the channel at the same time.

Taking the Bend Side of the Channel Middle   Perhaps the safest way to turn with a following current is to approach the turn on a course a little to the bend side of the middle of the channel (Fig. 9.7C). The eddies under the point and the increased current in the bend can be avoided, and the force of the current against the quarter can be used to assist the turn.

Two ships should not attempt to pass in a narrow channel in a bend. The ship with a head current should stop and wait for the other to clear the bend.

9.17   Orders to the Wheel (Under All Conditions)   Orders to the wheel and to the engine room telegraph must be given firmly and distinctly and repeated by the steersman or engine order telegraph operator in the exact words given as proof that they are understood and are being obeyed. A standard phraseology should be used for changes in course and speed to ensure a uniform result. In many commands to the steersman, the first word gives the direction so that the wheel can be started immediately, and the second gives the amount of rudder to be used.

"Right (left) standard rudder!" Standard rudder is the amount used to turn with a certain tactical diameter.

"Right (left) full rudder!" This is used when it is desired to make as short a turn as possible. The number of degrees to use for full rudder is always greater than that used for standard rudder. As the full throw of the rudder is about 35 degrees to each side, full rudder is set a few degrees less in order to ensure that the rudder will not jam hard over against the stops.

"Right (left) 5 (10, etc.) degrees rudder!" This command is used when a more gradual turn is desired than would be the case if either standard or full rudder were used.

"Right (left) rudder!" This order starts the wheel over in the desired direction immediately and must be followed by other orders as an obscure situation develops. It should seldom be necessary to use this order.

With an experienced steersman, all the foregoing orders may be followed by an order to steady on a certain compass course. The steersman will carry this out without further orders and report when steadied on the new course. With an inexperienced steersman or when the new course cannot be determined beforehand, the following orders are used:

"Rudder amidships!" This order further slows the swing and is a warning that the new course is being approached.

"Meet her!" This order requires opposite rudder to stop the swing.

"Steady" or *"Steady as you go!"* These orders are given when it is desired to keep the ship on the heading she has at that instant.

The object of these orders is to steady the ship on the new course without letting her swing past it with consequent loss of position and unnecessary use of rudder. The exact times at which the various orders should be given for each ship must be determined by trial and experience. One valuable point to note is that a ship with heavy weights near the bow and stern requires more rudder to start and is harder to stop because of the momentum acquired during the turn.

All orders to the steersman in regard to the course must refer to the compass by which he is steering at the time and must be in the form *"Course, zero, zero, five."* The steersman is not concerned whether the course is true or magnetic and must never be required to apply compass corrections of any kind. The officer of the deck should check the compass course upon assuming a new course and frequently thereafter.

Certain other orders to the wheel are used on occasion:

"Shift the rudder!" This is an order to change an equal amount from right to left rudder, or vice versa. It is often used while going ahead or backing in restricted waters to assist in a turn.

"Right (left) handsomely!" This order is used for small rudder angles to make slight changes of course. It is rarely used today and probably is unfamiliar to most steersmen.

"Nothing to the right (left)!" This order is given when the course to be made good is a shade off the course set and all small variations in steering must be kept to the right (left) of the compass course. It is frequently used to avoid obstructions, buoys, or passing ships.

The steersman must repeat all orders exactly as given and must report when they have been carried out. When he is relieved, he must report that fact to the officer of the deck and report the course being steered.

9.18   Orders to the Engine Order Telegraphs (Annunciators)   Orders to the engine order telegraphs have three parts:

1. The first part designates the engine, as "Starboard (port) engine" or "All engines," to put the annunciator man on the alert.
2. The second part gives the direction in which the engine order telegraph is to be moved, as "Ahead" or "Back."
3. The third part gives the speed at which the engine is to be moved.

Thus: "All engines ahead full"; "Port engine back two-thirds"; "Starboard engine ahead standard!"

Every order to the engine order telegraphs must be repeated word for word by the operator. When the engine room has acknowledged the order by the repeat-back system on the telegraph, and the shaft revolution indicators show the engines are in the process of carrying out the order, the operator should then report what the engine is doing. Thus, upon the order from the officer of the deck, "Starboard engine, back one-third," the operator repeats, "Starboard engine, back one-third, sir." At the same time, he rings up "back one-third" on the starboard engine order telegraph. When this is repeated back from the engine room on the engine order telegraph, he reports, "Starboard engine answers back one-third, sir."

9.19 Man Overboard   Over the years, the cry, "Man overboard," has become one of the most dreaded utterances to the ear of the mariner, for without quick action on the part of the ship's officers and crew, a man's life might well be lost. Therefore, the prudent watch officer, upon assuming his duties on the bridge, will rehearse in his own mind the actions he would take if such an event were to occur during his watch. The proper actions to be taken in the event of a man overboard depend on many factors, including the following:

1. The individual officer's experience and preferences for recovery techniques
2. The ship's maneuvering characteristics (single-screw, double-screw, turning radius, etc)
3. The status of the engineering plant
4. The side on which the ready life boat is rigged
5. The visibility
6. The wind direction and sea state
7. The proximity of other ships
8. The ship's location with respect to hazards to navigation

Depending on the circumstances, one of the recovery methods outlined in Fig. 9.8 might be used. Simultaneously, several routine actions are taken immediately when a man is reported overboard.

One or more, preferably more, life buoys should be thrown over at once. If a little presence of mind is exercised here, it is often possible to throw one of these very close to the man and, if possible, between the man and the ship. At the first alarm, a number of men (previously instructed through drills, etc.) go aloft to try to keep the man in sight, and as quickly as possible a quartermaster tracks the man with a pair of good binoculars.

The ordinary life buoy is so small that often the man in the water cannot see it, and it is of little or no assistance to the lookouts who are trying to

Method and Primary Use	Diagram (ship on course 090; numbers refer to the explanation)	Explanation	Analysis	
			Advantages	Disadvantages
WILLIAMSON TURN 1. Used in reduced visibility because it makes good the original track.	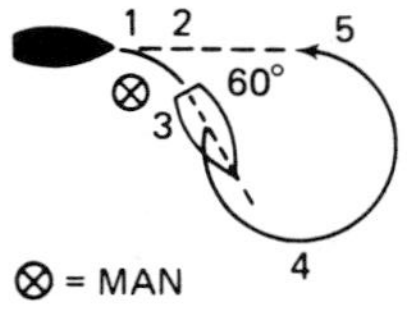 ⊗ = MAN	1. Put the rudder over full in the direction corresponding to the side over which the man fell. 2. When clear of the man, go ahead full on all engines, continue using full rudder. 3. When heading is 60° beyond the original course, shift the rudder without having steadied on a course. 60° is proper for many ships, however, the exact amount must be determined through trial and error. 4. Come to the reciprocal of the original course, using full rudder. 5. Use the engines and rudder to attain the proper final position (ship upwind of the man and dead in the water with the man alongside, well forward of the propellers).	1. Simplicity 2. Makes good the original track.	1. Slow 2. Takes the ship a relatively great distance from the man, when sight may be lost.
ONE TURN ("Anderson") Used by destroyers, ships which have considerable power available and relatively tight turning characteristics.	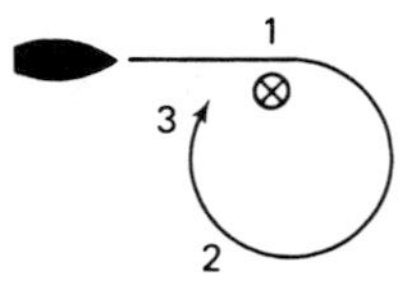	1. Put the rudder over full in the direction corresponding to the side over which the man fell. Go ahead full on the outboard engine only. When about two thirds of the way around, back the inboard engine 2/3 or full. Order all engines stopped when the man is within about 15 degrees of the bow, then ease the rudder and back the engines as required to attain the proper final position (as for the other methods). Many variations of this method are used, differing primarily in respect to the use of one or both engines, and the time when they are stopped and backed to return to the man and tighten the turn. The variation used should reflect individual ship's characteristics, sea conditions, personal preferences, etc.	The fastest recovery method.	1. Requires a relatively high degree of proficiency in shiphandling because of the lack of a straight-a-way approach to the man. 2. Often impossible for a single propeller ship.
TWO TURN (Race Track) Used in good visibility when a straight final approach leg is desired.	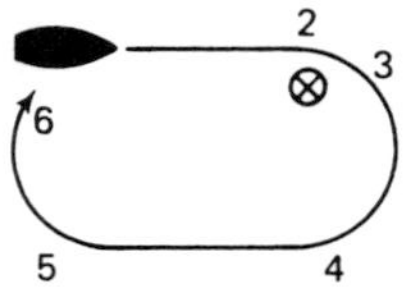	1. A variation of the one turn method which provides a desirable straight final approach to the man. 2. Put the rudder over full in the direction corresponding to the side over which the man fell. 3. When clear of the man, go ahead full on all engines, continue using full rudder to turn to the reciprocal of the original course. 4. Steady for a distance which will give the desired run for a final straight approach. 5. Use full rudder to turn to the man. 6. Use the engines and rudder to attain the proper final position (ship upwind of the man and dead in the water with the man alongside well forward of the propellers).	1. The straight final approach leg facilitates a more calculable approach. 2. The ship will be returned to the man if he is lost from sight. 3. Reasonably fast. 4. Effective when the wind was from abeam abeam on the original course.	Slower than the one turn method.

Fig. 9.8 Different methods of man-overboard recovery.

keep him in sight. This is a serious and often fatal defect. It is well to keep a number of these small life buoys about the deck to be thrown overboard on the instant by anyone who may be near them, but in addition there should be available packets of sea dye marker for daytime use and battery-operated water lights for nighttime. The latter are necessary to serve as markers not only for the man but to keep his spot in sight from the ship. At least 50 percent of all life buoys kept about the deck should be equipped with the battery-operated lights, and sea dye markers should be kept handy to each life buoy.

Ships fitted with a dead reckoning tracer should mark the trace at the time the man goes over. A course to steer back to this point on the chart can then be obtained. Loran-C should also be used when available.

Motor whaleboats or other lifeboats are kept ready at sea for instant lowering for use as lifeboats. Whatever the recovery method selected, while the ship is maneuvering to approach the man, the boat crew should be readying the boat to be put in the water as soon as the ship has slowed sufficiently. In most sea conditions, a boat may be lowered with reasonable safety from a ship at a speed of 4 knots.

One method of maneuvering to recover a man overboard is to go full speed astern as soon as the man is clear of the screw and to lower the boat as soon as speed has been reduced sufficiently. This method is especially effective when the ship was originally going at a slow speed. The boat in search of the man is guided by signals (semaphore-flags or hand held radios) from the lookouts aloft, provided they have succeeded in keeping the man in sight. Failing this, the boat cannot go far wrong if it goes back on a course opposite the original heading of the ship (down the ship's wake), for although the ship in backing will probably throw her head to one side, she will not usually gain a great amount of ground in that direction before coming to rest.

In weather too heavy to permit lowering a boat, the one method that can give hope of saving a man is to attempt to pick him up directly from the ship itself. Men should be standing by with heaving lines and additional life rings. In addition, the use of cargo nets over the side, attended by strong swimmers wearing immersion suits with safety lines attached, can be of great value.

Ships may use several different methods to approach a man in the water to pick him up, either directly, or with a boat. Three of the more common methods are discussed in Fig. 9.8.

For yachts, particularly those under sail, recent studies and tests indicate that a quick-stop recovery is by far the best method. Any procedure that requires the boat to sail away from the person in the water and then return reduces very much the chances of a successful recovery. The Seattle Sailing Foundation and the Naval Academy Sailing Squadron have conducted thorough tests that substantiate the above. The procedures to stop quickly vary widely with the type of boat, number of crew, and sail being carried but it is vital that a procedure be adopted and that it be rehearsed. Equally important is the major problem of bringing the victim back on board—a much more difficult operation than most of us imagine. With a full crew, it has been found best by the Naval Academy sailors to pull the person aboard by group strength. With husband and wife alone, for example, the Seattle Sailing Foundation recommends the use of a commercial device such as a Lifesling. Again, the key to avoiding a tragedy is training by actual practice.

9.20   Handling Very Large Ships   Most very large ships handle quite well, but the handler must adjust for the mass and the relatively limited power in proportion to the size of the ship. A 300,000 DWT VLCC (very large crude carrier) may have only twice as much horsepower as the average 30,000 DWT bulk carrier or tanker. The sea speed of the larger vessel may be nearly equal to that of the smaller vessel, but its backing power, particularly if it is steam turbine powered, will be much less effective. It may require as much as ten miles for such a vessel to come to a full stop (dead in the water) from full speed ahead.

Sometimes slewing the ship (turning the helm from hard over to hard over the other way before the vessel starts to swing) is used to reduce these large vessels' headway.

A very large ship may be damaged by a head sea without the master being aware, since he feels no strong pitching motion. Sagging, hogging, and racking stresses that smaller ships may ignore must be considered in heavy weather.

In going alongside a pier, care must be taken to land flat with minimum lateral way on, to avoid damage to both the large ship's hull and the pier. Doppler speed indicators are now available to the conning officer on the bridge. In traffic situations, small boats and other vessels should give these behemoths ample clearance since their maneuverability is comparatively limited. These large vessels are obliged to rely upon their steering systems to avoid close-quarter encounters, since it takes much too long for them to respond to their engines in order to slow or stop when proceeding at full speed at sea.

Handling Steamers in Heavy Weather

In the days of sail and in early steam vessels, most of which also had after sails, the conventional way to handle a ship when the weather was too heavy for her to proceed on her course was to bring her head up until she had the sea on the bow and to hold her there with the rudder and sail, with little or no resultant headway. If she fell off—as from time to time she did—and started to gather way, the hard down helm and after sail would bring her promptly back to meet the sea. Thus, she came up and fell off, making some little way through the water but none of it against the sea; in the main, she drifted steadily to leeward. For such bluff-bowed ships, this was, and is, the ideal way of riding out a gale. A modern steamer, however—whether a man-of-war, liner, or tramp—carries no sail and is commonly long and sharp-bowed. The propeller acts as a drag, tending to hold her stern-up to the sea, and this tendency is aggravated by the excess of draft that such steamers usually have aft. To hold such a steamer bows-on to the sea, she must be forced into it—not at great speed, perhaps, but sufficiently great to maintain steerageway. To do so can strain the ship severely, and there is grave doubt as to the wisdom of such a method of lying to. A steamer should run slowly before a sea or lie to with the sea astern or on the quarter.

9.21 The Approach of a Tropical Storm When a master is forewarned of the approach of a tropical storm, his first thought must be of the location of its center and its estimated track. The geographical position of his vessel with respect to the proximity of land or shoal water, and whether his vessel will be in the dangerous or navigable semicircle (see Chapter 18) of the storm, must be determined at once.

He should make an early decision and use all necessary speed to gain the safest possible geographical location before the storm is upon him. Once the center of the storm is near him, he should then be free to reduce speed and avoid damage to his vessel. It may then be desirable to proceed at dead slow engine speed, barely maintaining steerageway or even to lie to for several hours until the storm passes. It might also be desirable and safe to maintain a fair speed downwind.

If a master is unable to gain a satisfactory position with respect to shoal water in a tropical storm, he may be forced to oppose the winds with appreciable engine speed, accepting that risk of damages to avoid being pushed into shoal waters.

On the other hand, if arrival in the navigable semicircle of a tropical storm before the storm is upon him is his only concern, he should not force his vessel in any continued effort to do so but should ride out the storm as best he can.

9.22 Controlling a Ship in Very Heavy Weather The easiest position for a ship in a very heavy sea would be that which she would herself take if left at rest and free from the constraint of engines, helm, and sails. A ship left to herself in a seaway will usually fall off until she has the sea abaft the beam, the propeller acting as a drag and holding her stern-up. In this position, she will roll deeply, but easily, and will drift to leeward, leaving a comparatively smooth wake on the weather beam and quarter. In such a state, she lies a-*hull* or is said to be *hulling.*

If a ship rolls dangerously, she may be kept further away from the wind and sea either by using a drag over the stern or by turning over the engines just fast enough to give her steerageway. It seems to be established, as the result of experience, that a steamer may safely run with the sea either aft or quartering, *provided she runs very slowly.* Clearly, this is not "running" in the old sense of that term, according to which a vessel going before the sea was forced to her utmost speed with the idea of keeping ahead of the waves, these being expected to "poop" her if they overtook her. It is evident from the statements of a large number of shipmasters who have tried the experiment of slowing down or stopping when running before a heavy sea, that this maneuver, so far from resulting in the disaster that many seamen would expect from it, had an extraordinary effect of easing the ship and keeping her dry.

The explanation of this phenomenon would seem to be that a ship running a high speed through the water draws a wave after her that follows under the counter and rolls along toward the waist on either side, tending continually to curl over and break on board. This wave is reduced to insignificant proportions in running dead slow.

9.23 Roll and Pitch Another point entering into the behavior of a vessel going before the sea is that as she *rolls* and *pitches,* she buries her bow first to one side and then the other, increasing the pressure on the bow so buried. If she is being driven through the water, her head will be forced off, first to one side and then to the other, causing her to *yaw* badly with a continual tendency to *broach to.* This situation cannot be met by the rudder because, at the very time the bow is buried, the stern is lifted more or less out of the water, and the rudder momentarily loses its steering power. As the stern is lifted, the propeller begins to race—in itself a serious danger at high speed. There seems no question that the dangers connected with running—so far from being increased—are greatly reduced, if not altogether removed, by slowing or stopping.

It will of course be understood that in this matter, as in all other connected with seamanship, due regard must be given to the peculiarities of the individual ship and that the maneuver that is safest for a majority of ships may be dangerous for certain ones. Thus, a ship whose cargo might shift should not be allowed to roll excessively; nor should a warship whose heavy guns or missiles are carried high above the center of gravity. On whatever course the vessel may be kept, this rule may be regarded as having universal application; that, other things being equal, *the lower the speed at which she is run, the easier she will ride.*

9.24 Relationship between Ship and Waves Attention is invited here to an important relationship, not always recognized, between a ship and the waves in which she floats. For every ship (in a given condition as to trim, etc.), there is a perfectly definite *rolling period,* that is, a period in which she will make a complete roll *without regard to whether she is rolling 10 degrees or 40.* Likewise, in the case of a seaway, there is usually a fairly regular interval of time between the wave crests passing a given point. If the point is a ship in motion, her motion may increase or decrease the interval between the waves so far as she herself is concerned, but this will not change the *regularity* of the interval. If it happens that this interval coincides with that required for the ship to complete a roll, each wave as it passes her will add its rolling impulse to the accumulated effect of those which have preceded it, and the ship will roll more and more deeply until she reaches *the maximum roll of which she is capable.* She will not capsize (if properly designed and undamaged) because there are forces at work to resist the rolling, and these increase as the depth of roll increases until the rolling forces and the resisting forces balance. But she will continue to roll to the maximum limit until something is done to break up the synchronism between her period and that of the sea.

It is possible to make this break, *provided the ship has headway,* by changing her course or her speed, thus changing not the real, but the apparent, period of the waves. By running more nearly *into* the sea—meeting the waves—the apparent period is shortened; by running more nearly *before* it, the period is lengthened; but in either case, it is *changed* and will no longer coincide with the rolling period of the ship. The same effect is produced by a change of speed. If, therefore, it is judged from the violence of the rolling on a given course that the period of the waves is coinciding with that of the ship, the course or speed or both should be changed.

A ship making high speed in the direction of a heavy sea or swell may take a sheer and roll very severely. This misfortune has happened to destroyers during high-speed trials, with men being washed overboard and lost, as the ship, without warning, took a maximum roll. A moderate following sea, accompanied by a less obvious swell from a slightly different direction, can occasionally coincide or harmonize, producing a very large sea astern which, if the helmsman is not alert and experienced, can produce the sudden roll mentioned above. Vigilance by the conning officer and good steering are the obvious preventions—in addition, of course, to keeping men off the weather decks.

The length of the ship as compared with that of the waves is also a very important factor in the behavior of the ship, especially when she is running more or less with the waves or meeting them. It often happens that a small ship in a long sea will be perfectly comfortable whereas a larger and longer ship may be less so. The small craft climbs up and slides down the waves, accommodating herself to their slopes, and pitching only as the slope changes; but the longer craft, partially spanning the crests and the hollows of the waves alternately, one end being poised on the crest of one wave while the other end is buried in the adjoining one, may be making very heavy weather. Some years ago a large aircraft carrier in the Philippines was badly battered by a typhoon, but a destroyer escort, which passed through the same gale at very nearly the same place, was perfectly comfortable.

9.25 Bringing a Ship Bows-On If, when a steamer is before the sea or in the trough, it is decided to bring her up to it, bows-on, she should first be slowed until she barely has steerageway and then be brought up as gradually as possible. To put the wheel over with considerable speed and bring her up with a rush—slapping the sea in the face, as it were—could result in serious damage. After getting her up to the sea bows-on, the greatest watchfulness is required—first, to avoid falling off into the trough of the sea, as she will try to do the moment she loses way, and second, to avoid driving into the heavy, breaking seas, which will threaten her now and again.

There is reason to believe that many of the phenomenal ''rogue waves'' reported as having suddenly overwhelmed steamers in mid-oceans have been simply the exceptionally heavy waves that build up from time to time in any long-continued gale, and that their destructive power resulted from the fact that the vessels were driven into them instead of being allowed to drift before them and ride over unresistingly.

In lying to bows-on, an officer should always be kept at the engineroom telegraphs, and an engineer should be standing by below to obey bridge signals instantly. So long as the vessel heads up to it, the more slowly she turns over, the better. If a heavy sea is seen bearing down upon her, she should be stopped altogether. If she falls off, it will be necessary to increase the speed a little to bring her up, but she must be slowed again as soon as possible.

In twin-screw ships, the propellers do not have as much drag as in single-screws, and such ships can sometimes be held up the sea, without being driven into it dangerously, by turning over the lee screw very slowly. This is often the best way to lay a twin-screw ship to, although there is nothing in the nature of the case to prevent such a ship from riding easily with the sea astern or quartering.

9.26 Using a Sea Anchor or Drogue With small ships, and especially with yachts, sea anchors have been used with good results in very heavy weather. For yachts, the conventional sea anchor is a canvas cone held to shape by a metal ring. A recent design by Hathaway, Reiser, & Raymond involves a cone of heavy nylon webbing instead of canvas, sold as a Galerider. The September 1986 issue of *Yachting* contained an account of a test of Galerider that was highly successful.

9.27 The Calming Effect of Oil In view of the laws against ocean pollution and the fact that the really efficient vegetable oils are rarely available, mariners these days almost never use oil and the subject will not be discussed herein.

9.28 Summary We may sum up the various methods of handling a ship in heavy weather with the statement that the ship will usually be safest and most comfortable when stern-to, or nearly stern-to, the sea, and *drifting before it.*

If, by the use of sails, a drag, or any other means, she can be held bows-on, *while being still allowed to drift,* this is probably the best way to lay her to. If she cannot be held up without being forced into the sea, however, it will be because of the natural drag of the stern and propeller, and, in this case, advantage should be taken of this drag to hold her more or less directly stern-on, letting her drift in this position.

Even if the position she takes up in drifting is nearly in the trough of the sea, it will usually be found that she is easier in this position than in any other.

If the position she takes in drifting proves to be one in which she rolls dangerously, then she may run fast enough to steer, *but no faster,* and so keep the course that is found most comfortable.

Remember that it is the occasional large wave with the vertical face that presents the greatest danger. These rogue waves are much bigger than their fellows and can pitchpole a yacht or small steamer end over end or roll it over. A few people have survived this experience, which has been reported most often in the immense waves of the Roaring Forties in the Southern Hemisphere. These freak waves occur even in moderate seas with a frequency that is statistically predictable.

One final word of caution. The effect of "free surface" water in bilges and compartments is particularly important during heavy weather when a ship's stability is severely tested. Pumps must be kept operable to remove water; electrical switchboards must be kept dry. This points up to the need for making watertight closures well in advance of the onset of the worst part of the gale. To minimize free surface effect (see Chapter 3), it is particularly advisable when bad weather is expected to keep all tanks containing liquid either full or empty.

References

Blair, Carvel H. *Seamanship: A Handbook for Oceanographers.* Centreville, MD: Cornell Maritime Press, 1977.

Crenshaw, Jr., R. S. *Naval Shiphandling.* 4th ed. Annapolis: Naval Institute Press, 1975.

King, E. and Noel J., *Shiphandling* New York: D. Van Nostrand, 1952.

Van Dorn, William G. *Oceanography and Seamanship.* New York: Dodd, Mead & Co., 1974.

The Admiralty Manual of Seamanship. London, U.K.: Her Majesty's Stationery Office, 1983.

See also the References for Chapter 10.

Docking, Mooring, and Anchoring— Handling With Tugs, Anchors, and Alongside

Mooring Lines

The lines used to secure the ship to a wharf, pier, or another ship are called *mooring lines*. Five-inch manila or smaller nylon is used for mooring lines in destroyers or smaller vessels. Larger ships may use 8-in. or even 10-in. lines. The manila lines may be reinforced or replaced by heavier lines or wire hawsers when the ship is finally securing alongside. Nylon and other synthetic fiber lines are common now for all types of ships.

The mooring line that runs through the bull nose or chock near the eyes of the ship is called the *bow line*. The corresponding line aft is the *stern line*. These lines should lead well up the dock to reduce the fore-and-aft motion of the ship. Other mooring lines are either *breast lines* or *spring lines*. They are called *bow, waist,* or *quarter breasts* and *springs,* depending on the part of the ship from which they are run.

Breast lines are run at right angles to the keel and prevent a ship from moving away from the pier.

Spring lines leading forward away from the ship at an angle with the keel are *forward (bow, waist,* or *quarter) springs.* Those leading aft are *after (bow, waist,* or *quarter) springs.* Springs leading forward or aft prevent a vessel from moving aft or forward, respectively.

If a ship moves ahead or astern with lines out, a breast may become a spring, and spring lines may change their leads. In the U.S. Navy, to prevent confusion and to increase the efficiency of line handling, lines are numbered from forward aft, according to the position where they are secured aboard ship. A ship may use fewer or more lines as necessary, in which case the numbers are changed accordingly. The names are used after the ship is secured, and the use and lead of each line becomes definite. Figure 10.1 shows the names and numbers for seven mooring lines. A list of orders given to the men at the lines appears in Table 10.1, with explanations of each.

Lines can be of the greatest assistance in making or clearing a pier. Prior to a ship's coming alongside, the required lines with eye splices in the ends should be led through the chocks and outboard of and over the lifelines. Heaving lines that have been successfully passed should be made fast near the splice and not at the end of the bight where they will become jammed when the eye is placed over the bollard. Heaving lines should be passed as soon as possible; the heavy lines, the bights of which are necessarily hard to handle, may be run later when the vessel is farther up the pier and nearer her berth.

As a large ship works her way up the pier or into the slip, the lines should be *fleeted* (that is, moved) up the pier in short steps, thus keeping them in position for use.

If two bights or eye splices are to be placed over the same bollard, the second one must be led up and through the eye of the first and then placed over the bollard. This method, which makes it possible for either to be cast off independently of the other, is called *dipping the eye*.

The ship in Fig. 10.2(a) is lying off a pier with a bow breast line secured to a bollard. If the line is led to a winch and a strain put on it, the bow will swing toward the pier, and the stern will move out. It should be noted, however, that the stern does not go out as much as the bow comes in. Because the ship is not held rigidly at the pivoting point, the mass as a whole will respond to the force acting on the bow, and the resultant motion will be like that shown.

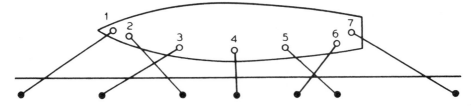

Fig. 10.1 Types of line: (1) Bow line, (2) after bow spring, (3) forward bow spring (4) waist breast, (5) after quarter spring, (6) forward quarter spring, and (7) stern line.

Table 10.1   Orders to the Men at the Lines

Command	Meaning
Pass one (or number one)	Send line number one over to the pier. Place the eye over the bollard or cleat but do not take a strain.
Slack (slack off) the bowline (number one):	Pay out the line specified, allowing it to form an easy bight.
Take a strain on one (or number one):	Put number one line under tension.
Take in the slack on three (or number three):	Heave in on number three line but do not take a strain.
Ease three:	Pay out number three enough to remove most of the tension.
Avast heaving:	Stop heaving (taking in).
Check three:	Hold number three line but not to the breaking point, letting the line slip as necessary.
Hold two:	**Take enough turns so that the line will not slip.**
Double up and secure:	Run additional lines or bights of lines as needed to make the mooring secure. Rig rat guards.
Single up:	Take in all lines but a single standing part to each station, preparatory to getting under way.
Stand by your lines:	Man the lines, ready to cast off or moor.
Take in one (or number one):	Retrieve line number one after it has been cast off. When used by the conning officer it means to slack one, cast it off, and then pull it back abroad. When used by the officers in charge on the forecastle it is preceded by the commands "slack one" and "cast off one" and means merely to retrieve line number one and bring it back on deck.
Cast off:	A command to those tending the mooring lines on the pier or on another ship to disengage or throw off the lines from over the bollards or cleats.

If, in the above case, the stern is also held by a line to the pier as shown in Fig. 10.2(b), the pivot is transferred to the stern, and the whole ship will move toward the dock. This requires much greater effort than turning the ship near her natural pivoting point, as in Fig. 10.2(a).

If the bow and quarter breasts are hove in at the same time, the ship will be breasted in bodily but at greater expenditure of work than in the preceding cases.

If the ship has way on, either ahead or astern, her momentum enters

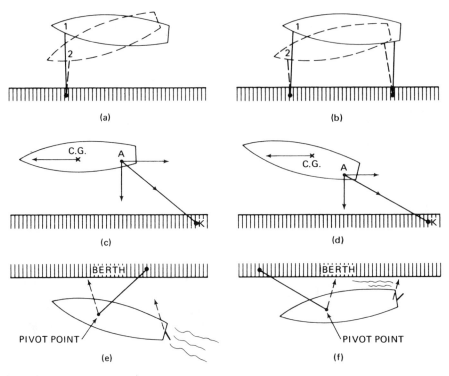

Fig. 10.2 Handling ship around a pier.

into the problem of her behavior. In Fig. 10.2(c), the ship is moving forward parallel to the face of the pier (with engines stopped and rudder amidships). The after quarter spring AK is taut. The motion of the ship will be that resulting from her momentum along the original course and the tension along AK. The tension on AK may be resolved into two components. One retards the ship along the line of her original course and thus directly opposes the momentum, and the other moves her toward the pier. The stern will swing in and the bow out. It is important to note, however, that the momentum, which is concentrated at the center of gravity forward of the pivot (A), opposes the turning and tends to keep the ship parallel. Thus, as a matter of fact, the ship does not turn much but comes in relatively parallel to the pier, as shown in Fig. 10.2(d).

The vessel in Figs. 10.2(c) and (d) could go ahead on her engine(s) and put her rudder left to throw her head in. Since the steering effect of the rudder is due to the discharge current against the rudder and since the stern cannot move to starboard because it is held by the spring, left rudder can have comparatively little turning effect. Right rudder, on the other hand, will help to throw the stern in.

If, in Fig. 10.2(a), the rudder is put left, it will throw the stern out and increase the rapidity with which the bow turns in. If put right, it will oppose the turning but not enough to overcome it.

In any case, if the line is made fast at the ship's natural pivoting point, and the engine(s) is turned over ahead or astern, the ship will spring in bodily. Her heading can be controlled by putting the rudder over, which throws the stern to either side, as desired. The ship swings under the influence of the rudder while coming bodily in on the spring, and it is often possible to come alongside quickly and smartly by using this line only, as shown in Fig. 10.2(e) and 10.2(f).

In securing alongside a dock, wharf, or pier, special attention must be paid to the state and range of the tide. When securing at high water, enough slack must be left in the lines to ensure that at low tide they will not part, carry away bollards, or, in extreme cases, list the ship to a dangerous degree or even capsize small vessels.

Landings, Departures, Handling Alongside

10.1 Making Landings The names *dock, pier, and wharf* are used almost interchangeably. These are all structures connected to the shore with enough water up to them for vessels to come in or alongside. A *pier* is built at right angles to the shore; a *wharf* is parallel. Both are sometimes called *docks,* although strictly speaking, a dock is a structure used for drydocking a vessel. The space between neighboring piers is called a *slip.*

Wharves and piers may be built on piles that allow a fairly free flow of water under them and in the slips between them. If their underwater construction is solid, there will be no current within the slips, but eddies of various sorts may be found. Warehouses or other buildings built on them may vary the effect of the wind on the upperworks of the docking vessel.

Wind and current at right angles to a pier are always more dangerous than those blowing or running, respectively, along its face. In coming alongside, the conditions of existing wind and current should be observed carefully and should be taken advantage of when possible. Several cases of going alongside under different conditions of wind and current will be discussed.

It is of initial importance in making landings to make a plan in advance that shows the approach course and the point at which to reduce speed and/or stop engines so as to avoid making the final landing with too much headway. This practice particularly applies if the wind or current are from astern.

10.2 Going Alongside—No Set On or Off the Pier (Single-Screw Vessel) A single-screw (right-handed) vessel can make a *landing to port* with little difficulty when there is no current or wind ("set") pushing the ship toward or away from ("on or off") the pier. The ship should be headed for a point a short distance outboard of the final position of the bridge when the ship is secured. The course of the approach should be at an angle of 10 to 15 degrees with the face of the pier, at a slow speed, and with the engines stopped when there is sufficient headway to reach the berth. Enough headway to steer should be retained when the ship is almost abreast of her berth, at which time the engine can be backed to stop the ship and swing her stern to port and then parallel to the pier. The ship can then be breasted in by the mooring lines and winches.

If a single-screw ship must make a *landing to starboard,* the angle of approach should be about 10 degrees. The speed should be less than that used for a port landing but still enough to keep the ability to steer. As the bow approaches the pier, the rudder should be put over to port (and, if necessary, the engine be given a kick ahead) to swing the bow away from, and the stern toward, the pier. Just before the ship is parallel to the pier, the engine should be backed to allow the sideways force from the propeller to counter the ship's swing so that she is stopped parallel to the pier abreast her berth. The point for which the ship should be headed during the approach should be the final position of the bridge when she is secured.

The port anchor may be dropped at short stay during the early part of the starboard approach. The anchor is then dragged over the ground to improve the ship's steering ability, reduce her speed, and give the master better control of the bow and the stern when the final landing is being made.* The difficulty at that time when a *close* landing is contemplated is that reversing the engine will force the stern away from the pier and the bow toward the pier.

The engines should be stopped later than they would be for a port landing. The dragging anchor will enable the ship to be stopped without much backing either in terms of power or time and may very well enable the master to lay the ship alongside her berth without any backing at all, or perhaps with just a touch astern.

If the engine *is* backed, every effort should be made to get a stern line out as soon as possible so that this line can be held and the stern prevented from swinging away from the pier.

10.3   Going Alongside, Port Side To—Being Set On to the Pier   The point for which the ship should be headed at the start of the approach should be farther away from the pier than the one used with no set. The angle of approach should be 20 to 30 degrees, and the speed of approach

---

*See Section 10.18.

should be greater than before, without in any way attempting a high-speed landing. The amount of set ought to be watched constantly. If it is apparent that the set is greater than anticipated and that, if the ship continues, she will strike the pier, there are four courses of action to choose from, as follows:

1. Head farther away from the pier.
2. Back clear and try again.
3. Stop with the ship parallel to the pier while there is still some open water between the ship and the pier.
4. Proceed at greater speed in order to reduce the time during which the ship is subject to wind and current.

The conditions near the berth, the proximity of the berth, and the course will determine what action is advisable. If there are ships alongside the pier ahead and astern the allotted berth, it is probably wise to head up or back clear and try again. If there is a clear space astern of the correct berth, it may be possible to make a landing short of it and, once alongside, move up to it. There is always the fourth choice, in which case the discharge current from the backing screw may cushion the impact somewhat if the pier is of solid (as opposed to pile) construction. The aim should be to stop the ship, preferably by backing the outboard engine only, parallel to the berth and about 30 feet from it, if the wind is blowing strongly toward the pier. If she is brought up much further out, she may gather excessive leeway before touching.

10.4   Going Alongside, Starboard Side To—Being Set On to the Pier   If a single-screw ship attempts a starboard landing with a set on to the pier and finds that she is too close, the four courses of action are still available, but the second should be changed to: Stop with the ship heading slightly away from the pier. In this position, she can back, and in so doing, the stern will swing away from the pier. The ship will parallel the pier, lose her headway, and the discharge current will cushion the impact. The first choice, to head up, is not as satisfactory as before because the original approach course should make a smaller angle of about 10 degrees with the face of the pier. There is not as great an angle through which to head up as is available in a port landing.

10.5   Going Alongside a Pier—Being Set Off   If the wind is blowing off the berth, it is essential to keep the bow well up to the pier until a line is passed. Once the bow has drifted outside the throw of a heaving line, the situation can seldom be righted except by a tug. It is therefore better to approach at a rather greater angle than in calm weather, to head initially for the nearer end of the berth and to get the bow line passed at the first opportunity. Should it be seen that the vessel is being set off the pier, the ship's head can be pointed well up into the pier and the approach made with more speed. The bow lines are gotten out, and when close to the pier, the rudder is put away from the pier. For a single-screw vessel, port side to, the landing is easily made by backing down on the screw. For a single-screw vessel making a pier to starboard, the approach should be made by snubbing the port anchor as previously described. In addition to snubbing the port anchor, a starboard quarter breast can be used to hold in the stern as the ship forges slowly ahead. In a twin-screw vessel, the outboard engine is backed.

10.6 Going Alongside—Current from Ahead When a current is running parallel to a pier, the ship should be headed into the current and then brought alongside. Slack water is the most favorable condition; yet a current, if not too great, can be made use of and the berthing accomplished without trouble, except in the case of the largest vessels. With current from ahead, a vessel can use more speed through the water without increasing its speed relative to the pier; as a result, it will have better rudder control.

The ship, making little headway along the face of the pier, is brought in fairly close and parallel. The vessel must not be canted in because she might come in too fast and cause damage. A forward bow spring is sent well ahead and up the pier.

When the ship is in the proper position relative to the pier, all forward motion relative thereto is stopped, and the vessel is slowly dropped back on the spring. The amount of tension on this spring determines the rapidity with which the ship will drift in toward the pier. The rudder may be used to swing the stern.

Should the current be very strong, the ship should go a little way above the pier and drop the outboard anchor. A forward bow spring should be run ashore. By veering chain and holding the spring, the ship will swing slowly in toward the pier. By using the rudder and adjusting the strain on the anchor chain, perfect control can be maintained. When the ship is alongside, a bow breast and forward quarter spring are got out as soon as possible.

10.7 Going Alongside—Current from Astern Making a pier with a *fair current* (current from astern) is difficult and should be avoided whenever possible. If there is swinging room and if other reasons do not forbid, much time and fuel will be saved and danger avoided by dropping an anchor, swinging with the current, and making the pier as previously described with the current from ahead. If this approach is not practicable, tugs should be used. If tugs are not available, the approach should be made as slowly as possible and as near to the pier as is safe. When about in position, the bow is canted out a few degrees from the pier. An after quarter spring is got out as soon as possible and the engines backed to keep from parting the line. Backing on the inboard engine of a twin-screw ship forces more water between the pier and the ship, thus cushioning her as she comes in. Care must be taken to prevent the stern from swinging away from the pier. The use of after spring lines and stern lines with the outboard engine backing will prevent this movement. A vessel having a stern anchor can drop it at short stay.

10.8 Clearing a Pier—No Wind and No Current Clearing a pier is less difficult than making a pier. The first step is to slack all lines carefully and observe the effect. If the ship does not drift out, it will be necessary to force the stern away from the pier.

In a single-screw ship with its starboard side to the pier, the engine is backed. This swings the stern rapidly to port. If the bow is forced into the pier, right rudder is used to clear it as the ship goes astern. When the stern is about 50 ft out, the bow will be pointed toward the pier. A quarter breast, which becomes a spring as the ship continues to go slowly astern, is now held. This action will bring the bow out. When pointed fair, the ship casts off and goes out ahead.

If the port side is to the pier, an after bow spring is used to allow the ship to go slowly ahead. Left rudder throws the stern well out. The ship casts off and backs down slowly with right full rudder until clear. As the stern gradually turns in toward the pier, it will be necessary to stop it when parallel to the pier and several beams' width out from it. The vessel now goes ahead with right rudder, and the bow falls off as required.

The easiest way for a twin-screw vessel to shove off from a pier is by holding the after bow spring and slacking off all other lines. The outboard engine is turned over, slow ahead, until the inboard propeller is clear of the pier. Fenders can be used, as necessary, on the bow. Once the inboard propeller is free, all lines are let go and both engines backed slow. The discharge current from the inboard propeller will breast the vessel out, particularly if the pier is a solid one. The conning officer should glance aft to note any tendency of his ship to start swinging either way. He should use the engines for steering until sufficient sternway is reached for the rudder to be used. The distance between the pier and the bow should be noted and the rate of turn regulated to prevent touching. The inboard screw discharge current tends to keep the bow off when it reaches it.

10.9 Clearing a Pier—Being Set On This is difficult situation. Since to go out ahead without the use of tugs or an outlying anchor is risky, the ship must be taken out astern. A single-screw ship with her starboard side to the

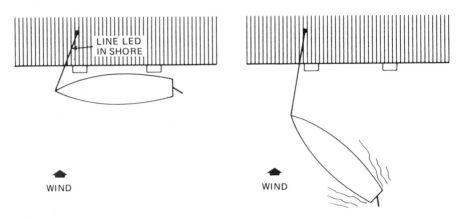

Fig. 10.3 Clearing a pier (being set on).

pier should go ahead on an after bow spring, or heave in on the bowline, and when the stern is well out, cast off and go astern full. (See Fig. 10.3.) If she is port side to, it is advisable to wait for a change in conditions.

If no tugs are available, no anchor has been dropped, and the after bow spring proves ineffective, it is possible for a small ship to cast her stern well out by running a line from right forward to a point well inside the pier. When the engine(s) is backed, the bow will be hauled into the pier, and the ship will pivot as she tries to align herself with the pull of the line. She will gather sternway more rapidly on slipping than she would do if an after bow spring were used, and she is therefore less liable to scrape her bow heavily on the pier before getting clear.

If only one tug is available to get the ship away from the pier in an onshore wind, she should tow outwards from a point fairly well forward, between the stern and amidships. As the tug begins to haul off, the ship should work her engines and rudder as necessary to swing the stern out. The ship then moves bodily outwards. In a single-screw ship, some head-way will be gained by the need to go ahead with the rudder hard over toward the pier.

A twin-screw vessel should first go ahead on the outboard engine, with the after bow spring held. This will throw the stern out against the set. Then the ship should cast off the spring and back immediately on both engines. The wash of the inboard engine will tend to keep her off, and the speed of the inboard engine can be varied to keep the bow clear.

10.10 Clearing a Pier—Being Set Off If the ship tends to drift out when all lines are slacked, the clearing of the pier is very simple. Continued slacking away on the lines will ease the ship off the pier. All lines are then cast off, and the ship can proceed.

10.11 Clearing a Pier—Current from Ahead All lines are eased off except the forwared quarter spring. The stern will come in, and the bow will go out where it will catch more of the current and swing. While going ahead very slowly to keep the stern and the propellers away from the pier, the bow will continue to swing. When far enough out, the ship may cast off all lines and proceed.

Should the stern not be sufficiently clear to go ahead on the engines, a bow breast should be kept under a light strain; when the ship is headed correctly, the breast should be checked while slacking the quarter spring. The stern will swing out and clear, and all lines can then be cast off and the engines put ahead. To use the bow breast in this manner, the bow must be farther out than the stern; otherwise, the ship will come back alongside.

Should the wind prevent the bow from falling off, it will be necessary to go out astern as previously described for a ship being set toward the pier.

10.12 Clearing a Pier—Current from Astern Holding an after bow spring and easing out on a quarter breast will let the stern swing outward. When the ship is pointed correctly, all lines are cast off, and the ship goes out astern.

10.13 Working into a Slip The best time for entering a slip is when the water is slack. The procedure is the same as in making a pier. In entering, an anchor under the forefoot for snubbing is of great assistance, since it gives greater steering control.

If there is a good current running, the docking should be done with tugs; if tugs are not available, the ship can make a landing at the end of the pier, heading into the current. The ship is then warped into the slip. The springs for this purpose should be as short as possible to reduce the radius of the swing and should be as nearly perpendicular to the keel lines as practicable to produce the best springing effect. To protect the ship's side and the pier, a *camel* or suitable fenders are placed at the knuckle of the pier where the pressure is localized. The camel will distribute this pressure over many of the ship's frames, thereby preventing their being crushed. The ship goes slowly ahead until the knuckle of the pier is amidships. The after bow spring is then held and the rudder thrown hard over toward the pier to aid in the turn. If, after entering the slip, the ship is being set off, the lines should be got out and walked up the pier in short steps as necessary to hold the ship in. If the ship is being set on, lines are run to the opposite side of the slip.

When backing into a slip, the same principles of spring use apply. The lines, especially the bow breasts, must be very strong, and good seamanship dictates that more than one be run. The additional lines, called *preventers*, are used alternately in the shifting of the lines for better leads. The vessel is dropped back until the knuckle of the pier is amidships, and with the quarter spring held, the bow breast is eased. When the ship is pointed correctly, the engine is backed slowly. Deck winches are a help and almost a necessity in the case of a single-scew ship backing to starboard.

The most difficult problem of all is making a landing on the upstream side of a slip when the wind and current are from the same direction and at right angles to a pier with a solid underwater structure and a large warehouse built upon it. Under these conditions, entering the slip at slow speed will invariably result in the ship's stern being swept across to the other side of the slip before it can be controlled, with almost certain damage to the ship, the pier, or other shipping. Such a landing is sometimes possible for a high-powered vessel if it enters the slip at a high enough speed for the stern to be out of the effect of wind and current before it can be swept across the slip and if the vessel then backs full to kill the headway. Such a maneuver requires expert judgment as to the instant of backing and perfect coordination with the engine room in order to avoid ramming the head of the slip.

10.14 Mooring to a Buoy   With the current from ahead, the ship should approach slowly, and the buoy should be kept on a constant bearing. If there is any wind, the buoy should be picked up on the lee bow so that the bow will drift toward it rather than away. In the case of a single-screw ship, it may be wiser to pick the buoy up and the starboard bow because of the tendency of the bow to drift to starboard when the engine is backed.

Most large ships moor by shackling the end of their chain, unbent from an anchor, to the ring of the buoy. Small ships may pass the end of the chain through the ring, haul it in, secure it on deck, and ride to the bight, but this practice is not recommended because the chain can be damaged where it is passed through the ring. If mooring is made habitually, a heavy wire mooring pendant with an eye and shackle on the end may be made up. In any case, a hook rope is first passed to hold the bow in position while the moor is being made, and a man is placed on the buoy to handle lines and shackle up. Under favorable conditions, the man can be lowered over the bow and the hook rope passed down to him, but it is better to send him to the buoy in a boat. The same boat can carry the hook rope and a messenger fastened to the end of the chain. The hook rope is secured first. Care should be taken not to put too much strain on it, or the buoy may be capsized and the man working on it thrown into the water. Next the messenger is run through the ring from underneath and brought back on deck to the capstan. The messenger is used to haul the end of the chain down to or through the ring. If shackle and pin are used, they can be taken in the boat or, preferably, lowered from the bow with lines, thus making it easier for the man on the buoy to handle them.

Some destroyers send out the bight of a heaving line in a boat. The bight has been cut and a ring and snaphook inserted. The man in the boat reeves one end of the heaving line through the ring on the buoy and snaps it to the other. The mooring party on the forecastle hauls the heaving line through the ring rapidly. A heavier messenger follows as the ship approaches the buoy. The anchor is secured and enough chain roused up to allow its end to be reeved through the bull nose and to hang down to the water. As the ship gets closer to the buoy, the messenger, which is made fast to the end of the chain, is hove in. The chain reeves up through the ring on the buoy and is hove up on deck and secured. Such a mooring can be made in a couple of minutes.

It is important in all moorings to bring the ship up to the buoy and not attempt to pull the buoy to the ship.

Large ships with heavy chains, such as cruisers, usually moor close to the buoy with a wire. The anchor chain is shackled to the wire and allowed to slide down it to be made fast to the ring on the buoy.

A buoy can be picked up with a fair tide under some circumstances. To do so requires skillful shiphandling and speedy work by the man on the buoy unless the ship has twin rudders. Swinging of the vessel may put a severe strain on the moorings. In some cases with the current from astern, time will be saved if it is possible to drop an anchor, swing, and then pick up the buoy.

The need for *veering chain* when moored to a buoy during adverse weather is most important. If the ship is snubbed up close, the pull is upward for the most part, tending to break the buoy loose from its moorings. In addition, the lack of substantial weight of chain permits the transfer of ship movements to the buoy to be horizontal at the same time as it provides a cushion for the surges. Scopes as great as 45 fathoms have been used to good advantage. Where circumstances permit, the chain to the mooring buoy should be veered to produce a catenary of such extent that the chain can never be straightened out by the ship's movements. The *Hammerlock Moor* can also be used at a buoy to control "horsing," but adequate chain must be veered before dropping the anchor to ensure that it is dropped well outside the anchor clump to which the buoy is secured. (See Section 10.27.)

10.15 Slipping a Mooring For this maneuver, a strong manila line or flexible wire is run through the buoy ring and back on deck for use as a slip rope. A strain is taken on it, and the chain is unshackled. Should the ship be riding to a bight of the chain, an easing-out line is used to ease the chain through the ring while the chain is being hauled in. The ship now rides to the slip rope, and unmooring is completed by letting the end of the slip rope go and reeving it through the buoy ring.

10.16   Mooring to Buoys, Bow and Stern   It is sometimes necessary to moor bow and stern to two mooring buoys in order to avoid any swing in a restricted space. When possible, the approach should be made against the current and on the side from which any wind or current present will tend to set the ship down on the line of buoys. The bow is moored to the upstream buoy in the usual manner. Meanwhile, another boat should be used to carry a line to the second buoy to hold the ship's stern from swinging off. This line should be no heavier than necessary so that it can be handled easily, and care must always be taken to keep it way from the screws. The end of a wire of sufficient strength may then be carried out and shackled to the buoy ring. The first line may be taken in or kept as a preventer and for use in unmooring. The final moor should be taut in order to prevent the vessel from ranging ahead or astern. This moor may be ensured by heaving in on the stern line with an after winch or by veering on the buoy chain, taking in the required amount of stern line and then heaving taut on the chain.

10.17   Winding Ship   It is seldom necessary to *wind ship* (turn a ship end for end) at a pier. When it must be done, the most satisfactory method is to use tugs, especially for large ships. Tugs give better control and assist the ship's engines to turn it. For small ships, or when no tugs are available, it is quite possible to wind ship by the use of its own engines or by taking advantage of the current.

It is safer to pivot on the bow and thus avoid possible damage to the rudder and screws against the pier. An after bow spring should always be held and the stern lines slacked or let go. With a current from astern, the stern will usually start out by itself. With a single-screw ship, starboard side to, backing down slowly will usually start the stern out. If it is port side to, going ahead dead slow on the after bow spring will have the same effect. With a twin-screw ship, backing the inboard screw or going ahead on the outboard one, or a combination of the two, should start the stern out. The swing is made on the after bow spring, but a forward bow spring on the other bow should be led from well aft to assist in controlling the swing and to take the strain after it is past 90 degrees, as shown in Fig. 10.4. The bow is kept clear of the pier by backing a little as needed. Should a strong current be running, a long after breast may be used to slow down the first part of the swing. During the latter part of the swing, the engines may be used to slow the swing and to prevent the ship from slamming into the pier. After the winding is completed, the ship can be spotted in position with the engines or by hauling her ahead of her original position.

10.18   Use of the Anchor in Shiphandling   A very important shipboard aid in shiphandling is the anchor, most commonly used in handling large,

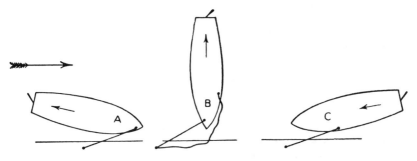

Fig. 10.4 Winding ship.

low-powered, single-screw vessels but a most useful device for all ships. The most common use of an anchor is to help a ship make a turn. If there is not sea room in which to turn with the aid of the propeller(s) and rudder(s) alone, and particularly if the wind or current is setting the ship down dangerously, then dropping an anchor and swinging to it is the quickest solution. The chain is held at short stay, the ship swings to the wind or current, the anchor is hove in, and the ship proceeds on its way. Ordinarily, no harm is done if the anchor should drag slightly; the bow will still be brought up into the wind.

The other major use of the anchor in shiphandling is normally restricted to large, low-powered, single-screw merchant-type vessels and is known as dredging. These ships are unusually sensitive to the effect of wind and often do not have the power or steering control needed to make a landing under unfavorable circumstances. An anchor dropped as the ship approaches the pier will keep the bow from being blown off, will greatly reduce drift or leeway, and will permit the use of greater power on the propeller, thus increasing the effectiveness of the rudder. Some of the ways an anchor can be used by such ships will now be discussed.

Suppose your heavily loaded, single-screw merchant ship is approaching a pier and will go alongside starboard side to. The ship answers the rudder sluggishly at low speed and will not respond at all if the propeller is stopped. The problem is to maintain steering control but still keep the speed of the deeply laden ship within safe bounds. To do so, the port anchor should be dropped while the ship is still a considerable distance from the pier (300 to 1000 yards is recommended, depending on circumstances). The anchor chain is held on the brake after enough chain has veered so as almost to stop the ship with the engine going ahead slow. This scope may be equal to about the depth of water plus 5 to 10 fathoms. The engines may now be ordered ahead at half speed or even two-thirds, but the ship's speed must remain low. The object is to drag the anchor at short stay and thus slow the ship's way, while, at the same time, permitting the ship's propeller to revolve to provide more rudder effect. A precaution to remember is not to veer too much chain. The ship may be stopped completely if the anchor really takes hold. The anchor should be taken aboard after all lines are doubled up.

There is no firm consensus among shiphandlers as to which anchor should be used in dredging; the lee anchor permitting the chain to pass under the ship's hull or the windward anchor. There are advantages and disadvantages to both techniques but, except in special circumstances, it is recommended that the windward anchor be used.

Anchors are also used under special circumstances in situations other than in making a landing. A single-screw ship may be required to stop suddenly in a crowded port or channel. To use the engines in backing will throw the ship's bow to starboard, which might be dangerous, but an anchor dropped at short stay will slow the ship and keep the bow under control. In an emergency, both anchors can be dropped and held—a procedure that has saved many a ship from a minor collision or grounding at close quarters.

There are occasions when a ship meeting another vessel in a narrow channel will not answer her rudder. Perhaps she has taken a sheer when in a canal because of bank cushion. Once again, dropping an anchor at short stay will usually provide the control over the ship's movements that had been lost.

Shifting anchorages or moving into more exact position in an assigned berth can be done easily with the anchor at short stay so long as the bottom is soft and clear of obstructions. This is a most useful procedure for a low-powered, single-screw vessel that has failed to make an accurate anchorage under adverse conditions. Instead of making a laborious retreat and a new approach, it simply drags its anchor to its proper position.

10.19 Handling Alongside Under Way Shiphandling alongside for the transfer of material and personnel is common to most big navies and sometimes takes place between merchant tankers. It presents no special problems, but a few techniques and guidelines may be helpful.

In approaching from astern another ship maintaining a steady course and speed, it is wise to measure her course as read by a compass. Since gyro compass differences of several degrees are not uncommon, it will be an advantage to know if there is one.

Depending on weather, the direction of sea and swell, and the officer's own degree of confidence, the approach should be made smartly, about 100 to 200 ft from the delivering ship—in general, the closer, the better in order to facilitate and expedite passing lines across. When the ships are hooked up, a reasonably close distance should be maintained—under good sea conditions, about 80 to 120 ft.

Following the guide ship's wake, the receiving ship should maintain a reasonable distance, perhaps 100 ft, as it goes alongside. By imagining that the guide ship is in the wake alongside, it will not be difficult to select the proper distance. If you are making 5 knots more than the guide, a rough thumb rule is to reduce to her speed as your bow passes her stern. It is better to overshoot a bit than be short since the lines can start over as you range ahead of, and then fall back to, your station. However, if you have overshot considerably and end up on the bow of the supplying ship, great care must be exercised. A reduction of speed without some alteration of the outward course to counteract the inward turning moment caused by interaction can cause the receiving ship to gain inwards and fall across the bow of the supplying ship.

It goes without saying that the best man should be on the wheel with a reliable officer to watch him and double check the execution of his commands and that casualty procedures should be known and rehearsed.

In maintaining station, the steersman must be given an exact course in degrees. He will soon find the amount of rudder needed to maintain a given course. Wind, sea, and the pull of replenishment lines between ships are all factors that vary widely.

The use of modern constant-tension wire highlines that exert a pull of 6 to 10 tons—often at considerable distances from the ship's pivot point—introduces a few special factors but no great problems for the shiphandler. If the difference between receiving and delivering ships is great in respect to size and if a heavy tension is exerted far abaft or far forward of the ship's pivot point, a considerable deflection of course may be experienced by one or both ships. This can be countered by the ship keeping station by carrying as much as 10 degrees of rudder to maintain course. In some cases, the receiving ship may have to steer a course 2 or 3 degrees off the guide's course. The guide may also be required to carry rudder in order to maintain its specified replenishment course.

When tension is applied during hook-up, commanding officers should keep each other informed of any special deflection experienced. Casting off constant-tension rigs (tripping pelican hooks or unshackling) should not take place until tension has been released.

Bow wave and stern suction effects are always possible on passing close aboard a large ship. As the bow approaches the guide, the submerged bow wave meeting the guide's hull or wake will tend to force the bow out; a good helmsman will expect this and counter it easily. The opposite effect—an attracting force between ship hulls as a result of stern suction caused by water being pulled into the propellers—is also a possibility if the stern is permitted to get too close to the guide. If this should happen, the engines should not be stopped or backed. Since it is important to maintain a minimum relative speed in relation to the guide, the helmsman should be coached to bring the ship out gradually.

In maintaining station in regard to speed, it should be remembered that a small ship may be affected by head seas and swells that will leave a larger guide unaffected. If an occasional large head sea tends to slow the small ship down, all that can be done is to crank up a few turns each time it happens, taking them off as the ship begins to move forward again.

When replenishment is concluded and all lines are reported clear, the receiving ship should increase speed quickly with gradual course changes to move it away from the guide's course. Its stern must be watched until well clear of the guide, and, of course, his bow should not be crossed until no possibility exists of embarrassing him.

10.20 Handling Destroyers (and Destroyer Types) More Naval officers learn practical shiphandling in destroyers (and destroyer types) than in any other vessel. This is especially true of conning alongside, as destroyers are often required to dock, go alongside tenders, or secure in nests at a mooring buoy. For this reason, it is well to note carefully some of the peculiarities of this type of handling. For the purposes of this discussion, destroyer type means today's cruisers, destroyers, and frigates, and range in size from 3,500 to 10,000 tons.

Destroyers are high-powered in comparison to their displacement and respond quickly to the engines. They have plenty of backing power. Destroyers have a narrow beam compared to their length; consequently, the propeller shafts are close together. The fact that most of the after deadwood has been cut away gives these ships a small turning circle. All (except the frigates) have twin screws and rudders.

Most destroyers have more surface exposed to wind forward than aft. This construction acts as a permanent head sail and gives the bow a tendency a fall off before the wind and the stern a tendency to back into it.

Going Alongside a Pier The light construction of destroyers makes it imperative to avoid heavy pressures and sharp blows on their hulls when going alongside. An additional danger in most of today's destroyers is the presence of a large, sensitive sonar dome hull-mounted on the bow. There is an understandable fascination in handling destroyers that often leads to the taking of unnecessary chances. A good destroyer officer is one who handles the power at his disposal daringly when he needs to do so but does not invite disaster by rashness. It happens occasionally that an engine will not follow the signal because of personnel error, and engine order telegraphs have been known to break down with the ship on full speed ahead or astern. Should such an accident happen when the commanding officer— merely to show himself to be a smart shiphandler—is charging into a landing at high speed and trusting to his backing power to stop in time, the result may be a smashed bow or worse, caused not by an effort to perform important service but merely by bravado. Situations are sure to occur when the extra power available must be depended upon; it is the height of folly to invite more of them. While a destroyer should always be handled with style and flair, it should never be risked imprudently simply to impress.

The light fittings, large power, and small lines of the destroyer make it especially important for the shiphandler to exercise care in warping or springing around piers. It is often necessary to work the engines in opposite directions in order to twist the stern in or out from a pier or landing. When doing so, the rudder(s) should be placed over full in the direction the shiphandler desires the bow to move.

The speed used in approaching a pier should be in keeping with the space available ahead or astern of the landing, and with weather and harbor conditions. Five knots is most often prudent. It often happens that the landing must be made with other vessels moored ahead and astern of the assigned berth, "parallel parking," so to speak. This situation usually requires a single tug.

The pier should be approached, slowly but steadily, at a slight angle (10 to 20 degrees) and the engines stopped with sufficient headway to overrun the landing slightly, that is, when it is certain that the ship's momentum is sufficient to carry the bow into heaving line distance. Heaving lines are passed as soon as possible, and the mooring lines hauled ashore. The engines are worked to bring the ship into a securing position, care being taken that springs and breasts are properly led and that neither bow nor stern is brought in too sharply since any localized pressure may result in damage to the thin hull. The use of a single tug on the bow, particularly for those destroyer classes with a bow-mounted sonar, is generally sensible. A second tug is seldom necessary in other than extreme conditions of weather.

When the current is running strong and parallel, or nearly parallel, to the pier, the wind may be considered of secondary importance, for the destroyer is long and narrow and, when placed at an angle to the axis of the current, will rapidly be carried toward or away from the pier in accordance with that angle. An exception to this rule is a destroyer type with a large, high structure, which will always feel the wind strongly.

If the wind or current is forcing the ship onto the pier, as will often happen if the pier is athwart the stream, it is important that the engines be maneuvered to keep the ship squared up with the pier as it drifts in with the current. Under such circumstances, fenders must be in place in sufficient numbers to prevent serious local damage to the hull. A tug on the bow is mandatory for a destroyer carrying a hull-mounted sonar in such a situation.

If the wind or current is running away from the pier, speed is necessary, and lines must be got out smartly. Once the lines are out, the stern must be brought in by springing on the bow line and by skillful use of engines and rudders. The best procedure is to move the bow close in, possibly under control of a single tug forward, then twist the stern in by opposing engines and putting the rudder over in the direction of the pier. Once close aboard the pier, securing the inboard shaft will cause the stern to "walk in" toward the pier, assuming inboard turning shafts.

Going Alongside a Ship at Anchor   This is very similar to going alongside a pier except that the conditions of wind and current are usually more favorable. The destroyer must keep clear of an overhanging stern or of any projections from the side of the vessel approached, and if possible, should select a part of the other ship's side where there are no projections. The greatest danger is from the yawing of the vessels at anchor. Destroyers yaw very freely when anchored and riding to wind or current.

There is rarely any difficulty in going alongside another vessel at anchor. The fact that she is at anchor makes it reasonable to suppose that there will be ample maneuvering room astern, except when her stern rides close to the beach. The approach should be made fairly well clear, with a slight cant inward, and the stern should be brought in and the bow carried out by backing the outboard screw and using the rudders as forward lines are passed. A spring leading forward from the after forecastle shock of the destroyer can be held and the ship breasted in easily by the current. Care must be exercised not to get the current on the inboard bow. Unlike the situation in going alongside a pier, the forward lines are the more important, for the stern will be taken care of by the wind or current to which the anchored vessel is riding. The engines and rudder can be used to assist in paralleling the two vessels as they draw together.

If a destroyer must approach a nest or tender at a wide angle, its bow should be distanced about its own beam width from the bow of the outboard destroyer or tender. The destroyer should then be stopped. A bow line should be sent across and held as a pivot. The approaching destroyer now goes ahead one-third or two-thirds on the inboard engine after the rudder has been put over hard—away from the nest. The powerful turning force of the discharge flow from the ahead propeller against its rudder is now utilized. The outboard engine is backed at the same speed and changed as necessary to prevent gaining head or sternway. This is a simple twist to bring the stern in toward the other ship, and should result in a gentle landing.

Anchoring

Letting go a single anchor is perhaps the simplest method of securing a ship to the bottom, and if the holding ground is good, she should ride easily in bad weather provided ample scope of chain is used. The disadvantages are that in a strong current or in a gale she may sheer considerably or swing to the combined effects of wind and current. It is therefore necessary to have an unobstructed area equal to a circle whose radius is the length of the ship plus the scope of chain used. If, for some reason, the anchorage does not afford such an area, the ship must be moored.

10.21 Letting Go In modern ships with heavy ground tackle, the anchors are commonly housed in the hawse pipe and secured by chain stoppers that engage the chain by a slip or pelican hook. (See Chapter 5.)

To ensure that an anchor will let go *immediately* after the housing chain stopper is released, prepare as follows: Connect up the windlass wildcat, slack and release the outboard housing chain stopper, and then engage the pelican hook of this stopper to the first horizontal chain link abaft the link previously engaged. Now release the friction brake, heave in until the windlass wildcat takes the strain, cast off the after chain stopper(s), walk out the anchor until the outboard housing chain stopper takes the strain and there is one link of slack chain abaft the stopper, set up the friction brake lightly to prevent the slack chain from going into the chain locker, and disconnect the windlass wildcat.

If the drift between the hawse pipe and the chain locker is considerable, it would be well to rouse up a few links of chain and lighten the slack forward to a point just abaft the stopper. Care must be taken that all is clear below decks and in the chain locker.

To let go, the bale shackle pin is pulled out, and then the bale shackle of the chain stopper is knocked off the pelican hook with a sledge.

Always bear in mind that anchors may be required unexpectedly when on soundings, in narrow channels, in restricted waters, or working around docks, etc. If they are ready for *instant* use, they may save worry and trouble. The anchor should always be let go with the ship moving slowly either ahead or astern so as to avoid paying the chain down on top of the anchor.

10.22 Anchoring in Deep Water If it becomes necessary to anchor in very deep water, it is absolutely essential that the ship be going dead slow. As the anchorage is approached at this speed, the usual practice is to walk out the anchor to within 5 to 20 fathoms from the bottom at the proposed anchorage, fasten the stopper to the chain, disengage the windlass—making the anchor ready for "letting go"—and then let go. Only enough headway to avoid paying the chain down on top of the anchor is maintained. The details of handling the windlass for anchoring in this way will vary with the type of windlass used, but it will be found that even when the ship is dead in the water and the anchor is let go with only a few fathoms of drop, the weight of the chain alone will cause it to run out violently. In extreme cases, where depths run to 40 and 50 fathoms, it may be advisable not to "let go'' but to "walk out" the chain by the windlass engine until the anchor is on the bottom and the necessary scope of chain is out.

10.23 Anchoring at High Speed If obliged to let go at a high speed, or if for any reason it does not seem safe to check the ship with a short scope, the chain should be allowed to run until the ship loses her way sufficiently to make it safe to snub her. There is no great harm in running out 75 or even 90 fathoms of chain and afterward heaving in to a shorter scope, and it should be remembered that if headway has to be checked by bringing up on the chain, the danger is less with a long scope than with a short one.

The danger connected with letting go while under considerable headway is often overlooked because the resulting damage does not necessarily show itself at once. The excessive strain may distort and weaken the links of the chain without actually parting them. The result is that the chain may give way at some time under a comparatively moderate stress. The practice of reducing the ship's headway by means of her ground tackle may introduce strains sufficient to cause fracture and will in any event be very apt to strain the chain beyond its maximum safe load, equal to the proof load.

10.24 Scope of Chain for Maximum Holding The scopes given in Table 10.2 are the optimum scopes for maximum holding. If longer scopes are used, the chain may be stressed beyond its safe service working load; if shorter scopes are used, the anchor will tend to drag before developing the full safe load on the chain. These figures substantially apply regardless on the size of the ship, provided that it is furnished with a properly balanced outfit of ground tackle and is given a safety factor of 4 on the ultimate strength of the chain. The scopes shown for the greatest depths could be obtained only by bending additional shots to the standard lengths of chain cable.

Table 10.2 Scope Table

Chains	Depth in Fathoms (outboard lip of hawse pipe to bottom)									
	5	*71/2*	*10*	*15*	*20*	*25*	*30*	*35*	*40*	*45*
Cast-steel chain (fathoms)	64	78	91	110	127	142	155	166	178	188
Die-lock N.E. steel chain or 1.25 manganese steel chain (fathoms)	74	90	104	127	146	164	178	192	204	216
Die-lock nickel steel chain (fathoms)	78	95	109	133	154	174	188	202	216	228

It is a common rule under ordinary circumstances to use a length of chain equal to five to seven times the depth of the water. The rule is satisfactory only in depths of water not exceeding 18 fathoms. This amount of chain is perhaps enough for a ship riding steadily and without any great tension on her cable. On the other hand, if conditions necessitate, a chain anchored in shallow depths should be veered to the maximum indicated in the scope table.

If greater holding power than that given by one anchor with the scope of chain shown in Table 10.2 is necessary, it is better practice to drop a second anchor with a moderate scope of chain than to rely upon the one anchor with a longer scope. Of course, in extreme cases when the greatest possible holding power is required, all anchors should be dropped and the chains veered with the greatest possible scope. If there is ample sea room, it would be better to reduce the scopes to the amounts shown in the table and accept the possibility of dragging anchor rather than risk breaking chain.

10.25 Weighing Anchor In heaving in, the windlass and chain can be relieved of considerable strain by a judicious use of the engines and rudder. The forecastle detail must keep the bridge fully informed as to how the chain "tends"; whether the chain is "taut" or "slack"; when the anchor is at "short stay"; when the chain is "up and down"; and when the anchor is "aweigh." As the anchor is hove in, the reports made to the bridge are "Anchor in sight, sir" and "Clear or foul anchor," as the case may be; "Anchor clear of the water, sir"; and "Anchor is up, sir." The captain will then direct, "Secure the anchor" or "Make the anchor ready for letting go."

If the chain tends across the bow, it may be cleared by stopping the windlass and going astern.

10.26 Foul Anchor Although modern double-fluke anchors are much less likely to foul than the old type, they occasionally give trouble in the following way: A ship may be greatly embarrassed by a lack of facilities for lifting the anchor to a point where it can be hung securely and where the chain can be handled conveniently. As a rule in such cases, a chain stopper should be put on the chain and the wildcat disengaged and the anchor let go; the wildcat is then reengaged and the anchor heaved in.

Under conditions where the anchor may be expected to foul, it is a good rule to "sight" it frequently; indeed, this precaution is advisable under any conditions when a ship remains at single anchor for a long time. It is especially important at the approach of bad weather if the ship has been lying for some time under circumstances making it probable that the anchor is foul. For sighting, this anchor may be weighed and another let go when the chain of the first is "up and down." If there is a scuba diver aboard, it is prudent to have him sight the anchor on the bottom. At the mouth of a river with a flow of silt the anchor should be sighted every few days.

An anchor sometimes becomes so well dug in or so fouled in rock or coral that it cannot be raised in a normal manner. If so, a wire strap around the crown may be needed. Anchorage charts often indicate locations where anchors have been lost (such as St. George's Channel, Bermuda). If necessary to anchor in such a place, it might be wise to consider fitting a crown strap and a buoyed work wire to the anchor before letting go. An anchor that has been lost with some chain attached can usually be recovered by the use of grapnels or an *anchor hawk*.

10.27 Riding to a Single Anchor   A vessel at single anchor in a strong tideway is likely to sheer considerably. Such a tideway brings the current first on one side and then on the other and drives the vessel across the stream until she is brought up sharply by her chain, often with a violent shock. This effect may be prevented in great measure if she is held with a steady sheer away from her anchor by putting the rudder over as far as may be necessary and keeping it there. The stern is thus driven over to one side, and the vessel is canted across the current and held there.

A ship is never in greater danger of dragging her anchor or parting her cable than when driving down with a slack chain, broadside on or partially so, to wind or tide. Such a situation may of necessity arise in anchoring or may come about in sheering, as described above. It frequently happens in squally weather, when a ship swings in one direction during a lull just in time to be caught by a strong squall on the beam and be driven bodily off. She may be brought up with the chain taut across the stem.

In lying at an anchorage where such situations may arise, the greatest watchfulness should be exercised. Steam must be kept on the steering engine and at the throttle, a man must be at the wheel, an ample scope of chain must be veered, and a second anchor should always be ready for letting go at a moment's notice even though there seems no chance of its being needed.

Whenever there is a possibility of the anchor dragging, a lookout should be posted to ensure instant notice of that fact. A *drift lead* is useful although not always to be trusted. This is a heavy lead kept on the bottom with its line made fast, but left hanging with considerable slack, to some place well forward that is convenient for observation. If the anchor drags, the line tautens and tends ahead. As long as the ship is fairly steady, a drift lead will usually give notice of dragging, but if she sheers about considerably, it cannot be relied upon. The farther forward it is used, the better, because the bow moves much less than the stern in sheering.

Good bearings of objects on shore are more reliable than the drift lead, and a range is best of all. Both of these, however, are less trustworthy when the ship is sheering about than when she is steady because even a range will open out when the ship swings and seeem to indicate that she is dragging. Such indications may be checked by watching the heading. Radar ranges to fixed objects ashore may also be used to detect dragging.

There are times when unexpected and unusual swells, seas, and currents set in toward an anchorage. In such cases, the only thing to do is to get up steam promptly and shift to a safe anchorage or stand out to sea. Sailing directions should always be carefully read and every effort made to obtain the latest weather reports.

There are also times when nearby ships will swing in opposite directions with little current or wind. In such cases, either each ship should heave in sufficient chain to avoid fouling or one or more boats should be placed at the stern to exert sufficient power to push the ships clear or hasten their swing.

It is always advisable to keep a detachable link on deck where it can be reached conveniently for sudden slipping if an emergency arises and to make sure that the pins can be driven out without difficulty. Tools for unshackling should be kept in a convenient place and never removed. A buoy and a buoy-rope at hand complete the preparations for slipping at short notice. In an exposed anchorage subject to sudden gales, these precautions, of course, are especially important.

If a vessel or other danger is seen drifting down upon you when lying at anchor in a tideway, giving the ship a cant with the rudder—thus bringing the current on the bow—and veering the anchor chain roundly ought to sheer her well across the tide and probably clear of danger.

If an anchor is known to have dragged in a clay bottom, it should be picked up as quickly as possible, for it is certain to be "shod" (balled in mud) and to have lost much of its proper holding power. In letting go to a bottom of this kind, it is important to give good scope from the very beginning to prevent even the minimal dragging commonly expected of an anchor as it digs down to get its hold.

The practice of bending two cables together to obtain a "long scope" is not recommended if such a scope would result in exceeding the safe limit given in Table 10.2. The fact must not be overlooked, however, that a defective link or shackle may result in disaster if only a single cable is in use, and that it may be wise to let go a second anchor whenever no chances can be taken. The vessel would then be moored.

Mooring with Anchors

10.28   Types of Mooring   There are two basic types of mooring: (1) The *ordinary moor,* in which the unobstructed area in which the ship will swing, is reduced to a circle with a radius only slightly larger than the length of the ship. For this taut moor, two anchors are let down at a considerable distance apart and with such scope of chain on each that the ship is held with her bow approximately midway between them. The anchors should be so placed with respect to any current that a straight line connecting them would be parallel to the direction of current flow. (2) A slack moor, known as a *bridle* or *hammerlock moor,* in which the bow of a ship is snubbed to prevent it from sheering in a current, gale, or hurricane. Under these conditions, the angle between the chains must be about 90 degrees and the anchors so placed that a straight line joining them would be perpendicular to the direction of current flow or expected wind.

10.29   The Ordinary Moor   In the ordinary moor, the ship stands against the current (wind) to the proper position and lets go the first anchor, which must always be the *riding* (upstream) *anchor* at that time. She veers on the riding chain, carefully laying it out so as to keep it taut and tending ahead while she drops down with the current (wind) to the position for letting go the *lee* (downstream) *anchor.* When that position is reached, the second anchor is let go. She now veers on the lee chain and heaves in on the riding chain, taking care to lay the lee chain out properly until she is riding midway between both anchors with the desired scope of chain to each.

A *mooring swivel* is frequently used to prevent the anchor chains from fouling one another when a moored ship swings with the wind or current. When the swivel is used, it is impossible to veer both chains.

10.30   The Bridle or Hammerlock Moor   In riding out a gale or hurricane, a vessel on a single anchor will often sheer violently back and forth across the wind (Fig. 10.5), and the rudder will have little effect in holding her with a steady sheer. This tacking back and forth is often called *horsing.* Violent horsing can be cut in half by dropping a second anchor underfoot with minimum scope to act as a *snubber,* but even such reduced horsing may become excessive in a violent storm. In such cases, it is a good idea to pick up the second anchor and redrop it at one extreme reach of a sheer, still using only a short scope, and then ride to this *bridle* (see Fig. 10.6). The two chains will now work together to snub the bow and hold it steady whether the chains lead from the hawse in an open "V" or whether they cross the stem in an "X." The horsing will be almost completely eliminated, and the main engines can be used with precision to offset the greater portion of the wind. Should the wind be from a hurricane or typhoon and the bottom sand or mud, it is sometimes feasible to permit the short-scope anchor to drag around as the wind veers or backs so that the open "X" or "V" of the bridle always faces the wind. Either position is satisfactory, but with preplanning as the hurricane approaches, it is naturally preferable to figure out which anchor should be used as the riding (long-scope) anchor

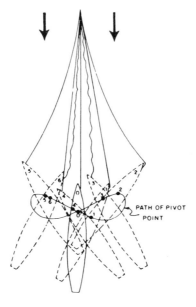

Fig. 10.5 Violent figure-eight horsing motion of a ship riding with a long scope of chain out to a single anchor during a high wind.

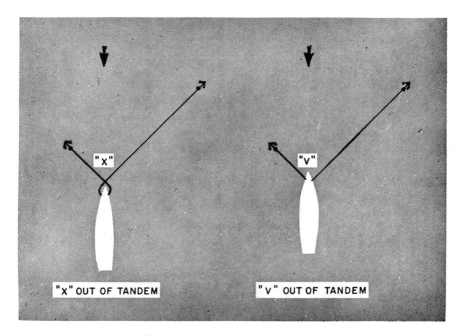

Fig. 10.6 Anchors acting as a bridle.

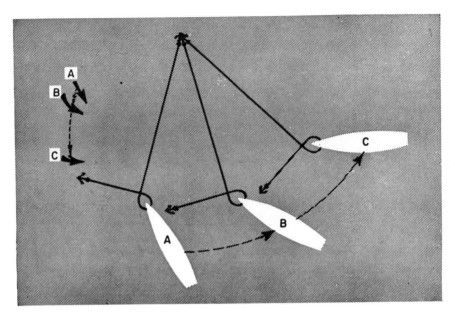

Fig. 10.7 Effect desired when short-scope anchor drags properly.

in order to ride out the entire wind shift with an open "V" hawse as the short-scope anchor drags around (Fig. 10.7).

10.31 The Mediterranean Moor The Mediterranean Moor (Med Moor) is essentially a method of mooring a ship perpendicular to a mole or pier using lines to secure the stern and two anchors to hold the bow in place. As the name implies, the Med Moor is used in Mediterranean ports where pier space is at a premium.

This type of moor has several advantages. First, it saves space in a harbor or port where pier space is limited. Second, it provides a strong moor for high winds and rough weather. Third, it eliminates many of the problems associated with mooring alongside in nests. Fourth, each ship has its own brow (gangplank) to the pier.

The Med Moor also has two major disadvantages. There is a strong possibility of anchors becoming fouled with other ships when trying to get under way. For this reason, it is often advisable to get under way in inverse order of entering port. The second disadvantage stems from the first in that it is difficult to get under way quickly in a crowded harbor.

This discussion will be limited to the destroyer, although cruisers and merchantmen also utilize the Med Moor. (Carriers, as a rule, usually anchor outside harbors because of the limited maneuvering space.)

Since the Med Moor is made perpendicular to the pier, it is important that the conning officer determine how far from the pier the anchors will be dropped. The first consideration is the length of the ship. The destroyer is about 390 ft long, or 130 yd. Next, it is necessary to determine the required scope of chain. The shortest chain on a destroyer is 105 fathoms. In making the Med Moor, a scope of chain must be chosen that will allow enough room from the pier for the ship to maneuver freely but still allow a margin for error. In general, 75 fathoms (or 150 yd) is chosen for a destroyer, a length that allows a reserve of 30 fathoms. Thus, the drop distance from the pier is seen to be equal to the length of the ship plus the scope of chain, or 280 yd. (See Fig. 10.8.)

With this distance determined, the conning officer takes a course approximately parallel to the pier, reducing speed so that the ship has only bare steerageway when it is approximately 50 yd short of the position abreast of the berth. At this point, the outboard anchor, or the one opposite the pier, is dropped from the wildcat. If the starboard anchor is dropped, right full rudder and a twist on the engines are applied to keep the anchor chain clear of the ship. The starboard anchor chain is veered until the ship reaches a point 50 yd from the opposite side of the berth. At this time, the other anchor is dropped. Since a destroyer has only one wildcat, it is necessary to drop the first anchor from it so that the scope of chain may be shortened at any time; the other anchor is dropped from the *compressor,* which is a movable constriction in the chain pipe that serves to check the anchor chain. Then the second chain is veered and the first taken in while the ship twists and backs into the berth.

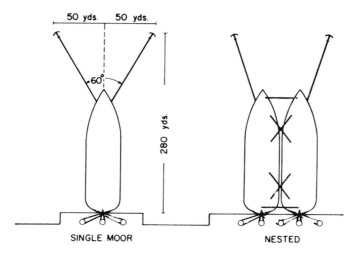

Fig. 10.8 Mediterranean Moor (Med Moor).

To obtain its final position, the ship backs gently against the catenary of the anchor chain on the wildcat. When the moor is completed, there should be an equal amount of chain to each anchor, and in an optimum situation, an angle of about 60 degrees between the chains. When the ship is close to the pier, the conn is generally shifted to the fantail so that the distance to the pier can be observed more accurately. The stern is secured to the pier with a stern line and quarter lines that are crossed under it. A stronger moor may be obtained by using the towing line as the stern line and reinforcing the quarter lines with wire. Once the stern line is secure, the moor is tautened by heaving in and equalizing the anchor chains. There should be moderate strain on the anchor chains, and they should be standing well out of the water so that a wind from the bow will not endanger the ship.

When getting under way, the brow and after lines are taken in, and the second anchor dropped is heaved on. If other ships are close aboard, lateral movement of the ship's stern can be controlled by a line to the pier aft and/or by the ship's engines. After the second anchor is aboard, the first anchor is heaved on; as it comes in, the bow is usually headed fair for leaving port. Since harbors requiring the use of a Mediterranean Moor are crowded and small, a pilot and necessary tugs are not only available but usually mandatory.

Destroyers often moor in a Med Moor nest, in which the first ship drops her inshore anchor only and then backs into a stern-first position against the pier. The other ships moor alongside with standard mooring lines to their neighbors. The last ship in drops her offshore anchor only and twists into the stern-first position.

In some harbors, such as the one of Barcelona, Spain, gales that send seas into the harbor entrance can cause a rapid rise and fall of the water level. Under such circumstances, a firmly moored ship may part her lines to the wharf, and the resultant fore-and-aft surging may carry away the brow. If circumstances warrant, it is recommended that the brow be removed and all lines to the wharf eased or taken in. A line or two tended on a winch will usually keep the stern under control as the ship surges. Nylon lines, because of their greater elasticity, should be of help.

There is one important precaution to take when Med-mooring a large ship. The stern line, holding the stern in close to the pier against the strain of the anchor chain, must never be led from the aftermost chock straight down to the pier. In bad weather, as the stern rises and falls, a straight, short lead to the pier either will part or will pull out or rupture the bollard. Instead, the stern lines should be led aft from each quarter chock well forward of the stern chock. These lines will be longer, have more "give," and make a smaller angle with the pier. In addition, of course, after spring lines should be led out from the stern chock, crossed, and secured well down the pier on each side to prevent the stern from moving side to side.

Shiphandling with Tugs

The size of modern vessels and the congestion of our harbors have encouraged the use of tugs to assist vessels to berth, unberth, and maneuver in confined quarters.

The direction of the tug's activities is normally the responsibility of the pilot or docking master. Nevertheless, every deck officer should acquaint himself with the dynamics involved.

Good communication between the ship and the tug is essential. The general use of VHF radio-telephone for this pupose has made the use of hand and whistle signals outmoded except as an emergency measure. It is however, appropriate for the tugs to acknowledge orders on their own whistles.

A tug's basic function is to assist the vessel to steer, to turn the vessel, to move it laterally, or hold it in position while it is heaving up or letting go its lines. In addition, the tug may be required to check a vessel's way, stop a vessel's sheer, slow the vessel's swing, or even propel it physically. In short, the tug permits the shiphandler to safely undertake maneuvers with a vessel that would otherwise be difficult, dangerous, or impossible without it.

10.32   Using Tugs Alongside   This common method of employing tugs in American ports uses the tug to push or back to move the bow or stern of the ship in the desired direction, or, when made fast forward or midship, to move the vessel laterally. If the tug is forward, however, the ship will have to turn its rudder toward the tug and go ahead on its engine to ''lift'' the stern.

A tug may make fast with as many as three lines: headline, springline, and sternline. If, however, the job will be mostly pushing, a headline alone may be sufficient.

If the tug must back for an extended period of time or maintain a position at right angles to the ship, it will probably require a sternline or quarterline (terms used interchangeably here). When the tug is working alongside the ship, the vessel will usually provide the ahead and astern propulsion. However, if the vessel needs to move along the face of a dock, it is sometimes more convenient to have the tug lay at an angle and push it ahead or astern.

10.33   Using Torque to Advantage   If a single-screw tug is secured to a ship with only a headline, in still water and with no way on the vessel, lying at approximately 90 degrees to the ship, the stern will move to port (assuming a right-hand propeller) when the tug backs its engine. It is obvious that if the shiphandler wishes the tug to maintain its angle of 90 degrees without having the tug put up a quarterline, then the ship must move in the same direction and at the same speed that the stern of the tug is moving. As long as the vessl's direction and speed of movement conform to the effect of torque on the tug, the tug will stay in position.

This is less complicated than it seems. There are occasions, especially if the ship's chocks and bitts are poorly located, or when the tug may only be required to back for a short time, that it is appropriate to use the tug this way. Also, if the tug has only one line up and will be required to shift, it will have only one line fast which can be cast off quickly.

10.34   Working the Tug Without a Line   Tugs can often work effectively without a line. A tug may assist a ship to depart from its berth by breasting the stem toward the dock to spring the stern open and then steer it as it backs its engine by pushing on either side of the stem as needed. A tug can also slip inside between the ship and the dock if the stern has been sprung open and then push the vessel right around as it gathers sternway. At tanker berths, it is common for tugs to work on the inshore side of the vessel between the dolphins to prevent it from landing heavily against the dock or to push it clear of the dock when it departs its berth.

10.35   Working Tugs on a Towline   Using tugs on a towline for docking a ship is seldom done in this country, though it is the prevailing method in Europe. Nevertheless, this method is quite useful for undocking and for other applications. In towline work, this would apply when the vessel is obliged to transit narrow bridges, locks, and channels and where the width of the waterway would prohibit using tugs fast alongside.

Compared to the alongside method, there are certain disadvantages. There are hazards associated with towline work that do not apply to tugs used alongside. If the ship uses its engine rashly, it can "trip" the tug, and if the tug comes into contact with the bow of a fast-moving ship while taking a towline from it, the tug can become "stemmed." In both instances, the tug can be capsized or sunk.

The mechanics of towline work seem fairly obvious. The tug pulls the ship (or the end of the ship it is fast to) in the direction that the pilot wishes. Hawser length is normally 100 to 150 feet. When the tug tows the ship, the vessel *must not* be allowed to overtake the tug. If the tug is towed stern first by the ship, this must be done slowly to avoid capsizing the tug.

The tug's wheelwash can also affect the ship. This may not be important if the vessel is just being pulled off of a dock or turned, but if the ship is being towed through locks or bridges it may be necessary to lengthen the tow line or reduce the speed of the tow.

10.36 Using Tugs in Current Current is an everyday reality for many shiphandlers. The current's direction and velocity may change at every tide, or it may be a river current whose direction is constant, but the velocity will change according to the height of the river.

When tugs are used in this situation, they are subject to the same forces that affect the ship. They must be "made up" to the ship in such a fashion that any maneuvering they do to stay in position will not *adversely* affect the vessel, or else, they must be secured to the vessel in such a way that they will not be required to maneuver.

Tugs may be used in many fashions: as *free agents* (i.e., with no lines), with a head line only, with two or three lines (head, stern, and perhaps a springline), on a towline, and "hipped up" (this means lashed firmly alongside the ship).

There are three basic situations involving current: current ahead, current astern, and cross-current. This seems simple enough but the ramifications can be extensive. Current ahead can be "dead" ahead or setting on or off of the dock. The cross-current situation can be equally complex.

10.37 Handling Dead Ships There are basically three different ways of handling dead ships:

1. With tugs alongside;
2. With tug and tailboat;
3. With tug alongside and lead boat.

When tugs are used alongside, if the ship is small it may require only one tug. In determining where the tug should make up, consideration should be given regarding which side of the ship goes to the dock and where the bow and stern should go. It is also important to consider what kinds of turns the tug will be required to make with the ship in tow alongside. It is best for the tug (especially if it is single screw) to be fast on the inboard side of a turn when a hard turn is made. The reason being, if the tug backs its engine, this will accelerate the swing without adding headway to the tow.

More tugs will be required to shift larger vessels. In some ports a minimum of three tugs are required. In this case, one tug will usually "hip up" aft to provide propulsion and two will be positioned forward for steering. Very large ships may require four or more tugs.

Tugs and tailboats or stern tugs are sometimes used for shifting dead ships, especially if locks, bridges, and narrow channels must be navigated. The stern tug must be ready to check the way on the ship so that it does not overpower the lead tug.

On lengthy shifts, it is sometimes practical to use a tug fast alongside aft with a tug ahead of the ship on a towline. This is a particularly effective way to use two tugs of moderate power to move a sizeable ship.

10.38   A New Generation of Tugs   A new generation of harbor tugs is much more versatile than the conventional single-screw or twin-screw tugs commonly encountered. These tugs include those fitted with flanking rudders, or steerable Kort nozzles, as well as the propeller-steered tugs more common in Europe of both "pusher" and "tractor" configuration. The virtue of these tugs lies in the fact that they can steer equally well when maneuvering ahead or stern. The PS "tractor" tugs are principally designed for towline work, and usually push stern first when required to do so. Since their rudder propellers are located forward, they are much less likely to become girded or stemmed than other types of tugs when a towline is employed.

10.39   Rules for Handling Tugs

1. A tug required to back on a headline must take out the slack before applying full power or risk parting the line; the delay must be allowed for.
2. It is easier and less hazardous for a tug to make up to a ship proceeding at moderate speed than one going full ahead.
3. A tug on a towline is vulnerable to tripping or capsize if a ship's engines are maneuvered rashly by a negligent shiphandler.
4. Conventional tugs are much more effective maneuvering ahead than astern unless proper lines are rigged to keep them in position.
5. Care should be taken when letting go the tug's lines, especially a towline from the stern of the ship. It is best to slow the ship and stop the engine to avoid fouling the propeller.
6. If a tug is fast forward, it should be advised ahead of time if the ship's anchor is to be used.
7. A ship making a bend with a tug fast alongside forward must reduce speed if the tug is to be of assistance.
8. If the ship has much freeboard, it may save some time in making the tug fast by passing it a heaving line especially if the wind is blowing hard. It is good manners, as well as good seamanship, to slack the tug's working lines back easily when it casts off instead of letting them go on the run and perhaps injure a deckhand.

9. The tug must be allowed to do the work; its effectiveness is more or less inversely proportionate to the speed at which the ship is maneuvered.

References

Blair, Carvel H. *Seamanship, A Handbook for Oceanographers.* Centreville, MD: Cornell Maritime Press, 1977.

Crenshaw, Jr. R. S. *Naval Shiphandling.* 4th ed. Annapolis: Naval Institute Press, 1975.

Danton, Graham. *The Theory and Practice of Seamanship.* London: Routledge & Kegan Paul, 1985.

Hooyer, H. H. *Behavior and Handling of Ships.* Centreville, MD: Cornell Maritime Press, 1983.

King, E. and Noel, J., *Shiphandling,* New York: D. Van Nostrand, 1952.

MacElrevey, D. H. *Shiphandling for the Mariner.* Centreville, MD: Cornell Maritime Press, 1983.

Reid, George H. *Shiphandling with Tugs.* Centreville, MD: Cornell Maritime Press, 1986.

Van Dorn, William G. *Oceanography and Seamanship.* New York: Dodd, Mead and Co., 1974.

The Admiralty Manual of Seamanship. London, U.K.: Her Majesty's Stationery Office.

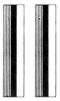

Towing and Salvage

The rescue of ships in distress and the refloating of those that have grounded is a highly specialized calling to which men devote their lives, but every seaman should have a basic knowledge and understanding of towing and salvage.

Salvage tugs equipped to tow, fight fires, pump out ships, and assist in groundings are on call near all the major shipping lanes and routes of the world. Sometimes they are at sea on station waiting for their clients. Their work is highly specialized, usually hazardous, and often profitable. Very long-range towing of huge floating offshore oil drilling rigs is another specialty that can only be mentioned in passing.

This chapter provides all that the average seafarer need know in order to tow or be towed in an emergency or to meet the emergency of a sudden grounding.

Towing

In recent years, the economy of towing operations has encouraged the increasing use of tug and barge units in coastal and nearby overseas trade. Tugs and barges can be quite competitive with conventional ships, especially over short routes handling bulk cargos, because of their reduced manning costs for a seven or eight man crew as well as their lower construction costs compared to those of a comparable ship of the same capacity.

The tug's principal function is that of prime mover, which—depending on circumstances—will be used to move barges, either by towing alongside (on the hip), towing astern, or pushing the barge ahead. The barges, of course, are the carriers. Those in offshore service are of various configurations, with raked bows, spoon bows, or model bows. They usually have an after rake fitted with two skegs, which are often adjustable, and help prevent the barge from yawing when under tow. If the barge is designed for pushing, there will also be a notch at the stern to accommodate the bow of the tug.

11.1 Alongside Towing Alongside towing ("on the hip") is a common method of handling a barge when docking, undocking, and transiting congested waterways. The tug will usually make up at the bow or the stern of the barge with its centerline inclined at an angle toward the barge to compensate for the offset position of the tug. The tug will make fast with several lines, usually a minimum of three—a head line, a spring line (also called a *tow strap),* and a stern line.

The operator must allow for the tendency of tug and barge units to "crab" sideways a bit because of the offset position of the tug. This tendency will vary according to the draft of the barge as well as which end of the barge is forward (with the stern forward, the tendency is less pronounced because of the skegs). The wake angle will often give an idea of the unit's true direction of movement.

11.2 Deep-Notch Towing Pushing "in the notch" is an increasingly common practice in offshore towing when weather and sea conditions are favorable. (The notch is the indentation at the stern of the barge into which the bow or stem of the tug fits to permit pushing.) This is probably the most efficient way for a tug to propel a barge, and is faster than conventional towing, since it eliminates the drag of the towing gear and the tendency of barges to yaw or sheer (see Fig. 11.1).

Tugs and barges navigated in this fashion (sometimes referred to as dual-mode ITBs) are suitably reinforced in the area of contact and have special gear to secure them together. The tugs are also well fendered.

Generally speaking, the deeper the notch, the more weather the tug and barge can withstand when in the pushing mode. Nevertheless, when sea conditions are too rough, the tug will be obliged to take the barge in tow; towing gear is usually prepared in advance for this contingency.

There are certain common characteristics of deep-notch tug/barge units operating in pushing-mode:

Fig. 11.1 Tug *Columbia* (5600 H.P.) pushing in the notch.

1. When the barge is light, the unit is much affected by wind conditions, and the tug captain must exercise great care when maneuvering the unit in confined waters when it is windy.

2. With the tug in the notch when the barge is loaded, the unit will often have a tendency to skid or slide sideways when making a turn. If this tendency is not anticipated by the captain, it could result in an accident or a grounding.

3. The tug should exercise care when backing its engines when the barge is deep-loaded and is just barely afloat, as the barge may behave erratically due to the tug's propeller wash.

4. When the tug is in the pushing mode it should be handled carefully, since the strain of maneuvering usually falls on the pushing gear. If this carries away it can result in an accident.

5. Most large deep-loaded barges have a pronounced tendency to sheer when towed. In confined waters when the barge is on a short hawser, this characteristic can be extremely dangerous. With the deep-notch tug/barge units (or dual-mode ITBs) this normally only occurs when the unit is crossing the bar, inbound or outbound,

when sea conditions are too rough to permit the tug to push the barge. A speed in excess of 3 to 3½ knots may be excessive in this situation. If the barge must be towed faster than is prudent, in order to overcome current, for example, then it is best to wait for sea conditions to abate in order to handle the barge from the notch.

11.3 Hawser Towing Towing astern, the most common method of navigation for tug and barge units—is employed in all oceans in all seasons. For this purpose, a tug may use either a hawser or tow cable. As a rule, hawsers are made of some synthetic fiber, usually nylon, although other synthetic lines (particularly those that float, such as polypropylene, polyethylene, and some blends like polydacron) are used by small tugs.

The tow hawser must be protected against chafing, either by securing a towing board to it or integrating a piece of chain where it passes over the stern of the tug. It is customarily shackled to a chain, wire rope pendant, or bridles secured to the bow of the barge.

Towing with a cable is much the same except that the cable is wound on the drum of a towing winch instead of secured to the tow bitts as a hawser is. On most commercial tugs, these winches are nonautomatic and do not pay out or recover cable when the load increases or decreases. Since the cable has little elasticity, a length of chain or nylon shockline is usually attached to the barge's bridle to help absorb some of the occasional heavy surge loads that the cable's catenary may not adequately compensate for.

The tow cable must also be protected against chafing, either by shackling it to a steel spool that slides back and forth across the tow span (known as a *Texas bar*) or securing it to a metal ''shoe'' where it crosses the stern of the tug.

11.4 Multiple Tows Multiple tows are frequently handled by oceangoing tugs. If the tug has a double-drum towing winch, and is towing two barges, they are usually connected to separate cables and the forward barge rides over the bight of the after barge's cable. With hawser tugs, the barges are usually connected by an intermediate hawser. With tugs fitted with only a single-drum winch or those tugs with double-drum winches that are towing more than two barges, the after barges may be connected to the barges ahead by an intermediate hawser, or an underwire. The underwire is connected to the towing bridals of both barges and rides beneath the leading barge.

Tugs should avoid allowing their tow cables to drag on the bottom in shallow water, as this could damage them. This concern does not normally apply to hawser tugs since their hawsers normally ride on or near the surface of the sea.

Most of the complications in multiple tows stem from the rigging and maneuvering involved in making or breaking tow and in entering and departing from confined waters.

11.5 Making and Breaking Tow Making and breaking tow are the processes involved in connecting up and getting underway with the barge, entering port, taking the barge "on the hip" or "on the head" (pushing), and docking it.

Making Tow If the barge is alongside a dock and must be maneuvered clear, the tug will usually "hip up" on the bow of the barge and connect its cable or hawser to the barge's bridle. Once the tug and barge unit is clear of the dock, the tug will drop the barge astern on a short hawser until it is clear of confined waters and then slack the cable or hawser to the desired length.

Breaking Tow Breaking tow is basically the reverse of the former procedure. The tug normally shortens up the hawser in an area clear of traffic before proceeding into the ship channel. Hawser length is restricted to 75 fathoms between tug and tow. However, if the captain decides that this length is insufficient, he may use a greater one. The amount of the cable or hawser used between tug and barge will depend on several factors, among them the width of channel, the amount of ship traffic expected, and sea conditions at the bar.

Once the tug and tow are inside the harbor, the tug will further shorten tow and then either make fast alongside the barge or disconnect and take it on the head for berthing.

Any successful marine operation requires a high order of seamanship, but there is a particular emphasis on shiphandling in towing operations; in no other area of maritime activity is this skill so essential, except perhaps in piloting.

11.6 The Towline Generally speaking, the longer and heavier the towline, the easier the towing will be. A decided dip or catenary gives the same advantage here as in the case of a vessel at anchor riding with a good scope of chain. The weight of the catenary acts as a spring, preventing tension variations from being thrown upon the towline in sudden jerks. It must be remembered that a tow line leads down, not up.

Wire rope has proved very satisfactory for heavy sea towing, its advantages being that it is convenient for casting off, takes up comparatively small space when stowed, and does not deteriorate if properly dried and oiled before stowing.

Nylon is satisfactory for light or moderate towing. It is heavy enough to give a good dip when used in sufficient length, but it is not too heavy for convenient handling. Nylon is popular because of its resiliency, ease of handling, and long life.

For towing a ship as small as 3000 tons in rough weather—and it must not be overlooked that rough weather may be encountered in almost any towing operation—the full length of an 8-in. nylon hawser or a 1½-in. diameter wire rope will be none too much.

Where the tow is a vessel whose displacement is comparable with that of a cruiser or aircraft carrier, the towline should be made up of 2½- or 2¼-in. diameter wire rope connected to a good length of her own anchor cable. The length needed will vary with circumstances, but it is far better to have too much than too little.

A point of some importance in towing in a seaway is to keep the ships in step. In other words, the length of the line should be such that the ships will meet the waves and ride over them together. If the length of the line allows one vessel to be in the trough of the sea and the other on the crest, the line will slacken for a moment and then tauten with a sudden jerk; if the ships meet the waves at the same time, however, the tension of the line will remain comparatively steady.

11.7 Securing the Line on the Towing Ship In securing the towline, consideration must be given to letting go in an emergency. For convenience in letting go, it is desirable to have a break in the line near the stern. It would be advisable to have a shackle connecting two parts of the line at or near this point, together with some arrangement like a pelican hook for slipping quickly. The possible whip of towlines and bridles when these are released at any point may be overcome by the use of preventers.

If the towing ship is comparatively large and has a chock at the stern, the line should be brought in through it. It is a good plan to use a short length of chain for the lead through the stern chock, shackling it outside to an eye in the end of the towing hawser and inside to a towing bridle. The chain through the stern chock not only takes the chafe but by its flexibility does away with the dangerous nip that might be thrown into the wire if the tow chanced to take a rank sheer onto the quarter.

Where the chain is not used for taking the chafe in the stern chock, the towline must be fully protected by chafing gear in the form of a long and bulky *pudding*. The stiffness of this pudding reduces the sharpness of the nip; without the pudding, the nip would be thrown upon the towline from time to time by the sheering of the ships. Manila should be wormed, parceled, and served. Canvas, hides, burlap, and old rope should be used on wire towlines.

If the strain is not too heavy, one pair of bitts may be used to secure the towing line. Figure 11.2(A) shows how it should not be secured. Since the greater strain comes on the left bitt, the bitt might be lifted and torn out. In Fig. 11.2(B), the greater strain is taken by the after bitt, and though the forward bitt has some strain, both should hold under ordinary conditions.

When one pair of bitts is not strong enough, the line can be taken to as many as three sets of bitts. To divide the strain, it is advisable to take one turn around the first set, two around the second, and three around the third, thus leaving the line free to render slightly and so equalize the strain.

If pelican hooks (see Fig. 11.3) are used for letting go, the strain is taken momentarily on the hook, relieving the shackle so that it can be disconnected and the towing hawser slipped at command. This arrangement entails practically no delay. This arrangement, with the pelican hook taking the steady strain of towing, offers the quickest emergency release.

If pelican hooks are not used, a strap may be attached to the wire or chain outside the shackle and a heavy purchase hooked to the strap and taken to a winch (Fig. 11.3C). In letting go, the strain is taken by the winch long enough to disconnect at the shackle, and then the strap is cut as ordered. A preventer must be used to prevent a dangerous whip upon letting go.

There are some conditions under which it is convenient to use a span on the towing ship. Its two parts are brought in through the quarter chocks. Generally, this makes it rather easier for the towing ship to steer, and this advantage may become important in cases where a small ship is dealing with a heavy tow. If the line leads from a chock directly over the rudder, it binds the stern in such a way that it can swing only in obedience to the rudder by dragging the tow with it. A large ship can take care of this situation by the power of her steering gear, assisted if necessary by the propellers, but a small ship with a heavy tow and the line leading through the stern chock will steer very sluggishly if she steers at all. Tugs specially fitted for towing have their bitts well forward of the rudder to allow the stern to swing; the fittings abaft the bitts allow the line to sweep freely across from one quarter to the other.

Spans may be made up of chain, wire, or line. Arrangements must be made for letting them go quickly in emergencies.

A convenient plan is to bring the tow line in through a quarter chock and bend a hawser from the other quarter to it at such a point outside that the two parts shall form a span of convenient length. The lines may be secured around bitts as previously described. This plan has the advantage that by letting go the second line we get rid of the span at once and have to deal only with the tow line itself.

(A)

AFT →

(B)

Fig. 11.2 Securing a towrope: (A) the wrong way, and (B) the right way. *(Official U.S. Navy photograph)*

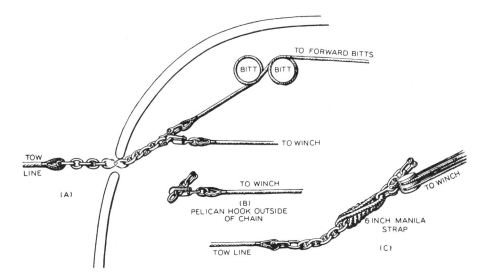

Fig. 11.3 Towing by bitts.

11.8 Towing Winches Most vessels designed especially for towing work (seagoing tugs, tug-supply boats, and salvage vessels) are fitted with hydraulic, electric, or engine-driven towing winches that carry the tow cable on a drum. Some of the winches are designed to maintain a constant tension on the tow cable automatically and will pay out and retrieve the cable as the load varies because of sea conditions.

Nonautomatic winches have proven successful, however. In their case, surge loads are compensated for by a nylon shockline or length of chain attached to the tow's bridles; either provides the necessary elasticity or catenary to absorb the surge loads.

Towing winches are heavily constructed and the foundations firmly secured well forward of the tug's rudders to permit it to maneuver. At sea, the tow cable may be secured to a spool on a tow span or pass through towing pins at the stern both to protect the cable and prevent it from leading over the side of the tug if the towed vessel takes a sheer.

Tow cables on larger vessels are usually 2- to 2½-in. diameter extra improved plowsteel and 2000 to 3000 ft in length. They are wound evenly on the drum of the towing winch by a level-wind device.

11.9 Securing the Line on the Towed Ship On board the tow, the hawser is usually secured to the anchor cable, although there may be many conditions under some other arrangement will be used. If the anchor cable is not used, at least a short length of chain is desirable to take the chafe in

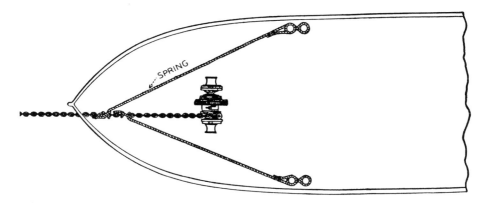

Fig. 11.4 Bow of towed ship.

the chock in the same manner as already described for securing the line on the towing ship. If the anchor cable is used, the hawser is secured or shackled to it and the cable veered away to the desired length; the windlass brakes are then set up and springs or chain stoppers used to take the real strain of towing (see Fig. 11.4). It is well to have a shackle between the windlass and the point at which the springs or chain stoppers are secured and to keep tools at hand for unshackling if it becomes necessary to let go in an emergency. Ordinarily, the tow should not be let go in this way, except in case of extreme emergency, because the line weighted with a considerable length of heavy anchor cable would sink immediately, hanging as a dead weight from the stern of the towing vessel. In this position, it would be extremely difficult to handle and in danger of fouling the propellers. This applies only when the tow is a vessel of some size and is towing by her anchor cables. When a large ship is towing a small one, it is evident that the natural way of casting off is for the tow to let go, leaving the line to be handled by the large ship.

11.10   Taking a Disabled Vessel in Tow at Sea   In good weather, this maneuver presents no special difficulty and calls for no extended discussion. The lines are run and secured as already described. The towing vessel starts ahead slowly on the course upon which the disabled vessel happens to be heading and uses every precaution to prevent a jerk on the line. Before changing course, it waits until both ships have gathered way and are moving steadily with a good tension on the tow line.

In bad weather, towing should not be attempted unless exceptional circumstances make it necessary. The running of lines in a heavy sea is attended by considerable difficulty, especially if the vessel to be towed is unable to assist by placing herself in a favorable position. Moreover, in really heavy weather, it would be necessary to proceed so slowly that little or no time would be lost by waiting for the weather to moderate.

Disabled vessels lie in different positions relative to the wind, depending on the size and position of the superstructure, the trim, and, perhaps, the drag induced by the damage sustained. If there is more superstructure forward than aft, the vessel will lie with the wind from abaft the beam to astern. Vessels with much superstructure amidships will lie with the wind abeam, and those with superstructure aft, such as tankers, will lie head into the wind. All such vessels make leeway—and, if lying at an angle to the wind, headway or sternway—of 1 to 3 knots. Vessels down by the head tend to head into the wind, and vice versa.

If a tug with a deckhouse forward and a flat stern is the towing vessel, she should approach downwind and just clear of the bow, except when the vessel to be towed lies head into the wind. In this case, the approach of the tug is still downwind but just ahead of the vessel, using the engines to keep her position and clear. Figure 11.5 shows how the tug is able to work close to the disabled vessel and still keep clear by a kick ahead at intervals.

In the following discussion, it will be assumed that one vessel is going to tow another and that the weather is rough enough to call for the use of all reasonable precautions but not rough enough to make towing impracticable. It may be assumed that the disabled vessel will be lying with the wind and sea a little abaft the beam, this being the position that a ship usually takes when lying in a seaway with engines stopped. The other vessel places herself on a parallel, heading either to windward or to leeward. In considering which of these positions is to be preferred, we must remember that considerable time will be required to run the lines and that during this time both vessels will be drifting. A light vessel will drift faster than one loaded, and the drift of a vessel in ballast trim often amounts to several knots. If the lighter vessel is to leeward, she will drift away from the other and make it very difficult to run the lines. It may be said that, as a general rule, if there is any important difference in the rate of drift of the two vessels, the lighter one should be to windward when the work of running the lines is begun. The towing vessel then places herself to windward if she is drifting faster than the disabled vessel, and to leeward if she is drifting more slowly and on the same heading as the vessel.

If the difference in the rate of drifting is considerable, the time available for running the lines after the work is once begun will be short at best. Every precaution should be taken to prevent delay, with a clear understanding being established between the ships and all preparations made before the towing ship takes her position. For communicating between two ships, megaphones or loud hailers are of the greatest value. Under any except the

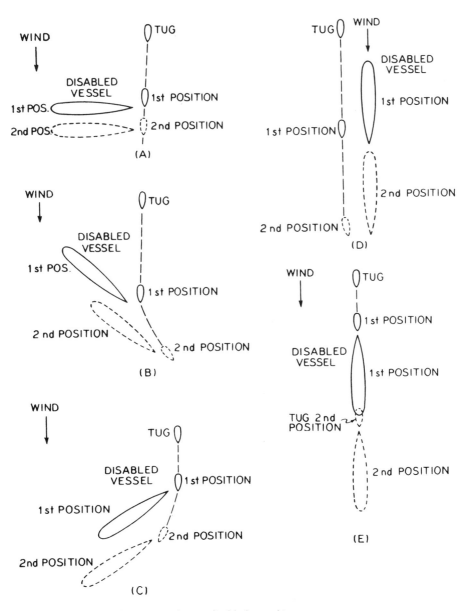

Fig. 11.5 Taking a disabled vessel in tow at sea.

Table 11.1   Code of Sound Signals for Towing

A short blast must not exceed 2 seconds in length. A long blast must not be less than 6 seconds in length.	
I am putting my rudder right.	1 short blast
I am putting my rudder left.	2 short blasts
Go ahead.	2 long
Stop.	1 long, 2 short
All fast.	2 long, 1 short
Haul away.	2 short, 1 long
Let go.	2 long, 5 short
Pay out more line.	1 short, 2 long
Avast hauling.	3 short
I am letting go (emergency).	5 short, 5 short, 5 short

most favorable conditions, they should make it possible to effect a thorough understanding of what is to be done and how. To a great extent, they also may take the place of signals between the two ships after the towing begins. A code of sound signals may be adopted and will be useful under many conditions (see Table 11.1). It is an excellent plan (when feasible) to send an officer on board the tow to remain there. He must be acquainted with the plan to be carried out and provided with a list of signals for handling the lines and the ships. Radio voice communications (VHF) or portable hand-held radios are the best communications devices of all.

11.11   Handling Lines and Getting Under Way   The first line to be run will be a light one by means of which the heavier ones can be hauled across. A new 3-in. manila or an equivalent floating synthetic fiber is a convenient size to begin with. If a boat is to be used, it should be lowered with the crew and the greater part of the line in it and made clear as quickly as possible. the line should be payed out as the boat pulls away for the other ship.

The line may be floated alongside the disabled ship without much difficulty. The best way to do so will depend upon circumstances, but a common way is to float a good length of the line by life belts, casks, or any other means and to steam slowly around the disabled vessel, dragging this snare astern and causing it to foul the disabled vessel. If proposing to take up a position on her weather bow, it is a good plan to steam along to leeward fairly close aboard, cross the stern, and come around parallel to her heading, thereby causing the line to foul her stern. This approach will entail a little trouble in shifting the vessel forward, but it leaves the towing ship in position without further maneuvering. Similarly, if proposing to take a position on the lee bow, the tow vessel should pass along to windward, cross the stern, and come around to leeward. The line should then be picked up without difficulty.

There may be special circumstances when it will be desirable for the disabled vessel to run lines, but under ordinary circumstances it is more convenient for the towing vessel to run them. Once the first line is across, the heavier lines are run and made fast to the anchor cable of the vessel to be towed. A good length of cable is paid out—20 to 45 fathoms is none too much for heavy work—and the line made secure on both ships as has been described. Chafing gear is used liberally wherever it is needed. In the meantime, full instructions about starting are given to the chief engineer, and when all is ready, the engines are started ahead as slowly as possible and stopped the moment the line begins to tauten out. Then a few more turns are made and so on until the inertia of the tow is overcome and both ships are moving slowly with a steady tension on the line. The revolutions are then increased little by little and the course changed gradually, as necessary. When the tow is finally straightened out and moving steadily, the speed is worked up to that at which it is thought wise to continue.

In all changes of course, the tow puts her rudder at first to the side opposite that of the leader and so steers around into the leader's wake.

After settling down to a steady rate of towing, the lines should be examined, the strain divided as evenly as possible, chafing gear renewed wherever necessary, etc. Hands should be stationed night and day to watch the lines on both ships, with axes and unshackling tools ready for slipping hurriedly, if that is necessary. It is well to have a light messenger line between the ships for hauling messages across and for use in running a new line in case of necessity. This line should be left slack and should have ample length to allow for the fact that, if the towline parts, the leading ship will forge ahead considerably before she can be stopped.

11.12 Groundings Salvage in its broadest sense includes the salvage (recovery) of cargo, the removal of wrecks, and the refloating of grounded ships. Only the matter of grounded ships will be discussed here since the salvage of cargo and the removal of wrecks involve highly specialized techniques not of major interest to seafaring men as a whole.

The first thing to do on going aground is to think the problem through and avoid taking hasty action. The ship should not be backed full for a prolonged period and should not be lightened before a careful plan has been made. In the meantime, the crew must make ready to lay out an anchor. Hasty disposal of weight may result in the ship's being driven further up on the beach and/or cause it to broach. It is often wiser to add weight by flooding certain compartments. Using the engines unwisely can foul the intakes and condensers and can wash more sand under the hull. If possible, an anchor should be laid out to seaward so that the ship may wait for a salvage vessel with beach gear. Soundings must now be taken all around the ship to determine what part of it is grounded and the loss in draft. The average loss in draft times the tons per inch immersion as taken from the ship's curve will give the total loss of buoyancy in tons. This weight is the problem. The loss of buoyancy must be reduced to the point that the pull of beach gear and tugs will be sufficient to refloat the ship.

Salvage men have calculated that a pull of about 30 percent of the remaining lost buoyancy is required to refloat a ship that is aground on a sandy bottom with a gentle slope; 50 percent when the bottom is hard or gravelly; 60 to 80 percent when it is coral; 80 to 150 percent when it is rocky. A large amount of weight will probably have to be removed from the ship to reduce the lost buoyancy to a manageable amount.

Personnel, fuel, and water can be removed more easily and quickly than stores, cargo, ammunition, spare parts, and guns. The decision to remove any or all of these weights, as well as when to move them, will depend on a number of factors. In all probability, the determining factor in offshore groundings will be the weather, although the state of the tide at grounding and the time of the next tide, or perhaps the next spring tide, may be equally important. In some parts of the world, the range of the tide is so great that ships grounding at part tide are refloated at high tide. Where the rise and fall of the tide is not that great, the hour and date of the next spring tide may be the deciding factor as far as time is concerned.

Some other physical conditions must also be known and weighed. Is the ship fully loaded? What compartments, bottoms, and tanks have been holed? What kind of bottom is under the ship? Currents can scour the sand from under a ship in one place and pile it up in another. While all the physical conditions are being compiled and analyzed, it is wise to send out additional anchors to hold the ship in her grounding position.

11.13 Planning and Methods The planning must be done carefully so that the weights to be moved, the equipment to be used, and the dredging to be done will be coordinated and completed at the end of the time available. Some fuel and water will be required for engines. All of the removed weight cannot come from the double bottoms and fuel tanks, or the stability of the ship may be adversely affected. Many men are required to handle stores, spare parts, cargo, and ammunition. They must have deck space to handle these items, and there must be space alongside for the barges to receive the stores, fuel, etc. The plan must coordinate the times for removing weights, for laying out the beach gear on deck, for dredging alongside, and for receiving barges.

The following measures may be undertaken.

1. Remove fuel.
2. Remove water.

3. Remove cargo.
4. Remove stores.
5. Remove spare parts.
6. Remove ammunition.
7. Remove guns or missiles.
8. Transfer some men.
9. Dredge and scour alongside.
10. Tunnel under the ship.
11. Rig beach gear.
12. Expel water from holed compartments.
13. Use services of salvage vessels.
14. Use services of tugs.
15. Twist the ship.

When large ships are stranded, a trench can be dredged along each side of the ship if the bottom is sandy or muddy. The trenches should be made deep enough to receive a large part of the sand or mud upon which the ship is resting. If this sand or mud can be crumbled and moved into the trenches, the ship may be floated in her grounded position. This method is successful only occasionally.

European salvage men have had some success with scouring the bottom from under the ship. A small vessel with her propeller well immersed is secured to the grounded ship in such a position that the discharge current from her propeller scours the sand from under the other ship. Sometimes the engines of the grounded ship itself have been used to remove sand and mud from under it, but care must be taken that a new shoal is not formed astern. The engines cannot be operated astern for very long because sand may be washed under the ship and the problem of refloating made more difficult.

After trenches have been dredged, divers with high-pressure hoses are used to start the movement of sand and wash away the remaining sandy supports. Divers are also used to tunnel under the ship so that chains can be rigged to hold the pontoons in place.

It is probable that certain compartments were flooded when the ship grounded. These compartments can be nearly freed of water by forcing air into them. Care must be taken so that the pressure of the air does not rupture the compartment. The pressure of the air should be a little higher than the pressure of the water at the relevant distance below the surface.

11.14 Beach Gear Useful equipment available to a grounded ship is known as *beach gear*. It is, in reality, a development of the older methods of laying out anchors and cables for salvaging ships. Present-day beach gear consists of the following:

1. An 8000–lb Ells anchor, fitted with a crown line and buoy, for breaking loose and recovery
2. 15 fathoms of 2¼-in. chain attached to this anchor
3. Two or three 100-fathom wire cables of galvanized plow steel
4. Shackles
5. Wire stoppers
6. A four-sheave wire tackle.

The anchor, sometimes backed by a second one, is planted well out and in the direction the ship will have to move when it is refloated. The end of the second wire is led through a chock or an opening cut in the side of the grounded ship. The tackle is laid out on deck and aligned with the wire so that the pull will be straight, with no nip or bend in the wire. The hauling part of the tackle is now led to a ship's winch or to a salvage winch installed to supplement the ship's gear. In the salvage of the *Missouri,* nine sets of beach gear were used in addition to three sets laid out from each of two salvage vessels that were pulling too. Each set of beach gear can exert a pull of 45 to 60 tons.

11.15 Use of Tugs Tugs are usually the first vessels called to assist a stranded ship. Until fairly recently (within the last generation), however, their power was ordinarily comparatively limited—usually less than 1600 horsepower. This was often insufficient to refloat a large ship that was hard aground. For this reason, tugs often served in an auxiliary capacity or handled the barges fitted with beach gear. But things have changed in recent years. There are now plenty of 3000 to 5000 horsepower tugs around, and some tugs have as much as 9000 horsepower. Many have hydroconic bottoms and Kort nozzles, and can generate bollard pull in excess of 200,000 pounds. These powerful tugs can provide a competitive alternative to standard salvage operations using beach gear.

However, even less powerful tugs can prove useful. In some instances, a vessel may refloat itself by either discharging ballast, or taking advantage of a favorable tide. In this case, it may be prudent to have even a small tug standing by to assist the vessel in manuevering in order to avoid stranding again. If heavy weather makes up, a tug with a tow line up may keep a vessel from broaching or "climbing the beach."

If tugs are not successful in refloating a vessel, or if it has suffered severe bottom damage, arrangements must be made to have a salvage vessel provide the additional gear and services necessary including pumps, compressors, divers for underwater welding and explosives, as well as beach gear.

The beach gear is often handled directly aboard the salvage vessels, and includes powerful winches to heave the cables on the anchors. In this case, the salvage tug is secured directly to the stranded ship with its own tow cable.

It is very probable that the lost buoyancy of a large ship will be so great that she exerts a pressure on the bottom of hundreds of tons. The sand under her has been packed so tightly that it has the consistency of low-grade concrete. We may say that the ship exerts a powerful suction on the bottom. One of the ways of breaking this suction has already been mentioned, namely, the crumbling of the sand under the ship into dredged trenches alongside. After much of the weight of lost buoyancy has been removed and all preparations completed to refloat the ship, large tugs are used to twist the ship and thus break the suction. Small tugs are useful to hold large tugs and salvage vessels in position to exert their best pull.

The salvage plan should include the measures necessary to ensure the safe voyage of the refloated ship to the nearest base or shipyard. Anchors and chains must be returned, the holed compartments should be patched and shored, and the stability and trim of the ship must be satisfactory. If her engines cannot be used, she will have to be towed. These measures may require the reloading of fuel, water, stores, and even ballast to prevent further disaster.

11.16 Using Tugs in Emergencies Most emergencies affecting vessels in pilotage waters fall into one or more of these five categories: (1) fire; (2) holed or sinking; (3) stranded (discussed above); (4) loss of power; and (5) loss of steering.

Tugs are suitable for assisting in most of these situations. If they are fitted with firefighting gear, their capabilities may be enhanced.

Fire. While fire may not be the most common emergency, it is potentially the most dangerous. It is often essential to remove the vessel from its berth. Ships normally have "fire wires" hung over the side, fore and aft, for tugs to make fast to—for this purpose.

Before approaching the ship, the tug should have its towing gear ranged, fire hoses led out, and the crew dressed in oilskins or fire-fighting gear.

The tug will normally back up to the ship to take it in tow astern. Fire hoses can be played upon the ship to reduce the heat and protect the crew while they are securing the towline to the fire warp. Other vessels can also help by directing their fire monitors or hoses in such a fashion that they will cool the area. The tug should slack 200 to 250 feet of tow hawser before taking an *easy* strain in order to avoid parting the fire warp.

If tugs are secured at both bow and stern of the ship, they can control the vessel well. If only one tug is used, it is probably best secured forward, unless the vessel is trimmed heavily by the bow.

Once the vessel is clear of the dock, it is often desirable to ground it. This should be done in an area where the bottom is flat and soft so that the vessel will not be damaged when the tide drops.

Vessel Sinking or Holed.   If the vessel is sinking or holed, it may need the assistance of a tug to put it aground (as quickly as possible), but tugs have sometimes been used to breast a vessel against a dock to keep it from capsizing or sliding into deeper water where the bottom slants downward away from the dock.

If a tank vessel is holed and leaking flammable products, the tug should stay clear of this area. The fumes could cause a galley or engine room explosion. In this instance, the tug might be able to approach the vessel from the weather side, but even this may be hazardous.

Loss of Power or Steering.   Loss of power is a dead ship situation and the tug must take the vessel in tow. In the case of a small ship in protected waters, the tug may make-up "on the hip." The vessel may be towed stern first if one of the anchors is dragged to provide directional stability. A tug can probably best assist a vessel to steer on a towline. However, it can also assist made-up alongside forward, or by pushing the stern of the ship.

11.17   Rescuing the Crew of a Wreck at Sea   There are no hard and fast rules for rescuing the crew of a wreck; only what is considered the best practice by experienced and capable seamen may be stated. So many elements control the application of the general rules—such as sea, wind, urgency of immediate assistance, maneuverability of the assisting ship, and the training and experience of the boat crews—that each case must be decided according to circumstances.

After having made contact and established communications, find out how urgent the case is and how much help may be expected from the crew of the wreck. If it is nighttime, the weather conditions indicate an improvement in, or at least no worse, weather the next morning, and the master of the disabled ship feels he can hold on and the rescue ship feels it can maintain contact, it is wise to wait for daylight.

Under any circumstances, when the rescue begins, the comparative drift of the two ships and whether or not there is any wreckage about the disabled ship must be determined. If there is wreckage, it must be decided how it will hamper the boat work. If the rescue ship drifts faster than the disabled ship, it should go to windward; if the opposite is the case, it should go to leeward.

Before the rescue work begins, the rescue boat should be equipped with two sharp hatchets in brackets, one at the bow and one at the stern; one ring life preserver with stout heaving lines made fast, two spare life jackets stopped with sail twine under each thwart; and two spare oars, if a pulling boat.

If the weather is very rough, extreme precautions must be taken in lowering the boat and getting her clear. The ship should be held with the sea on the bow to give a lee for the boat and to reduce rolling as much as possible. The crew, with its life belts on, is lowered into the boat. Frapping lines are used around the falls to steady the boat, and fenders are rigged to prevent her from being stove in if she swings in too heavily.

Assuming that the boat gets off and makes the trip to the wreck in safety, the officer in charge must decide how he will establish communication and take off the passengers and crew. It is out of the question to go alongside to windward, but if he goes alongside to leeward, not only is there a risk of being stove by the wreckage likely to be found floating under the quarter, but there is the much more serious danger of being unable to get clear of the side again. A ship lying in a seaway with engines stopped drifts to leeward at a rate that is always considerable and may amount to several knots. A boat alongside such a ship to leeward is in exactly the same position as if she were alongside a dock against the face of which a strong current is setting. As a rule, the boat must never be brought directly alongside the wreck. She may either lie off to windward, keep well clear, and hold up head to sea, or lie off to leeward and hold on with a line from her bow to the wreck. If she is obliged to go alongside, her stem may be allowed to touch, with all being ready to back off if she shows a disposition to get broadside on. The people on board the wreck must put on their life belts and go down a line one at a time, hand over hand, to be hauled into the boat. The most favorable point for working will usually be under the lee quarter or the lee bow, but this depends upon the way the wreck is lying with reference to the sea. It is sometimes possible for people to lower themselves, or be lowered, to the boat from head booms or from an overhanging main boom when they cannot be rescued in any other way. So serious is the question of avoiding actual contact with the wreck that many officers consider it best for the rescue ship to go to windward and drop its boat down with a line with only two or three men aboard, or drop down an unmanned rubber boat.

Salvage for Boatmen

An active boatman, especially one who ventures offshore, should know something about salvage procedures, both for his own safety as well as for that of others who might require assistance.

In this instance, the term *light salvage* is applicable because even though the basic procedures are much the same as in commercial salvage, the gear is handier and the vessels smaller. There are three common situations for which a knowledge of salvage will be useful: grounding or stranding, a breakdown at sea, or sinking. Most accidents (excluding fire) fall into one or more of these categories.

11.18 Grounding In the case of grounding, the remedy is to refloat the vessel by pulling it into deeper water. In order to do this, the salvor must overcome *ground effect,* the resistance caused by the vessel's weight resting on the bottom. It is often overcome by having another vessel tow the grounded vessel off the beach. In this case, it might be prudent for the assisting vessel to get its own anchor down to weather so that it can hold its bow to the wind or sea and avoid going ashore itself.

If no outside assistance is available, a vessel may often be refloated by *kedging off* with its own anchors, which have been carried out into deeper water. It may be necessary to use several anchors in series on the anchor line to get sufficient holding power to heave against.

The amount of *heaving power* can be increased either by attaching a block and tackle to the anchor line or by rigging a multiple purchase through shackles or loops tied in the anchor line and heaving the line on the anchor winch. Lightening the vessel by removing stores or ballast can also be of help.

If a vessel is very hard aground, it may be necessary to rig a *dead man* to heave against. If there is a sand or mud bottom, a number of oil drums (chained together with their tops cut out) can be jetted onto it with a centrifugal pump; these will provide quite good holding power. On a rocky bottom, it may be necessary to fabricate a large grapnel anchor or to have a diver spot one of the boat's anchors where it will not easily come adrift.

Pulling power can be considerably increased by using a chain fall or "come along" on the anchor line, compounding the fall by using block and fall on the hauling part of the tackle, which is made fast to the anchor line. In some cases, skids and rollers placed beneath the hull can also be useful.

In heavy commercial salvage, it is assumed that the vessel will best come off the way she went on. Such is not necessarily the case in light salvage, for if there is a heavy breaking sea on the reef where the boat is stranded and a quiet lagoon beyond the reef (as there often is), it may be easier to take the boat right across the reef.

Deep-draft vessels, such as sailboats, can often be heeled down on their side far enough to be floated, either by rigging a weight on the boom swung over the side or by heaving the mast down with the halyard until the vessel is afloat on its side.

Before refloating a vessel, it is wise to check for any hull damage that might cause the vessel to sink when it is towed into deeper water.

11.19   Rescue Towing   A breakdown at sea as a result of mechanical fail-ure (or dismasting in the case of a sailboat) is usually remedied by a tow from an assisting vessel. This operation is usually simple enough, provided that the boat's deck fittings (bitts or cleats) are strong enough for the towline to be secured to them.

The towline, of course, should be strong enough to withstand the strain and long enough to allow the surge loads from swells to be absorbed by the tow hawser without undue shock to either of the vessels or the line itself. If such is not the case, it may be necessary to bend the towline to the anchor line of the vessel being towed. Generally speaking, the towline should be long enough for the bight of the line to remain in the water at all times. It must be well secured aboard both vessels and protected against chafing, especially where it passes through chocks or over the edge of the deck.

It may be convenient to rig a bridle from the stern of the towing vessel to make steering easier. If vessels are poorly fitted with cleats or bitts to make fast to, it may be necessary to run a strap right around the vessel and secure it in place with lashings.

During heavy weather, the nearest port may not always be the best choice if it is too far to windward. A better choice would probably be to go down wind, even if the port is farther away. Breaking inlets should also be avoided whenever possible.

11.20   Sinking   A vessel begins to sink when water enters the hull faster than the pumps can remove it. The remedy is obvious: simply reverse the process. In order to do so, either the pumping capacity must be increased or the leak must be reduced.

The nature and location of the leak will often determine the best method of controlling it. Broken pipelines can be repaired with rubber hose and clamps or underwater epoxy tape; small holes can either be plugged or sealed with fast-setting hydraulic cements, or underwater epoxy com-pounds. Large holes may best be sealed with plywood patches and foam rubber patches held in place by toggle bolts or by bolts passed through the hole and second piece of plywood on the other side (sandwich patch). A life jacket or cushion can be stuffed into a large hole as an emergency measure and secured in place by wedges or lashings until a more perma-nent patch can be made.

Most successful light salvage efforts are the result of a combination of good seamanship and having the necessary material and equipment avail-able. To this end, the prudent boatman should carry whatever tools might be required in an emergency, a towline able to serve as a spare anchor rode, and perhaps a portable pump that can move large volumes of water. Such anticipation might save a boatman's life as well as his vessel.

References

Brady, Edward M. *Tugs, Towboats & Towing.* Centreville, MD: Cornell Maritime Press, 1967.

Brady, Edward M. *Marine Salvage Operations.* Centreville, MD: Cornell Maritime Press, 1960.

Cady, Richard A. *Marine Hawser Towing Guide.* Centreville, MD: Cornell Maritime Press, 1978.

Plummer, Carlyle J. *Shiphandling in Narrow Channels,* 3rd ed. Centreville, MD: Cornell Maritime Press, 1978.

Reid, George H. *Primer of Towing.* Centreville, MD: Cornell Maritime Press, 1975.

Reid, George H. *Boatmen's Guide to Light Salvage.* Centreville, MD: Cornell Maritime Press, 1979.

Reid, George H. *Shiphandling with Tugs.* Centreville, MD: Cornell Maritime Press, 1986.

12

Boat Handling and Helicopter Operations

Boat Handling

As ship's boats are normally designed for a variety of purposes, their handling will be discussed in terms of the circumstances in which they are to be used.

The powerboats of a ship, including landing craft, do the greatest part of their work in port or off the beach, running from ship to shore. Under these circumstances, it is a normally safe and simple matter to hoist and lower them with a crane or boom. When hoisting or lowering at sea or at anchor during rough seas, however, certain precautions must be observed in order to prevent the boat from being stove in, swamped, or the crew thrown overboard. If these precautions for operations in rough seas are understood and observed *at all times,* there should be no difficulty in hoisting and lowering boats under more favorable conditions.

With the exception of those boats provided with their own davits, large boats and heavier landing craft are hoisted and lowered by means of boat cranes or booms that hook on the slings rigged in the boat. The slings are attached to hoisting eyes that are built into the strongest sections of the boat. Davits used for many of the smaller boats can be considered as nothing more than two cranes that perform the same job in a slightly different manner.

Ships have devices for hoisting and lowering boats. When hoisted (or lowered) by a ship's crane, the boat's hoisting slings are used. When hoisted at the davits, the boat's fore-and-aft shackles are used. The Raymond releasing hook is a standard release device used for attaching or releasing the davit falls from the davit shackles installed in the boat. It is a swivel hook with a tripper hinged at the bill of the hook. The tripper is so weighted at its outer end that when the boat is waterborne and the load is removed from the hook, it automatically tumbles, thus throwing the boat shackle out of the hook and releasing the boat.

When the boat is not waterborne, the load on the hook prevents the tumbling of the tripping device. To speed up "hooking on" prior to lifting the boat, the weighted end of the hook is provided with a lanyard which is passed through the shackle and held taut in order to, first, prevent tumbling of the tripper, and, second, hold the shackle in the hook prior to hoisting. This is not difficult in a flat calm, but normally a ship is rolling when the boat rises and falls. Consequently, many boat crews wear hard hats or helmet liners. The bow hook should be strong, agile, and steady in order to do his job and to avoid a swinging hook both while hooking on and after release.

12.1 Boat Davits Gravity, crescent, quandrantal, and radial or round bar are the usual types of davits. (See Fig. 12.1) With the *gravity-type davit,* the boat is carried in two cradles mounted on rollers. The rollers ride along two parallel tracks at right angles to the ship's side. After the gripes are released, a brake is released. This action permits the boat and the entire assembly to roll down the tracks by gravity, stopping with the lifeboat suspended over the ship's side. Tricing lines swing the boat against the ship's side and hold it in position until frapping lines are passed around the falls and secured, thus holding the boat in position to receive people aboard. After this, the tricing lines are cast adrift by tripping the pelican hooks before the boat is loaded. The next action is that of releasing the brake, which causes the boat to be lowered to the water (See Fig. 12.2). A falls tensioning device on modern gravity davits maintains a constant and safe tension on the boat during lowering and hoisting.

The *crescent davit* is a type of hinging-out davit used on all classes of Naval vessels. In this type of davit, the arms are crescent-shaped and are moved in and out from the ship's side by means of a sheath screw, which may be operated by handcrank or by power.

With *quandrantal-type davits,* the boat is carried on chocks under the davits. The davits themselves stand upright with the tops curved in toward each other so that the ends come directly above the hoisting hooks of the

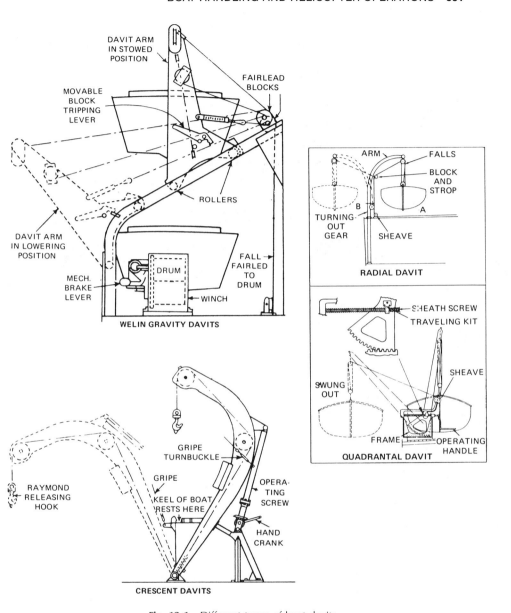

Fig. 12.1 Different types of boat davits.

Fig. 12.2   A 26-foot plastic-hulled motor whaleboat being lowered from gravity davits. (*Official U.S. Navy photograph*)

boat. The davit, which pivots, is turned outboard by a crank operating a worm gear.

With *radial* or *round-bar davits,* the boat is carried in chocks under the davits. Like the two preceding types, these also pivot. Chapter 12 includes a detailed description of the use of radial davits.

Two commercial davits are the *Rottmer* and the *Steward.* These feature releasing hooks in each end of the boat to which the falls are attached. Hinged on pins, the hooks are held engaged by a locking device. A jointed shaft running the length of the boat is connected to both locking devices or releasing devices. This can be so configured that each fall can be separately released, the preferable alternative when the boat is launched or recovered when the ship is underway. Upon throwing a lever attached to this shaft, the hooks are capsized and the boat is released.

The *Mills chain-releasing mechanism* is also common in the merchant navy. The gear-release handle is conveniently located on deck at the after end of the boat. When this handle is pulled, trigger hooks with ball weights (to which the boat falls are made fast) drop. The boat is then free fore and aft. Before the releasing gear can work, the boat must be waterborne.

A new davit, the *Miranda,* is used with the new covered lifeboats described later in this chapter. The Miranda system uses fixed ramp arms, winch, motor, and the boat in its own launch/recovery cradle. This allows the boat to be launched when the ship is heeled as much as 30 degrees.

The cradle permits people to be loaded while the boat is still in its cradle in the davit. The launch and recovery are controlled by the helmsman within the boat, who also controls the release gear.

Davits are used to swing the boat to the lowering position and then, after it has been hoisted, to swing it back on board. The actual raising and lowering could be done by manning the boat falls with sufficient men. However, the falls are usually taken to some source of power to raise the boat and then to a belaying point, such as a cleat or the gypsy head of a winch, to lower it.

As vessels are modernized, davits like the Welin Crescent Davits are the most frequent choice. This davit (Fig. 12.3) operates like a hinge and can be totally hand powered or powered by hydraulics. The advantages of such davits compared to radial davits lie in their ability to increase the speed of launching while cutting down the size of the crew needed to launch.

As the radial davit is the most difficult to use, it will be discussed in detail. Many of the boat safety procedures and skills mentioned (such as passing a stopper) can also be used in all boat operations involving a great variety of other davits or cranes.

The radial davit provides a rapid and simple method of swinging out small boats such as a motor whaleboat. Prior to swinging the boat out, the boat plug is checked and reported to the man in charge as being in place. If the boat is resting in chocks, it is hoisted clear of the deck, and all preparations are made to swing it out. When it is clear of the deck, the boat is shifted aft so that the bow will clear the forward davit. This davit is rotated and the bow pushed out so as to clear the side. The rear davit is then rotated and the stern pushed over the side. The boat is then ready for lowering.

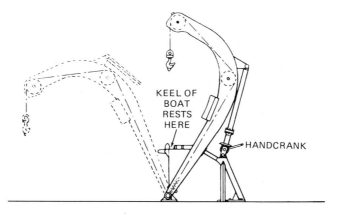

KEEL OF
BOAT
RESTS
HERE

HANDCRANK

Fig. 12.3   Welin Crescent Davit.

Care must be taken in hoisting the boat out of the chocks. To hoist it clear, it is advisable to hoist the stern first so as to avoid any danger of striking the propeller or rudder against the deck. After the stern has been hoisted clear, the commands are "avast heaving" and then "pass the stopper." The hauling part is then stopped off as shown in Fig. 12.4 by means of a rolling hitch, a half hitch, and two or more turns against the lay, and by holding the bitter end of the stopper and the fall firmly together by hand. When the stopper has been passed and secured, the command "walk back" is given, and the strain is gradually released on the hauling part and taken up by the stopper. When all the strain has been transferred to the stopper, the order "up behind" is given. The men on the hauling part move forward with the slack of the fall to the davit where the line is belayed on a cleat or bitts at the command "belay." Figure 12.5 shows the proper manner of doing this. Emphasis is placed upon passing a round turn first and a half hitch last. It is well to mention here that many seamen prefer to pass two round turns first, instead of one, for added protection. This procedure places the weight of the boat on the whole cleat rather than on just one of the horns, which could conceivably shear off. When the after fall is properly belayed, the bow of the boat is raised and secured in like manner.

After the boat has been lifted clear of the chocks, the order "launch aft" is given, and the boat is moved aft far enough to let the bow or stem of the boat clear the forward davit. When it is clear, the order "launch

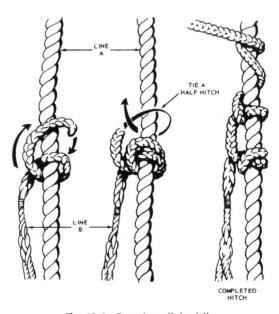

Fig. 12.4 Stopping off the fall.

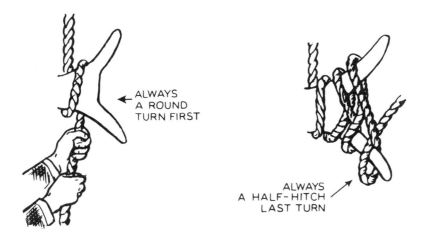

ALWAYS A ROUND TURN FIRST

ALWAYS A HALF-HITCH LAST TURN

Fig. 12.5   Securing the fall to the cleat.

forward and bear out'' is given. Then, as the bow is pushed out, and the boat is pushed forward, the bow passes over the side and between the davits. When it is far enough forward for the stern to clear the after davit, the command ''bear out aft'' is given, and the stern is pushed over the side of the ship. The davits are then placed at right angles to the ship, and the boat is ready for lowering. The davits are fixed in their outboard position by guy lines to the davit heads.

12.2   Lowering and Hoisting Boats by Radial Davit   *Lowering Away* Because the placing of the boat in the water from a ship that is anchored or moored is normally a simple operation, lowering away will be discussed only while under way, as this maneuver is the most dangerous and difficult. The proper use of the rope known as the *sea painter* and the rudder or sweep oar is essential to keep the boat from being thrown against the side of the ship. The use of the sea painter will be described later in this chapter.

In lowering a boat in heavy weather, steadying lines called *frapping lines* (Fig. 12.6) must be used. One end of the frapping lines is secured to something solid on deck. The bight is passed around the falls, and the end is brought back on deck and tended by a turn or two. The purpose in using the frapping lines is to keep the boat from swinging wide as the ship rolls. Another means of accomplishing this purpose is the use of *traveling lizards* (Fig. 12.6). The traveling lizards are kept in hand in the boat, after a turn has been taken around a thwart. Under no circumstances are the lizards to be secured in the boat. It is also possible to use frapping lines and lizards in conjunction.

When ready to lower, the man in charge takes a position between the

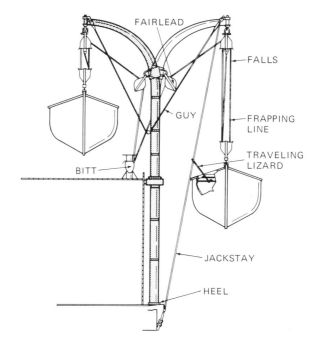

Fig. 12.6 Use of frapping lines and traveling lizard.

davits. When lowering by means of radial davits, only the most experienced men should be used on the cleats when slacking the falls. Care must be taken to prevent the lines from jumping the cleats. At the command "lower away together," the men on the cleats remove all the turns but the round turn (leaving two turns if falls are nylon) and then gradually pay out the falls, hand over hand. The boat should go into the water on an even keel or slightly by the stern. If the sea is rough, the boat should be held clear of the water until a trough appears in which to set it down. If the boat is set down on the crest of a wave, the hoisting gear will be subjected to a heavy strain when the sea drops out from beneath the boat. As soon as the boat is waterborne, the command "up behind" is given. At this order the men on the cleats remove the final turns and slack the lines so that the boat will ride immediately to the sea painter.

The coxswain of the boat must require his crew to wear lifejackets and hardhats and to keep both hands on the *monkey* (safety) *lines* in case the boat should fall. Small boat fenders should be rigged between the boat and the ship. He will have his engineer start the engine during lowering to be sure that it is warmed up. As soon as the boat is waterborne, the man in charge of lowering will order that the *after* falls be cast off, followed by the *forward* falls. The coxswain then sheers off and orders the bow hook to let go the sea painter.

To prevent the lower block from tumbling, a nontumbling block is used, that is, one designed to keep from turning over as it is hoisted back on board and the weight of the boat is no longer on it. However, care must be taken in bringing even this type of block back on board. If the hauling part is pulled, parts of the falls will not pass through the sheaves, and the block will turn over.

Another safety factor is the swivel hook attached to the lower block. This swivel permits the removal of twists in the falls. If an attempt is made to raise the boat without removing the turns, the grind of the turning block may shear the shank off the hook. If not, the friction on parts of the falls will be so great as materially to increase the difficulty of raising the boat.

One thing to be stressed is the necessity of using the lanyard (if fitted) in hooking and releasing so that the hands are kept clear of the block. In addition to the danger of fingers' being caught between the hook and the ring, there is the danger of a hand being mauled between the heavy block and the boat should a swell raise the boat unexpectedly. In hooking on, the lanyard should always be led through the hoisting ring and then used to draw the ring on the hook and to hold the hook close until the boat is clear of the water and the weight of the boat is on the hook. To prevent the hook from accidentally tripping, the lanyard should be bent around the shank of the hook.

Hoisting In   All preparations should be made in advance for receiving a boat that is to be hoisted in. The davits should be swung out over the side at right angles, and the blocks should be lowered near the water from the davits, crane, or boom. The sea painter should be dropped by means of a light line. The most important point is to be sure that the painter is secured to the boat at the proper time.

When the boat is in position, the coxswain should order his men to hook on the blocks, being sure to hook on with the forward block first. When this operation has been accomplished, he reports this fact to the man in charge of the hoisting-in detail. The man in charge must never commence hoisting until the coxswain affirms that the blocks are hooked.

When all is in readiness for hoisting, the man in charge gives the command "set taut." The men on each winch then take the slack out of the falls. Because it is often difficult for the winch men to tell when the slack is out of the falls, the order "heave around together" and then "avast heaving" is given as soon as the slack is out and the falls are taut. The proceedings are then stopped, and the man in charge checks to see that all is in readiness for hoisting, that is, that there are no dips or turns in the falls. When everything is ready, he gives the order "heave around together." If one end of the boat is hoisted faster than the other, the command is given, "avast heaving forward (aft)"; when the boat is again level, the command is "heave around together."

If possible, the boat is stopped at deck level to disembark the personnel. When the boat has been hoisted high enough to clear the rail, the order is given "avast heaving" and then "pass the stopper." When stoppers are passed and secure, the tension on the hauling part of the falls is eased off by the command "walk back together," at which the men on the winches slack the falls by rotating the turns around the gypsy heads. When the stoppers have taken the strain, the command "up behind and belay" is given. On this command, the men at the winches throw off the turns and quickly take the slack to the cleats, where it is belayed. Speed is essential, for at this time the weight of the boat rests entirely on the stoppers. Once the falls have been belayed, the stoppers are removed and the boat swung in.

12.3   Lowering and Hoisting Boats by Crane or Boom   When this method is used, a lee is first made, and it is preferable to have no way on the ship. Steadying lines are secured to the bow and stern of the boat and tended by the boat handling detail on deck. The *safety runner* is also rigged. The boat is then lowered until just clear of the water and at the proper moment dropped quickly into it. As soon as the boat is waterborne, the ring of the slings is run clear of the hook by a pull on the safety runner. Figure 12.7 illustrates the use of this safety runner. When the ship is rolling or pitching, steadying lines should be used on the crane blocks. The boat's engine should be running before the boat takes the water. Round fenders should be hung over the bow and quarter of the boat.

When all preparations have been made for hoisting, including handling the slings from the bight of the safety runner, the boat is worked up under the crane. The bow line, stern line, and steadying lines are passed and the crane block lowered. The slings hang slack in the bight of the runner while the legs are shackled to the hoisting chain bridle of the boat.

When hoisting in a seaway using a crane or boom, there are three principal difficulties to be overcome, as follows:

First, after hooking on and hoisting has commenced, the boat may retouch the water, as the ship rolls, with a violent jerk that might prove destructive to hoisting gear. To avoid such damage, advantage should be taken of a quiet moment. When the ship has begun to roll toward the boat or the boat is on the crest of a wave, the block is quickly lowered, the ring of the slings is run onto the hook by the safety runner, and hoisting is commenced.

Second, the rolling of the ship may cause the boat to swing into the side of the ship as it is being hoisted. This danger is met by the use of

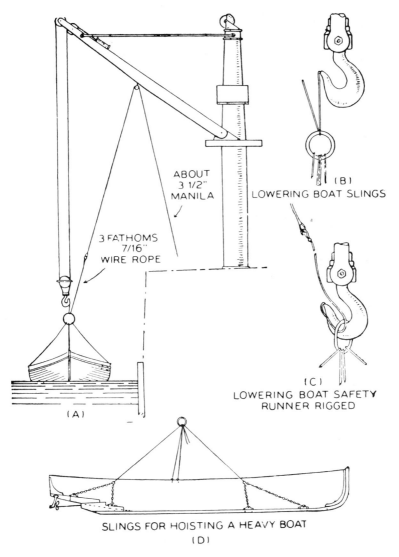

ABOUT
3 1/2"
MANILA

3 FATHOMS
7/16"
WIRE ROPE

(A)

(B)
LOWERING BOAT SLINGS

(C)
LOWERING BOAT SAFETY
RUNNER RIGGED

SLINGS FOR HOISTING A HEAVY BOAT
(D)

Fig. 12.7 Safety runner in use with boat sling.

fenders hung over the side of the boat. By properly tending the steadying lines and taking in and holding the slack as necessary, the swing will be somewhat reduced. The action of the steadying lines is similar to that of frapping lines. Where the boat is making headway through the water or the ship is pitching badly, a long bow line and stern line should be used to help reduce the surge fore and aft as the boat is being hoisted.

Third, after hoisting and swinging in, difficulty is sometimes encountered in plumbing the boat into the chocks. It is advantageous, especially if the boat is to stow close to the side of the ship, to have four steadying lines, two forward and two aft. These lines should lead from opposite sides of the boat at the bow and stern so as to cross each other, thus providing a better lead for steadying the boat into position.

Figure 12.8 shows a lifeboat being hoisted aboard by means of a gravity davit. With this type of davit, the problem of plumbing the boat directly into its chocks is eliminated. Many other problems encountered when using either cranes or booms are also eliminated.

12.4   Use of the Sea Painter   The sea painter is made fast by toggle, for quick release, close to the center of the inboard side of the forward thwart and leads out over the gunwale on the inboard side of the boat. It is rigged so as to facilitate sheering the boat off from the side of the ship when it is necessary to get away. On many occasions, it is necessary to hold the boat alongside the ship in order to embark additional personnel. For this operation, many seamen recommend that a lanyard be attached to a bow shackle or ring at the stem and then passed around the painter and hauled tight to help hold the boat alongside.

12.5   Enclosed Lifeboats and Life Capsules   Many newly built vessels and vessels as they are modernized are being equipped with enclosed lifeboats. Life capsules and enclosed lifeboats are part of the standard equip-

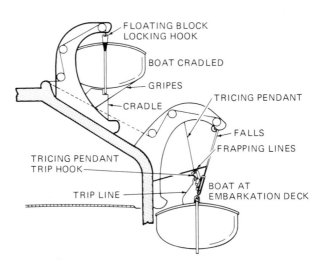

Fig. 12.8   Hoisting life boat aboard using a gravity davit.

ment of oil platforms. These emergency boats have a number of features in common. They are completely enclosed in order to give the crew protection from fire and weather as they leave a burning vessel or rig. To enhance this protection provided by an enclosed vessel, there are spray nozzles provided from an engine-driven pump that spray a protective screen of cooling water over the craft. This cools the fire-retardant fiberglass shell. A compressed air tank supplies air to the survivors and engine if it is found necessary to shut down the ventilators in a fire. This supply is limited to approximately ten minutes and is designed to provide a slight positive pressure to prevent the intrusion of fumes and fire gasses. In case of a capsize, the ventilators, which are provided with automatic shut-offs, will close. For passing through fire, the ventilators can be closed by hand.

Most of these emergency craft are provided with some means of self-righting if they capsize. Because of the high probability of possible capsize, especially during a launch under poor conditions, these craft are provided with safety belts for the survivors. It is important for the person in charge of the craft to insure that the persons under his charge are belted in, for their own safety and the real danger that the vessel will not right if persons who are thrown about in the cabin upset the balance and defeat the self-righting feature. In addition, most of these type of craft are equipped with a steering mechanism, watertight doors and hatches, nonskid deck surfaces, a diesel engine and, are painted International Orange.

Survival capsules have many of the same features as the enclosed lifeboats, and are either round or oval in shape, depending on their capacity. The biggest difference is in the single fall and Rottmer releasing hook in the center. While this makes the capsule easier and faster to launch from oil rigs, the vessel that comes upon one of these capsules must remember never to use the releasing hook if the craft is to be towed. The use of the hook could cause the capsule to capsize. A bow towing bridle is provided for this purpose.

As with the enclosed lifeboat, when getting ready to launch, all survivors should be belted in and all doors, access hatches, and ventilators should be closed. This will aid in insuring that the capsule will right itself. A more recent addition to these craft, added after some problems with righting, is an inflatable air bag at the top which can be activated from the inside of the capsule. This provides extra bouyancy for righting if the capsule capsizes.

12.6 Launching and Recovering an Enclosed Lifeboat from a Ship The enclosed lifeboat is launched in a different manner from the regular gravity-davit-launched boat. A Miranda Gravity Davit, Fig. 12.9, is frequently used. The difference between this davit and older davits is that the boat is launched in a cradle and the entire launching procedure is done from in-

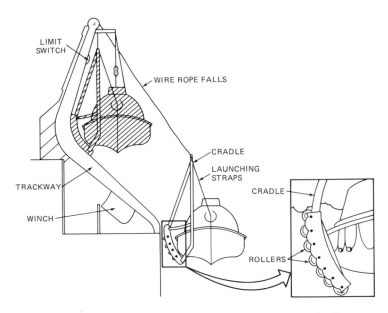

Fig. 12.9 The Miranda Gravity Davit, showing the cradle and rollers.

side the boat. The cradle holds the boat during its descent along inclined trackways and then down the side of the ship. To insure the proper operation of these rollers, they must be inspected and lubricated at regular intervals.

To launch this craft, it must be boarded in a stowed position. The person in charge of the launch then insures that all are seated and properly seat-belted, and all gear is properly stowed. The launch is then started and sustained by maintaining a steady pull on the control wire. When the craft is waterborne, a pin is removed which allows the disengaging lever to open the release hooks. These boats are lifeboats and not designed for launching as ship's boats would be. The engine should be prepared during launch as would be done on any motor-driven lifeboat.

To recover the lifeboat, the cradle must be positioned below water level. The recovery pendants must be taken out of their stowed location and one taken through each end hatch. The link end of the pendant is secured to the lifting hook. The snaphook of the pendants is then secured onto the fall wire above the cradle. When both of the pendants are attached, the boat can be hoisted. It is important not to exceed the hoisting weight restrictions with these davits. Any persons in excess of these restrictions must climb a ladder to board the vessel. The boat is then raised to embarkation level and the personnel remaining aboard disembark. When the boat is at the embarkation level, the hanging-off jib is now dropped from the davits and the hanging-off pendants attached to the lifting plates. The boat's weight is then transferred to the hanging-off pendant by pulling the control wire and, if necessary, using the hand pay-out on the winch. Once the weight is transferred to the hanging-off pendant, the recovery pendant is removed and replaced in its stowage place aboard the lifeboat. Secure the launching pendant to the lifting hooks and replace the gripes on the keel pegs. The boat should now be hoisted into the fully stowed position. Once fully stowed, remove the hanging-off pendants and replace the hanging-off jibs in their stowed position.

12.7   Launching and Recovering an Enclosed Lifeboat From Oil Rig/Platform Davits   The davits installed aboard oil rigs and drilling platforms differ from those installed aboard ships in that the boat remains hanging over the water when fully stowed. If there is a choice when launching, always launch the leeward boat to insure that the boat will drift away from the platform. The danger with launching the windward boat comes if the boat is not able to be moved away from the rig immediately, as it then could drift under the rig and become fouled. It is important that the persons in the boat use a compass when leaving the rig in case of fire, as the visibility, limited in the enclosed boat or capsule at best, is even more limited. It would be wise to mark the best escape course right near the steering station, and leaving the area in the blind must be practiced.

To launch one of these craft, the launch team first releases the gripes, and then all persons embark. Just as in the shipboard enclosed boat, all lowering procedures are done from this point on from the inside of the boat. The person in charge must insure that once all are aboard, all doors, hatches, vents, and rowing ports are closed. Once this is done, all persons must fasten their safety belts. Again, as in all motor boat launches, the engine should be started on the way down. The control wire is pulled and the tension on this wire must be held until the boat is afloat. Once afloat, the control wire is released; the releasing hook lever is thrown and both fore and aft gear releases together are thrown. The boat would then leave the rig on the predetermined course.

To recover a boat, such as after a drill, an operator must be on deck. This person pays out the falls to the boat if needed. The release hooks should be checked before approach to insure they are ready to receive the falls. Safety pins are not installed right away, in case the boat must release if there is a problem with the hook up. The crewmen in both forward and after hatches now hook up the falls. The operator on the rig's deck must check to see whether the brake and the main disconnect switches are on. The switch or button which starts the winch is now pushed and the operator watches the boat as it is hoisted. Once the boat is clear of the water, the safety pins can be inserted in the releasing gear.

The operator must be cautious as the boat reaches the stowed position. The limit switches, which prevent the winch from driving the boat into the stops, have been known to fail. When the limit switch stops the motor, the persons in the boat then disembark. The davit is then hand-cranked to bring the boat into its final stowed position. The boat is properly secured when the davit bumpers are against the boat's deck. To determine whether or not the boat is properly secured, rock the boat back and forth. If the boat rocks, it is not secured. The control wire must be fed through the fitting in the top of the boat. Properly secure this wire in position and then insure that all gear is stowed as required. Taking time now could save valuable seconds later.

12.8 Launching and Recovering a Survival Capsule from Oil Rig/Platform Davits The survival capsules on oil rigs are similar in many respects to the enclosed lifeboats, but there are some important differences. First, there is only one fall wire, so it is very important that the lower seats are filled first and all occupants are evenly distributed about the capsule. As in the other enclosed survival craft, all openings must be secured and all personnel must use the seat belts provided. The capsule is lowered to the water when the person in charge orders the person at the hook to open the center hatch and remove the safety pin. That person then pulls the launch handle and the capsule begins a controlled descent. The engine should be started either prior to or simultaneous with this step. When the capsule is in the water, the fall is unhooked by releasing the wire from the lever inside the boat. As in the previous enclosed lifeboat launch, the course away from the rig should be marked near the steering station and the craft steered immediately away from the rig. If needed, the safety systems may be activated to protect the capsule.

To recover the capsule, the hook and its safety pin must be reset. The person at the winch then lowers the falls to the proper height for pickup. The instructions posted at the winch will give the proper procedures to reset the launch mechanism. When the capsule is positioned under the fall, the person assigned to pick up the hook will be in the center hatchway and will pick up the lifting ring and shove the ring into the hook. The winch operator then commences to raise the capsule when the hook-up is made. The capsule must be stopped about six feet from the boarding deck. The crew must now turn the capsule to insure it is properly positioned before it is secured. When the capsule is properly positioned, it is raised until stopped by the limit switch apparatus. This should occur just before it reaches the final stowed position. If the capsule's steel flange bearing plates are lined up with the main beams of the platform, the operator will then hand-crank the capsule to its final position. The crew then leaves the capsule, and the person-in-charge must insure that the safety pin is re-inserted in the launch release handle and that the capsule is in all respects ready for use.

12.9 Life Raft Davits While inflatable rafts were briefly mentioned in another chapter, there are a number of vessels with very large inflatable rafts which must be launched on davits. These rafts are built much sturdier than the rafts normally found aboard ship. These are so strong that they can hold their full load while being lowered into the water. The instructions here are general and, as with any safety system, you must check out the specific instructions for the installation aboard your ship. The inflation and preparation instructions for the particular raft are followed before the davit is attached. In order to launch one of these rafts, it must be positioned where the davit can be attached. To prepare the davit, locate the crank handle for the falls, which, if stowed, must be installed. After the falls are attached, rotate the crank handle until the falls reach the stop. If necessary, the handle is now stowed. The raft should be positioned over the side of the ship in the boarding position and personnel now board the raft. The total weight should not exceed the limit stenciled on the raft. The personnel in the raft should be positioned so as to evenly distribute the weight. The person in charge now kneels at the opening, lifting the flap which covers the release handle, and pulls the handle to release the raft from the platform. The handle is then pulled a second time to release the brake and when the handle is let go, the raft will then begin to move down. When you are close to or afloat on the water's surface, pull the lanyard attached to the releasing gear to cock the hook for automatic opening. If the hook fails to open automatically when the raft is afloat, then give the lanyard a firm pull to release the raft.

To reset the davit to launch additional rafts, press down and hold the brake weight, painted orange, and move the lever to the ''on'' position. Use the quick return wheel, on the upper part of the davit, to raise the falls until the yellow mark on the fall is in line with the yellow line on the davit. Pull the hook in with the retrieval line and attach the hook to the next raft container. You would then start over again with the procedure outlined above.

12.10 Handling a Powerboat A Navy powerboat crew usually consists of a *coxswain*, a *boat engineer*, a *bow hook*, and a *stern hook*. The coxswain is in command of the boat, subject to the supervision of any regularly assigned boat officer or the senior line officer present in the boat. The engineer operates and cares for the engine. The bow hook handles forward lines and falls when making fast or letting go, casts off the sea painter, and acts as forward lookout when under way. The stern hook handles the stern lines and falls and keeps an eye out aft when under way.

Boats in the Merchant Marine are in charge of an Able Bodied Seaman or lifeboatman and as large a crew as the type of boat requires. Since lifeboat falls on merchant boats are lever released, there is no need for a bow hook or stern hook. In the following paragraphs, the term coxswain refers to the person actually handling the boat.

Steering a powerboat is much the same as handling a single-screw ship, although the reactions of the boat to the engines and rudder are more pronounced. When under way in choppy seas, speed should be reduced somewhat, not only to avoid shipping seas, but also to reduce the strain on the hull and on the machinery caused by the racing of the screw when the stern rides clear of the water. Boats may be swamped if they are run too fast against the seas. When heading into the sea, it is possible to make fair speed by careful nursing, that is, by watching the seas and slowing, or even stopping for a moment, as heavier seas bear down upon the boat. As with ships, the boat may sometimes be made to ride much more easily if, instead of plunging head-in into the sea or running directly before it, a course is made with it on the bow or quarter. If running more or less across the sea, it is well to head up momentarily to meet heavy waves.

A large motor launch or landing craft has a high bow, and turning against the wind and sea is difficult. A large turning circle therefore may be expected and should be allowed for in confined waters. Attention must be paid to weight distribution, especially in a head sea. Too much weight forward may cause the bow of the boat to plunge into the waves and possibly swamp; too much aft will cause the boat to fall off. When the boat is running before a heavy sea, weights aft will reduce yawing, but too much weight aft will cause the bow to ride too high.

Wind and current should be observed and allowed for when leaving the ship or landing; in reduced visibility, so should the compass course and time to destination, in order that the proper course may be steered. In approaching any object in the water that might be damaged or injured by contact, such as a seaplane or target drone, always maneuver for a position such that, when the boat is stopped, it will be separated from the object. A coxswain should be careful to slow in passing small open craft, men working on floats, or divers and swimmers so as not to give them his wash. Neglecting to do so can often prove dangerous to others who are near or in the water. Never pass a pier head or a bow or stern of an anchored ship too closely.

12.11 Making a Landing In making a landing, whether at a pier or a ship's accommodation ladder, it is a common mistake to keep too much way on the boat (conditions of load and trim materially affect momentum). The landing should be approached at such an angle and at such a speed that, should the engine fail to back, control of the boat can be still maintained; it can be sheered away by rudder action alone without damage. The engines may, and often do, fail to respond promptly. In a right-handed screw, the backing throws the stern off to port—a fact that should be taken into consideration when determining the angle of approach. In coming alongside a ship's accommodation ladder in a current or heavy sea, care must be taken not to catch the current or sea on the outboard bow, as doing so will sweep the bow in forward, and perhaps underneath, the lower platform of the accommodation ladder. Under these circumstances the boat may be swamped or damaged (Fig. 12.10a). The landing should be made with the aid of a boat line from forward, the boat being kept off a little from the side until the line is fast and then eased in by the rudder.

A powerboat coming alongside in a rough sea or in a strong current should always be required to take a boat line. Crews of powerboats frequently make their landings at an accommodation ladder with the aid of

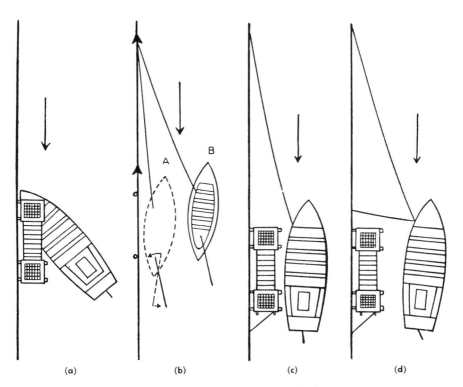

Fig. 12.10 Action of sea painter in landings.

boat hooks alone, taking hold of anything that is within reach and holding on, often with great difficulty and with the ever-present danger of a man falling over-board between the ship and the boat.

A boat lying at the accommodation ladder in a current and secured by a boat line made fast to a cleat on the inboard bow of the boat can be controlled by a touch of the rudder, which sheers the stern out or in and thus catches the current on one bow or the other (Fig. 12.10b). If a ship is rolling in an open roadstead or riding with the wind ahead and swells surging aft alongside her, the boat will rise and fall dangerously at the lower platform and any contact between the two many damage or capsize the boat. The need of a long boat line—in effect, a sea painter—is here emphasized. By using a boat line in combination with the breast line and by judicious use of rudder and engines, the boat may lie alongside the accommodation ladder without coming into contact with it (Figs. 12.10c and d). Fenders should always be carried and used freely. See Fig. 12.11 for a rigged accommodation ladder.

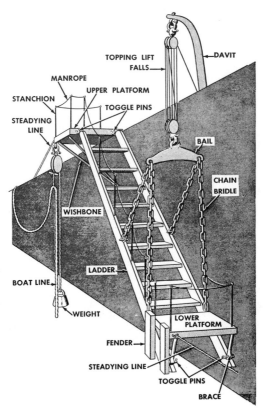

Fig. 12.11 Accommodation ladder.

12.12 Embarking and Disembarking It is sometimes impossible, because of heavy seas, to make a landing at the accommodation ladder. In this case, the passengers may come in over the boat boom. The rudder of the ship is put over to one side or the other, preferably to the side opposite that of the anchor. The ship will yaw back and forth but will usually yaw more on the side away from the rudder, thus creating a partial lee under her quarter. During each weather yaw of the ship, the boat pulls under the quarter by means of a long bow line previously rigged, and boat passengers can climb up cargo nets hung for this purpose from the boat boom or from the ship's side. As the ship yaws back, the boat drops back on the painter and awaits the next lee.

Another method of embarking is by means of a cargo net rigged under a crane or boom. As the boat comes under the crane or boom, the net is lowered and seized by the passenger, who is then swung aboard. When the ship is so equipped, the airplane whip of a crane should be used because of its fast hoisting speed. This method is applicable when under way in a heavy sea, but only as a last resort because timing must be precise and the disembarking passenger is in constant peril.

The cargo net is also used for the embarkation of a large number of persons or troops at sea from the ship to a number of boats or landing craft. Cargo nets of sufficient length are hung over the side to reach into the boats. Each boat comes alongside and is held there while the foot of the cargo net is hauled into it and kept there until the men who are hanging on the net drop into the boat.

Personnel may be transferred from the boat to the ship in like manner, but care must be taken in a heavy sea that the foot of the cargo net is taken into the boat to prevent personnel from falling between the boat and the ship and being crushed.

In the event of an emergency, such as having to recover a number of people struggling in the water, cargo nets hung over the side of the ship may expedite the operation.

12.13 Securing Boats Boats are usually secured to boat booms (Fig. 12.12), their bows to guesswarps and their sterns to a boat securing line that leads from the end of the boom well aft to the ship's side to help hold them apart and keep them parallel to the ship. Sufficient slack should be allowed for roll and pitch when securing.

In a heavy sea or storm, the boat boom may become unstable because of the roll and pitch of the ship, making it impractical to secure boats to it. In this situation, the boats may be secured in tandem from astern or hoisted aboard for the duration of the blow. In either event, fenders should always be used and precautions taken against lines chafing.

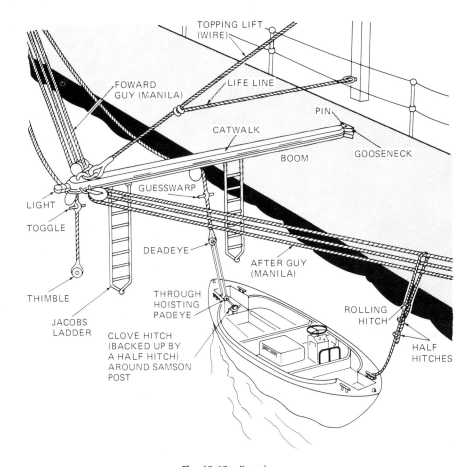

Fig. 12.12   Boat boom.

12.14   Handling a Boat under Oars   Boats that are fully oar-propelled are not as common today as they once were, but handling a boat under oars is still required for certification as a lifeboatman in the Merchant Marine. Many lifeboats found aboard merchant vessels, however, are equipped with hand-propelling gear (Fig. 12.13) instead of oars.

The latter type of propulsion involves a propeller, stern tube, stern gland, and gears but instead of using an engine, power is furnished by pushing and pulling lever handles fore and aft. The bottom ends of the lever handles fit into sockets connected to a bar on each side of the boat. These two bars move cranks on the sides of the gear box near the boat's stern. Gear boxes on hand-propelled boats must be kept free of water. In cold weather, this water can freeze and make it impossible for the gears to rotate

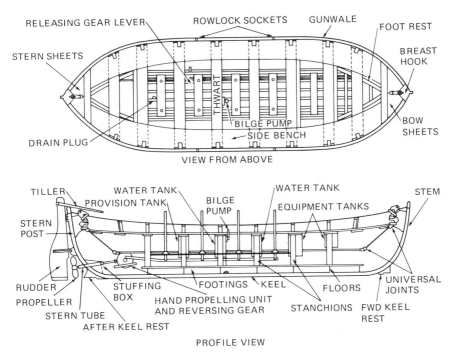

Fig. 12.13 Hand-propelled lifeboat.

and propel the boat. The bars, cranks, and levers for hand-propelled boats must be kept clear when stowing gear, or the boat may be without a means of propulsion at a critical moment. The boat equipped with hand-propelling gear handles similarly to a power-driven boat.

On the other hand, a boat under oars, if properly handled by an experienced crew, possesses much the same maneuverability as a powerboat and, in the case of the whaleboat, considerably more seaworthiness. The standard commands shown in Table 12.1 should be used when handling a boat under oars.

Large boats propelled by oars, such as the whaleboat, are normally steered by a *sweep oar*. A sweep oar is somewhat larger than an oar used to propel the boat. The coxswain using this oar can steer the boat with a great deal more maneuverability than the standard tiller offers, depending on how much leverage is used or how deep the oar is set.

Boats under oars may also be steered by the use of a tiller (rudder); however, except for use in extremely heavy seas or during long periods of time, a tiller possesses no advantages over a sweep oar, nor is it as efficient.

Table 12.1   Commands for Handling a Boat under Oars

Command	Meaning
Stand by the oars	Lift oars off the thwarts, place blades flat on the forward gunwales, push oars forward until handle is over respective thwart.
Up oars	Lift oars to vertical position. Trim blades fore and aft with handle resting on footings.
Shove off the bow	Bowman lets go boat rope or sea painter or hauls in boat painter. Shoves off bow using boat hook.
Let fall	Let oars fall into rowlocks using crook of outboard arm to control the oars. Trim oars horizontally with blades trimmed fore and aft. Bowmen up oars before command of "let fall" or put out oars as soon thereafter as possible.
Give way	Move blades of oars forward and dip about half way into the water and start stroke. At end of stroke, blades are feathered fore and aft and pushed forward and another stroke is made.
Oars	Complete the stroke and level the oars horizontally with the blades trimmed fore and aft.
Back water	Row backwards.
Hold water	Complete the stroke, stop rowing, dip blade about half way into water, and hold water to stop the way on the boat.
Stern all	When rowing in ahead motion, complete the stroke, then commence to back-water, gradually increasing the depth of immersion of the blades.
Way enough	When rowing in ahead motion, complete the stroke, raise oars with crook of elbow to about 30 degrees, swing blades forward, and place oars in the boat.
Toss oars	Complete the stroke, come to "oars," raise the oars smartly to the vertical, rest handles on the footings, and trim blades fore and aft.
In bows	The bowmen complete the stroke, swing their oars forward, and boat the oars, then stand by with boat hooks or to receive the sea painter or boat rope.
Boat the oars	From "oars" or from "toss oars," place the oars in the boat with blades forward.
Out oars	Place oars in rowlocks directly from the boated position or from "stand by oars" position.
Stand by to give way	Term used in racing. The blades are pushed to forward position and slightly dipped ready for an instant start.
Give way port, back-water starboard (or vice versa)	The orders are followed to turn the boat without making way ahead or astern.
Give way port, hold water starboard (or vice versa)	This command will result in turning the boat with slight headway.
Trail oars	At this command, the blades of the oars are brought alongside the boat and left trailing in the water, in single-banked boats fitted with swivel rowlocks.

12.15 Handling a Boat under Sail It is beyond the scope of this book to describe the handling of the numerous yachts, pleasure craft, and small commercial vessels that use sail as motive power. Ship's boats are workboats; they are not designed to sail and none carry sails, except incidentally. Stowage considerations forbid the use of false keels and special ballast. Because of this, ship's boats must depend upon their beam for stability and always have a tendency to make leeway unless fitted with a centerboard. The treatment of handling a boat under sail in this volume is at best rudimentary. It is included here so that if an emergency arises where the handling of a ship's boat under sail is required, you will have some familiarity with the terms and skills. The sections which follow are not meant to be in-depth coverage on the handling of a boat under sail, but enough to get you started. For a thorough knowledge of sail seamanship, practice is required and also study of the forces involved in sailing as outlined by any text on the subject.

The direction of the wind is that from which it blows. *To windward* is into the wind; *to leeward* is down the wind. A *lee shore* is the shore to leeward. The *weather side* is that side exposed to the wind; the *lee side* is the opposite side. Naturally a boat heels away from the wind, so that the lee side is *down* and the weather side *up*. When the rudder is amidships, the tiller or helm is also. (While the terms "helm" and "tiller" have been officially banned in connection with modern ships, they are still applicable to sailboats and will be used here in accordance with original practice.) The coxswain may put his tiller up to windward and have *weather helm;* if he puts it down, he has *lee helm*. When a boat turns her head into the wind, as if she were going to tack, she is said to *luff*. The opposite of this is *wearing away*.

When sailing with the wind on one side, a puff of wind may strike the sail, causing the boat to heel and possibly capsize. To prevent this, the coxswain may luff by putting his helm down until she turns into the wind; the sails then cease to *draw* and the boat comes back to an upright position.

It may be necessary in a heavy squall to let the sheets go; therefore, in a small boat, *never belay the sheets*. A *sheet* is a line that controls the foot of a sail (Fig. 12.14).

When a sheet is hauled in and the boom or foot of the sail is nearly fore and aft, the sheets are said to be *hauled aft*. In *setting the jib aback* or *backing the foresail*, the weather sheets are *flattened aft*. This maneuver may be required to give more turning effect in tacking and is also performed in *heaving to*. When sails are brought more nearly parallel to the centerline of the boat, they are *trimmed in;* the opposite is *easing off* or *starting the sheets*.

A boat cannot sail directly into the *eye of the wind,* but depending on the boat and rig, sails at an angle of from four to six points off it. She must

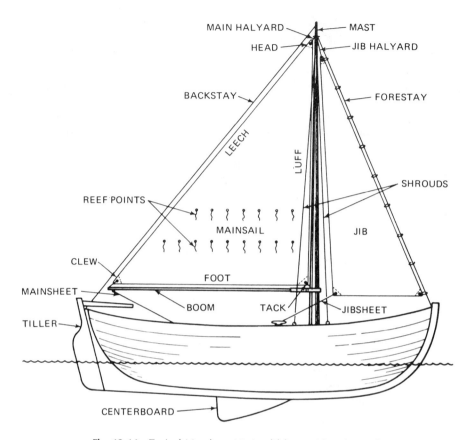

Fig. 12.14 Typical Merchant Marine lifeboat with sail rigged.

thus make a zigzag course upwind on legs of direction called *tacks*. This process is called *beating to windward*. She is said to be sailing *close-hauled* or *on the wind* on each of these tacks.

A sailboat is said to be on the *starboard tack* when the wind is coming over the starboard side, and on the *port tack* when the wind is coming over the port side. When a boat is not sailing as close to the wind as possible with advantage, she is said to be *sailing free*. When the true wind is within two points on either quarter, she is said to be *running before* the wind. If, when sailing free, the wind is still forward of the beam, she is said to be on a *close reach;* if the wind is from abaft the beam, she is said to be on a *broad reach*. The *apparent wind* is the wind striking the sails that is generated by a combination of the boat's speed through the water and the *true wind*. Figure 12.15 illustrates these terms.

Tacking is bringing the boat on the opposite tack, head through the

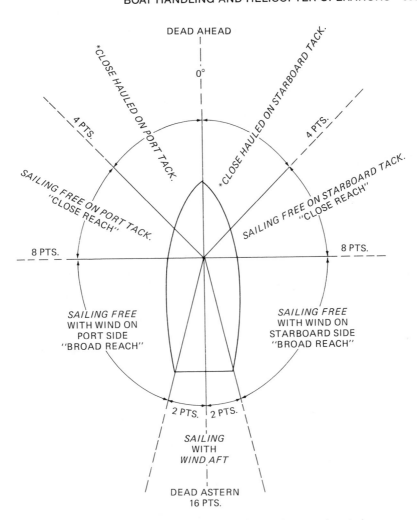

Fig. 12.15   Sailing terms for various positions relative to the wind.

wind. *Wearing* consists in turning the boat from one tack to the other tack, stern through the wind. During this procedure, as the wind comes aft and the sails are trimmed flat, the boom is carefully allowed to swing to the opposite side. The boom is then said to have been *jibbed over*. Should the boat be sailing free and alter her course so as to bring the wind on the opposite side, thereby carrying the stern through the wind, she has been *jibed*, as in *jibing around a buoy*.

To do her best under sail, a boat must be *trimmed* in accordance with her build and rig. To effect this condition, the trim of the boat and sails must be altered, as necessary, to meet the varying conditions of sailing.

In sailing on the wind, a properly designed and trimmed boat should carry a slight weather helm; that is, she should have a slight tendency to come into the wind. If too much weight is carried forward, the boat trims by the head and the stern rises, offering less lateral resistance *aft* to the water. A deeper bow, on the other hand, offers greater lateral resistance to the water and, in addition, increased pressure from the bow wave. These forces form a couple that tends to cause the boat to luff; to counteract it, an excessive weather helm is necessary. Too much weight aft causes a corresponding tendency to fall off.

If the sails are too flat forward, lee helm is necessary to counteract the tendency to fall off; if too flat aft, weather helm is necessary.

In addition, as the boat heels, the forward component of the force of the wind on the sail acting on the center of effort is displaced to leeward of the keel line, thereby producing a leverage that tends to make the boat luff. This tendency is especially noticeable in a tall sloop rig, which endeavors to *work out from under* when struck by a sudden gust as she is making headway close-hauled.

When running before the wind, weights should be carried aft to decrease yawing, but doing so may decrease the speed if overdone.

After the boat has been under way for some time, the sail or halyards may stretch, or, in wet weather, may shrink. This situation calls for appropriate setting up or slacking off on the halyards to correct the set of the sail.

12.16 Close-hauled—on the Wind On the wind, a boat should carry a little weather helm. The sails should be kept well full, sheets not too flat, but everything drawing and the boat alive. It is a common mistake to get the sheets so flat that the boat, while pointing high, actually makes a course to leeward of that which she would make if kept away a little with sheets eased accordingly; and it is of course clear that, if kept away, her speed will be greater than when jammed up into the wind in the hope of stealing a fraction of a point. A boat of good draft with a deep keel and centerboard, and yachts designed for racing, with fin-keels 10 feet below their normal water line, will lie amazingly close to the wind with little leeway. Ship's boats, however, are not constructed on yachting lines and cannot be held up in the same way. The shape of the sail when close-hauled is very important; the leech should be almost flat, and some boats, to accomplish this, have battens which fit in pockets in the leech of the sail. A little curve or belly should be allowed in the luff. The cut of the sails, the way they are laced to the yards and booms, and the tautness of the halyards all affect the shape of the sails when drawing.

The sails being properly set, the luff of the sails is kept just short of trembling, with weather helm enough to let the helmsman "feel" that she wants to come into the wind. As the wind will vary more or less (in apparent, if not real, direction), it is necessary to be watchful and bring her up or keep her away from time to time in order that she may always be at her best. The sails should be kept fuller in rough than smooth water, as it is more important that the boat be kept *going* so as to be always under command of the rudder. If a heavy breaking sea is seen bearing down upon her, she should be luffed to meet it and kept away again as soon as it has passed. If she loses way she becomes helpless at once. It is dangerous to be caught by a heavy sea on the beam; and, if the course to be made in rough water would bring the boat into the trough, it is the best plan to run off for a time with the sea on the quarter, then bring her up with it on the bow, and so make good the course desired without actually steering it at any time.

For a moderate squall, the boat should be luffed sufficiently to shake the sails without spilling them, thus keeping enough headway to retain control. If the wind becomes stronger, she must be luffed more decidedly and the sheets eased off. The sheets may, of course, be let go, and in an emergency this must be done at once, in addition to putting down the helm. For this reason it is a universal rule in boat sailing that the sheets should never be belayed or left untended in any weather.

12.17   Sailing Free   A boat sails her fastest on this point of sailing. The tendency to luff is strong, especially if the wind is fresh and the boat or sails are improperly trimmed. In a squall the situation is quite different from that in sailing close-hauled. Here the wind cannot be spilled by a touch of the tiller and the only prudent thing to do is to slack the sheets while luffing. In this procedure care must be taken not to jam the helm down hard for it causes the boat to heel dangerously to leeward, and as it turns into the wind the lee quarter and rail may go under, the end of the boom trip in the water, and the boat capsize.

The same thing may happen in jibing if the boat is allowed to fill away too quickly on the new tack. The force of the wind would be much reduced by running off, but the trouble with this is that, if it comes too strong, there is no recourse but to lower the sail, and the chances are that it will bind against the shrouds and refuse to come down. Moreover, there is always danger that the wind will shift in the squall, and the mainsail may jibe with dangerous force.

The gaff-headed rig has the advantage over the tall triangular rig on this point of sailing, but the gaff-headed mainsail must be tended more carefully, as the efficient angle to the apparent wind exists within narrower limits than that of the jib-headed rig. In general, in sailing free the gaff-headed rig must be trimmed closer than a jib-headed rig in order to maintain its most efficient angle. This requires close watching of the apparent wind at all times. Underwater resistance may be somewhat reduced by partially raising the centerboard, if the boat be so equipped.

The tall jib-headed rig gains power as the wind hauls forward and the low gaff-headed rig gains power as the wind draws aft.

12.18   Running before the Wind   In a fresh breeze, this is the most dangerous point of sailing, because of the chance of an unintentional jibe. The danger increases if the boat yaws. From this follows the rule to keep the weight fairly well aft, though never at the extreme after end when running before the wind. Very careful steering is required; and, if the sea is heavy, the boom may jibe in spite of all the care that can be taken unless lashed to the lee rail or shroud by a "lazy guy."

Squalls are not as dangerous before the wind as when close-hauled or reaching, unless they are accompanied by a shift of wind. To reduce sail quickly in a gaff-headed boat, to meet this emergency, the peak of the mainsail may be dropped.

In running before the wind, the foresail is sometimes set on the side opposite the mainsail, a temporary boom being rigged by using a boat hook or an oar. A boat sailing in this way is sailing "wing and wing."

If the sea is rough, it is well to avoid running with the wind dead aft. To make a course directly to leeward, the wind may be brought first on one quarter and then on the other, the mainsail being clewed up or the peak dropped each time the course is changed, if the breeze is strong enough to make jibing dangerous.

A serious danger in running before a heavy sea is that of "broaching to." The boat will yaw considerably, the rudder will often be out of water, and the sails will be becalmed in the trough of the sea. The situation here is much like that of a boat running in a surf; and, as in that case, the yawing will be reduced by keeping the weights aft and by steering with an oar. The jib should always be set with the sheet flat aft. It helps to meet and pay her off if she flies to, against the helm. A drag towed over the stern is also helpful.

Another danger in running is that the boom may dip as she rolls and thus capsize the boat.

12.19   Tacking   In tacking, the same principles apply to a boat as to a ship. An after sail tends to bring her head into the wind and a headsail to keep her off; but all sails, so long as they draw, give her headway and so add to the steering power of the rudder.

It is clear that a short full boat will turn to windward better than a long narrow one and will require a much shorter distance for coming around.

Thus a short boat is preferable to a long one for working up a narrow channel.

When about to tack, the coxswain should let her fall off a little to fill the sails and gain good headway, and he should watch for smooth water and avoid luffing into a breaking wave. The rudder should not be suddenly put hard over, but should be put over enough to have a good effect at first and then more and more as the boat swings; by the time the boat is swinging rapidly the rudder should be over about 30 or 35 degrees and held there.

Under ideal conditions, a boat, close-hauled but with good way on, shoots into the wind as the tiller is eased down, making a good reach to windward and filling away on the new tack, without a moment losing headway. The main boom is hauled amidships in a two-masted boat and nearly amidships in a single-masted boat, and as the jib and the foresail lift, their sheets are let go. The boat comes head to wind and as she pays off on the new tack the sheets are hauled aft and she is steadied on her course. Under less favorable conditions, such as a heavy head sea or a very light breeze, tacking is not so simple.

If the boat gets in "irons," the jib sheet must be held out on the old lee bow to pay her head around. Care must be taken not to make a "back sail" of the mainsail. If she gathers sternway, the rudder is shifted, and if necessary, an oar is gotten out to help her around. The statement is sometimes made that it is lubberly to use an oar in a boat under sail. The lubberly part is the getting into a position where an oar is needed.

Carrying the weights forward is favorable for tacking, but when a boat has sternway she may be helped around by putting a few of the crew on the (new) lee quarter, where, by increasing the immersion of the full lines of the counter, they may add to the resistance and cause the bow to fall off.

Attention may again be called to the fact that in squally weather a boat is in a dangerous position whenever she is without headway, because she can be neither luffed nor kept away in the event of being struck by a heavy gust. If, through ignorance or carelessness, the sheets are belayed at such a time, the danger is greatly increased.

12.20 Wearing In beating to windward, boats ordinarily go about by tacking, because in tacking they turn into the wind and gain ground to windward. In wearing around they turn away from the wind, losing more or less distance to leeward according to circumstances; still it is often possible to wear in winds so strong or water so rough that tacking ship's boats is impossible. It is often necessary to resort to wearing when maneuvering in close quarters, such as clearing a dock or avoiding a collision.

In wearing, the helm is put up and the mainsheet eased off in order to help in bearing away and to get the maximum effect of the mainsail in increasing headway. When the wind comes nearly aft the sheets are rounded in smartly in such a manner that both the sail and the stern pass through the wind at the same time. As the sails jibe over, the sheets are eased off slowly and gradually. Care should be taken at this point, especially with a sloop rig, that the boat not be allowed to come up on the new tack too quickly, as this may bring about a dangerous heel to leeward.

The details of the maneuver may vary considerably, according to the conditions of wind and sea and peculiarities of the boat as to rig and trim. In boats of more than one mast, it is best to sail dead before the wind, trim in the sails, jibe them, and ease them out on the new tack in the order of jib, foresail, and mainsail.

In a fresh breeze, as jibing is dangerous, the mainsail should be doused, brailed up or the peak dropped before the wind comes aft, and set again in time to bring her to the wind on the new tack.

12.21 Remarks on Jibing A sail is "jibed" when it is allowed to swing from one side to the other, the wind being aft or nearly so, and the sail full first on one side and then on the other. This may be done intentionally, as in wearing or in simply changing course, or it may come unexpectedly from a shift of wind or from the yawing of the boat. As it necessarily involves a violent swing of the sail, it puts a heavy strain upon the spars and rigging; it endangers everyone in its path and causes the boat to lurch more or less steeply to leeward. At this point the boat shows a strong tendency to luff on the new tack, and if not met with the rudder the boat may be knocked down and capsized.

It is important in jibing that the sails be trimmed flat before the stern of the boat is brought into the wind, and after the boom has jibed over, the sheets should be started slowly and gradually. The trimming of the sheets should be so timed with the swinging boat that the helmsman does not have to check his swing and wait for the sails to be trimmed in, nor should the boat be allowed to run with the sheets flat aft. In either case the boat loses speed, and loss of speed is loss of control.

12.22 Reefing When an open boat begins to ship spray and water over the lee rail, it is time to reef. A boat that is decked over may run with her lee rail awash; but when an open boat heels her gunwale close to the surface of the water, it must be remembered that a fresher puff may bear the gunwale lower without warning, and that the moment it dips, the boat will almost certainly fill and capsize.

The details of reefing will depend upon the rig, but a few general rules may be laid down. The crew should be stationed before beginning, and should all be required to remain seated. The boat is then luffed, but not to the point where steerageway and control are lost. One hand lowers the halyards of each sail as much as necessary, another hauls down on the luff and shifts the tack. The sheet is hauled in a little to let the men get hold of and gather the foot. The clew earing, followed by the points, are then passed, and the halyards manned. The sail is then hoisted and the sheets trimmed as the boat fills away on her course.

If the boat has more than one sail, it is a good plan to reef them one at a time.

12.23 The Motor Lifeboat Prudent seamanship requires that a boat always be kept ready for immediate use as a lifeboat. Aboard all men-of-war and many passenger liners, a boat of the motor whaleboat type is used as the ready lifeboat.

Men-of-war so equipped have two of their boats rigged as ready lifeboats, one on either side to expedite lowering. Smaller men-of-war and most auxiliaries have only one boat rigged as a lifeboat. Passenger liners like large men-of-war have two small boats rigged, normally situated on either side forward of the boat deck. The sea painter is kept rigged, and lowering the boat becomes only a matter of releasing the gripes. Most Navy lifeboats are rigged for lowering by radial davits, as shown in Fig. 12.16, whereas most merchant ships use gravity davits. It must be pointed out that boats of the Merchant Marine are in themselves lifeboats and, as such, are rigged for immediate use. Thus, with but few exceptions, all boats aboard merchant ships may be used as ready lifeboats with no special preparations.

Since the gravity davit does not require that the boat be swung out to facilitate speed in launching, only the use of the radial davit will be discussed in any detail. As a general rule, the davits are swung outboard, and

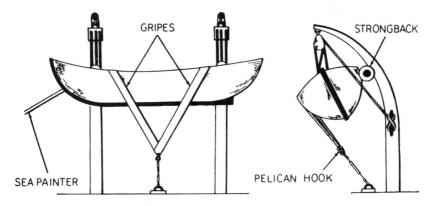

Fig. 12.16 Ready lifeboat.

the boat is griped against a spar, called a *strongback* or *pudding spar,* spanned between the davit arms. The boat is griped up against two puddings (fenders) built up around the spar. The V-shaped gripes (made of line or wire covered with canvas to prevent chafing) have their upper ends shackled to eyes in the strongback or pudding spar or to each davit head. The lower end of the V is attached to the deck by means of a turnbuckle equipped with a pelican hook. The turnbuckle is used to take up any slack and keep the boat snug against the puddings. A pelican hook is used for quick release.

In order to keep the weight of the boat from resting upon the falls, wire pendants (preventers) are run from the davit heads to the hoisting eyes of the boat. These pendants are also equipped with pelican hooks to facilitate quick release. Aboard auxiliaries and merchant ships, the lifeboat usually rests upon chocks directly beneath the davit. To secure this boat in its chocks for sea, clamps equipped with a turnbuckle are used. The lower end is secured to the deck, and the clamp is fitted over the gunwale. Several quick turns of the turnbuckle constitute all that is required to release the clamp and make the boat ready for instantaneous lowering.

12.24   Handling Boats under Severe Conditions   The proper handling of boats under severe weather conditions is an art in itself, calling for judgment and skill that can only be acquired by practical experience. Some seamen have every opportunity to gain this knowledge through experience and are able to handle boats under the most severe conditions. The sea can be, and often is, unforgiving, however, and even experienced seamen are lost each year because they took chances. No boat should confront severe weather or sea conditions unless it is necessary.

The coxswain of a boat is responsible for the lives of those aboard, and it is therefore he who must ensure that the boat is seaworthy and operated in a safe manner. Safe operation is what places the most burden on the coxswain because that feat requires knowledge, skill, practice, and judgment.

To understand the factors that effect the boat is essential. Waves make up the major pressure on the hull, although wind also contributes if a vessel has high freeboard. Waves are caused by wind pressure on the water, and these wind-raised waves depend on several factors. The size and height of a wave depend on the wind speed, the distance over which the wind has blown (known as *fetch*), and the length of time the wind has been blowing. When the waves pass out of a storm area, they advance as *swells*. Swells are not regular and are lower in height and longer in length then the waves that produced them. During heavy weather, the many different wave systems give the watersurface a complex and irregular pattern. These wave systems cross each other at angles, producing mountainous seas.

If you are running into a sea, the bow of the boat will be driven into the waves with increasing force, instead of being lifted as is normal. This action causes the boat to take a tremendous pounding. The propeller is alternately submerged and then out of the water, with the result that the engine is loaded one moment and racing wildly the next. Consequently, the boat comes under extreme stress, and steps must be taken to reduce it. The easiest way to do so is to slow down. This will cause the bow to lift with the waves, as the natural force of buoyance is again allowed to function. The seas should be taken slightly off the bow, preferably at an angle approaching 45 degrees. Doing so will cause the boat to roll and pitch, but the combination is far easier on the boat than the violent motions of pitching alone.

If unable to make headway under these conditions, it is advisable to lay to. Most power-driven vessels left alone turn their stern into the wind. Since this is a highly dangerous position, enough power should be used to keep the bow up into the wind, adjusting the speed so that the boat makes neither headway nor sternway.

The use of a sea anchor (described in Chapter 9) would be advisable here, but only if the coxswain knows what he is doing. An improperly used sea anchor could worsen the situation. In all cases, the center of gravity must be held as low as possible by keeping all occupants down, on or near the bottom of the boat. Doing so will make the boat more stable and reduce the chance of capsizing.

Running in a *beam sea,* or *in the trough,* is acceptable only under conditions of comparative calm. In a beam sea, the waves are acting directly on the vessel's sides and, in rough enough water, could roll it over. If the required course puts you in the trough and the action of the boat becomes excessive, it is best to change course so that the seas are off the bow or quarter. In order to make the desired course, it will be necessary to run a zig-zag course, taking the seas off the bow for awhile and then off the quarter.

A boat is said to be *running before the sea* when she sails in the same direction that the seas are running. Close attention to the rudder is required, as the turning action of the hull is difficult to control. The force of the water acting on the stern can cause the boat to yaw wildly from side to side. On powerboats, the rudder and propeller can be lifted clear of the water if the stern is picked up by an approaching wave. If the boat is yawing at the time the stern is lifted clear of the water, the boat will go completely out of control and could be thrown broadside into the trough and rolled over by the next wave. This phenomenon is known as *broaching* and must be avoided at almost any cost.

The secret of avoiding a broach is to keep yawing under control *at all times.* Sideways motion can be kept to a minimum only when the rudder is in the water. This is precisely why the use of a steering oar is preferable to a rudder in heavy seas. In a power-driven vessel, the rudder can be kept in the water by slowing down as the wave approaches the stern and allowing it to pass under. The power is then increased slightly until the next wave approaches the stern, when it is reduced long enough to let that wave pass under. By careful use of the throttle and the rudder, yawing can be kept to a minimum. (It must be remembered that any yaw can quickly become a broach.)

Another danger is *pitchpoling,* that is, flipping end over end. To prevent it, control of engine speed in a heavy following sea is essential. Unless a boat is slowed down when a giant wave approaches the stern, the boat will be picked up by the wave and find itself racing down the forward face of the wave at a greatly increased speed. While this might seem like good fun, it could become highly dangerous if the boat races forward and plows into the trough, burying the bow well under in the process. The following wave might well pick up the stern and, with the bow deeply set in the water, flip the boat end over end.

Both broaching or pitchpoling will cause, at the very least, serious injuries to the boat's occupants.

One other problem caused by seas breaking into the boat is called *swamping.* This must be guarded against by continual bailing. Failure to do so will slowly cause loss of freeboard and increase the chance of sinking.

12.25 Landing through a Surf—General Because of the hazards of the sea, any seaman is likely to find it necessary to take almost any kind of ship's boat or raft ashore through a surf. He may have a green or exhausted crew whose lives as well as his own depend on his performance; therefore, it behooves every seaman to learn all he can of the subject both by study and actual experience whenever the opportunity offers.

A surf never looks as dangerous from seaward as it actually is, especially from a small boat. When there is any possibility of a surf, a beach should be approached with caution, and care should be taken to remain well outside the breakers until ready to make an attempt at running the surf. If there is any possibility of help from the shore, it should be awaited before running a heavy surf. If no help is available and it is necessary to run the surf unaided, two principles should be kept in mind. First, the boat must be kept end on to the surf to avoid broaching and capsizing. Second, the boat must be able to meet and resist the breakers to keep them from driving her toward the beach out of control or, in extreme cases, driving her under or throwing her end over end.

Methods of running the surf vary with the height of breakers, type of beach, set of current, weather, type and trim of boat, gear available, and experience and condition of crew. Since the means and methods to be used must be decided after a consideration of all these factors, their very nature precludes the statement of anything other than general principles. Only those methods considered safest and simplest will be discussed here.

To understand the dangers in landing through surf, you should be familiar with the characteristics of surf. Surf is caused by winds, local or distant. The nature of the surf, however, depends on the character of the waves that approach the shore line and on the manner in which these waves are changed as they go from deep water into shallow water.

There are three main breaker types, as follows:

Plunging Type The back of the wave continues to be well rounded, but the front of the wave becomes so concave that the crest of the wave suddenly falls forward and breaks. This type of wave occurs mainly on beaches where the bottom as a steep slope.

Spilling Type Both sides of the wave grow more concave as the wave advances, until the wave is so steep and deep that it breaks down by spilling. This type usually occurs on flat beaches.

Surging Type This type usually occurs on the steep beaches. It neither plunges nor spills but surges into a peak that it maintains up the beach face until it subsides.

In addition to the ratio of wave height to wave length, the beach slope, winds, currents, and the presence of an offshore bar will also influence breaker characteristics.

When waves run from deep into shallow water, the *period,* or time between successive crests, will not change to any extent. As the length and speed of the wave decreases, the height increases.

Studies show that a wave will break on a beach when the wave face slope becomes 90 degrees. This usually occurs at a depth of water between one and one and one-half times the height of the wave. However, the presence of a bar may cause the waves to break in deeper water. Such a presence would be indicated by a single line of breakers at high tide and by several diminishing lines at low tide.

Waves usually approach the shore at an angle. When they do, they break at an angle to the shore line, and a current is set up parallel to the beach. This *longshore current* is very treacherous when landing a boat through surf and is largely responsible for the tendency to broach. As the boat advances into the surf zone, the velocity of this longshore current increases as a result of three factors: increasing breaker height, increasing angle of the breaker with the beach, and steeper beach slopes. The velocity of the longshore current decreases with increasing wave period.

A *rip current* is a narrow seaward-moving water current that returns to deep water the water carried landward by waves. It can be very useful to the boat handler when approaching the beach because it tends to flatten the surf and allow for an easier passage.

12.26   Landing through a Surf with Oars   The most important consideration for the inexperienced coxswain is the necessity for remaining outside the breakers for a long enough time to study the surf carefully. Care must be exercised to ensure that the boat is kept far enough outside the outermost line of breakers to avoid being caught unexpectedly by a sea. One will find that the large seas come in a more or less regular sequence, usually three or four in a series. Then follows a period of smaller seas during which there is another build-up. It is during this time that the entrance into the line of breakers must be made.

Having determined the period of the seas and decided on the run in, it is necessary to wait until the last sea of the large series breaks just inshore of the boat and then turn so as to present the bow seaward and back in. As each succeeding wave overtakes the boat, it may be necessary to go ahead to meet it. In doing so, the oarsmen are usually faced so that the coxswain may make the best use of them to control the speed and direction of the boat. Too much emphasis cannot be placed on the full utilization of the oars in steering the boat. It is possible for the boat to be kept headed directly into the seas by having first one side and then the other give way as may become necessary. As each sea passes, it is necessary to "stern all" and gain more distance toward the beach. With each overtaking sea, the boat will be carried shoreward a considerable distance, even though the oarsmen are pulling against it. If even the smaller seas are of dangerous size, it will be necessary to impart a great deal of way to the boat in order to give it sufficient inertia to overcome the power of the sea and avoid broaching.

Broaching is most apt to occur when the seaward end of the boat is lifted by an onrushing wave, depressing the shoreward end in the relatively calm, motionless water immediately in front of the wave. Under these circumstances, one end of the boat is deeper than the other and embedded in stationary water whereas the other end has a tremendous force acting on it. It is apparent that this force applied to one side or the other of the seaward end of the boat will create a powerful turning moment, one arm of which is equal to about the length of the boat. Thus, it is also obvious that a great amount of power is necessary to overcome the forces that tend to cause broaching.

Considering the weight of the boat constant, since buoyancy is also a paramount factor, this power can be met only by rowing strongly against each oncoming wave. Weights should be located in the bow (seaward end) of the boat, but not in the extreme end. Oarsmen should use a short, fast, powerful stroke so that they may back-water with as little delay as possible as each sea passes.

It should now appear that the seaward end of the boat is the most important and the one on which adverse forces are apt to be most dangerous. Hence, it follows that the problem would be less difficult if there were some means of holding the bow steady while the overtaking seas pass. In practice, there are two very handy devices for accomplishing this—the *drogue* and the *surf-line*. Both of these, however, should be used only by experienced surfmen.

A drogue is a conical-shaped bag about 2 ft wide across the mouth and 4½ ft long. It is towed mouth foremost by a 2½-in. line, which is secured to the mouth by means of a bridle. A small line known as the tripping line is made fast to the apex, or pointed end. When towed mouth foremost, the drogue fills with water and offers considerable resistance; when towed by means of the tripping line, the resistance becomes negligible, and the drogue passes through the water easily.

When a drogue is used in a boat landing through a surf, it must be carefully tended by men in the bow so that there is always a strain on the towing line when a sea overtakes the boat. When the sea passes, it is desirable to ''stern all,'' and the tripping line is hauled taut so that the drogue passes easily through the water. The coxswain and men tending the drogue must be alert to slack the tripping line well in advance of the arrival of the next wave in order to allow it to fill with water and exert the greatest resistance to keep the bow pointed seaward. A drogue is especially recommended when any current is setting parallel to the beach.

A surf-line consists of a 2½- or 3-in. line made fast to an anchor just beyond the outermost line of breakers. This line should be about 150 fathoms long. The line, coiled in the boat free for running, is payed out by men in the bow so that there is always a strain on it when the boat is overtaken by a sea; as the sea passes, the line is again payed out.

A surf-line exerts a more positive force on the bow of a boat landing through a surf, but it is not recommended when there is any appreciable current setting parallel to the beach. The reason, of course, is that the farther the boat progresses (i.e., the longer the scope), the more it will be carried down by the current. Hence, there will actually come a time when the boat will be carried broadside to the waves or nearly so and be in grave danger of capsizing. Another disadvantage of the surf-line is that it actually stops the progress of the boat toward the beach each time the men in the bow hold it to permit a sea to pass under the boat.

12.27   Landing through a Surf with Power   Landing through a surf with a power-driven vessel is very much like landing with an oar-propelled vessel. The major difference is that the propellers and rudder must be protected, and therefore the vessel must be brought in bow first. Again, the coxswain should lay outside the breaking point of the in-rolling waves and make his approach at a low speed. As the last big wave of a pattern runs in and passes the center of gravity of the boat, lifting the forebody, full ahead throttle must be applied to bring the boat riding in just behind the breaking wave. The throttle is used to control the position on the wave and the tendency to override.

The tendency to broach in the longshore current must be counteracted—a difficult thing to do since the boat will be making very little speed through the water.

The wrong position for the boat on a wave is to place its center of gravity forward of the crest. In this position, the boat may be overrun by the wave, swamped, and broached.

12.28 Entering an Inlet   There are numerous small inlets from the sea that have to be run by small vessels. These can be dangerous, and it takes skill to handle them. The skill of the coxswain, the construction of the boat, and the inlet itself will all affect the way in which the inlet should be entered. The conditions change with the weather and the state of the tide, and the dangers of broaching, pitchpoling, and swamping are ever present.

As a wave approaches a narrow inlet, its height increases rapidly and breakers form over the shallowest areas, indicating the location and size of sand bars. Since these sand bars are constantly shifting, they thwart all attempts to identify the navigable channel with buoys.

The same techniques used in running the surf are used when running an inlet. Again, a drogue can be used, but only by an experienced boat handler. If the inlet is not familiar, get local help. It is essential to take time and watch how the water breaks before attempting a run. To get in, high power may be required to maintain the proper attitude in relation to the seas. Therefore, if the vessel doesn't respond quickly to the demands for power, the run should not be attempted.

12.29 Beaching and Retracting the LCVP   *Beaching*   The most interesting and important phase of LCVP (or LCM) operation is the run to the beach. In the surf, the coxswain and crew are really put to the test. There are a number of factors to be kept in mind when the student coxswain goes into the surf for the first time. These will be discussed roughly in the order in which they occur during a landing operation.

The coxswain should make certain that each crew member is in his place as he makes ready for the run. All men must wear life jackets when the LCVP is launched since there may be no time to slip them on in an emergency. Even a champion swimmer can drown quickly if he happens to be knocked out for even a moment.

As the beach is approached, the rolling ground swell that starts to rise several hundred yards out from the shore determines the size of the surf. Once the boat is inside the breaker line, its course should not be changed. Therefore, it should be lined up with the spot on the beach where it is to be landed before it enters the surf.

The LCVP, handled by an expert, can cope with a 12-ft surf, but a 6- to 8-ft surf is high enough to cause plenty of trouble, especially for the beginner. The speed of the boat must be regulated so that it rides into the beach *just behind the crest* of a comber. If the boat is right on the crest, it will be set down *hard* on the sand when the wave crashes and ebbs.

The boat should be kept *at right angles* to the surf. It is likely to broach if this rule is not observed. Usually the surf goes in parallel to the beach, and if the boat hits the sand head on, it will ground safely.

The exact spot at which the coxswain aims his boat should be chosen with care. Since the LCVP was designed primarily to run aground on a sand beach, both coxswain and forward lookout must keep a sharp eye for underwater obstacles, for example, any large stones or outcropping of rocks that might damage its hull or ramp.

If the boat should run aground on a sand bar some distance from the beach, the engine should be run slowly in forward speed until the hull is floated partly free by the next breaker, at which time the engine speed should be increased. If the boat is not freed, the engine speed should be cut and another attempt made when the next incoming wave lifts the boat.

It is unwise to assume that the water is shallow all the way to shore if the boat grounds some yards out. Unless word is received from the beach party, the unloading of troops should not be attempted. The water may be 10 ft deep a few yards inshore from a sand bar that has stalled the boat.

After clearing all bars, the LCVP should be run on the beach at a good speed to ensure a good hold on the sand. When properly beached, the boat is at right angles to the surf and its keel is grounded along its entire length. In this position, the boat is not likely to broach while loading or discharging cargo.

The engine should be kept turning over fast enough to hold the boat well up on the beach. When the water recedes and the screw loses its bite between breakers, the engine should be idled down.

Should the engine fail or some mishap occur when the boat is within the surf line but not aground, the first thing to do is drop a stern anchor. This helps to hold the stern at right angles to the breakers if the line is payed out carefully. Since the boat must be allowed to surge toward the beach with each comber, the line should be snubbed only when the boat touches the beach, to prevent broaching. The flow of the tide is something to take into consideration if the boat must be beached for any length of time.

Several precautions may be taken to keep from broaching. *First,* be sure that the breaking seas are kept dead astern. Otherwise the stern will fall off to port or starboard as the water dashes against it. *Second,* drive well up on the beach so that the entire length of the keel is aground. *Third,* speed up the engine in forward gear as incoming waves float the boat. *Fourth,* see that the antibroaching lines are thrown to the beach party at once. Figure 12.17 shows how these lines are used to prevent broaching.

No hard and fast rule can be laid down for the use of the antibroaching lines. The coxswain must think and act intelligently to allow for wind, different types of beaches, and other factors influencing broaching. Usually, however, it is wise to line up the bow with some object on the beach so that it becomes immediately apparent whether the bow or stern is moving. In this case, the rudder should be put *in the direction in which the stern is swinging.* Then the engine should be speeded to drive the boat higher on the beach to bring the stern around. If, despite all precautions, the boat should be broached and the surf is not too high, it is sometimes possible to free it by engine power alone.

Retraction   When retracting from the beach, the coxswain tackles the most difficult part of the landing operation. It is during retraction that the beginner at boat handling is likely to broach or to damage the rudder, screw, or skeg.

The coxswain will be most successful in getting away from the shore and safely beyond the breaker line if he observes the following:

1. The rudder should be set amidships before attempting to retract. For this purpose, the engine of an LCVP should be run about half speed ahead. The discharge current or wash from the screw will force the rudder into an amidships position.
2. The bow should be lined up with an object on the beach to make it easier to note any swing of the boat soon enough to correct her movement and hold her straight.
3. The engine should be shifted into reverse and a wave awaited to float the hull. When flotation is achieved, the engine should be accelerated. Nearly always the boat will move backward a short distance.
4. When the wave recedes, the engine should be prevented from racing needlessly as the screw loses its bite in the water; doing so will prevent the rudder and skeg from digging into the sand.
5. If the bow begins to swing, the steering wheel should be turned *in the direction of the swing* to bring the bow back. The wheel should then be turned back before this return swing is completed or the bow will move too far and require more maneuvering.

Fig. 12.17 Beaching an LCVP.

6. Once the LCVP is floating free and has passed all outer sandbars, it should be backed at right angles to the surf until outside the breaker line.
7. Once the boat is through the breakers and on the crest of a wave, the rudder should be put over hard and the engine shifted into forward and accelerated. Doing so will cause the boat to pivot quickly and take the next sea on the bow.

12.30   Beaching and Retracting the LCM   Most of the general rules laid down for running to the beach with an LCVP are observed when piloting the larger tank lighter, the LCM. The boat is kept at right angles to the surf and is driven ashore just behind the crest of a wave. It should be grounded well up on the beach along the entire length of its keel and the engines kept running with enough speed to hold it firmly beached while loading or unloading.

Once the coxswain is familiar with it, he will find that the tank lighter is easier to retract than the smaller, single-screw LCVP because its twin-screw design gives better control over the bow's tendency to fall off to port or starboard when backing through the surf. To retract, the rudders are put amidships, both engines are reversed, and the boat is backed off slowly.

If the bow falls off to starboard, there is no need to spin the wheel. The coxswain simply speeds up the port engine in reverse until the swing is corrected. He must ease off on the throttles, however, as soon as the bow begins to come back to starboard; otherwise, it might continue its swing and fall off to port.

Like the LCVP, the LCM can broach in a few seconds, but because of its greater size, it is apt to be more difficult to salvage. The same precautions observed with the LCVP will help keep the LCM at right angles to the surf.

Helicopter Operations

12.31   The Helicopter at Sea   The helicopter is of marked significance to mariners, performing a variety of useful or vital services in its capacity as a physical link between ships and between ship and shore. Some of the many tasks regularly performed offshore by helicopters are the following:

1. At-sea pickup and transport of emergency medical cases.
2. Search and rescue.
3. Transport of supplies and personnel.
4. Icefield reconnaissance.
5. Planeguard duty for navy aircraft carriers.
6. Antisubmarine search and attack.
7. Coast and Geodetic Survey support.
8. Minefield reconnaissance and minesweeping.

A responsible mariner will inform himself of the helicopter's capabilities, limitations, and requirements, for he can expect to work closely with this unique machine at some stage, perhaps on short notice. (See Figs. 12.18 and 12.19.)

Life or health is frequently at stake in helicopter operations. Those awaiting help may be jeopardized by the failure, delay, or inefficiency of a helicopter mission. Participants or bystanders may be endangered should there be an accident, not necessarily a crash, during such a mission. Consequently, knowledge of and adherence to prescribed operating and safety procedures and the development of informed judgment are required of those working with or near helicopters.

12.32 Helicopter Types In general configuration, the four most common helicopter types are the following:

Single rotor—A helicopter having two or more large horizontal rotor blades rotating about a single vertical axis near its center of gravity. There is also a small, vertical, sidefacing rotor at the tail used to counteract the torque effects of the large rotor and to provide control about the yaw axis.

Fig. 12.18 An HH 3F twin-turbine helicopter gives crewmen a lift with the heavy navigational aids they are assembling for an offshore site. Its primary work, search and rescue, is facilitated by the unique navigational computer it carries. (*Official U.S. Coast Guard photograph*)

Fig. 12.19 The HH 52A, or S 62, with a cruising speed of 98 mph and a loading capacity of more than 3000 lb, can operate from water, land, ice, snow, swamp, mud, or practically any other surface. (*Official U.S. Coast Guard photograph*)

Tandem rotor—A helicopter having two sets of horizontal blades placed near opposite ends of the fuselage. Since these rotors rotate in opposite directions, no vertical antitorque propeller is required.

Contrarotating twin rotor—A helicopter having two separate rotors that intermesh. These two rotors are on the same horizontal axis. No tail rotor is required, and the plane has a standard tail.

Advancing blade concept (ABC) rotor system—A helicopter having two coaxial, counterrotating rigid rotors. No tail rotor is required.

Helicopters may be either single-engine or multi-engine. The transition from reciprocating engines to gas turbine engines in recent years has markedly improved helicopter performance.

12.33 Helicopter Characteristics Helicopters perform many demanding tasks under difficult conditions. Since they are as vulnerable to misuse as any complex machine, respect for their characteristic limitations is as important as proper use of their capabilities.

Lift for flight is achieved by the speed of rotation of the rotor rather than the forward speed of the vehicle as in the conventional airplane. Consequently, hovering, sideward, and backward flight are all possible, but within definite limits.

Helicopters are characterized by relatively slow airspeed. Although top speeds up to 280 knots (or more) can be reached by modern helicopters, many older models cruise at speeds less than 100 knots. The most frequent as well as most critical helicopter operations take place at very slow speeds and low altitudes. These include takeoff and landing, hovering, and flight operations around a ship.

In case of failure of one engine in flight, a twin-engine helicopter may be able to use the remaining good engine to continue flight or to make a powered landing. A single-engine helicopter, however, must land in the event of engine failure. However, under most flight conditions the helicopter can be brought to a controlled landing, by the process of *autorotation*. This is a maneuver in which the helicopter's forward motion, descent, and proper pilot action cause the rotors to continue to turn sufficiently to produce enought lift for ''gliding'' flight.

For operations over water, the twin-engined helicopter is preferred, as the second engine gives it an improved margin of safety. The U. S. Coast Guard is replacing its present fleet of HH-52 single engine helicopters, with the HH-65A, which has been named the ''Dolphin.'' This helicopter has been designed for a short-range recovery mission which would take it 150 nautical miles out to the target vessel, allow 15 minutes of search time, and 15 minutes to hover and then return to its base. It is designed to take aboard three persons in addition to the crew. Unlike previous rescue helicopters, it is not designed to land on the water. Figure 12.20 shows this new helicopter.

Modern helicopters of moderate to large size, particularly those operated by the U.S. Coast Guard and the U.S. Navy, are equipped for instrument flight and can operate over water in weather of moderate severity. Older helicopters and the smaller models of current helicopters have very limited ability to operate at night over water or under conditions of low visibility. Unless equipped with the proper instruments and radios for instrument flying, even the best helicopter pilot is running a great risk when he undertakes helicopter flight without a visible horizon.

Fig. 12.20   A U.S. Coast Guard HH-65A helicopter. A new generation of helicopter search and surveillance.

The useful operating range of a helicopter is primarily influenced by wind velocity and rate of fuel consumption, the latter depending on the engine power setting used. Range and endurance vary with different helicopter models and the conditions under which each is operated. Sustained high-speed flight or sustained hovering markedly reduces flight endurance because of the high power settings required. A typical endurance figure for normal flight conditions, however, would be about two to three hours, with perhaps another hour available if the plane is provided with auxiliary fuel tanks. Hovering, slow flight, and lateral flight are valuable helicopter characteristics. Sideward and backward flight are limited to a few knots airspeed, except for the tandem rotor helicopter, which can accomplish sideward flight of up to about 30 knots. A helicopter normally must hover facing into the wind; with the wind abeam or aft, slow ground speed or hovering is possible only if the wind is very light.

In hovering over a deck, the action of the rotors pushes air downward to the surface. The air then flows outward and circulates back into the rotors from the top. This downwash has considerable velocity, and its effects should be anticipated. For personnel working on a deck near or under a hovering helicopter, the wearing of helmet and goggles is advisable. Assorted objects, including loose articles of clothing, in the vicinity are likely to be hazards. Objects may be blown overboard or, if light enough, (for example, hats) can be captured by the recirculating air pattern and pulled into the helicopter blades, causing them damage.

In hovering over the water, the downwash blows spray at a high enough velocity to reduce the efficiency of personnel should any be in a boat near the helicopter. With regard to turbine-powered helicopters, a further potential hazard exists in that the ingestion of foreign objects into the engine's air intake is almost certain to result in engine failure. Shipboard personnel must be aware of this hazard and make every effort to reduce the foreign object damage (FOD).

Many modern helicopters are amphibious, being capable of landing in water in light to moderate seas. If some lift is provided by the rotors, considerable waterborne stability can be achieved. Conversely, with no rotor lift, waterborne stability will be reduced. If the helicopter rolls or pitches very much in this condition, the tips of the rotor blades may touch the water, with possibly perilous consequences.

Even for helicopters designed to operate on water, a water landing is a dangerous operation. If there is to be a pick-up at sea, the preferred method is to use a powered hoist with a strong, flexible steel cable. A hook at the free end of the cable permits the attachment of devices such as a net, basket, Stokes litter, light cargo bag, or a harness or sling for lifting a man into the helicopter. Some helicopters are rigged with external cargo hooks underneath, at the center of gravity, for the attachment of heavy cargo in cargo nets or on pallets in slings.

In the United States, the most common lifting method is by rescue basket. It is the safest method of personnel removal, since it is dangerous to use the rescue sling for an unconscious person. If the rescue sling—a loop of webbing sometimes padded into a horsecollar shape—is used, it is important to insure that the bight of the loop should always be placed at the back of the man to be hoisted and that the ends are passed up to the hook under each arm. A common and dangerous mistake occurs in placing the bight over the chest.

12.34 Wind Wind velocity and turbulence are major factors in helicopter operations and must be taken into account at all times by the pilot and by shipboard personnel working with a helicopter. The presence or absence of relative wind can determine or limit the helicopter's ability to take off or hover safely with a heavy load, particularly in hot, humid weather, which reduces helicopter performance.

A helicopter can fly in forward flight with somewhat more load than it can safely support in hovering flight because of the increased lift provided by the relative wind created by the helicopter's forward motion. In a practical sense, this means that sometimes a helicopter will be able to maintain station over the deck of a ship only if the ship maneuvers to provide the necessary relative wind velocity. With insufficient wind velocity, the helicopter may not be able to hover or may operate with an inadequate margin of safety to cope properly with turbulence or an emergency.

The relative wind with respect to the ship should, if possible, satisfy several conditions. Preferably, it should provide a clear, overwater, upwind approach to the position at which the ship-helicopter operation, such as hoisting a man, will take place. To minimize turbulence, the wind should reach the helicopter after having passed around as little superstructure as possible. The wind direction should permit the helicopter to face into the wind, or nearly so, while maintaining its hover over the ship. This helicopter heading should permit a clear view of the ship by the pilot and the hoist operator, both of whom are normally stationed on the helicopter's right-hand side so as to have adequate visual reference for accurate positioning. If a clear deck or level space exists aft, it can be seen that these conditions will be well satisfied if the ship takes an upwind course and speed that establishes the relative wind at an angle of about 10 to 30 degrees on the port bow and at a relative velocity of over 10 knots. The helicopter pilot and the hoist operator then have the ship in full view during the approach and hover. If the helicopter must operate at a point other than the after end of the ship, a relative wind close to broad on the ship's beam is usually preferable. In the case of a ship dead in the water, less flexibility exists, and the pilot must determine whether safe operations are possible.

When the helicopter is traveling point to point, wind direction affects performance and navigation. A helicopter cruising at 60 knots airspeed directly into a 30-knot wind can achieve, at most, one half its no-wind range, and its ground speed will be only 30 knots. Any crosswind component reduces range, even for a round-trip flight, because of the necessity to crab into the wind to maintain the desired track. Wind effects on the ground speed of a helicopter must be kept in mind by the controlling personnel of the ship from which it operates.

12.35 Sustained Operations with Helicopter All vessels that operate with helicopters regularly should prepare, with the help of aviation personnel, a "Helicopter Operations Bill"; this bill details stations and defines duties and responsibilities for various operations such as launching, landing, and refueling, and emergencies such as deck crash, fire, and man overboard. Explicit safety precautions should be part of the bill or issued as a separate directive for wider promulgation.

12.36 Emergency or Occasional Operations with Helicopter The vessel that only occasionally works with a helicopter or has to do so in an emergency must know what to do. Although transfer of supplies and personnel is now quite common in the oil and mineral industry, the vessel is most likely to operate with a helicopter when the transfer of personnel by hoist becomes necessary. If a U.S. Coast Guard helicopter is involved, the ship can expect to be contacted by radio (HF, VHF, or UHF) and informed by the pilot of his intentions and requirements for ship actions. Such brief instructions obviously cannot substitute for previous indoctrination of ships' personnel. If the helicopter is unable to establish radio contact, the degree of urgency and pilot's discretion will determine whether or not a message drop, large writing on a blackboard, or other communication will permit enough information exchange for the personnel transfer or other mission to be safely accomplished. Fuel limitations may preclude time-consuming attempts to communicate at length by other than radio, or to engage in prolonged hovering over the ship. Consequently, ship action that immediately demonstrates familiarity with helicopter operations by steering a good course and by manning the appropriate deck area with properly equipped personnel will save valuable time and may make the difference between mission success and failure.

12.37 Safety Precautions Safety procedures and precautions have been printed in many manuals but the most readily available source is the "Coast Pilot." The information printed here has been provided by the U.S. Coast Guard, and vessels of all sizes should have it readily available.

Helicopter Evacuation of Personnel Helicopter evacuation for a patient and for the flight crew and should be attempted only in event of very serious illness or injury. The doctor on shore should be provided with all necessary information concerning the patient so that an intelligent evaluation can be made of the need for evacuation. Most rescue helicopters can proceed less than 150 miles offshore (a few new helicopters can travel 250 to 300 miles out to sea), depending on weather conditions and other variables. The vessel must therefore be prepared to proceed within range of the helicopter and should be familiar with the necessary preparations prior to and after its arrival.

When requesting helicopter assistance, it is necessary to do the following:

1. Give the accurate position, time, speed, course, weather conditions, sea conditions, wind direction and velocity, type of vessel, and voice and CW frequency for your ship.
2. If not already provided, give complete medical information including the ambulatory state of the patient.
3. If you are beyond helicopter range, announce your diversion intentions so that a rendezvous point may be selected.
4. If there are changes to any data reported earlier, advise the rescue agency immediately. Should the patient die before the arrival of the helicopter, be sure to inform the rescue crew.

Preparations prior to the arrival of the helicopter include the following:

1. Provide continuous radio guard on 2182 kHz or specified voice frequency, if possible. Helicopters usually cannot operate CW.
2. Select and clear the most suitable hoist area, preferably aft, with a minimum 50-ft radius of clear deck. Secure loose gear, awnings, and antenna wires. Trice up running rigging and booms. If hoist is aft, lower the flat staff.
3. If the hoist is to take place at night, light the pick-up area as well as possible. Be sure not to shine any lights on the helicopter to avoid blinding the pilot. If there are any obstructions in the vicinity, put a light on them to alert the pilot of their positions.
4. Point searchlights vertically to help the flight crew locate the ship and turn them off when the helicopter arrives on the scene.
5. Be sure to advise the helicopter of the location of the pick-up area in advance so that the pilot may make his approach to aft, amidships, or forward, as required.
6. Since the high noise level under the helicopter will make voice communications on deck almost impossible, prepare a set of hand signals for the crew who will assist.

The hoist operations are as follows:

1. If possible, have the patient moved to a position as close to the hoist area as his condition will permit; time is important.
2. Normally, if a litter (stretcher) is being used, it will be necessary to move the patient to the special litter lowered by the helicopter. Be prepared to do so as quickly as possible, making sure that the patient is strapped in, face up, with a life jacket on (if his condition permits).
3. Be sure that the patient is tagged to indicate what medication, if any, was administered to him and when.
4. Have patient's medical record and necessary papers in an envelope or package ready for transfer with him.
5. Again, if the patient's condition permits, *be sure* he is wearing a life jacket.
6. Change the vessel's course to permit the ship to ride as easily as possible with the wind on the bow, preferably the port bow. Try to choose a course that will keep the stack gases clear of the hoist area.
7. Reduce speed to ease ship's motion, but maintain steerageway.
8. If radio contact with the helicopter is not available, invite the helicopter in, when the ship is ready, with a "come on" hand signal, or at night with flashlight signals.
9. Allow the basket or stretcher to touch deck prior to handling in order to avoid static shock.
10. If a trail line is dropped by the helicopter, use it to guide the basket or stretcher to the deck, keeping it free at all times. This line will not cause shock.
11. Place the patient in the basket, sitting with his hands clear of the sides, or in the litter, as described above. Signal the helicopter hoist operator when ready for the hoist. Patient should signal by a nodding of the head if he is able.
12. If it is necessary to take the litter away from the hoist point, unhook the hoist cable and keep it free for the helicopter to haul in. Do not secure the cable or trail line to the vessel or attempt to move the stretcher without unhooking.
13. When the patient has been strapped into the stretcher, signal the helicopter to lower the cable, attach the cable to the stretcher sling (bridle), and then signal the hoist operator when the patient is ready to be hoisted. Steady the stretcher so that it will not swing or turn.
14. If a trail line is attached to the basket or stretcher, use it to steady

the patient as he is hoisted. Keep your feet clear of the line, and keep the line from becoming entangled.

12.38   Coast Guard Droppable, Floatable Pumps   Many vessels in distress and taking on water will receive their first assistance in the form of droppable, floatable pumps delivered by helicopter or surface vessel. The most commonly used pump comes complete in a sealed aluminum drum about half the size of a 50-gal oil drum. A single lever on top opens it up. Don't be smoking at the time as there may be gas fumes inside the can. The pump will draw about 90 gal/min. There should be a waterproof flashlight on top of the pump for night use. Operating instructions are provided inside the pump container.

12.39   Joint Rescue Operations   When a helicopter and surface vessel jointly engage in the rescue of personnel in the water, maximum coordination is essential since any interference might imperil those awaiting rescue as well as both the helicopter and surface vessel. In no way should competition be permitted to develop. The first to arrive at the exact site of rescue would normally be in charge of the operation, but the procedures outlined in the *Merchant Ship Search and Rescue Manual (MERSAR)* and the *National Search and Rescue Manual* should be followed.

Although the superior speed, search, and rescue capability of a trained helicopter team should be recognized, the helicopter and surface vessel may be able to perform rescues simultaneously. Alternatively, one or the other might better stand by, ready to render assistance but remaining clear so as to provide ample maneuvering room to the other. If the surface vessel stands clear, it should be aware of the helicopter requirement of making an upwind approach to a point of rescue and should avoid blocking the helicopter's approach and takeoff path.

References

Chapman, W. *Piloting, Seamanship, and Small Boat Handling.* New York: American Book-Stratford Press, 1979.

Cornell, M., and Hoffman, A. C. *American Merchant Seaman's Manual.* Centreville, MD: Cornell Maritime Press, 1981.

Rousmaniere, John. *The Annapolis Book of Seamanship.* New York: Simon and Schuster, 1983.

Turpin, Edward A., and MacEwen, William A. *Merchant Marine Officer's Handbook.* Centreville, MD: Cornell Maritime Press, 1965.

White, Lawrence A. *The Coast Guardsman's Manual.* Annapolis, MD: Naval Institute Press, 1976.

Merchant Ship Search and Rescue Manual (MERSAR). New York: Unipub, 1980.

13

Ice Seamanship

With the increasing activity in both the Arctic and Antarctic, an understanding of ice seamanship in its broad sense is becoming more important. This activity includes the finding of oil, gas, and minerals in the Arctic in commercial quantities, the advent of tourism in the Antarctic, the support of polar science and research, and Naval training in strategic ice-pack areas.

13.1 General In sea-ice areas today a vessel either operates singly or is aided by icebreaker escort. As a rule, an unreinforced ship should never attempt to negotiate more than three-tenths ice concentration by itself, this estimation being based on how the ice lays. In other words, if it is necessary to break through other than the smallest concentrations of ice, or *brash ice,* icebreaker assistance is usually required. A vessel with an ice classification, with its increased power and built-in protection from ice damage, has far greater capability in the ice than an unreinforced ship. The trend now is to employ only ice-classified vessels and to request icebreaker escort for only the most difficult ice passages, that is, about six-tenths concentration and above. The characteristics of the ice—its hardness, temperature, thickness, amount of snow cover, and salt content—as well as its disposition must be taken into account.

13.2   Polar Ice   Two kinds of ice confront the mariner in the polar regions: (1) *glacial ice*, or icebergs of land origin, and (2) *field ice*, of sea origin.

Glacial ice is formed from the accumulation of snow that has gradually changed form as it is compressed into a solid mass of large granular ice. This process produces a structure quite different from that of sea ice. Air entrapped in the ice forms tiny high-pressure air pockets of high density, giving the ice a milky appearance and causing it to effervesce as it melts. Since it is formed over land, glacial ice is essentially salt free.

Icebergs are produced when the buoyant forces of water act to break off sizable pieces of ice from the seaward terminus of glaciers. The following data about icebergs at sea comes from the International Ice Patrol. Mariners in areas where bergs are found should be aware of the signs of their presence. These signs may prove of assistance but are only supplementary to a good lookout. The only sure sign of an iceberg is an actual sighting. Too much reliance on any other indication of the presence or absence of bergs can be dangerous.

Bergs in the warm waters of the Gulf Stream give off cracking sounds as they melt. When a *growler* is calved, that is, when a quantity of ice is sloughed off from the side of a berg, a thunderous roar may be heard as it falls into the water. In warm water, these noises occur frequently but cannot be relied upon as a sign of danger. The presence of several growlers and smaller pieces of detached ice often indicates that a berg is in the vicinity, and probably to windward. (Bergs have been located in thick fog by this means.) If one must transit ice-infested waters, it is probably best to pass to windward of a berg during a period of low visibility or at night to avoid any undetected growlers. The presence of an iceberg has no appreciable effect upon the temperature (or salinity) of the water surrounding it. Sudden changes in the temperatures of the surface water, therefore, do not necessarily signify that ice is near at hand.

Icebergs can be sighted at various distances, depending upon the state of visibility, the height of the berg, and the height of the observer. Large bergs can usually be seen on a very clear day at a distance of 18 miles by an observer with an eye height of 70 ft. In clear weather, but with a low-lying haze around the horizon, the tops of bergs have been seen at 9 to 11 miles. If the sun is shining, it may first appear as a luminous white mass. Without the sun, it takes the appearance of a dark, somber shape. In light fog or drizzling rain, a berg is visible at 1 to 3 miles. There is a tendency to overestimate the distance, believing that one can see further than is actually the case. In a dense fog, a berg cannot be seen at any appreciable distance ahead of the ship. In a light, low fog, an observer can see a berg from aloft sooner than from deck. On a clear, dark, starlit night, a lookout will not pick up a berg at a greater distance than one-fourth of a mile, but if its bearing is known, an occasional light spot, caused by the swell breaking against it, is discernible with binoculars at a distance of a mile. With a full moon and favorable conditions, a berg can normally be seen at greater distances, possibly three miles. Much depends on the relative positions of moon, berg, and ship. Note also that echoes from the ship's whistle are not to be relied upon, both because the shape of the berg may prevent any echo and because echoes are often obtained from fog banks.

Careful tests by the International Ice Patrol have proved that radar cannot provide positive assurance of an iceberg presence. Since sea water is a better reflector of radar signals than ice, an iceberg or growler inside the area return on the radar scope may go undetected. The average range of radar detection of a dangerous growler or very small iceberg, if it is detected at all, is only four miles. Although radar remains a valuable aid for ice detection, its use cannot replace the traditional caution exercised in the vicinity of the Grand Banks while transiting south of the estimated limits of all known ice.

Upon sighting a berg, no matter how great the temptation, it should never be approached close aboard by any vessel, except, at times, by an icebreaker.

The International Ice Patrol was established as a result of the sinking of the *Titanic* by an iceberg in the western North Atlantic in 1912. It is financed by maritime interests of many nations and operated by the U.S. Coast Guard. The positions and tracks of icebergs that present dangers to shipping in the Atlantic are continuously plotted by ships and planes of the Coast Guard. Ships are alerted through broadcasts and notices. The Ice Patrol broadcasts a bulletin twice each day as well as a daily radio-facsimile chart to inform ships of the movement of bergs. Mariners should note that, in spite of the best efforts of the Ice Patrol, icebergs may still drift unnoticed into the usual shipping routes near the Grand Banks.

Icebergs should be avoided by vessels at all times, but field ice, which is composed of frozen seawater, must often be crossed or negotiated. To do so most efficiently, the weakest sections of ice should be traversed or a course should be chosen that will take the ship through the areas of highest water-to-ice ratio. As field ice is so important to polar operations, an understanding of its development, distribution, physical characteristics, movements, deterioration, and mechanics is necessary.

Sea ice is never a solid, homogenous mass, except in sheltered sounds and embayments. Rather, it is constantly being broken into floes as variations in temperature, wind, and current create cracks and channels. These same forces propel the sections or pieces of ice apart and together in an accordion-like manner that alternately increases and decreases the pressure in the pack.

The term *icebreaking* is actually a misleading term of how a passage is opened through sea ice; the mechanics of the process are better described as *ice displacement*. Ice forward of the icebreaker is shoved aside to accommodate the underwater portion of the vessel. Where the ice coverage is too solid to permit lateral displacement, it is necessary to shove the ice over and under adjacent layers.

Only those pieces of ice too large to be readily shoved aside are broken. Breakage is accomplished either by the shock of impact or by a cleaving action in which the bow rises up and cuts through because of its weight and the leverage applied at the bow section by the buoyancy of the depressed stern. The broken pieces must still be forced into nearby ice-free areas, or the icebreaker will be impeded in its progress. Occasionally, ice is forced under the hull where it is caught in the propeller stream and driven astern. Under such circumstances, a piece of ice may become entangled with a propeller, sometimes resulting in a broken blade or shaft. The friction of the ice against the under part of the vessel may also bring the icebreaker to a halt.

The cushioning effect of snow can prevent the upraised bow from returning to the water or ice-free area beneath the icebreaker hull. As a countermeasure, liquid ballast (usually sea water) can be transferred laterally between heeling tanks to impart a rolling motion to the icebreaker, thereby breaking the snow's sticky grip. Sometimes, however, even this method, combined with the sudden application of full-astern power, is of little use. In such cases, depending upon the situation, the use of explosives or just waiting until a shift in tide or wind direction may be the only course of action remaining.

13.3 Icebreaker Techniques An icebreaker, with the aid of its helicopters searching ahead, attempts to locate the easiest paths through the jigsaw-puzzle pattern of ice floes. Ease of transit, however, is not the only criterion. Compromises must be made in order that the courses taken never stray further than 45 degrees from a direct one to the destination, unless, of course, such a course is only of very short duration.

With its barrel-like hull and no keels to impinge against the ice, an icebreaker rolls hideously in rough seas. Before the advent of antiroll devices, everyone boasted of a record roll at one time in the 60 degree-range. In the ice, however, where the vertical movement of the seas is dampened, an icebreaker ride is an entirely different affair. While in light to moderate ice, there is an almost imperceptible rising and lowering of the bow as the vessel rides up to break the larger floes. The ride and motion are pleasant.

If charging and backing tactics must be employed as a result of heavy ice conditions or pressure, the effect is like riding a freight train over a broken track. When in solid, homogeneous ice, where these tactics are employed, the bridge controllers are advanced to full ahead (with all diesel-generators on the line). The engines respond with a roar, the ship charges ahead, and momentum builds up. Bow metal grinds against hard ice, and the ship slows. The bow rises sharply as the icebreaker comes to a complete stop after an advance of about one length. The propellers are then reversed and the ship backs off for another charge. It is a slow operation that is hard on machinery.

13.4 Basic Channel-Cutting Methods   To cut a channel through an area of *fast ice* (homogeneous or solid) in a sound or embayment, either of two basic methods may be used, but first a plan should be evolved that will take into account the general effect of wind, tide, and access into a desired location. For an excellent example, let us take the situation at McMurdo Sound in the Antarctic. There, two or three icebreakers are employed to carve a yearly channel in December that will accommodate the thin-skinned supply ships scheduled to come later. The 25- to 40-mile channel is cut in the shape of a huge V, with the open end to the north at the entrance and its center axis aligned as much as possible in the direction of the prevailing southerly winds, due regard being given to the Coriolis effect. This channel design faciliates the escape of the broken ice, or *brash*. In spite of these precautions, clogging of the channel by ice rubble sometimes reaches serious proportions. The icebreakers themselves may have difficulty negotiating the ice conglomerate that accumulates when northerly winds blow or when there are extended periods of calm. At such times, the situation can be improved only by a slow process of attrition in which the icebreakers work up and down the channel, breaking large ice chunks into smaller ones and stirring up the ice debris with screw currents to promote melting. (See Fig. 13.1.)

If only one icebreaker is available to carve the channel—perhaps because its partner is occupied in reworking ice that is clogging the channel—it should alternately charge the ice at 30 to 40 degrees to port of the axis and then to starboard, employing a third blow straight ahead along the axis. This is known as the *herringbone pattern*.

The other basic method requires two icebreakers. They make two straightforward, parallel cuts, about three ship-widths apart. The intervening ice breaks up under this attack, yielding a channel of greater width than that provided by the herringbone pattern. The method also has the advantage of being about three times as fast. (See Fig. 13.2.)

13.5   Preparation for a Polar Cruise

Preparing the Crew   The polar training program initiated for the crew should include damage control procedures, the effects of low temperatures upon materials, the classification of sea ice, ice terminology, survival in-

Fig. 13.1 U.S. icebreaker *Staten Island* clearing ice from McMurdo Sound channel that leads to main U.S. logistic station in the Antarctic. *(Official U.S. Navy photograph)*

Fig. 13.2 Two U.S. Coast Guard icebreakers using railroad-track method for cutting ice channel into McMurdo Sound, Antarctica. *(Official U.S. Navy photograph)*

structions and precautions, and ice and sea life reporting. It is helpful to use references such as reports of previous expeditions and operations, ice atlases, and sailing directions for the areas where the ship will be operating. Polar shiphandling and operation manuals, books, and films, together with instructions for the operation of shipboard equipment in cold weather and ice observing and reporting techniques, are other valuable aids for the program.

The psychological effect of constant travel through ice should be considered. The relentless noise from the engines and broken ice hitting the hull will cause strain in the crew. All personnel should be on the alert for the effects of this stress; to relieve it, the crew must be kept active.

Navigational Aids   The navigator should obtain up-to-date charts of the areas to be navigated, including the latest information on pertinent topographic features, points of land, prominent peaks, islands, and other configurations of harbors or operational areas. In areas where navigational aids are normally found, the mariner must be aware of the real possibility that they will not be on station, that is, where they are supposed to be, having been destroyed by ice and not replaced. In polar areas, he should realize that celestial navigation during the summer months depends solely upon altitude sights of the sun, and that piloting is performed mainly by use of radar and the gyro compass instead of lighthouses and other customary navigational aids.

Ice atlases portray average ice conditions for each month of the year and are valuable, not for depicting conditions during a certain year, but for showing the trend of ice growth and deterioration throughout the year. From studying them, one will see that the maximum growth in distribution or area covered is attained in the Arctic and Antarctic, during March and September, respectively, and that the sea-ice areas have reached the greatest shrinkage in the Arctic and Antarctic, during September and March, respectively. The reason is that the cumulative effect of the sun or lack of sun has reached its maximum at these times. Usually polar operations are conducted early in the summer season before much disintegration has occurred. The only advantage of early operations is that if a vessel experiences trouble, one has the assurance that conditions will inevitably become better. The disadvantage, however, is that a vessel may be damaged needlessly by heavy ice.

Sailing Directions (Planning Guides), a series of publications obtainable from the Defense Mapping Agency Hydrographic/Topographic Center, Washington, D.C., gives general information on ice conditions, together with useful advice on piloting, currents, meteorology, flora and fauna, and natives (if any). An account of ship exploration within an area or region is also discussed. The principal help provided by this resource lies in its descriptions and photographs of navigational landmarks and warning of navigational hazards in an area. The *Antarctic Sailing Directions* of the Defense Mapping Agency gives unusually descriptive information on whaling, sealing, and exploration, and even provides the ingredients for an acceptable trail ration. The *Sailing Directions* of other countries—particularly Canada for the Arctic, and Argentina, Chile, and Great Britain for the Antarctic—provide additional information of value. Some of the charts produced by these countries may offer a more convenient scale for navigating.

Current and future ice conditions are developed for the Arctic by Canada and the United States, and for the Antarctic by the latter country. Ships operating in these regions and the shore facilities associated with them are informed of the ice conditions by the Naval Polar Oceanography Center, in Suitland, Maryland. For the purposes of forecasting sea ice, this Center defines Arctic as the Arctic Ocean and all adjacent seas extending southward to the southern limit of the seasonal ice cover, including partial ice cover. This includes the Bering Sea, Sea of Okhotsk, Norwegian Sea, Northern Sea of Japan and the Labrador Sea. The Antarctic is the Southern Ocean extending northward to the northern limit of seasonally ice-covered and partially ice-covered waters. There are many different reports, or products, as they are termed, prepared by this Center, to give the mariner accurate information on the ice conditions in the area of his operations. A number of these forecasts and analyses are produced on a routine basis, while other more specific information on ice is only produced as needed. Sea ice products are produced in three scales, Global, Regional, and Local. Global scale products make up the bulk of these and are disseminated as mailed charts and as facsimile broadcasts. Only the ice edge data from these charts are disseminated in message format. Regional scale products are disseminated as facsimile and mailed charts. Local scale products are almost entirely disseminated as message reports. Direct support to deployed units will be regional or local scale products, depending on the data sources available and are almost always disseminated by message.

The routine products are produced on varying schedules. The global routine products are three weekly charts covering the Eastern and Western Arctic Analysis/Forecast and Antarctic Analysis. There are also two weekly messages, one covering the Eastern and the other the Western Arctic. Three twice-monthly 30-day forecasts are issued, for the Eastern and Western Arctic, which come out in the form of a chart, and for the Ross Sea, which is in message format. The final products in this group are two annual booklets which give the Eastern and Western Arctic Seasonal Outlook. There are two routine regional scale charts which are issued three times weekly. These are the Alaska Regional Analysis and the Great Lakes Analysis. There are no routine local scale products.

All sea ice information on the chart products is in the World Meteorological Organization (WMO) symbology, known as the Egg Code. The Egg Code is available to the mariner in numerous official sources including the *Pre-Sail Information Booklet* issued by the Naval Polar Oceanography Center. The charts also differentiate between actual and estimated information and indicate the seven-day ice edge forecast.

The sea ice data messages consist of a series of plain language and latitude/longitude pairs. By plotting these latitude/longitude pairs and connecting them an approximate reproduction of the sea ice chart is possible. The beginning of the message is always the ice edge line. This is followed by a period and groups of latitude and longitude pairs which describe concentration boundaries. Included in this portion is information on the ice concentration and the estimated age of the ice. These messages do not carry the detail found in the mailed charts. The messages use sets of abbreviations whose detailed definitions can be found in the *Sea Ice Observation Handbook, Handbook For Sea Ice Analysis and Forecasting,* and abbreviated definitions are in the *Pre-Sail Information Booklet* issued by the Naval Polar Oceanography Center.

Preparing the Vessel While the ship is in drydock, all underwater openings must be examined to ensure that they are unobstructed and that the individual valves work efficiently. Since ringbolts, scupper guards, and other hull projections may be damaged by sea ice, these should be removed if possible.

It is necessary to provide timbers, joists, lumber, and iron cut to various shapes and sizes; an assortment of nuts and bolts; packing and washer material; and oakum, quick-drying cement, and other patch material for repairing holes and fractures to the shell plating. For a steel vessel, the most useful equipment is a portable welding outfit. Further needs are diving equipment, ice anchors and explosives.

To combat cold, snow, topside ice, and sea ice, special stores must consist of cold-weather clothing and footwear, ice axes, explosives, detonators, fuses, antifreeze liquid, hardwood mallets, heavy hammers, snow shovels, extra storage batteries, and sufficient storage battery acid for cold-weather operations (125 percent normal allowance). If the ship is to operate in the Antarctic, it is necessary to carry the following mooring equipment aboard: 8-ft long wooden planks, old railroad ties, or sections of telephone poles *(deadmen);* 6-ft long manila or steel-wire straps for use with the deadmen; hardwood toggles or fids for use as mooring triggers; shovels and ice chisels for digging holes in the bay ice (large, powered posthole diggers have been used to speed the digging process); and a number of spars or telephone poles to serve as fenders when mooring against an ice edge. Supplies, equipment, or cargo should never be stored against the sides of the vessel in a hold in a way that might deny access to damaged plating.

Ship's gear and equipment should be examined and placed in top operating condition for the difficult voyage ahead—the gyro compass, fathometer(s), and radar(s) being of utmost importance in this regard. The magnetic compass should be compensated.

To determine whether the vessel meets ice strengthening and power requirements, the ice classification rules provided by the appropriate classification society should be referred to, as described in the following section.

13.6 Ice Classification of Vessels With the exception of naval vessels or vessels operated by military or quasi-military agencies, ships are classified with regard to their ice-navigating capabilities by various classification societies. The specific systems of classification employed by these societies are usually based on an extensive one developed by Sweden and Finland. In the United States, the American Bureau of Shipping is responsible for assignment of ice classifications. In general, their regulations for ship construction, strength, and engine power are as follows:

Shell Plating, Frame Spacing, Stringers, and Strength Members Thickness of shell plating, frame spacing, stringers, and strength members is based on the ice pressure that will be encountered in a specific area of operation.

Propellers, Shafts, etc. Propellers must be of forged steel or other material of equal strength. The diameters and thicknesses of propellers and shafts must be increased over standard dimensions by various assigned percentages.

Rudder Head, Pintles, etc. Diameters and cross sections must be increased by various assigned percentages. Increases are also required in the strength of the steering engine.

Engine Horsepower Horsepower must be above standard values by various assigned ratios.

Main Injection Valves and Steam Chests Main injection valves and steam chests on steam vessels must be fitted with steam connections to keep from freezing and to remove ice if choked.

Shape of Bow and Stern There are no specific regulations for the design of the bow and stern except that self-propelled ship-shaped vessels must be suitably designed for navigation in ice.

13.7 Topside Icing On a voyage into high latitudes the first indication that there is a difference from operations in more temperate climates may be the freezing of spray on the topside of the vessel. Such a phenomenon occurs when the wind is strong enough to blow spray on the ship from wave crests and from the water stirred up by the passage of the ship. It may also occur during fog (including "frost smoke") in freezing temperatures. This kind of icing, sometimes known as *glaze ice,* has high density and great powers of adhesion.

Ice tends to form high up on the ship, on masts and rigging, resulting in loss of freeboard and stability. Therefore, a vessel with considerable freeboard and metacentric height, together with minimum topside area in the form of masts, rigging, and superstructure offers the greatest margin of protection against such icing. When a large area of ice builds up, particularly around and ahead of the foremast, it may act as a sail and hamper the ship's maneuverability.

Typical conditions for the formation of glaze ice are air temperatures of 20° to 25°F with a Force 6 (or above) wind and sea temperatures of 30° to 34°F. If air temperatures fall below 0°F (-17.7°C), the ice cannot adhere because it will strike the ship in the form of small, dry crystals.

There are a number of ways to reduce the effects of this kind of icing. One is to reduce the high topside area upon which the ice will adhere. Thus, a tripod mast may substitute for a normal mast and rigging, and light alloys or fiber glass may replace normal construction materials. Another way is to eliminate as much rigging as possible. Wire ropes may replace rail, and all movable rigging such as derricks or cranes should be lowered to their extreme extent. Electric coils may be installed in important apparatus.

When serious icing conditions prevail, a course downwind should be taken, if possible, so as to reduce substantially the amount of spray being driven over the ship.

Many ice-removal methods may be employed when glaze ice has accumulated on the ship. The most common is by manual means, using mallets, chippers, clubs, scrapers, shovels, and stiff brooms. Care should be observed not to damage an underlying metal surface. Fiberglas whip antennas and antenna and stay insulators are very fragile.

Other methods, though less effective, are the use of hot-air heaters, rock salt (corrosive to metal surfaces), and ice-phobic coatings or anti-icers.

13.8 Operations and Navigation in Sea-Ice Areas Before entering ice, the ship should be trimmed down by the stern in order to prevent low-riding ice from striking the propeller(s). When approach is made to an ice boundary for the first time, care should be taken to enter the perimeter in the lee, insofar as that is possible, particularly if there are growler-size chunks or pieces of heavy ice bobbing up and down from waves or a stiff wind. Usually, entry may be made safely by skirting around long ice tongues or choosing entry at a point that has protection from ice to windward. A thorough preliminary reconnaissance through observations from the crow's nest and use of the radar will assist such an entry. Remember that the effect of wind and swell decreases in proportion to the distance of the ship from the ice edge. Retracting the pitometer sword prior to ice entry is recommended.

After ice entry is made, the conning officer will be required to make innumerable decisions about speed and course. If the situation requires it, the best way for him to view the ice conditions ahead is to position himself as high in the ship as possible. He will see that the channels between individual ice floes never follow a straight line and that some end up in cul de sacs. Choosing the correct channel and maintaining a course that will keep the vessel clear of ice contact or breaking through the least ice possible is a job that will keep him occupied constantly. Although many course changes will be necessary, he must remember not to allow the vessel to stray too far from the desired base course, or he may find the vessel actually doubling back on its track. A good rule to follow is never to permit the course to vary more than 45 degrees from the base course. (See Fig. 13.3.)

In order to get the "feel" of the ship when navigating in ice, he must proceed at a very slow speed at first and then work up to a greater speed when the reaction of the ship in ice becomes better known. Weak sections in the ice should be chosen and approached at a slow speed. When contact is made, power should be increased. If it is necessary to strike an ice floe, it should never be hit with a glancing blow as this will swing the bow in the direction of least resistance and tend to swing the vulnerable propeller(s) toward the floe. If heavy ice halts the ship, the rudder should be kept amidships and the propeller(s) turned over "ahead." This action should clear the ice astern so that the ship will be able to back down for another attempt at going ahead.

Dense field-ice areas should never be entered by a single ship without icebreaker assistance if it can be avoided. Plane and helicopter reconnaissance is a great help in selecting navigable areas before they are actually reached by a vessel. *Water sky* is another aid that has been employed frequently in both the Arctic and Antarctic. This is the dark appearance on the underside of a cloud layer caused by the reflection of a surface of open water surrounded or bounded by ice. When the underside of a cloud layer produces a yellowish-white glare, the phenomenon is known as *ice blink*. Thus the selection of a base course towards "water sky" rather than "ice blink" ensures that the ship will approach open water or, at worst, light ice concentrations.

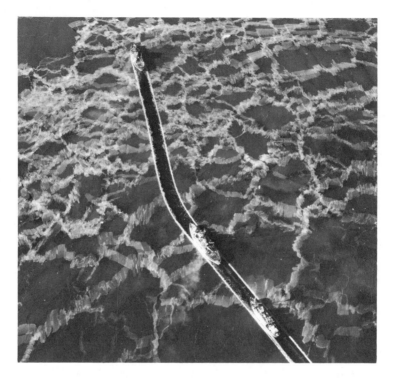

Fig. 13.3 *USS Edisto, USCGC North Wind,* and *RRS John Biscoe* transit pack off Palmer Gerlasche Strait. *(Official U.S. Navy photograph)*

If the ship becomes involved in heavy ice and cannot move in any direction, one or more of the following procedures may be employed for getting free:

1. Go full speed astern and then full speed ahead. By putting the rudder first to one side and then to the other, it may be possible to get the stern to move slightly to one side so that the bow will shift a little. If this occurs, going astern should release the vessel from the grip of the ice.
2. *Sally* the ship by having the crew run first to one side then to the other on signal. However, this ploy will be ineffective for a large ship. Shifting heavy weights and ballast and swinging out boats on booms are other alternatives in heeling the ship.
3. If the foregoing methods fail, bury a large spar or deadman in the ice on the quarter or astern and then winch the ship sternwards by purchases with the engines put on full astern.

4. Employ explosives as a last resort, planting charges at strategic points of ice pressure just off the bows. "Shaped charges" are useful for creating holes through the ice to enable the explosive charge to be placed beneath the ice surface. (Sometimes the shaped charges alone will cause a stress point that will open a large crack.) Close down radio transmissions to avoid prematurely setting off explosions. Have the crew seek cover during the blast and keep engines on full ahead. Beware of ship damage caused by use of explosives.

Because of the numerous course and speed changes during ice operations, accurate dead reckoning is almost impossible. Automatic dead-reckoning devices cannot be employed since it is impracticable to introduce an accurate speed component (ice damages the propeller of a "speed log"); therefore, reliance must be placed on either a "Dutchman's log" or use of radar. In the Dutchman's log method, the speed is estimated by noting the time taken for the ship's stern to come abreast of a chip of wood thrown overboard from the ship's bow. Then with the formula, $S = D/100T$, the ship's speed S, in knots, may be estimated, using D as the length of the ship, in feet, and T as the noted time, in minutes, for the observations. However, the ship's radar will be far more accurate in estimating speed.

Because of the constant daylight in these extreme latitudes, celestial positioning during the summer months when ice operations become practicable is entirely dependent upon altitude sights of the sun, the position being obtained by crossing sun lines that are taken at intervals at least two hours apart. However, each set of observations should consist of at least three or more integrated sextant observations so that a mean may be determined. Frequently, the fact that there is a poor or indeterminate horizon makes celestial observations difficult. Because of the low horizontal component of the earth's magnetism—being zero magnitude at the magnetic poles—the magnetic compass has little value for navigation in the polar regions, although it is surely better than nothing if the gyro compass fails. Although the gyro compass loses its directive force at the geographic poles and is subject to errors, it is still invaluable for bearing reference and the ship's course. It should be checked against sun azimuths several times daily and corrected in accordance with latitude versus speed tables or diagrams.

The development of satellite navigation systems as well as other sophisticated electronic aids has simplified polar navigation in recent years (see Fig. 13.4).

13.9 Escort by Icebreakers Escort by icebreaker(s) is necessary for cargo or similar ships, especially those not having an ice classification, when traversing field-ice areas greater than three- or four-tenths ice concentration.

Fig. 13.4 Satellite photograph of ice conditions surrounding Antarctica. *(Official U.S. Navy photograph)*

The resulting formation may consist of a single icebreaker escort and one ship, an icebreaker and several ships, or two or more icebreakers and several ships.

Icebreakers perform escort duties in several ways: (1) aiding vessels over only very difficult stretches of ice, as in the St. Lawrence approaches during the height of winter or as in the Soviets' North Sea Route during summer; (2) remaining with vessels during the major portion of the polar voyage, as is necessary in the high latitudes of the Arctic Polar Basin and the Antarctic seas; or (3) keeping a channel open for passage and only returning to free a vessel that has encountered difficulties, as in the Hudson River.

The objective of the ice convoy is to get its vessels through a stretch of ice in the fastest time, yet in a safe manner. Basic considerations in the success of any ice convoy are, first, the prevailing ice conditions, and second, the type and number of vessels to be conducted. This means that an ice convoy should be formed basically of ships whose dimensions, construction, and engineering allow them to operate safely in the prevailing ice conditions.

As the leading vessel with the others dispersed behind it in a column, the icebreaker must set the course and speed of the convoy. It must select those courses that will get the convoy through the weakest sections of ice in the general direction of the final destination. It can do so with helicopter help or by conning from its crow's nest or high con. Compromises must usually be made in turning to new courses, making them gradual enough and straight enough so that following ships will have little difficulty in conforming. The character and pattern of ice floes and the fact that the icebreaker, as a result of its relatively short length, tends to follow the path of least resistance, make the channel behind the icebreaker a meandering one that is often difficult for long ships to follow. Another difficulty is that the ice-free path cleared by the wide beam of the icebreaker, while at first adequate, tends to close rather quickly, making it necessary for the following ships to keep closed up. (See Fig. 13.5.)

Before icebreaker-escort operations commence, the captain of the icebreaker should be informed of the following characteristics of each vessel

Fig. 13.5 *USCGC Polar Sea* transits polar pack. *(Official U.S. Coast Guard photograph)*

to be escorted: length; turning radius; tonnage as loaded; draft; horse-power; steam or diesel; direct or electric drive; turbine or engine; number of propeller shafts; special ice-strengthened features included in its ice classification; maneuverability aids such as a variable pitch propeller(s) and bow thruster; and the ice experience of the captain or master. Such data will determine the vessel's position in a multiple-ship convoy and be of help to the icebreaker captain in knowing how a vessel will respond to various ice situations.

A vessel must be subject to the orders given by the captain of the ice-breaker, obeying them promptly without question. It must maintain its position in a formation to the best of the conning officer's ability, and he must not allow the vessel to venture into the ice on its own accord. Vessels are to be guided by voice and whistle signals, if these are prescribed, repeating them to acknowledge that they are understood and will be executed. Convenient whistle signals are: one short blast—Stop; one long blast—Come Ahead; several short blasts—Back. Vessels should be ready in all respects for towing and should have repair facilities for possible ice damage. They should promptly notify the icebreaker captain of ship damage, engine casualties, besetment, or difficulty in maintaining proper station in the convoy.

Once the ice convoy is under way, the following thumb rules are helpful:

1. In making course adjustments to remain in proper station, the amid-ships section or the stern of the ship must not be swung against heavy ice. These are the vulnerable portions of the ship.
2. Aids for maintaining station in the formation should be employed. A stadimeter, radar, or range finder will help the ship handler in this respect.
3. When a formation turn is made, the ship should be started swinging so that its bow will turn just inside the kick of the ship ahead, ensuring that it will remain in the cleared channel at the completion of the turn. (All course changes should be as gradual and minimal as possible.)

In the event a vessel is brought to a stop because of ice and attempts to extricate it prove fruitless, the only recourse is to await help from the icebreaker. In most cases, the icebreaker will advise all other ships in the convoy to keep headed on course (with no way), if possible. After an initial survey of the situation, the captain of the icebreaker will back down either to break the ice just ahead of the vessel if it is stopped by a concentration of ice just ahead of the bow, or to clear the ice from the lee side of the vessel if it is more seriously blocked. In any case, just before the icebreaker begins to move the critical piece of ice that blocks progress, the engines of the beset vessel should be put ahead full in order to take advantage of the release from pressure when it comes.

The following precautions should be observed when an icebreaker breaks out a beset ship:

1. When employing the backing-down method to free a ship's bow from ice, the icebreaker must be careful not to allow her powerful screw currents to turn the bow of the other ship away from the desired course, and not to place its own propellers and rudder against heavy ice.
2. In clearing ice from the lee side of the beset ship, the icebreaker should be aware of the danger presented by the bow of that ship blowing against its own side. Also, the icebreaker must avoid pushing heavy ice chunks against the thinner hull of the ship it is aiding.

When towing a vessel of an ice convoy, the techniques are much the same as in conventional towing except that the beset ship must be towed either in the icebreaker's stern notch or with a short scope (50 to 100 ft) of towing hawser. This precaution is necessary so that ice closing behind the icebreaker's stern does not hinder the progress of the bow.

The *notch method,* which is employed by older icebreakers equipped with a stern notch, is recommended only for light-tonnage vessels in which the bow is relatively low. Larger ships with higher bows impose too much of a burden on the stern when turning and the bow will not remain in the notch satisfactorily. In the notch method, the bow of the tow is brought into the notch by the towing engine and snugly secured against chafing gear. To help prevent the tow's bow from jumping or swinging out of the notch, two preventer lines should be taken from the tow's bow, from either side, and then crossed at the notch and secured to bitts on either quarter of the icebreaker.

The *short-scope method,* which has been found to be the most satisfactory in the majority of cases, permits towing at a distance of 50 to 100 ft behind the icebreaker's stern, but only with the added danger of the tow overriding the icebreaker if the latter suddenly strikes heavy ice or incurs an engine casualty. The powerful propeller wash from the icebreaker will tend to prevent damage by swinging the tow's bow to one side or other and also by slowing the momentum of the tow. Since it may sometimes be necessary for the tow to back down full and swing clear of the icebreaker's stern promptly, ready communications or whistle signals should be set up beforehand.

13.10 Anchoring and Mooring The only difference in anchoring and mooring in ice-cluttered waters as compared to ice-free waters is the degree of readiness required to weigh anchor on short notice. When operating in areas off the ice shelves of the Antarctic, which include about 75 percent of the periphery of that continent, the extreme depths will preclude the possibility of anchoring. Low sections of the ice shelf or stretches of fast or bay ice—which is smooth, thick, and exists in one unbroken strip—fortunately provide convenient piers against which to moor.

Because many of the embayments and harbors in the polar regions have never been charted, the selection of an anchoring site depends upon the results of preliminary soundings conducted by boats sent ahead of the ship on the way to an anchorage. A further precaution in entering such an anchorage would be letting the anchor out to about 10 fathoms and holding it there while the ship cruises slowly ahead.

The employment of ice anchors to moor a ship to an ice edge is not advised during the summer months. Their bearing surface is small and usually not sufficient to hold in soft summer ice. Experience has shown that deadmen, if employed as shown in Fig. 13.6, provide greater holding power and make weighing easier and quicker with the toggle release. When laying

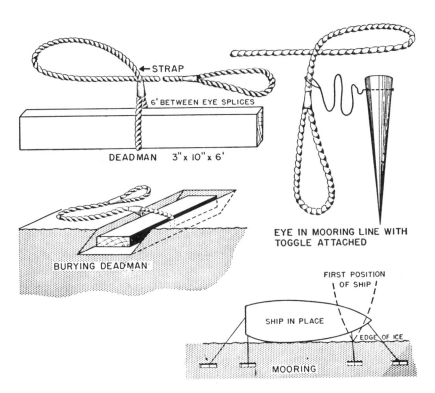

Fig. 13.6 Mooring to ice shelf.

out deadmen, it is very important for the trench for each to be slotted at an angle so that the pull on a mooring line will tend to bury the deadman ever deeper in the ice. Once the deadmen have been positioned in their trenches, each is covered with snow and small pieces of ice, and if freezing air temperatures prevail, fresh water is poured over the ice conglomerate so that it will quickly freeze.

When the ship is satisfactorily moored against a straight, crack-free ice edge, all overboard discharges of water from the ship should be either blanked off or diverted by canvas or wooden overlays to spread down the ship's sides; otherwise, the erosive effects of the streams of water on ice alongside in the vicinity of a hatch may render that site unsafe for unloading or loading.

The best way of ensuring that the ice remains safe during unloading operations is to post an ice patrol with the responsibility of continuously examining access roads and ice in unloading zones. Members of this patrol should have full authority for keeping areas as clean and free of trash, oil, and foreign matter as possible since dark material increases the melting effect of the sun. Metallic objects, moreover, will often melt their way so deeply into the ice that they cannot be recovered.

Large amounts of cargo should never be allowed to accumulate in one location on the ice because of the possibility of sudden ice break-up.

Roads, particularly when air temperatures are above freezing, become dark and deeply rutted from embedded foreign matter and continued use. For this reason, routes or access roads over an ice surface may require frequent changing.

The ice patrol should not only maintain a log or journal that notes every development and detail relating to the strength and safety of the ice in the proximity of a ship but should also be fully cognizant of the "ice mechanics" affecting the cracks and anomalies of the ice.

13.11 Boat Operations   The following rules should be observed when operating boats with internal combustion engines in polar regions:

1. The first boat ashore should carry survival gear for all personnel to be landed.
2. Fuel, lubricating oil, and boat equipment should be checked each time before leaving ship. Fuel tanks should be filled full to prevent condensation and freezing.
3. When operating in sea ice, a bow lookout should be stationed to warn of nearby ice.
4. Use caution when approaching ice. Proceed at slow speed, avoiding any contact with ice as much as possible. If contact is unavoid-

able, push against the ice at slow speed so that it will be swung to one side.

5. Warm up engines very slowly. Keep engine heaters in place when the boat is not in use. Maintain circulation water at a minimum—just enough to prevent overheating of engines. When a boat is hoisted out of the water, drain the engine block. If an engine has a closed-circuit cooling system, ensure that the cooling liquid does not freeze by adding antifreeze liquid if necessary.

6. After a landing is made, never shut down the engines. Coxswains should never leave their tillers unattended. When there is drifting ice about, the boat should always be ready to move quickly.

7. When a boat goes into the water, ensure that the drain plugs are in place. When a boat is hoisted out of the water, likewise make sure that the drain plugs are out of the drain holes. The drain plugs may be frozen in place unless these chores are performed each time.

References

Bowditch, Nathaniel. *American Practical Navigator,* vol. 1. Washington, D.C.: Defense Mapping Agency Hydrographic Center, 1980.

MacDonald, Edwin A. *Polar Operations.* Annapolis, MD: Naval Institute Press, 1970.

Naval Arctic Manual (ATP 17 A). Washington, D.C.: U.S. Government Printing Office, 1970.

Pre-Sail Information Handbook. Washington, D.C.: Naval Polar Oceanography Center, 1986.

Sea Ice Observation Handbook 1984. Washington, D.C.: Naval Polar Oceanography Center, 1984.

Climatology of the Cold Regions: Northern Hemisphere, Volume 1, Northern Hemisphere, Volume 2, and Southern Hemisphere. Washington, D.C.: U. S. Army Corps of Engineers, 1967–1969.

Weather. Oceanography. and Ocean Pollution

14

The Atmosphere and Its Circulation

14.1   Introduction   Man lives at the bottom of a sea of air—the atmosphere—that changes by the day, the hour, and even the minute. The state of the atmosphere at a given time and location is what man calls *weather*. *Climate,* on the other hand, is a description of weather conditions for any area over a period of years. Temperature, humidity, precipitation, cloudiness, wind, and atmospheric pressure are major elements described. *Meteorology* is the science that deals with the nature of the atmosphere, its changes, and the reasons it changes.

During this century, meteorology has developed along scientific and mathematical lines so that today much is understood about existing local conditions and their causes in all parts of the world. Experience is necessary in forecasting weather, but modern developments have done much to put the subject on a more scientific basis.

The present discussion of weather is directed to those who need to (1) understand the advice of professional meteorologists so as to make full use of existing weather facilities, (2) develop the ability to interpret weather conditions with limited or no outside information, (3) supplement official broadcasts with personal observations so that intelligent decisions can be made on the basis of both. This section, therefore, will present some of the fundamental concepts of the physical processes that cause weather, along with descriptive weather information. It should provide a basis upon which to build one's own knowledge through observation.

The *United States Coast Pilots* and the *Sailing Direction Planning Guide* published by the National Ocean Survey and Defense Department, respectively, contain descriptive material of the weather and climate to be found along our own coasts and in many other parts of the world. These publications should be read by those operating in the areas concerned. The monthly *Pilot Charts* published by the Hydrographic Center of the Defense Department also contain a mass of useful information concerning prevailing winds, fog, ocean currents, and average weather conditions. Special articles on hurricanes, waterspouts, fog at sea, icebergs, and other phenomena appear on the backs of many of these charts.

The *U.S. Navy Marine Climatic Atlas of the World* is a series of studies on meteorological and oceanographic climatology at the surface of, and upper air over, the ocean areas of the world. Users will find this series of publications extremely helpful to their seagoing operations.

14.2 The Atmosphere   The *atmosphere* is the mixture of gases that envelops the earth and extends to an indefinite height. It is dense enough at 600 miles above the earth to yield auroral effects; its extreme upper limit would be at about 18,600 miles, where a gas molecule would no longer be held in orbit by the earth's gravitational attraction.

The atmosphere is divided by its vertical temperature structure into layers that form a series of concentric shells, as shown in Fig. 14.1. The two significant layers are the *troposphere* and the *stratosphere,* which are separated by the *tropopause,* the level at which temperature stops decreasing with height. The tropopause is higher over the equator than at the poles, higher in summer than in winter, and higher over stormy areas than over regions of settled weather.

The features of the troposphere are as follows:

1. Temperatures decrease an average of 1°F for each 300 ft of altitude.
2. It has both horizontal and vertical air circulation.
3. It is the region where such phenomena as storms, precipitation, changing weather conditions, and nearly all clouds are confined.
4. About three-fourths of the mass of the atmosphere is contained in the troposphere.
5. Its average upper limit is about 7 miles above the earth's surface, but this limit varies from about 10 miles at the equator to about 5 miles at the poles.
6. It contains water vapor in varying amounts.
7. It is compressed and therefore quite dense as compared with the

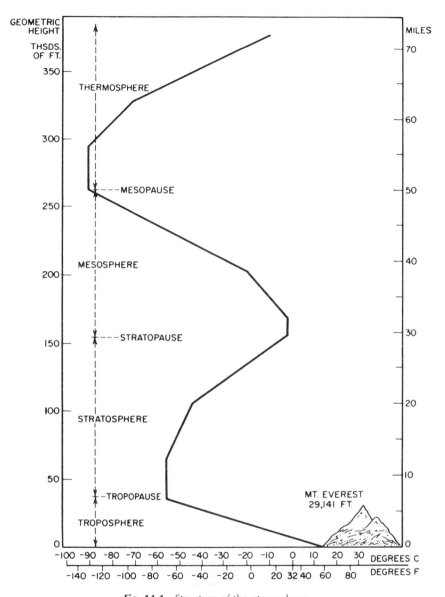

Fig. 14.1 Structure of the atmosphere.

stratosphere. In the lower levels of the troposphere, atmospheric pressure decreases approximately 1 in. of mercury for each 1000 ft of altitude.

8. Flying conditions may be poor. Icing, rough air, poor visibility, cloud ceilings, and thunderstorms are common in the troposphere.

The essential characteristics of the stratosphere are as follows:

1. A nearly constant temperature exists for a considerable distance upward from the base of the stratosphere, after which the temperature increases with height.
2. Vertical air motion occurs only in shallow waves, although strong winds exist.
3. Very little water vapor is found in the stratosphere; clouds are virtually nonexistent.
4. Favorable flying conditions prevail.

14.3 Composition of Air   Figure 14.2 shows the approximate percentages by volume of the principal constituents of the air. Throughout the troposphere, air is composed of a mixture—not a chemical compound—of about 78 percent nitrogen, 21 percent oxygen, less than 1 percent water vapor, 1 percent argon, and less than 1 percent carbon dioxide. There are traces of a number of other gases, dust, smoke, and salt particles that are important in weather processes. Each atmospheric constituent except argon is important: oxygen to animal life and combustion, nitrogen as a dilutant for oxygen, carbon dioxide to plants, and water vapor to the formation of various weather phenomena.

The gaseous constituents of the stratosphere and their percentages of the total are the same as in the troposphere, with the exceptions of water vapor and ozone. Water vapor is virtually nonexistent in the stratosphere. Ozone (triatomic oxygen) is concentrated in very small but still significant

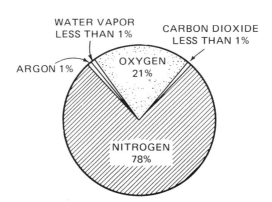

Fig. 14.2 Air is a mixture of gases, in which nitrogen predominates. Each has a function, but water vapor is the most important in weather and climate phenomena. The percentages by volume are indicated, but the percentage of water vapor may vary from less than 1 to about 5 percent.

amounts in the layer 12 to 20 miles above the earth. Because of its absorptive capacity, it is important to the radiation balance of the upper atmosphere and protects living things on the earth from excessive ultraviolet radiation from the sun. It does, however, present serious problems for high-flying aircraft because of its poisonous effects and its degradation of such materials as rubber.

Even at high levels and far inland, air contains large numbers of salt particles that have been carried away from the sea by the winds. Together with other so-called hygroscopic particles, such as soot and smoke, these provide important nuclei necessary for the formation of raindrops. Such particles also affect visibility and are a factor in sky coloring.

The amount of water vapor that air can hold varies with temperature and pressure. Although water vapor usually constitutes only about 1 percent of the air, it may be present in any amount ranging from next to nothing to 4 or 5 percent. When air temperature increases by 20°F, the capacity of air to hold water vapor approximately doubles; therefore, air at 80°F can hold 16 times as much water vapor as air at 0°F.

Air is considered to be *saturated* when it contains the maximum possible amount of vapor at the existing temperature and pressure. The term is rather misleading, as saturated air, even at warm temperatures, never consists of more than a small percentage of water vapor by volume. *Relative humidity* is the ratio of the amount of water vapor actually measured to that which the air could hold at saturation given the existing temperature and pressure. *Dew point temperature* is the lowest temperature to which air can be cooled, at constant pressure, before *condensation* begins.

14.4 Heating and Cooling of the Atmosphere Heat is transferred in three ways: by *radiation*, by *conduction*, and by *convection*. The sun sends forth a constant flow of energy that reaches the outer limits of the atmosphere in the form of *short-wave radiation*. From 35 to 40 percent of this incoming radiation is reflected back to space, while the remainder, except for a small part absorbed in the atmosphere, is absorbed by and heats land and water on the earth's surface. Some of this earth-trapped energy is reradiated as *long-wave radiation*. Part of it heats the atmosphere; the remainder returns to space. By absorbing the outgoing long-wave more readily than the incoming short-wave radiation, water vapor and carbon dioxide, the principal heat-absorbing constituents of the atmosphere, cause the atmosphere to warm. In the presence of clouds, they reflect the long-wave radiation back toward earth, trapping the heat like the glass of a greenhouse.

If the loss of energy from the earth's surface and atmosphere did not balance the incoming solar radiation, the earth would get ever colder or, worse, become incandescent since the temperature would rise on an average of around 3°F per day if all the solar radiation were trapped and none reflected.

Radiation is not the only means by which the atmosphere is heated. Air in immediate contact with warmer water or land surfaces is heated by means of *conduction*. Conduction alone is effective in heating that portion of the atmosphere that is in contact with earth. *Convection,* on the other hand, which involves both horizontal and vertical movement of air, can carry heated portions of surface air to the upper levels of the troposphere. When a mass of air at the earth's surface becomes heated by conduction, it expands and becomes lighter. It then rises and is replaced by colder, heavier air from above, which is heated in turn and eventually also rises to upper levels as a result of convection. The processes of convection, conduction, and radiation are shown in Fig. 14.3.

14.5 Atmospheric Pressure The total weight of the atmosphere is enormous. If that weight were replaced by the same weight of ordinary water, a layer of water 34 ft deep would cover the earth.

At sea level, the average pressure exerted by the atmosphere amounts to 14.7 psi, a pressure equivalent to the weight of a column of air 1 in. in cross section extending from sea level to the upper limit of the atmosphere. Pressure decreases with height in the atmosphere; at 18,000 ft it is only about half that at sea level and at 36,000 ft, one quarter.

Oxygen decreases proportionately with altitude so that normal human respiration exists only to about 13,000 ft. At 30,000 ft, unconsciousness will

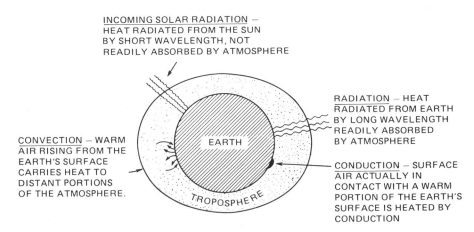

Fig. 14.3 Radiation, conduction, and convection—the means by which the atmosphere receives heat.

set in in little more than a minute. At about 52,000 ft, man, in a manner of speaking, drowns in his own water vapor, because at this height and at normal body temperature his lungs become filled with carbon dioxide and water vapor, there not being sufficient atmospheric pressure for any oxygen to enter. Above 63,000 ft, this pressure is so low that body liquids begin to boil at ordinary blood temperature.

In meteorology, atmospheric pressure is usually expressed either in terms of the length in inches, of a column of mercury or in millibar units. (A pressure of 14.7 psi is equivalent to 29.92 in. of mercury or to 1013.25 millibars.) These units will be considered later in connection with barometers.

Atmospheric pressure at any location constantly changes and varies from place to place. These variations are caused by changes in temperature. When air is warmed, it expands and becomes less dense, and the atmospheric pressure is correspondingly reduced. Conversely, when air is cooled, it contracts and becomes more dense. Consequently, cold masses of air over a region will increase its atmospheric pressure readings.

Lines drawn on a map through points on the earth having the same atmospheric pressure at the same time are known as *isobars*. These lines of equal pressure reveal the distribution of the overall pressure force. A quantity known as the *horizontal pressure gradient* indicates the change of pressure per unit distance in a horizonal direction perpendicular to the direction of the isobars. In Fig. 14.4 the isobars are seen to be spaced closer together in the southeast portion of the high-pressure area than in the northwest. When isobars are close together, the situation is known as a *steep,* or *strong,* pressure gradient.

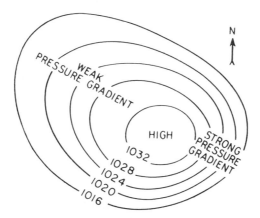

Fig. 14.4 An area of high pressure centered at "high." In the southeast quadrant of this "high," the isobars are close together, and the pressure gradient is therefore strong; at the center and to the northwest, the gradient is weak.

14.6 Wind Speed and Direction Wind speed is determined primarily by the pressure gradient. Strong gradients cause strong winds.

Hills, trees, buildings, and other objects on land retard the speed of wind more than water surfaces do. If there are strong winds crossing exceptionally rough terrain, the earth's frictional effect can be detected as high as 3000 ft; ordinarily, however, the effect does not exist over land and water surfaces at heights exceeding 1500 ft.

Wind direction depends chiefly upon the direction of the pressure gradient and the rotation of the earth. First let us consider the effect of the pressure gradient. Figures 14.5(a) and (b) show the tendency of air to flow from a high-pressure area to one of lower pressure. This flow of air, or wind, tends to blow parallel to the pressure gradient, that is, at right angles to the isobars. Because of the rotation of the earth, however, the wind, or air in motion in any direction, is deflected to the right in the Northern Hemisphere (since the observer's horizon at any point rotates to the left, or counterclockwise, with reference to a point in space) and to the left in the Southern Hemisphere (since the observer's horizon at any point rotates to the right, or clockwise).

Deflection caused by the earth's rotation is known as the *Coriolis effect.* Figure 14.6(a) shows a disk rotating to the left, counterclockwise. Let us assume that air starts to move in a straight line from A toward points B and C, with B located just off the edge of the disk and C located at the edge of the disk. Assume, also, that point C on the disk rotates 30 degrees to the left during the time that it takes the air to move from A to B. Figure 14.6(b) shows the curved path that the air would now take over the rotating disk

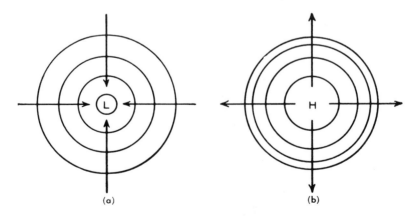

(a) (b)

Fig. 14.5 (a) Air flows toward regions of low pressure (L). Were it not for the apparent deflective force caused by the earth's rotation, air would tend to flow directly toward points where pressures are the lowest. (b) Air flows away from regions of high pressure (H). Wind direction would be parallel to the gradient, as shown, were it not for the earth's rotation.

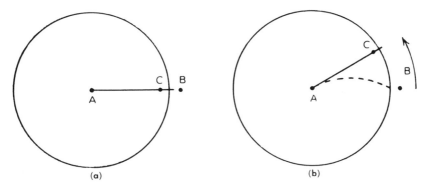

Fig. 14.6   Demonstration of Coriolis force: (a) Air starts to move from point A, located on a disk that is rotating counterclockwise toward point B, which is located just off the disk. As the air leaves point A, it is also headed toward point C on the edge of the disk. (b) The disk rotates through an angle of 30 degrees as the air moves across the disk from A to B. The air, because it is headed toward B, does not reach point C. Though it moves directly from A to B, its path appears as a curved line to an observer on the disk.

to reach B. To see this clearly, cut out a disk of paper and fasten it with a thumbtack to the center of a board. Print a B on the board just off the disk. Place a pencil point at the center of the disk, and while rotating the disk slowly in a counterclockwise direction, draw a line slowly toward B. The pencil line will curve as shown in Fig. 14.6(b).

The Coriolis force acts perpendicularly to the direction of air movement, or pressure gradient. It is strongest in polar regions, zero at the equator, and varies at intermediate latitudes as the sine of the latitude. When its effect and the pressure gradient are balanced, wind will flow parallel to the isobar.

A third important factor that helps determine wind speed and direction is *friction*. The degree of friction retarding air movement depends upon the nature of the surface over which the air is moving. Its effect is least over water and greatest over mountainous terrain (Fig. 14.7).

Friction causes surface winds to flow toward low pressure across the isobars instead of parallel to them, as they would do were the pressure gradient and Coriolis forces in balance. Since friction decreases with increasing altitude, the winds gradually shift with altitude until, above the friction layer, they blow directly along the isobars, their speed increasing gradually as the friction decreases.

14.7   General Winds of the Earth   Uneven heating of the earth's surface causes differences in atmospheric pressure, and these, in turn, cause winds. Equatorial regions receive considerably more heat than polar areas and the

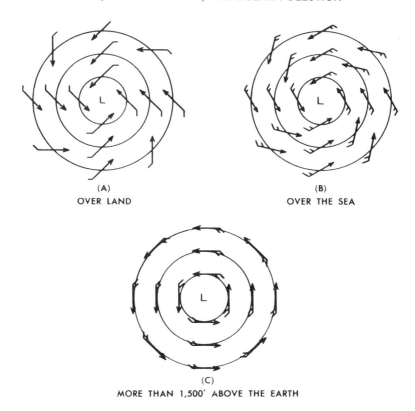

(A)
OVER LAND

(B)
OVER THE SEA

(C)
MORE THAN 1,500' ABOVE THE EARTH

Fig. 14.7 With similar conditions of pressure gradient, wind velocities are greater over the sea than over land; at elevations above 1500 ft, wind velocities are greater than at the surface. It is also apparent from the figures that the wind blows parallel to the isobars at elevations above 1500 ft; it makes an angle of 10 to 20 degrees over the sea; over the land, it makes an angle with the isobars that averages about 30 degrees.

higher latitudes, as shown in Fig. 14.8, and receive it more directly. This excess of heat at the equator is the basis of a definite world wind pattern. On a nonrotating globe of homogeneous surface, the system would be simple. The atmosphere, having been warmed and expanded over the hot equatorial belt, would rise and flow poleward at the higher levels of the troposphere, thereby increasing polar surface pressures, decreasing equatorial surface pressures, and setting up a pressure gradient. The pressure gradient, in turn, would cause air to flow away from the poles and along the earth's surface to the equator. This simple circulation pattern, shown in Fig. 14.9, is impossible, not only because of the influence of the earth's rotation, but because the world wind system is further complicated by the contrasting temperatures of continents and oceans and by many other local

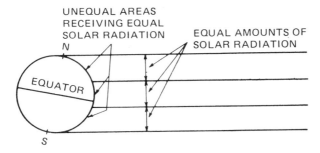

Fig. 14.8 The sun's rays reach the earth's surface more obliquely in polar regions than in the tropics, thus causing unequal heating of the earth's surface. It will be noted that equal amounts of insolation affect unequal areas of the earth's surface.

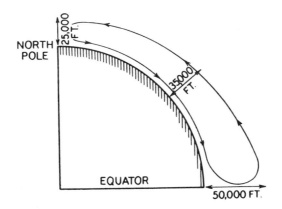

Fig. 14.9 Theoretical pattern of wind circulation caused by the unequal heating of the earth's surface. Actually, this scheme is considerably modified because of the rotation of the earth and the influence of oceans, continents, and other factors. *(After Rossby.)*

causes that we will now consider one by one, beginning with the Northern Hemisphere. (See Fig. 14.10.)

14.8 The Doldrums The girdle of low atmospheric pressure in the region of the equator where the trade winds from the Northern and Southern Hemispheres converge is known as *the doldrums,* or *meteorological equator.* This zone shifts slightly north and south with the seasons, its mean position being somewhat north of the equator. It is characterized by light and variable surface winds as well as frequent dead calms. Warm temperatures and their associated rising air currents are quite general. Cloud types are the mushrooming cumulus and cumulonimbus (thunderhead). The air

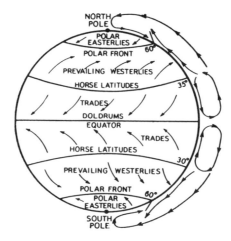

Fig. 14.10 General pattern of world winds.

is sultry, the sky is often overcast, and showers and thunderstorms are frequent. Average annual rainfall is heavier than that of any other latitudinal belt.

14.9 Subtropical High-Pressure Belt, or Horse Latitudes Air rising over the doldrums flows poleward in the high levels of the troposphere, but it does not blow directly north. The Coriolis effect causes it to be deflected to the right so that it becomes a southwest wind. (Wind direction is always expressed as the direction *from which* the wind is coming.) In fact, at about 35 degrees north latitude, the deflecting effect of the earth's rotation causes the wind at high levels to blow approximately from west to east. This deflection of the wind to the right makes the air tend to pile up, or densify, resulting in a ring of high pressure that extends around the earth at these latitudes. The cooling of the air as it flows northward at high levels and its consequent shrinking and sinking contribute to this high-pressure belt, which is characterized not only by descending air currents but by cloudless skies. At the earth's surface, the winds are light and variable. The weather in the horse latitudes is generally fine and the air humidity comparatively low—a marked contrast to the weather in the doldrums. It was, in fact, because of their persistently fine weather that the horse latitudes were so named; the lack of rainfall meant that horses had to be thrown overboard from sailing ships to help preserve diminishing supplies of water.

14.10 The Trade Winds Since surface pressure conditions are high in the horse latitudes and low in the doldrums, we would expect to find wind blowing from the high- to the low-pressure region, and so it does. The so-called *trade winds* blow from the horse latitudes to the doldrums and are the most persistent in direction and force of any wind in the world. Captains of early sailing vessels, notably Christopher Columbus, learned to take advantage of the trade winds on their voyages to the New World. Were it not for the rotation of the earth, these winds would blow directly from north to south. Since the deflective effect turns them to the right, however, they become the northeasterly trade winds (in the Northern Hemisphere only, of course).

14.11   The Prevailing Westerlies   Surface air also flows northward from the high-pressure region of the horse latitudes. The Coriolis effect deflects it to the right so that it becomes a southwesterly wind. The prevailing southwesterlies of the temperate zone, or middle latitudes, are not nearly so consistent as the trades of lower latitudes. The reason is that the region of the prevailing westerlies is subject to the paths of innumerable storms throughout the entire year, these storms being the product of winds from all points of the compass. Only occasionally are the trades interrupted by storms—the hurricanes or typhoons that occur only during a certain season of the year.

14.12   The Polar Cap of High-Pressure and Prevailing Northeasterlies
Wind at the higher levels of the atmosphere flows poleward, where it descends and tends to build up a region of high pressure at the earth's surface. Winds at surface levels, therefore, tend to blow southward but are deflected toward the right by the Coriolis effect and become the prevailing northeasterlies of the polar regions. At the junction of northeast and southwest lies a region of disturbed weather conditions—cloudiness, precipitation, and gusty winds.

14.13   The Southern Hemisphere   The Coriolis effect in the Southern Hemisphere, as previously mentioned, causes deflection of moving air to the left instead of to the right as in the Northern Hemisphere. Hence, trades south of the equator blow from the southeast rather than from the northeast; prevailing westerlies blow from the northwest rather than southwest; and polar winds blow from the southeast instead of from the northeast. Since the Southern Hemisphere presents a predominantly water surface largely unsubject to the complicating effects cause by great land masses, the prevailing winds are not only much more constant in direction but have higher average speeds than those of the Northern Hemisphere. In fact, the region of prevailing westerlies in the Southern Hemisphere is known as the *Roaring Forties* because of the comparatively high winds speeds found between 40 and 50 degrees south latitude.

14.14   The Jet Stream   The jet stream was discovered toward the end of World War II when American bombers flying to Japan encountered headwinds that often caused them almost to stand still with relation to the ground. Studies since then, along with reports from satellites and high-flying aircraft, have established the fact that the winds in the upper troposphere of each hemisphere have relatively narrow bands of strong winds called *jet streams.* They are centered just below the tropopause (30,000 to 60,000 ft) in mid-latitudes, but both latitudinal position and height vary considerably. The jet streams resemble rapidly flowing, meandering rivers, flowing between banks of relatively stagnant air. The average wind direction is from west to east, but an individual jet will usually show north-to-south wave patterns, often of large amplitude. Jet streams in the tropical regions, which are weaker and not always detected, flow from east to west. Although wind speeds of up to 300 knots have been measured in jet streams, the customary speed is in the 100- to 150-knot range. These jet streams play an important role in the development and movement of surface storms and are associated with clear air turbulence.

14.15   Heating and Cooling of Land and Water   The general pattern of global wind circulation at the earth's surface is considerably modified by the uneven heating of the continents and oceans. During the daytime, land areas are usually much warmer than they are at night because the heat absorbed during the day penetrates only a short distance and is readily reradiated to open space. The balance between incoming and outgoing heat occurs at about two hours past noon. After that time, land areas begin to lose heat by radiation faster than they receive heat from the sun. Likewise, there is a considerable annual variation in land temperature; it is much colder during winter, of course, than in summer. Land does not conduct nor convect heat well; it is also not fluid so that absorbed heat is reradiated at the same location.

The effect of the sun's heat upon ocean surfaces is much different from that upon land because of the heating qualities of water. Water is a good absorber, and the absorbed heat can be mixed to a great depth mechanically through convection. Since water is also a good conductor, it is effective as a means of moderating the atmosphere. Moreover, since water has a heat capacity two or three times that of land, it can absorb great amounts of heat without reaching the high daytime ground temperatures of a desert and; it can give up comparable amounts of heat without getting cold. Water evaporates continuously from the oceans, a heat loss that keeps oceans from getting too warm in summer. The vapor carries the latent heat to the air to be released elsewhere.

14.16   Permanent and Semipermanent High and Low Centers   In winter, the continental land masses of North America, Asia, and Europe are much colder than the waters of the North Atlantic and Pacific oceans. The result is the building up of high-pressure areas over the continents and the deepening of low-pressure areas over the adjacent oceans. (See Fig. 14.11; see also Fig. 14.12.) The low lying between Canada and the Scandinavian peninsula is known as the *Icelandic low*. The counterpart low area in the Pacific is known as the *Aleutian low*. These low areas are associated with cloudiness, rain, drizzle, sleet, snow, fogginess, and strong winds. The stormy weather of these regions is not unlike the stormy weather of any other section, but it is more widespread, persistent, and intense.

It must be borne in mind that the Aleutian and Icelandic lows do not represent a continuation of one and the same low-pressure system. Rather, they are regions where low-pressure systems either form or arrive from other places to remain for a time. The lows may move on or die out and be replaced by other lows. The Aleutian and Icelandic centers shift to various nearby positions and at times are replaced by high-pressure areas.

Semipermanent high-pressure areas in the Northern Hemisphere are located in the Atlantic near the Azores and in the Pacific off the coast of California. A lesser center is found in the vicinity of Bermuda. In the Southern Hemisphere, semipermanent high centers are located in the Pacific west of Chile, the Atlantic west of Africa, and the Indian Ocean. These high centers represent intensifications of the ring of high pressure that lies between the trades and the prevailing westerlies in both the Northern and Southern Hemispheres.

The semipermanent lows and highs affect the general global wind circulation and have a decided effect on the weather in many parts of the world. They also have a direct relation to the direction and velocity of the currents of the oceans (see Figs. 17.2 and 19.12). Having considered the general pattern of world wind circulation, pressure, and heat distribution, it is now appropriate to look at the seasonal winds.

14.17 The Monsoon Winds Monsoon winds develop in response to the annual variation in temperature between continents and oceans (see Figs. 14.13 and 14.14). These differences in temperature (and therefore in pressure) cause semiannual reversals of the wind direction in the regions affected (see Figs. 14.15 and 14.16). The results are quite marked in the Indian Ocean, China Sea, and south and southeastern Asia.

During the winter season, air flows outward from the interior of the continent of Asia toward the regions of lower pressure over the warm waters of the Indian Ocean and Australia. In India and southeastern Asia at this time, the prevailing winds come from the northeast and are dry because of their origin and their descent over the southern slopes of the east-west Himalaya range; it is the season of fine weather in this part of the world and extends from October to April. After the winds cross the equator, they are deflected toward the left and become northwest winds.

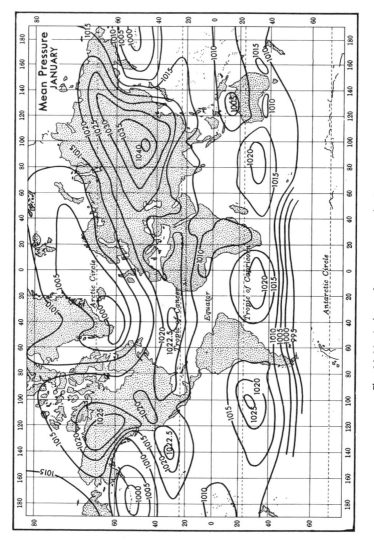

Fig. 14.11 Isobars of mean pressure for January.

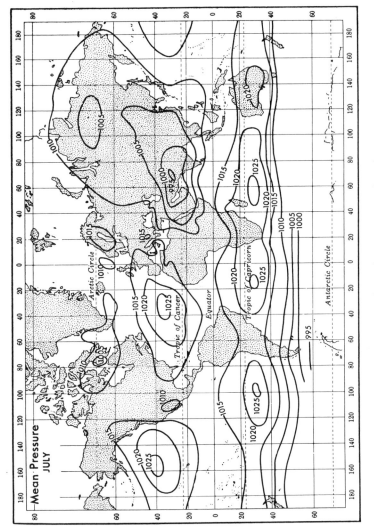

Fig. 14.12 Isobars of mean pressure for July.

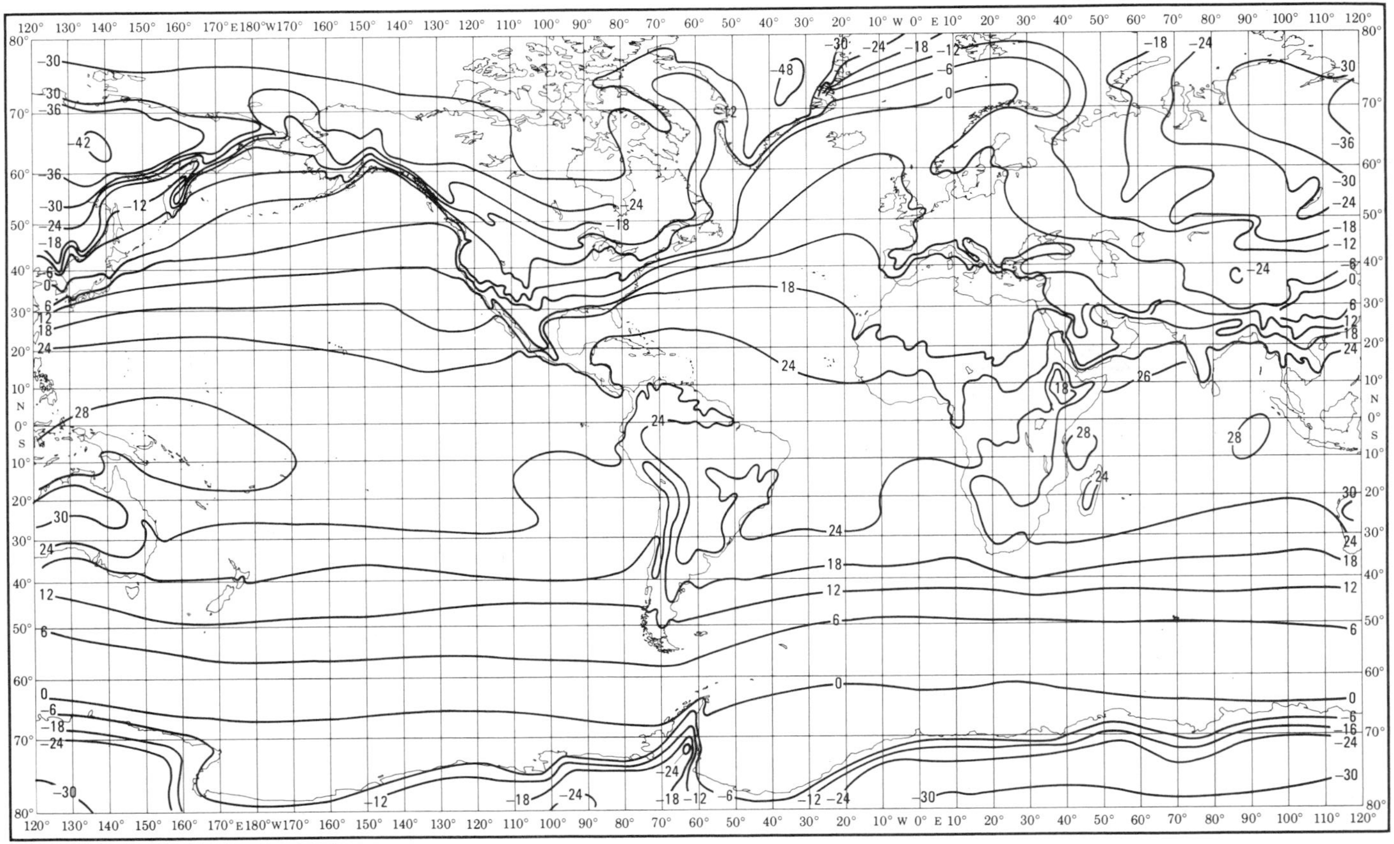

Fig. 14.13 Mean air temperature for January.

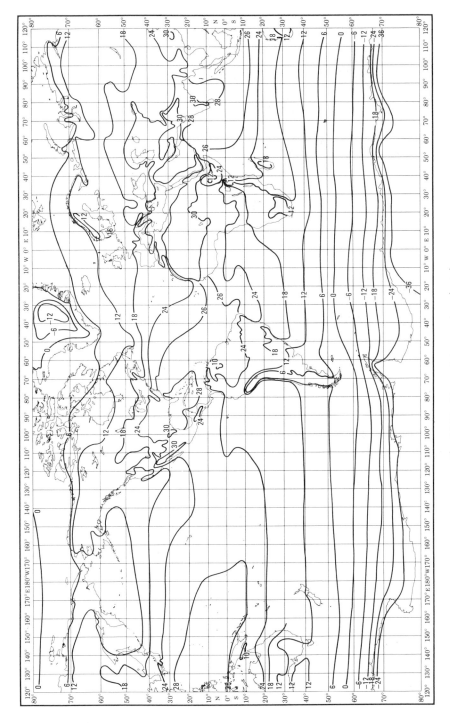

Fig. 14.14 Mean air temperature for July.

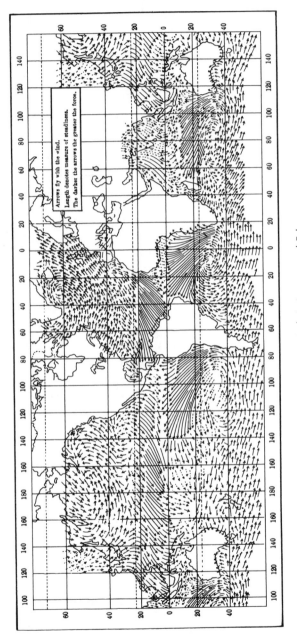

Arrows fly with the wind.

Length denotes measure of steadiness.

The darker the arrows the greater the force.

Fig. 14.15 Ocean winds in January and February.

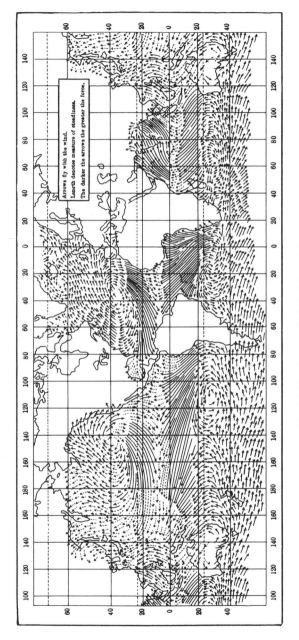

Within the figure legend box:

Arrows fly with the wind.
Length denotes measure of steadiness.
The darker the arrows the greater the force.

Fig. 14.16 Ocean winds in July and August.

During the warmer portion of the year, the conditions are reversed. The wind flows from the relatively high-pressure area of Australia and the Indian Ocean to the area of low pressure that prevails over the continent of Asia. The southeast trades south of the equator cross to the Northern Hemisphere and are then deflected toward the northeast, becoming the winds of the southwest monsoons experienced by south and southeast Asia. As the moist ocean winds reverse themselves and move inland over India and adjacent areas, they bring heavy squalls, rains, and occasional cyclones (as Atlantic hurricanes do). The summer monsoon usually occurs at any time from May to September. During this period, there is considerable local variation in the winds and rain, but, in general, it is the rainy season for this part of the world. In areas where the winds are deflected upward by the Himalayas, very heavy rainfall is reported. Cherrapunji, India, has an average annual rainfall of 35½ ft, most of it falling during the summer monsoon.

Many other parts of the world have similar seasonal reversals in wind direction that are associated with dry and rainy seasons. A mild monsoon wind reversal is noted in the states bordering the Gulf of Mexico, and there are monsoon-type winds in parts of Australia, central and south Africa, and South America.

14.18 Land and Sea Breezes   In the tropics and higher latitudes, particularly in the warmer seasons during the day, land along coasts and around inland lakes is usually warmer than the adjacent water. As the air overlying the land is heated, expands, and rises, cooler air flows onshore from the surface of the adjacent water to replace it. Such sea breezes may penetrate inland for distances of 25 miles or more, extend 25 miles or more offshore, and extend 1500 to 2000 feet above ground during maximum heating. The effect near inland lakes usually prevails for distances of only a few miles. The seabreeze actually undergoes a clockwise rotation during the day in many places (in the Northern Hemisphere) as a result of the coriolis force, so that, for instance, by late afternoon it blows in toward shore obliquely with the land on its left.

Over land surfaces at night, loss of heat by radiation causes land surfaces to become cooler than water surfaces, and a reversal of wind direction takes place. Since the contrast between land and water temperatures at night is not as great as during the day, the nighttime land breezes are usually not as strong as the sea breezes of daytime.

14.19 Mountain and Valley Breezes   The solar heating that takes place over mountain slopes and summits during daytime results in convection. Since the warmed air rises along the slopes, the general flow of air is upward. At night, radiation brings about a chilling of the mountain slopes with a resultant cooling of the ambient air. The cool, dense air then drains down the slopes and into the valleys. Strong winds are sometimes noted, particularly in narrow canyons.

14.20   Gravity or Drainage Winds   During the cold season, strong high-pressure areas of dense, cold air build up over plateaus and inland areas sheltered by mountains. Usually, this air will seep down the slopes and arrive at coastlines as a gentle or moderate breeze. The approach of a low-pressure system, however, may cause the cold air to be accelerated through mountain gaps and valleys to arrive at the coast with strong, gusty winds, an effect that is most pronounced when the cold air must pass through a narrow valley or through an opening where several valleys converge. The most famous wind of this type worldwide is the *bora,* a cold, north-northeasterly wind that blows over the northern shores of the Adriatic at speeds over 80 mph and with recorded gusts of 135 mph. Other well-known gravity winds are the *mistral* of Southern France and the *Tehuante-pecers* and *Papagayos* on the west coasts of Mexico and Central America.

15

Clouds, Thunderstorms, Stability, and Fog

15.1 Introduction A knowledge of the various kinds of clouds, how they form, and what they indicate is indispensable to those at sea or in the air, or to anyone who must deal with the weather and its changing conditions. Because clouds offer visual evidence of changing atmospheric conditions, they can be read as signs of approaching weather, particularly if they are periodically observed to note alterations in structure or type.

Aviators soon learn to distinguish the clouds associated with rough and smooth air and those that will coat their planes with ice. Seamen also quickly learn which clouds foretell squalls or rain.

In general cloudiness is greater at night than in the daytime over land, and greater in the winter than in the summer.

Clouds—as seen from the earth's surface—are divided into three groups according to structure and height. *Cirrus clouds* are feathery and silklike; *stratus clouds* form a more or less uniform flat layer over most or all of the sky; *cumulus clouds* are the heap-shaped, lumphy masses that develop vertically.

In respect to height above ground, cirrus clouds occur only in the upper troposphere; stratus clouds appear only at low levels, although certain *stratiform* clouds are present in the middle troposphere (and only there).

Cumulus clouds may extend from near the ground to the cirrus level. The principal types of clouds are grouped by height as follows: *cirrus, cirrostratus,* and *cirrocumulus* at 20,000 to 40,000 ft; *altostratus* and *altocumulus* at 6000 to 20,000 ft; and *stratus, stratocumulus, nimbostratus,* and *cumulus* below 8000 ft; and *cumulonimbus,* which extends through all of these layers.

Cloud forms are divided into ten types. In addition, there are many subtypes and combinations, but these need not be discussed here. (The *International Cloud Atlas,* published by the World Meteorological Organization, contains detailed descriptions and excellent photographs of all cloud forms.)

Figure 15.1 illustrates twelve cloud varieties. Nimbostratus is not included because it is too difficult to photograph. A low, formless, and rainy layer of a nearly uniform dark gray color, it is feebly illuminated, seemingly from the inside. Its precipitation takes the form of continuous rain or snow.

15.2 The Weather Significance of Clouds Cloud types, of themselves, are significant only if consideration is given to the method and timing of their development, to the structural changes taking place at any one time, and particularly to the sequence in which they occur.

Cirrus clouds may be the first sign of an approaching storm, but only if they are increasing in number and are succeeded by cirrostratus clouds. ("Storm" here is taken to mean a well-developed low-pressure area with strong surface winds and generally overcast skies containing rain or snow.) If a storm is approaching, these cirrostratus clouds must thicken and be succeeded by altostratus. When the altostratus clouds are succeeded by nimbostratus, the precipitation that started with the altostratus will continue—often with fog present. Strong storm winds will occur if both altostratus and nimbostratus are present. The end of these winds will be signaled by breaks in the low clouds and patches of blue sky to the west. Since storms in the mid-latitudes ordinarily move from west to east, their approach is indicated by clouds from the west and their passage by clearing conditions in the west.

Cumulus clouds indicate rising air currents, caused by uneven heat at the earth's surface. Air may also be driven upward when deflected by a hill or mountain or when wind blows against a colder and denser air mass. An air current continues to ascend as long as its temperature is warm compared to that of the surrounding air.

The formation of cumulus clouds early on a summer morning means that the air is quite moist and convection has begun. The clouds are likely to become more numerous by afternoon, building up to high levels, and afternoon thunderstorms are likely. If the cumulus clouds do not appear until late in the morning, the air contains less water vapor, the afternoon

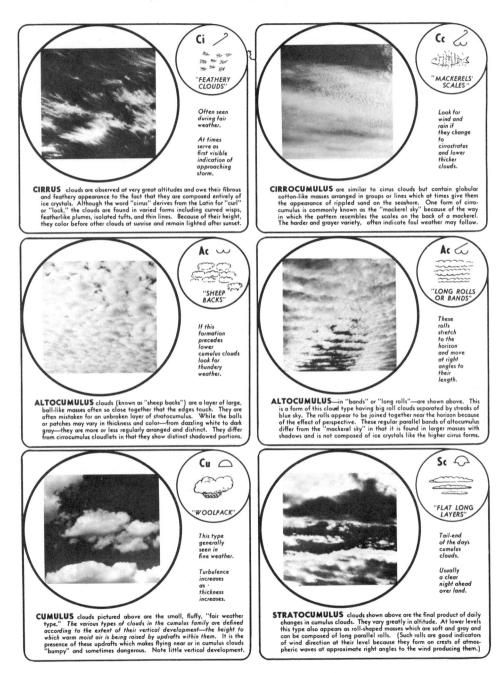

Ci

"FEATHERY CLOUDS"

Often seen during fair weather.

At times serve as first visible indication of approaching storm.

CIRRUS clouds are observed at very great altitudes and owe their fibrous and feathery appearance to the fact that they are composed entirely of ice crystals. Although the word "cirrus" derives from the Latin for "curl" or "lock," the clouds are found in varied forms including curved wisps, featherlike plumes, isolated tufts, and thin lines. Because of their height, they color before other clouds at sunrise and remain lighted after sunset.

Cc

"MACKERELS' SCALES"

Look for wind and rain if they change to cirrostratus and lower thicker clouds.

CIRROCUMULUS are similar to cirrus clouds but contain globular cotton-like masses arranged in groups or lines which at times give them the appearance of rippled sand on the seashore. One form of cirrocumulus is commonly known as the "mackerel sky" because of the way in which the pattern resembles the scales on the back of a mackerel. The harder and grayer variety, often indicate foul weather may follow.

Ac

"SHEEP BACKS"

If this formation precedes lower cumulus clouds look for thundery weather.

ALTOCUMULUS clouds (known as "sheep backs") are a layer of large, ball-like masses often so close together that the edges touch. They are often mistaken for an unbroken layer of stratocumulus. While the balls or patches may vary in thickness and color—from dazzling white to dark gray—they are more or less regularly arranged and distinct. They differ from cirrocumulus cloudlets in that they show distinct shadowed portions.

Ac

"LONG ROLLS OR BANDS"

These rolls stretch to the horizon and move at right angles to their length.

ALTOCUMULUS—in "bands" or "long rolls"—are shown above. This is a form of this cloud type having big roll clouds separated by streaks of blue sky. The rolls appear to be joined together near the horizon because of the effect of perspective. These regular parallel bands of altocumulus differ from the "mackerel sky" in that it is found in larger masses with shadows and is not composed of ice crystals like the higher cirrus forms.

Cu

"WOOLPACK"

This type generally seen in fine weather.

Turbulence increases as thickness increases.

CUMULUS clouds pictured above are the small, fluffy, "fair weather type." *The various types of clouds in the cumulus family are defined according to the extent of their vertical development—the height to which warm moist air is being raised by updrafts within them.* It is the presence of these updrafts which makes flying near or in cumulus clouds "bumpy" and sometimes dangerous. Note little vertical development.

Sc

"FLAT LONG LAYERS"

Tail-end of the day's cumulus clouds.

Usually a clear night ahead over land.

STRATOCUMULUS clouds shown above are the final product of daily changes in cumulus clouds. They vary greatly in altitude. At lower levels this type also appears as roll-shaped masses which are soft and gray and can be composed of long parallel rolls. (Such rolls are good indicators of wind direction at their level because they form on crests of atmospheric waves at approximate right angles to the wind producing them.)

Fig. 15.1   Cloud chart. (*Courtesy of* All Hands *magazine*)

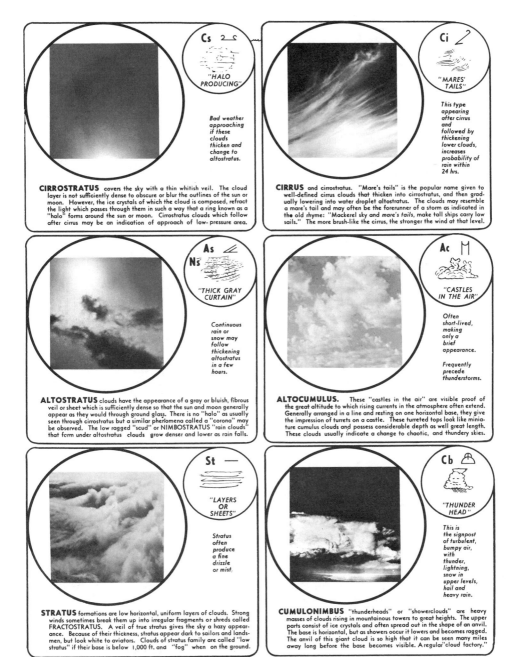

Cs "HALO PRODUCING"

Bad weather approaching if these clouds thicken and change to altostratus.

CIRROSTRATUS covers the sky with a thin whitish veil. The cloud layer is not sufficiently dense to obscure or blur the outlines of the sun or moon. However, the ice crystals of which the cloud is composed, refract the light which passes through them in such a way that a ring known as a "halo" forms around the sun or moon. Cirrostratus clouds which follow after cirrus may be an indication of approach of low-pressure area.

Ci "MARES' TAILS"

This type appearing after cirrus and followed by thickening lower clouds, increases probability of rain within 24 hrs.

CIRRUS and cirrostratus. "Mare's tails" is the popular name given to well-defined cirrus clouds that thicken into cirrostratus, and then gradually lowering into water droplet altostratus. The clouds may resemble a mare's tail and may often be the forerunner of a storm as indicated in the old rhyme: "Mackerel sky and *mare's tails*, make tall ships carry low sails." The more brush-like the cirrus, the stronger the wind at that level.

As Ns "THICK GRAY CURTAIN"

Continuous rain or snow may follow thickening altostratus in a few hours.

ALTOSTRATUS clouds have the appearance of a gray or bluish, fibrous veil or sheet which is sufficiently dense so that the sun and moon generally appear as they would through ground glass. There is no "halo" as usually seen through cirrostratus but a similar phenomena called a "corona" may be observed. The low ragged "scud" or NIMBOSTRATUS "rain clouds" that form under altostratus clouds grow denser and lower as rain falls.

Ac "CASTLES IN THE AIR"

Often short-lived, making only a brief appearance.

Frequently precede thunderstorms.

ALTOCUMULUS. These "castles in the air" are visible proof of the great altitude to which rising currents in the atmosphere often extend. Generally arranged in a line and resting on one horizontal base, they give the impression of turrets on a castle. These turreted tops look like miniature cumulus clouds and possess considerable depth as well great length. These clouds usually indicate a change to chaotic, and thundery skies.

St "LAYERS OR SHEETS"

Stratus often produce a fine drizzle or mist.

STRATUS formations are low horizontal, uniform layers of clouds. Strong winds sometimes break them up into irregular fragments or shreds called FRACTOSTRATUS. A veil of true stratus gives the sky a hazy appearance. Because of their thickness, stratus appear dark to sailors and landsmen, but look white to aviators. Clouds of stratus family are called "low stratus" if their base is below 1,000 ft. and "fog" when on the ground.

Cb "THUNDER HEAD"

This is the signpost of turbulent, bumpy air, with thunder, lightning, snow in upper levels, hail and heavy rain.

CUMULONIMBUS "thunderheads" or "showerclouds" are heavy masses of clouds rising in mountainous towers to great heights. The upper parts consist of ice crystals and often spread out in the shape of an anvil. The base is horizontal, but as showers occur it lowers and becomes ragged. The anvil of this giant cloud is so high that it can be seen many miles away long before the base becomes visible. A regular "cloud factory."

Fig. 15.1 Cloud chart (*continued*)

will exhibit comparatively few formations, and their tops will not reach to great heights. In the late afternoon, these clouds will usually disappear, and by evening the sky will be clear. If the land or sea surfaces are sufficiently warm, however, convective currents will persist. Then, if moisture is still available in the air, the clouds will continue to build up to great heights, and thunderstorms are likely even at night.

The operational significance of the principal cloud types to the weather will now be examined.

Cirrus Clouds Arranged in filaments or strands that are scattered and not increasing (known as *mares' tails*), these clouds have no weather-related meaning except to signify that any bad weather is far distant. Cirrus clouds in thick patches, often anvil-shaped, mean that showers are nearby. Such clouds are formed from the tops of thunderstorms. Cirrus clouds shaped like hooks or commas signal the approach of a warm front—almost certainly if they are followed by cirrostratus clouds. They also indicate the presence and location of jet streams. None of the cirrus types have serious significance except for what use may be made of their jet stream identification.

Cirrostratus Clouds When in a continuous sheet and increasing, these clouds signify the approach of a warm or occluded front with attendant rain, snow, or stormy conditions. If they are increasing but not continuous, a storm passing to the south of the observer is signified, and no bad weather will occur. Other than the reduced visibility they create, cirrostratus clouds have no flight significance.

Cirrocumulus Clouds These clouds are rare and of mixed significance. In some areas, they foretell good weather; in others, bad. Good weather areas include England, New England, and the West Coast of the United States. Bad weather areas stretch across southern Europe, particularly Italy. In the tropics, these clouds have no significance. They also have no flight significance except that they involve somewhat more turbulence than cirrus and cirrostratus.

Altostratus Clouds Of all clouds, these are the most reliable weather indicator and the greatest help to the aviator or seaman. Altostratus clouds nearly always indicate that the air aloft is being pushed upward over a surface frontal system. Impending rain or snow of the steady all-day type may be expected if the overcast cloud layer progresses continually over a station and thickens. Another important clue given by altostratus clouds—particularly at sea where reports are scarce—is their indication of new storm development. Altostratus clouds often signal formation of a pressure low long before it is apparent from surface-level isobars or wind. Flight conditions in altostratus clouds are usually not dangerous. Turbulence is generally light, and icing will become serious only if prolonged flight through them is required. What is important to pilots and surface observers is their indication of an approaching warm front, with its associated rain, low ceilings, poor visibility, and possibly heavy icing in the lower clouds.

Altocumulus Clouds   In general, these clouds are significant only when followed by thicker, high-cloud forms or lower cumuliform clouds. Altocumulus clouds are sometimes arranged in parallel bands in advance of warm fronts, on the forward and lateral edges of altostratus sheets, and near the core of the jet stream. North of this banded type, altostratus and precipitation may be encountered; if the altostratus is moving southward, precipitation may be expected. When altocumulus occurs in the form of turrets rising from a common flat base, it is frequently the forerunner of heavy showers and thunderstorms. For flight operations, altocumulus clouds are characterized by only mild turbulence and only light to moderate icing. When they are associated with thunderstorms, of course, flight hazards increase markedly.

Stratocumulus Clouds   These clouds form from degenerating cumulus clouds and are usually followed by clearing at night and fair weather. The *roll stratocumulus,* with its washboardlike undersurface, characteristically occurs in cold weather over both land and water whenever the air is cooled from below and mixed by winds of 15 knots or more. This cloud yields no more than a light steady rain and possibly fine snow. Stratocumulus will persist for long periods under proper air-to-land or air-to-sea temperature relations. It rarely presents serious flight hazards. Since its layer is thin, a flight path can be easily taken above or below it. It does cause icing, however, an effect that must be taken into account during takeoffs and landings, or when prolonged flight is required in the cloud layer. Also, visibility may be seriously reduced in stratocumulus precipitation.

Stratus Clouds   These clouds have little weather significance. Other than a light drizzle, no precipitation can be anticipated from them unless it comes from unseen higher clouds, a possibility especially when the stratus forms ahead of a warm front. On continental west coasts, such as California, the absence of stratus in summer is more significant than its presence since it implies offshore flow and higher maximum temperatures (80s and 90s instead of the usual 60s and 70s). Stratus clouds are a hazard to flight because of the low ceilings they create, but they do not interfere with surface operations. Radar ducting and extended radar ranges normally accompany stratus.

Nimbostratus Clouds These dark clouds with their heavy rain or snow are of little help as a forecasting device, since bad weather is already at hand when they are overhead. It can be assumed, once nimbostratus has formed, that existing wind and weather conditions will persist for several hours. For flight operations, nimbostratus are hazardous because of their occasional heavy turbulence, low ceilings, and heavy icing. They also make surface operations difficult.

Cumulus Clouds When detached and of limited vertical development, these clouds are called *fair weather cumulus* and have practically no effect upon flight operations. If they swell and develop vertically into dome-shaped protuberances with a cauliflowerlike pattern at the top, deep layers of convection are created, and showers and thunderstorm development are likely. This type of cumulus cloud is very turbulent; above the freezing level, it can cause the heaviest aircraft icing of any formation. However, since cumulus clouds usually cover no more than about 25 percent of the sky, they can easily be circumnavigated. They affect surface operations only by the gusty winds that accompany showers.

Cumulonimbus Clouds These clouds may extend from near the surface to higher than 65,000 ft. The immediate implication of a cumulonimbus that has developed to the thunderstorm stage is heavy rain, lightning, gusty winds, and possibly hail. Tornadoes are also associated with thunderstorms and derive their energy from them. Cumulonimbus is the most dangerous cloud for flight operations because its turbulence may cause loss of control or structural damage. Surface operations can also be disrupted by sudden gusty winds, hail, lightning, waterspouts, and rough seas.

15.3 Cooling and Warming Rates of Air Clouds result chiefly from ascending air currents. When air rises, it encounters regions of lower pressure and expands. This expansion causes the air to be cooled. The cooling rate for rising and expanding unsaturated air of 5.5°F per 1000 ft is known as the *dry adiabatic rate* of cooling. An adiabatic cooling process is one in which no heat is added or taken away from a mass of air by exchange with the environment; the air cools only because of expansion.

Descending air is compressed and warmed at the dry adiabatic rate of 5.5°F per 1000 ft. Since warming of air keeps its relative humidity below 100 percent, the dry adiabatic rate will always apply to descending air.

If rising air cools to the dew point and condensation starts, a cloud will appear, signaling a release of the heat of condensation, which is about 600 calories per gram of the water vapor condensed. If the cloud continues to rise, the cooling rate will be about 2.7°F for every further 1000 ft of ascent since the 5.5°F cooling rate for unsaturated air is balanced against the 2.8°F heating rate caused by the heat of condensation. The 2.7°F cooling rate is known as the *wet adiabatic,* or *saturation adiabatic.*

15.4   Foehn, or Chinook, Winds   These winds illustrate the effects of the adiabatic heating and cooling of air. A *foehn* is a warm, dry wind that blows down the side of a mountain range. When atmospheric pressure conditions are higher on one side of a range than on the other, air is caused to flow upward, over, and down the range toward the area of lower pressure on the leeward side. An example of such conditions is found in the Rockies when pressure is high over the north Pacific and low in the northern plains states. Fairly warm, moist air then flows inshore and ascends to higher ground. If at first the air is not saturated, it cools at the dry adiabatic rate of 5.5°F for each 1000-ft rise in elevation. Once it becomes saturated, clouds form and the cooling rate decreases to about one-half the dry adiabatic rate. Under these conditions, rain or snow is very likely. Once the air reaches the region overlying the backbone of the Rocky Mountain range, it begins its descent at the dry adiabatic rate to the eastern areas of Montana and Wyoming, where it is known as a *chinook wind.* Here it is much warmer and drier at any elevation than at a corresponding elevation on the western slope because the net cooling rate on the windward side is less than the heating rate on the leeward side. The chinook wind is so pronounced at times that it can rapidly and completely melt and evaporate heavy blankets of snow east of the Rockies. Figure 15.2 illustrates the formation of a chinook wind.

Fig. 15.2   The formation of a chinook wind: Saturated air at a temperature of 60°F ascends a mountain range. Clouds and rain occur on the windward slopes. When the air reaches the summit, its temperature has decreased to 44°F. Descent on the leeward slopes results in the warming of the air so that its temperature increases to 77°F, 17 degrees higher than at the corresponding level before ascent.

Another example of the foehn wind is the Santa Ana of Southern California during winter, often producing high-speed wind in the river valley of that name.

In Europe, this type of wind is known as a foehn and is common on the north slope of the Alps. Warm, moist winds from the Mediterranean are forced to ascend the southern slopes of the Alps when pressure is low over central Europe. As the wind descends to lower ground north of the Alps, it becomes the warm, dry foehn.

15.5 Cloud Formation The discussion of the chinook wind illustrated one way in which clouds form: *orographic ascent* (rising air induced by the presence of mountains). Three other ways in which clouds form are as follows:

1. *Convection:* Consider the case of cumulus clouds that form over an island during the daytime. As the land areas become warmer than the surrounding water surfaces, they heat the overlying air and cause it to expand and become less dense. When natural buoyancy causes the less dense air to rise, it is replaced by cooler, denser air that flows inshore from the colder sea surfaces. If the rising air current continues to ascend, it will eventually cool to the *dew point,* or temperature at which it is saturated with water vapor. The relative humidity is then 100 percent, and any further rising and cooling of the air results in the condensation of some of the water vapor into visible cloud particles. That cumulus clouds have flat bases is apparent if they are viewed from an airplane or in a diagonal direction from the earth; the flat base marks the elevation at which the rising air currents cooled to the dew point. Typical cumulus clouds have rounded, clear-cut tops (Fig. 15.3); these tops mark the full height of the ascending air currents that caused the clouds to form. At elevations below the cumulus cloud base, the air cooled at the dry adiabatic rate. Throughout the cloud mass, the rising air column cooled at the wet, or saturation, adiabatic rate. Cumulus clouds, once formed, may be carried horizontally for considerable distances by winds, but without the support of rising currents, they eventually tend to return to the invisible vapor form from which they had their genesis.

2. *Overrunning Air Currents:* Now consider what happens when a current of cool air from the east converges with a current of warm air from the south. As you look at Fig. 15.4, note that you are facing west with north to the right and south to the left. The current of cool air is moving away from you as indicated by the circle with a cross representing the *tail* of an arrow moving with the wind. The southern current is warmer and therefore lighter than the eastern current. When these two currents meet, they do not mix. The warmer current is deflected upward by the heavier, denser air, as indicated in the figure, which actually shows what is known as a *warm front.* (Fronts, together with air masses, will be discussed in Chap. 17.) Many

Fig. 15.3 Cumulus formation. (*Official U.S. Navy photograph*)

types of clouds are formed when one air current overruns another and then rises, expands, and cools adiabatically. Four such types—cirrus, cirrostratus, altostratus, and nimbostratus—are shown in Fig. 15.4.

3. *Turbulence:* Figure 15.5 shows how clouds may be formed as a result of turbulence. Wind blowing over the earth's surface, particularly over rough terrain, causes upward and downward currents as high as 1500 to 2000 ft above the surface and sometimes higher. Obviously, if the air contains much water vapor, adiabatic cooling of the rising currents may result

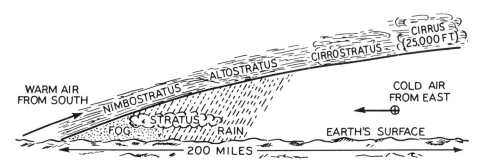

Fig. 15.4 A vertical cross-section through the air looking west. The cirrus clouds shown may be 25,000 ft above the earth's surface and 200 miles north of the place where the warm current began its ascent over the cooler wedge of air.

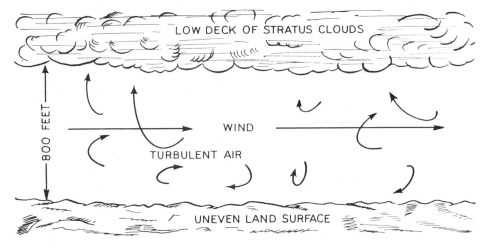

Fig. 15.5 Stratus formation: These clouds may form when fresh to strong winds of high humidity blow over rough terrain. Friction with the ground surfaces causes upward air currents that expand, cool, and produce stratus or stratocumulus clouds.

in their dew point being reached and the formation of clouds. These clouds will be either stratus or stratocumulus and are usually not rain-producing. Their tops will ordinarily not extend more than about 4000 ft above the ground since turbulence caused by surface friction does not often exist above this elevation.

Wind speed often determines whether clouds or fog will form. As will be seen later, gentle or light winds often produce fog when they flow over cold surfaces. If the wind velocity is moderate to strong, the friction of air and ground so stirs up the air that clouds are more likely to form than fog.

15.6 Stability, Instability, Conditional Instability, Inversion Why are cumulus cloud tops low and rather flat on some days, whereas at other times the tops grow to great heights, sometimes building up to great cumulonimbus domed masses? The relative stability of the air is the answer to this question, and the processes involved are as follows:

If a volume of air rises for any reason—as, for instance, in one of the ways described in Section 15.5—it can do one of three things after the initial force that started it upward is removed. It may remain at the height to which it was forced; it may sink back to a lower level; or it may continue its journey upward. What it does depends on its *stability*. If the air is in a condition of neutral stability, it will remain at the elevation to which it was pushed; if the air is stable, it will tend to drop back; but if the air is unstable, it will continue its journey upward.

The temperature of the atmosphere, on the average, is 1°F colder at each additional 300 ft of elevation above the earth. Since this is only an average figure, it is known as the *vertical temperature gradient*. The existing lapse rate at any place and time may be either greater or less than 1°F per 300 ft. Sometimes the temperature is warmer at increased elevations, and such a condition is known as an *inversion*.

Conditional instability is the term applied to air that is stable when cooling takes place at the dry adiabatic rate but unstable when cooling occurs at the wet adiabatic. Conditional instability is quite common and is the basis of much cloudiness and precipitation.

Figures 15.6, 15.7, and 15.8 graphically illustrate stable, unstable, and conditionally unstable conditions; flat cumulus and cumulonimbus clouds are shown on the appropriate diagrams. In Fig. 15.6 it will be noted that

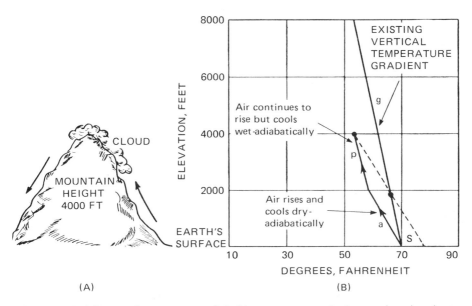

Fig. 15.6 Stability: (A) shows a current of air rising over a mountain. It expands and cools at the dry adiabatic rate (5.5°F/1000 ft) until it reaches an elevation of 2000 ft where the air becomes saturated. Rising from 2000 to 4000 ft, it cools at the wet adiabatic rate (about 2.7°F/1000 ft). Now refer to graph (B). Let us assume that line g represents the existing vertical temperature gradient. Line a shows the rate of decrease in the temperature of the rising air current as it cools at the dry adiabatic rate. Line p shows the rate of decrease of the temperature of the rising air current as it cools at the wet adiabatic rate. Looking back at (A), it will be noted that the mountain forces the air current only to a height of about 4000 ft. Referring again to (B) it will be noted that at all heights the temperature of the rising column is less than its environment, and therefore stable. Hence upon reaching the leeward side of the mountain the air current will tend to descend.

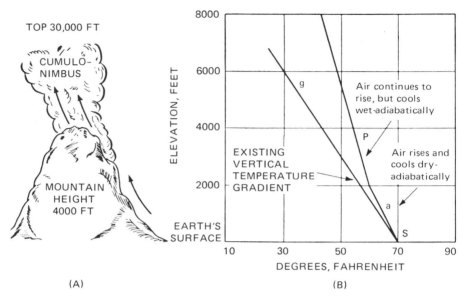

Fig. 15.7 Instability: Again, (A) shows a current of air ascending a mountain slope. Expansion and cooling occur at the dry adiabatic rate up to 2000 ft where the dewpoint is reached and a cloud base forms. Above 2000 ft, cooling takes place at the wet adiabatic rate. Referring to (B), we note that the existing vertical temperature gradient is represented by line g. This temperature gradient is steeper than the one shown in Fig. 15.6. Lines *a* and *p* show the rate of temperature decrease while the air column is cooling at the dry adiabatic and wet adiabatic rate, respectively. It will be noted that at any height the temperature of the rising air column (shown by line a-p) is greater than the air through which it is rising (shown by line g). Therefore, once the air begins to ascend the mountain slope, it will tend to continue upward as long as it continues to be warmer than its environment.

the cloud top does not extend to a great height because the air column that forms the cloud does not tend to continue upward beyond the level to which it is forced by the mountain. In Figs. 15.7 and 15.8, the cloud top reaches a great altitude because its air column continues to rise after being forced to 4000 feet by the mountain. In Fig. 15.7(B), any slight upward motion of the air at S will result in a rising air column; the column will continue to rise as long as it is warmer than its environment.

Figures 15.9(A) and (B) show surface and elevated temperature inversions, respectively. Inversions at the earth's surface develop at night over land surfaces. These radiate the heat absorbed during the day, and, if skies are clear and winds are light, the earth becomes cooler than the air in contact with it. This air is then cooled by conduction, and the inversion is formed. It disappears when the sun rises and reheats the surface, which in turn reheats the air. Ground fog is often the result. Inversions at levels near

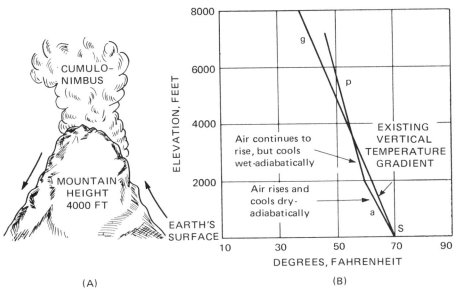

Fig. 15.8 Conditional instability: Note that the existing vertical temperature gradient, g, is steeper than in Fig. 15.6, but not so steep as in Fig. 15.7. Air having this type of temperature gradient is stable for air columns rising and cooling at the wet adiabatic rate. In this case, as air ascends the mountain slope, at 2000 ft it has expanded and cooled to the dewpoint where a cloud base forms. Between 2000 and 4000 ft, the rising air column expands and cools at the wet adiabatic rate. If the air column rises to just above 4000 ft, it will be warmer than its environment and will continue upward. Had the air column contained less moisture, it would have continued to a higher elevation than 2000 ft at the adiabatic rate, and cumulonimbus might not have formed.

the earth's surface act as lids through which air rising from below finds it difficult to penetrate. As a result, there is a spreading out of smoke and other restrictions to visibility at the base of the elevated inversion.

Inversions near the earth's surface are important not only because of their relation to fog but also to air pollution, a problem that increases linearly with increasing population density. In areas like coastal Southern California, for example, there are persistent inversions that trap man-made pollutants. The topography of this region, which allows for no low-level escape of the smog to the east, aggravates the problem. Health and economy are adversely affected. Occasionally, lethal smogs have developed when a strong inversion and light winds have persisted for several days. Notable examples occurred in Donora, Pennsylvania, in 1948, and in London in 1952. In these cases, a dense fog combined with smoke and other pollutants became concentrated to a toxic level. Inversions generally indicate radar ducting. Normal radar ranges are extended when a transmitter is lo-

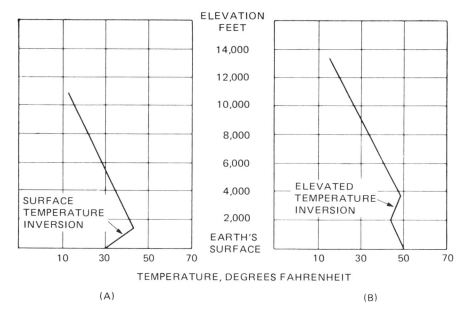

Fig. 15.9   Graph (A) shows a temperature inversion at the earth's surface. Surface inversions are characterized by stability and poor visibility; common at night, they are often associated with ground fog. Graph (B) shows an elevated inversion, the base of which is known as a "lid." It is difficult for air from below to penetrate the base of a lid; any smoke, fog, dust, or haze present tends to spread out at the base of an elevated inversion.

cated below the inversion. Radar transmitters located above the inversion experience reduced ranges.

15.7   The Thunderstorm   Thunderstorms are spectacular, violent local storms produced by cumulonimbus clouds and are characterized by squalls, gustiness, turbulence, heavy showers, thunder and lightning, and often hail, which is sometimes as large as 4 in. in diameter. The strong, gusty surface winds are of serious concern to surface craft and to aircraft on the ground; the strong vertical currents in and below the cumulonimbus cloud offer danger to flight. Up and down drafts may be so violent as to put dangerous strains and stresses on a plane's structure and even cause loss of control in large aircraft. Visibility is invariably poor in a thunderstorm, ceilings are low, and landings difficult to make. Airplanes may also be seriously damaged by hail; lightning may affect radio antennae, Pitot tubes, and other protruding equipment; icing of the planes surfaces and fuel system is likely. Deck cargo and superstructure damage is possible on surface craft. Violent downdrafts at sea during storms have recently been found to have been the cause of the loss of small sailing ships and yachts.

These windbursts are sometimes referred to as "bombs," because the storm center deepens at an explosive rate, more than a millibar per hour for at least 24 hours.

Thunderstorms form in a number of ways, but all require warm, unstable air of high moisture content and some type of lifting or trigger action. Tropical oceanic regions experience these conditions all year long. The air parcel must be lifted to a point at which it is warmer than the surrounding air, after which it will continue to rise freely until, at some point aloft, the air parcel has cooled to the temperature of the surrounding air. Lifting may occur in several ways, from heating, the presence of mountains, or fronts.

15.8 Life Cycle of the Thunderstorm The life cycle of the thunderstorm is short, often lasting from only one to two hours, and consists of three stages.

In the *cumulus stage,* the air in the cloud is warmer than the outside air, and thus the cloud is accelerated upward. At this stage, only updrafts exist within the cloud. These updrafts increase with elevation, and the cloud builds rapidly to heights well above the level at which freezing occurs. During this process, cloud droplets, raindrops, and snowflakes accumulate rapidly. When the heavier elements of this accumulation can no longer be supported by the updrafts, rain and snow begin to fall through the cloud. When the frictional drag exerted by them turns an updraft into a downdraft, the snow melts and heavy rainfall reaches the ground. This is the beginning of the mature stage of the thunderstorm.

In the *mature stage,* there are updrafts and downdrafts side by side within the cloud. The falling rain and snow coming from the colder air aloft cools the downdraft, which spreads out horizontally over the ground as a chilly pool of air. Sharp, strong gusts are characteristic of the arrival of the downdraft at the ground; gusts at sea of over 80 knots have been recorded. During the mature stage, the downdrafts gain over the updrafts, and the storm reaches the dissipating stage.

During the *dissipating stage,* the cloud exhausts its water supply, the rain intensity decreases, and finally the cloud dissolves into irregular lumps, or *scud,* at low levels and dense patches and streaks of cirrus at high levels.

The preceding description applies to a single thundercloud cell. Usually, there are several of these cells in a cluster, each cell being from 1 to 6 miles in diameter. The stage of development of these cells will vary from young to old. Since there is a strong tendency for new cells to form on the forward side of the downdraft of an old cell, the life span of a cluster will be much longer than that of an individual cell.

15.9 Thunderstorm Patterns Thunderstorms occur in more or less distinct patterns, which can be categorized as the air mass and frontal varieties.

Air mass thunderstorms form within a uniform mass of air that provides the necessary warm, humid, and unstable conditions required for storm development. They occur over land or water almost everywhere in the world, although rarely at high latitudes. Since their formation depends on air heated at the surface, they occur over land most frequently in the afternoon hours, usually on hot, sultry days when winds are light. Strong winds prevent thunderstorm formation by breaking up the vertical currents. Over the oceans, thunderstorms are more frequent at night because sea surface temperatures remain almost as warm at night as during the day.

Since temperatures at the upper levels of air over the ocean drop a considerable amount throughout the night because of radiation, however, there is the same type of temperature contrast between warm surface air and cooler upper air as is found over land during summer afternoons. Many persons who have gone to sea may recall clear days and evenings that have been followed by showers before daybreak. Although thunderstorms are most common during the warmer months over land, they occur at sea with greater frequency during the colder months.

Another way in which air mass thunderstorms form is known as the *orographic.* Thunderstorms occur quite commonly on the windward slopes of mountains. The upward deflection of the air by the mountains furnishes the trigger action that may result in thunderstorm activity. Even in relatively flat country, such as the middle western states, thunderstorm activity may break out when air ascends only a few hundred feet in the vicinity of low rolling hills. Over ocean areas not subject to lifting caused by sea temperature differences, wind blowing across an atoll or small island may have enough lift to trigger a cloud—a common sight on a clear day.

Frontal thunderstorms occur along warm fronts, cold fronts, and prefrontal squall lines at any time of day or night; they usually form in a line along the leading edge of the front. Both warm and cold front thunderstorms result when moist, warm, unstable air is forced to rise over cold air lying beneath the frontal surfaces. Squall line thunderstorms form anywhere from 50 to 300 miles ahead of cold fronts under special atmospheric conditions. These thunderstorms are similar to those formed by a cold front, although they tend to be a little more intense and menacing in appearance. Tornadic activity sometimes occurs in conjunction with squall lines.

15.10 Forecasting and Tracking Thunderstorms Thunderstorms are forecast by use of data from upper air soundings; the essential problem is determining the stability of the air mass (Figs. 15.6, 15.7, and 15.8) and whether or not there will be enough heating or lifting to trigger the required instability. Forecasting thunderstorms is beyond the scope of the layman, although he can often anticipate air mass thunderstorms with fair accuracy by observing the degree and time of development of cumulus clouds in his vicinity (Section 15.2). Once formed, thunderstorms are tracked by reports from the network of weather stations, radar stations, and satellites.

15.11   Tornadoes   Although the tornado is the least extensive of all storm types, it is the most violent and sharply defined. Tornadoes occur in other parts of the world but are most common in the United States, particularly in the plains and southern areas. "Tornado Alley," from Oklahoma north-northeast to Iowa, has more tornadoes than any other area in the world.

Tornadoes average only a few hundred yards in diameter and move at a speed of 25 to 40 knots along paths that range in length from a few hundred feet to 300 miles, with an average of 25 miles. In the Northern Hemisphere, the wind of the tornado whirls counterclockwise and speeds approach 400 miles per hour. The tornado may be recognized by its funnel-shaped snout that probes downward to the earth from a cumulonimbus cloud. The cloud mass of the funnel is composed of condensed vapor, although it also contains much dust and debris picked up in the course of its journey. A *mammatus sky*—one with many dark bags hanging down from its cloud base—often gives warning of impending tornado formation; it is also known as a *tornado sky*.

The tornado funnel may or may not reach ground but does little damage unless it does so. Since the pressure within the tornado is very low, a building literally explodes when struck by one because the normal pressure within the building pushes its walls and ceiling outward toward the region of low pressure. A 20- by 40-ft house, for example, has a 68-ton outward force exerted on its roof during an overhead passage of an average-sized tornado. The violent winds of the funnel then complete the destruction of the house and scatter its parts in every direction.

15.12   Waterspouts   Tornadoes over water are called *waterspouts*. Although not as violent as tornadoes, they can capsize boats and also damage property when they move over land. The waterspout is composed of water droplets formed by condensation, not of sea water drawn up by the funnel, although some sea spray will be carried aloft as the unusually salty rainwater following the passage of the waterspout testifies. The extremely low pressure at the center of a waterspout creates a mound of water as high as 2 ft at its center.

15.13   Fog   *Fog* is a cloudy mass of suspended water droplets with its base on the ground. Although its substance is the same as that of a cloud, the process of cloud and fog formation are different. Clouds form chiefly because air rises, expands, and cools. Fog results from the cooling of air that clings to or near the earth's surface. This lowering of air temperature at or near ground level may occur in a number of ways, as described for the following fog types:

Advection Fog   These fogs form when warm air sufficiently high in water vapor content flows over cooler land or water surfaces. The cool surface chills the overrunning air, and the water vapor tends to condense on particles of dust, smoke, or salt even before the relative humidity reaches 100 percent. The fog will be light, moderate, or dense, depending upon how far over the cooler surface the warm air travels. Dense fog is likely if the relative humidity approaches 100 percent or if the warm air travels great distances.

Tropical air moving far northward in winter will cross ground or water that is near freezing, or frozen, and often snow covered. If wind speeds are 15 knots or more, the warm air that is cooled will be mixed throughout a layer some 1000 ft thick. An inversion forms at the top of the mixed layer, and a stratus deck forms near the top. As the tropical air continues northward, the mixed layer becomes saturated at lower and lower levels until the stratus layer finally reaches the surface. A fog layer of this kind will be very thick and persist day and night. Such fogs are very common in the higher oceanic latitudes.

Advection fog is rare over land in summer, but at sea it is very common whenever warm, moist air is advected over cold currents in high latitudes. Favored regions for fog formation, summer or winter, are those in which cold and warm ocean currents abut one another.

Radiation, or Ground, Fog   This fog is a nighttime phenomenon over land. At night, since only outgoing radiation exists at the earth's surface, the topsoil temperature gradually decreases, as does the temperature of the air in contact with it. Cooling raises the relative humidity of the air, until, at some point during the night, the relative humidity becomes high enough for condensation to occur and a mist to form at ground level. This mist deepens and thickens into a fog. Light winds, clear skies, moist air, and long nights are the requirements for formation of radiation fog. It is a shallow fog through which the sky is usually plainly visible, but it makes aircraft landings and takeoffs difficult and can sufficiently obscure landmarks to complicate navigation. Sometimes it forms soon after sunset; at other times a sustained drop in temperature throughout the night is required for it to form.

Radiation fog usually dissipates within an hour or so after sunrise. If mixed with smoke, a particularly common phenomenon in winter, it forms a greasy *smog* (smoke and fog) that may not be dissipated until later in the morning.

Steam Fog, or Arctic Sea Smoke   Steam fog occurs when very cold air passes over much warmer water. The difference in vapor pressure causes rapid evaporation from the water surface into the air. The vapor immediately condenses into water droplets and soon fills the air with fog. Steam fog is usually very shallow and looks like tufts of whirling smoke coming out of the water. If there is an inversion not too far above the water surface, the air between the surface and the inversion will fill up with this "smoke" and become a dense fog. Although steam fog is most common in artic regions, it also occurs frequently over inland bodies of water, lakes, and rivers whenever cold fall and winter air moves southward.

Frontal Fog Fog sometimes forms ahead of warm fronts and behind cold fronts when rain falls from the warm air above the frontal surfaces into the colder air beneath. Evaporation from the falling warm raindrops causes the dewpoint temperature of the cold air to rise until condensation takes place. If the winds are strong, or the cold air unstable, stratus or stratocumulus clouds will form instead of fog.

Inversion Fog This type of fog is typical of subtropical west coasts—California, for instance. *Upwelling* of cold water is common along west coast, and the air over this cold water experiences correspondingly lower temperatures and higher relative humidity. Upwelling is caused by winds blowing from land to sea that draw the surface water of the sea along with them. Deeper cold water upwells to replace this surface water. Above the cool, moist layer of air thus produced lies a temperature inversion that keeps the moist air from rising. Fog forms as a result—as in the advection process—and very frequently offshore. At night, as the land cools, the fog works inland.

Ice Fog Ice fog—a fog made up of ice particles—occurs at temperatures of $-30°C$ or colder, most frequently in inhabited areas subject to artificial heating. Aircraft running up their engines in temperatures of $-40°C$ or lower will quickly cause an airport to be covered with ice fog. Even reindeer, after some exercise, can find themselves surrounded with an ice fog caused by evaporation of body liquids that condense and freeze in bitterly cold air.

15.14 Fog at Sea Fog is rare at the equator and in the subtropics except along the coasts of California, Chile, and northwest and southwest Africa. On the other hand, it is a common phenomenon of middle and high latitudes, particularly in spring and early summer. In the northwestern Atlantic, the Newfoundland Banks is a region off the coast of Canada where the Gulf Stream and the Labrador current meet. Air warmed by the Gulf Stream overruns the cold water of the Labrador current, and dense fog banks result. Likewise, in the northwestern Pacific, fog is common off the coast of

Asia where air warmed by the Japanese current overruns the cold Kamchatka current.

During spring and summer, warm, moist air currents that flow *from land to sea* frequently produce fog over coastal waters. A shift in wind direction tends to push the fog back over the adjoining land. During fall and early winter, it is the air blowing *from sea to land* that tends to produce fog over coastal areas. Such fog may drift back to sea with a reversal of wind direction.

In the north Pacific Ocean and Bering Sea, wide expanses of dense fog are common; at times the fog may extend as high as 4000 ft or more. Such fogs are caused by air moving northward from high-pressure areas centered in the Pacific Ocean at about 35 to 40 degrees north latitude. This air eventually reaches its saturation temperature after passing over the colder waters to the north and becomes sufficiently chilled for its density to increase to the point that it loses its tendency to rise.

In the Aleutians, such fog may persist even when winds are quite strong, although when fog-laden wind flows around and over land obstructions, clear spots may be found to leeward. The sun is not effective in dissipating this type of fog, which is at a minimum during fall and spring months. In winter, arctic sea smoke is also common and may sometimes build up to elevations of several thousand feet above the surface.

15.15 Weather Modification Of mankind's many dreams for improving his lot upon earth, few have been as widespread and pesistent as that of controlling weather. It was not until World War II that it was demonstrated in the laboratory that clouds could be modified and some precipitation produced by scientific means. Since then, greatly increased research activity in the field of weather modification has demonstrated that we still do not have enough knowledge of fundamental atmospheric processes and cloud physics to know how to bring about successful weather modification. The potential benefits to mankind are great; of primary interest are the ability to increase precipitation, to dissipate low stratus and fog, and to modify severe weather, particularly thunderstorms and tropical cyclones.

What must be learned is how to reap the benefits of weather modification while, at the same time, avoiding activity that might affect the climatic controls of heat-moisture balances and general atmospheric and oceanic circulations. Misguided action that might affect climates has too many potential hazards—flooding of heavily populated coastal plains, turning fertile areas into deserts, and destruction of insect and animal life, to name but a few.

Weather modification experiments to date involve attempts to alter the life cycle of a cloud or a cloud system by seeding it with such substances as water, dry ice, silver iodine, carbon black, and other chemicals. The object is (1) to cause small cloud droplets to coalesce and reach a size large enough to fall to earth, or (2) to seed that part of a cloud composed of supercooled water droplets (droplets still in liquid form but in equilibrium at temperatures below freezing). The seeding agent provides nuclei upon which the supercooled droplets can collect to be transformed to ice particles. These ice particles, because of the vapor pressure differences between ice and water droplets, will then collect neighboring water droplets and grow to a size large enough to fall toward the ground.

Although progress in weather modification has not been rapid, these statements can be made with accuracy:

1. Under special conditions, and to a limited degree, rainfall can be increased from individual cumulus clouds.
2. Clouds can be modified by artificial means, either increased in size or dissipated. Supercooled clouds 30 by 70 miles in size have been dissipated.
3. Evaporation processes can be altered over water surfaces, and there is evidence that they might also be altered over land covered with vegetation.
4. There is evidence that modification of the electrical charge in the lower atmosphere may affect precipitation from cumulus clouds.

Various interesting weather modification studies are in progress, but environmental and legal considerations will continue to keep them limited.

16

Weather Elements, Instruments, and Reports

16.1 Introduction In order to determine and describe the conditions of the atmosphere or weather at any given time and place, various *weather elements* must be observed and measured. Reports of these observations are quickly made available for the use of seamen, airmen, forecasters, and others concerned. Some weather elements are estimated or determined visually; others are measured with the aid of instruments (some of which are carried aloft by balloons in order to determine pressure, temperature, moisture, and wind conditions through the many strata of the atmosphere). Still other elements are measured by satellites in space.

16.2 Cloud Observations Cloud observations include the types of cloud that are present, the proportion of the sky that they cover, and the height of their bases. Twenty-seven variations of the ten basic cloud types can be identified. For example, cumulus clouds may be of the relatively flat-topped type common to fair, settled weather, or they may extend to a considerable height, thereby indicating unstable atmospheric conditions with the possibility of storminess. When cloud types and their variations are observed and reported adequately, many useful inferences may be drawn concerning present weather conditions and imminent changes. Such forecasting is particularly valuable at sea, where surface weather reports are scarce.

16.3 Visibility *Visibility* means the greatest horizontal distance in a given direction at which it is just possible to see and identify with the unaided eye (1) by day, a prominent dark object at the horizon, and (2) at night, a known light source. Every weather station maintains a ''visibility weather chart'' that shows the distance and direction of various permanent landmarks or other reference points used to determine visibility. In open seas, the determination of visibility is much more difficult—the usual point of reference being the horizon; at other times, nearby land or other ships. Needless to say, visibility is of prime importance in navigation at sea and to landing aircraft.

A definite relationship exists between general weather conditions and visibility. When air is warmer than its underlying surface, it tends to be stable, and poor surface visibility may result from fog, haze, smoke, drizzle, or dust. Poor visibility is often associated with clouds of the stratus type that are formed under such conditions. If a surface is warmer than its overlying air, horizontal visibility at the surface tends to be good since particles that might restrict visibility are carried upward by the surface air as it expands and rises when heated by the warmth below. Any clouds that might form would be of the cumulus type.

Fog, rain showers, and falling snow are three of the most serious hazards to visibility because they can cause it to deteriorate with startling rapidity. Fog may be anticipated when temperature and dewpoint values begin to approach one another, especially when the air contains considerable foreign matter, such as salt, dust, smoke, or haze.

16.4 Atmospheric Elements Affecting Vision A weather report always includes a reference to the state of the atmosphere in terms of the presence, absence, or likelihood of any type of precipitation or other obstructions to vision. It is possible to record and report some 100 different types of weather, ranging from cloudless skies to heavy thunderstorms with hail. Other typical conditions reported within existing weather codes include various degrees of squalls, lightning, rain, snow, showers, drizzle, fog, and the like, as well as dust, haze, smoke, and so on. Frequently more than one type of weather will occur at once. Definitions of some of the more commonly reported weather elements follow.

Dust Dust consists of minute dry particles of matter (especially earth) that are picked up and carried along by the wind. Distant objects take on a more or less grayish or tan appearance in its presence, depending on the amount accumulated. Although there is always some dust in the air, appreciable amounts are usually of local origin. Blowing dust is reported when sheets or clouds of it are carried along by a strong wind, at times making even fairly nearby objects disappear altogether.

Haze   Haze is composed of very finely divided particles of matter from land areas or of salt particles from the sea, both of which are much more minute than dust particles. Haze gives distant objects a pale blue or sometimes yellow appearance. At a far enough distance, their details disappear, and the objects stand out in silhouette fashion.

Smoke   Particles resulting from combustion are known as smoke. Except for its odor, it might be confused with fog, dust, or haze, especially when present in only light amounts. It is common in the vicinity of cities, especially to leeward of industrial areas, and gives a reddish tinge to the sun's disk at sunrise and sunset.

The following types of *hydrometeors* (defined as water in solid or liquid form that falls through air) are noteworthy in meteorology:

Drizzle   Drizzle is composed of minute liquid droplets so numerous that they seem to fill the air as they fall. This form of precipitation originates in stratus clouds. Drizzle particles not only seem to float in air but to follow even its slightest motions. Drizzle is characteristically associated with fog and poor visibility. When its droplets instantly freeze to objects that they strike, it is known as a *freezing drizzle.*

Rain   Rain is a steady falling from clouds of drops of water considerably larger than those in a drizzle. The drops are usually sparser as well. The intensity of rain—as opposed, technically, to a shower—does not change rapidly. When drops instantly freeze to objects that they strike, it is known as freezing rain.

Showers   This form of precipitation, associated with cumuliform clouds, is characterized by beginning and ending suddenly. Showers, usually of short duration, often occur in a series with periods of fair weather between individual showers. They are indicative of unstable atmospheric conditions, and the form of precipitation may be either snow or rain. Light snow showers are sometimes known as *snow flurries.*

Hail   Hail is almost exclusively a phenomenon of violent or prolonged thunderstorms. It consists of ice pellets or stones with diameters ranging from $1/5$ to 4 in. or more that fall either detached from one another or fused in irregular lumps. They may be transparent or composed of alternately clear and opaque, snowlike layers.

Snow   This form of precipitation from clouds consists mainly of white or translucent ice crystals in branched hexagonal shapes of myriad variety, but these are often mixed with simple ice crystals.

Sleet   In the United States, sleet is defined as small ice pellets or frozen rain. In England, the International Weather Code, and popular parlance, it is also defined as a mixture of rain and snow.

16.5 Atmospheric, or Barometric, Pressure   Atmospheric pressure is one of the most important variables used to forecast weather. It is particularly significant when considered in connection with the direction and speed of prevailing winds and the types and sequences of attendant clouds. Average pressure values reveal much about the climatic characteristics of a region. Since human beings cannot normally feel changes in pressure, it is a variable that cannot be estimated. It must be measured instrumentally with an aneroid barometer, a mercurial barometer, or a barograph.

The *aneroid* (liquid-free) *barometer* is a small, convenient instrument and the one now most commonly used by ships and land stations. (See Fig. 16.1.) It consists of a corrugated metallic vacuum chamber or cell that is prevented from collapsing by means of an internal strong steel spring. One side of this cell is designed to respond to variations in atmospheric pressure by expanding and contracting, these motions being magnified by a system of levers and transmitted to a hand on the dial of the instrument. Temperature differences are compensated for by means of a bimetallic link of brass and steel. To ensure their accuracy, aneroid barometers must be periodically tested and compared with standard mercurial instruments.

Mercurial barometers—formerly the world-wide standard at land stations—are direct-reading instruments, but correction for temperature, gravity, and elevation above sea level must be applied as well as an individual correction unique to each instrument. The mercurial barometer is essentially a glass tube with one end closed. The tube is filled with mercury and inverted so that its open end projects into a well or cistern of mercury that is left exposed to the atmosphere. The column of mercury in the tube then lowers until its weight just balances the weight of a corresponding column of the atmosphere being exerted on the surface of the mercury in the cistern. The height of the mercury column in the tube as measured from the surface of the mercury in the cistern is an indication of the atmospheric pressure at any given time. When the atmospheric pressure increases, the column of mercury rises; when it decreases, the column declines. (See Fig. 16.2.)

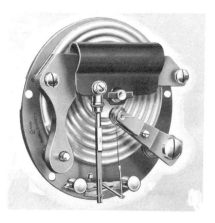

Fig. 16.1   Aneroid barometer. (*Courtesy of Taylor Instrument Companies*)

In nautical terminology, the mercurial barometer was commonly called "the glass," a contraction of "weather glass." High pressure was known as a "high glass"; low pressure, as a "low glass." A high glass was usually associated with fair weather conditions; a low glass, with cloudiness, rain, increased windness, and stormy conditions in general.

The scale on European mercurial barometers is usually calibrated in terms of millimeters. In the United Staes, inches are still frequently used, and readings may be made to thousandths of an inch by means of a vernier scale. The value in inches is then converted to *millibar units*. This unit has been adopted in scientific meteorological work because it represents a

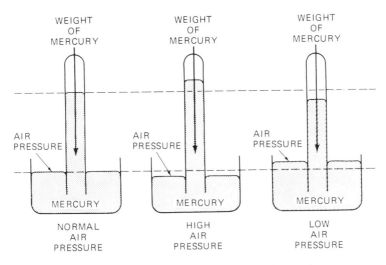

Fig. 16.2 The principle of the mercurial barometer.

force rather than a *length* and is therefore a more accurate reflection of the parameter being measured. Isobars on weather maps (see Chapter 14, Section 14.5) are therefore drawn in terms of millibars rather than inches. One millibar is equivalent to 1000 dynes/sq cm, and 1000 millibars are equivalent to 29.53 in. of mercury. The standard atmospheric pressure at sea level of 29.92 in. of mercury therefore equals 1013.25 millibars (see Fig. 16.3).

Barographs (Fig. 16.4) are instruments that afford a continuous record of atmospheric pressure; they consist of two parts. In the first, the motion of a series of small aneroid cells is magnified and transmitted to a pen by means of a system of levers. In the second, a card mounted on a drum is rotated slowly on a vertical axis by means of a clock mechanism. The pen

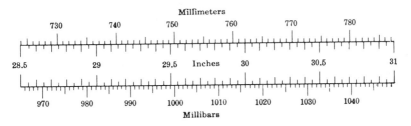

Fig. 16.3 The relationship between the millimeter, inch, and millibar scales, the latter being used in weather maps. (European barometers are commonly fitted with millimeter scales, whereas those in the United States and England are scaled in inches.)

Fig. 16.4 A microbarograph. (*Courtesy of Friez Instrument Div., Bendix Aviation Corp.*)

traces a continuous record of the barometric pressure on this card. The barograph is a most useful instrument on land because it not only gives present readings but, even more important, it indicates whether pressure values are rising or falling and the rate of their changes. Obviously, this instrument has limited usefulness at sea because a ship's forward motion and pitch and roll will cause unrealistic readings.

One of the most significant elements of a weather report is the "pressure tendency" during the three-hour period prior to the report. The tendency reflects both the character of the pressure change—that is, whether it is rising or falling, etc.—and the net amount of the change to the tenth of a millibar. The barograph trace shows the pressure tendency at a glance.

The barograph, like all aneroid barometers, must be checked frequently against other instruments. The card on the drum may record the pressure for four or seven days, depending on the type of barograph in use. Figure 16.5 shows a typical barograph trace. It will be noted that pressure values are indicated along the vertical scale; time units, on the horizontal scale. The time lines are curved because the pen that records pressure value is pivoted.

16.6 Temperature Air temperature is measured by thermometers or other devices and graduated in degrees Fahrenheit (freezing at 32°F, boiling at 212°F) or in degrees Celsius (freezing at 0°C, boiling at 100°C). To be representative, air temperatures near the surface msut be measured under

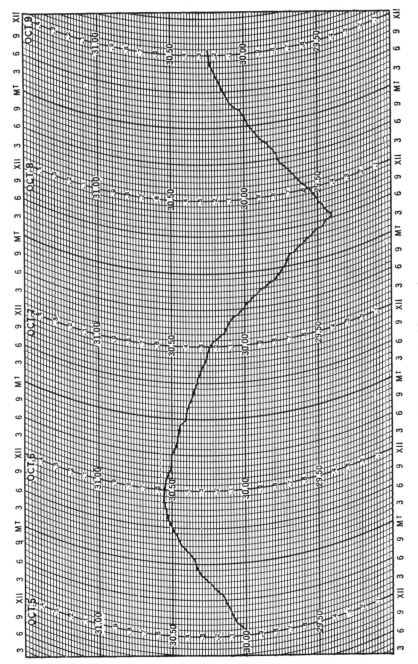

Fig. 16.5 Typical barograph trace.

conditions in which no influences are exerted on the thermometer except that of free air.

Thermometers at land stations are exposed in white shelters with insulated roofs and louvered sides that are raised 5 to 6 ft off the ground. At sea, temperature measurement in a shelter is not satisfactory because conditions at any one location in a ship are not constant. For example, at any time a surge of heat may issue up from below decks, or the prevailing wind may carry off heat in a different direction. There is also the problem of temperature differences on leeward and weather sides.

Temperature and humidity measurements are made aboard ship with a *sling psychrometer* or a portable *aspiration psychrometer*. (see Section 16.7.) The sling psychrometer makes use of two thermometers mounted on a single backplate. The backplate has a short chain and handle mounted at its top to prevent the observer from making direct contact with the thermometers and to allow him to swing them about to cause the required evaporation. The portable aspiration psychrometer consists of two thermometers within a tubular shield and is artificially ventilated by means of a battery-driven fan attached to the top of the instrument. These psychrometers are taken to the exposed windward side of the ship for readings.

The *thermograph* is an instrument that continuously records air temperature. A commonly used thermograph is one that uses a bimetallic strip as the sensor. Two thin, curved sheets of metal of widely different thermal expansion characteristics are welded together. When the temperature changes, the two metals expand unequally, and the curvature of the strip changes. This change is transferred through levers to a pen that moves up and down on a card wrapped around a drum. The drum is driven slowly around a vertical axis by a clock mechanism. The values shown by an instrument such as this are constitutionally subject to error, but if the thermograph is checked frequently against a good mercurial thermometer, its errors may be determined and corrected.

A *maximum thermometer* is one that shows the highest temperature recorded since the instrument was last read and set. It is similar to an ordinary thermometer except that the bore has a constriction in it just above the bulb (in this, it is like the clinical or fever thermometers used by doctors). When the mercury in the bulb warms and expands, it will flow past the constriction and rise in the bore but will not flow back into the bulb when the temperature decreases. To force the mercury back into the bulb, it is necesary to whirl or shake the thermometer.

A *minimum thermometer* is one that shows the lowest temperature recorded since it was last read and set. It is an alcohol thermometer with a small glass index in the alcohol column that looks like a two-headed pin. The surface of the alcohol, the *meniscus*, holds the top of the pin by means of surface tension. As the alcohol moves downward with lower temperature, the index is dragged down. When the temperature rises, the alcohol moves upward but the index does not so that its top end still shows the lowest temperature reached.

16.7   Dewpoint and Relative Humidity   The water vapor content of the air may be measured by means of psychrometer readings. A psychrometer, as previously mentioned, consists of two thermometers, one of which is called the *dry-bulb,* the other the *wet-bulb.* There is no difference between the two thermometers, except that the bulb of one—the wet-bulb—is fitted with a piece of cotton wick. When a reading is desired, the wick is moistened. A sling psychrometer is then whirled or the motor of an aspiration psychrometer is started. If the air is saturated with water vapor, as during a dense fog, there will be no evaporation from the wet-bulb, and the two thermometers will read the same. When the air is not saturated, evaporation will take place from the wet-bulb. Since evaporation is accompanied by cooling, the reading of the wet-bulb thermometer will be lower than the reading of the dry-bulb. For any given air temperature, the greater the difference in the dry- and wet-bulb readings, the lower will be the dewpoint and relative humidity. In order to establish the exact dewpoint and relative humidity values, it is necessary to make use of mathematically calculated tables usually referred to as *psychrometric tables.* The dry-bulb temperature and the difference between the dry- and wet-bulb readings are the two quantities that are entered in these tables.

16.8   Wind Direction   The wind direction is the direction *from which* the wind blows, not that *to which* it is blowing. This direction may be roughly estimated, or it may be determined by means of a wind vane since wind vanes always point toward the direction from which the wind is blowing. Vanes may be wired to an indicator in a weather office or any other location so that the wind direction may be known at a glance. In most weather offices, a continuous record is made of wind direction.

In order to estimate *true wind direction* from the appearance of the sea, the crests of small ripples are considered to be perpendicular to the wind direction. In strong winds, foam streaks show the direction reliably. At night and during heavy rains when ripples or foam streaks cannot be seen, it may be necesary to determine the *apparent wind direction* in order to calculate the true wind. The apparent wind is the resultant of the true wind and the ship's movement. Wind vanes on board ship register apparent wind.

To determine true wind direction and velocity from the values of apparent wind direction and velocity and the true course and speed of the vessel, any one of several methods may be used—the plotting or maneuvering board, a direct-reading instrument, or the true wind computer. The maneu-

Table 16.1   Beaufort Scale of Wind Force

Beau-fort No.	Knots (mph)	Description	Effect at Sea	Effect Ashore
0	Less than 1	Calm	Sea like a mirror.	Smoke rises vertically.
1	1–3 (1–3)	Light air	Ripples with the appearance of a scale are formed but without foam crests.	Does not move wind vanes, but wind direction shown by smoke drift.
2	4–6 (4–7)	Light breeze	Small wavelets, still short but more pronounced; crests have a glassy appearance and do not break.	Wind felt on face; leaves rustle; ordinary vane moved by wind.
3	7–10 (8–12)	Gentle breeze	Large wavelets. Crests begin to break. Foam of glassy appearance. Perhaps scattered white-caps.	Leaves and small twigs in constant motion; wind extends light flag.
4	11–16 (13–18)	Moderate breeze	Small waves, becoming longer; fairly frequent whitecaps.	Raises dust and loose paper; small branches are moved.
5	17–21 (19–24)	Fresh breeze	Moderate waves, taking a more pronounced long form; many whitecaps are formed. (Chance of some spray.)	Small trees in leaf begin to sway; crested wavelets form on inland waters.
6	22–27 (25–31)	Strong breeze	Large waves begin to form; the white foam crests are more extensive everywhere. (Probably some spray.)	Large branches in motion; whistling heard in telegraph wires; umbrellas used with difficulty.
7	28–33 (32–38)	Moderate gale (high wind)	Sea heaps up and white foam from breaking waves begins to be blown in streaks along the direction of the wind. Spindrift begins.	Whole trees in motion; inconvenience felt in walking against wind.
8	34–40 (39–46)	Fresh gale	Moderately high waves of greater length; edges of crests break into spindrift. The foam is blown in well-marked streaks along the direction of the wind.	Breaks twigs off trees; generally impedes progress.
9	41–47 (47–54)	Strong gale	High waves. Dense streaks of foam along the direction of the wind. Sea begins to roll. Spray may affect visibility.	Slight structural damage occurs (chimney pots and slate removed).
10	48–55 (55–63)	Storm	Very high waves with long overhanging crests. The resulting foam in great patches is blown in dense white streaks along the direction of the wind. On the whole the surface of the sea takes a white appearance. The rolling of the sea becomes heavy and shocklike. Visibility is affected.	Seldom experienced inland; trees uprooted; considerable structural damage occurs.
11	56–63 (64–73)	Violent storm	Exceptionally high waves. (Small and medium-sized ships might for a long time be lost to view behind the waves.) The sea is completely covered with long white patches of foam lying along the direction of the wind. Everywhere the edges of the wave crests are blown into froth. Visibility affected.	Very rarely experienced; accompanied by widespread damage.
12	Above 63 (73)	Hurricane	The air is filled with foam and spray. Sea completely white with driving spray; visibility very seriously affected.	

vering board is the most commonly used method. The ship's course and speed are plotted from its center; the apparent wind is plotted from the end of the ship's course and speed. An arrow drawn from the center to the end of the apparent wind provides the true wind direction and velocity. The other methods, less commonly used, are a direct-reading anemometer that has been modified to display true wind, and the true wind computer, which consists of a set of movable plastic discs that permit essentially the same calculations as the maneuvering board.

Table 16.1   Beaufort Scale of Wind Force (*Cont.*)

Wind Speed (knots)	Wind and Sea Scale for Fully Arisen Sea*				Average Period	Average Wave Length	Minimum Fetch (nautical miles)	Minimum Duration (hours)	Average Wave Height[b] (maximum)
	Wave Height–Feet								
	Average	Significant Average 1/3 Highest	Average 1/10 Highest						
0	0	0	0	—	—	—	—	—	—
2	0.05	0.08	0.10	0.5	10 in.	5	18 min		
5	0.18	0.29	0.37	1.4	6.7 ft	8	39 min		
8.5	0.6	1.0	1.2	2.4	20	9.8	1.7 hrs	2(3)
10	0.88	1.4	1.8	2.9	27	10	2.4	
13.5	1.8	2.9	3.7	3.9	52	24	4.8	3½(5)
16	2.9	4.6	5.8	4.6	71	40	6.6	
18	3.8	6.1	7.8	5.1	90	55	8.3	
19	4.3	6.9	8.7	5.4	99	65	9.2	6(8½)
20	5.0	8.0	10	5.7	111	75	10	
22	6.4	10	13	6.3	134	100	12	
24.5	8.2	13	17	7.0	164	140	15	9½(13)
26	9.6	15	20	7.4	188	180	17	
28	11	18	23	7.9	212	230	20	
30.5	14	23	29	8.7	258	290	24	13½(19)
32	16	26	33	9.1	285	340	27	
34	19	30	38	9.7	322	420	30	
37	23	37	46.7	10.5	376	530	37	18(25)
40	28	45	58	11.4	444	710	42	
42	31	50	64	12.0	492	830	47	
44	36	58	73	12.5	534	960	52	23(32)
46	40	64	81	13.1	590	1110	57	
48	44	71	90	13.8	650	1250	63	
50	49	78	99	14.3	700	1420	69	29(41)
51.5	52	83	106	14.7	736	1560	73	
54	59	95	121	15.4	810	1800	81	
56	64	103	130	16.3	910	2100	88	37(52)
59.5	73	116	148	17.0	985	2500	101	
>64	>80	>128	>164	18	~	~	~	45(—)

* To attain a fully arisen sea for a certain wind speed, the wind must blow at that speed over a minimum distance (fetch) for a minimum time (duration). When winds are 50 knots or more, the required fetch and duration for a fully arisen sea rarely occur. The wave heights shown in the last column, "Average Wave Height" represent what will be found on the average at given wind speeds.
Wave heights refer only to wind waves, and swells from distant or old storms are nearly always superimposed on the wind-wave pattern.
Practical Methods of Observing and Forecasting Ocean Waves, Pierson, Neuman, James, H.O. Pub. 603, 1955.
[b] H.O. 118A.

16.9   Wind Speed   Wind speed may be estimated, or it may be measured by means of an *anemometer*. It can be expressed in knots, miles per hour, meters per second, or in Beaufort force numbers. The Beaufort scale of wind force, shown in Table 16.1, is useful in estimating wind forces (see Section 19.5). Experienced seamen become expert at estimating wind speed and direction by observing waves, funnel smoke, flags, and even sounds. Ninety percent of all wind information concerning the high seas comes from merchant ships with no wind observation equipment.

16.10 Upper-Air Winds Some ship-and-shore meteorological stations are equipped to determine the direction and force of the wind at various heights above the earth's surface. This information is important to airmen for navigation purposes and fuel consumption planning. Weather forecasters also require upper-air wind data because it indicates sources of air masses and other processes that determine cloudiness, precipitation, and other weather conditions.

Pilot balloon (PIBAL) observations are used to get upper-air wind data. Small rubber balloons are inflated with hydrogen or helium in a manner that defines their rate of ascension. After a balloon has been released, it is watched through the telescope of a *theodolite,* an instrument that resembles a surveyor's transit. By means of scales on the theodolite, the azimuth and the vertical angle of the balloon are determined at 1-min. intervals. Since the balloon has an assumed rate of ascension based on atmospheric density and vertical wind velocity, its height can be known within reasonable accuracy at all times. Applying the principles of trigonometry, the height, azimuth, and vertical angle readings can then be used to compute the wind speed and direction through each successive layer.

Balloons with radio transmitters attached are tracked with radio direction-finding equipment. Other balloons with radar reflectors attached are tracked with radar. Wind measurements obtained by these two methods are called RAWINS. Aboard ship the radar reflector method is the one most frequently used. Obviously, the ship's course and speed must be taken into account. Satellites also observe and measure upper winds with specialized sensors. These measurements are of specific value to forecasters, but they are not normally available to other parties.

16.11 Ceiling The *ceiling* is defined as the vertical distance between the earth's surface and the lowest layer of clouds that cover more than one half the sky. Ceiling values, which are of great importance in aviation, may be estimated or measured. If they are estimated, previous values, weather trends, and conditions reported from surrounding areas must all be considered. Aircraft reports obtained in "let downs" or in level flight at the base of cloud decks are an important source of ceiling information.

Many shore stations are equipped with a *ceilometer,* an instrument used to detemine ceiling conditions both at night and during the day (see Fig. 16.6). The height of the cloud base is determined by trigonometry from the known baseline and the projector beam angle.

16.12 Ocean Surface Temperature Observations from ships at sea include the temperature of the water at the surface, which is obtained either

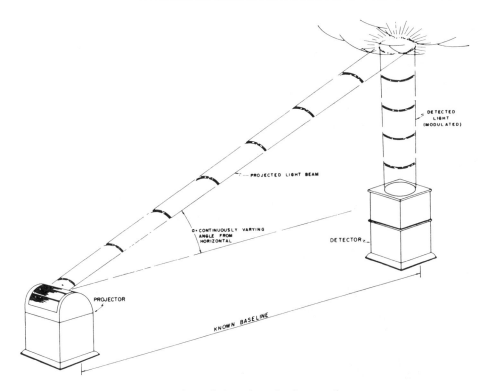

Fig. 16.6 Typical installation of rotating beam ceilometer.

by a thermometer reading at the condenser intake or by measuring the temperature of the water brought on deck in a bucket. Sea surface temperatures are also provided by infrared sensors on satellites. Surface water temperature is important in the forecasting of fog, clouds, mixed layer depth, and other phenomena.

16.13 Marine Automatic Weather Stations To fill the gaps in key ocean areas, seagoing automatic weather stations are deployed. The U.S. Navy pioneered one verison called NOMAD (Fig. 16.7), which has been tested in the Alaskan Gulf, Gulf of Mexico, and of the Virginia Capes. These bouys measure winds, temperature, humidity, and pressure and automatically transmit the data on a set schedule. Some of them measure oceanographic data such as wave, swell, and sea temperature and transmit these as well.

16.14 Upper-Air Temperature, Humidity, and Pressure—Radiosondes
The *radiosonde* is an instrument containing sensors to determine the pressure, temperature, and humidity of the upper air. Only a limited number of land stations and ships are equipped to make this type of weather obser-

Fig. 16.7 Naval oceanographic meteorological automatic device (NOMAD).

vation, which is known as RAOB. A built-in battery-operated radio trans-mitter transmits the measurements to a receiver located at a meteorological station. The instrument is carried aloft by a balloon to heights consistently near 100,000 ft and many times between 100,000 and 150,000 ft. When the balloon bursts, the radiosonde descends by parachute to prevent dam-age to property on the ground, and is sometimes recovered, repaired, and reused. Data obtained by RAOBs are used immediately to prepare weather charts and forecasts.

Weather reconnaissance flights often use a *dropsonde* to obtain upper-air data. This instrument, which is similar to the radiosonde, is parachuted to earth from the aircraft. The aircraft orbits within signal-reading distance of the dropsonde and collects the data that it transmits.

16.15 Rocketsondes With advances in technology, and need for high-level atmospheric information increase rapidly. Environmental factors are of importance in the design, launching, and reentry of missiles and space systems, for example, the conditions of density, temperature, and wind in the 100,000- to 350,000-ft layer. (Radiosondes and Rawins give the informa-tion from surface to 100,000 ft.)

Rocketsondes provide density, wind, and temperature information in the vertical—reliably to 200,000 ft, less reliably at higher altitudes. Sensors used to measure these weather elements continue to be improved with each technological advancement in electronics and solid-state research.

16.16 Weather Satellites The latest means of obtaining information about the state of the atmosphere is from weather satellites, which operate in two ways. Some circle the earth at altitudes of over 400 miles and transmit pictures of the earth and its cloud cover along a path 750 to 1000 miles wide. Others are placed in an earth-synchronous orbit at about 22,000 miles above the equator; they are stationary with respect to a chosen longitude and provide pictures of almost half the earth. Figure 16.8 illustrates how the cloud patterns of storms can now be seen in their entirety. In addition to daylight pictures, weather satellites are equipped with infrared radiometers that make it possible to determine cloud patterns at night by sensing the differences in heat radiation from the earth and from the clouds.

Fig. 16.8   The earth as seen by the applications technology satellite from an altitude of 22,240 statute miles. (*Courtesy of NASA*)

Operational use is now being made of these pictures, which show the configuration and location of tropical and extratropical cyclones, the presence or absence of clouds, the location of jet streams, the vertical temperature and wind structure of the atmosphere, land and sea surface temperatures, the state of the sea, and polar ice coverage.

The particular value of satellites in tropical areas is their ability to discover hurricanes and typhoons in the incipient stage. Reconnaissance aircraft are then sent to the suspicious areas to make a thorough investigation. The satellites can also track the progress of these cyclones.

Another use of satellites is as collectors and transmitters of data from outlying weather stations (manned or automatic), weather and oceanographic buoys, and instrumented balloons floating freely at known atmospheric levels. Weather satellites have been placed in orbit by many nations. Any ship may obtain their pictures easily with inexpensive receiving equipment.

16.17 Transmission of Weather Observations By international agreement, all ships of all nations use the same weather code for transmitting weather reports. After each weather observation has been made, it is encoded for radio transmission. The code is designed to reduce the transmission time, to prevent errors and misunderstanding, and to make the data compatible for computer use. Each coded message consists of a variable number of five-digit groups of numbers. The number of groups used will depend upon the complexity of the data and how much of it the ship decides to transmit. A vast revision of the code went into effect in January of 1982, and experience has shown that many modifications can be expected in the next five or so years. The code format, however, can be obtained from the observing forms or observing manuals.

16.18 The Use of Weather Reports Ship and land stations, regardless of their location, simultaneously observe and record weather conditions every six hours, starting at midnight Greenwich time. These reports are transmitted by landline or radio to collection and control centers, where, in the shortest possible time, they are used for the preparation of the weather charts from which forecasts are made. These forecasts are then transmitted on assigned frequencies and at specified times to all parties capable of receiving them.

In addition to the forecasts, a general description of each weather map is also broadcast, along with selected surface reports from which any ship may prepare its own weather map if it so desires. Advancements in radio facsimile have made it possible to broadcast facsimiles of weather maps in picture form. Many merchant ships and a great number of military ships are equipped to receive this form of transmission.

Complete weather broadcast schedules for various parts of the world are contained in the following publications: *Worldwide Marine Weather Broadcasts and Marine Weather Services Charts,* published by NOAA; and *Information for Shipping,* Publication No. 9. TP 4 (Volume D), published by the World Meteorological Organization.

NOAA weather radio broadcasts are made on one of seven high-band FM frequencies ranging from 162.40 to 162.55 MHz. These broadcasts are continuous, containing current and forecast weather, basic marine weather information, and warnings or watches of potentially severe weather. The National Weather Service has more than 350 of these broadcast stations throughout the United States and reception range is usually 20 to 40 miles.

16.19   Criteria for Wind Warnings

Wind Warning Terminology in Common Usage by NOAA and the U.S. Navy   Warnings of winds associated with closed cyclonic circulations of tropical origin are expressed in the following terms:

Type of Warning	Corresponding Wind Speed
Tropical depression	Winds up to 33 knots
Tropical storm	Winds of 34 to 63 knots
Hurricane/typhoon	Winds of 64 knots or greater

Warnings of winds associated with weather systems located in latitudes outside tropical regions, or by systems of tropical origin other than closed cyclonic circulations, are expressed in the following terms:

Types of Warning and Advisory	Corresponding Wind Speed
Small craft advisory	Winds up to 33 knots (for use in coastal and inland waters only)
Gale warning	Winds of 34 to 47 knots
Storm warning	Winds of 48 knots or greater

Wind Warning Terminology Used by NOAA for Coastal Warning Displays   Warnings of winds for coastal display purposes are issued by NOAA in accordance with the following criteria:

Types of Warning	Corresponding Wind Speed
Small craft warning	Winds up to 33 knots
Gale warning	Winds of 34 to 47 knots
Storm warning	Winds of 48 to 63 knots
Hurricane warning	Winds of 64 knots or greater

17

Weather of the Middle Latitudes

17.1 Introduction The middle latitudes of the Northern Hemisphere, those lying between the tropical and polar regions, have a temperate climate unusually favorable to man. Just as there are more people in the mid-latitudes, there is also more "weather." Weather in the tropics and polar regions tends to occur in more or less dependable patterns, but such is not the case in the mid-latitudes. It is in these latitudes that the masses of air moving northward from the tropics and southward from the polar region tend to converge and create various types of fronts. The reaction of these air masses with each other and with the land and water surfaces of the earth causes the constant weather changes that characterize the middle latitudes of both hemispheres. Widespread areas of low and high pressure drift eastward in the prevailing westerlies of these latitudes and contribute greatly to these changes.

This chapter deals with the air masses, fronts, and high- and low-pressure systems of the middle latitudes; the preparation and use of weather maps; and the general principles involved in forecasting weather from surface maps and from local indications. In addition to surface weather maps, professional meteorologists construct and use many other kinds of maps, charts, and graphs that show pressure, humidity, temperature, and wind conditions in the upper portions of the atmosphere—data that is used both for forecasting and for aircraft operation. New instruments and techniques for gathering and interpreting atmospheric conditions at various elevations above the earth's surface has enabled the meteorologist to forecast changes far more effectively than he ever could using surface weather maps only.

17.2 The Meaning and Classification of Air Masses An *air mass* is defined as a large body of air whose physical properties, particularly temperature and moisture distribution, are nearly homogeneous in the horizontal. One of the most important elements of forecasting is recognizing the various air masses that affect the weather picture, determining their characteristics, and predicting their behavior.

When a large body of air remains for some time over a particular place, it acquires the characteristics of that region, known as the *source region.* For example, air that stands for several days or weeks over northern Canada during the winter becomes extremely cold. It will have a low moisture content, not only because of its coldness but because of the absence of water at the earth's surface from which vapor could be received. It would be described as a "cold, dry mass of polar continental air." On the other hand, a body of air that stagnates over the Gulf of Mexico for any length of time will acquire not only the warmth of those waters, but a large content of water vapor as well because of the ready evaporation induced by that warmth and the capacity of warm air to sustain it. Such a body of air would be described as a "warm, moist mass of tropical air." In this case, the source region, the Gulf of Mexico, is tropical maritime.

Air masses are classified according to their sources, for example: arctic, polar, and tropical. They are further classified according to their moisture content. Masses whose source regions are over the ocean are known as *maritime air masses* and are moist, or high in water vapor content. Those originating over land areas are known as *continential air masses* and are relatively dry, or low in water vapor content. A further classification depends on whether an air mass, once it starts to move about, is warmer or colder than the surface over which it is moving. For example, a mass that moves northward over the Gulf states from the Gulf of Mexico would be classed as a warm mass in winter because the air mass is warmer than the cold land. In summer, however, the mass would be classed as cold because the land surfaces are then warmer than the air mass. (See Fig. 17.1.)

17.3 Weather in Warm and Cold Air Masses Warm and cold air masses may occur in either summer or winter months. The weather associated with them is a function of the temperature differential between the air mass and the underlying surface. A cold air mass will absorb heat and moisture from

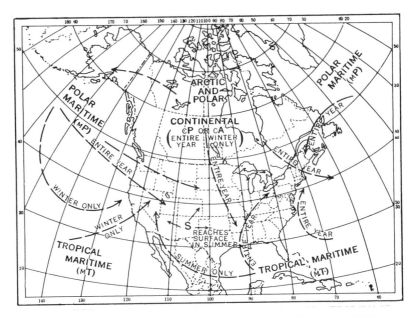

Fig. 17.1   Air mass types that visit the United States. (*Courtesy of CAB*)

below, and this heat and moisture will be conducted to higher levels. The typical weather associated with a cold air mass is good visibility, turbulent and gusty winds, cumuliform clouds, showers, and, in severe cases, thunderstorms. Conversely, a warm air mass will surrender heat to the surface, and the coldest air is found in the layers nearest the ground or water. This stable stratification means that there is no tendency for the air to rise and mix, and the associated weather consists of layer-type clouds, fog, drizzle, poor visibility, and steady or calm winds.

17.4   Oceans, Ocean Currents, and Weather   The oceans and their currents have a very strong stabilizing influence on temperatures over most of the world because of water's great specific heat capacity. The moderating influences of the oceans are carried around the world by air masses as well as by ocean currents. Figure 17.2 shows the general pattern of ocean currents throughout the world. The direction of their flow tends to coincide with the prevailing winds of the world (see Figs. 14.15 and 14.16).

Ocean currents distribute huge quantities of warm and cold water over thousands of miles. The warm currents prevent the great north-south temperature contrasts we would otherwise have. In the North Atlantic, the Gulf Stream is the predominant example. Opposed to it is the cold Labrador current, which starts in the Arctic Ocean and passes south and southeast-

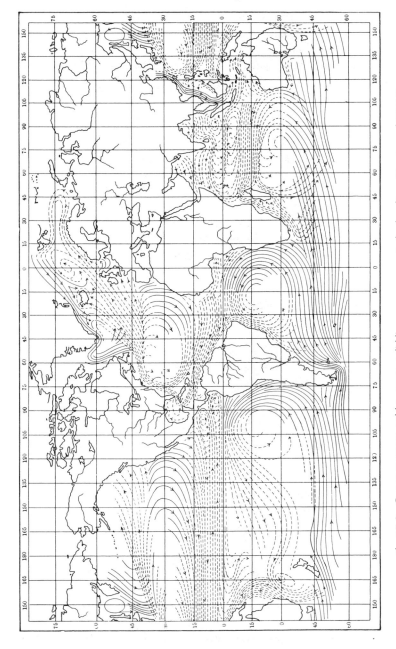

Fig. 17.2 Ocean currents: cold currents, solid lines; warm currents, broken lines (*Courtesy of NOAA*).

471

ward past the Grand Banks. In the North Pacific, the current system is quite similar. The Japan current brings warm water toward the Gulf of Alaska, whereas a cold current runs along the east coast of Asia. In the Southern Hemisphere, the cold polar current runs mainly from west to east, although there are numerous northward branches along the west coast of South Africa and both coasts of South America. The general effect in the Northern Hemisphere is to have cold east coasts and warm west coasts north of 40 degrees north latitude and warm east coasts and cold west coasts south of this latitude.

The Gulf Stream offers a good textbook case of how ocean currents affect weather and climate. It flows from the Caribbean through the Straits of Florida, where it unites with the Antilles current. The combined current flows northward at three to four knots along the Atlantic coast as far as Nova Scotia and Newfoundland. The Gulf Stream air masses usually do not penetrate the East Coast because of the prevailing westerly winds, but the warm waters of the Gulf Stream serve as an active breeding ground for many of the severe storms that cause heavy rains, snows, and strong winds over the seaboard states. The Gulf Stream also serves as a path for many hurricanes.

At the Grand Banks of Newfoundland, where the Gulf Stream meets the cold Labrador current, the world-famous fogs occur. Soon after passing the Banks, the Gulf Stream current divides into several branches. One flows toward the south coast of Greenland, where it greatly modifies the climate of the southwest coast—sufficiently, in fact, for Eric the Red to lead his fellow Norsemen there to settle. Another branch flows toward Iceland, where it ameliorates the climate somewhat before losing itself in the Norwegian Sea. The main branch of the Gulf Stream passes straight eastward, dividing again soon. The southern branch turns southeastward, skirting the coasts of southwest Europe and Africa as a now-cold current before returning to the tropics to warm up and start the long journey over again. The northern branch, hurried along by the strong winds of the Icelandic Low, washes the shores of west and northwest Europe with the warmest waters to be found anywhere at latitudes this high. The current passes into the North Sea and along the west coast of Norway, contributing a strong moderating influence on Norway's climate and throwing off eddies of warm water into the Norwegian Sea to influence the weather there. The current then goes past North Cape as far as Murmansk, famous from World War II as an ice-free port. One flagging branch of the current keeps the west coast of Spitzbergen ice-free in summer, a coast only 800 miles from the North Pole. Even after the current sinks below the fresher waters of the Arctic Sea, it still provides enough heat through the ice to make the area much warmer than comparable Antarctic latitudes.

17.5   Fronts   Adjacent air masses with different qualities of temperature and humidity do not tend to mix readily. Since the cold masses are heavy and the warm masses light, the warmer of two converging currents tends to overrun the colder. A *polar front* is defined as the surface between the converging southwesterly winds of middle latitudes—with their moist, warm air masses—and the prevailing northeasterly winds of polar regions—with their cold, dry air masses. The winds from the south ascend over the cold northeasterlies. A *frontal surface,* then, is the boundary between two masses of air of dissimilar properties. A *surface front* is the area where this boundary intersects the ground. In general, there are four kinds of fronts: *cold, warm, occluded,* and *stationary.* All types are watched closely on weather maps because the poorest possible weather conditions occur in their vicinity, with frequent and rapid changes from one type of weather to another taking place.

17.6   Warm Fronts   Figure 17.3 shows a west-east, vertical cross section through the atmosphere. To the right is a mass of cool air in which the wind is blowing from the southeast; on the left is a warm air mass in which the wind is from the southwest. Even though the cold air mass has southeast winds, it is moving northeastward because it is being overtaken by the faster-moving warm air from the southwest. As the currents converge, the warm stream of air is forced to ascend the cool barrier. It is assumed here that the system as a whole is drifting from west to east, as is customary for atmospheric disturbances in the temperate zone of the middle latitudes. It is further assumed that the warm current has a reasonably high relative humidity. The slope of the wedge is greatly exaggerated in the figure in order to show clearly the process involved. Actually, the ratio of slopes of warm fronts averages about 1 mile in the vertical to 100 miles in the hori-

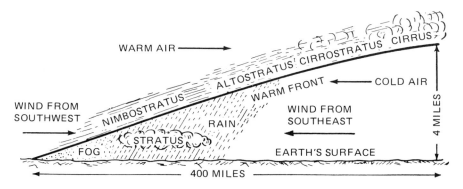

Fig. 17.3   Temperature, cloud, and precipitation phenomena.

zontal, but it can sometimes be as high as 1 to 300 miles. As the warm air rises over the wedge of cold air, it expands and cools adiabatically, resulting in the formation of the various cloud types shown.

The situation just described is quite typical of the warm fronts that occur in the United States and other portions of the middle latitudes. Warm front areas often cover hundreds of square miles, regardless of whether they are over land or sea. The ceilings are low because of the widespread presence of nimbostratus clouds, and visibilities may be poor because of the presence of rain or drizzle and fog. When temperatures in the cloud and rain areas approach freezing, icing on ships and aircraft is prevalent.

Warm front flying is usually smooth, except when unstable warm air is involved. In this case, thunderstorms or other turbulent cloud masses will form in the warm air above the frontal surface. In fact, any cloud type may appear along a warm front, depending on various atmospheric conditions. During late fall and early spring, frozen rain may form in the rain curtain beneath the front whenever raindrops falling from above are frozen in the cold air of the wedge.

17.7 Cold Fronts A west-east, vertical cross section through the atmosphere illustrating a typical cold front of the middle latitudes appears in Fig. 17.4. At the left of the figure, a wedge of cold air is shown advancing from the northwest. It is underrunning and forcing upward a stream of slower-moving, warm, moist air that flows from the southwest. The system as a whole is drifting toward the east. As in the illustration of the warm front, the wedge is exaggerated to clarify the processes involved. Cold fronts are usually steeper than warm fronts, with slopes ranging from 1/50 to 1/150. Even when the slopes are similar to those of warm fronts, the leading edge

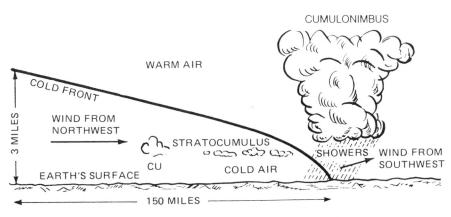

Fig. 17.4 Cold front wind: temperature, cloud, and precipitation phenomena.

of the cold front is much steeper because of the effect of surface friction on the advancing cold air.

As in the case of the warm front, weather is poor along the cold front, but it is a different type of weather, because the greater steepness and speed of the cold front makes it force the warm air upward more violently. The resulting formation of clouds is cumulus rather than stratus, and the cumulus cloud tops commonly reach considerable heights and often develop into cumulonimbus. Precipitation takes the form of rain showers and often heavy hail or snow flurries. The cloud and precipitation areas of a cold front are narrow horizontally as compared with those of a warm front. The accompanying air is usually rough to an altitude of 6000 ft, and it may be turbulent to heights of 20,000 ft or more if thunderstorms are present, which they frequently are. At levels where the temperature drops to or below freezing, aircraft icing will be encountered, and visibilities and ceilings are unfavorable for contact flight.

Stratocumulus or cumulus clouds will often form immediately behind the front over mountainous or moist areas as a result of the rapid movement of cold air over ground previously heated by the warm air ahead of the front.

Before considering occluded fronts, let us examine the nature of the *extratropical cyclone* (one occurring outside the tropics) and note the relationships that exist between its various kinds of air masses and fronts.

17.8 Extratropical Cyclones An extratropical cyclone—also known as a *depression,* a *low-pressure area,* or simply as a *low*—is a low-pressure system that occurs outside (hence "extra") the tropics and that is *colder* within its center than without. (Lows or depressions are systems or areas in which the atmospheric pressure is lower than that of surrounding areas.) Since tropical cyclones are lows that are *warmer* within their centers than without, they will be discussed separately.

Figure 17.5 shows the air masses, fronts, clouds, precipitation, and winds that made up an extratropical cyclone. The figure represents an idealized model of the low in one particular stage of its development. The center diagram presents a plan view; The top diagram presents a vertical section taken through the line A-B of the plan view; and the bottom diagram presents a vertical section taken through the line C-D. In the plan view, we note a warm front in which warm air from a so-called warm sector is converging with and rising over the cold air to its right. We also note a cold front in which the cold air at the left is underrunning the air in the warm sector. The broken arrow pointing to the right indicates that the entire formation—that is, the low and the air masses—are moving toward the right, or east. The shaded portion shows where rain is occurring. Cloud types are not shown in a plan view.

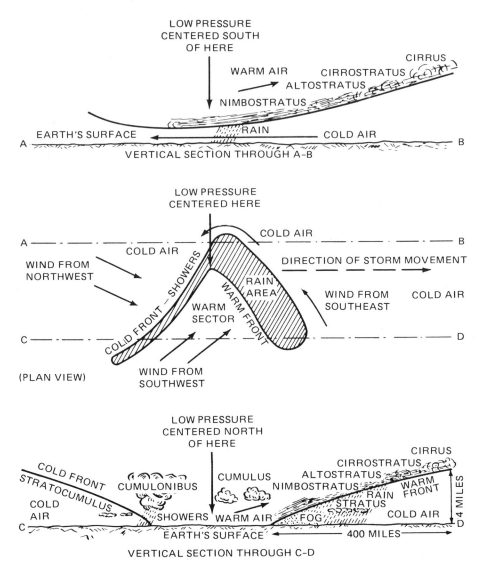

Fig. 17.5 A plan view and two vertical sections of an extratropical cyclone. Hatched area in plan view shows where rain occurs. (*After Bjerknes*)

The vertical section through C-D, shown in the bottom diagram, helps explain what is happening in the upper air. It will be noted that cumulonimbus clouds appear at the cold front (altocumulus clouds could also be present there) and that a variety of stratus and cirrus clouds attend the advance of the warm front. The broad area of rain at the warm front and the narrow band of rain at the cold front are evident. In the cross section through A-B, the warm air does not reach the earth's surface at all but rides up over the cold air that is sweeping around toward the west.

17.9   Formation and Occlusion of Extratropical Cyclones   The life history of a depression, or low, is shown in Fig. 17.6. A *stationary front* is any warm or cold front that has ceased moving. In the polar front shown in Fig. 17.6(a), the cold air flowing toward the west while warm air flows toward the east has created a stationary front. In Fig. 17.6(b) the front has ceased to be straight, possibly because pressure is being exerted at the left side of the figure by a mass of cold air to the north. A definite cold and warm frontal system has developed, and the arrows show that the wind has commenced to blow in a counterclockwise direction around a center of lower pressure. The hatched areas indicate that cloudiness and precipitation have begun. This development is known as a *wave* that has formed along the stationary front, and the wave will move from left to right along the front in much the same manner as an ocean wave. The cyclone has reached a normal stage of development in Fig. 17.6(c), in which the cold front advances faster than the warm front, and in Fig. 17.6(d) it has overtaken the warm front in the vicinity of the center of the depression. The dying out or *occlusion* of the cyclone has now begun. The process from this stage onward resembles, in fluid motion, the breaking of an ocean wave. Further occlusion takes place in Figs. 17.6(e) and (f); cloudiness and precipitation continue but in diminishing amounts. Occlusion, if it continues, results in the obliteration or filling up of the depression.

Two distinct types of occluded fronts are shown in Figs. 17.6(g) and (h). In the *cold-front occlusion* of Fig. 17.6(g), when the cold front catches up with the warm front, the air to the left is colder than the air to the right and therefore underruns the latter, squeezing the warm sector above ground level. Precipitation continues at and behind the surface front, the usual form along cold fronts being showers. In the *warm-front occlusion* of Fig. 17.6(h), the air to the left is not as cold as the air to the right. The cool air, therefore, rises over the cold air and occludes the warm air as shown. The precipitation continuing at and ahead of the surface front is the steady rain or drizzle typical of warm fronts.

17.10   Extratropical Cyclone Weather   Assume that the low shown in Fig. 17.7 is moving east-northeast at 600 miles per day and that its center passes north of a ship at point A. The first indication of the approaching storm will be a falling barometer, which will continue to fall, ever more rapidly, until the warm front passes. Along with the pressure fall, cirrus clouds usually appear, and these thicken in a few hours to cirrostratus. If the overrunning air is unstable or turbulent, cirrocumulus will occur along

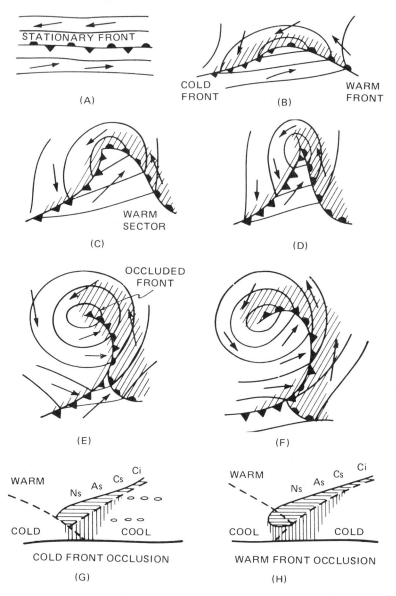

Fig. 17.6 Development of a depression. Hatched areas indicate precipitation. Solid half circles represent a warm front; solid triangles, a cold front; alternating solid half circles and triangles on the same side, an occluded front; and alternating solid half circles and triangles on opposite sides, a stationary front. The side of the front on which the symbols are placed indicates the direction toward which the front is moving.

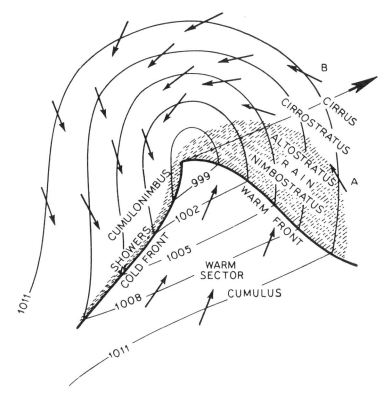

Fig. 17.7   Extratropical cyclone. Shaded areas indicate rain or showers.

with the cirrostratus, forming the "mackerel sky" so often mentioned in sailing-ship lore. Winds are southerly and increasing. The waves start to build up, along with the wind, and are superimposed on a southwesterly swell moving out from the area of the storm center.

When the warm front is about 300 miles away, altostratus clouds are predominant; sometimes they are mixed with altocumulus. Precipitation—rain or snow—can start at any time when the warm front is 200 to 300 miles distant. Winds and waves continue to increase, with the winds backing more and more into the southeast. After the precipitation starts, the rain or snow becomes heavier, the clouds thicker and lower (becoming nimbostratus, and sometimes stratocumulus). Often, there is low stratus or fog when falling rain saturates the cold air underneath the front, and there may be cumulonimbus clouds above the front. Winds and waves continue to build, with winds up to 45 knots in a strong storm and waves 25 to 35 ft high with an occasional monster of some 50 ft.

As the warm front passes, the winds shift from southeast to southwest; the temperature rises rapidly; cloudiness decreases or vanishes altogether; precipitation stops; the barometer steadies and remains so throughout the warm sector. Winds will usually be lighter and seas lower.

As the cold front now approaches, the southerly wind flow increases and cumuliform clouds of the kind appearing in Fig. 17.8 will darken the horizon to the west and northwest. When the front arrives, there are heavy showers, often thunderstorms, strong gusty winds, and confused seas. The wind shifts sharply from south or southwest to a direction between west and north; the barometer rises rapidly; the temperature drops sharply; and usually there will be rapid clearing after the cold front passes. Waves will now come from the northwest and increase rapidly—sometimes reaching swells of up to 35 ft in six hours. The seas will then subside gradually, although it will sometimes be as long as two days before they drop below 10 ft.

Suppose now that the low center passes south of a ship located at point B in Fig. 17.7. Since point B will not encounter the warm and cold fronts, the weather sequence will be quite different from that at point A. The first indications of the approach of the low will be cirrus clouds, a shift in wind direction to the east, and a downward trend of the barometer. As the low moves closer, cirrostratus clouds replace the cirrus, the wind continues from the east, and the barometer continues downward. Presently, altostratus clouds replace the cirrostratus clouds; a steady, light rain begins; the wind continues from the east; the barometer falls further. As the low progresses east-northeastward, the wind shifts to the northeast and then to the north, with nimbostratus clouds replacing the altostratus. Eventually, the wind shifts to northwest; the barometer begins to rise; the sky gradually clears; the precipitation ceases. The low has passed to the eastward, and fine, clear weather prevails.

The description just presented is that of a purely theoretical low. Actually, lows vary as much as people do. Some are of great diameter, well over 1000 miles; some are relatively small, 400 to 500 miles. Some produce heavy precipitation; others, little. Although cloud forms may not follow the conventional pattern, wind, temperature, and pressure nearly always do, particularly at sea.

17.11   Distribution and Movement of Lows   Since extratropical cyclones (lows) form along fronts, they occur with greatest frequency in the higher mid-latitudes where the cold and warm air masses meet along the *polar* and *Arctic fronts*. (The polar front is a semicontinuous front circling the globe all year, moving north and south and constantly affecting the mid-latitudes; the Arctic front is a winter front only and infrequently affects mid-latitudes.) In the Northern Hemisphere, there is a maximum frequency of lows at 50 degrees N in winter, 60 degrees N in summer. In the Pacific there is a broad band of frequent cyclone activity from southeast Asia to the Gulf of Alaska. In the cold season, these storms become very intense and usually move northeastward to accumulate in the Gulf of Alaska. Some storms that form on the mid-Pacific polar front take a more southerly track and reach coasts as far south as southern California.

In the Atlantic, the most common region for low development is the Virginia coast and the general area east of the southern Appalachians. These, often called "Hatteras storms," are frequently very intense. They move northeasterly along the Gulf Stream and eventually stagnate near Iceland or in the waters between Greenland and Labrador.

The rate of storm movement in summer is about 500 miles per day; in winter, it is somewhat faster, probably averaging 700 miles, but there are many variations. At times, an extratropical cyclone may slow down and remain stationary over an area; at other times an area may be subjected to a series of lows that move along quickly one after another. Lows are more stormy and sharply defined in winter than in summer.

17.12 Anticyclones An *anticyclone* (Fig. 17.9) is an area of high pressure, or *high;* its name is derived from the fact that the wind within it blows clockwise and outward, instead of counterclockwise and inward as in a cyclone.

Fig. 17.8 Cold front cloud. (*Official U.S. Navy photograph*)

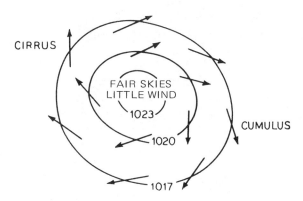

Fig. 17.9   An anticyclone and associated weather elements.

Subtropical anticyclones, centered around the world at 30 degrees latitude, are very persistent at all times of the year and move little or not at
all. *Migratory anticyclones,* on the other hand, alternate with lows in a regular parade across the oceans and across continents. In North America, the
most likely regions for initial development of highs are Alaska and that portion of western Canada to the east of the Rocky Mountains. These highs
move southeastward toward the Atlantic Coast, lost their identity as they
reach the warm Atlantic waters and become absorbed in the subtropical
anticyclone. In Asia, they develop over Siberia and move into the western
Pacific.

Cool or cold but fair weather is typical of migrating highs. Their rate of
movement and size are fairly comparable to those of lows. They may be
thought of as atmospheric mounds of cold, dense air that have broken
away from their northern source regions to drift southward and thereby
lessen the pressure that builds up in polar areas.

17.13   Preparation of Surface Weather Maps   Surface weather maps are
prepared four or more times daily at forecasting centers. The techniques
involved are beyond the scope of this book, but the maps themselves
should have been discussed sufficiently by now to enable the reader to
understand and use them. On land, they are available in daily newspapers;
at sea, they are available over several types of broadcasts. Some ships still
plot their own.

Surface weather maps do not indicate existing conditions in the upper
air, such as the direction and velocity of the wind at various heights, cloud
levels, turbulence, regions where airplane icing may occur, air stability,
temperature and humidity values, and other phenomena important to the
forecaster and airplane pilot. Therefore, auxiliary maps and diagrams must

be prepared to complement the surface map. The most useful of these are the constant pressure charts, which show conditions at several selected upper levels along a constant pressure surface. For example, the 500-millibar charts show wind, temperature, and humidity conditions along this pressure surface, whose elevation varies from about 16,500 to 19,500 ft. Constant pressure charts are used in forecasting to determine the movement of weather systems, wind flow at high levels, jet stream location and intensity, and the development and intensity of pressure systems.

Electronic computers have replaced individual mapmakers in preparation of these charts and can do an almost flawless job. The computer is programmed to use mathematical procedures not only for their development but their analysis. It is able to make projections for 12, 24, 36, 48, and 72 hours into the future.

17.14   Preparation of Forecasts   Once all weather charts have been analyzed and prognostic charts prepared, the forecaster has several things to consider before finalizing his forecast, including the following:

1. Displacement of fronts and pressure systems
2. Deepening and filling of pressure systems
3. Development of new pressure systems
4. Properties of existing air masses and the changes that might occur with displacement
5. Local influences, such as mountains, bodies of water, and industrial activity

Empirical rules derived from local observations as well as climatological rules must be taken into account. Finally, the forecaster makes room for his own experience as a contributing factor and proceeds to make a forecast.

17.15   Use of Weather Maps and Forecasting at Sea   The seaman can do much to help himself even if his only weather information is what he can see or measure from his own bridge. Before radio came into use, the master of a ship had to rely on whatever conclusions he could draw from the appearance of the sky, movement of upper clouds, backing and veering of the wind, pressure changes, changes in the state of the sea, and changing visibility. Many seamen became, and many still are, relatively expert at forecasting weather changes simply by relying upon their own observations. Naturally, without a knowledge of the state of the upstream weather, there are bound to be some disappointing results (which occur even when forecasters do know the upstream weather). Lacking other information, the seaman can improve upon his local knowledge by asking other ships in the general area to send their position, present weather, barometric reading, and wind direction and force. With this data he can make a two- or three-point sketch to give him a rough estimate of the pressure pattern and intensity of the pressure systems in his area, and possibly, the location of fronts.

Frequently, ships can receive broadcasts of other ships' weather reports, weather maps in coded form, as well as forecasts of weather conditions for the area of concern. Ships equipped with radio facsimile equipment can copy a great variety of weather and oceanographic charts.

If forecasts are available, a ship usually need not make its own since weather offices ashore have many more reports with which to reach conclusions and professional meteorologists to do the forecasting. There will be many times, however, when a ship may find itself in an area not adequately covered, and it will be to its advantage to make a weather map by using its own observations and applying such usually reliable forecasting rules as the following:

1. The *rule of persistence* calls for an extrapolation into the future of the same rates of movement and changes in intensity of pressure systems that have occurred in the past. The rule is quite reliable for up to six hours, with a gradual loss of reliability thereafter.
2. Troughs of low pressure tend to move with an eastwardly component to the position of the preceding ridge of high pressure, but the speed of movement can be quite variable.
3. Lows with a warm sector tend to move in a direction parallel to the warm sector winds and isobars and with a speed of about 80 percent of the warm sector winds.
4. When a low has a large "open" warm sector, *deepening* (decrease of central pressure) may be expected.
5. The rate of deepening will usually increase with the narrowing of the warm sector (cold front approaching the warm front) and decrease when the occlusion process begins.
6. When a low has nearly occluded, it moves less rapidly; the movement of very large occluded lows is very slow and irregular.
7. Small lows caught in the circulation of a large system tend to follow the main system.
8. A large low with no fronts will tend to move in the direction of the strongest winds in the circulation.
9. Frontal depressions tend to occur in families, each low following approximately the path of its predecessor but displaced somewhat towards a lower latitude.
10. Lows tend to move around large, warm highs in the direction of the air flow around their boundaries.
11. Occluded cyclones tend to weaken slowly, particularly when over a relatively cool surface.

12. Ridges of high pressure between lows tend to move in the same direction and the same speed as the lows themselves.
13. Speed of fronts is determined largely by the wind component perpendicular to the front.
14. A front parallel to the isobars either moves slowly or is stationary.
15. Frontal precipitation increases in intensity as the wind shift across the front becomes sharper.
16. Weather activity in cold fronts in subtropical latitudes is more active than in warm fronts. This behavior is reversed in polar latitudes.

After the above rules have been considered and the shipboard forecaster has an idea of what his weather map should look like, he is ready to make a forecast.

If there is a low approaching, the forecaster determines where its center will pass in relation to his own position and anticipates whatever typical low-pressure-center weather conditions are customary for that position. Approaching cold and warm fronts are treated similarly. By obtaining temperature readings of air and water for the area, he can estimate the probability of fog occurrence. From the isobaric pattern, he can calculate wind speed and direction. These data will provide the necessary information for marking a forecast of sea state.

18

The Tropical Cyclone

18.1 Introduction Tropical cyclones are cyclones of tropical origin in which the barometric pressure steadily decreases from the periphery to a minimum at the center, where the winds spiral inward from all sides (counterclockwise in the Northern Hemisphere) and where the temperature at the center is warmer than at the edges. When winds of cyclonic circulation reach a strength of 64 knots or more near the center, the cyclone will, depending upon its location, be called a *hurricane* (Atlantic, Gulf of Mexico, eastern Pacific), a *typhoon* (western North Pacific), a *baguio* (Philippines), a *willy-willy* (western Australia), or simply a *cyclone* (Indian Ocean). Tropical storms involve the same atmospheric phenomenon, but of lesser intensity, with winds of 34 to 64 knots. Tropical depressions have winds of less than 34 knots.

Mature tropical cyclones are extraodinarily violent. They usually do not involve as large an area as many temperature-zone storms, nor do they have the sharply concentrated, irresistible force of tornadoes, but they are the most dangerous and destructive of all storms. From hurricanes alone, in an active season, damage may approach two billion dollars, and hundreds, often thousands, of lives and homes may be destroyed. Some coastal cities have been completely demolished, never to be rebuilt. It is obvious that ships at sea must make every effort to avoid tropical cyclones of hurricane or typhoon intensity.

Even a well-found ship may be in danger of foundering. Masts and superstructures are especially vulnerable to the extreme violence of wind and sea. Personnel may be lost overboard or seriously injured by objects adrift. Lifeboats and other exposed small craft, even aircraft, are almost certain to be carried away by the wind and sea. The prudent seaman will find it well worthwhile to study the nature of the tropical cyclone and to avoid it in any way possible. Many ships in service for years have never encountered one; if ordinary precautions are used, most ships should never have to pass through a violent one.

18.2 Areas Affected   The regions in which tropical cyclones form are shown in Fig. 18.1A, and the speeds at which they move are shown in Fig. 18.1B. Tracks are indicated in the Pacific and Indian Oceans both north and south of the equator and north of it in the Atlantic Ocean. It will be noted that the tropical cyclone is entirely absent in the Atlantic south of the equator as well as in the Arctic and Antarctic Oceans.

Tropical cyclones usually form over the ocean in latitudes between 5 and 20 degrees north and 5 and 20 degrees south. Once formed, they may travel distances of hundreds or even thousands of miles before losing their force and finally dissipating; they are the most persistent of all storms, sometimes living for three to four weeks. Many tropical cyclones move near to, or cross over, continental coastal areas, but South America, Europe, and Africa are free from such visitations. In North America, the east and west coasts of Mexico and the Central American countries and the states of the Gulf and Atlantic coasts may be affected. China, Japan, India, and the northwestern and northeastern portions of Australia are other regions subject to the tropical cyclone.

Tropical cyclones of the eastern North Pacific may be encountered from May through December off the western coasts of Mexico and Central America. Hurricanes of this region can be as violent but usually not so large as those of the North Atlantic.

In the western North Pacific, the tropical cyclone may occur during any month of the year, but the months of greatest frequency are July, August, September, and October. There are over twice as many tropical cyclones per year in the West pacific as in the Atlantic, and more of these become giant storms.

18.3 Frequency of Tropical Cyclones   In the Atlantic, tropical storms and hurricanes occur with greatest frequency during August, September, and October. Figure 18.2 shows the monthly frequency for a 101-year period ending in 1986 (excluding two tropical storms and one hurricane that

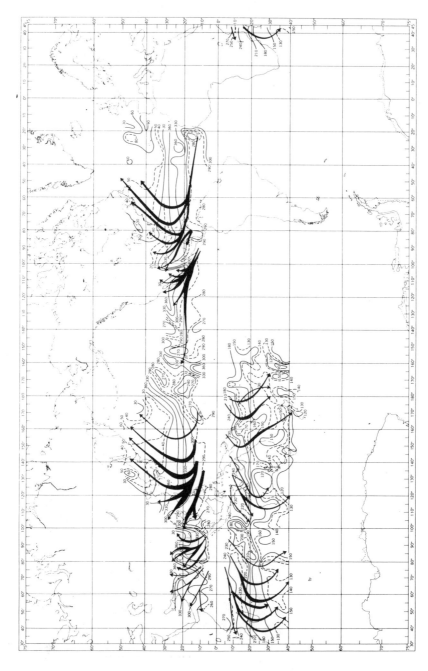

Fig. 18.1A Preferred storm tracks for tropical storms (represented by black arrows). The width of arrow indicates approximate frequency of storms; the wider the arrow, the higher the frequency. Isolines on base map show resultant direction toward which storms moved (isogons). Data for entire year have been summarized for this figure. (*Mariners' Worldwide Climatic Guide to Tropical Storms at Sea*, U.S. Navy.)

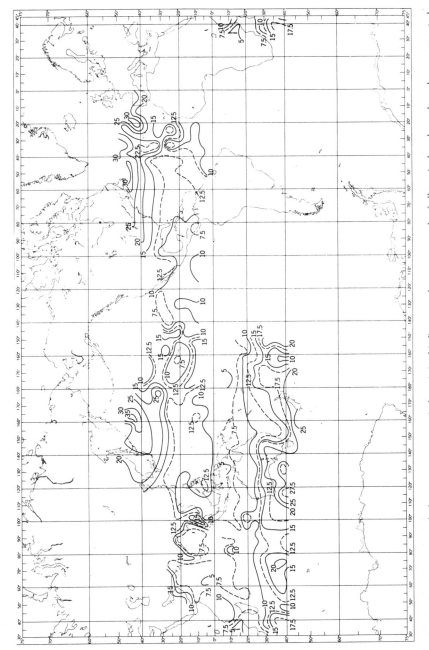

Fig. 18.1B Average speed of storm movements (in knots). In this figure, scalar mean speeds of all tropical cyclones have been computed for the entire year. *(Mariners' Worldwide Climactic Guide to Tropical Storms at Sea*, U.S. Navy.)

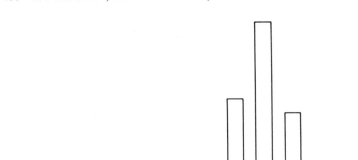

MONTH	MAY	JUN	JUL	AUG	SEP	OCT	NOV	DEC
NUMBER	14	54	65	197	292	176	44	5

Fig. 18.2   The total number of tropical storms and hurricanes in the North Atlantic, by month, for the period 1886–1986.

occurred in February and March). Figure 18.3 shows the annual frequency during the same period (note that the number per year is quite erratic, ranging from 1 to 21). This figure also shows that there was a maximum, of sorts, in the early part of the period, with another one starting in the early 1930s. The increased frequency in the thirties has tended to maintain itself ever since, and more of the storms have been hurricanes. The average annual number of tropical storms and hurricanes during the 101 year period is less than eight and a half, and between nine and ten for the past 30-year period. The increased number of tropical storms and hurricanes may be associated with a gradual warming of the atmosphere and sea during the period.

In the Bay of Bengal and the Arabian Sea, tropical cyclones are more likely to be encountered during May and October than in other months, whereas in the South Pacific and South Indian Oceans, the season extends from September to May, with the months of January, February, and March exhibiting the greatest frequencies.

18.4   Formation of the Tropical Cyclone   It is fortunate that typhoons, hurricanes, and other tropical cyclones are comparatively few in number as compared with their nontropical cousins. There are often as many of the latter on a weather map in one day as there are hurricanes in a season or two.

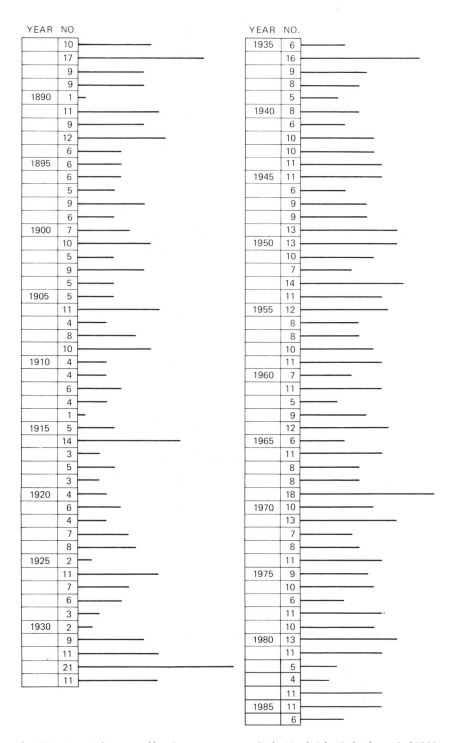

Fig. 18.3 Tropical storm and hurricane occurrences in the North Atlantic for the period 1886–1986.

Meterologists have not been able to unravel the mysteries of tropical cyclone formation, although the tropical cyclone is the nearest thing to a simple heat engine to be found among atmospheric disturbances. Day after day in tropical regions, conditions look just right for cyclones to form from existing disturbances in the trade wind belt—temperatures of air and water are warm enough, there is plenty of moisture, and the winds are of the right speed. Yet, only once in 10 times are tropical cyclones born from these fertile-looking patterns, and when they do form, the manner varies from one storm to the next.

The mean latitude of storm formation moves poleward in the first half of the season and then retreats equatorward. Early- and late-season cyclones form mostly in the belt from 5 to 15 degrees in the Northern Hemisphere; at the height of the season, they form in the belt between 10 and 25 degrees. In the Atlantic, some formations occur between 25 and 30 degrees, with a northern limit of 35 degrees. The great majority of tropical cyclones undergo their principal development in the northeast trade wind current, not in the doldrums or equatorial trough, as had been thought for so many years.

In addition to the north-south shift in tropical cyclone formation, there is an east-west pattern, particularly so in the Atlantic. Here, a majority of early season (May and June) storms originate in the Gulf of Mexico and western Caribbean. In July and August, the areas of most frequent origin shift eastward, and by September they are located over the large area from the Bahamas southeastward to the Lesser Antilles, and thence eastward to south of the Cape Verde Islands, near the coast of Africa. After mid-September, the principal areas of origin shift back to the western Caribbean and Gulf of Mexico.

18.5 Tropical Cyclone Movement   Tropical cyclones are notorious for their erratic movement. There is a general similarity of movement in the early stages of storm development along the ESE-WNW axis, and all cyclones have a tendency to move toward higher latitudes eventually. There is no longitudinal regularity in any turn to the north, however, and in all track samples there are *benders, loopers, double loopers,* and *wobblers.* (A bender is characterized by rapid reversals or changes of course; a looper by a change of course exceeding 360 degrees either clockwise or counterclockwise; a wobbler by a constantly changing direction of movement in a general direction.) Also, tropical cyclones undergo sudden accelerations (as much as 1500 percent in 24 hours) and sudden decelerations; sometimes, after stopping suddenly, they will hold position within a 50-mile circle for as long as three days.

The mean speed of tropical cyclone movement south of 30 degrees N varies, by area, between 12 and 16 knots. Occasionally, when the subtropical highs are exceptionally strong, hurricanes and typhoons south of 30 degrees N will move toward the west at 20 to 25 knots.

North of 30 degrees N, the speed of storm movement is much less predictable. The speed range is from 0 to 70 knots, and acceleration can be pronounced. Disastrous and unexpected results have occurred when hurricanes that were loafing along off the Virginia Capes have suddenly spurted and roared up the coast at maximum speed.

Hurricanes and typhoons favor movement over the warmest waters. The Gulf Stream is a good example.

18.6   General Nature of Tropical Cyclones   The average mature tropical cyclone carries hurricane-force winds (64 knots, or 75 mph) over an area slightly exceeding 100 miles in diameter and gale-force winds (34 to 64 knots) over an area 400 miles in diameter. In large hurricanes, these areas may extend to over 200 miles for hurricane-force winds and 600 miles for gale-force. In a few huge Pacific typhoons, the area of hurricane-force winds has exceeded 300 miles, with the gale-force winds covering an area of over 1500 miles. A gale force wind 600 miles from the hurricane center does not necessarily mean that winds near the center will be of remarkably high speed. Small storms may be the most violent. For instance, the infamous Florida Keys hurricane in 1935 had a path of destruction only 40 miles wide.

The strongest winds of hurricanes and typhoons have probably never been measured, because wind measuring devices are not designed to stand much more than 125 knots, after which they stop functioning or are blown away. Reconnaissance planes have often reported winds in the 130- to 150-knot (150- to 175-mph) range; actually measurements at land stations have been made that were as high as 150 knots; and in the Florida Keys hurricane mentioned, engineers estimated that the winds must have been in the 170- to 215-knot (200- to 250-mph) range to account for the damage done.

An estimate of the maximum surface wind in a cyclone can be obtained by the empirical formula,

$$V_{max} = K\sqrt{1010 - P_c}$$

where:

V_{max} = maximum *sustained* surface wind speed, in knots
K = constant, given variously by several authors as 14, 15, or 16
P_c = central (minimum) pressure of the cyclone, in millibars

A feature of the wind that helps to account for much of the damage it does is its gustiness. Since momentary gusts can exceed the steady winds by 30 to 50 percent, a wind of 100 knots may have momentary gusts of 150 knots.

Winds in a tropical cyclone do not blow in circles around the eye (the low pressure center); instead, they blow inwardly at an angle of anywhere from 20 to 30 degrees all the way from the outer limits of the storm toward the wall of the eye. The angle grows less and less as the eye is approached, and the winds blow stronger. At the wall of the eye, the winds do indeed blow in a circle and at their very strongest, creating phenomenal seas. The 20- to 30-degree inflow accounts for the fact that birds, butterflies, and helpless ships may be driven into the eye and destroyed by the abrupt energy change from maximum to minimum that makes its fabled calm highly deceiving.

It is typical for the strongest winds to occur to the right of the direction of movement, looking "downstream" (the direction of forward movement). On the right side, the forward motion of the storm is added to the observed wind velocity, and on the left, it is subtracted.

The steepest pressure gradients in the world, barring tornadoes, occur in tropical cyclones of the lower latitudes. One ship in the Caribbean experienced a pressure fall of 1.34 in. (40.5 millibars) in 20 min. In the 1935 Florida Keys hurricane, one estimate gave a pressure gradient of 1 in. in 6 miles. The lowest sea-level barometric pressure readings for the whole world have been recorded in hurricanes and typhoons. The lowest reading at sea was 26.18 in. (886.56 millibars); the land record is 26.35 in.

The eye of the tropical cyclone is unique among atmospheric phenomena. At the edge of the eye, the winds are at their strongest. Then, within a distance of as little as a few hundred feet, it is possible to have the winds fall off from 100 knots to 10. In the eye, the dense, dark clouds disappear, although there are usually some low clouds present. The average diameter of the eye is about 14 miles, but it can be as small as 4 miles and as large as 100.

The strong winds of tropical cyclones generate some of the highest ocean waves known. In an average hurricane, waves of 35 to 40 ft are common; in giant storms, they can build up as high as 45 to 50 ft, and there have been reports of waves 60 to 90 ft in height. The highest waves are found on the right side of the storm along the direction of movement because the stronger winds are found there and have more time in which to push against the water since both waves and storm are moving in the same direction.

Waves move more slowly than the winds that create them but still move much faster than the cyclone itself. As the waves move out of the storm area, at perhaps 45 to 50 knots, they become swells and continue on ahead of the storm for hundreds or even thousands of miles. A characteristic of hurricane or typhoon swells is their long period (length of time from crest to crest or trough to trough) of 15 to 30 seconds as compared to the normal period of 4 to 6 seconds.

Storm surge occurs along exposed coastal areas as surface water is piled up, driven by the wind. When the surge coincides with high tide, high water can be 20 ft above normal on the right forward side of a strong tropical cyclone. On the left forward side of the same cyclone, water is driven away from shore, and lower than normal tides occur.

Rainfall is heavy in tropical cyclones. Over water, it has been calculated that the fall will be about 11 in. at any one location during their passage. Over land, because of its added lifting effect, tremendous amounts of rainfall have been recorded, like the 49.13 in. in 24 hours at Paishih, Taiwan, or the 96.5 in. in four days in Jamaica.

Tropical cyclones live longer than any other storms. Their average life is nine days, but many have lived for three to four weeks; the recordbreaker logged five weeks during a grand tour from Africa to the Bahamas to Cape Hatteras to the Azores.

18.7   Hurricane Advisories and Storm Signals   During the hurricane season, the U.S. Navy, NOAA, and the U.S. Air Force work together to provide the coastal areas of the United States and shipping interests with timely storm warnings. NOAA is responsible for warning civilian interests and merchant shipping; the Navy and Coast Guard for their own coastal activities and ships at sea; and the Air Force for both Air Force and Army installations.

Weather satellites play an important role in the discovery of incipient tropical cyclones and in tracking them during their later and more destructive stages. Satellite information is still not detailed enough to replace that obtained by aircraft, but the future holds great promise of satellites doing the whole job of detection and tracking.

The Department of Defense and NOAA have reconnaissance responsibilites. They are frequently called upon to investigate areas of possible hurricane formation. Once a tropical system is located, the hurricane hunter planes and satellites give it almost a 24-hour-per-day examination, sifting out all the facts on surface and upper winds, clouds, state of the sea, pressure, the location of the eye, and of the center of the eye. Without this information, forecast stations would not be able to forecast any better than they did thirty years ago. Small storms would be missed for days or forever; intensities would be misjudged; movement predictions would be very inaccurate. Hurricane reconnaissance is a difficult, dangerous job, but one that has saved many lives and prevented much damage.

A similar arrangement is in effect in the western Pacific, except that typhoon warnings are issued for all civilian and military interests from the Joint Typhoon Warning Center (Navy and Air Force), located in the U.S. Naval Oceanography Command Center, Guam.

SMALL CRAFT, GALE, WHOLE GALE AND HURRICANE WARNINGS

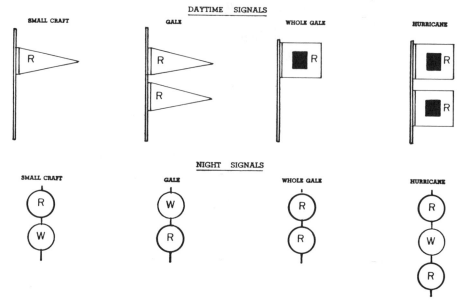

Fig. 18.4 Storm and hurricane wind displays for small craft.

In addition to hurricane and storm communiques by radio, a system of flags and lights (Fig. 18.4) is displayed at many points along the United States seacoasts when winds dangerous to navigation are forecast for that coastal section. Explanations of the various warnings follow:

Small Craft Warning   One red pennant displayed by day and a red light over a white light at night indicate that winds up to 38 miles an hour (33 knots) and/or sea conditions dangerous to small craft are forecast for the area.

Gale Warning   Two red pennants displayed by day and a white light above a red light at night indicate that winds ranging from 39 to 54 miles an hour (34 to 48 knots) are forecast for the area.

Whole Gale Warning   A single square red flag with a black center displayed during daytime and two red lights at night indicate that winds ranging from 55 to 73 miles an hour (48 to 63 knots) are forecast for the area.

Hurricane Warning   Two square red flags with black centers displayed by day and a white light between two red lights at night indicate that winds of 74 miles an hour (64 knots) and above are forecast for the area.

18.8   Locating a Tropical Cyclone by Local Signs   *First Indications* The long-period, heavy swell of the hurricane arrives well before its cloud formations. The first clouds directly connected with hurricane circulation are cumulonimbus (thunderstorm). There are active bands of these along a line several hundred miles ahead of the storm, the distance varying with the size of the storm. Following their appearance, and the day before the storm arrives, the tropical pattern goes out of phase. The thunderstorms of the previous day are missing; the usual cumulus clouds are suppressed; there are bright skies and above-normal temperatures. Then, the barometer starts to drop, and the wind may come from an unusual direction. In the trades, a north wind is a most unusual direction and ordinarily a danger sign.

Convincing Signs A drop in barometric pressure of 3.4 millibars (0.10 in.) or more within a 24-hr period, particularly if it occurs within 3 to 6 hr, is a significant indication of the possible approach of a tropical cyclone. It should be kept in mind in this connection that, in the tropics, there is a very regular, twice-daily rise and fall in barometric pressure over a range of 2 millibars (0.06 in.).

It is also significant if there is an increase in wind speed of 25 percent or more in a limited area in the normal trade wind flow, especially if the wind flow changes cyclonically, say, from easterly to a more northerly direction. Also, any wind south clockwise to north is a danger signal.

The significant cloud pattern starts with cirrus. These seem to converge in the direction from which the storm is approaching, a characteristic most noticeable at sunrise and sunset. The cirrus clouds are followed by cirrostratus, which produce solar and lunar halos and brilliant ruby and crimson skies at sunrise and sunset. Next come the altostratus, often mixed with altocumulus. The steady rain accompanying the altostratus is yet another indication, because rain in the tropics is usually the showery type. As the center of the storm gets closer, the clouds change at lower levels to cumulus; the barometer falls more rapidly; the wind increases; the seas grow mountainous; and finally, an ominous black wall of clouds approaches, called the *bar* of the storm.

18.9   Handling Ships in a Tropical Cyclone   The following rules apply in handling ships in a tropical cyclone (see Chapter 9):

1. Determine the bearing, distance, and track of the cyclone from the official warnings or from your own calculations if there are no warnings. From this information, you can plan how best to avoid the dangerous semicircle on the right side of the cyclone, looking downstream in the direction of movement. Relationship to shoal water must be considered.

2. If near a cyclone and you have no warnings, determine its bearing by (a) the direction from which the swells are arriving, and (b) by adding 115 degrees to the direction from which you observed true wind to be blowing.
3. If the wind gradually hauls to the right (clockwise), the ship is in the dangerous semicircle. If it hauls to the left, you are in the safe or navigable semicircle. (See Fig. 18.5.)
4. If the wind remains steady in direction, increases in speed, and the barometer continues to fall, you are directly in the path of the storm.
5. Use your radar, if available. A continuous knowledge of the center of the storm will be helpful in maneuvering.
6. Do not try to outrun or cross the front (or "T") of a mature tropical cyclone; to do so usually means trouble. The main difficulty arises from the front-running swells, which build rapidly in size with the approach of the center. These can cut down ship speed by several knots at the same time that the storm keeps roaring along at its previous pace or speeds up.
7. If Sea Surface Temperature charts are available, avoid the areas of warmest water. When tropical cyclones are moving slowly, at 10 knots or less, they tend to use these areas as a path.
8. If the ship is actually caught within the cyclone circulation, even its fringes, the following steps should be taken:

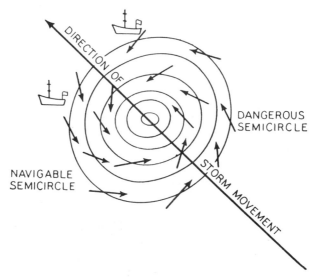

Fig. 18.5 A ship hove-to in the dangerous semicircle will note the wind shift to the right (clockwise); the wind will shift to the left (counterclockwise) if the ship is in the navigable semicircle.

(a) If you are dead ahead of the center, bring the wind on the star-board quarter (160 degrees relative) and "make best speed" on this course. Doing so is the quickest way to take the ship away from the center and into the safe semicircle. When well within this semicircle, bring the wind 130 degrees relative and continue making best speed.

(b) If the ship is in the safe or navigable semicircle, bring the wind on the starboard quarter (130 degrees relative) and make best speed.

(c) If it is in the dangerous semicircle, bring the wind on the star-board bow (45 degrees relative) and make as much headway as possible.

(d) If it is behind the cyclone center, steer the best riding course for keeping a distance from the center, remembering the tendency of cyclones to curve northward and eastward eventually.

18.10 Handling Sailing Vessels in a Tropical Cyclone   (Northern Hemisphere) While making a preliminary study of the storm (Fig. 18.6), sailing vessels should be hove to on the starboard tack.

If the wind shifts to the right, the vessel is in the dangerous semicircle but on the proper tack. It must then attempt to work away from the track of the storm center, close-hauled on the starboard tack. If it is necessary to heave to, do so on the same tack.

If the wind hauls to the left while hove to on the starboard tack, the vessel is in the navigable semicircle and heading away from the track of the storm center. In this case, the wind should be brought on the starboard quarter and run as long as possible. If it is necessary to heave to, do so on the port tack; try to make as little headway as possible.

If the wind direction remains the same while hove to on the starboard tack and the barometer falls steadily, it is likely that the vessel is ahead, and in the path, of the hurricane, assuming that the storm is circular in shape rather than elliptical. The vessel should run with the wind on the starboard quarter and hold the compass course thus noted until the barometer begins to rise.

18.11 Storm Surge: The Most Deadly Killer   Many factors are involved in the formation and propagation of a storm surge, such as the strength of the storm, bottom conditions where the surge comes ashore, and the position of the storm center in relation to the shore.

Storm surge begins over the deep ocean. The low pressure and strong winds around the hurricane's eye raise the ocean surface a foot or two higher than the surrounding ocean surface, forming a dome of water as much as 50 miles across. As the storm moves into shallow coastal waters,

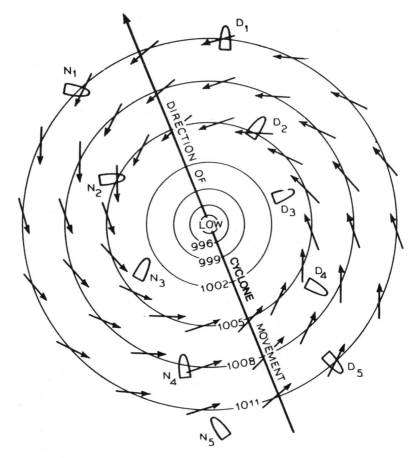

Fig. 18.6 Rules for lying to by sailing ships in the Northern Hemisphere (note that the wind draws aft for both vessels N and D).

decreasing water depth transforms the dome into a storm surge that can rise 20 feet or more above normal sea level, and cause massive flooding and destruction along shorelines in its path. The stronger the hurricane, the higher the storm surge will be. This is unquestionably the most dangerous part of a hurricane. Nine out of ten hurricane fatalities are caused by the storm surge. Just as the storm surge is superimposed on the normal tides, the high wind-driven waves of the hurricane are superimposed on the storm surge. The result is an extremely effective battering ram, capable of smashing structures to rubble, eroding long reaches of beach and under-mining poorly anchored buildings. During the infamous hurricane Camille in 1969, a 25-foot storm surge inundated Pass Christian in Mississippi. Lesser

Table 18.1   Hurricane Scale (Saffir/Simpson).

Category	Central Pressure (Millibars)	Winds (MPH)	Storm Surge Above Normal
1	980 or more	74–95	4–5 feet
2	965–979	96–110	6–8 feet
3	945–964	111–130	9–12 feet
4	920–944	131–155	13–18 feet
5	less than 920	more than 155	more than 18 feet

heights are more usual but still extremely dangerous. The highest and most dangerous portion of the storm surge usually extends from near the center of the hurricane some 50 miles along the coast in the quadrant of the hurricane where winds are blowing toward shore.

A hurricane disaster-potential scale is shown in Table 18.1. Developed by consulting engineers and the National Hurricane Center, and made available to public safety officials when a hurricane is 72 hours from landfall.

References

Crutcher, H. L., and Quayle, R. G. *Mariners Worldwide Climatic Guide to Tropical Storms at Sea.* NAVAIR 50-1C-61. Washington, D.C.: Government Printing Office, 1974.

Harding, E. T., and Kotsch, W. J. *Heavy Weather Guide.* Annapolis: Naval Institute Press, 1965.

Haurwitz, B., and Austin, J. M. *Climatology.* New York: McGraw-Hill, 1944.

Pettersen, S. *Introduction to Meteorology.* 2nd ed. New York: McGraw-Hill, 1958.

Ibid. Weather Analysis and Forecasting. 2nd ed. New York: McGraw-Hill, 1956.

International Cloud Atlas. World Meteorological Organization. Geneva: WMO, 1981.

Manual for Ship's Surface Weather Observations, Commander, Naval Oceanography Command. Bay St. Louis, MS, 1981.

National Data Buoy Office Pamphlet. Bay St. Louis, MS: U.S. Department of Commerce, NDBO, 1981.

Tropical Cyclones of the North Atlantic Ocean, 1871–1977. U.S. Department of Commerce, NOAA. Asheville, NC: Government Printing Office, 1978.

U.S. Navy Marine Climatic Atlas of the World. Commander, Naval Oceanography Command. Washington, D.C.: Government Printing Office, 1981.

U.S. Standard Atmosphere. U.S. Department of Commerce, NOAA. Washington, D.C.: Government Printing Office, 1976.

Weather Service Observation Handbook No. 1 (WSOH-1), Marine Observations. U.S. Department of Commerce, NOAA. Washington, D.C.: Government Printing Office, 1981.

19

Oceanography

The seaman encounters aspects of nature rarely dealt with ashore. Understanding these oceanic phenomena involves numerous scientific disciplines, for *oceanography* spans the fields of biology, chemistry, geology, and physics, with particular emphasis on their interrelationships. A knowledge of oceanography will help the mariner to use the marine environment to his advantage. His operations are strongly affected by wind, waves, currents, fog, and storms; the physics of the ocean helps explain these facts of life at sea. The shape of the ocean floor, of beaches, and of harbors, the holding ground for anchors, the location of bars and shoals can best be understood from a geological perspective. Marine corrosion, the perpetual enemy of ship hulls and machinery, is chemical in nature. Fouling and sonar interference result from biological processes. Whether transporting passengers, hauling cargo, launching aircraft, hunting submarines, catching fish, or sailing for pleasure, the seaman will profit by any effort he makes to understand oceanographic principles. The references at the end of this chapter suggest titles of suitable texts to help him in his study.

Size and Shape of the Oceans

19.1 Depths and Areas The three oceans—Atlantic, Pacific, and Indian—cover 71 percent of the earth's surface to an average depth of 12,400 ft. The largest and deepest is the Pacific, with an area of 52,400,000 square nautical miles (nm). The Atlantic is the next largest in area (31,000,000 square nm) and shallowest in mean depth. The Indian Ocean has the smallest area (21,800,000 square nm) with a mean depth intermediate between the Atlantic and Pacific. The southern parts of the oceans are larger than the northern parts; a hemisphere with a pole at 47° S, 177.5° E (near New Zealand) is 90-percent covered with sea water. The portions of the three oceans surrounding Antarctica are sometimes considered as a fourth ocean—the Antarctic or Southern Ocean. Uninterrupted by continents, its currents and wind circulate all the way around the globe. Chilled by the frigid air, Antarctic water becomes denser, sinks to the bottom, and flows slowly northward to form the deepest layer of all the other oceans.

19.2 Bottom Topography The land margins of the world's oceans follow a common topographic pattern. Starting at the shore line, the bottom slopes very gently over the *continental shelf* out to the *shelf break.* (See Fig. 19.1.) The average width of the continental shelf is 37 nautical miles, but it varies from less than a nautical mile off the California coast to over 900 nautical miles off northern Siberia. The shelf break depth varies from 165 to 1500 ft, with an average of about 430 ft. A figure of 100 fathoms (600 ft) or 200 m (656 ft) is often taken as the depth at the edge of the shelf break since one or the other of these two contours appears on most marine charts and in many parts of the world falls close to the actual shelf break depth.

Definition of the shelf is important to the Law of the Sea. From 1958 to 1982, a series of United Nations conferences developed a treaty covering, among other points, the right of coastal states to the shelf. The treaty defines the seaward limit of the shelf as the 200 meter depth contour. The adjacent state may explore and exploit natural resources within that limit. The United States refused to sign the treaty, and in 1983, by Presidential Proclamation, claimed sovereign rights and jurisdiction over an Exclusive Economic Zone (EEZ). The EEZ runs not to the 200 depth meter contour but rather to a line distant 200 nautical miles seaward of the continental United States, Alaska, and U.S. islands. In many locations, the U.S. definition covers a wider area than that of the U.N.

To define the 200 meter contour accurately and worldwide will require extensive additional surveying and charting. Until these are accomplished the mariner will have to rely on his depth finder and knowledge of oceanography to determine whether or not his vessel is over the shelf.

Fig. 19.1 Principal submarine topographic features.

Seaward of the shelf break, the *continental slope* drops more sharply towards the *abyssal plain*. On some coasts (Mexico's Gulf of Tehauntapec, for example), the slope continues down into a trench; on others (such as the northeastern United States), it gives way to a less steep *continental rise*. To illustrate these features, the scale of Fig. 19.1 has been vertically exaggerated. When one attempts to visualize the relief of the actual sea bottom, this distortion can be misleading. The average steepness of the world's continental slopes is 4 degrees, with those in the Pacific generally steeper than those in the Atlantic and Indian Oceans. On land, a 4-degree slope (7-ft drop in a 100-ft run) is hardly the spectacular sight suggested by the vertical exaggeration of the figure. It is considerably more dramatic, however, than the slope of the continental shelf, whose average of 0.1 degrees provides a gradient of about 2 in. in 100 ft. Submarine canyons are a permanent feature of both shelf and slope. Many equal the Grand Canyon in size. Some, like the Congo Canyon, are associated with rivers; some, like the huge Monterey Canyon, extend seaward from bays; some have no apparent continental topographic connection.

The continental shelf, slope, and rise together comprise the *continental margin,* one of the three major morphological divisions of the seabed. The ocean *basin floors*—extensive abyssal plains lying 10,000 to 20,000 ft below sea level with slopes of less than 0.1 degrees—make up the second division. These give way in some areas to low hills with a relief of a few hundred feet. More rugged features result from volcanic activity. Some of these rise above the sea surface as *volcanic islands,* whereas others are covered with a thick pile of limestone and the skeletons of reef corals and other marine animals and plants. The later are the coral *atolls* of the Pacific and Indian oceans. Volcanoes that do not break the sea surface are called *seamounts* or *sea knolls.* Most have conical or irregular peaks, but many (termed *guyots* or *tablemounts*) have broad flat tops. These once stood at sea level before the seamount slowly sank, over millions of years, beneath the waves. The boundary between the ocean basin and the continential margin may, as mentioned above, take the form of a deep *trench.* Trenches can extend for several thousands of miles in length with widths measured in no more than tens of miles. They hold the ocean's greatest depths—the Mariana Trench is the deepest of them all at over 36,000 ft—and are most numerous in the Pacific, particularly along the coasts of South America, Central America, and the Aleutian Islands. Fourteen Pacific Ocean trenches are deeper than 21,000 ft; the Atlantic Ocean has only two; the Indian Ocean, only one.

The third division of the seabed includes the midoceanic *rises* and *ridges.* Figure 19.2 shows the ridge that winds down the middle of the Atlantic. Close examination reveals a central rift valley flanked on either side by symmetrical ridges. In a few locations, like Iceland and the Azores, the ridge reaches the surface; elsewhere its crest is hundreds of fathoms deep.

Fig. 19.2   Atlantic Ocean floor. *(Courtesy of* National Geographic Magazine; © 1968 *National Geographic Society)*

East and west of the crest, depths gradually increase as the ridge descends to the floor of the abyssal basins.

In recent decades, geophysicists have traced a system of ridges and rises across all the oceans (Fig. 19.3). They now realize that these constitute the boundaries of *tectonic plates*. Each continent rests on a plate—a section of the Earth's *lithosphere*. The plates in turn float on the denser, semiliquid mantle. At the center of each midocean ridge, molten *magma* rises through the rift where it cools and solidifies to form additions to the adjacent plates, one on each side of the rift. The plates drift slowly apart, a few inches each year, carrying their continents with them. Satellite measurements have confirmed the rate of continental drift derived from more conventional geological data. The outer edges of the plates meet in one of two ways. In

Lithosphere plates of the Earth.

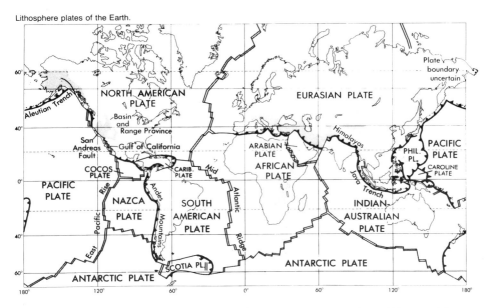

Fig. 19.3   Lithosphere plates of the Earth. Each continent rests on a plate. Mid-ocean ridges and rises mark plate boundaries.

some cases, for example on the Pacific coast of South America, one plate slides below the other with the accompaniment of earthquakes and volcanoes and the formation of a trench. In others, the collision of the plates causes both to buckle and form continental mountain systems like the Alps or the Himalayas. The theory of *plate tectonics,* here summarized very briefly, makes fascinating reading. Fuller explanations will be found in the introductory texts listed at the end of this chapter.

19.3   Exploring and Working at the Ocean Bottom   Knowledge of water depth has long been essential to the mariner. Within the last century, it has become important to the scientist and engineer as well. The ability to place machinery and sometimes men near the ocean bottom has become a vital factor in naval warfare, oil and mineral exploration and extraction, cable laying, salvage, treasure hunting, and fishery research. Technological progress has been rapid, particularly in the years since World War II.

Water depths were originally measured by *lead line.* Transmission of sound energy by sea water, however, permits a faster and more accurate measurement. Modern instruments called *echo sounders* measure the time required for an acoustic pulse to travel from a hull-mounted transducer to the sea bottom—where it is reflected—plus the time for the echo to travel back to the transducer. At an average velocity of about 4,800 ft/sec, a pulse completes its round trip to a depth of 240 ft, for example, in 0.1 sec. The echo sounder electronically interprets these short time intervals as depths, which are then displayed on various types of recorders. To study the structure of sediments that exist below the water bottom interface, scientists generate stronger and lower frequency pulses by exploding underwater charges. The resultant echoes are processed to yield seismic reflection profiles. High-frequency, short-pulse echo sounders can also give information on sediment, pollutants, or biota suspended in the water.

Recent developments use both sonic and electromagnetic energy to measure depths over large areas rather than just beneath a survey ship. *Sidescan sonar* projects a sound beam in a fan-shaped pattern from a towed "fish." This image shows both bottom topography (ridges, trenches, etc.) and sunken objects like ships, aircraft, and pipelines. GLORIA (Geological LOng Range Inclined Asdic) yields a "sonograph" up to 30 nautical miles wide. SWATH (BS^3, or Bathymetric Swath Survey System) projects multiple beams from a surface ship to produce a contour map of the sea floor. So accurate and detailed are SWATH charts that the U.S. Navy and the National Oceanic and Atmospheric Administration (NOAA) disagree on the appropriate security classification to be assigned.

Satellite altimeters use radar to measure the distance to the sea surface. These readings, together with gravity measurements, locate the *geoid* (undulating surface of the ocean) and indirectly reveal the depth of the water below the satellite. This technique has discovered and mapped seamounts in areas rarely visited by survey ships. The ABS (Airborne Bathymetric Survey) system under development by the U.S. Navy will use three different sensors: laser, multispectral scanner, and electromagnetic profiler. These will measure depth over a swath beneath a P-3 aircraft using satellite GPS (Global Positioning System) for location. Designed for use in depths down to 200 feet, day and night, the complete system is scheduled to become operational in 1990. All of these new systems will increase not only the accuracy but also the area coverage of ocean bathymetry.

More detailed information on the sea bed is obtained by physically bringing a sample to the surface with a corer, grab, or dredge. The first reliable deep-ocean cores were taken by the *Challenger* Expedition in the early 1870s. Although these penetrated only 2 ft, they provided 85,000 years of geological history. It was 1945 before cores over 100 ft long were obtained. In 1961, a Project Mohole test drill went to 1,030 ft (producing 10-million-year sediments). The *Glomar Challenger* drilled to a record 3,321 feet in water 20,146 feet deep. In 1985 a new drill ship, *JOIDES Resolution*, took over the Joint Oceanographic Institutions for Deep Earth Sampling (JOIDES) project.

Samples can also be collected and material retrieved by a variety of manned submersibles or remote-controlled vehicles. The latter, termed

ROVs (Remote Operated Vehicles), include robots like ANGUS, the U.S. Navy's Surface Towed Search System (STSS), and Hydro Products' RCV series, the "swimming eyeball." STSS has sonars, television, and still cameras to find and identify aircraft wreckage or other submerged objects. ANGUS (Acoustically Navigated Underwater Survey System) has been used to study the biology and geology of the mid-Atlantic rift. Manned deep-submergence vehicles (DSV) are particularly suited to the recovery of items previously located by search vehicles. *Alvin* discovered a lost nuclear weapon 2,500 feet deep in the Mediterranean, and more recently explored the wreck of the *Titanic* in 12,500 feet off Newfoundland. *Trieste II* worked at 8,500 ft searching for the lost submarine USS *Thresher* and at over 10,000 ft searching for the USS *Scorpion*. Other DSVs used for exploration include *Trieste I, Aluminaut, Cyana, Archimede, Autec, Turtle,* and Commandant Cousteau's *Soucoupe*. Figure 19.4, a schematic summary of modern oceanographic research tools, includes DSVs and a drill ship as well as devices for investigating the water column above the sea floor.

Water and Its Role in Shaping the Environment

Water has unique chemical and physical properties. As its symbolic representation H_2O indicates, its molecule is made up of two hydrogen atoms bonded to a single oxygen atom. The asymmetrical form of this bond gives the molecule positively and negatively charged zones—a geometry that is responsible for water's unusual behavior. This, together with its abundance, gives water a predominant influence on the earth's environment and life forms. Here we shall discuss those of greatest oceanographic impact.

19.4 Properties of Sea Water Water is very nearly a universal solvent, and the oceans contain in solution at least a trace of virtually every element. The major dissolved constituents are chloride (55 percent), sodium (31 percent), sulfate (8 percent), magnesium (4 percent), calcium (1 percent), and potassium (1 percent), these percentages being approximate. The constituents occur in virtually the same relative proportion throughout all the world's oceans—evidence of thorough horizontal and vertical mixing. If 1 kg (about 2.2 lb) of ocean water were evaporated, we would recover about 35 g (1.2 oz) of solid material, including all dissolved constituents. Thus, the salinity is said to be 35 parts per thousand (abbreviated 35‰). This figure varies by only a few parts per thousand in open seas; near shore and in estuaries, the salinity is lower. Inside Chesapeake Bay, for example, salinities range from 5 to 30‰. Salinity is significant for a number of reasons, the most important for the mariner, perhaps, being its corrosion of iron and steel, which accelerates as the salinity increases. Salinity distribu-

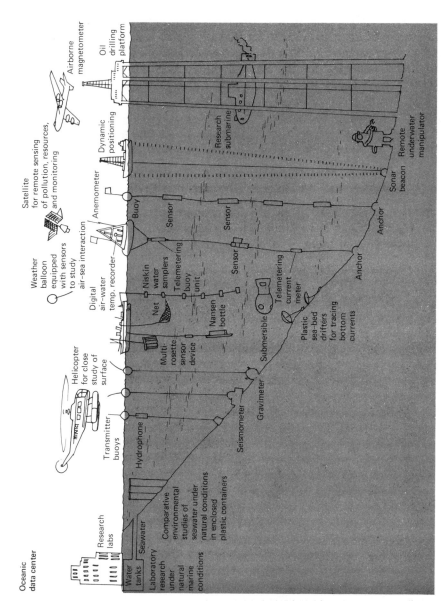

Fig. 19.4 Modern oceanographic research tools for investigating sea bottom and overlying waters.

510

tion, moreover, affects the flow of geostrophic oceanic currents that are driven by differences in density.

The thermal properties of water are anomalous in that changes of temperature or of state (ice—liquid—vapor) require more heat than almost any other liquid or solid. In winter, seawater gives up great amounts of heat to the colder atmosphere without a large change in water temperature. If the temperature is finally lowered to the freezing point, the water continues to give up heat (which warms the atmosphere) without any further drop in temperature until the heat of fusion has been removed. Thus, the winter temperatures of coastal areas are warmer than those of inland areas at the same latitude. In summer, the reverse is true. Melting ice absorbs large quantities of heat from the atmosphere, thereby reducing its temperature. Once the ice is melted, seawater continues to absorb many calories for each degree of temperature increase, and air temperature continues to drop. For this reason, summer temperatures of coastal areas are cooler than inland temperatures. Areas remote from the sea have severe climates—hot summers and cold winters—compared to areas near the ocean, where the annual temperature is warmer and the temperature range smaller. Mean air temperatures in Siberia, for example, range from 15°F (-10°C) in January to 40°F (4.5°C) in July; in northern Scotland, at about the same latitude, the range is from 35°F (1.7°C) to 39°F (4°C). Chapter 14 explains these relationships in more detail.

Large-scale flows of ocean water carry their stored heat with them. North-flowing currents like the Gulf Stream and the Kurushio transport large amounts of heat from regions near the equator, which absorb relatively more solar heat, to those nearer the poles, which absorb less solar heat. The Brazil and East Australia Currents play a similar role in the Southern Hemisphere.

A ship, like any other floating object, displaces a volume of water whose mass equals that of the ship. Since water density (mass per unit volume) changes with temperature and salinity, a vessel has a greater draft in brackish water than in the open sea and a greater draft in warm water than in cold water. Sea water becomes more dense as temperature drops until it cools to, or nearly to, the freezing point. Since ice is less dense than water, it floats on the surface, where it acts as an insulator and slows the chilling of the water beneath it. Deep water bodies, as a result, do not freeze down to the bottom, and marine plants and animals can continue to live through the winter.

Water in Motion

19.5 Wind Waves Wind waves can be approximated by a sine curve, as shown in Fig. 19.5. *Wavelength L* is the distance between two successive

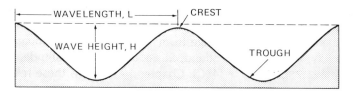

Fig. 19.5 Wave parameters.

crests; *height H* is the vertical distance from trough to crest. *Still water level* (SWL) is half-way between crest and trough, and *amplitude* is the vertical distance from crest to SWL. *Period T* is the time required for two successive crests to pass a *fixed* point. (An observer on a moving ship will measure a different time between crests—one not equal to the period.) Water particles on the crest move forward, in the direction of wave travel. Particles at SWL move vertically up and down. Particles in the trough move backwards.

Phase velocity or *celerity* can be computed by the formulas

$$V \text{ (ft/sec)} = \frac{L \text{ (ft)}}{T \text{ (sec)}}$$

or

$$V \text{ (knots)} = \frac{L \text{ (ft)}}{T \text{ (sec)}} \times 0.6$$

In nature, waves rarely, if ever, have a true sinusoidal shape. In the *generating area*, where energy is transferred from wind in the atmosphere to waves in the sea, the surface appears confused. Waves seem to appear and disappear with little pattern. If one measures wave height as it varies with time, however, it is possible by a process termed *Fourier analysis* to determine that the sea consists of the sum of a number of sine waves, each with a different height, period, length, and direction. The mathematical description permits the oceanographer to forecast wave behavior.

Not only does the wave shape move, but also the water particles within it. These have a rotary motion. In deep water, the particles move in circles (Fig. 19.6), the diameter of which decreases exponentially with depth below the surface, the short wave lengths damping out faster than long wave lengths. Submariners thus experience less motion at deep submergence than at periscope depth. Near the surface, depth control is easier when surface waves are moderate, with wavelengths of 50 to 100 ft, than in a gale, where wavelengths may reach 300 to 400 ft. In shallow water, the particle circles flatten into ellipses, and the motion extends all the way to

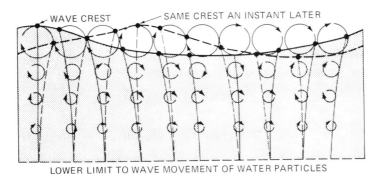

Fig. 19.6 Cross-section of deep water wave in motion. Circles represent the orbit of water particles in the wave. At the surface, orbit diameter equals wave height. At a depth equal to 0.5 wavelengths, orbit diameter is only 0.04 that at the surface.

the bottom. A bather can observe this by noting the back-and-forth movement of sand particles on the bottom as waves approach a beach.

The height, length, and period of a sea are determined by the wind. Three wind characteristics are important: (1) *velocity;* (2) *duration,* or time during which the wind blows; and (3) *fetch,* or distance across the open ocean over which the wind is unchanged in speed and direction. For each wind speed, there is a maximum amount of energy that can be transferred to the sea. Energy exceeding this maximum will result in breaking waves that dissipate the excess as turbulence. When energy input equals energy dissipation, the waves stop growing, and the sea is at its "fully developed" state. To reach this stage, minimum values of both fetch and duration are required. Table 16.1 of Chapter 16—an extension of the well-known Beaufort scale—lists these minimum values for a wide range of wind speeds. As an example, a fully developed sea under a wind of 20 knots results only if the wind has blown across a 75-mile, or longer, fetch for at least 10 hr. The waves will have an average height of 5 ft, but about one-third of the waves will average higher—8 ft—and one-tenth will average higher still—10 ft. The *significant height* is, by definition, the average of the highest third. This is the value that an experienced seaman will normally report as the height of the sea described above. Evidently, one subconsciously eliminates small waves from his mental averaging, thus producing an estimated height somewhat greater than the true statistical average.

Just as a fully developed sea consists of a mixture of waves of different heights, it also includes a mixture of waves of different periods. Both height and period depend on wind velocity. For any given wind speed, waves of a certain period contain most of the energy (i.e., have the greatest heights). This period can be estimated as

$$T' \text{ (sec)} = 0.4W\text{(kts)}$$

where W is the wind speed in knots at a height of about 65 feet above sea level. For a 30 knot wind, therefore, waves with a 12 second period will be highest, and will have a wavelength of about 730 feet. Waves of both longer and shorter periods and wavelengths will be present, but their heights will be lower.

Occasionally, when all the component sine waves crest simultaneously at a point, a giant, or *rogue wave,* may occur with a height twice the significant height. A sea of 30-ft waves in a fresh gale may spawn a 60-ft giant with a near-vertical, breaking face. This can pitchpole a yacht or endanger a ship. In April 1966, the liner *Michaelangelo* was struck by a giant wave that killed three passengers and damaged the ship's bridge 80 feet above the waterline. Fortunately for the mariner, few weather systems support the development of fully aroused seas for wind speeds over 40 knots. An exception is the Southern Ocean, where the prevailing westerlies blowing across an unlimited fetch create the "Roaring Forties" and the infamous seas that roll past Cape Horn. It was in the Pacific, however, that the USS *Ramapo* recorded the highest wave ever reliably reported, a mountainous 112 ft.

Ship weather reports include not only wave height, but also wave period. The National Climatic Center has found that most observers tend to underestimate the period, probably because many wave trains are generally present at the time of observation. The Center recommends the following averaging procedure for determining correct value of wave period: Select a distinctive patch of foam or a small floating object at some distance from the ship. As the object falls astern select a new one. Note the elapsed time to the nearest second between moments when the object is on the crest of the first and of the last well-formed wave of the group. Also note the number of crests that pass under the object during the interval. Continue the observation until at least 15 waves have been timed. Add the elapsed times of the various groups together and divide the total by the number of waves to obtain the average period.

19.6 Swell As explained above, wind waves are created in a generating area in which wind energy is transferred to the water. Waves within this area are referred to as *sea.* Eventually, the waves find themselves outside the generating area, either because the wind has stopped blowing or because the wave's travel (velocity times time) has taken it out of reach of the wind. Their profiles become smoother, more closely resembling a sinusoid, and they are then called *swell.* Because their height diminishes very gradually, swells can travel thousands of miles. A yacht off Southern California may be rolling to a swell generated by a storm southeast of New Zealand.

19.7 Wave Celerity Wave celerity, or phase velocity (V), governs several aspects of wave behavior. In deep water, V can be computed from either wavelength L or period T.

$$V(\text{kts}) = 1.3 \sqrt{L(\text{ft})} = 3.0T(\text{sec})$$
$$V(\text{ft/sec}) = 2.3 \sqrt{L(\text{ft})} = 5.1T(\text{sec})$$

Thus, deep water waves of different periods travel at different velocities. The energy of a train of deep water waves travels at a speed equal to one-half its celerity, so that longer period waves have higher travel speeds.

An observer at a distance from a storm, outside the area where wind is generating the waves , first notices low, long-period "forerunner" swells. These have travelled fastest, and consequently reach the observer first. The highest swells arrive later, for their period, and therefore speed of travel, are lower. Thereafter, wave height decreases as swells of still shorter period and lower speed finally arrive. Thus the confused waves of a storm sea are filtered or sorted out as they leave the generating areas at differing speeds to become a smoother, more uniform swell.

As waves enter shallow water, their velocity becomes dependent only upon water depth H, so that the formulas become

$$V(\text{knots}) = 3.4 \sqrt{H \text{ (ft)}}$$
$$V(\text{ft/sec}) = 5.7 \sqrt{H \text{ (ft)}}$$

Waves approaching a beach thus travel at a reduced velocity with a shorter wavelength. Water depth below the troughs, moreover, is less than that below the crests. Since the crests therefore travel faster than the troughs, the leading edge of each wave becomes steeper and the trailing edge more gentle. When the wave reaches a water depth slightly greater than wave height and the wave steepness (ratio of height to wave length) approaches about $\frac{1}{7}$, the wave breaks and becomes surf. Breaker height depends upon the offshore height of the wave or swell, its wavelength, and the underwater topography.

Direction of wave travel also changes as the wave enters shoal water because of a phenomenon called *refraction*. Refraction tends to align the wave crests parallel to a straight shoreline, to concentrate wave energy on headlands, and to reduce wave height in bays. Details of water flow in the surf zone are not completely understood. It takes on complicated forms, including *longshore currents,* which set parallel to the beach, and *rip currents,* in which water carried shoreward by breaking waves finds its way back to deep water in fast, narrow jets. Longshore and rip current velocities may be as great as 3 knots.

Most inlets and river mouths have a bar or shoal across the entrance. Here the shoaling effect can produce high waves that sometimes break, particularly in an onshore wind. Experience shows that breaker height—

difficult to measure at best—is usually underestimated by observers on the seaward side. "Crossing the bar" in bad weather can turn into a dangerous operation. Chapter 12 gives advice on entering breaking inlets and handling small craft in the surf.

19.8 Wave Forecasts Oceanographers use several methods to forecast behavior of sea, swell, and surf. Since the physics of energy transmission from wind to waves is not yet fully understood, the schemes are at least partly empirical. The forecaster starts his work with a surface wind forecast. From this he outlines fetch areas. Knowing how long a given wind has been blowing at forecast time, he can estimate how much longer it will continue. These arguments—wind speed, duration, and fetch length—allow the forecaster to enter a nomograph giving expected wave heights and periods. The wave forecasts in turn lead to swell forecasts. Shoaling and refraction diagrams can assist in predicting changes in wave height and direction that will occur as a wave train approaches land. Other rules, somewhat less reliable, predict the characteristics of surf, longshore currents, and rip tides, all important variables for amphibious operations.

The reader can find a summary of current wave prediction methods in Chapter 3 of Bishop (1984). This is an active area of oceanographic research. The ability of satellite altimeters to measure surface wind speed and wave height greatly increases the volume of data available for analysis.

19.9 Seismic Sea Waves A submarine earthquake, by suddenly changing the elevation of the ocean surface, can cause a *seismic sea wave* or *tsunami* (sometimes incorrectly called a *tidal wave*). Wavelengths measured in miles with heights of only a few feet give the waves a gentle slope unnoticeable at sea. Traveling at speeds as high as 500 knots, the waves cross long distances with little loss of energy. Nearing land, they enter shoal water and experience a sudden reduction of velocity and wavelength. Since the energy contained in each wave remains constant, the height of each crest increases as the distance between successive crests diminishes. Funnel shaped topography may concentrate the wave energy still more with an even greater increase in wave height.

A 1946 earthquake in the Aleutian Trench caused a well-documented tsunami. Nearly five hours later, waves at Hilo, Hawaii, 1800 nautical miles to the south, reached more than 30 ft above mean high water. At Scotch Cap on Unimak Island, 100 nautical miles north of the quake, a lighthouse was wrecked by a wave over 100 ft high. In 1883, the volcanic explosion of Krakatoa in Sundra Strait created a tsunami of similar height. Energy from this wave was detectable in the English Channel after crossing the Indian and Atlantic Oceans.

19.10   Tides   The *tide* is a wave caused by gravitational attraction of the sun and moon. Since the attraction between two objects increases as the objects draw closer together, the ocean water on the side of the earth directly under the moon is attracted more strongly than water 90 degrees away, where the moon is either rising or setting. Water on the opposite side of the earth from the moon is attracted even less. Because of the differences in magnitude of these attractive forces, water is pulled away from the earth on the moon side and the earth is pulled away from the water on the far side. The result is two bulges of water, one on each side of the earth, with the earth rotating inside the bulges (Fig. 19.7). If the earth was completely covered by an ocean, with no continents, a point on the earth would experience a high tide as it passed under one bulge, then a low tide as it passed under the shallow area 90 degrees away, followed by a second high tide and a second low tide. One lunar day (24.8 hr) after the first high tide, the bulge would again be over the same point, and another high tide would occur.

The sun's gravitational attraction is superimposed on that of the moon. The sun's mass is greater than the moon's, but the sun is much more distant. As a result, the sun's attraction is only about half that of the moon. When sun, moon, and earth all lie in a straight line at the time of new and full moons, their gravitational attractions are additive, and *spring tides* result. High tides are higher than average and low tides lower. At the times of the first and last quarters, sun and moon are "in quadrature," that is, 90 degrees apart, and their gravitational pulls are out of phase. *Neap tides* result, with high tides lower than average and low tides higher. (See Fig. 19.8.)

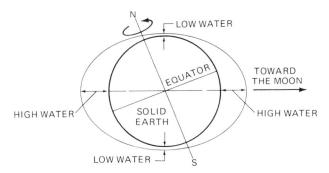

Fig. 19.7   Theoretical equilibrium configuration of a water-covered earth resulting from the moon's differential gravitational forces. One bulge of the water envelope is located at the sublunar point; the other at the antipode. *(From* American Practical Navigator, *vol. 1, 1977)*

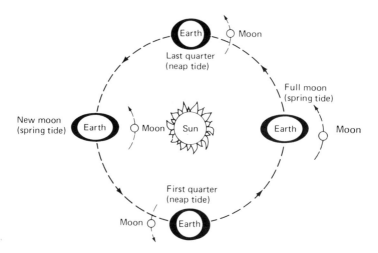

Fig. 19.8   Spring and neap tides. Tidal amplitude is greatest at springs when sun, moon, and earth are in line. Amplitudes are least at first and last quarter.

The sun and moon not only occupy different rotational positions with respect to the earth; they also move north and south of its equator and move closer to and farther away from its orbit. The simple pattern of tides described above becomes more complex. Some parts of the earth have one high and one low tide daily (*diurnal tides*); others have two equal high tides and two equal low tides each day (*semidiurnal tides*); some have two highs of unequal height and two lows of unequal height (*mixed tides*).

The "equilibrium tidal theory" just described ignores the existence of the continents and the bathymetry of the oceans as well as the fact that the oceans' waters are in continuous motion. These factors further modify the tides from a simple double bulge oriented toward the moon. The "dynamic tidal theory" attempts to explain the results of these parameters, but a completely satisfactory theory has yet to be evolved.

Figure 19.9 shows the complex changes at several ports. The change in range from neaps (on 3 and 19 September) to springs (on 13 and 25 September) is particularly noticeable at Port Adelaide and at Pei-Hai. These occur at approximately, but not exactly, the lunar phases predicted by equilibrium theory. The differences of several days demonstrate its shortcomings.

Tides are not predicted on the basis of either of these theories, but rather by a harmonic analysis of tidal records collected over long intervals at stations all over the world. At least a year's observations are desirable, although less reliable predictions can be made from shorter records. Most of the maritime nations publish annual tide tables in two parts. The first

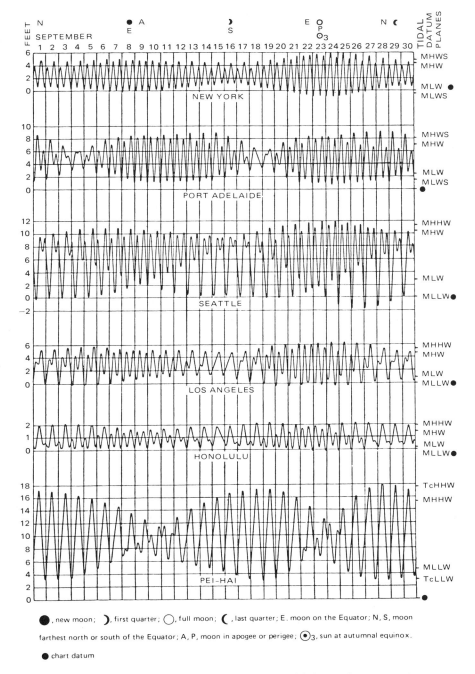

Fig. 19.9 Tidal variations during a month. Definitions of tidal datum planes: MHWS = Mean high water, springs; MHW = Mean high water; MLW = Mean low water; MLWS = Mean low water, springs; MHHW = Mean higher high water, MLLW = Mean lower low water; TcHHW = Tropic higher high water; TcLLW = Tropic lower low water. *(From* American Practical Navigator, *vol. 1, 1977)*

part consists of predicted times and heights of daily high and low waters for a number of reference stations, including many of the major ports. The second part contains differences in times and heights of high and low tides for several thousand "subordinate stations," each with respect to one of the reference stations. The tables contain instructions for their use. No particular work form is necessary, but the format of Fig. 19.10 may be helpful.

The tables are accurate insofar as they predict the "astronomical tide" caused by the sun, moon, and local topography but do not, and are not intended to, take into account the water level changes caused by meteorological conditions. Variations of several feet are therefore common. Both hurricanes and extratropical cyclones, moreover, can cause "storm surge." Low barometric pressure, onshore winds, and heavy rain can combine to cause higher tide levels than those predicted, particularly in estuaries or other semi-enclosed water bodies. If such conditions occur at the time of a high spring tide, flooding of coastal areas may occur. The reverse situation may cause unusually low water levels. The U.S. National Weather Service has developed models from which they issue storm surge predictions. Additional information on surges, including prediction methods, is available in Chapter 4 of Bishop (1984).

19.11 Tidal Currents The vertical motion of the tides is accompanied by horizontal water flow called *tidal current.* Motion from the ocean towards the land is termed the *flood;* motion towards the sea, *ebb.* Between these comes *slack water,* when current velocity is zero. High tide does not necessarily coincide with slack water. The term "high water slack" should be avoided; it is better to speak of "slack before flood" or "slack before ebb." The time interval between high tide and slack before ebb varies, depending upon whether the tide wave in the body of water is a *standing wave* or a *progressive wave,* a fact that is not always recognized. "Bowditch" (see references) advises: "One should exercise extreme caution in using general rules. The belief that slack occurs at local high and low tides and that the maximum flood and ebb occur when the tide is rising or falling most rapidly may be approximately true at the seaward entrance to, and in the upper reaches of, an inland tidal waterway. But generally this is not true in other parts of inland waterways. When an inland waterway is extensive or its entrance constricted, the slacks in some parts of the waterway often occur midway between the times of high and low tide. Usually in such waterways the relationship changes from place to place as one progresses upstream, slack water getting progressively closer in time to the local tide maximum until at the head of tidewater (the inland limit of water affected by a tide) the slacks occur at about the times of high and low tide."

Tidal current tables are published in a format similar to that of the tide tables. The one shown in Fig. 19.11 is useful for calculating times and veloc-

NAVIGATION DEPARTMENT   DIVISION OF NAVAL COMMAND AND MANAGEMENT

COMPLETE TIDE TABLE

Date: Jan. 2, 1975

Substation	Yonkers
Reference Station	New York
HW Time Difference	(+)1^{h}09^m
LW Time Difference	(+)1^{h}10^m
Difference in height of HW	(−)0.8ft.
Difference in height of LW	0.0ft.

Reference Station   Substation

HW	2231	4.6ft.		2340	3.8ft.
LW	0516	(−)0.6ft.		0626	(−)0.6ft.
HW	1138	4.9ft.		1247	4.1ft.
LW	1749	(−)0.9ft.		1859	(−)0.9ft.
HW					
LW					

HEIGHT OF TIDE AT ANY TIME

Locality: Yonkers   Time: 1000   Date: Jan. 2, 1975

Duration of Rise or Fall:	6^{h}21^m
Time from Nearest Tide:	2^{h}47^m
Range of Tide:	4.7ft.
Height of Nearest Tide:	4.1ft.
Corr. from Table 3:	1.8ft.
Height of Tide at:1000	2.3ft.

Fig. 19.10 U.S. Naval Academy tidal work form. *(From* American Practical Navigator, *vol. 1, 1977)*

NAVIGATION DEPARTMENT   DIVISION OF NAVAL COMMAND AND MANAGEMENT

COMPLETE CURRENT TABLE

Locality: The Battery   Date: Feb. 3, 1975

Reference Station: The Narrows

Time Difference:	Slack Water:	$(+)1^h 30^m$
	Maximum Current:	$(+)1^h 35^m$
Velocity Ratio:	Maximum Flood:	0.9
	Maximum Ebb:	1.2

| Flood Direction: | $015°$ |
| Ebb Direction: | $195°$ |

Reference Station: The Narrows   Locality: The Battery

			0000	F
2355	2.0F		0130	1.8F
0305	0		0435	0
0621	2.0E		0756	2.4E
1005	0		1135	0
1222	1.5F		1357	1.4F
1516	0		1646	0
1839	1.9E		2014	2.3E
2216	0		2346	0
2400	F		2400	F

VELOCITY OF CURRENT AT 1500

Int. between slack and desired time:	$1^h 46^m$	
Int. between slack and maximum current:	$2^h 49^m$	(Ebb)(Flood)
Maximum current:	1.4kn	
Factor, Table 3	0.8	
Velocity:	1.1kn	
Direction:	$015°$	

DURATION OF SLACK

Times of maximum current:	0756	1357
Maximum current:	2.4kn	1.4kn
Desired maximum:	0.3	0.3
Period — Table 4:	35^m	46^m
Sum of periods:		81^m
Average period:		40^m
Time of slack:		1135
Duration of slack: From: ____1115____ To: ____1155____		

Fig. 19.11 U.S. Naval Academy current work form. *(From* American Practical Navigator, *vol. 1, 1977)*

ities of currents. Tabulated data, in general, are for surface currents in mid-channel. In estuaries and tidal rivers, bottom currents may differ from surface currents. Near the mouth, bottom currents usually begin to flood earlier and flow more strongly. Cross-channel variations also exist; in a straight channel, currents are weaker and shift their direction near shore earlier than they do in midstream. In a winding waterway, stronger currents are encountered on the concave shore (*bend*) and weaker on the convex (*point*). Current tables are usually based on less observational data than tide tables and are hence not only more limited in coverage but more subject to meteorological deviations. A safe assumption, however, is that abnormally high tidal ranges at a given location cause abnormally strong currents.

19.12   Oceanic Circulation   Tidal currents have widths of a few tens of miles at most and flow for perhaps one or two hundred miles. In the oceans, by contrast, currents are wider, longer, and deeper. Together, the various currents of the world make up a system of oceanic circulation driven not only by gravitational attraction but more significantly by winds and by pressure differences caused by changes in salinity and temperature. The earth's rotation also plays a major role.

Surface currents are primarily driven by the world's surface winds. As explained in Chapter 14, the tropical regions between 30 degrees north and 30 degrees south latitude are dominated by the northeast trade winds above the equator and the southeast trades below. Currents driven by the trades meet near the equator to create *equatorial drift currents* flowing westward across all three oceans. (Unlike winds, which are named for the direction *from* which they blow, currents are named by the direction *towards* which they flow. The northeast trades thus drive a southwesterly current.) Blocked by continents to the west of the oceans, these currents are deflected to the north in the northern oceans and to the south in the southern oceans. (See Fig. 17.2.) This pattern of current deflections results from the Coriolis force or acceleration that diverts moving objects—fluid or solid—to the right in the Northern Hemisphere and to the left in the Southern. The currents continue their poleward motion until they reach the prevailing westerlies in the middle latitudes, which force them eastward back across the ocean basins. Currents in higher northern latitudes are affected by topography as well as by winds. Those in the Southern Ocean, unchecked by land masses, follow the westerlies of the Roaring Forties clear around the Antarctic continent in what is known as the *west wind drift*. (See Fig. 19.12.) A comparison of Fig. 19.12 with Figs. 14.15 and 14.16 will illustrate the interrelationship of winds and surface currents.

The effects of the wind are restricted to the relatively shallow layers of the ocean. The deeper waters are also in motion, although their influence on the mariner and his ship is less significant. Deep currents are driven primarily by pressure gradients caused by variations in salinity and temperature. A column of warm, dilute sea water weighs less than a column of equal height of cold, saltier water. Between the base of these two columns exists a pressure gradient. Pressure is higher under the denser water and lower under the lighter water. As a consequence, water at depth flows down the gradient, from high to low pressure. Like wind-driven currents,

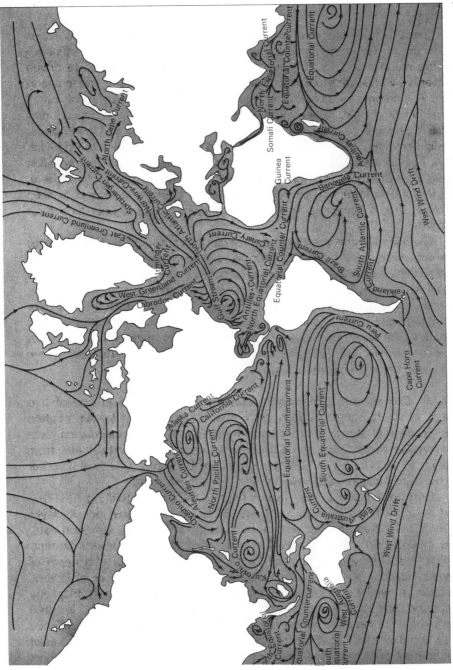

Fig. 19.12 Major ocean surface currents. Flow is clockwise in the Northern Hemisphere; counterclockwise in the Southern. The phenomenon of *westward intensification* strengthens and concentrates currents on the western boundaries of the oceans, particularly in the Northern Hemisphere.

these *thermohaline flows* are subjected to Coriolis deflection (right in the Northern Hemisphere, left in the Southern). Bottom topography plays a role with respect to deep currents that is similar to that of the continents with respect to surface currents.

The direction and velocity of surface currents are available in pilot charts, current atlases, and oceanographic texts. The mariner should remember that all these report *average* values of turbulent flow. By definition, *turbulent flow* is irregular, varying continuously in both direction and magnitude. The set and drift experienced on a given day's run in the Gulf Stream, for example, may differ significantly from the mean values printed on that month's pilot chart. Predictions tend to be more accurate on the west sides of ocean basins, where currents are strongest, than in midocean, where the mean current velocity is low.

19.13 Current Measurements Currents are measured in one of two ways. In the *Lagrangian approach,* a float is released at a known position and recovered later at another known position. A simple calculation gives the average current direction and velocity over the time and distance from launch to recovery. The *Eulerian approach,* by contrast, utilizes a sensor to measure direction and velocity at a given fixed point.

Drift bottles and *buoys*—which float on the surface (see Fig. 19.13)— and *Swallow floats*—which are ballasted to follow a given density layer at intermediate depths and are traced accoustically—give Lagrangian data. The Swallow float helped reveal the presence of the Cromwell Current, which flows eastward across the Pacific below the Equator at a depth of several hundred feet. Eulerian current meters utilize a number of factors, including propeller effect, Doppler effect on sound velocity, electromagnetic induction, and drag effect. Meters may be tethered from buoys, lowered from ships, or mounted at the bottom. The latter are advantageous, since they avoid spurious readings caused by the motion of the buoy or vessel but present problems in deployment, relocation, and recovery. A recent development is digital storage of current data in a microcomputer memory inside the current meter's pressureproof body. Such an instrument needs no cable or other connection with the surface. Another advance allows oceanographers to compute current speed from satellite altimetry data.

19.14 Upwelling and El Niño Strong winds blowing parallel to a shoreline cause surface water to flow not only downwind but also, because of the Coriolis effect, across the wind. In the Northern Hemisphere, the Coriolis motion is to the right; in the Southern Hemisphere, to the left. If the Coriolis transport is offshore, the surface water is replaced by colder water "upwelling" from greater depths. The deep water typically is rich in *nutri-*

Fig. 19.13 Launching a telemetering buoy from the R/V *Chain*. The buoy is used to trace currents and to return data by radio to a research vessel. *(Courtesy of Woods Hole Oceanographic Institution)*

ents—decay products from dead marine life that have drifted down from the upper layers. These "fertilize" the upper layers, causing plankton "blooms," which in turn support huge populations of fish.

The Peru current, driven by the southeast trades, flows north along the Pacific coast of South America. Surface water motion has a westerly, offshore component because of the Coriolis effect. The resultant upwelling is responsible for a multimillion-ton anchovy catch, one of the world's largest. The rich marine life supplies food for sea birds—pelicans, boobies, cormorants—whose colonies are so numerous that their droppings, or *guano* are a profitable source of fertilizer. Occasionally, during the southern summer, the trades are replaced by westerly winds. Upwelling stops, and a nutrient-poor countercurrent from the equator raises water temperatures dramatically. Occurring in December, the event is called *El Niño* for the Christ child. The anchovy die or follow the cold water out of the fishing grounds, and the purse seiners' nets come aboard empty. To aggravate the financial disaster, the guano birds starve. Their decaying carcasses generate enough hydrogen sulfide to turn ships's hulls black in the *Callao Painter* phenomenon.

El Niño of 1982–83 was unusually severe. Oceanographers and climatologists have come to realize that this phenomenon is not confined to Peru, but also involves abnormal conditions across the entire tropical Pacific Ocean. Indirectly, these same changes are linked through the global atmosphere and oceans to droughts, floods, storms, and other disasters throughout the world.

Temperature and Salinity Distribution

A knowledge of the temperature structure of the oceans is important in the fishing industry, antisubmarine warfare, and particularly weather forecasting and climatology. Figure 19.14 shows the global distribution of yearly averaged sea surface temperature. It reflects the concentration of solar heat input in equatorial regions that produces high temperatures at mid-latitudes and a gradual poleward decrease (see Fig. 14.8). At a given latitude, however, there is usually an East-West variation in temperature resulting from heat transfer by ocean currents. Warm currents flowing poleward along the western boundaries of the oceans cause higher than average temperatures on the East coasts of the continents. In the Florida Straits, for example, annual sea temperature is about 1.7°F (1°C) higher than the average for 26

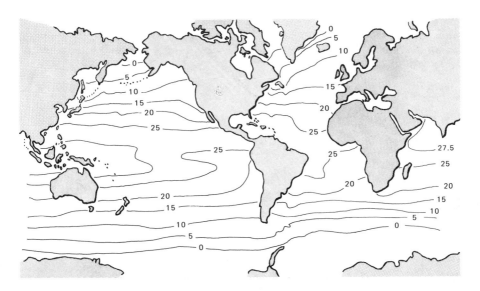

Fig. 19.14 Yearly-averaged ocean surface temperatures (degrees C).

degrees north latitude. Cape Bojador, across the Atlantic on the Sahara coast, is 3.2°F (1.8°C) lower than the average for 26 degrees north.

Salinity is important as a tracer for water circulation and as an aid in finding water density. Salinity, temperature, and depth together determine water density, a quantity which in turn allows oceanographers to calculate pressure gradients and current speed and direction.

19.15 Temperature Variation with Depth In low (tropical) and mid-latitudes, the vertical temperature structure of the oceans is marked by three layers. Near the surface is a region of nearly constant, relatively warm water that is termed the *mixed layer.* As the name implies, wind waves and swell cause enough vertical mixing to prevent the build-up of a temperature gradient. The *bottom layer,* far below the direct reach of solar heating, is uniformly cold. Between these two layers is the thermocline, a region in which temperatures grow colder as depth increases.

By contrast, in high latitudes (near the poles) the temperature is uniformly cold from top to bottom.

Figure 19.15 shows typical temperature variation with depth at high, mid, and low latitudes. At high and low latitudes, the summer profiles closely resemble those of winter. In the mid-latitudes, however, the surface layers are warmed in summer by the returning sun. The surface temperature rises and surface water becomes less dense. Coupled with the decrease in storm activity, the resulting increase in vertical stability reduces the thickness of the mixed layer. The thermocline in summer therefore spans a greater temperature and depth range than in winter.

The day-to-night change in *isolation* (heating from the sun) similarly creates a diurnal thermocline, which is superimposed on the mixed-layer trace. Typically, its magnitude is 1°F (.56°C) and its depth, 20 to 30 ft.

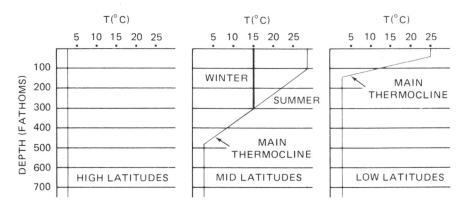

Fig. 19.15 Idealized variation of temperature with depth.

19.16   Measuring Temperature at Sea   Surface water temperature can be measured by a ship's thermometer installed in a cooling water intake. More accurate readings can be taken by collecting a sample by bucket from a forward position, well clear of any discharges. The water should then be stirred with an accurate thermometer, out of wind and sun, until a constant reading is obtained. Oceanographic thermometers, fitted with a bail for lowering over the side and a small reservoir to hold the water sample, are also available.

Remote sensors on satellites can also measure surface temperature. A combination of infrared and microwave radiometers yield temperatures day and night on an all-weather basis with an accuracy of 2° F or better. Their lower accuracy (which is continually being improved) is compensated for by their wide-area coverage, and satellite temperature data is now a reliable input to weather forecasts worldwide.

Subsurface temperatures can be measured by thermometer, thermistor, or bathythermograph (BT). The conventional *bathythermograph* consists of a temperature sensor and a pressure sensor; the former moves a stylus while the latter moves a carriage bearing a graduated chart. As the device is lowered into the water, pressure and temperature variations produce a plot of temperature versus depth. The BT may be used to depths of 900 ft. The ship must slow to 10 knots for optimum results. Hull-mounted BTs allow submarines to obtain similar plots by sinking from periscope depth to deep submergence. The conventional BT is being replaced by the more accurate, and expendable, XBT. Dropped over the side, this device telemeters temperature information along a thin wire to a recorder on the ship. Since the sinking rate of the unit is known, instrument depth may be determined as a function of time. At the end of the drop, the wire breaks and the XBT falls to the bottom. XBTs that can measure temperatures down to 5000 ft are under development. An air-dropped XBT relays data via a buoy to a recorder in the aircraft.

When water samples are needed to supplement temperature data, oceanographers use bottles (Nansen, NIO, or Niskin) equipped with twin reversing thermometers (Fig. 19.16(A)). A series of bottles are fastened at intervals to a wire cable and lowered into the water by special oceanographic winches capable of paying out and hauling in 36,000 feet of wire cable. When the entire cast has been lowered into the water, a *messenger* (small brass weight) is attached to the cable and released. When this messenger hits the first bottle, it trips a latch, causing the bottle to flip into reversed position and release another messenger (Fig. 19.6(B)). The new messenger travels down the wire to release the latch on the second bottle. The process continues until all bottles have been reversed. When a bottle is reversed, valves at each end close to trap a water sample. At the same time, the column of mercury in the twin reversing thermometers separates

Fig. 19.16(A) Attaching a Nansen bottle with reversing thermometers to a hydrographic wire. The bottle collects a water sample at a preset depth, and the thermometers record the temperature at that depth. (*Courtesy of Woods Hole Oceanographic Institution*)

at a restriction that prevents a subsequent change in temperature reading. One of the thermometers is protected against pressure; the other is not. The unprotected instrument will have a higher reading than the other. The difference in readings is related to the depth, thereby allowing water temperature at the sample depth to be obtained as well as the depth at which the sample was taken.

Another temperature measuring instrument, the *thermistor chain,* is a long cable containing temperature-sensitive devices called thermistors. The chain is towed behind a ship and readings at 100 to 200 different depths are relayed to the ship. CTD (conductivity-temperature-depth) probes contain

Before   At the   After
                          reversing

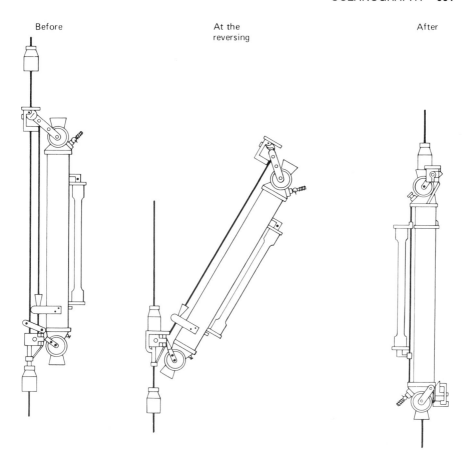

Fig. 19.16(B)   Three positions of the Nansen bottle and messengers.

sensors for each of these parameters, which taken together can also indicate salinity. These measurements are transmitted continuously to the ship
over an electric cable as the CTD is lowered. Data can either be read on
meters or stored on magnetic tape for insertion directly into computers for
later analysis.

Practical Results from Oceanography

The application of knowledge gained through oceanography, in combination with the allied fields of meteorology and hydrography, has proven valuable to society in general and to the mariner in particular.

19.17   Improvement of Charts   Today's maps of the ocean bottom are about equal in accuracy and degree of detail to land maps drawn 200 years ago, a lag primarily caused by difficulties in obtaining a sufficient number of accurate soundings. Before 1935 each charted depth was the result of an individual sounding by leadline. The advent of the continuous-recording echo sounders, SWATH sonars, air-borne depth sounders, and satellite depth-finding have made available multitudes of accurate soundings at precisely known positions. Even small boats can carry automated depth finders and automated plotters. The blank spaces on the world's charts are rapidly disappearing. The need for accurate bathymetric charts, however, continues to increase with the increasing depth of submarine operations. It is not enough merely to chart submerged hazards projecting into the paths of surface vessels; seamounts or shallow areas within the upper thousand or two feet can endanger deep-diving submarines. Hydrographers have made dramatic progress but still have years of work ahead.

19.18   Ice Predictions   Construction of the Distant Early Warning (DEW) Line across arctic North America in the late 1940s brought many ships into sea-ice areas for the first time. Annual damages exceeded $1 million in the early years. More recently, discovery and development of the Northern Slope oil fields have created a commercial need for knowledge of ice conditions. Programs pioneered by the U.S. Navy Oceanographic office have been expanded by the Naval Weather Service and NOAA. Using aerial and satellite observations augmented by current, wind, and other environmental information, they provide accurate ice forecasts for both the Arctic and Antarctic. These allow planners and operators to decide when it is possible to sail into polar areas under ice-free conditions and when to return to avoid the danger of being iced in. In areas where ships may be driven onshore by strong winds, forecasters advise them when to proceed and when and where to seek shelter. Information of this type will help icebreaker/tankers follow the route of the S.S. *Manhattan* through the Northwest Passage to carry oil to the ports of the northeastern United States.

19.19   Optimum Track Ship Routing   The Optimum Track Ship Routing (OTSR) system combines meteorology and oceanography to produce useful operational forecasts. The goal of OTSR is to recommend routes that will results in the least steaming time that is consistent with existing weather and will avoid areas of possible storm damage. All oceans are covered by the service. Developed by the U.S. Naval Oceanographic Office, the system was turned over to the Naval Weather Service in 1958. Several commercial organizations provide OTSR service for the merchant fleet.

Action starts with a request from the ship naming ports, operating speed, and dates. The voyage must exceed 1500 miles to make OTSR worthwhile. The weathermen who do the routing know ship characteristics as related to various types of seas; a destroyer and a tanker bound for the same port may receive different routing instructions. The ship router bases his work on three types of charts: detailed weather and oceanographic analyses for the day of departure; prognostic sea state charts out to three days; and prognostic charts showing locations of storm centers and storm tracks from three days out to the port of destination. The ship sends a daily situation report that includes position, state of the sea, weather, and comments on the day's routing results. The router updates his weather and sea state charts each day and modifies the ship's track as necessary. A moderate following swell, for example, can add a knot to speed made good and may justify a change in route.

A survey by the Military Sealift Command showed an annual saving of about $1 million from OTSR. Three-fourths was attributed to shorter sailing times; the remainder to damage avoided. Other evaluations show an average reduction of voyage time of 10 percent, or a savings of $15 to $40 thousand for a Pacific crossing at 1981 fuel prices.

Higher fuel prices make optimum routing even more economical. Bishop (1984) Chapter 12 includes detailed results of a cost-saving experiment as well as other information on OTSR.

19.20 Search and Rescue (SAR) Setting up a search for a raft, a boat dead-in-the-water, or personnel in lifejackets require an assumption of the last known position and the corresponding time. Oceanographic knowledge then can help predict subsequent positions on which to pattern the search. Forecasting techniques are based upon current direction and velocity together with estimates of down-wind drift as a function of the shape and size of the floating object and the wind direction and velocity. Temperature predictions help in estimating the survivors' physical condition. Forecasts provide estimated position and position error probability for specified search times. SAR techniques are described in Bishop (1984) Chapter 12.

19.21 Improvements in Fish Catch Biological and fishery oceanographers have learned a great deal about the reaction of marine life to varying sea temperatures, the productivity of ocean areas as a function of vertical and horizontal currents, and the travel of spawn. Operational systems have been developed to determine the most productive areas, to direct fishing fleets to them, and to regulate the catch for optimum long-range production. Oceanographic fronts (lines of change in water temperature or color) are especially good fishing areas for Pacific tuna and albacore. Since 1960, the government has prepared and distributed charts showing such areas. As technology improved, additional sensors were incorporated into the program, and today data comes from ships, buoys, and satellite measurements of surface temperature and color. Figure 19.17 shows a representative chart.

On the United States East Coast, the location of the Gulf Stream and its warm-core eddies is especially important in planning fishing trips and setting bottom lines and traps. The National Oceanic and Atmospheric Administration uses satellite data to prepare charts showing these features and transmits them by telecopier. To make this information available to small craft lacking telecopiers, the National Weather Service and the Sea Grant Marine Advisory Service have developed ways to relay the data by voice radio to reach a wide group of users, both commercial and recreational. A swordfish boat from Cape May, for example, can save hours and dollars by fishing in a warm core eddy west of the Gulf Stream rather than continuing east to reach the Stream proper.

Knowing the vertical temperature profile is also helpful to fishermen. A National Marine Fisheries Service investigation found that tuna longlines set above the thermocline took significantly fewer fish than those below the mixed layer. Figure 19.18 shows that, for some species, a deep thermocline is less favorable to the purse seiner than a shallow one.

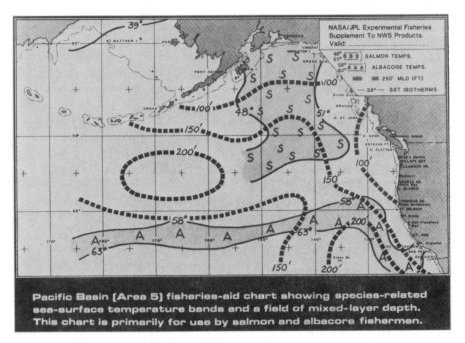

Fig. 19.17 Fisheries-aid chart prepared by NASA and NOAA (National Weather Service). MLD is the abbreviation for mixed layer depth; SST, for sea surface temperature.

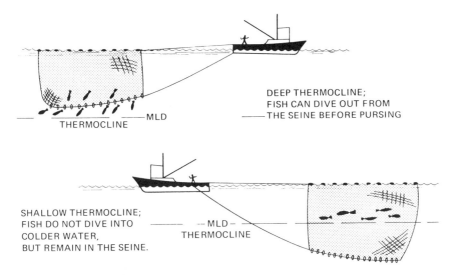

Fig. 19.18 Schematic example of the effect of changes in mixed layer depth (MLD) on purse seining for pelagic fish.

19.22 Antisubmarine War (ASW) Environmental Prediction The purpose of the Navy's ASW environmental prediction system is to provide fleet commanders and ASW units (air, surface, and submarine) with forecasts of oceanographic conditions for use in finding enemy submarines, for routing convoys through areas where their detection by enemy submarines will be least likely, and for making weapons settings. These forecasts can also be used by submarines in offensive missions.

Figure 19.19 shows the environment with which ASW forecasters must deal. From left to right, the first column shows a typical bathythermograph trace of temperature versus depth. The temperature of the mixed layer is constant down to 400 ft. Temperature then decreases sharply in the main thermocline until it reaches the nearly constant temperature of deep water (about 35°F, or 20°C). The second column plots sound velocity versus depth. Sound velocity increases with depth in the mixed layer because of increased pressure. The temperature effect becomes dominant in the thermocline, and velocity begins to decrease with depth. At about 2000 ft, the pressure effect exceeds the temperature effect, and sound velocity begins to increase again. The depth of minimum sound velocity, about 2000 ft, is the axis of the *deep sound channel* (or *Sofar channel*), in which sound is trapped. Ship noise travels for hundreds of miles, and small explosions have been heard at a distance of 12,000 miles.

Figure 19.19 shows various noise sources in the oceans: ship's noise,

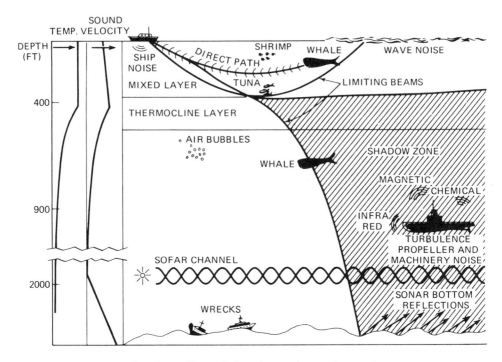

Fig. 19.19 The antisubmarine warfare environment.

marine life noise, submarine machinery noise, and surface wave noise. Whales or large fish can cause a sonar return resembling that of a submarine. In the thermocline, most sound beams are bent upward, giving a large area, known as the *shadow zone,* in which a submarine can hide. Direct-path sonar beams can pick up submarines in the mixed layer. Longer ranges into the shadow zone can be obtained through bottom reflection of the sound (or *bottom bounce*), but effective use of this technique requires a detailed knowledge of the sea floor.

The submarine puts energy into the water in the form of machinery and propeller noise. It also gives off chemical, infrared, magnetic and other detectable signals that may resemble those from bottom wrecks, large fish or whales, air bubbles, and distant surface ships. The problem of separating the submarine's signals from the confusion of background noise is formidable. Since the submarine can change depth at will and can evade at speeds in excess of those of many surface ships, the problem of locating a high-speed evading target in three dimensions becomes even more difficult.

Identical sonar equipment in different locations vary widely in the distance at which they can pick up targets of equal signal strength because of environmental effects. These effects can be forecast, but fleet operators do not want to make computations based on unending volumes of surface temperatures, BTs, and layer depth predictions. They want a ready answer to the question, "At what range will my sonar system acquire a target in my immediate area today?" The Naval Weather Service has devised a system for forecasting detection ranges for each of the sonar systems now in use. The approach is to calculate composite propagation-loss profiles for a series of points representative of predetermined acoustical regimes. Each regime is an area reasonably homogeneous as to water mass, bathymetry, and bottom-bounce acoustical loss. Both power-limited and raypath-limited ranges are predicted. The choice depends upon the spatial relationship of the transducer and target: whether they are in the same layer, lie across a layer boundary, or are both in a duct. Range variability expected within each regime is also calculated. The system is adaptable to both active and passive detection systems. The resulting sonar ranges are given by Acoustic Sensor Range Prediction (ASRP) for fixed-wing aircraft. The Ship Helicopter Acoustic Range Prediction System (SHARPS) supports other fleet users.

19.23   Trends in Oceanographic Research   In 1985, the Ocean Sciences Advisory Committee of the National Science Foundation prepared a plan for the coming decade. It called for an integrated global approach extending the growing understanding of planet-wide processes. These include ocean circulation, climate, biological productivity, flux of elements and compounds between organisms and their environment, and plate tectonics. It called for increased funding of basic research projects, improvement of instrumentation and replacement of aging research vessels, and continuation of the Ocean Drilling Program.

The National Academy of Sciences has urged a similar program with emphasis on long-term continuity. Satellites and supercomputers will be central to such a program. Satellite remote sensing provides global, synoptic observations that can be input to computer models leading to "significant advances in understanding the state of the Earth, its changes, feedbacks, interactions, and global trends on timescales of years to centuries."

The satellite phase of the ten-year plan will be executed by cooperative efforts of the National Aeronautics and Space Administration (NASA), the U.S. Navy and Air Force, the National Oceanic and Atmospheric Administration (NOAA), and the National Science Foundation (NSF). Four new satellites are planned. (Fig. 19.20) NROSS (Navy Remote Ocean Sensing System) will be launched in 1989. From a sun-synchronous polar orbit it will observe surface winds, sea surface temperature, waves, eddies, and fronts. In the same year, NASA will launch TOPEX (The Ocean Topography Experiment). Its primary purpose is to measure sea surface elevation with an

Proposed missions, sensors, and scientific measurements for the next decade

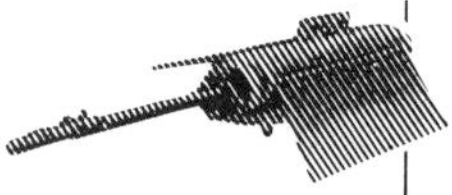

Proposed Mission and Timing	Primary Sensors	Variables of Major Research Importance
NROSS 1985 start, 1989 launch	Scatterometer, altimeter, microwave radiometer	Surface winds and temperature, ice sheet topography
TOPEX 1986 start, 1989 launch	Precision altimeter and tracking system	Ocean surface topography for surface currents
OCI 1987 start, 1990 launch	Ocean color imager	Ocean color for surface chlorophyll
GRM 1988 start, 1991 launch	Satellite range rate and magnetometer	Global geoid and magnetic field

Fig. 19.20 New programs proposed by the Satellite Planning Committee of Joint Oceanographic Institutions, Inc. The Committee, which includes members from ten of the leading U.S. research organizations, presented this plan in 1984.

accuracy of a few centimeters over most of the world's oceans. OCI (Ocean Color Imager), scheduled for 1990 launch, will measure worldwide biological productivity, and GRM (Geopotential Research Mission) will observe gravity and magnetic fields.

References

General Oceanography:

Bhatt, J. H. *Oceanography: Exploring the Planet Ocean.* New York: D. Van Nostrand Co., 1978. (Qualitative and descriptive, for the general reader. Covers biological, chemical, geological and physical oceanography.)

Thurman, Harold V. *Introductory Oceanography,* 3rd ed. Columbus, OH: Charles E. Merrill, 1981. (More detailed, requiring a basic scientific background.)

Physical Oceanography:

Bishop, Joseph M. *Applied Oceanography.* New York: John Wiley and Sons, 1984. (A review of physical oceanography, with application to practical problems like oil spills, ocean dumping, marine resources, and military uses.)

Bowditch, Nathaniel. *American Practical Navigator.* Washington, D.C.: Defense Mapping Agency Hydrographic Center, 1977 (Volume I, Part 6, is especially slanted for the navigator.)

Harvey, J. G. *Atmosphere and Ocean.* Los Angeles: Artemis Press, 1976. (Outstanding, nonmathematical blending of physical oceanography and meteorology.)

Satellite Oceanography

Badgley, Peter C., ed. *Oceans from Space.* Houston: Gulf Publishing Co., 1969. (Basic information on remote sensing plus information on early satellite developments.)

Cracknell, Arthur P., ed. *Remote Sensing Applications in Marine Science and Technology.* Dordrecht, Holland: D. Reidel Publishing Co., 1982. (Proceedings of NATO Advanced Study Institute. Contents range from highly technical to more general discussions of satellites and their applications.)

Stewart, Robert H. *Methods of Satellite Oceanography.* Berkeley: University of California Press, 1985. (Principles of interaction of electromagnetic radiation with atmosphere and ocean; techniques and instruments. Intended for scientists and engineers of various backgrounds. Requires some physics and Calculus.)

20

Ocean Pollution

20.1 Introduction The oceans at first glance seem an ideal disposal site for the wastes of civilization. We have learned, however, that even their vast volumes can be harmed if pollutants are dumped at sea or in waters flowing into the sea. This chapter describes the most common types of marine pollutants, explains why they are harmful, and suggests ways for the seaman to avoid contributing to oceanic pollution. This is a wise objective, and not merely from a moral viewpoint. Most maritime nations have adopted laws protecting the environment. Ships' crews, oil drillers, and others found guilty of polluting harbors, coastal waters, or the high seas may be fined or even imprisoned.

The effect of a pollutant depends on several factors, including: (1) how much of the substance enters the environment; (2) its inherent toxicity; (3) how long it persists before breaking down into harmless compounds, and (4) whether it remains localized or disperses throughout a large volume. Spreading is fastest and dilution greatest in the open ocean, slowest with least dilution in enclosed harbors. Estuaries are particularly vulnerable. They have a special two-layered circulation pattern which traps pollutants rather than carrying them out to sea.

20.2 Pollutants in the Ecosystem An *ecosystem* comprises the living and nonliving components of a natural habitat together with the complex relationships that link them together. The marine ecosystem includes (1) sea water; (2) dissolved elements, nutrients, and other compounds; (3) green plants utilizing solar energy to convert water and carbon dioxide into living matter; (4) animals subsisting on plants and on other animals; and (5) bacteria and fungi that decompose organic matter, converting dead organisms and waste back to nutrients and other inorganic compounds. An important interrelationship among these components is the *food web*. Figure 20.1 illustrates the web of trophic (feeding) links that support the herring. This ecosystem takes the form of a pyramid: vast numbers of tiny organisms make up the base, or lowest trophic level, with a much smaller number of much larger organisms at the peak.

Pollutants can disturb not only the food web but other aspects of the marine ecosystem as well (Table 20.1). Dissolved oxygen (DO), for example, is essential if animals are to survive in an aquatic environment. Some fish, such as carp, require relatively low levels of DO; others, like salmon, require more. If pollution lowers the DO in a local area, fish and other mobile organisms can move out. These that cannot, like oysters and clams, may not survive. Organisms linked to these shellfish in the food web are

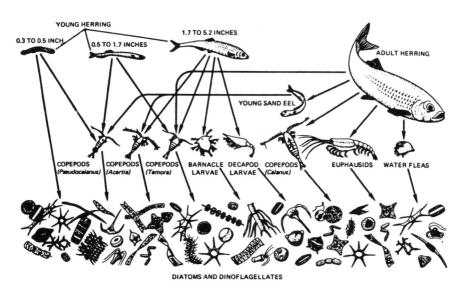

Fig. 20.1 The food web takes the form of a pyramid. Vast numbers of microscopic plankton form the base, tapering upward to a few adult herring at the top. Pollutants can enter or interrupt the web at any level. (*From* The Life of the Ocean, *McGraw-Hill Book Co.*)

**Table 20.1   The Relationship of Pollution to Important Factors
in the Water Environment**

Factor	Function	Disrupting Agent

Light	food web
	mobility
		silt-dredging, land
		   erosion, colored chemicals,
		   humic acids

Temperature	reproduction
	food web
	metabolism
		industrial and power
		   plant discharges,
		   sudden changes in air temperature,
		   overland runoff

Dissolved
   oxygen
	metabolism	biodegradation of
		   organic material

Plankton	food web
	oxygen production
		oil, chemicals,
		   organic wastes, water temperature,
		   self-annihilation

likewise threatened. This type of pollution is quantified as *biological oxygen demand* (BOD) and *chemical oxygen demand* (COD). The former is a measure of how many decomposing (oxygen-removing) organisms are contained in a volume of water; the latter, how much inorganic oxygen-removing material.

Bioconcentration or *bioaccumulation* is a process involving pollutants ingested by organisms low in the food web. Substances like DDT are retained in the tissues of these organisms and passed on to animals at the next higher trophic level when they feed on the DDT-contaminated prey. At each level, more and more DDT is retained until creatures high in the food web may contain enough of the pollutant to interfere with their metabolism or reproduction.

20.3 Oil Pollution   Oil enters the ocean directly or indirectly from a number of sources: pumping bilges, accidental spills, leaks from industrial plants, shipping accidents, and intentional dumping of crankcase drainings. It has many harmful effects. Oil fouls fish's gills, inhibiting the uptake of oxygen. By covering small organisms it essentially eliminates them from the ecosystem; by settling to the bottom it blankets fish eggs and benthic animals. Decomposition of oil depletes the DO supply, and a surface oil film impairs the solution of atmospheric oxygen. Oil gives fish an unpalatable flavor and kills seabirds by coating their feathers.

Oil can be removed by a variety of methods. Sludge formers, such as clay, cause the oil to sink. However, this approach transfers the problem from the water surface to the bottom of the ocean. Emulsifiers break up the oil mass into fine droplets and enable dispersal. The increased surface area permits more rapid decomposition by bacteria. When the sea is sufficiently calm, "skimmers" and mechanical corrals can be used. These are particularly useful in harbors. Booms floating on the surface, towed by boats, localize the spill and permit pumping the oil to storage. Shown in Fig. 20.2 is a mechanical boom. A recently developed method that appears to hold promise is the endless-belt squeegee. A plastic foam belt absorbs the oil as it passes through the oil spill. The oil-ladened belt is then put through a wringer and the oil squeezed out.

In polar regions, decomposition in the water environment takes place at a very slow rate. Other means are necessary to cope with spills. One of these is to burn the oil floating on the surface. Straw or tiny glass beads spread on the oil surface act as wicks to facilitate combustion.

To help cope with large-scale spills, the U.S. government has prepared a series of planning guides. These discuss, for a number of different coastal areas, likely movement of oil at sea, relevant meteorological and environmental data, and probable impact on sea birds, fisheries, and other marine resources. (See Fig. 20.3). Initially they were prepared by NOAA (Bishop, 1980), but responsibility for the series has been transferred to the Federal Emergency Management Agency (Bishop *et al.* 1981). Additional informa-

Fig. 20.2 A lightweight aluminum boom for containing oil spills (*Courtesy of Reynolds Metal Company*)

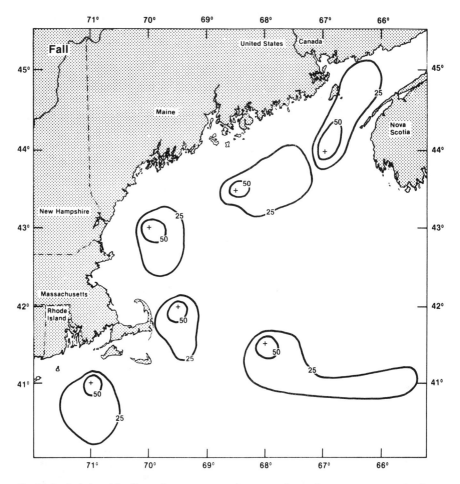

Fig. 20.3 Relative risk ellipses for autumn conditions. Each set of contours surrounds a hypothetical oil spill marked by a cross. On a climatological basis, each point on the contour marked 50 has a 50% probability of being affected by the spill. (*From Federal Emergency Management Agency* Climatological Oil Spill Planning Guide. No. 2)

tion on oil spills, including modeling techniques, is available in Bishop (1984). See references.

20.4 Heavy Metal Pollution Heavy metals enter the oceans from discharge of industrial wastes, leaching of ship bottom paint, and burning of fossil fuels, as well as from natural weathering of continental rocks. Metals that are toxic to marine organisms, and possibly through bioconcentration to human beings as well, include tin, mercury, cadmium, silver, nickel, selenium, lead, copper, chromium, arsenic, zinc, and manganese. These are particularly dangerous because they are produced in large quantities, are toxic even in low concentrations, and persist for long periods without biological or chemical change. In the 1950s, Minimata Bay in Japan became contaminated with mercury from industrial waste. Over 100 people died of "Minimata Disease" before the cause was discovered and the discharge stopped. Tributyl tin, a component of modern antifouling bottom paint, is the topic of both controversy and research. It has proven highly effective in keeping ships unfouled, but is suspected of damaging shellfish beds in the vicinity of shipyards.

20.5   Pollution from Mineral Extraction   Pollutants can enter the marine environment from oil and gas extraction operations; sand, gravel, and shell recovery; and seabed mining of manganese nodules and polymetallic sulfide ores. Offshore oil and gas exploration and drilling on the continental shelf pose the greatest threat, both through underwater noise and possible leaks and spills. Benthic (bottom-dwelling) organisms are particularly susceptible, but fish, marine mammals, and sea turtles can also be affected. Although recovery of manganese nodules is still in the experimental stage, there is concern that the process will stir up large quantities of sediment. When this resettles on the sea floor it will blanket and probably destroy nearby benthic organisms. Research is necessary to discover how serious the problem is, together with ways to reduce the damage.

20.6   Radioactive Pollution   Radioactivity can damage or destroy cells in animal tissue. Natural background radiation exists from cosmic rays and from radioactive compounds in the soil, but at a level that has little effect on human beings. The near-cessation of atmospheric nuclear explosion tests has reduced another source of radioactive fallout into the ocean. Bioconcentration of dissolved radioactive salts, however, is potentially dangerous. Elevated levels of radioactive zinc, for example, have been detected in sea animals off the coast of Oregon. The source was probably the plutonium production plant at Hanford, Washington, with outfalls in the Columbia River (Fig. 20.4).

Although nuclear-powered submarines have been lost at sea, there has been no intentional disposal of radioactive material on the sea bed. The U.S. Department of Energy, however, is conducting research on the feasibility of burying high-integrity waste cannisters tens of meters into deep ocean sediments. The goal is to retain the radioactivity within multiple barriers (waste form, cannister, clay sediments, and ocean water) until the radionuclides decay to innocuous levels.

Fig. 20.4 Cooling tower of Trojan Nuclear Power Plant on the Columbia River. The Environmental Protective Agency (EPA) regulates ocean disposal of low-level radioactive waste and monitors the disposal areas. (*EPA—Documerica, Gene Daniels; courtesy of U.S. Environmental Protection Agency*)

20.7 Pesticide Pollution Ever-growing human populations demand increased food production, a goal reached in part through the development and widespread use of pesticides. These include herbicides, fungicides, fumigants, rodenticides, and insecticides. These have proven, unfortunately, to have damaging environmental side-effects. DDT, a *chlorinated hydrocar-*

bon, has been effective not only in reducing crop losses but also in controlling insect-carried disease. Together with its long-persisting decay product DDE, however, DDT has not stayed on the farmlands where it was applied. After runoff into rivers and thence to estuaries and oceans, it entered the marine food web. Bioconcentration began at the lowest trophic levels, increasing as it passed up the web. Oceanic fish and sea birds travel long distances and soon DDT could be detected in marine animal tissue across all the world's oceans. In the United States, ospreys and brown pelicans came close to extinction before the use of DDT was prohibited by federal law. The insecticide is still used in many third world countries, however, who now face difficult choices among health, hunger, and protection of the environment. Chemical companies are trying to develop safer pesticides, and the U.S. Environmental Protection Agency (EPA) monitors progress closely. A truly satisfactory pesticide, that kills only pests without harming other organisms, has yet to be developed.

20.8 Waste Disposal When large quantities of sewage sludge and industrial waste are produced in coastal locations, traditional practice has been to dump them offshore. The low cost of transportation by tanker or barge and the apparent absence of harmful effects combined to make this approach seem reasonable and economical. Dump sites 12 miles offshore in the New York Bight, for example, have annually received millions of tons of sludge from treatment plants in New York and New Jersey. Farther offshore, Deep Water Dumpsite (DWD)106—one hundred and six nautical miles southeast of Sandy Hook—has received toxic industrial wastes from the chemical plants of New York, New Jersey, and Delaware.

A continuing monitoring program conducted by NOAA suggests that shallow-water nearshore dumping has serious environmental consequences. Toxic chemicals can injure or destroy fish and shellfish and render them inedible. Nutrients (compounds of nitrogen and phosphorus) are always present in sewage and have more complicated effects. An excess of nutrients causes an explosive but transitory growth of phytoplankton in a "bloom" which lasts only until the plankton have taken up all the nutrients. Lacking a further supply of this essential for their metabolism, the plankton suffer an equally massive die-off followed by decomposition. The latter process removes DO from the water with the result of heavy animal mortality (see Section 20.2). The end result of too many nutrients can thus be an area devoid of both plants and animal life. Dumping in carefully selected areas of deeper water farther offshore, however, using proper techniques, may result in dilution of pollutants to acceptable levels.

The Environmental Protection Agency regulates offshore dumping. The EPA is investigating how to pretreat sludge before dumping in order to prevent unacceptable levels of pollution. The present trend is to reduce the

Fig. 20.5 In the words of pioneer enviornmentalist Rachel Carson, ''Everything goes somewhere.'' This folded newspaper was photographed 15,000 feet down on the bottom of the Western Atlantic Ocean.

volume dumped and to dispose of it farther offshore. The ultimate goal is complete elimination of offshore waste disposal (Fig. 20.5).

Incineration at sea by specially equipped ships has been proposed as an environmentally safe way to dispose of toxic wastes. Research is necessary to determine whether harmful material is completely degraded or merely shifted to the atmosphere for eventual return to the oceans. As of 1986, the procedure had not been approved by U.S. authorities.

Ships at sea generally have no alternative to overboard disposal of refuse and sewage wastewater. When far offshore, this probably causes insignificant harm except for plastic material. Since they float indefinitely without degrading, bottles, bags, cups, and other plastic items remain in the ocean until they drift ashore or are ingested by marine animals, birds, or fish. On the beach they create unsightly litter; if swallowed they generally kill the host involved. Until degradable plastics are developed, discarded plastic items should be segregated for disposal ashore after reaching port whenever possible. Lost or abandoned gill nets, made of monofilament webbing, likewise drift at sea for long periods, dooming the fish that become entangled in the nets. A combination of international regulations and improved technology are needed to reduce both of these types of plastic pollution.

In recent years, most ocean-going vessels have been equipped with collecting, holding, and transfer (CHT) systems. In coastal waters and in port, the CHT system retains sanitary wastewater for later discharge to a shore sewage plant. A few ships and craft have treatment or incinerating systems. Providing adequate shore disposal systems, especially for small boats, remains a problem in areas removed from major ports.

20.9   Solid Waste Disposal   The United States generates nearly half a million tons of trash daily. Disposal of this mass of plastics, metals, paper, and garbage without environmental damage is a major task. Incineration, pyrolysis, and sanitary landfall are the methods generally used. The first two involve either burning or heating the waste, while the latter consists of burying waste material beneath a layer of soil. Careful engineering can prevent pollutants from leaving the landfill, but poor procedures can allow runoff to carry them into waterways. A particularly dangerous type of toxic chemical, PCB (polychlorinated biphenyls), has been found in U.S. coastal waters, principally near large cities. Through bioconcentration in fish and shellfish, it can endanger human health. Until production was banned in 1977, PCB's were widely used in heat transfer and hydraulic fluids, lubricants, and as transformer dielectrics. Disposal in leaky landfills or illegal dumping elsewhere of this highly stable chemical has caused a pollution problem that will last for years.

20.10   Dredging   Because of silting of existing harbors and the construction of deeper channels, dredging is a continuing coastal activity and a potential threat to the environment. The dredge's cutter head or bucket can stir up fine sediment around the dredge itself. This silt and clay, if polluted, reintroduces pollutants that had settled out. Even if unpolluted, they can smother shellfish beds when the particles eventually settle on the bottom again. Proper dredging procedure and the use of turbidity curtains around the dredge, however, can prevent significant damage. (See Huston and Huston, 1976, for recommended dredging techniques). A far greater hazard involves the placement of the dredge material itself. This process can reintroduce pollutants and, since the volumes of spoil are measured in millions of cubic yards, create major changes in the sea bottom. These hazards can be avoided, although at considerable cost, by containing the spoil in a diked enclosure or by ocean dumping well offshore.

20.11 National Marine Pollution Program (NMPP) The upsurge of environmental interest that swept the country in the 1960s and 1970s led to a number of new policies, laws, and agencies. These were eventually coordinated in the National Ocean Pollution Planning Act (PL 95-273) in 1978. Under the Act, NOAA developed a five-year plan, to be revised periodically, covering all federal research, development, and monitoring programs for the Great Lakes, estuaries, and oceans. Annual NOAA publications (*NMPP Agency Program Summaries* and *NMPP Catalog of Federal Projects*) report status and progress. In a typical year, the federal budget includes about 100 million dollars for the overall program. The largest shares go to the Department of Interior (Minerals Management Service, Fish and Wildlife Service, and Geological Survey), EPA, Department of Commerce (NOAA), and Department of Energy. Investigations of pollution associated with offshore oil and gas production and with offshore dumping usually receive the largest shares of funds. Smaller amounts are normally allocated for habitat-related, non-point source, accidental discharge, and marine transportation studies.

20.12 Practical Advice from the U.S. Naval Ship System Command And the Citizens Program for the Chesapeake Bay:

Industrial and Chemical Wastes

DO: Store hazardous waste materials (mercury, solvents, etc.) in suitable containers for ultimate shore disposal.
DON'T: Discharge these materials overboard or into ship drains.
DON'T: Leave bottom paint scrapings in a drydock. Sweep them up and dispose of ashore before the dock is reflooded.

Solid Wastes

DO: Use incinerators for combustible trash.
DO: Make sure trash discharged overboard will sink.
DON'T: Discharge any solid trash overboard within 50 miles of land.

Oil and Oily Wastes

DO: Observe all regulations concerning handling of fuel oils and prevention of fuel oil discharges.
DO: Report all accidental oil discharges.
DO: Inspect oil storage tanks weekly for signs of leakage.
DO: Inspect oil lines, transfer equipment, and any other oil-related gear for leaks periodically.
DON'T: Allow oil to accumulate in bilges or boilers.

DON'T: Fill fuel oil tanks above 95 percent of capacity.

DON'T: Discharge oily wastes overboard or into ship bilges.

Detergents

DO: Use phosphorus-free detergents in the galley and for general scrubbing.

Small Boats

DO: Discharge heads into holding tanks for shore pumpout whenever possible.

DON'T: Pump heads overboard in less than 20 feet of water or in a marina.

DON'T: Throw trash overboard.

DON'T: Let paint scrapings reenter the water when cleaning the bottom in a marine railway.

References

Baum, B., and Parker, C. *Solid Waste Disposal.* Vols 1 and 2. Ann Arbor, Mich.: Ann Arbor Science Publishers, 1973.

Bishop, J. M. A Climatological Oil Spill Planning Guide, No. 1, New York Bight. NOAA, Environmental Data and Information Service, Washington, D.C., February 1980.

Bishop, J. M., Harrigan, A., and Melle, V. A Climatological Oil Spill Planning Guide, No. 2, Gulf of Maine/Georges Bank. Federal Environmental Planning Agency, Washington, D.C., June 1981.

Bishop, J. M. *Applied Oceanography.* New York: John Wiley, 1984.

Conner, W., Aurand, D., Leslie, M., and Amr, A. *Disposal of Dredged Material Within the New York District.* McLean, VA: The Mitre Corp., 1979.

Detwyler, T. *Man's Impact on the Environment.* New York: McGraw-Hill, 1971.

Huston, J. W. and Huston, W. C. *Techniques for Reducing Turbidity Associated with Dredging.* Report D-76-4. U.S. Army Waterways Experiment Station, 1976.

Manahan, S. E. *Environmental Chemistry.* Boston: Willard Grant Press, 1979.

Menard, H. W. and Schreiber, J. L. *Oceans: Our Continuing Frontier,* (pages 190–207). Del Mar, CA: Publisher's Inc., 1976.

Murdoch, W. *Environment.* Sunderland, Mass.: Sinauer Assoc., 1975.

Odum, E. *Ecology.* New York: Holt, Rinehart and Winston, 1975.

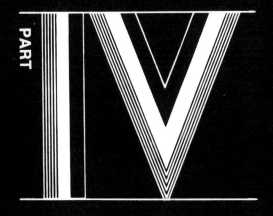

PART **IV**

Rules
of the Road

Introduction to the Rules of the Road

21.1 **History** The need for uniform Rules of the Road arose when steam vessels with higher speeds than sailing vessels appeared on the trade routes of the world. The modern Rules date from 1863, in which year Great Britain and France adopted uniform regulations for the prevention of collisions at sea.

The Congress of the United States approved a law on April 29, 1864, containing rules similar to those already adopted by Great Britain and France. About 1885, Belgium, Denmark, Germany, Japan, and Norway accepted the same rules as Great Britain, France, and the United States.

In 1889, the President of the United States called a conference of all maritime nations to draw up rules and regulations for the safety of lives and property at sea. The conference approved the *International Rules of the Road,* 1889, which were accepted and used by all maritime nations until a 1948 revision was adopted and put into effect in 1954.

An international conference was held in the spring of 1960. As an outgrowth of this conference, the 1948 Rules were changed in many ways. The most significant revision concerned conduct in restricted visibility. A new rule was adopted to provide for safe navigation by a vessel that detects another vessel outside of visual or audible range. Though not mentioning radar specifically, this rule—when considered together with the annex entitled "Recommendations on the Use of Radar Information as an Aid to Avoiding Collisions at Sea"—resolved several important questions concerning vessels navigating with the aid of radar.

The effective date of the 1960 International Rules was September 1, 1965. They were enacted by the United States as Public Law 131, 88th Congress, on September 24, 1963, and declared effective on the date indicated by Presidential proclamation. Other countries by similar process made the rules effective on the same date.

The most recent revision of the International Rules is an outgrowth of an international conference held in London in 1972 under the auspices of the Intergovernment Maritime Consultative Organization, or IMCO. In 1982, IMCO changed its name to IMO—International Maritime Organization.

The International Regulations for Preventing Collisions at Sea, 1972 (72 COLREGS), came into force generally on July 15, 1977, but for the United States particularly on July 27, 1977, under the provisions of Public Law 95-75. The 72 COLREGS supersede the 1960 regulations.

The rules were reorganized in the 1972 revision and a number of editorial improvements are evident. The rules provide: (a) better guidance in determining safe speed and risk of collision, (b) recognition of vessels constrained by draft and of air-cushion vessels, (c) controls for operation in or near traffic separation schemes adopted by IMO, (d) technical details for lights, shapes, and sound-signaling devices in separate annexes, (e) new sound signals for overtaking situations in narrow channels, and (f) a number of changes concerning lights, shapes, and fog signals.

IMO has since approved a number of relatively minor amendments to the 72 COLREGS which went into effect in 1983.

The International Rules made provision for any local rules that nations might wish to exercise in waters under their jurisdiction that are not part of the High Seas. For U.S. waters, such a code has been long established.

The *Inland Rules of the Road* were first approved by Congress on June 7, 1897, and made effective October 7, 1897. Over the years, many additions and amendments resulted in an unwieldy collection of rules governing the inland waters of the United States. Chief among them were the Inland Rules, the Great Lakes Rules, the Western Rivers Rules, their associated Pilot Rules and Interpretive Rulings, and the Motorboat Act of 1940.

This hodgepodge was complex enough to make a complete understanding of collision avoidance regulations by mariners plying U.S. waters almost impossible. The added burden of learning an almost entirely different set of rules for waters just across some imaginary boundary line from inland waters compounded the problem.

For many years, there was an active effort to unify the inland rules and regulations into a simple and coherent system and to make them conform closely to international regulations. With the signing of the 72 COLREGS in 1972 and the enactment of the implementing legislation in 1977, this movement gained momentum. The Rules of the Road Advisory Committee, composed of experienced mariners from all segments of the maritime community, was established by the Coast Guard. After eight years of hearings and discussions, the Advisory Committee developed a proposal to unify the inland rules. That proposal became the basis for the Inland Navigational Rules Act of 1980.

The Inland Navigational Rules Act of 1980 (Public Law 96-591) was signed into law on December 24, 1980. The new *Inland Navigational Rules* parallel the 72 COLREGS very closely and supersede the old Inland Rules, the Great Lakes Rules, the Western Rivers Rules, their respective pilot rules and interpretive rulings, and parts of the Motorboat Act of 1940.

The new rules went into effect on all inland waters of the United States except the Great Lakes on December 24, 1981. The effective date for the Great Lakes was March 1, 1983.

21.2   Inland Navigational Rules   As has already been mentioned, the new Inland Navigational Rules, sometimes referred to as the "unifed rules," have taken old rules from various sources and combined them in a simple, logical, and much more understandable order. Many of the old provisions remain, but many more have been discarded. Although the new Inland Navigational Rules are often identical (with minor editorial changes) to the 72 COLREGS, in some cases existing rules and practices have been retained as being more appropriate for local situations and more consistent with safety because of special problems. These differences between inland and international rules will be pointed out throughout this discussion.

The Inland Navigational Rules are statutory and are divided into five parts, as are the 72 COLREGS. Part A deals with applicability, responsibility and definitions. Part B contains steering and sailing rules and consists of three subparts for the conduct of vessels: in any condition of visibility; in sight of one another; and in restricted visibility. Part C contains the rules on lights and shapes. Part D contains the rules and definitions for sound and light signals. Part E has only one rule, exemptions. In addition, five annexes have been established by regulation: two on technical details; one on additional signals for fishing vessels; one on distress signals; and one on pilot rules.

One of the special pilot rules in Annex V is a provision of specific interest to mariners: the operator of a self-propelled vessel 12 meters or more in length must carry on board and maintain for ready reference a copy of the Inland Navigational Rules. Appendix 4 contains the entire set of rules and mariners keeping a copy of this volume handy comply with that requirement of the rules.

21.3 Applicability The Inland Navigational Rules, or unified rules, are designed to prevent collisions on the navigable waters of the U.S. and should be understood and followed by the operators of vessels who ply these waters. The Inland Rules have teeth in that it is not necessary to have a collision to run afoul of them. Rule 38 states that whoever operates a vessel in violation of the rules or any regulation issued thereunder, is liable to a civil penalty of not more than $5,000 for each violation. The unified rules basically apply to all vessels on U.S. waters inside the lines, called Demarcation Lines (see below), which separate inland waters from the waters on which the COLREGS apply. There are exceptions, however, as they also apply to U.S. vessels on the Canadian waters of the Great Lakes to the extent where there is no conflict with Canadian Law. The Inland Rules don't apply, however, on all Alaskan waters and on designated waters of Puget Sound, New England and southern Florida, where the COLREGS apply. When navigating in these waters, mariners should consult their charts to see which rules apply.

Other exceptions exist. Although the vast majority of the Inland Rules apply uniformly in inland waters, there are a few special situations, notably in Rule 14 (Head-on Situation), Rule 15 (Crossing Situation) and Rule 24(i) (Towing), which apply only on the Great Lakes and their connecting tributaries, the Western rivers and waters specified by the Secretary of Transportation as follows:

Tennessee-Tombigbee Waterway and Tombigbee River

Black Warrior River

Alabama River

Mobile River above the Cochrane Bridge at St. Louis Pt.

Coosa River

Flint River

Chattahoochie River

Apalachicola River above its confluence with the Jackson River

21.4 Demarcation Lines The COLREGS Demarcation Lines are listed under Title 33 of the U.S. Code of Federal Regulations. The specific geographic locations are promulgated through the Federal Register and by the Coast Guard. These lines generally follow the high water shoreline, but where there is an entrance to a harbor, or mouth of a river or bay, the line is drawn directly across the opening. The Demarcation Lines appear on applicable charts but should not be confused with Boundary Lines, which are used to determine where the laws relating to vessel inspection, equipment and manning apply. Except as noted above, the Inland Rules apply to the waters inside the demarcation lines and the COLREGS apply to the waters outside the lines.

21.5 Responsibility The "Rule of Good Seamanship" and the "General Prudential Rule" have been retained intact in the Inland Rules under Rule 2, the "Responsibility Rule," which is the same as that in the 72 COLREGS. The Rule of Good Seamanship requires compliance with all the rules and with "the ordinary practice of seamen." The General Prudential Rule directs the mariner to avoid blind adherence to the rules right into the jaws of collision but does not apply in every case where it merely suits the convenience of a vessel to use it. As noted, all other rules should be strictly followed in most cases. The object of the rules is to prevent and not cause collisions. There has always been and will always be a huge variety of operating situations. In order to cover *all* of them, Rule 2(b) exists. It should be obeyed when collision is imminent and both vessels must take further action to avoid impact or to lessen its effects. Until this point is reached, the other Steering and Sailing Rules should be applied. See Section 24.7 for a more detailed discussion.

21.6 Ability to Maneuver Both sets of rules are based, *in part,* on the premise that certain vessels are unable to maneuver as quickly and as easily as other types of vessels. The more maneuverable vessel is required, therefore, to keep clear of the less maneuverable. An example is the rule that requires power-driven vessels to keep out of the way of sailing vessels except when the sailing vessel overtakes the power-driven vessel or when the power-driven vessel cannot safely exit from a narrow channel or fairway. In the latter case, the sailing vessel must not impede the other vessel's passage. See Chapter 23 for a detailed explanation.

21.7 Give-way and Stand-on Vessels The old terms "burdened" and "privileged" vessels were often used to indicate which vessel must give way and which vessel must hold its course and speed when there was a risk of collision. The terms were expressive but misleading because each vessel is required by the rules to act in a certain manner. For example, "When two power-driven vessels are crossing so as to involve risk of collision, the vessel which has the other on her own starboard side shall keep out of the way . . . " (Int. and Inl. Rule 15). Hence, the terms "stand-on" and "give-way" have been adopted from the International Regulations to describe the status and actions required of vessels in approach situations where the risk of collision exists.

21.8 Shifting Responsibility In many cases, the courts have ruled that, when two vessels are approaching each other so as to involve risk of collision, the original responsibilities under the law cannot be changed by the subsequent movements of either vessel until the collision is so imminent that both must take appropriate action under Rule 17 (both sets of rules) or until the risk of collision exists no longer. In other words, no subsequent change in bearing or distance, after risk of collision is involved, will alter the fact that one of the vessels must keep clear and the other hold her course and speed. Of course, the time may come when there is no right of way, and, therefore, each vessel must take measures to avoid the collision that is imminent. When the risk of collision exists no longer, the Rules apply no longer, and a different situation may then arise.

21.9 Assumptions In order that a collision may be avoided after risk of collision exists, it is necessary that the movements of one vessel—the stand-on one—must be known so that the other vessel—the give-way one— may change her course and speed, if necessary, to keep clear. A vessel has the right to assume that the other vessel will obey the Rules of the Road, will be navigated with care and attention, will keep to its own side of a channel, etc. However, the assumption does not hold when it becomes evident that the other vessel is not being navigated with care and attention. For example, a stand-on vessel in a crossing situation should not hold its course and speed until collision results. Justice Longyear, in the MILWAUKEE suit, said, ''It is true, that, prima facie, each has the right to assume that the other will obey the law. But this does not justify either in shutting his eyes to what the other may actually do, or in omitting to do what he can to avoid an accident, made imminent by the acts of the other.'' Although this is a very old case, the precepts remain valid. Accordingly, Inland Rule 17(ii), applicable on COLREGS waters since 1977, allows the stand-on vessel to take action to avoid collision as soon as it becomes evident that the give-way vessel is *not* taking appropriate action under the Rules.

21.10 Jurisdiction When collision between vessels occurs in navigable waters used in interstate commerce, the case can be heard in the Federal courts sitting as courts in admiralty. The district courts are the trial courts, the circuit courts hear appeals, and the Supreme Court may hear the final appeal. If the collision occurs on waters wholly within a state, the state courts have sole jurisdiction. If the collision occurs on waters in or between two states which empty into the sea, there is concurrent jurisdiction. Either the Federal or state court may hear the case.

When a vessel runs into a pier or bridge through negligence or bad seamanship, the admiralty courts have no jurisdiction. On the other hand, if a bridge or draw damages a vessel because of improper construction or operation, the case can be heard by an admiralty court.

21.11 Legal Personality A merchant ship is liable *in rem* (against a thing) for the faults of her master, officers, or men (perhaps a lookout) operating the ship. She can be sued in an admiralty court, attached, and sold to satisfy a judgment. The owners are not otherwise liable in such suits unless they have contributed to the fault by neglect, privity, or knowledge.

A British Sovereign cannot be sued because one of his vessels—that is, a naval vessel—has collided with a merchant vessel unless he has granted such privilege. Congress has approved such suits against the Federal government, but a U.S. naval vessel cannot be seized and thus placed out of commission or sold to satisfy a judgment.

21.12 Division of Damages Originally, U.S. courts held that where both vessels are in fault in a collision, the liability of each vessel is one-half the total loss, regardless of the degree of fault. In recent years, there has been a tendency away from this practice of unequal fault/equal responsibility, and in 1975 a decision was handed down by the Supreme Court that ". . . damage is to be allocated among the parties proportionately to the comparative degree of their fault. . . ." However, if the fault of one is great and that of the other minor, nonstatutory, and noncontributory, the courts may not inquire fully into the minor fault, or they may disregard it and order the full costs to be paid by the vessel with the major fault.

21.13 Anchorages A vessel has a right to anchor. The only question is, where can she anchor legally? Certain water areas are designated by the Secretary of Transportation as anchorages. It is improper, although not unlawful, to anchor outside these areas in restricted waters, save in an emergency. A vessel has a right to anchor in large, navigable water areas such as Chesapeake Bay or on soundings off the Coast. But Rule 9(g) states that every vessel must avoid anchoring in a narrow channel if the circumstances of the case permit.

Channels are primarily for traffic and not for anchorage. It is sometimes necessary to anchor in a narrow channel—in a thick fog—but the anchorage should be shifted to an authorized anchorage as soon as possible. While the vessel remains in the narrow channel, every precaution to prevent collision should be taken in addition to sounding proper sound signals and showing proper lights, including (a) use of a short scope of chain, (b) keeping power on the anchor engine, (c) stationing a watch in the engine room and keeping steam up to the throttle, (d) stationing a watch on the bridge, and (e) posting extra lookouts.

Of course, if the channel is well lighted, marked, and wide and there is plenty of room for other vessels to pass, a vessel may remain at anchor there without violation of the statute. An example is the Hudson River off 96th Street, New York. Even so, she should anchor to one side of the channel and be particularly careful that: (a) her anchor lights are showing, (b) a trained lookout is posted, (c) proper signals are sounded in a fog, and (d) the anchor ball is hoisted by day.

Attention must be called to Inland Rule 30, which permits the Secretary of Transportation to designate "special anchorage areas" where vessels not more than 20 meters in length may anchor and are not required to exhibit an anchor light. Such areas are usually near yacht clubs or marinas and are intended primarily for pleasure craft, secured for the night. The rules also permit vessels less than 7 meters in length to anchor anywhere without showing lights as long as they are not near a navigable channel.

After the vessel has anchored in accordance with her legal rights, she must exhibit prescribed lights, sound correct fog signals when necessary, and post a watch on deck. Sufficient trained lookouts must be stationed to inform the officer in charge of the ship of the approach of other vessels or objects that might require action.

An anchored vessel is presumed to be without fault if a moving vessel collides with her unless the moving vessel can prove that the anchored vessel was at fault. The moving vessel must proceed lawfully in moving through an anchorage ground. Tides and current do not excuse her.

The anchored vessel may be found in fault if she has failed to anchor in a legal position, show the proper lights, or sound the proper fog signals. She may also be found in fault if she: (a) anchors without necessity in a narrow channel; (b) swings to the tide and obstructs the channel substantially; (c) anchors on a frequented fairway when a safer anchorage is available; (d) fails to move from a channel when possible; (e) fails to move when warned that her position is dangerous; (f) anchors where approaching vessels rounding a point sight her suddenly and belatedly; (g) fails to veer chain or use her helm when such action might prevent a collision, the moving vessel having done all in her power to avoid a collision; (h) anchors so close to another anchored vessel as to foul her when swinging; or (i) fails to shift anchorage when dragging dangerously close to another anchored vessel. The vessel that anchored first should warn the one that anchored last if the berth chosen will foul the former's berth.

Vessels that drag should take every measure possible to stop dragging, such as dropping a second anchor. Anchored vessels are not required to keep steam up unless weather, ice, or good seamanship demands it. An anchored vessel is not required to take unusual precautions to avoid collisions with moving vessels.

A moored vessel alongside a wharf may be found in fault if she projects into the channel and thereby obstructs it and contributes to a collision. A slight projection may not cause her to be found at fault if passing vessels can pass her safely using reasonable care. If the moored vessel unnecessarily obstructs the slip in which she is secured so that other vessels using the slip cannot evade collision by exercising reasonable care, she may be found at fault. A moored vessel alongside a wharf or slip is not required to show anchor lights, to sound fog signals, or to post a lookout. She must, however, house her anchors in the usual, secure manner so that passing vessels will not be damaged by them. In some areas she may be required by custom or local regulation to show a white light at each projection or extremity and normally should of her own accord in congested waters.

Finally, anchorage may be regulated by state or local authorities, provided such ordinances or laws do not conflict with Federal statutes and maritime law as interpreted by U.S. courts.

21.14 Exemptions The Inland Navigational Rules Act of 1980 exempts many vessels from having to comply with the technical Annexes of the rules with respect to the position, visibility, and color specifications of lights. For instance, if the keel of the vessel was laid before the enactment date (December 24, 1980) and the vessel complies with the lighting regulations in effect at that time, lights don't have to be repositioned because of the conversion to the metric system. Moreover, if the vessel is less than 20 meters in length, it is permanently exempt from having to display the masthead and sternlight of Rule 23 as long as it carries an all-round white light. Other exemptions deal with the repositioning of lights and the requirements for sound signal appliances.

Some vessels, particularly those of the Navy and Coast Guard, are built for a special purpose, such as a submarine, and can't comply with the rules for lights because of their construction. As long as they conform as closely as possible to the requirements, such vessels can be issued a certificate of alternative compliance by the appropriate Secretary.

21.15 Traffic Separation Schemes—Vessel Traffic Services

INTERNATIONAL RULE 10—TRAFFIC SEPARATION SCHEMES

(a) This rule applies to traffic separation schemes adopted by the organization.

(b) A vessel using a traffic separation scheme shall:

(i) proceed in the appropriate traffic lane in the general direction of traffic flow for that lane;

(ii) so far as practicable keep clear of a traffic separation line or separation zone;

(iii) normally join or leave a traffic lane at the termination of the lane, but when joining or leaving from the side shall do so at as small an angle to the general direction of traffic flow as practicable.

(c) A vessel shall so far as practicable avoid crossing traffic lanes, but if obliged to do so shall cross as nearly as practicable at right angles to the general direction of traffic flow.

(d) Inshore traffic zones shall not normally be used by through traffic which can safely use the appropriate traffic lane within the adjacent traffic separation scheme.

(e) A vessel, other than a crossing vessel, shall not normally enter a separation zone or cross a separation line except:

(i) in cases of emergency to avoid immediate danger;

(ii) to engage in fishing within a separation zone.

(f) A vessel navigating in areas near the terminations of traffic separation schemes shall do so with particular caution.

(g) A vessel shall so far as practicable avoid anchoring in a traffic separation scheme or in areas near its terminations.

(h) A vessel not using a traffic separation scheme shall avoid it by as wide a margin as is practicable.

(i) A vessel engaged in fishing shall not impede the passage of any vessel following a traffic lane.

(j) A vessel of less than 20 meters in length or a sailing vessel shall not impede the safe passage of a power-driven vessel following a traffic lane.

The 72 COLREGS provide detailed instructions to vessels using the IMO-approved traffic separation schemes (TSS). These traffic separation schemes are located at heavily traveled sea lanes throughout the world, including the seaway entrances to the major ports of the United States. The TSS boundaries are printed on the appropriate chart of the area. Vessels should adhere closely to the requirement of each TSS.

The Inland Rule covering vessel traffic services (VTS) is very brief and requires vessels using the VTS to comply closely with the regulations in force for the particular area concerned. VTS is operational in such ports as Puget Sound, San Francisco, the Houston Ship Channel, and New Orleans and Berwick Bay, Louisiana. Pamphlets describing detailed directions for vessels are issued by the Coast Guard district in which the VTS is located.

21.16 Bridge-to-Bridge Radiotelephone Passing signals required by the rules may be made by radiotelephone on the Bridge-to-Bridge frequency (156.65 Mhz). Rule 34(h) of the unified rules states that a vessel reaching an agreement with another vessel in a meeting, crossing or overtaking situation by using the radiotelephone in accordance with the Bridge-to-Bridge Radiotelphone Act, is not required to sound the prescribed whistle signals. This provision is applicable only in waters covered by the Inland Rules since there is no equivalent in the COLREGS. Only larger vessels or certain vessels engaged in carrying passengers for hire, vessels 26 feet or longer, and certain dredges and floating plants are required to have the capability.

21.17   Reports of Collisions   With few exceptions, U.S. vessels that have sustained or caused any accident involving loss of life, material loss of property, or any serious injury to any person, or have received any material damage affecting their seaworthiness or efficiency, are required to report the accident within five days or as soon thereafter as possible to the commander of the Coast Guard District where the vessel belongs or where the accident took place. This is usually done by means of a written report.

21.18   Sea Manners   The expression *sea manners* is understood by seamen to mean a consideration for the other vessel and the exercise of common sense under certain conditions when vessels meet. A tug with a tow is difficult to maneuver. A large ship is more difficult to maneuver than a smaller one. A convoy or a formation of naval vessels is more difficult to maneuver than a single ship. All of these vessels are required to obey the Rules of the Road. No vessel is exempt. If a vessel disobeys the Rules, she is liable. Accordingly, seamen are not advised to disobey the Rules of the Road to show sea manners but to obey them. The Rules of the Road apply when there is a risk of collision. Before that moment, there is enough time and plenty of opportunity for a single vessel to avoid a tug with tow, a convoy, or a formation of naval ships. Small vessels can keep clear of large ones.

The rules caution sailing vessels against hampering large power-driven vessels in narrow channels and prohibit power boats under 20 meters from hindering large vessels navigating a narrow channel. These are but two common cases calling for sea manners. Sea manners should be applied where conditions indicate, and in all waters.

22

Lights and Shapes

The basic purpose of lights is to warn vessels of the presence or approach of other vessels and to help determine the course and target angle (the relative bearing of one's own vessel from the target) of vessels underway. White lights are visible at a greater range than colored lights, and many vessels carry two white lights on the fore and aft centerline, the masthead, and the after masthead lights. These lights serve not only to help determine the course and target angle but to give an immediate indication of any *change* in course.

By observing the lights or shapes displayed by an approaching vessel, the mariner can determine which vessel has the responsibility to keep out of the way of the other. As will be discussed in later chapters, this responsibility will be determined by the different right-of-way categories or the approach situation between vessels in the same category.

The sections dealing with lights and shapes in both the COLREGS and the unified rules are in most cases identical. For instance, Rule 20, dealing with the application of lights is the same in both sets of rules:

INLAND AND INTERNATIONAL RULE 20—APPLICATION

(a) Rules in this part shall be complied with in all weathers.

(b) The Rules concerning lights shall be complied with from sunset to sunrise, and during such times no other lights shall be exhibited, except such lights as cannot be mistaken for the lights specified in these Rules or do not impair their visibility or distinctive character, or interfere with the keeping of a proper look-out.

(c) The lights prescribed by these Rules shall, if carried, also be exhibited from sunrise to sunset in restricted visibility and may be exhibited in all other circumstances when it is deemed necessary.

(d) The Rules concerning shapes shall be complied with by day.

(e) The lights and shapes specified in these Rules shall comply with the provisions of Annex I of these Rules.

Under both sets of rules, Inland and International, lights are *required* to be shown in restricted visibility as well as at night. Lights may also be shown at any other time when deemed necessary. Certain lights are required only when a vessel is under way and "making way through the water." Making way refers to motion that is a result of a vessel's propelling machinery (or sails), including the motion after the engines are stopped—up to the time when a vessel is actually dead in the water.

To avoid needless duplication, only the Inland Rules will be presented here. The differences that exist between the two sets of rules will be brought out in each discussion. Minor differences in format, wording, and spelling are ignored. All illustrations apply to both sets of rules unless otherwise stated.

22.1 Definitions of Lights

(a) "Masthead light" means a white light placed over the fore and aft centerline of the vessel showing an unbroken light over an arc of the horizon of 225 degrees and so fixed as to show the light from right ahead to 22.5 degrees abaft the beam on either side of the vessel, except that on a vessel of less than 12 meters in length the masthead light shall be placed as nearly as practicable to the fore and aft centerline of the vessel.

(b) "Sidelights" mean a green light on the starboard side and a red light on the port side, each showing an unbroken light over an arc of the horizon of 112.5 degrees and so fixed as to show the light from right ahead to 22.5 degrees abaft the beam on its respective side. On a vessel of less than 20 meters in length the side lights may be combined in one lantern carried on the fore and aft centerline of the vessel, except that on a vessel of less than 12 meters in length the sidelights when combined in one lantern shall be placed as nearly as practicable to the fore and aft centerline of the vessel.

(c) "Sternlight" means a white light placed as nearly as practicable at the stern showing an unbroken light over an arc of the horizon of 135 degrees and so fixed as to show the light 67.5 degrees from right aft on each side of the vessel.

(d) "Towing light" means a yellow light having the same characteristics as the "sternlight" defined in paragraph (c) of this Rule.

(e) "All-round light" means a light showing an unbroken light over an arc of the horizon of 360 degrees.

(f) "Flashing light" means a light flashing at regular intervals at a frequency of 120 flashes or more per minute.

(g) "Special flashing light" means a yellow light flashing at regular intervals at a frequency of 50 to 70 flashes per minute, placed as far forward and as nearly as practicable on the fore and aft centerline of the tow and showing an unbroken light over an arc of the horizon of not less than 180 degrees nor more than 225 degrees and so fixed as to show the light from right ahead to abeam and no more than 22.5 degrees abaft the beam on either side of the vessel.

The COLREGS make no mention of a special flashing light.

22.2   Types of Shapes   The various day shapes displayed by a vessel to indicate the constrictions under which it is operating at any given time are shown in Fig. 22.1.

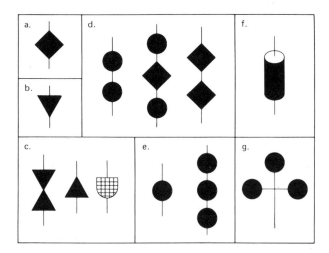

Fig. 22.1   Day shapes: (a) Diamond, for towing; (b) cone, for vessel under sail and towed by machinery; (c) cones and basket, for display by fishing vessels; (d) balls and diamonds, for special operations (to indicate the clear and the obstructed side); (e) balls, for vessels anchored or aground; (f) cylinder, for vessel constrained by her draught (COLREGS only); and (g) balls, for minesweeper.

22.3 Visibility

The lights prescribed in these Rules shall have an intensity as specified in Annex I to these Rules, so as to be visible at the following minimum ranges:

(a) In a vessel of 50 meters or more in length:
a masthead light, 6 miles;
a sidelight, 3 miles;
a sternlight, 3 miles;
a towing light, 3 miles;
a white, red, green or yellow all-round light, 3 miles; and
a special flashing light, 2 miles.

(b) In a vessel of 12 meters or more in length but less than 50 meters in length:
a masthead light, 5 miles; except that where the length of the vessel is
less than 20 meters, 3 miles;
a sidelight, 2 miles;
a sternlight, 2 miles;
a towing light, 2 miles;
a white, red, green or yellow all-round light, 2 miles; and
a special flashing light, 2 miles.

(c) In a vessel of less than 12 meters in length:
a masthead light, 2 miles;
a sidelight, 1 mile;
a sternlight, 2 miles;
a towing light, 2 miles;
a white, red, green or yellow all-round light, 2 miles; and
a special flashing light, 2 miles.

(d) In an inconspicuous, partly submerged vessel or object being towed:
a white all-round light, 3 miles.

The special flashing light is omitted in the 72 COLREGS.

22.4 Power-Driven Vessels Under Way All power-driven vessels under way in Inland and COLREGS waters are required to show a masthead light, sidelights, and a sternlight. An after masthead light higher than the forward one is required for vessels 50 meters and upward in length (see Fig. 22.2) but is optional for vessels less than 50 meters in length. A power-driven vessel less than 12 meters in length does not have to show a masthead light or sternlight but can display an all-round white light instead.

In addition to the aforementioned lights, an air-cushion vessel operating in the nondisplacement mode is required to show an all-round flashing yellow light. It must flash at regular intervals at a frequency of 120 flashes or more per minute, a frequency significantly higher than that of lighted aids to navigation.

Fig. 22.2 Power-driven vessels under way, showing after masthead light.

Instead of the second masthead light and sternlight, a power-driven vessel on the Great Lakes may carry an all-round white light. This rule is retained from the old Great Lakes Rules because the higher all-round light is more visible in the prevalent low-lying fogs in the area. No comparable rule exists in the 72 COLREGS.

Another difference between the Inland Rules and the COLREGS is that the COLREGS state that a power-driven vessel of less than 7 meters in length and whose maximum speed does not exceed 7 knots may show an all-round white light. Such a vessel shall, however, show sidelights if it can.

22.5 Power-Driven Vessels Engaged in Towing Power-driven vessels towing on inland and COLREGS waters carry just about identical lights and shapes. They all display sidelights and a sternlight. Towing vessels 50 meters in length or greater display an additional masthead light.

Vessels towing astern, in addition to the above lights, must display two towing masthead lights if the length of the tow is 200 meters or less (see Fig. 22.3). If the length of the tow exceeds 200 meters, three towing masthead lights must be exhibited (see Fig. 22.4). These towing masthead lights can be carried either on the forward or after mast. Also, a yellow towing light is displayed in a vertical line above the sternlight. A diamond day shape is required only when the length of the tow exceeds 200 meters (see Fig. 22.1a).

Vessels towing alongside (Fig. 22.5) or pushing ahead (Fig. 22.6) display the two masthead lights plus two yellow towing lights in a vertical line. The second towing light replaces the sternlight but is carried only in inland waters. When a pushing vessel and a vessel being pushed ahead are rigidly connected in a composite unit, they are regarded as one vessel and show the lights prescribed for such a vessel.

INTERNATIONAL
Towing (length of tow not exceeding 200 meters)

Fig. 22.3 Power-driven vessels less than 50 meters long, towing astern with length of tow less than 200 meters.

571

INTERNATIONAL
Towing (length of tow exceeding 200 meters)

Fig. 22.4 Power-driven vessels less than 50 meters long, towing astern with length of tow exceeding 200 meters.

Fig. 22.5 Power-driven vessel with after masthead light, towing alongside.

Fig. 22.6 Power-driven vessel, pushing ahead (inland waters only).
Y = yellow signal

A vessel engaged in a towing operation that renders her unable to deviate from her course, displays, in addition to the lights required for a vessel towing, three all-round lights in a vertical line: red-white-red. In daytime, a ball-diamond-ball (black) sequence is required in a vertical line (see Fig. 22.1d).

22.6 Vessels Being Towed A vessel or object being towed astern is required to show sidelights and a sternlight in both sets of rules. When the length of the tow exceeds 200 meters, a diamond shape is required. An inconspicuous or partly submerged object is required to display a number of all-round white lights if at all possible; the number depends on its size. Where it is impracticable for a vessel or object being towed to show a sidelight, sternlight, or an all-round white light, all possible means shall be taken to light the vessel or object towed or at least to indicate its presence. (See Fig. 22.7.)

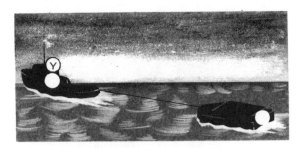

Fig. 22.7 Tug, with tow astern, displaying yellow towing light.
Y = yellow signal

A vessel being pushed ahead that is not part of a composite unit is required to show sidelights and a special flashing light at the forward end. (The special flashing light is not required by the 72 COLREGS.) A vessel being towed alongside is required to show a sternlight and sidelights at the forward end. A number of vessels being towed alongside or pushed ahead in a group are lighted as one vessel.

On the Great Lakes, western Rivers and other waters designated by the Secretary of Transportation (see Section 21.3), vessels pushing ahead or towing alongside are required to display only sidelights and two yellow towing lights. There is, of course, no comparable rule in the 72 COLREGS.

22.7 Sailing Vessels Underway   In inland and COLREG waters, a sailing vessel underway exhibits sidelights and a sternlight. In addition to the above lights, a sailing vessel underway may exhibit two all-round lights in a vertical line near the top of the mast—the upper one, red; the lower one, green (see Fig. 22.8). Sailing vessels less than 20 meters in length can combine the sidelights and sternlight in one lantern carried near the top of the mast. The optional red and green vertical lights cannot be displayed in conjunction with the combined lantern.

A sailing vessel less than 7 meters in length shall, if practicable, show sidelights and a sternlight or the combined lanterns, ''but if she does not, she shall have ready at hand an electric torch or lighted lantern showing a white light in sufficient time to prevent collision.''

A vessel proceeding under sail when also being propelled by machinery must exhibit forward, where it can best be seen, a conical shape, apex downwards.

A vessel under oars may exhibit the lights prescribed for sailing vessels, but if she does not, she must have ready at hand an electric torch or lighted lantern showing a white light, which must be exhibited in sufficient time to prevent collision.

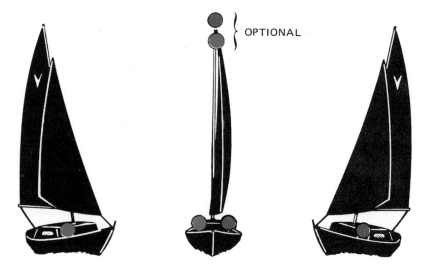

Fig. 22.8 Sailing vessel under way.

22.8 Vessels Engaged in Fishing Fishing vessels are divided into two broad categories: trawlers and vessels fishing by any other method. Trawlers drag behind them, usually at short distances, a conical-shaped dredge net or similar apparatus. Sometimes trawlers work in pairs, with the net stretched between them, requiring additional caution on the part of other mariners. A vessel engaged in trawling in both inland and COLREGS waters displays two all-round lights in a vertical line—the upper one, green; the lower one, white. (See Fig. 22.9). Sidelights and a sternlight are shown only when under way, making way. Annex II (both sets of rules) provides for

Fig. 22.9 Vessels engaged in trawling, under way and making way.

additional lights to be shown by vessels trawling in close proximity, as follows:

(a) Vessels when engaged in trawling, whether using demersal or pelagic gear, may exhibit:

(i) when shooting their nets: two white lights in a vertical line [see Fig. 22.10];

(ii) when hauling their nets: one white light over one red light in a vertical line;

(iii) when the net has come fast upon an obstruction: two red lights in a vertical line.

(b) Each vessel engaged in pair trawling may exhibit:

(i) by night, a searchlight directed forward and in the direction of the other vessel of the pair;

(ii) when shooting or hauling their nets or when their nets have come fast upon an obstruction, the lights prescribed in (a) above.

Vessels fishing by means other than trawling often use long lines or nets that sometimes extend for miles and severely hamper their maneuverability. Such vessels display two all-round lights in a vertical line—the upper one, red; the lower one, white (see Fig. 22.11). Sidelights and a sternlight are shown only when under way, making way. When outlying gear extends more than 150 meters from the vessel, an all-round white light is displayed in the direction of the gear.

Vessels engaged in fishing with purse seine gear may exhibit two yellow lights in a vertical line (see Fig. 22.12). These lights must flash alternately every second and with equal light and occultation duration and should be exhibited only when the vessel is hampered by its fishing gear.

A vessel engaged in fishing or trawling during daylight hours is required to show two cones, point to point; a vessel less than 20 meters in length

Fig. 22.10   Vessel trawling, under way, making way, and shooting her nets.

Fig. 22.11 Vessels engaged in fishing, under way but not making way.

Fig. 22.12 Vessel engaged in purse seining, hampered by her gear, under way but not making way. Y = yellow signal

may substitute a basket. A vessel engaged in fishing, other than trawling, with outlying gear extending more than 150 meters horizontally from the vessel must also show a cone point up, in the direction of the gear. (See Fig. 22.1c.)

22.9 Vessels Not Under Command A vessel not under command is required to show two all-round red-over-red lights in a vertical line wherever best seen (see Fig. 22.13). In addition, sidelights and a sternlight are required only if making way through the water. By day, two balls must be shown in a vertical line wherever best seen (see Fig. 22.1d). The lights prescribed for a vessel not under command are not required for vessels less than 12 meters in length.

22.10 Vessels Restricted in Ability to Maneuver A vessel restricted in her ability to maneuver (special operations)—except a vessel engaged in mineclearance operations—is required to show three all-round lights in a

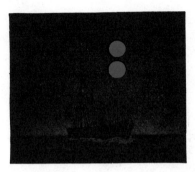

Fig. 22.13 Vessel not under command, not making way.

vertical line wherever best seen: red-white-red (see Fig. 22.14). A vessel making way through the water must also show masthead lights, sidelights, and a sternlight (the after masthead light is optional for a vessel less than 50 meters in length). During the day three black shapes must be displayed in a vertical line wherever best seen: ball-diamond-ball.

When the vessel is at anchor, the red-white-red lights or ball-diamond-ball shapes are shown in addition to the light(s) or shape for a vessel at anchor. (See Fig. 22.1d.)

A vessel engaged in dredging or underwater operations, when restricted in her ability to maneuver, is required to show the three all-round lights in a vertical line wherever best seen: red-white-red. When an obstruction exists, she must also show red-over-red all-round lights on the obstructed side and green-over-green lights on the clear side, all displayed below the red-white-red lights (see Fig. 22.15). Such a vessel, when making way through the water, must also show masthead lights, sidelights, and a sternlight (the after masthead light is optional for a vessel less than 50 meters in length).

Fig. 22.14 Vessel restricted in her ability to maneuver, not making way.

Fig. 22.15   Vessel engaged in dredging or underwater operations, restricted in her ability to maneuver, with obstruction to starboard.

During the day, the ball-diamond-ball shapes must be displayed in addition to two balls in place of the red lights on the obstructed side and two diamonds in place of the green lights on the clear side. These are also the only day shapes shown when at anchor. (See Fig. 22.1d.)

Such a vessel, when at anchor, shows only the red-white-red lights, and if an obstruction exists, the two red and two green lights.

Whenever the size of a vessel engaged in diving operations makes it impracticable to exhibit the shapes described above, a rigid replica of the International Code flag "alpha" not less than 1 meter in height must be exhibited. Measures must be taken to ensure all-round visibility.

A vessel less than 12 meters in length, except when engaged in diving operations, is not required to exhibit the lights or shapes described above.

22.11   Vessels Engaged in Mineclearance Operations   A vessel engaged in mineclearance operations is required to show three all-round green lights, one at the foremast head and one at each end of the fore yard. She is also required to show all the other lights prescribed for a power-driven or anchored vessel of her length. (See Fig. 22.16.) During the day, three balls are shown in the same position as the three green lights (see Fig. 22.1g). The lights and shapes indicate that it is dangerous to approach within 1000 meters of the mineclearance vessel.

22.12   Pilot Vessels   All vessels under way in pilotage duty are required to show white over red all-round lights in a vertical line at or near the masthead, sidelights, and a sternlight (see Fig. 22.17).

A pilot vessel at anchor is required to show the white-over-red lights in addition to the anchor light(s), or a ball during the day. A pilot vessel when not engaged in pilotage duty must exhibit the lights or shapes prescribed for a similar vessel of her length.

Fig. 22.16 Vessel engaged in mineclearance operations.

22.13 Vessels at Anchor or Aground A vessel at anchor is required to show two white lights (all-round), one in the fore part of the vessel and the other near the stern and lower than the forward light (see Fig. 22.18). A vessel less than 50 meters in length may substitute one all-round white light wherever best seen. During daylight hours, a black ball is displayed where it can best be seen (see Fig. 22.1e). Vessels of 100 meters and upward in length are required to illuminate their decks with working lights or the equivalent (optional for smaller vessels).

A vessel less than 7 meters in length, when at anchor not in or near a narrow channel, fairway, or anchorage, or where other vessels normally navigate, is not required to exhibit the lights or shapes described above.

A vessel aground is required to show the anchor lights for a vessel of her length and two all-round red lights in a vertical line wherever best seen (see Fig. 22.19). During daylight hours, three black balls in a vertical line are displayed (see Fig. 22.1e).

Fig. 22.17 Vessels under way in pilotage duty.

Fig. 22.18 Vessel at anchor, 50 meters or more in length.

Fig. 22.19 Vessel aground, less than 50 meters in length.

A vessel less than 12 meters in length, when aground, is not required to exhibit the lights or shapes described above.

In inland waters only, a vessel less than 20 meters in length, when at anchor in a special anchorage area designated by the Secretary of Transportation, is not required to show anchor lights or shapes.

22.14 Vessels Constrained by Their Draft (COLREGS Waters Only) A vessel constrained by her draft in COLREGS waters may show three all-round red lights in a vertical line, or a black cylinder day shape, wherever best seen, in addition to the lights required by a vessel of her length (Fig. 22.20). During daylight hours, a cylinder may be displayed, as shown in Fig. 22.1f. There is no provision for a vessel constrained by her draft in inland waters.

22.15 Special Inland Lights Annex V of the Inland Rules—Pilot Rules—contains provisions for special lights in inland waters only. One such rule authorizes a flashing blue light for Federal or state law-enforcement vessels engaged in direct law-enforcement activities.

Another section describes the white lights to be placed on barges moored at a bank or dock. When a moored barge projects into a channel and reduces the navigable width to less than 80 meters or when it is not parallel to the bank or dock, the lights are placed on the two corners far-

Fig. 22.20 Vessel constrained by her draft (COLREGS only).

thest from the bank. Groups of barges are lighted on one barge at the upstream and one at the downstream end of the group.

Dredge pipelines are marked by equally spaced, yellow flashing lights. Two red lights mark the two ends in a channel where the pipeline is separated to allow vessels to pass.

22.16 Seaplanes

INLAND AND INTERNATIONAL RULE 31—SEAPLANES

Where it is impracticable for a seaplane to exhibit lights and shapes of the characteristics or in the positions prescribed in the rules of this part she shall exhibit lights and shapes as closely similar in characteristics and position as is possible.

22.17 Distress Signals Rule 37 of both sets of rules states that a vessel in distress and requiring assistance shall use or exhibit, either together or separately, the following signals described in Annex IV to the regulations:

(a) A gun or other explosive signal fired at intervals of about a minute.

(b) A continuous sounding with any fog-signaling apparatus;

(c) Rockets or shells, throwing red stars fired one at a time at short intervals;

(d) A signal made by radiotelegraphy or by any other signaling method consisting of the group . . . ——— . . . (SOS) in the Morse Code,

(e) A signal sent by radiotelephony consisting of the spoken word "Mayday";

(f) The International Code Signal of distress indicated by N.C.

(g) A signal consisting of a square flag having above or below it a ball or anything resembling a ball;

(h) Flames on the vessel (as from a burning tar barrel, oil barrel, etc.);

(i) A rocket parachute flare or a hand flare showing a red light;

(j) A smoke signal giving off orange-colored smoke;

(k) Slowly and repeatedly raising and lowering arms outstretched to each side;

(l) The radiotelegraph alarm signal;

(m) The radiotelephone alarm signal;

(n) Signals transmitted by emergency position-indicating radio beacons.

In addition to the above distress signals, the Inland Rules provide for the exhibition of a high-intensity white light flashing at regular intervals from 50 to 70 times a minute. Attention is drawn to the relevant sections of the International Code of Signals, the Merchant Ship Search and Rescue Manual and the following signals:

(a) A piece of orange-colored canvas with either a black square and circle or other appropriate symbol for identification from the air,

(b) A dye marker.

Figure 22.21 illustrates approved distress signals.

Since January 1, 1981, boats over 16 ft in length have been required to carry aboard some type of Coast Guard-approved visual distress signal for day use, night use, or day-and-night use. Table 22.1 shows the devices and options available, the time of day for which they are approved, the quantity

Table 22.1   Visual Distress Signals

Device	Number Required	C.G. Number
Day Use:		
Floating orange smoke	3	160.022
Hand-held orange smoke	3	160.037*
Orange flag with black ball and square	1	160.072
Night Use:		
Electric distress signal	1	160.013
Day-and-Night Use:		
Hand-held red flare	3	160.021
Pistol-projected parachute red flare	3	160.024
Hand-held, rocket-propelled parachute red flare	3	160.036
Red aerial pyrotechnic flare	3	160.066

*For the 5-min smoke; for the 15-min smoke, the number is 160.057.

Fig. 22.21 Distress signals. The use or exhibition of any of these distress signals except for the purpose of indicating distress and need of assistance, and the use of other signals which may be confused with any of the above signals is prohibited.

required and the C.G. number that must appear on each device. Boats less than 16 ft in length do not have to carry a day distress signal but must carry a signal for use when underway at night. It should be kept in mind that whatever pyrotechnics are carried, their expiration dates should not have been reached.

22.18   Signals to Attract Attention

INLAND AND INTERNATIONAL RULE 36—SIGNALS TO ATTRACT ATTENTION

If necessary to attract the attention of another vessel, any vessel may make light or sound signals that cannot be mistaken for any signal authorized elsewhere in these rules, or may direct the beam of her searchlight in the direction of the danger, in such a way as not to embarrass any vessel. See Sections 7.17 and 7.18 in Chapter 7.

22.19   Additional Station or Signal Lights

INLAND RULE 1(C)

(c) Nothing in these Rules shall interfere with the operation of any special rules made by the Secretary of the Navy with respect to additional station or signal lights and shapes or whistle signals for ships of war and vessels proceeding under convoy, or by the Secretary with respect to additional station or signal lights and shapes for fishing vessels engaged in fishing as a fleet. These additional station or signal lights and shapes or whistle signals shall, so far as possible, be such that they cannot be mistaken for any light, shape, or signal authorized elsewhere under these Rules. Notice of such special rules shall be published in the Federal Register and, after the effective date specified in such notice, they shall have effect as if they were a part of these Rules.

International Rule 1(c) is identical except that the last sentence is omitted.

22.20   Distinctive Lights Authorized for Submarines

In accordance with Rule 1(c), International and Inland Rules, the Secretary of the Navy has authorized the display of a distinctive light by U.S. Naval submarines in international water and in the inland waters of the United States. The light will be exhibited in addition to the presently prescribed navigational lights for submarines.

The normal navigational lights of submarines have been found to be easily mistaken for those of small vessels when in fact submarines are large deep draft vessels with limited maneuvering characteristics while they are on the surface. The authorized light promotes safety at sea by assisting in the identification of submarines.

U.S. submarines may therefore display an amber rotating light producing 90 flashes per minute visible all around the horizon at a distance of at least 3 miles, the light to be located not less than 2 feet, and not more than 6 feet, above the masthead light.

22.21   Vessels of Special Construction or Purpose

INLAND RULE 1(E)

(e) Whenever the Secretary determines that a vessel or class of vessels of special construction or purpose cannot comply fully with the provisions of any of these Rules with respect to the number, position, range, or arc of visibility of lights or shapes, as well as to the disposition and characteristics of sound-signaling appliances, without interfering with the special function of the vessel, the vessel shall comply with such other provisions in regard to the number, position, range, or arc of visibility of lights or shapes, as well as to the disposition and characteristics of sound-signaling appliances, as the Secretary shall have determined to be the closest possible compliance with these Rules. The Secretary may issue a certificate of alternative compliance for a vessel or class of vessels specifying the closest possible compliance with these Rules. The Secretary of the Navy shall make these determinations and issue certificates of alternative compliance for vessels of the Navy.

(f) The Secretary may accept a certificate of alternative compliance issued by a contracting party to the International Regulations if he determines that the alternative compliance standards of the contracting party are substantially the same as those of the United States.

International Rule 1(e) is the same as the Inland Rule for all intents and purposes. Lights for Coast Guard and Navy vessels of special construction are promulgated in the Federal Register and listed in the Code of Federal Regulations.

23

Responsibilities Between Vessels—Right of Way

23.1   Right of Way Between Different Categories of Vessels   This section will consider the right of way between different categories of vessels underway, namely:

Category	Special Light Array
Not under command	Red-over-red
Restricted in ability to maneuver (includes mineclearance vessel)	Red–white–red Three green lights
Constrained by draft	Red–red–red
Engaged in fishing (includes trawling)	Red-over-white Green–over–white
Sailing vessel	Red-over-green (optional)
Power-driven vessel includes: pilot vessel towing vessel	None White-over-red Towing masthead lights and yellow towing light

This table is applicable to both inland and COLREGS waters with one exception—there is no provision for a vessel constrained by her draft in inland waters.

(f) The term "vessel not under command" means a vessel which through some exceptional circumstance is unable to maneuver as required by these Rules and is therefore unable to keep out of the way of another vessel;

(g) The term "vessel restricted in her ability to maneuver" means a vessel which from the nature of her work is restricted in her ability to maneuver as required by these Rules and is therefore unable to keep out of the way of another vessel; vessels restricted in their ability to maneuver include, but are not limited to:

(i) a vessel engaged in laying, servicing, or picking up a navigation mark, submarine cable, or pipeline;

(ii) a vessel engaged in dredging, surveying, or underwater operations;

(iii) a vessel engaged in replenishment or transferring persons, provisions, or cargo while underway;

(iv) a vessel engaged in the launching or recovery of aircraft;

(v) a vessel engaged in mineclearance operations; and

(vi) a vessel engaged in a towing operation such as severely restricts the towing vessel and her tow in their ability to deviate from their course.

Rule 18 of both sets of rules gives the hierarchy, or order of ranking, of responsibilities between vessels. Both rules are identical except that the International Rule has an additional subparagraph to make provision for vessels constrained by their draft.

INLAND RULE 18—RESPONSIBILITY BETWEEN VESSELS

Except where Rules 9, 10, and 13 otherwise require:

(a) A power-driven vessel underway shall keep out of the way of:

(i) a vessel not under command;

(ii) a vessel restricted in her ability to maneuver;

(iii) a vessel engaged in fishing; and

(iv) a sailing vessel.

(b) A sailing vessel underway shall keep out of the way of:

(i) a vessel not under command;

(ii) a vessel restricted in her ability to maneuver; and

(iii) a vessel engaged in fishing.

(c) A vessel engaged in fishing when underway shall, so far as possible, keep out of the way of:

(i) a vessel not under command; and

(ii) a vessel restricted in her ability to maneuver.

(d) A seaplane on the water shall, in general, keep well clear of all vessels and avoid impeding their navigation. In circumstances, however, where risk of collision exists, she shall comply with the Rules of this Part.

An additional subparagraph in International Rule 18 states:

(d)(i) Any vessel other than a vessel not under command or a vessel restricted in her ability to maneuver shall, if the circumstances of the case admit, avoid impeding the safe passage of a vessel constrained by her draught, exhibiting the signals in Rule 28.

(ii) A vessel constrained by her draught shall navigate with particular caution having full regard to her special condition.

As has been pointed out, the Inland Rules do not contain any reference to a vessel constrained by her draft. The developers of these rules felt that such a general rule was open to interpretation and might lead to abuses resulting in dangerous situations. Nevertheless, Rule 18 catalogs the responsibilities between vessels and lists which vessels must keep out of the way of other vessels. Its first part relates to other privileges and duties that take precedence over it: Rule 9, Narrow Channels; Rule 10, Traffic Separation Schemes, COLREGS waters only; and Rule 13, Overtaking.

23.2 Exceptions to Right of Way Provisions Between Categories The rules make exceptions to the right of way provisions discussed in the previous section. Inland and International Rule 9, the rule for Narrow Channels, provides that:

(b) A vessel of less than 20 meters in length or a sailing vessel shall not impede the passage of a vessel that can safely navigate only within a narrow channel or fairway.

(c) A vessel engaged in fishing shall not impede the passage of any other vessel navigating within a narrow channel or fairway.

(d) A vessel shall not cross a narrow channel or fairway if such crossing impedes the passage of a vessel which can safely navigate only within that channel or fairway. The latter vessel shall use the danger signal prescribed in Rule 34(d) if in doubt as to the intention of the crossing vessel.

(g) Every vessel shall, if the circumstances of the case admit, avoid anchoring in a narrow channel.

International Rule 10 provides specific instructions to vessels operating in or near a traffic lane, as noted below. These traffic separation schemes are not applicable in inland waters, but the vessel traffic services that are their equivalent provide specific operating instructions for each area.

INTERNATIONAL RULE 10—TRAFFIC SEPARATION SCHEMES

(a) This rule applies to traffic separation schemes adopted by the organization.

(h) A vessel not using a traffic separation scheme shall avoid it by as wide a margin as is practicable.

(i) A vessel engaged in fishing shall not impede the passage of any vessel following a traffic lane.

(j) A vessel of less than 20 metres in length or a sailing vessel shall not impede the safe passage of a power-driven vessel following a traffic lane.

Rule 13, which is the same for both inland and COLREGS waters, states that any vessel overtaking any other vessel shall keep out of the way of the vessel being overtaken.

23.3 Sailing Vessel Approaching Sailing Vessel

INLAND AND INTERNATIONAL RULE 12—SAILING VESSELS

(a) When two sailing vessels are approaching one another, so as to involve risk of collision, one of them shall keep out of the way of the other as follows:

(i) when each has the wind on a different side, the vessel which has the wind on the port side shall keep out of the way of the other;

(ii) when both have the wind on the same side, the vessel which is to windward shall keep out of the way of the vessel which is to leeward;

(iii) if a vessel with the wind on the port side sees a vessel to windward and cannot determine with certainty whether the other vessel has the wind on the port or on the starboard side, she shall keep out of the way of the other.

(b) For the purposes of this rule the windward side shall be deemed to be the side opposite to that on which the mainsail is carried or, in the case of a square-rigged vessel, the side opposite to that on which the largest fore-and-aft sail is carried.

The inland rule is exactly the same as that for the 72 COLREGS. The rule also conforms closely to yacht racing rules. Another important aspect of this rule is its specification that whenever a mariner is in doubt as to which is the give-way vessel in an approach situation, he is to assume that he is and keep out of the way of the other vessel.

24

Approach Situations Between Power-Driven Vessels in Sight

General Provisions—Inland and International Rules

24.1 Risk of Collision The stand-on or give-way status of two power-driven vessels approaching each other is determined by the approach situation—head-on, crossing, or overtaking. For any of the three approach situations to exist, two vessels must be approaching so as to involve risk of collision, and they must be in visual contact, which does not include tracking by radar. The situations apply in fog and other conditions of restricted visibility, *but only after the vessels have sighted each other*. (See Fig. 24.1.)

Both the International Rules and the Inland Rules prescribe certain "Steering and Sailing Rules" that must be followed when two vessels are approaching each other ". . . so as to involve risk of collision . . ." Justice Longyear, in the MILWAUKEE suit, said. "Risk of collision begins the very moment when the two vessels have approached so near each other and upon such courses that by a departure from the rules of navigation . . . , a collision might be brought about."

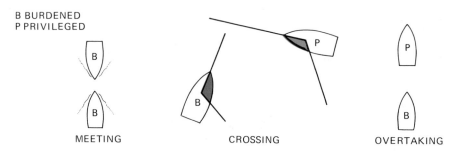

Fig. 24.1   Approach situations between power-driven vessels.

INLAND AND INTERNATIONAL RULE 7—RISK OF COLLISION

(a) Every vessel shall use all available means appropriate to the prevailing circumstances and conditions to determine if risk of collision exists. If there is any doubt, such risk shall be deemed to exist.

(b) Proper use shall be made of radar equipment if fitted and operational, including long-range scanning to obtain early warning of risk of collision and radar plotting or equivalent systematic observation of detected objects.

(c) Assumptions shall not be made on the basis of scanty information, especially scanty radar information.

(d) In determining if risk of collision exists, the following considerations shall be among those taken into account:

(i) such risk shall be deemed to exist if the compass bearing of an approaching vessel does not appreciably change;

(ii) such risk may sometimes exist even when an appreciable bearing change is evident, particularly when approaching a very large vessel or a tow or when approaching a vessel at close range.

Both sets of rules state that risk of collision is considered to exist "if the compass bearing of an approaching vessel does not appreciably change." Risk of collision can also exist with an appreciable bearing drift when the approaching vessels are at close range. Although a steady compass bearing is the surest way to verify a risk-of-collision situation, other means are at hand; a vessel is required to use every one of them, especially radar, if on board and operational. If there is any doubt whether a risk of collision exists, vessels should assume such to be the case and act accordingly.

24.2   Proper Lookout

INLAND AND INTERNATIONAL RULE 7

Every vessel shall at all times maintain a proper lookout by sight and hearing as well as by all available means appropriate in the prevailing circumstances and conditions so as to make a full appraisal of the situation and of the risk of collision.

The importance of a proper lookout cannot be overstated. The courts have long attached great importance to maintaining a proper lookout and have asserted in various decisions:

(1) "Lookout is a person who is specially charged with duty of observing lights, sounds, echoes, or any obstruction to navigation."

(2) "Lookouts, who must be kept on all vessels, must be persons of suitable experience, properly stationed on vessel, and actually and vigilantly employed in the performance of that duty."

(3) "Lookout should be placed as low and as far forward as possible." This is a requirement in clear weather as well as in fog if failure to comply can result in any one of the following:
(a) the lookout does not have a clear, unobstructed view
(b) the lookout's ability to hear signals is impaired
(c) the lookout will sight a danger earlier if placed forward (as when leaving a blind slip)

(4) "Lookout . . . should have no other duties."

(5) The circumstances will dictate the number of lookouts required. The number must be sufficient to detect any reasonably foreseen danger from any direction.

(6) A lookout astern is required when backing.

(7) Lookouts must have a direct and positive means of communicating what they observe to the conning officer. A lookout cannot wear headphones, as his ability to hear signals would be impaired.

24.3 Safe Speed In order to take proper and effective action to avoid collision, every vessel in inland and COLREGS waters in all conditions of visibility is required by Rule 6 to proceed at a safe speed. Safe speed is not defined by the rules, but several factors, listed below, must be taken into consideration when determining it:

1. State of visibility
2. Traffic density
3. Maneuverability of vessel
4. At night, presence of background lights
5. State of wind, sea, and currents
6. Proximity of any hazards to navigation
7. Available depth of water

Determining a safe speed is a judgmental decision, but the result must be a speed that will allow the vessel to be stopped within a distance appropriate to the prevailing circumstances and conditions. It has been said that any moving vessel involved in a collision was not proceeding at a safe speed. Although not always true, this after-the-fact appraisal can serve as a reminder that excessive speed will increase the possibility of a collision.

Rule 6 also lists some safe-speed considerations for vessels equipped with operational radar:

1. Range scale in use
2. Effect on radar detection of sea state, weather, or other sources of interference
3. Possibility of not detecting small vessels
4. Number, location, and movement of vessels detected by radar
5. Radar's more exact assessment of existing visibility

24.4 Action to Avoid Collision International and Inland Rule 8 states that action to avoid collision should be positive, that is, obvious enough to be seen readily by the other vessel and also taken in a timely manner. The rules should be obeyed early on to avoid the immediate risk of collision and to give the other vessel an opportunity to understand a situation. Slowing or stopping is always a good way to gain more time to assess the situation. More often than not, however, the best avoiding action is a large course change that will ensure that the vessels pass at a safe distance. Any action should be carefully monitored until the vessels are free and clear of a collision course.

24.5 Give-Way Vessel Duties

INLAND AND INTERNATIONAL RULE 16—ACTION BY GIVE-WAY VESSEL

Every vessel which is directed by these rules to keep out of the way of another vessel shall, as far as possible, take early and substantial action to keep well clear.

There it is again—early and substantial action. Hanging on—waiting for a situation to clear of itself—is not only a violation of the rules but a sure way of getting into embarrassing circumstances.

24.6 Stand-On Vessel Duties Rule 17, Action by the Stand-on Vessel, is the same in both sets of rules. It requires the stand-on vessel to maintain her course and speed until it becomes apparent that collision can no longer be avoided by the action of the give-way vessel alone (in extremis). However, a provision of the rule allows the stand-on vessel to take avoiding action as soon as it becomes apparent that the give-way vessel is not taking appropriate action in compliance with the rules. Its intent is not to allow the stand-on vessel to maneuver at will but only when the give-way vessel is obviously failing to live up to her obligation to keep clear. A vessel that takes action under this provision in a crossing situation is advised against altering its course to port.

In no way does Rule 17 relieve the give-way vessel of her obligation to keep clear.

24.7 Responsibility   Just about all experienced mariners are familiar with the "Rule of Good Seamanship" and the "Rule of Special Circumstances," the latter often called the "General Prudential Rule." Both these rules are found in Inland Rule 2, the Responsibility Rule, which is identical to the 72 COLREGS rule. Although this rule was mentioned briefly in Chapter 21, a more detailed discussion in this chapter is appropriate when we consider the action to be taken by vessels in the three basic approach situations.

INLAND AND INTERNATIONAL RULE 2—RESPONSIBILITY

(a) Nothing in these Rules shall exonerate any vessel, or the owner, master or crew thereof, from the consequences of any neglect to comply with these Rules or of the neglect of any precaution which may be required by the ordinary practice of seamen, or by the special circumstances of the case.

(b) In construing and complying with these rules, due regard shall be had to all dangers of navigation and collision and to any special circumstances, including the limitations of the vessels involved, which may make a departure from these rules necessary to avoid immediate danger.

Rule 2(a) embodies the "Rule of Good Seamanship." The following list contains specific actions that may be required by good seamanship (all quotations are from U.S. court rulings on the Inland Rules.):

1. Speed in good visibility
   (a) must comply with local regulations.
   (b) must not create swell or suction that would cause damage to other vessels.
   (c) must be such that the vessel is completely under control.
2. Vessels must not pass unnecessarily close to pier ends.
3. Vessels must be properly manned and steered.
4. Vessels must not navigate with defective equipment.
5. Vessels have the "responsibility to utilize available weather reports so that [they] can operate in a manner consistent with foreseeable risk."
6. Vessels moored must have sufficient mooring lines.
7. "A navigator is chargeable with knowledge of the maneuvering capacity of his vessel. He is bound to know the character of his vessel and how she would turn in ordinary conditions."
8. "When a vessel is known to be about to enter or leave a dock, other vessels should keep well clear and avoid embarrassing her maneuvers."

9. "In waters well frequented by small tows . . . the law requires that a ship should have a competent person standing by in the forecastle ready at a moments notice to let go the anchors."

Any condition that causes a deviation from the norm may require additional precautions. The following factors may necessitate additional precautions:

1. Adverse weather conditions
2. Unusual conditions of loading or trim
3. Failure or degradation of any equipment important to safe navigation
4. Traffic density
5. Proximity of navigational hazards
6. Availability of external aids to navigation
7. Transport of dangerous cargo or cargo which poses a threat to the environment

Rule 2(b), the "General Prudential Rule," recognizes that the rules cannot cover every situation and that special circumstances may require a departure from the other rules in order to avoid "immediate danger." It is not implied that the other rules do not apply to close-quarters situations. The meaning is that in some situations, in the face of immediate danger, obedience to a rule may cause a collision. One of the more common of such situations is the approach of a third vessel. A vessel may approach two (or more) other vessels in such a way that she must stand on with respect to one, and give way to the other. If she cannot conform to the steering and sailing rules by handling the approaches one at a time, "special circumstances" should be deemed to exist.

Other situations for which the rules provide no specific guidance include approach situations where one or both vessels are entering a slip, maneuvering around piers, or backing. In either case, at least one vessel is not on a steady course. Even though both sets of rules provide a signal for a vessel backing, and the Inland Rules provide a signal for a vessel leaving her slip, there are no directions on how to maneuver a vessel if an approaching vessel cannot be avoided without one of the two taking action. Such situations involve "special circumstances," and the rules for the head-on, crossing, or overtaking situations do not apply.

Often, the best initial action to take under "special circumstances" is to slow or stop and sound the in-doubt, or danger, signal. Once signals have been exchanged in inland waters, or the intention of the other vessel has become clear, it should then be safe to proceed.

The "General Prudential Rule" has also modified the requirement for the stand-on vessel in inland waters. U.S. courts have ruled that the stand-on vessel is legally maintaining course and speed when maneuvering for any of the following reasons:

1. "Stopping her engines and checking her speed preparatory to landing"
2. "Following a channel course that of necessity curves around bends"
3. Stopping to pick up a pilot
4. Making "such necessary variations in her course as will enable her to avoid immediate danger arising from natural obstructions to navigation."

24.8 Maneuvering and Warning Signals It is with these signals that the most significant difference occurs between the Inland Rules and the 72 COLREGS. The Inland Navigational Rules Act of 1980 retained the signals of "intent and reply" from the old rules because they are so firmly embedded in the maritime customs of the United States. The drafters of the rule also believed these signals to be much safer for use in the confined waters of the U.S. than the "action" signals required by the 72 COLREGS.

For inland waters only, Inland Rules 34(a) and 34(c) provide that:

(a) When power-driven vessels are in sight of one another and meeting or crossing at a distance within half a mile of each other, each vessel underway, when maneuvering as authorized or required by these Rules:

(i) shall indicate that maneuver by the following signals on her whistle: one short blast to mean "I intend to leave you on my port side"; two short blasts to mean "I intend to leave you on my starboard side"; and three short blasts to mean "I am operating astern propulsion".

(ii) upon hearing the one or two blast signal of the other shall, if in agreement, sound the same whistle signal and take the steps necessary to effect a safe passing. If, however, from any cause, the vessel doubts the safety of the proposed maneuver, she shall sound the danger signal specified in paragraph (d) of this Rule and each vessel shall take appropriate precautionary action until a safe passing agreement is made.

(c) When in sight of one another:

(i) a power-driven vessel intending to overtake another power-driven vessel shall indicate her intention by the following signals on her whistle: one short blast to mean "I intend to overtake you on your starboard side"; two short blasts to mean "I intend to overtake you on your port side"; and

(ii) the power-driven vessel about to be overtaken shall, if in agreement, sound a similar sound signal. If in doubt she shall sound the danger signal prescribed in paragraph (d).

International Rule 34(a) and 34(c) provide that:

(a) When vessels are in sight of one another, a power-driven vessel underway, when maneuvering as authorized or required by these rules, shall indicate that maneuver by the following signals on her whistle:
 —one short blast to mean "I am altering my course to starboard";
 —two short blasts to mean "I am altering my course to port";
 —three short blasts to mean "I am operating astern propulsion."
(c) When in sight of one another in a narrow channel or fairway:
 (i) a vessel intending to overtake another shall in compliance with Rule 9(e)(i) indicate her intention by the following signals on her whistle:
 —two prolonged blasts followed by one short blast to mean "I intend to overtake you on your starboard side";
 —two prolonged blasts followed by two short blasts to mean "I intend to overtake you on your port side".
 (ii) the vessel about to be overtaken when acting in accordance with Rule 9(e)(i) shall indicate her agreement by the following signal on her whistle:
 —one prolonged, one short, one prolonged and one short blast, in that order.

The signals required by International Rule 34(c) are a special case, for they are actually signals of intent and assent. In contrast, the one- and two-blast signals of International Rule 34(a) are rudder-action signals, informing other vessels that a change of course is being executed. They are required of a power-driven vessel whenever a vessel of any type or category is in sight. The one- and two-blast signals of the Inland Rules neither signal a change in course nor an intention to change course; they merely enable vessels to agree on which side they will pass in the head-on, crossing, and overtaking situations.

Both sets of rules provide for optional light signals to supplement the whistle signals. When used in inland waters, the light signals must be synchronized with the whistle signals.

24.9 The In-Doubt Signal

INLAND AND INTERNATIONAL RULE 34(D)

34(d) When vessels in sight of one another are approaching each other and from any cause either vessel fails to understand the intentions or actions of the other, or is in doubt whether sufficient action is being taken by the other to avoid collision, the vessel in doubt shall immediately indicate such doubt by giving at least five short and rapid blasts on the whistle. Such signal may be supplemented by a light signal of at least five short and rapid flashes.

The use of the in-doubt, or danger signal is the same for both sets of rules. Both the give-way and the stand-on vessels are *required* to sound the five-blast in-doubt signal any time the intentions of another vessel in sight are not understood or when there is doubt whether the other vessel is taking sufficient action to avoid collision.

Overtaking Situation

24.10 Overtaking Situation Defined Rule 13 of the Inland and International Rules clearly defines the overtaking situation.

Inland and International Rule 13—Overtaking

(a) Notwithstanding anything contained in Rules 4 through 18, any vessel overtaking any other shall keep out of the way of the vessel being overtaken.

(b) A vessel shall be deemed to be overtaking when coming up with another vessel from a direction more than 22.5 degrees abaft her beam, that is, in such a position with reference to the vessel she is overtaking, that at night she would be able to see only the sternlight of that vessel but neither of her sidelights.

(c) When a vessel is in any doubt as to whether she is overtaking another, she shall assume that this is the case and act accordingly.

(d) Any subsequent alteration of the bearing between the two vessels shall not make the overtaking vessel a crossing vessel within the meaning of these rules or relieve her of the duty of keeping clear of the overtaken vessel until she is finally past and clear.

The rules do not prescribe the side on which the overtaking vessel should pass. In confined waters, good seamanship suggests that the passing shall be to port if safe and practicable, since the vessel ahead is required to keep to the starboard side of a fairway or channel. The overtaken vessel may be forced to move to starboard if she meets another vessel head on. Such a move to starboard might be awkward, if not dangerous, to the overtaking vessel trying to pass to starboard.

In situations where the overtaken vessel gives a whistle signal of agreement to the other vessel's proposal, such agreement should not be given when it is dangerous to pass. The overtaken vessel similarly should not agree to an overtaking proposal if she herself is planning a maneuver, such as a turn to make a berth or pick up a pilot.

An overtaking vessel must anticipate changes of course by the overtaken vessel for the purpose of following the channel or avoiding rocks, shoals, or other vessels. Sailing vessels, in particular, must be given a wide berth in order that they may make the necessary tacks to follow a channel.

The general practices of good seamanship and the definitions for the overtaking situation are the same for both inland and COLREGS waters. The differences arise in the signals required of vessels during the passing.

24.11 Overtaking Situation in COLREGS Waters The overtaking situation in open waters under the 72 COLREGS is very simple. The overtaking vessel sounds one or two short blasts if she turns right or left to avoid the overtaken vessel. If she makes no course change in the passing, she sounds no signal. The overtaken vessel maintains course and speed and sounds no signal.

The overtaking situation in narrow channels or fairways is more complicated when the vessel to be overtaken has to take action to permit safe passing. Then the vessel intending to overtake is required to sound the following signals:

—two prolonged blasts followed by one short blast to mean ''I intend to overtake on your starboard side''
—two prolonged blasts followed by two short blasts to mean ''I intend to overtake on your port side''

The overtaken vessel, if in agreement, sounds one prolonged, one short, one prolonged, and one short blast and then takes steps to permit passing. If she thinks the proposal is dangerous, she sounds five short blasts. The overtaking vessel should not attempt passing until an agreement is reached, nor does agreement relieve her of her obligation to keep out of the way until well past and clear. The signals are not limited to power-driven vessels.

24.12 Overtaking Situation in Inland Waters The overtaking situation in inland waters is much simpler than for COLREGS waters. In all cases, a power-driven vessel wishing to overtake sounds one short blast if she intends to overtake to starboard and two short blasts if she intends to overtake to port. The latter vessel signals her agreement by sounding a similar signal. If she does not think the proposal is safe, she must sound the doubt signal. The overtaking vessel is not permitted to pass the vessel ahead until the overtaken vessel answers with the same signal. ''The signal of an overtaking vessel must be repeated if not responded to, and the possibility of collision avoided, if necessary, by slackening speed or changing course.'' The vessel ahead is not obligated to maintain course and speed until she agrees to the proposal of the overtaking vessel.

Head-on Situation

24.13 Head-On Situation Defined The head-on situation is defined by Rule 14 of the Inland Rules as follows:

Inland Rule 14—Head-on Situation

(a) Unless otherwise agreed, when two power-driven vessels are meeting on reciprocal or nearly reciprocal courses so as to involve risk of collision, each shall alter her course to starboard so that each shall pass on the port side of the other.

(b) Such a situation shall be deemed to exist when a vessel sees the other ahead or nearly ahead and by night she could see the masthead lights of the other in a line or nearly in a line or both sidelights and by day she observes the corresponding aspect of the other vessel.

(c) When a vessel is in any doubt as to whether such a situation exists, she shall assume that it does exist and act accordingly.

(d) Notwithstanding paragraph (a) of this rule, a power-driven vessel operating on the Great Lakes, Western Rivers, or waters specified by the Secretary, and proceeding downbound with a following current shall have the right-of-way over an upbound vessel, shall propose the manner of passage, and shall initiate the maneuvering signals prescribed by Rule 34(a)(i), as appropriate.

The definition of the head-on situation in both sets of rules is the same—the masthead lights are in line or nearly in line or both sidelights can be seen. Since the white masthead lights are often in view long before the sidelights are visible, it is prudent to maneuver before the colored lights of the other vessel come into view. The definition of a head-on situation is more strictly applied in open waters than in restricted waters. Two vessels traveling in opposite directions in a narrow, crooked channel will eventually pass in a head-on situation even though they initially sight each other on crossing courses. Both sets of rules also require a vessel in doubt as to whether a head-on situation exists to assume it does and act accordingly. However, the actions required by the two sets of rules are considerably different.

24.14 Head-on Situation in Inland Waters When two power-driven vessels are in a head-on situation, a passing agreement must be made by whistle signals or by radiotelephone. Other than on the Great Lakes, Western Rivers, or waters specified by the Secretary of Transportation (see Section 21.3), either vessel may initiate the signals of proposal and agreement. One vessel sounds one short blast to propose a port to port passage; the other vessel agrees to such a passage with the same signal. When two vessels meet head-on such that it is impractical or unsafe for them to pass port to port, and a starboard to starboard passage appears safer, then the exchange of signals will consist of two short blasts meaning, "I intend to leave you on my starboard side", followed by a two short blast signal of agreement. These exchanges of signals are required whenever the CPA

(Closest Point of Approach) is within one-half mile, including situations in which both vessels can pass safely without a course change by either one.

Unless it is necessary to avoid immediate danger, a vessel should not alter course until her signal of proposal has been answered with the same signal. If the other vessel crosses the signal, that is, answers one blast with two or two blasts with one, the courts require the initiating vessel to sound the danger signal and stop her engines, even reversing them if the proximity of the other vessel requires it. A vessel that answers two short blasts with the danger signal, and then sounds one short blast without stopping or reversing, is guilty of cross signals—even if the original proposal was an unsafe one. After stopping, the vessels must exchange signals before they pass each other. The same procedure, rather than repeating the signal, is recommended when the other vessel does not answer a proposal.

On the Great Lakes, Western Rivers and other waters specified by the Secretary of Transportation, Rule 14(d) provides for a different set of arrangements for power-driven vessels meeting head-on. Vessels must still agree on the manner of passing, but a vessel proceeding downbound with the current has the right-of-way over a vessel proceeding upbound, shall propose the manner of passage, and initiate the appropriate passing signals.

24.15 Head-on Situation in COLREGS Waters   In a head-on situation both vessels are required to alter course to starboard in order to pass port to port. No provision is made for a starboard to starboard passage, which implies that such a passage is proper only when there is no risk of collision. Any course changes must be accompanied by the appropriate one- and two-short blasts signals when in sight of each other. There is no equivalent rule to 14(d) and radiotelephone passing agreements are not mentioned.

Crossing Situation

24.16 Crossing Situation Defined   The crossing situation is defined by Rule 15. The first part of the rule is exactly the same in the Inland Rules and 72 COLREGS:

(a) When two power-driven vessels are crossing, so as to involve risk of collision, the vessel which has the other on her own starboard side shall keep out of the way and shall, if the circumstances of the case admit, avoid crossing ahead of the other vessel.

The crossing situation is any approach situation that is neither a meeting nor an overtaking situation. If vessel B in Fig. 24.2 is in any doubt as to whether she is overtaking or crossing vessel A, she is required by the rules to assume that she is overtaking and keep out of the way. If vessel D is in

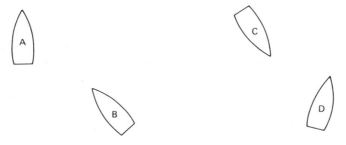

Fig. 24.2 The crossing situation.

any doubt as to whether she is meeting or crossing vessel C, she should assume that it is a meeting situation and alter course to starboard for a port-to-port passing.

Of the three approach situations, the crossing situation is the one that most severely tries the souls of mariners. One vessel is obliged to stand on, the master gritting his teeth as he watches the give-way vessel doggedly proceed. The other vessel, the give-way vessel—certain that to pass ahead is the easiest and safest thing to do—may attempt to do so. Out of such circumstances, collisions are born.

However, the latest revisions to both the COLREGS and the Inland Rules have greatly clarified the situation. In both jurisdictions, the vessel to the right has the right of way, keeping in mind the hierarchy of vessels in Rule 18. In the unified rules only, however, there is a special rule for the Great Lakes, Western Rivers, and waters specified by the Secretary of Transportation which requires any vessel crossing a river to keep out of the way of a power-driven vessel ascending or descending the river. In any case, the give-way vessel is required to take early and substantial action to stay well clear but must avoid passing ahead of the other vessel. Often, the best maneuver is to alter course to starboard and pass astern of the other vessel. Other options include slowing, stopping, reversing, altering course boldly to port, or any combination of the above. Whatever option is taken, it should be taken early on and be positive enough to be understood clearly by the other vessel.

The stand-on vessel maintains course and speed. If, however, she is in doubt that the give-way vessel is taking timely action to meet her obligations to keep clear, she must sound the doubt signal of five short blasts and then maneuver to avoid a close-quarters situation, avoiding, if at all possible, a course change to port. If the stand-on vessel finds herself in extremis, where action by the give-way vessel alone is not sufficient to prevent collision, then she must maneuver to prevent it herself.

Up to this point, the requirements placed on vessels in the crossing situation in both inland and COLREGS waters are the same. It is in the execution of the action with regard to sounding mandatory sound signals that the differences occur. The meaning and use of the backing signal of three short blasts, however, is the same in both sets of rules.

24.17 Crossing Situation in COLREGS Waters In COLREGS waters, the give-way vessel sounds the appropriate rudder or backing signal required by the rules as she maneuvers. In some cases, as when she only slows or stops her engines in order to keep clear, no whistle signal is required.

The stand-on vessel sounds no signal unless it is a doubt signal, whereupon it must maneuver under the provisions of Rule 17, sounding the appropriate one-, two- or three-blast signal.

24.18 Crossing Situation in Inland Waters In inland waters, the whistle signals in the crossing situation are signals of intent and agreement. Two power-driven vessels approaching a crossing situation that will result in a CPA of one-half mile or less must always exchange signals. As a rule, the give-way vessel sounds one short blast—"I intend to leave you on my port side"—and then slows, stops, reverses, or alters course to do so. The stand-on vessel responds with one short blast even if she doesn't change course or speed.

The Inland Rules provide for a two-blast signal in the crossing situation—"I intend to pass you on my starboard side."—but this is not the normal situation. If the other vessel agrees, she replies with two short blasts and watches uneasily as the give-way vessel passes ahead of her.

The rules do not require the give-way vessel to initiate the proposal although it normally does so. Either vessel can initiate the exchange, but the other must assent. If she does not assent, she should sound the doubt signal, stop her engines, and not proceed until an agreement has been reached. Cross signals—answering one blast with two, or two with one—are not permitted.

Signals in Inland Waters

24.19 Radiotelephone Exchange of Signals—Inland Waters As has been noted, vessels in inland waters that reach an agreement in a head-on, crossing, or overtaking situation by using the radiotelephone do not have to exchange whistle signals.

24.20 Approaches in a Narrow Channel Both sets of rules require vessels proceeding along a narrow channel or fairway to keep to the right side. A vessel less than 20 meters in length or a sailing vessel shall not impede a vessel that can safely navigate only in such a channel. A vessel fishing shall not impede any vessel navigating in a narrow channel. Rule 9(d) in both sets of rules states the following:

(d) A vessel shall not cross a narrow channel or fairway if such crossing impedes the passage of a vessel which can safely navigate only within that channel or fairway. The latter vessel shall use the danger signal prescribed in Rule 34(d) if in doubt as to the intention of the crossing vessel.

Rule 9(a)(ii), Inland Rules only, states the following:

. . . a power-driven vessel operating in narrow channels or fairways on the Great Lakes, Western Rivers, or waters specified by the Secretary, and proceeding downbound with a following current shall have the right-of-way over an upbound vessel, shall propose the manner and place of passage, and shall initiate the maneuvering signals prescribed by Rule 34(a)(i) [one or two blasts], as appropriate. The vessel proceeding upbound against the current shall hold as necessary to permit safe passing.

24.21 Bend Signal Both sets of rules require a vessel nearing a bend in a narrow channel to sound one prolonged blast when another vessel approaching from the other direction may be obscured by the bank or other obstruction. Vessels that hear this signal must respond with the same signal.

24.22 Inland Slip Whistle In inland waters only, a power-driven vessel leaving her dock or berth is required to sound one prolonged blast.

25

Law in Fog
and Restricted Visibility

25.1 Conduct of Vessels in Restricted Visibility Rule 20(c) of both Inland and International Rules states that the lights prescribed by the rules are to be exhibited in restricted visibility. Rule 35 of both rules states that the required sound signals are to be sounded in or near an area of restricted visibility. The primary rule for the conduct of vessels in restricted visibility, however, is Inland and international Rule 19 (the same for both). The rule applies to vessels not in sight of one another when navigating in or near an area of restricted visibility.

The key words here are "not in sight" and "in or near." The rule applies not only when a vessel is *in* an area of reduced visibility—such as a fog bank, heavy rainstorm, or smoke cloud—but *near* one in which another vessel may be hidden from sight. Such proximity means that navigational lights should be turned on, the ship's speed reduced, and fog signals commenced even though the ship may be steaming in bright sunlight.

INLAND AND INTERNATIONAL RULE 19

Conduct of Vessels in Restricted Visibility

(a) This Rule applies to vessels not in sight of one another when navigating in or near an area of restricted visibility.

(b) Every vessel shall proceed at a safe speed adapted to the prevailing circumstances and conditions of restricted visibility. A power-driven vessel shall have her engines ready for immediate maneuver.

(c) Every vessel shall have due regard to the prevailing circumstances and conditions of restricted visibility when complying with Rules 4 through 10.

(d) A vessel which detects by radar alone the presence of another vessel shall determine if a close-quarters situation is developing or risk of collision exists. If so, she shall take avoiding action in ample time, provided that when such action consists of an alteration of course, so far as possible the following shall be avoided:

(i) an alteration of course to port for a vessel forward of the beam, other than for a vessel being overtaken; and

(ii) an alteration of course toward a vessel abeam or abaft the beam.

(e) Except where it has been determined that a risk of collision does not exist, every vessel which hears apparently forward of her beam the fog signal of another vessel, or which cannot avoid a close-quarters situation with another vessel forward of her beam, shall reduce her speed to the minimum at which she can be kept on course. She shall if necessary take all her way off and, in any event, navigate with extreme caution until danger of collision is over.

The conduct of a vessel in fog must be determined by adherence to requirements in the following general areas:

1. Navigation lights (see Chap. 22)
2. Speed
3. Obtaining early warning of risk of collision
4. Action to avoid an approaching vessel that has been detected only on radar
5. Action to avoid an approaching vessel that has not been visually sighted but whose fog signal has been heard
6. Fog signals

25.2 Speed in Fog   The determination of safe speed for vessels in any condition of visibility is covered by Rule 6 and discussed in Chap. 24. When visibility is restricted, however, the need for safe speed is particularly relevant. There is no hard and fast rule to determine safe speed in reduced visibility, but the check-off list of Rule 6 can be of great help. A visibility of only five miles or less is a reasonable starting point at which to consider adjusting present speed. As the visbility decreases, so should safe speed.

25.3 Other Considerations   Inland and International Rule 19(c) requires mariners to be particularly mindful of existing visibility when considering or establishing, in addition to safe speed, the following: proper lookout, risk of collision, action to be taken to avoid collision, conduct in narrow channels, and conduct in vessel traffic services.

25.4 Obtaining Early Warning of Risk of Collision The rules make it clear that vessels must at all times maintain a proper lookout—not just visually and aurally but by every means available, including radar should it be available. If it is, the rules require long-range scanning to obtain early warning and plotting to provide "systematic observation" of detected objects. The rules further caution that assumptions are not to be made on scanty information, particularly scanty radar information.

The rules make it obvious that radar is not a substitute for a proper lookout by sight and hearing. Nevertheless, the courts have ruled that dependable radar equipment must be turned on and intelligent and reasonable use made of it.

The radar plot required by the rules includes plotting on a radar deflection plotter fitted over the scope as well as plotting directly on the scope. "Systematic observation" means making use of the plotting teams found on most Naval vessels as well as the computerized collision-avoidance systems that process radar bearing and range data and display the results.

The Port and Waterways Safety Act of 1972, as amended, requires every self-propelled vessel of 1600 or more tons to have a marine radar system on board when operating in U.S. waters. International protocol contains similar provisions. Furthermore, the 1978 Port and Tanker Safety Act requires ships over 10,000 tons, when they carry bulk oil or hazardous materials in U.S. waters, to be equipped with some sort of electronic relative-motion analyzer (ERMA). This type of collision-avoidance system provides tremendous advantages in tracking and analyzing multiple contacts; if properly used in conjunction with traditional measures, it should lead to a great improvement in navigational safety.

25.5 Actions When Radar Contacts Are Made Just as is true of a visual bearing, the radar bearing of an approaching vessel that remains fairly constant is indicative of a collision course and requires immediate and substantial action by the observing vessel to avoid a close-quarters situation. If the vessel is not in sight, however, the in-sight requirements for the three approach situations are not applicable. Course alterations in this situation should not be to port if the vessel is forward of the beam (unless overtaking) nor towards the vessel if it is abeam or abaft the beam.

25.6 Actions When a Fog Signal Is Heard Rule 19(e) requires a vessel hearing a fog signal of another vessel apparently forward of the beam to reduce its speed to bare steerageway and proceed with caution unless it has been carefully determined that no risk of collision exists. Such a determination can best be made with certainty with a properly tuned radar that has not been degraded by sea return or weather so long as its information is plotted and analyzed over a period of time.

25.7 In-Doubt/Danger Signal in Restricted Visibility Although the rules state that the five-blast signal of doubt is intended for vessels in sight of one another, requirements of the "Responsibility Rule" could be considered to allow for its use in fog even though the vessels are not in sight. In such a situation, it certainly would be prudent to sound the danger signal if doing so might prevent a collision.

25.8 Fog Signals Neither the rules nor the courts have attempted to establish a distance that defines restricted visibility for the purpose of sounding fog signals. Textbook writers have long recommended the visibility of sidelights as a guideline, which, in both sets of Rules, is presently 3 miles for vessels of 50 meters and upward in length.

The Rules prescribe three types of devices for sound signals: whistle, bell, and gong. The equipment required is determined entirely by the

Table 25.1 Fog Signals

Key: — prolonged blast (4–6 sec)		Bell	5-sec rapid ringing
. short blast (1 sec)		Gong	5-sec rapid sounding
		S	Distinct stroke on bell

Inland and International Signal and Interval[1]			
Power-driven vessel making way through the water		—	2 min
Power-driven vessel underway but stopped		— —	2 min[2]
Vessel not under command		—..	2 min
Vessel restricted in her ability to maneuver (underway or at anchor)		—..	2 min
Vessel constrained by her draft (International Rules only)		—..	2 min
Vessel engaged in fishing		—..	2 min
Vessel engaged in towing or pushing		—..	2 min
Vessel towed (or the last vessel in a tow, if manned)		—...	2 min
Sailing vessel		—..	2 min
Pilot vessel (optional)		....	

Vessel at anchor < 100 m	Bell[3]	1 min
≥ 100 m	Bell, Gong	1 min
may in addition sound	. — .	as required[4]

Vessel aground < 100 m	SSS Bell SSS	1 min
≥ 100 m	SSS Bell SSS Gong	1 min
may in addition sound	"appropriate whistle signal"	as required

[1] A vessel less than 12 m in length shall not be obliged to give the mentioned signals but, if she does not, shall make some other signal at intervals of not more than 2 min.

[2] 2 sec between blasts.

[3] Not required in a "special anchorage area" in inland waters by a vessel less than 20 m in length, or a barge, canal boat, scow, or other nondescript craft.

[4] Used by a vessel at anchor to give warning to an approaching vessel of her position and of the possibility of a collision.

length of a vessel, not by its sailing or power-driven status. The size of the vessel will be indicated by the frequency and audibility of the whistle signal, with the signals sounded by larger vessels usually being of lower frequency and greater audibility than those of smaller vessels.

INLAND AND INTERNATIONAL RULE 33—EQUIPMENT FOR SOUND SIGNALS

(a) A vessel of 12 meters or more in length shall be provided with a whistle and a vessel of 100 meters or more in length shall, in addition, be provided with a gong, the tone and sound of which cannot be confused with that of the bell. The whistle, bell, and gong shall comply with the specifications in Annex III to these Rules. The bell or gong or both may be replaced by other equipment having the same respective sound characteristics, provided that manual sounding of the required signals shall always be possible.

(b) A vessel of less than 12 meters in length shall not be obliged to carry the sound signalling appliances prescribed in paragraph (a) of this Rule but if she does not, she shall be provided with some other means of making an efficient sound signal.

The fog signals for inland and COLREGS waters are the same with two exceptions. One, the Inland Rules do not provide for a vessel constrained by her draft, and two, they do not require vessels less than 20 meters in length and barges, canal boats, and other nondescript craft in specially designated anchorages to sound fog signals.

Table 25.1 summarizes the fog signals prescribed in both sets of rules.

26

Radar for Collision Avoidance

The Rules make it clear that a quick look at the radar is not enough, as follows:

INLAND AND INTERNATIONAL RULE 7(c)

Assumptions shall not be made on the basis of scanty information, especially scanty radar information.

The reason is that observation of only the direction of relative motion (DRM) can be misleading. Consider the following two examples in which the positions of a radar contact have been marked with a grease pencil at 6-min intervals. The vessel making contact is heading north at 20 knots; radar presentation is stabilized, north-up. In the first example (Fig. 26.1), if the range rings were at 2-mile intervals, the speed of relative motion (SRM) would be 40 knots, and the contact would be on a nearly reciprocal course at a speed of approximately 20 knots. If the range rings were at 2-mile intervals, the SRM would be 20 knots, and the contact would be dead in the water. With the range rings at 1000-yd intervals, the SRM would be

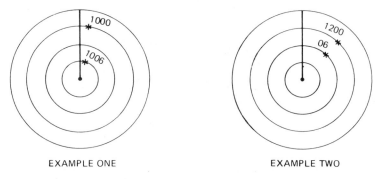

EXAMPLE ONE   EXAMPLE TWO

Fig. 26.1 Two examples of scanty radar information.

10 knots, and the vessel, proceeding at approximately 10 knots, would be overtaken.

The vector diagrams in Figs. 26.2 and 26.3 illustrate two possibilities for the second example in Fig. 26.1. Figure 26.2 illustrates a case with a low SRM (represented by the length of the relative motion vector). The situation is one in which the detecting vessel is gradually overtaking its contact. Fig-

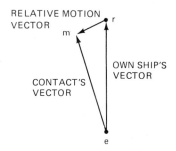

Fig. 26.2 A case with a low SRM.

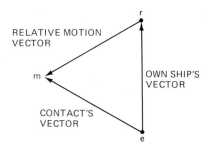

Fig. 26.3 A case with a high SRM.

ure 26.3 illustrates a case with a high SRM, in which the contact's course is nearly at a right angle to that of the detecting vessel.

In these two examples, knowledge of the speed of relative motion was required to differentiate between the possibilities represented by the direction between the two radar positions marked on the scope. Rough estimates may be made by comparing the detecting vessel's own speed with the SRM. The Rules require "systematic observation of detected objects"; the positions must be related to time in order to determine the speed of relative motion.

A radar contact's course, speed, CPA range, and CPA bearing can be obtained by transferring data to a maneuvering board or radar plotting sheet. With some sacrifice in accuracy, the same information can be obtained by methods used directly on the radar scope or reflection plotter. In many circumstances, the loss of accuracy is insignificant when the result is more timely action. In addition, less attention is directed away from the scope where new contacts or changes of course by contacts might be observed. By simply extending the direction of relative motion past the center of the scope, the range and bearing of the closest point of approach (CPA) may be obtained. (See Fig. 26.4.)

The course and speed of a contact may be estimated by constructing a small triangle, using the relative plot as one side. In Fig. 26.5, the contact's position has been marked at 6-min intervals. The length of the *er* side of the triangle, which is the vector for the detecting ship's course and speed, is ⅒ of its speed in knots (each side of the triangle represents miles traveled in 6 min). The length of the vector must be measured using the range scale on the radar scope. The direction of *er* is parallel to the heading marker. The *em* side of the triangle represents the contact's course and speed. The contact's speed is obtained by measuring the length of the *em* vector and multiplying by 10. An alternative method of constructing the same triangle is shown in Fig. 26.6.

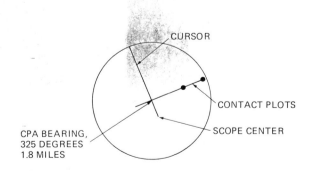

Fig. 26.4 Determining range and bearing of CPA.

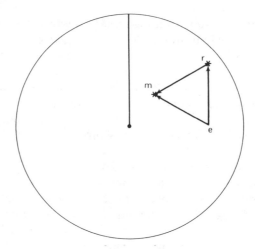

Fig. 26.5 Estimating the course and speed of a contact.

A similar method, called the *ladder method,* allows the observer to make an approximate solution quickly and then refine it after more observations. The "ladder" represents the distance the detecting ship travels from the time of the first observation used. The contact's course is obtained in the same manner as in the previous method. Each solution for the contact's speed involves taking the distance traveled over different time intervals. For example, in Fig. 26.7, the time intervals are 7 and 11 min.

The effect of a planned course change can be calculated by another method used directly on the scope or reflection plotter. In Fig. 26.8, the relative plot with 6-min intervals is employed. The length of *er* and *er'* represent the distance traveled in 6 min. The vector *rr'* represents the planned course change by the detecting ship. By the construction shown, the new

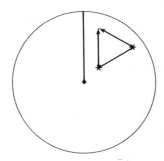

Fig. 26.6 Alternative method of constructing the same triangle.

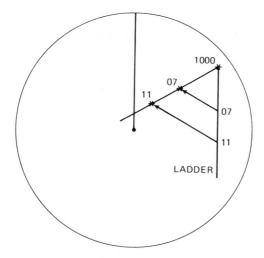

Fig. 26.7 The ladder method.

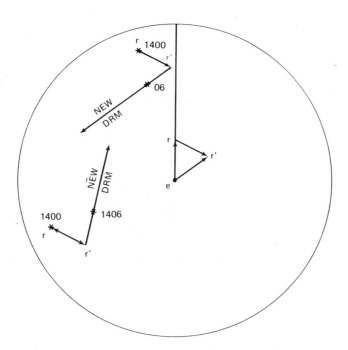

Fig. 26.8 Calculating the effect of a planned course change.

direction of relative motion (DRM) after the course change may be obtained. Note that this method does not require previous solutions of the contacts' courses and speeds.

References

Bassett, Frank E., and Smith, Richard A. *Farwell's Rules of the Nautical Road.* 5th ed. Annapolis: Naval Institute Press, 1977.

Tate, William H. *A Mariner's Guide to the Rules of the Road.* Annapolis: Naval Institute Press, 1980.

27

Maritime Buoyage System

27.1 Maritime Buoyage System Buoys are moored floating markers in various sizes, shapes, and colors which guide ships in and out of harbors and channels and warn them away from hidden dangers. Although they are valuable aids to navigation, they can never be followed blindly, as they can drag their moorings or be set adrift. Until a few years ago, there were many different buoyage systems in use around the world. Then in 1982, most of the maritime nations of the world, including the United States, signed an agreement sponsored by the International Association of Lighthouse Authorities (IALA). This agreement established a system knows as the IALA Maritime Buoyage System and provided rules which apply to most fixed and floating navigational marks. Within the system, there are two International Buoyage Systems, Regions A and B. The U.S. falls within Region B and it will be the only one discussed in this Chapter. In 1983, the Coast Guard began modifying U.S. aids to navigation, converting them to the IALA Maritime Buoyage System, with completion expected in 1989. Figure 27.1 shows the IALA Maritime Buoyage System and modifications used in the U.S.

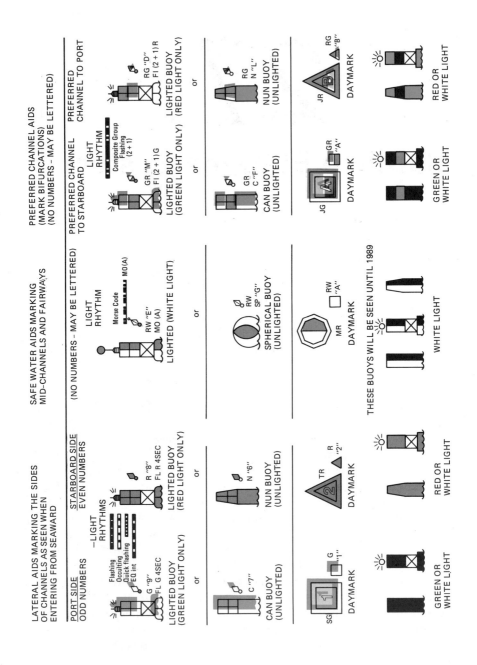

LATERAL AIDS MARKING THE SIDES OF CHANNELS AS SEEN WHEN ENTERING FROM SEAWARD

PORT SIDE
ODD NUMBERS

—LIGHT RHYTHMS

Flashing
Occulting
Quick flashing
EQ int

G "9"
FL G 4SEC

LIGHTED BUOY
(GREEN LIGHT ONLY)

or

C "7"

CAN BUOY
(UNLIGHTED)

G "1"
SG

DAYMARK

GREEN OR
WHITE LIGHT

STARBOARD SIDE
EVEN NUMBERS

R "8"
FL R 4SEC

LIGHTED BUOY
(RED LIGHT ONLY)

or

N "6"

NUN BUOY
(UNLIGHTED)

R "2"
TR

DAYMARK

RED OR
WHITE LIGHT

SAFE WATER AIDS MARKING MID-CHANNELS AND FAIRWAYS

(NO NUMBERS - MAY BE LETTERED)

LIGHT RHYTHM

Morse Code   MO(A)

RW "E"
MO (A)

LIGHTED (WHITE LIGHT)

or

RW
SP "G"

SPHERICAL BUOY
(UNLIGHTED)

RW
"A"
MR

DAYMARK

THESE BUOYS WILL BE SEEN UNTIL 1989

WHITE LIGHT

PREFERRED CHANNEL AIDS
(MARK BIFURCATIONS)
(NO NUMBERS - MAY BE LETTERED)

PREFERRED CHANNEL TO STARBOARD

LIGHT RHYTHM

Composite Group Flashing (2+1)

GR "M"
FI (2+1)G

LIGHTED BUOY
(GREEN LIGHT ONLY)

or

GR
C "F"

CAN BUOY
(UNLIGHTED)

GR
"A"
JG

DAYMARK

GREEN OR
WHITE LIGHT

PREFERRED CHANNEL TO PORT

RG "D"
FI (2+1)R

LIGHTED BUOY
(RED LIGHT ONLY)

or

RG
N "L"

NUN BUOY
(UNLIGHTED)

RG
"B"
JR

DAYMARK

RED OR
WHITE LIGHT

27.2 Types of Marks There are five types of marks used in the Maritime Buoyage System:

a. Lateral Marks—Indicate the port and starboard hand sides of channels.

b. Cardinal Marks—Used in conjunction with the compass to show that navigable waters lie to the named side of the mark.

c. Isolated Danger Marks—Erected on, or moored directly on or over, dangers of limited size.

d. Safe Water Marks—Used to indicate that water is safe for navigation all around the position, such as mid-channel.

e. Special Marks—Used to call attention to an area or specific feature.

27.3 Meaning of the Mark The meaning of a mark depends upon its color, shape, and/or topmark by day, and the light color and/or phase characteristic by night. Numbering or lettering of buoys is an optional feature, and in the U.S., fairway and channel buoys are always numbered odd to port and even to starboard, approaching from seaward. The meaning of IALA marks is as follows:

a. Shape—There are five basic buoy shapes, as shown in Fig. 27.2: can, nun, spherical, pillar, and spar. Except for pillar and spar buoys, the shape of the buoy indicates the correct side on which to pass. Can buoys are sometimes referred to as cylindrical and nun buoys as conical. The term "pillar" is used to describe any buoy which is smaller than a lighthouse buoy and which has a tall, central structure on a broad base. The side on which to pass depends on the meaning of the mark and/or its color.

b. Topmarks—The IALA system uses can, nun, spherical, and X-shaped topmarks only. Topmarks on pillar and spar buoys are particularly important to indicate the side on which they are to be passed and are used whenever practical.

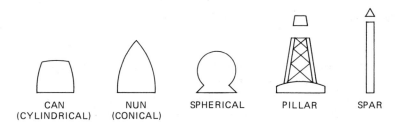

Fig. 27.2 Types of buoys.

c. Lights—On lighted buoys, a red light marks the starboard side of the channel entering from seaward while a green light marks the port side. Yellow lights are for special marks and white lights are used for other types of marks. The phase characteristic of the light, such as flashing, quick flashing, or group flashing, helps to identify the buoy.

27.4   Lateral Marks   Lateral marks are generally used for well-defined channels. They indicate the route to be followed and are used in conjunction with a "conventional direction of buoyage," defined in one of two ways:

a. Local Direction of Buoyage—The direction taken when approaching a harbor, river estuary, or other waterway, from seaward.
b. General Direction of Buoyage—A direction determined by the buoyage authorities, following a clockwise direction around continental landmasses, given in the Sailing Directions and indicated on a chart by a symbol.

27.5   Cardinal Marks   A cardinal mark is used to indicate the best navigable water by compass direction, as seen in Fig. 27.3. It is placed in one of the four quadrants (north, south, east, or west) from the best water and takes its name from the compass point in which it was placed. A cardinal mark may be used to:

a. Indicate that the deepest water is an area on the named side of the channel.
b. Indicate the safe side on which to pass a danger.
c. Draw attention to a feature in a channel, such as a bend, junction, branch, or end of a shoal.

27.6   Isolated Danger Mark   An isolated danger mark is erected on, or moored above, a danger of limited extent with navigable water all around it. For example, it can indicate an offshore shoal or an islet separated from the coast by a narrow channel. The most important feature of an isolated danger mark is a black double sphere topmark by day, as shown in Fig. 27.4.

27.7   Safe Water Mark   A safe water mark, Fig. 27.5, indicates that navigable water is all around the mark, such as a midchannel or landfall buoy. Red and white vertical stripes are used for safe water marks and whenever practical, a pillar or spar buoy used as a safe water mark will carry a single red sphere topmark.

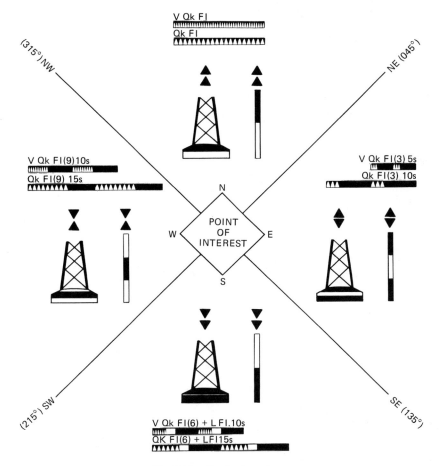

Fig. 27.3 Cardinal marks.

27.8 Special Mark A special mark, Fig. 27.6, may be used to indicate a special area or feature and is yellow in color. The shape is optional but must not conflict with a lateral or safe water mark. When a topmark is carried it takes the form of a single "X". Examples of special areas or features indicated by these marks are:

a. Traffic separation zones
b. Spoil grounds
c. Military exercise areas
d. Cables or pipelines, including outfall pipes

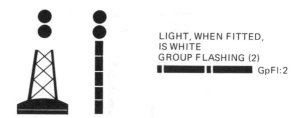

LIGHT, WHEN FITTED,
IS WHITE
GROUP FLASHING (2)

GpFl:2

Fig. 27.4 Isolated danger marks.

TOPMARK
(ALWAYS FITTED* IF BUOY
IS NOT SPHERICAL)

SHAPE: SPHERICAL
OR
PILLAR OR SPAR

LIGHT, WHEN FITTED,
IS WHITE
ISOPHASE OR OCCULTING,
OR LONG FLASHING EVERY
10 SECONDS

Iso
Occ
LFl.10s

Fig. 27.5 Safe water marks.

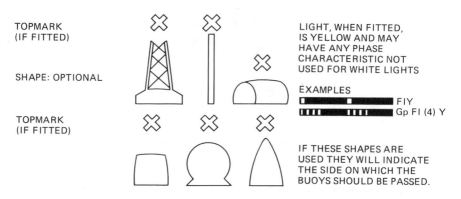

TOPMARK
(IF FITTED)

SHAPE: OPTIONAL

TOPMARK
(IF FITTED)

LIGHT, WHEN FITTED,
IS YELLOW AND MAY
HAVE ANY PHASE
CHARACTERISTIC NOT
USED FOR WHITE LIGHTS

EXAMPLES

Fl Y
Gp Fl (4) Y

IF THESE SHAPES ARE
USED THEY WILL INDICATE
THE SIDE ON WHICH THE
BUOYS SHOULD BE PASSED.

Fig. 27.6 Special marks.

27.9 Daymark Unlighted aids to navigation (except unlighted buoys) are called daymarks, as shown in Fig. 27.7. An example of a daymark is a single pile with a mark on top or a spar supporting a cask. Daymarks marking channels are colored and numbered like channel buoys, and many are fitted with reflectors that show the same color a lighted buoy would show at night in the same position.

SAFE WATER   SPECIAL MARK

REGION B   REGION B   REGION B   REGION B
PREFERRED   PREFERRED   STARBOARD   PORT HAND
CHANNEL   CHANNEL   HAND
STARBOARD   PORT

Fig. 27.7 Daymarks.

27.10 Intracoastal Waterway The Intracoastal Waterway (ICW), often called the inland waterway, is a channel in which a light-draft vessel can coastal navigate from the Chesapeake Bay almost to the Mexican Border, remaining inside natural or artificial breakwaters for most of the trip. Every buoy, daymark, or light structure marking the ICW has part of its surface painted yellow.

27.11 ICW Buoys Red buoys and daymarks are to the right, green to the left, in the ICW, proceeding from the Chesapeake Bay to the Gulf of Mexico. As in other channels, red buoys have even numbers, green buoys odd numbers, and lights follow the standard system. Because of the huge number of buoys in the ICW, they are numbered in groups that usually contain no more than 200 buoys. At certain natural dividing points, numbering begins again at 1.

Appendices

Appendix 1

Rope and Cordage

Rope is a term that includes both fiber and wire rope. Seamen, however, ordinarily refer to fiber rope as *line* and wire rope as *rope* or *wire*. More exactly, a line is a piece of rope, fiber, or wire, that is in use or has been cut for a specific purpose—for example, *lifeline, heaving line, lead line*. There are, nevertheless, a few lines with the word *rope* in their titles—*wheel rope, foot rope, bell rope.*

A1.1 Fiber Rope Fiber rope is made from natural fibers (manila, hemp, sisal, cotton) and synthetic or man-made fibers (nylon, dacron, polyester, polypropylene, etc.) The strength of fiber ropes depends in part on the lengths of the individual fibers.

Manila Manilla rope is made from the fibers of the abaca plant and is the strongest and most expensive of the natural fibers. In the past, manila was used whenever great strength was required, but its use is now limited to general purpose work (such as messengers, riding lines, and lashings). Manila has largely been replaced by synthetic fiber lines in most applications.

Sisal Sisal, made from the agave plant, was once a common natural fiber line used on shipboard. Of the natural fibers, it is next in strength to manila, being rated at 80 percent of manila's strength.

Hemp Hemp rope, made from the fiber of the stalk of the hemp plant, is now rarely used. Usually it was tarred. Aboard ship, the most commonly used hempen cordages were marline and ratline. *Marline* (two-strand, left-lay, tarred) was used for seizing, worming, and serving ropes. *Ratline* (three-strand, right-lay, tarred) is used in circumferences ranging from ¾ to 1½ in.

for lashings, servings, and the snaking on small ships such as destroyers. *Snaking* is the netting between the gunwales and one of the lifelines, intended to keep objects from washing overboard.

Cotton Cotton line, made from the fibers of the cotton plant, may be of three-strand, right-lay or of braided construction. A hollow-braided (without core) line, called a *signal halyard,* was formerly used to fly signal flags. In the Navy, nylon now serves that purpose, because it resists weather and stack gases much better. Other braided cotton lines with cores are used for heaving lines, lead lines, and so on. Three-strand, right-lay cotton line is used for fancy work and lashings. This is called *white line.* The most common sizes are ⅜ and ⅝ in. in circumference.

Nylon Nylon (Fig. A1.1) is a synthetic fiber of great strength, elasticity, and resistance to weather. It comes in twisted, braided, and plaited construction, and it can be used for almost any purpose except for lashings,

Fig. A1.1 Eight-inch nylon hawser faked down. (*Official U.S. Coast Guard photogarph*)

highlines, and other purposes where its slippery surface and elasticity is detrimental.

Nylon is expensive, costing almost three times as much as manila of the same size. It has several advantages over manila, however. It is almost three times as strong and lasts five times as long. Then too, its greater strength permits using a line about two-thirds as large. For these reasons, nylon is more economical. In the Navy, the use of nylon is authorized for towlines, mooring lines, and signal halyards.

One feature of nylon that can be a disadvantage in some applications is its elasticity. Under load, it will stretch up to 40 percent of its original length. This stretch is evidenced only in the standard three-strand nylon line, not in the double-braided or plaited lines. A degree of elasticity of this amount is not desirable in a line to be used as a boat fall or for a boom guy purchase.

Nylon rope of twisted construction is available in sizes up to 12 in. in circumference and of double-braided construction (Fig. A1.2 in sizes up to 12 in. in circumference. Double-braided line consists of an outer portion, or cover, of tightly braided fibers over a closely braided core. Approximately 50 percent of the strength is in the core. Size-for-size, double-braided line is about 1.2 times as strong as twisted nylon.

Nylon line in eight-strand plaited construction is available in sizes up to 12 in. in circumference. It is only slightly less strong than the double-braided line and stands up to hard usage and abrasion better. Plaited synthetic lines are becoming increasingly popular with merchant marine users.

Other Synthetics   Dacron has about 80 percent of the strength of nylon but will stretch only about 10 percent of its original length. Polyethelene and polypropylene are only half as strong as nylon, size for size, but they float in water—a feature that makes them desirable for use on ring buoys. Also, size for size, they are 25 percent lighter than nylon, making them very easy to handle.

A1.2 Construction of Fiber Rope   The steps in constructing twisted or plain laid fiber rope are about the same, regardless of the type of fiber used. The *fibers* are combed smooth; an emulsion of oils is added to soften, lubricate, and preserve them; and then they are spun into *yarns* or *threads*. Threads are twisted into *strands*, and the strands are twisted into *rope*. Ropes are twisted together to form *cables*. (See Fig. A1.2.) Threads are twisted to the right, and successive twists are taken in opposite directions. The direction in which the strands are twisted determines the lay of the rope. Most rope used aboard ship is three-strand, right-lay. If two lines are bent together, one being right-lay and one being left-lay, and put under strain, they would unlay each other and part because of their opposite twist.

(A) Double-braided
Nylon Rope.

(B) Rope in Coil.

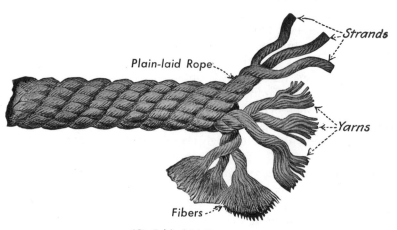

(C) Cable-laid Rope.

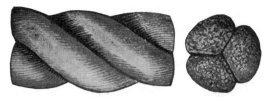

(D) Cross Section, Three-strand Rope.

Fig. A1.2   Fiber rope.

Large line is measured by circumference, but *small stuff* (i.e., line 1¾ in. in circumference and smaller) is identified by the number of threads. The largest small stuff is 24-thread. Large line (starting with 2 in.) is manufactured in ¼-in. gradations.

Braided Line Braided lines have certain advantages over twisted ropes. They will not kink or flex open to admit dirt or abrasives. The construction of some braids, however, makes it impossible to inspect the inner yarns for damage. The more common braided lines are hollow-braided, stuffer-braided, solid-braided and double-braided.

Hollow-braided lines usually consist of an even number of parallel, tape-like groups of small yarns braided into a hollow, tube-like cord. This type of construction in cotton formerly was used for signal halyards—a purpose now served largely by three-strand and double-braided nylon. Other uses are parachute shroud lines and shot lines for line-throwing guns.

Stuffer-braided lines are manufactured in a similar manner, except that the braid is formed around a highly twisted yarn core which rounds out and hardens the rope. This type of construction in cotton is used for sash cord (heaving lines).

Solid-braided lines are fashioned in various ways. One familiar construction is that used for lead lines, taffrail log lines, and the like. This braid is of large yarns, either single or plied, tightly braided to form a hard, relatively stiff rope that will not kink, snag, or swell in water.

Double-braided line is, essentially, two hollow-braided ropes, one inside the other. The core is made of large single yarns in a slack braid. The cover also is made of large single yarns but in a tight braid that compresses and holds the core. This line is manufactured only from synthetics, and about 50 percent of the strength is in the core. Double-braided line is used for mooring lines, towlines, signal halyards, dressing lines, and many other purposes.

Plaited Line Plaited line is made of eight strands, four right-twisted and four left-twisted. These strands are paired and worked like a four-strand braid (Fig. A1.3). Thus there are two pairs of right-laid strands and two pairs of left-laid strands formed into a rope that is more or less square. Plaited line has many uses including towlines, ship mooring lines, messengers and dressing lines.

A1.3 Care of Natural-Fiber Rope Unlike synthetic line, natural fiber line does not recover after being stretched. Therefore, no attempt should be made to put a maximum strain on a fiber line. This is especially true when loading a line that has seen continuous service with moderate strains, or on one that has been out close to its breaking point at sometime.

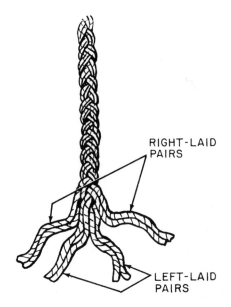

RIGHT-LAID
PAIRS

LEFT-LAID
PAIRS

Fig. A1.3 Plaited Line

The safety of a natural fiber line decreases comparatively rapidly with use, depending on the amount of strain with which it has been loaded. Manila line, for example, has a five year usable life span. After five years, it cannot be trusted for any use other than lashings, mats, and fenders. The age of the line can be determined from a paper tape inside the strands of natural fiber line, upon which is printed the name and location of the manufacturer and the date that it was made.

Rope tends to contract when wet and, unless allowed to do so freely, may be injuriously strained. It is for this reason that running gear is slacked in damp weather. On the other hand, advantage may be taken of this tendency by wetting the rope when lashings must be tautened.

Some practices that should be avoided or observed are as follows:

Never:

1. Stow wet or damp line in an unventilated compartment or cover it so that it cannot dry. Mildew will form and weaken the fibers.
2. Subject line to intense heat or unnecessarily allow it to lie in the hot sun. The lubricant will dry out, thus shortening the useful life of the line.
3. Subject a line to loads exceeding its safe working load. To do so

may not break the line, but individual fibers will break, reducing the strength.

4. Allow line to bear on sharp edges or run over rough surfaces. The line will be cut or worn, reducing the strength and useful life.
5. Scrub line. The lubricant will be washed away, and caustics in strong soap may harm the fibers.
6. Put a strain on a line with a kink in it.
7. Try to lubricate line. The lubricant you add may do more harm than good.
8. Let wear become localized in one spot.
9. Unbalance line by continued use on winch in same direction.

Always:

1. Dry line before stowing it.
2. Protect line from weather when possible.
3. Use chafing gear (canvas, short lengths of old fire hose, etc.) where line (or wire) runs over sharp edges or rough surfaces.
4. Slack off taut lines when it rains. Wet lines shrink, and if the line is taut, the resulting strain may be enough to break some of the fibers.
5. Coil right-laid rope to the right (clockwise).
6. Inspect a line before using it. Overworked or overstrained line will have a bristly surface. Mildew can be seen, and it has a peculiar, unpleasant odor. Untwist the line so that the inner parts of the strands can be seen. If they have a dull grayish look, the line is unsafe.
7. Give line the care it deserves. Someday your safety may depend on it.
8. Use chafing gear or occasionally "freshen the nip" to prevent or reduce localized wear.
9. Reverse turns on winches periodically to keep out the kinks.
10. Lay right-laid lines clockwise on reels or capstans and left-laid lines counterclockwise until they are broken in.
11. When opening a new coil of line, place the coil so that the end is at the bottom. Cut the stoppers and pull the end up through the tunnel. The line should uncoil counterclockwise.

A1.4 Care of Nylon and Other Synthetic Rope Most of the tips for the care of natural-fiber rope should be observed with nylon line. However, nylon is not subject to mildew, and it may and should be scrubbed if it becomes slippery because of oil or grease.

A coil of nylon rope, unlike other fiber rope, is not opened by pulling the end up through the eye of the coil. It should be unreeled in the same manner as wire rope.

Normally, plain-laid nylon rope is right-handed and should be loaded on capstans and reels in a clockwise direction. Cable-laid nylon rope is left-laid and should be loaded on capstans or reels in a counterclockwise direction.

Constantly coiling twisted nylon rope in the same direction tends to tighten the twist or unbalance the lay. To alleviate this condition, such rope should occasionally be coiled down against the lay. Braided nylon, having no lay, can be coiled down or coiled on a gypsy head in either direction without becoming unbalanced. One manufacturer recommends stowing braided line in a figure eight, but not as a rigid requirement.

When a synthetic line is put under load, it stretches. When the load is removed, the line recovers to its original length. However, complete recovery takes time. If a line has been highly loaded for a long period of time, the total recovery may take as much as a month. Fortunately, most of this recovery does take place in the first several minutes after the line is unloaded. This characteristic of synthetic line is called "memory." Because of "memory" there is one situation which should be avoided when working with synthetic line—SYNTHETIC LINE SHOULD NOT BE STOWED ON A POWERED STOWAGE DRUM/REEL. If a synthetic line has been under load and then is put on a powered stowage drum/reel where each wrap and each layer is tightly wound on the drum before the line has recovered its original length, then the line will continue to recover and shrink tighter and tighter on the drum. In several cases, this has caused steel drums to suddenly collapse and at the same time blow the flanges off.

With rope and cable-laid nylon, a stretch of one-third its length is normal under safe working loads. A stretch of 40 percent of its length is the critical point because it parts at a stretch of 50 percent. With double-braided nylon, the critical point is reached when the line is stretched 27 percent of its length. Double-braided nylon parts when the stretch is 30 percent. The elongation of nylon may at times be a disadvantage, but it can be halved by doubling the lines. Nylon can stand repeated stretching with no serious effects.

Sharp, cracking noises, caused by readjustment of the strands, are heard when applying a load to new cable-laid hawers. Wet hawsers under strain emit steamlike vapor. Nylon rope that has been under heavy strain may develop glazed areas where it has worked against bitt and chock surfaces. This condition may be caused by paint or the fusing of the fibers. In either case, the effect on the rope's strength is negligible.

Plain-laid nylon has a tendency to elongate around bitts when loaded.

To minimize this extension, take a round turn around the part of the bitts nearest the chock before making figure eights.

New cable-laid nylon hawers tend to be stiff and difficult to handle. To alleviate this condition, put the cables under tension for 20 min at 30-percent extension; for example, under tension, 100 ft of cable would measure 130 ft.

Nylon rope can hold a load even though a considerable amount of its yarn has been abraded. Where such a condition is excessive but localized, the chafed section may be cut away and the ends spliced together.

When nylon lines become iced-over in use, they should be thawed carefully at moderate temperatures and drained before stowing.

If a nylon line becomes slippery because of oil or grease, it should be scrubbed down. Spots may be removed by cleaning with light oils such as kerosene or diesel oil, or with liquid soap and water.

Because nylon rope, on parting, has stretched 50 percent of its length, it parts with a decided snapback. Keep your men and yourself out of the direct line of pull when heavy strains are applied.

A synthetic line parting under tension will snap back at a speed near that of sound, and reaction time to clear the area is nonexistent. Therefore, whenever possible, line handlers should be positioned clear of the danger area, approximately 90 degrees from the tension force, (Fig. A1.4).

Do not use a single part of plain-laid rope for hauling or hoisting any load that is free to rotate. If use of a single part of rope is essential, use a cable-laid hawser.

Do not stow nylon rope in strong sunlight. Cover it with a tarpaulin. In stowage, keep it away from heat and strong chemicals.

Employ only nylon rope stoppers for holding nylon hawsers under load.

Do not use wire or spring-lay rope in conjunction with nylon rope in the same chock or on bitts or bollards.

Extreme care should be exercised when easing out nylon line around bitts and cleats under heavy load. Since nylon's coefficient of friction is lower than that of manila and it may slip on easing out, keep an extra turn on the bitt or cleat.

When rigging nylon or other rope for heavy strains, do not attach fair-lead blocks or other equipment to padeyes or other fittings that have not been tested for the load. Untested padeyes have pulled away under heavy strain and injured and killed men in the vicinity.

Personnel who work with natural-fiber lines soon learn how to judge the tension in such lines by the sounds they produce. Unfortunately, although synthetic lines under heavy strain thin down considerably, they give no audible indication of stress, even when about to part. For this reason, a

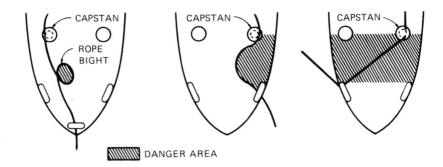

AREA WITHIN A BIGHT WHERE A PERSON SHOULD NOT STAND

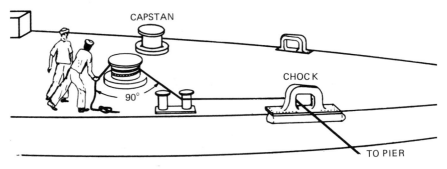

SHOWING LINE HANDLER AND SAFETY OBSERVER 90° FROM TENSION FORCE

Fig. A1.4 Safe work area.

tattletale cord should be attached to a synthetic line when it is subjected to a load which may exceed its Safe Working Load (SWL). A tattletale cord is a bight light small stuff such as 6 thread hung from two measured points on the working line. The line, when tensioned to its SWL, will stretch to a certain percentage of its length. When this point is reached, the tattletale becomes taut, warning that there is danger of exceeding the line's SWL. Figure A1.5 shows a tattletale cord on a three-strand nylon line.

If a line is loaded beyond its SWL, it may part. A line may repeatedly be brought to its SWL without impairing the line or reducing its useful life. From the standpoints of safety and economics, it makes sense to take precautions not to surpass the SWL of a line. Use tattletale cords and every other guide available to ensure that SWLs are not ignored. Lengths of tattletale, cords, distances between suspension points, and the percentage of stretch to critical points for various lines are shown in Table A1.1 (Remem-

A. UNDER NO TENSION

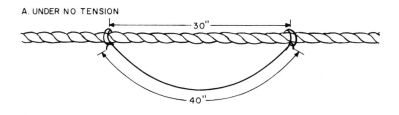

B. STRETCHED TO SAFE WORKING LOAD

Fig. A1.5 Tattletale cord on a twisted nylon line.

ber: The critical percentages listed do not show a correlation between the lengths of tattletale cords and the distances between suspension points.)

When nylon hawsers are employed on capstans for heavy towing or impact loading, take six turns on the capstan and two turns over-laying the last four turns to reduce the hazard of sudden surges.

The remarks concerning unreeling, storage, and cleaning of nylon rope apply to other synthetic fiber ropes as well. Other synthetics do not have nylon's coefficient of elasticity, however, and with them stretch should not exceed manufacturer's recommended limits. Like double-braided line, eight-strand plaited lines may be coiled down either to the left or right as desired. Although nylon is still used widely for anchor lines and mooring lines, it has been partly supplanted for halyards and sheets by the other synthetics. Special prestretched dacron and braided synthetic-fiber lines are popular among boatmen.

Table A1.1 Dimensions for Tattletale Cords

Type of Line	Length of Cord (Inches)	Distance (Inches)	Critical Stretch (Percent)
Nylon (Three Strand)	40	30	40
Nylon (Double Braided)	48	40	20
Nylon (Plaited)	40	30	40
Polyester (Three Strand)	40	34	20
Polypropylene (Three Strand)	36	30	20

A1.5 Wire Rope In order to understand this discussion on wire rope, the reader must first know the terms used.

Nominal breaking strength The nominal breaking strength is the value on which designs should be based.

Acceptance breaking strength The acceptance breaking strength is the minimum value on which compliance with the specification is determined.

Bright wires Bright wires are wires in ropes or strands that are uncoated.

Core The core is the foundation member (a twisted fibrous material, a wire strand, or an independent wire rope) around which the strands are laid.

Filler wires Filler wires are small-diameter auxiliary wires for supporting and positioning main wires. Filler wires are sometimes included in the actual wire count and identification of the rope construction.

Galvanized (or coated) wire ropes and strands Galvanized wire ropes and strands are wire ropes or strands made of zinc-coated (galvanized) wires.

Galvanized (zinc-coated) wires These wires are zinc-coated at finished size.

Lang lay In a lang-lay wire rope, the direction of lay of the wires in the strand and of the strand in the rope is the same. As a result, the rope gives the appearance that the wires are diagonal to the axis of the rope. The wires and the strands may run to the right—*right lang lay* (commonly called *lang lay*)—or to the left—*left lang lay* (on specific orders only).

Lay The word *lay* is used by the wire rope industry in two different ways:

1. The lay is the manner in which the wires in a strand or the strands in a wire rope lay (twisted).
2. The lay is the distance parallel to the longitudinal axis in which a wire makes a complete turn (spiral or helix) about the axis of the strand or a strand about the axis of the rope. It is also called the *lay length* or the *pitch*.

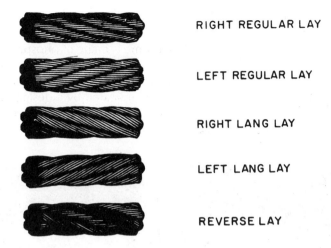

RIGHT REGULAR LAY

LEFT REGULAR LAY

RIGHT LANG LAY

LEFT LANG LAY

REVERSE LAY

Fig. A1.6   Lays of wire rope.

As shown in Fig. A1.6, wire rope is laid up in various ways:

Right regular lay: Wires in the strands are twisted to the left; strands in the rope are twisted to the right.

Left regular lay: Wires in the strands are twisted to the right; strands are twisted to the left.

Right lang lay: Both wires in the strands and strands in the rope are twisted to the right.

Left lang lay: Both wires in the strands and strands in the rope are twisted to the left.

Reverse lay: Wires of alternate strands are twisted to the right; those in the other strands are twisted to the left.

A1.6 Construction of Wire Rope   Wire rope is composed of three parts—wires, strands, and core. The basic unit is the *wire*. A predetermined number of wires of proper size are fabricated in a uniform geometric arrangement of definite pitch or lay to form a *strand* of required diameter. The required number of strands are then laid together symmetrically around a *core* to form the rope.

Cores are of three general types: fiber, wire strand, and independent wire rope. The core affords support to the strands wound about it. Fiber cores are adequate for most types of service, because they not only provide the necessary foundation but also add to the flexibility and elasticity of the rope. For service where high operating pressures are encountered or in cases where resistance to heat, additional strength, or minimum stretch is a prerequisite, either a strand core or an independent wire rope core is recommended.

Most wire rope is made of steel, but some is made of phosphor-bronze. Much of the steel rope is galvanized. Other variations in construction are in the number of wires in the strands and of the strands in the rope. (The number of wires and strands in a rope are indicated by a designation such as 6 × 19, that is, six strands of nineteen wires each.) Some of the more common types of ropes and their uses follow (see also Fig. A1.7).

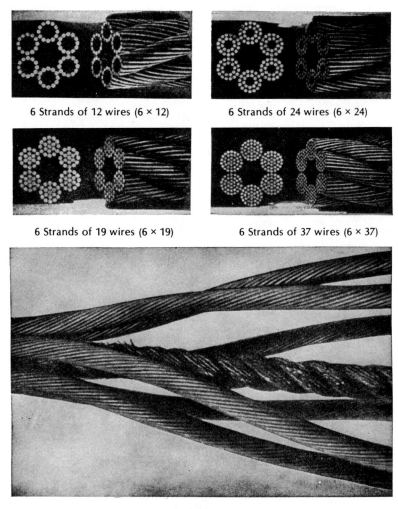

6 Strands of 12 wires (6 × 12)   6 Strands of 24 wires (6 × 24)

6 Strands of 19 wires (6 × 19)   6 Strands of 37 wires (6 × 37)

Wire Rope Unlaid, Showing Hemp Core

Fig. A1.7 Types of wire rope.

Galvanzied-Wire Rope   Galvanized-wire rope should be used if the rope is likely to corrode because of the presence of moisture, as for the standing rigging of a ship. Because the zinc coating is rapidly removed by wear, it should not, in general, be used for hoisting.

Uncoated-Wire Rope   Uncoated-wire rope should be used where it is protected from moisture, as in a building, and for more or less continuous hoisting. It may be used where it is exposed to moisture, as for derrick guys, if a protective coating is applied at regular intervals.

Phosphor-Bronze Wire Rope   Phosphor-bronze wire rope has lower strength than steel-wire rope; therefore its working loads should be lower. The sheaves should also be larger than those for steel rope. It is nonmagnetic and often used on small vessels.

Six-by-Seven   Only the galvanized type is specified. This construction is the stiffest of all the varieties. Not suitable for general hoisting, it is applicable mainly for permanent standing guys.

Six-by-Nineteen   When made of ungalvanized steel wire, this rope is of great strength and principally used for heavy hoisting, particularly on derricks and dredges. It is the stiffest and strongest construction of the types listed that are suitable for general hoisting purposes.

Six-by-Twenty-Four   This construction has almost the same flexibility as the 6 × 12 construction but is stronger. It is used primarily in the larger sizes, where the strength of a 6 × 12 rope of the same size will not be satisfactory, and where extreme flexibility is the major consideration.

Six-by-Thirty-Seven   When made of ungalvanized steel wire, this construction is very flexible, making it suitable for cranes and similar machinery where sheaves are of necessity smaller than desirable. It may be used for heavy hoisting, especially when conditions are unusually severe.

Six-by-Twelve   This construction for the fiber core of each strand as well as for the fiber core of the rope itself is more flexible than the 6 × 37 or 6 × 19 but not nearly as strong.

Spring-Lay   A special type of wire rope that is a combination of wire and fiber, spring-lay is designated as 6 × 3 × 19 because it is composed of six main strands laid around a fiber core. Each main strand consists of three performed wire strands and three fiber strands laid alternately around a fiber center. The function of the fiber parts is to provide a cushion for the wire strands, resulting in a rope having great flexibility and elasticity. Spring-lay is normally used for mooring lines and, on tugboats, for alongside towing and berthing vessels. Because it is a combination of wire and fiber, rules for the care of both wire and fiber rope apply when dealing with spring-lay. Uncoil it in the same manner as wire rope. It is also spliced the same as wire rope.

A1.7 Care of Wire Rope   Wire rope needs better care than hemp or manila and far better care than it usually receives on shipboard. It should be kept on a reel when not in use. A single kink in the finest wire rope practically ruins it at once. In receiving a line and transferring it from one reel to another, care should be taken to unreel it, instead of slipping off the successive bights over the end of the reel. Figure A1.8 and A1.9 illustrate the right way and the wrong way of dealing with wire rope under various conditions.

A wire hawser should be gone over thoroughly every month or two with a standard lubricant preservative. It is important that the lubricant, whatever its composition, be thin enough to penetrate into the interstices of the rope and yet have consistency enough to adhere to the wire for a reasonable length of time, after which it should be renewed. Care must be taken to ensure covering the rope all around. A hawser used for towing should be relubricated after use while it is being reeled up.

Wherever wire rope is to be worked over a sheave, the diameter of the sheave and the speed of running become very important factors. The larger the sheave and the lower the speed, the better. All manufacturers of wire rope prescribe a minimum diameter for sheaves, and their guaranteed breaking strains and estimated safe-working loads are for these minimum diameters and for moderate speed. High speed increases the wear upon the rope, not only by the friction on the sheaves but still more by the friction of the wires upon each other.

The diameter of the sheave over which the rope is worked should never be less than 20 times that of the rope itself; and the less flexible the rope, the larger should be the sheave.

It is important that the score of the sheave be of such size as to carry the rope without excessive play and, above all, without friction against the sides of the score. Metal sheaves are not required to be lined with wood or leather.

As the wear of the rope over a sheave increases more rapidly with the speed than with the load, it is better, when an increased output is demanded, to increase the load rather than the speed.

The turns of the rope should never be allowed to overlap on the drum of the winch.

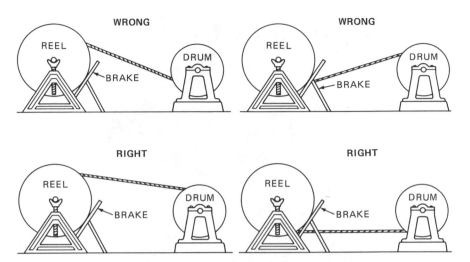

NEVER LOOP THE ROPE OFF THE REEL FROM THE SIDE

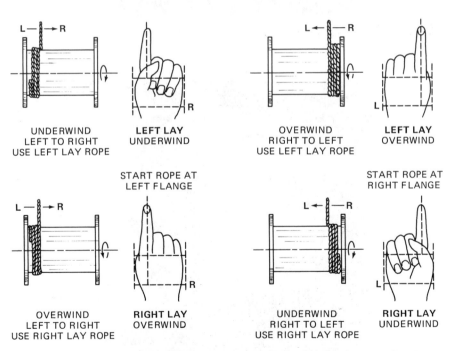

Fig. A1.8 By holding the right or left hand with index finger extended, palm up or plam down, the proper procedure for applying left- and right-lay rope on a smooth drum can be easily determined.

Fig. A1.9(A) Incorrect way to remove wire rope from reel. (*Courtesy of Bethlehem Steel Corporation*)

Fig. A1.9(B) Correct way to uncoil wire rope. (*Courtesy of Bethlehem Steel Corporation*)

Fig. A1.9(C)   Correct way to remove wire rope form reel. (*Courtesy of Bethlehem Steel Corp.*)

Fig. A1.9(D)   Another correct method of removing wire rope from a reel.

Fig. A1.9(E) Incorrect way to uncoil wire rope. (*Courtesy of Bethlehem Steel Corporation*)

By far the most unfavorable conditions to which wire rope can be subjected are those when it runs over sheaves that give it a reverse bend like the letter S. It passes over one sheave with a bend to the right and immediately swings around another with a bend to the left.

Wire role should be condemned when the outside wires are worn down to one-half their original diameter, or when it is apparent from broken wires or other abnormal indications that it has been subjected to excessive strain or to a sharp bend resulting in a pronounced kink. Wire rope should be replaced whenever the total number of fishhooks (broken wires) in one lay exceeds 4 percent of the total number of wires in the rope. For example, a 6 × 19 wire rope contains 114 individual wires; if five broken wires are encountered in one lay of the rope, replace it. (One lay is the length of rope needed for one strand to complete one spiral around the rope.) Figure A1.10 shows the results of improper care.

Tables A1.2 through A1.6 presents significant characteristics and specifications for various types of rope and wire.

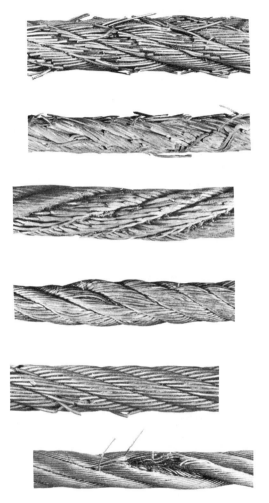

(A) Sheaves too small. This rope was forced to travel continuously over sheaves whose diameters were too small. This caused severe bending fatigue. Result—broken wires, ruined rope.

(B) Drum abrasion and abuse caused this. The rope was scuffed over and over against previous wraps on a flat-faced drum. Its life ended long before it should have.

(C) Kinking caused this. This dog-leg, or kink, was finally straightened out of this rope—but notice the uneven wear at the point where the kink had been. Beware of dog-legs! They're expensive.

(D) Uneven drum winding is a frequent rope-wrecker. This rope was wound unevenly time after time onto a drum. Result—it is crushed and flattened. The service cost of this rope was unnecessarily high. WATCH how the rope winds!

(E) Acids did this. This rope was attacked by high sulfur content in the water and crude oil through which the rope operated. A heavily internally lubricated rope will resist the action for a time.

(F) Foul play "killed" this rope. While in operation, this rope met with an accident that mashed and cut many of its wires. Result— a ruined rope, and many a rope dollar wasted that could have been saved.

Fig. A1.10 Results of improper care of rope. (*Courtesy of Le Tourneau-Westinghouse Co-Operator*)

WALL ROPE WORKS
NEW BEDFORD CORDAGE CO
BEVERLY, NEW JERSEY 08010

Table A1.2　Natural and Synthetic

DESCRIPTION	NATURAL FIBERS				NYLON FILAMENT TYPE		POLYESTER	
	MANILA		SISAL		Made from Hexamethalene diamine and adipic acid, which are made from coke, air and water, from petroleum products and or from Furfural, an agricultural by-product. This compound is extruded through fine orifices to form fine filaments (6 denier) twisted into rope. Figures below apply to Nylon 6-6 Nylon-6 (Golden Nyline) behaves very similarly, but is more sensitive to heat and exhibits more elongation		Polyester fiber is made from Ethylene Glycol, used in large quantities as an anti-freeze, and terephthalic acid, a chemical made from petroleum. This is extruded into 5.8 denier filaments, twisted into yarn plied and twisted into rope.	
	3' to 6' long leaf fibers from the Abaca plant, a close relative of the Banana, spun into yarns and twisted into rope.		2' to 4' long leaf fibers from the Agave Sisalana plant which resembles the century plant, spun into yarn and twisted into rope.					
ROPE DIAMETER	1''	2''	1''	2''	1''	2''	1''	2''
STRENGTH CHARACTERISTICS								
Tensile Strength Dry (For comparisons of other sizes, see tensile strength tables for each type of rope)	9,000 lbs.	31,000 lbs.	7,200 lbs.	24,800 lbs.	25,000 lbs.	92,000 lbs.	22,000 lbs.	80,000 lbs.
Wet Strength Compared to Dry Strength	Up to 120%	Up to 120%	Up to 120%	Up to 120%	90 – 95%	90 – 95%	100%	100%
Strength per unit of Weight, or "Breaking Length". (Tensile strength lbs. per ft.)	33,000	29,000	26,700	23,000	96,000	97,000	72,000	64,000
Ability to absorb shock loads, expressed as foot-pounds of energy absorbed per pound of rope.　DRY	1,800	1,800	1,400	1,400	15,660	15,660	7,300	7,300
WET	1,120	1,120	950	950	15,000	15,000	7,300	7,300
Repeat Loading Characteristics	POOR	POOR	POOR	POOR	GOOD	GOOD	EXCELLENT	EXCELLENT
Individual Filament or Fiber Strength (Grams per Denier)	5.0 – 7.0	5.0 – 7.0	4.0 – 5.0	4.0 – 5.0	8.0 – 9.0	8.0 – 9.0	7.5 – 9.0	7.5 – 9.0
WEIGHT & DENSITY CHARACTERISTICS								
Pounds per 100 Ft.	27.0	108.0	27.0	108.0	26.0	95.0	30.5	118.0
Specific Gravity of Fiber	1.5 – 1.6	1.5 – 1.6	1.25	1.25	1.14	1.14	1.38	1.38
Ability to Float	No	No	No	No	No	No	No	No
ELASTICITY – STRETCH								
Permanent Elongation at Working Loads (20% of Breaking Strength)	4.8%	4.8%	4.9%	4.9%	8.0%	8.0%	6.2%	6.2%
Working Elasticity (Temporary stretch under load) at Working Loads (20% of Breaking Strength)	5.0%	5.0%	5.0%	5.0%	16.0%	16.0%	5.9%	5.9%
Elongation at 100% Load (at break) for broken-in ropes	13%	13%	13%	13%	35%	35%	20%	20%
Individual Filament or Fiber Elongation	2 – 3%	2 – 3%	2 – 3%	2 – 3%	16 – 18%	16 – 18%	10 – 12%	---
SURFACE CHARACTERISTICS								
Coefficient of friction, new ropes on steel. Rendering qualities – Ability to ease out smoothly under load over bitts	Excellent		Excellent		Poor		Good.	
Hand (Feeling of rope to the touch)	Some harshness due to hairs. After use considerable harshness due to broken fiber ends.		Fairly harsh due to nature of fiber and hairs. After use quite harsh due to broken fiber ends.		Smooth. After use becomes fuzzy with a softer feel.		Smooth & Hard. Not slippery. After use becomes fuzzy with a softer feel.	
WATER ABSORBED INTO FIBER (Some water will be held between fibers of all ropes)	Up to 100% of weight of rope		Up to 100% of weight of rope		Up to 9%		Less than 1%	
RESISTANCE TO ROT, MILDEW & ATTACK BY MARINE ORGANISMS (Some marine organisms will attach themselves to any submerged object, including synthetic ropes)	Poor		Very Poor		100% Resistant		100% Resistant	
DETERIORATION								
Due to aging (stored ropes, ideal conditions)	About 1% per year		About 1% per year		Zero		Zero	
Due to exposure to sunlight	Some slight		Some slight		Some slight		Almost none	
RESISTANCE TO CHEMICALS								
To Acids	Very poor		Very poor		Fair–except to concentrated sulphuric & hydrochloric acids.		Very good to excellent	
To Alkalis	Very poor		Very poor		Excellent		Very good–except to concentrated Sodium Hydroxide at high temperatures	
To Solvents	Good		Good		Good		Very good to excellent	
WEAR								
Resistance to surface abrasion	Good		Fair		Very Good		Excellent	
Resistance to internal wear from flexing	Good		Very Good		Excellent		Very good to excellent	
Resistance to cutting (toughness)	Good		Poor		Excellent		Very good to excellent	
HIGH & LOW TEMPERATURE PROPERTIES								
Melting Point	Loses strength rapidly over 180° F.		Loses strength rapidly over 180° F.		482° F. Progressive strength loss above 300° F.		500° F. Progressive strength loss above 300° F.	
Low temperature properties	No change		No change		No change		No change	
Flammability	Burns like wood		Burns like wood		Burns with difficulty		Burns with difficulty	

Fiber Rope Characteristics

WDS–113 Revised – Nov. 77
Reprinted 10/80 2M

POLYETHYLENE
...de from polymers and copolymers of ethylene, a natural ...s or petroleum derivative. ...is extruded to 600 denier (12 mil) filaments, twisted in...yarn, plied and twisted ...o rope.

POLYPROPYLENE
MONOFILAMENT & PLURAL FILAMENT & PARAPRO

Made from a derivative of propane, a product of natural gas or petroleum. Monofilament is extruded to filaments of 600 denier (12 mil). Plural filament is extruded to filaments of 280 denier (8 mil). These are twisted into yarn, plied and twisted into rope.

BLENDS

POLY-PLUS — 100% Polypropylene core with single cover of blended polyester (52%) and polyethylene (48%) both by weight, plied and twisted into rope.

POLYCRON — 100% Polyethylene core with double cover of Polypropylene yarns veneered with Dacron, plied and twisted into rope 1.5 16'' dia. and larger are identified by a black Polyethylene core.

LST
LST is our trade name for ropes having a cover of polyester and a core of blown Monofilament Polypropylene encased within a sleeve wrap. (Available in 1¼'' dia. and larger).

LST-WB
Contains a double cover of Polyethylene Yarns veneered with polyester and a core of blown monofilament Polypropylene yarns enclosed within a sleeve wrap. (Available in 1¼'' dia. and larger).

	POLYETHYLENE		POLYPROPYLENE		POLY-PLUS		POLYCRON		LST	LST-WB
	1''	2''	1''	2''	1''	2''	1''	2''	2''	2''
	2,600 lbs.	47,700 lbs.	14,000 lbs.	52,000 lbs.	15,000 lbs.	56,500 lbs.	14,000 lbs.	60,000 lbs.	73,000 lbs.	65,000 lbs.
	100%	100%	102–105%	102–105%	100%	100%	100%	100%	100%	100%
	66,000	75,500	77,800	75,500	69,800	68,000	53,000	63,000	91,000	74,000
	4,600 / 4,600	4,600 / 4,600	9,300 / 9,300	9,300 / 9,300	8,600 / 8,600	8,600 / 8,600	8,300 / 8,300	8,300 / 8,300	9,000 / 9,000	8,000 / 8,000
	FAIR	FAIR	EXCELLENT	EXCELLENT	VERY GOOD	VERY GOOD	GOOD	GOOD	GOOD	GOOD
	5.5 – 7.0	5.5 – 7.0	6.0 – 7.5	6.0 – 7.5	---	---	---	---	5.0 – 9.0	5.0 – 9.0
	18.5	72.5	18.0	69.0	21.5 (Varies with Rope Size)	83.0 (Varies with Rope Size)	26.5 (Varies with Rope Size)	95.0 (Varies with Rope Size)	80.0 (Varies with Rope Size)	83.6 (Varies with Rope Size)
	.95	.95	.91	.91	Varies with Rope Size	Varies with Rope Size				
	Yes	Yes	Yes	Yes			No	No	Yes	Yes
	5.8%	5.8%	3.8%	3.8%	5.9%	5.9%	4.7%	4.7%	7.0%	6.5%
	5.9%	5.9%	8.9%	8.9%	7.1%	7.1%	5.1%	5.1%	3 – 4%	4.5%
	22%	22%	24% (MULTI)	24% (MONO)	27%	27%	21%	21%	20%	20%
	11 – 14%	11 – 14%	16 – 20%	14 – 18%	---	---	---	---	---	---
	...ood but requires extra ...raps.		Poor		Good		Good		Good.	Good.
	...mooth and very slippery. ...fter use becomes slightly ...arsh due to broken fiber ...nds.		Smooth but not slippery. After use becomes harsh due to broken fiber ends.		Smooth & Hard. After use bristles and fuzz appear but little harshness.		Smooth & Hard. Not slippery. After use becomes fuzzy but not harsh.		Smooth & Hard. Not slippery. After use becomes fuzzy with a softer feel.	Smooth & Hard. Not slippery. After use becomes fuzzy but not harsh.
	Zero		Zero		Almost Zero		Almost Zero		Less than 1%	Less than 1%
	100% Resistant		100% Resistant		100% Resistant		100% Resistant		100% Resistant	100% Resistant
	Zero		Zero		Zero		Zero		Zero	Zero
	Some black resists best		Some black resists best		Very slight		Almost none		Almost none	Almost none
	...xcellent except to conc. ...ulphuric		Excellent		Good to excellent		Excellent except to conc. nitric		Good	Very good to excellent
	...ood		Good		Excellent		Excellent		Very good to excellent	Very good – except to concentrated Sodium Hydroxide at high temperatures
	...ood		Good		Good to excellent		Good to excellent		Very good to excellent	Very good to excellent
	...ood		Good		Very Good		Very Good		Very Good	Very Good
	...ery Good		Very Good		Very Good		Very Good		Very Good	Very Good
	...ood		Good		Very Good		Very Good		Very Good	Very Good
	...0° F. Softens above ...0° F. ...comes brittle below –150°F ...rns with difficulty		330° F. Softens above 300° F. No change Burns with difficulty		Progressive strength loss above 250° F. Some brittleness below –150° F. Burns with difficulty		Progressive strength loss above 250° F. Some brittleness below –150° F. Burns with difficulty.		Progressive strength loss above 250° F. No change Burns with difficulty	Progressive strength loss above 250° F. Some brittleness below –150° F. Burns with difficulty.

Table A1.3   Ropes of Twisted Construction

Size Circumference (inches)	Minimum Breaking Strength (pounds)—Fiber Type				
	Natural		Synthetic		
	Sisal	Manila	Poly-propylene	Polyester	Nylon
¾	480	600	1,100	1,500	1,500
1	800	1,000	1,700	2,500	2,500
1⅛	1,080	1,350	2,150	—	3,000
1¼	1,400	1,750	2,500	—	4,500
1½	2,120	2,650	3,700	5,000	5,500
1¾	2,760	3,450	4,800	—	7,000
2	3,520	4,400	6,000	8,000	8,400
2¼	4,320	5,400	7,000	—	11,500
2½	5,200	6,500	9,000	13,000	14,000
2¾	6,160	7,700	11,000	—	16,000
3	7,200	9,000	13,000	18,500	22,000
3½	9,600	12,000	16,500	25,000	28,500
3¾	10,800	13,500	19,500	—	33,000
4	12,000	15,000	21,500	31,000	37,500
4½	14,800	18,500	26,000	—	46,000
5	18,000	22,500	32,000	48,000	57,000
5½	21,200	26,500	38,000	—	68,000
6	24,800	31,000	44,000	68,000	81,000
6½	—	—	50,000	—	90,000
7	32,800	41,000	60,000	88,000	110,000
8	41,600	52,000	75,000	110,000	137,000
9	51,200	64,000	94,000	140,000	170,000
10	61,600	77,000	115,000	165,000	200,000
11	72,800	91,000	—	—	240,000
12	84,000	105,000	—	—	280,000

Table A1.4 Ropes of Braided Construction

Size Circumference (inches)	Minimum Breaking Strength (pounds)			
	Double-Braid Nylon	Poly-propylene	Plaited Polyester	Nylon
¾	1,650	—	—	—
1	2,750	—	—	—
1⅛	3,300	—	—	—
1¼	5,000	—	—	—
1½	6,650	—	—	—
1¾	8,300	—	—	—
2	11,000	—	—	—
2¼	15,000	—	—	—
2½	17,500	—	—	—
2¾	20,800	—	—	—
3	25,000	14,000	22,300	27,000
3½	35,000	16,800	27,800	33,500
3¾	40,000	—	—	—
4	45,000	23,000	37,000	46,500
4½	60,000	28,500	47,200	56,500
5	70,000	34,000	55,000	70,000
5½	90,000	40,000	63,000	82,800
6	100,000	48,000	80,500	98,000
6½	120,000	—	—	—
7	—	61,000	100,000	131,000
8	—	81,500	133,000	170,000
9	—	105,000	168,000	212,000
10	—	118,000	195,000	245,000

Table A1.5 Comparison of Breaking Strengths of Various General-Purpose Wire Ropes (Uncoated)

Rope Type	Rope Size (inches) Breaking Strength (pounds)							
	1/4	3/8	1/2	5/8	3/4	1	1 1/4	1 1/2
6 × 7, IPS/FC	5290	11,720	20,600	31,800	45,400	79,400	122,000	172,000
6 × 19, IPS/FC	5480	12,200	21,400	33,400	47,600	83,600	129,200	184,000
6 × 19, IPS/WSC or IWRC	—	13,120	23,000	35,800	51,200	89,800	138,800	197,800
6 × 19, CRS/IWRC or IWRC	—	15,100	26,000	41,200	58,800	103,400	159,800	228,000
6 × 19, CRS/IWRC	—	—	22,800	35,000	49,600	85,400	129,400	180,500
6 × 37, IPS/FC	5180	11,540	20,400	31,600	45,200	79,600	123,000	175,800
6 × 37 and 6 × 61 IPS/WSC[b] or IWRC[b]	5560	12,400	22,000	34,000	48,600	85,600	132,200	189,000
6 × 37, CRS/IWRC	—	—	20,400	31,300	44,400	77,300	118,300	166,000
8 × 19, IPS/FC	4700	10,480	18,460	28,600	41,000	72,000	111,400	158,800
6 × 37 and 6 × 61, EIPS/WSC or IWRC	6400	14,280	25,200	39,200	55,800	98,200	152,200	216,000
6 × 91, EIPS/IWRC	—	—	—	—	—	—	—	—

Table A1.5 Comparison of Breaking Strengths of various General-Purpose Wire Ropes (Uncoated) (Cont'd)

Rope Type	Rope Size (inches) Breaking Strength (pounds)						
	1¾	2	2¼	2½	2¾	3	3½
6 × 7, IPS/FC	—	—	—	—	—	—	—
6 ×19, IPS/FC	248,000	320,000	400,000	488,000	584,000	—	—
6 × 19, IPS/WSC or IWRC	266,000	344,000	430,000	524,000	628,000	—	—
6 × 19, EIPS/WSC or IWRC	306,000	396,000	494,000	604,000	722,000	—	—
6 × 19, CRS/IWRC	—	—	—	—	—	—	—
6 × 37, IPS/FC	238,000	308,000	386,000	472,000	568,000	670,000	898,000
6 × 37 and 6 × 61, IPS/WSCᵇ or IWRCᵇ	256,000	330,000	414,000	508,000	610,000	720,000	966,000
6 × 37, CRS/IWRC	—	—	—	—	—	—	—
8 × 19, IPS/FC	—	—	—	—	—	—	—
6 × 37 and 6 × 61, EIPS/WSC or IWRC	292,000	380,000	478,000	584,000	700,000	828,000	1,110,000
6 × 91, EIPS/IWRC	—	—	—	554,000	666,000	786,000	1,054,000

ᵃ Subtract 10 percent for zinc-coated (galvanized) wire rope.
ᵇ 6 × 61 rope available only in sizes 2 inches and above and only in regular lay.

LEGEND: IPS—Improved Plow Steel.
E—Extra, as EIPS.
CRS—Corrosion-resistant Steel.

FC—Fiber Core.
WSC—Wire Strand Core.
IWRC—Independent Wire Rope Core.

Table A1.6 Breaking Strengths of Various Marine Wire Ropes

Rope Type	Rope Size (inches) Breaking Strength (pounds)											
	¼	⅜	½	⅝	¾	1	1¼	1½	1¾	2	2¼
Marine											
6 × 6, IPS/FC[a]	—	9,960	17,520	27,000	38,600	67,600	—	—	—	—	—
6 × 12, GIPS/FC	3,020	6,720	11,820	18,320	26,200	46,000	71,200	101,400	136,600	176,400	—
6 × 12, PhB/FC	1,470	3,220	5,640	8,740	12,240	—	—	—	—	—	—
6 × 24, GIPS/FC	—	9,540	16,800	26,000	37,200	65,600	101,400	144,600	195,000	252,000	—
Spring Lay											
6 × 3 × 7, G	—	—	8,940	13,900	19,920	—	—	—	—	—	—
6 × 3 × 19, G	—	—	—	—	—	35,000	54,400	77,800	105,400	137,000	212,000

[a] Subtract 10 percent for zinc-coated (galvanized) wire rope.

LEGEND: IPS—Improved Plow Steel. PhB—Phosphor Bronze.
G—Galvanized. FC—Fiber Core.

Appendix 2

Knotting and Splicing

A2.1 Knots, Bends, and Hitches Except among seamen, the term *knot* is ordinarily used as an all-inclusive term covering the more specific meaning that they reserve for it plus bends and hitches. To be more specific, *knots* are used to form eyes or to secure a line around a cord or object. *Bends* are used to secure lines together. *Hitches* secure lines to, or bend a line around, objects such as a ring, spar, or stanchion. In many cases, however, the functions of knots, bends, and hitches overlap; for example, the versatile bowline can be used for all three purposes.

A2.2 Knots Figure A2.1 shows the more common and useful knots, which may be described as follows:

Overhand Knot The overhand knot (A) is formed by passing the end of the line over the standing part and through the eye. This knot is seldom used alone but rather as the first move in tying a few other knots, such as the square knot.

Square Knot The square or reef knot (B) has a multitude of uses, chiefly in lashing situations where the line is passed around an object, heaved taut, and secured.

Bowline The bowline (C) also is a knot with many uses. It is employed whenever a loop is needed, such as in making a temporary eye in a mooring line.

Running Bowline The running bowline (D) can be used when a running eye is needed. It is made by tying a bowline around the standing part.

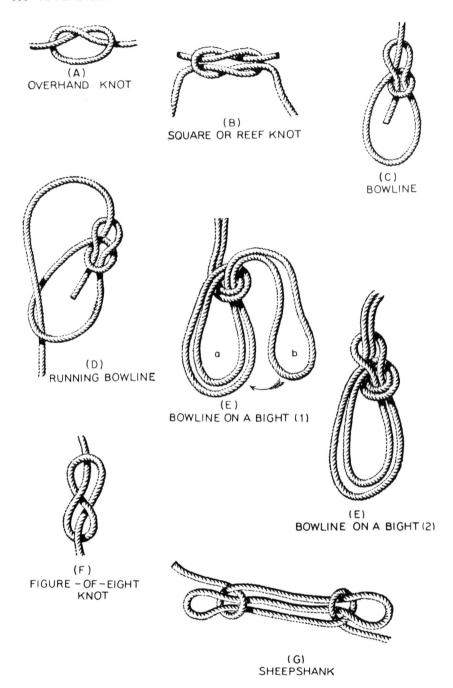

Fig. A2.1   A few of the more common knots.

Bowline on a Bight   The bowline on a bight (E) is used when greater strength than that given by a single bowline is necessary or when the end of the line is unavailable. This knot is tied with the line doubled. Form an eye as when making the single bowline; then pass the bight through the eye and around the two loops thus formed.

Figure-of-Eight Knot   The figure-of-eight knot (F) is used to prevent a line rove through a block from unreeving. It can also be used temporarily to keep an unwhipped line from unlaying.

Sheepshank   The sheepshank (G) is used to shorten a rope or to compensate for a weak spot in a line. The weakened spot should be in the center of the three parallel parts.

French Bowline   The French bowline (Fig. A2.2) may be employed to send a man over the side to work when he may have to use both hands, or it can be employed to hoist an unconscious man. The man sits in one eye, and the other goes around his body. The weight of his body in the one eye pulls the other eye taut and keeps the man from slipping out of the knot. The French bowline is tied in the same way as the ordinary bowline

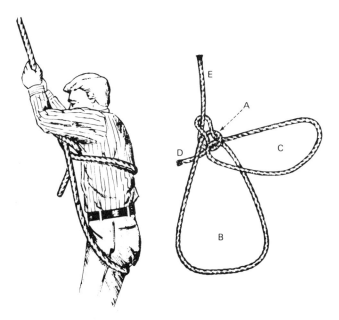

Fig. A2.2   The French bowline.

except that the end is run through the eye the second time before passing it around the standing part and back through the eye.

A2.3 Bends Bends are used to join two lines together. Various useful types are shown in Fig. A2.3.

Becket or Sheet Bend The becket or sheet bend is made by passing the end of one line through the eye or bight of the other, around the eye, and under itself. The single-becket bend (A) is used with lines of the same, or nearly same, size; the double-becket bend (B) is used with lines of different sizes.

Double Carrick Bend The double carrick bend (C) may be used to join two lines, if the ends are seized to the standing parts after tying the knot. This knot has more applications in fancy work, however. Note that the ends should come out at opposite corners of the knot.

Two Bowlines Using two bowlines (D) is a convenient way of bending two hawsers together, but they are somewhat bulky. Moreover, under great strain, they tend to part where the lines join.

Reeving-Line Bend The reeving-line bend (E) connects two hawsers in such a way that they will reeve through an opening, offering as little obstruction as possible. It is made by taking a half hitch with each end around the other hawser and seizing the ends to the standing parts.

Fisherman's Bend There are two different knots called fisherman's bend. One (F) is a variation of the reeving-line bend, but it should not be used on mooring hawsers. It may jam in a chock. It is used on fishlines and other lines that must pass through relatively small openings. The ends need not be whipped to the standing parts. The second fisherman's bend (G) is used for securing a line to a buoy or a hawser to the ring or jew's harp of an anchor. The end should be seized to the standing part.

A2.4 Hitches Hitches are used to bend a line to a ring or to, or around, a spar or stanchion. Various types of hitches are shown in Fig. A2.4.

Timber Hitch The timber hitch (A) may be used to haul an object, such as a spar, that has a fairly rough surface. It cannot be used on metal pipes and rods. To tie, the end is passed around the object, around the standing part, and then several times around itself.

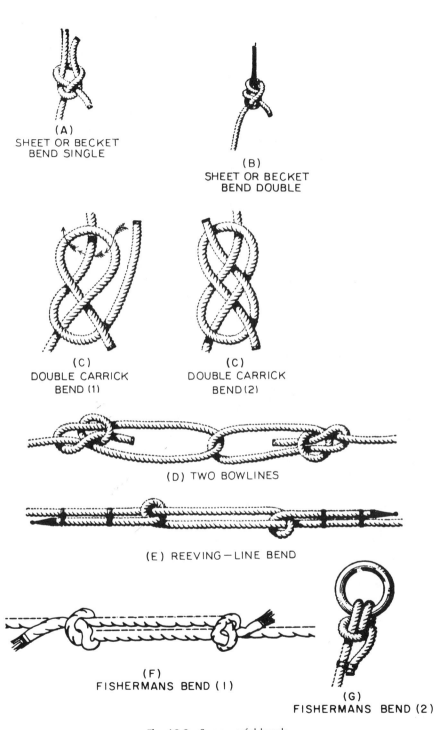

(A)
SHEET OR BECKET
BEND SINGLE

(B)
SHEET OR BECKET
BEND DOUBLE

(C)
DOUBLE CARRICK
BEND (1)

(C)
DOUBLE CARRICK
BEND (2)

(D) TWO BOWLINES

(E) REEVING—LINE BEND

(F)
FISHERMANS BEND (I)

(G)
FISHERMANS BEND (2)

Fig. A2.3 Some useful bends.

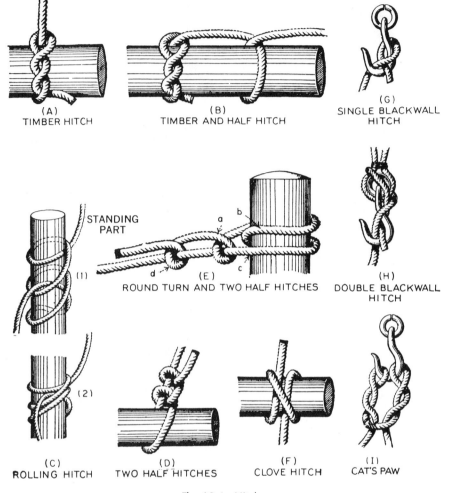

Fig. A2.4 Hitches.

Timber and Half Hitch Adding a half hitch to the timber hitch (B) gives better control, and the combination is less likely to slip than the timber hitch alone. Unless you can slip the half hitch over the end of the object, tie it before making the timber hitch.

Rolling Hitch The rolling hitch (C), sometimes called the *taut-line hitch,* is used when the line is to be bent to a round object or to another taut line. It is the basic hitch in one method of passing a stopper (See Fig.

A2.6). To tie, take a turn around the object and pull tight. Take a second turn; this turn must cross the first. Pull taut and add a half hitch.

Two Half Hitches Two half hitches (D) can be used to bend a line to a ring, spar, or stanchion. When tying, pass the end around the standing part twice—both times in the same direction.

Round Turn and Two Half Hitches To ensure that the line will not slip along a spar or stanchion when the angle of pull is acute, take a round turn before tying the two half hitches (E).

Clove Hitch The clove hitch (F)—one of the most useful hitches—is probably employed more often than any other knot to secure the end of a line. It will hold as long as there is a strain on the line, but once the strain is removed, the hitch should be checked and tightened to prevent the end from pulling out when the strain is reapplied. To make the hitch more secure after tying it, add a half hitch around the standing part.

Blackwall Hitch The blackwall hitch (G) is used to bend a strap to a hook. To tie, make a loop with the end under the standing part. Slip the loop up over the hook and pull it tight around the back of the hook. The double blackwall hitch (H) is made in the same manner; just lay up a second loop before slipping the line up over the hook. Tighten the double blackwall hitch as shown.

Cat's Paw The cat's paw (I) is used to shorten a line. Take two bights, twist them in opposite directions as many times as necessary, and slip them over the hook.

A2.5 Securing the End of a Rope Figure A2.5 shows several knots worked in the end of a rope by unlaying the rope and using the strands. Knots of this kind may be used to keep a rope from unlaying or for ornamental purposes. Before unlaying, place a temporary whipping below the point of the knot.

Wall Knot Form a bight with the frist strand (A), and pass the second strand around it. Pass the third strand around the end of the second and through the bight of the first. Pull taut.

Wall and Crown After tying the wall knot, top off with a crown (B). Lay strand 1 across the wall knot and strand 2 across 1. Number 3 goes over number 2 and under number 1.

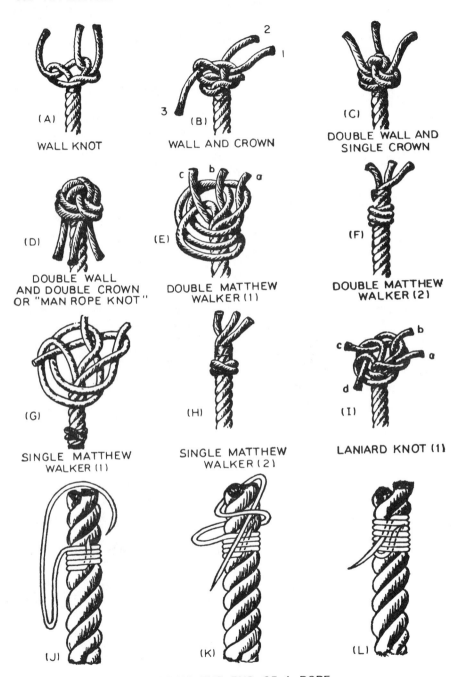

(A) WALL KNOT

(B) WALL AND CROWN

(C) DOUBLE WALL AND SINGLE CROWN

(D) DOUBLE WALL AND DOUBLE CROWN OR "MAN ROPE KNOT"

(E) DOUBLE MATTHEW WALKER (1)

(F) DOUBLE MATTHEW WALKER (2)

(G) SINGLE MATTHEW WALKER (1)

(H) SINGLE MATTHEW WALKER (2)

(I) LANIARD KNOT (1)

(J) (K) (L) WHIPPING THE END OF A ROPE

Fig. A2.5 Securing the end of a rope.

Double Wall and Single Crown   Tie a single wall and crown, leaving some slack in it. Pass each strand through the wall knot again, following the part nearest (C).

Double Wall and Double Crown   Double the parts of the knot forming the crown as well (D). This knot also is called the *man-rope knot.*

Double Matthew Walker   Pass strand "a" around the standing part and through itself, thus forming a knot; pass strand "b" around the standing part and through itself and the knot in strand "a"; pass strand "c" around the standing part and through itself and the knots in strands "a" and "c." When (E) is pulled taut, the result is (F).

Single Matthew Walker   The single Matthew Walker (G and H) is a cross between the wall knot and double Matthew Walker. Each strand goes through itself and one eye formed by another strand.

Laniard Knot   The laniard knot (I) is a single Matthew Walker tied in a four-strand line.

Whipping   A whipping prevents a rope from unlaying. To make a temporary whipping, lay a length of stout cord along the line and take several turns around it and the line (J). Lay the other end of the cord along the line (K), and wrap the cord around it and the line. Pull taut (L). The whipping should be about as long as the diameter of the rope.

Sailmaker's Whipping   The sailmaker's whipping is made with a sail needle and a length of twine. Push the needle through the line where the inboard end of the whipping will be. Pull all but a short length of the twine through the line. Wrap the twine around its end and the line, as for the temporary whipping. Then pass the needle through a strand close to the end of the turns. Haul taut. Run the needle through the next strand—but at the other end of the whipping. Haul taut. Run the needle through the last strand, again at the opposite end of the whipping. Haul taut, and secure the whipping by passing the needle through the rope a couple of times.

A2.6   Passing a Stopper   A *stopper* is used to hold a line under tension while the hauling part is being transferred from the gypsy head or capstan to the bitts or cleat where the line is to be belayed. There are several ways of passing a stopper. Two methods for stopping fiber line (Fig. A2.6) and two methods for stopping wire rope (Fig. A2.7) will be illustrated.

The first method for stopping fiber line (A) employs the first two turns of a rolling hitch *passed against the lay of the rope* and backed up by a half

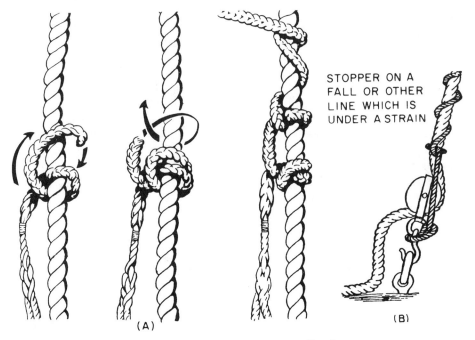

STOPPER ON A
FALL OR OTHER
LINE WHICH IS
UNDER A STRAIN

(A)

(B)

Fig. A2.6 Two methods for stopping fiber line.

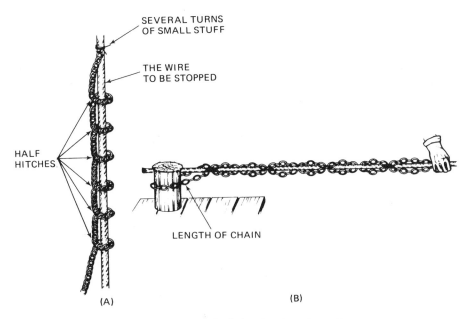

SEVERAL TURNS
OF SMALL STUFF

THE WIRE
TO BE STOPPED

HALF
HITCHES

LENGTH OF CHAIN

(A)

(B)

Fig. A2.7 Two methods for stopping wire rope.

hitch passed some distance away from the above two turns, as illustrated, to prevent the stopper from jamming. Several additional turns are then made around the taut line against the lay to complete the stopper. The second method (B) is used on smaller lines such as boatfalls. Smaller lines tend to kink and bind the first hitch of a stopper, making it almost impossible to remove the stopper. For this reason, a half hitch backed up by several turns with the lay is used.

The stopper methods employed for fiber line tend to jam when used on synthetic line. The preferred method of stopping a synthetic line is with a synthetic, criss-cross stopper. This is applied by passing the legs of the stopper criss-cross fashion around the line and then twisting the last section together to hold the stopper.

For stopping wire rope, a chain stopper should be used. There are two methods by which this can be done as well. The first method (A) uses a chain stopper with a short length of small stuff bent on the end link. The stopper consists of six or more half hitches made with the chain along the wire. The small stuff on the end is intended to keep the chain stopper taut until the strain is picked up. The second method (B) is used primarily to stopper wire rope and spring-lay mooring lines. To apply the stopper, a bight of a length of chain is dropped over the bitt or fitting on which the wire is to be belayed. The two ends are then criss-crossed over and under the wire, as shown, at least six times. The ends are held taut by hand or secured by several turns of small stuff until the wire is belayed.

With all the stopper hitches it must be remembered that the strain must be put on the stopper *slowly*. Throwing the turns off the gypsy so that the stopper abruptly takes the strain might result in a parted stopper at worst or at best a jammed stopper hitch. The command ''Back easy'' is used to direct that the turns on the gypsy be eased out until the stopper has the strain. When it is ascertained that the stopper has the strain, the command ''Up behind'' is given, directing the turns to be thrown off the gypsy and belayed as quickly as possible.

A2.7 Passing a Strap   At times it is necessary to clap a tackle on a rope or the hauling part of another tackle to increase the pull. For this purpose, an endless strap or selvage is used in one of the following ways:

First Method   In the first method, shown in Fig. A2.8(A), the strap is wrapped tightly around the rope. The end toward the direction of pull is then passed through the other end and slipped over the hook.

Second Method   In the second method, Fig. A2.8(B), the center of the strap is held against the hawser and both ends wrapped around it. The ends cross each other. Slip the hook through both ends.

(A) (B) (C)

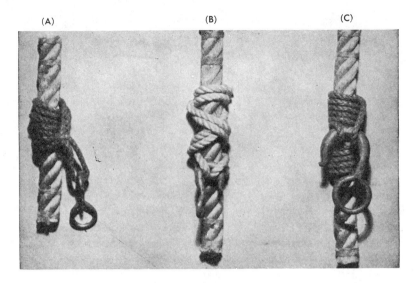

Fig. A2.8 Passing a strap.

Third Method In the third method, Fig. A2.8(C), the loop of one end of the strap is spread, and the other end is wrapped around the hawser inside the loop. The hook is then slipped through both ends.

A2.8 Splicing Twisted Fiber Rope Splices are used to make permanent eyes and permanent repairs in ropes. There are three general types: *eye, short,* and *long.* Several variations of these three exist for splicing wire rope.

When splicing fiber rope, the usual practice is to take three or four tucks with each strand. Better looking but less secure is the *taper splice,* wherein one tuck is taken with each full strand; half of each strand is cut away and the second tuck taken; and half of the remaining part of each strand is cut away and the third tuck taken.

When splicing large lines, it is a good idea to whip the strands and the line at the point at which the strands will be unlaid.

Eye Splice To make an eye splice, the line is first unlaid 6 or more inches, depending on its size. The center strand is then tucked under any strand of the rope as shown in Fig. A2.9(A). Next, the strand to the left of the center strand is tucked under the next strand up the line from the strand the center one is under (B). The line is then turned over and the last strand tucked under the remaining strand (C). The remaining tucks are made by passing the working strands over one of the standing strands and under the next.

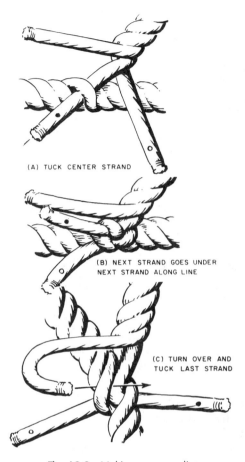

(A) TUCK CENTER STRAND

(B) NEXT STRAND GOES UNDER
NEXT STRAND ALONG LINE

(C) TURN OVER AND
TUCK LAST STRAND

Fig. A2.9 Making an eye splice.

If the line is large it may be necessary to use a *fid*—a round, pointed tool for opening the strands of fiber rope. Figure A2.10 shows a fid and tools for splicing wire rope.

Short Splice The short splice almost doubles the size of the line at the point of the splice; therefore, it can be used only in line that does not have to pass through a block or other small opening. To make one, both ends must be unlaid 6 or more inches. The two ends are then married, with the strands from each end alternating (Fig. A2.11). Until one attains some skill in splicing, it is a good practice to seize the strands at the marriage.

Take any strand of either rope and pass it over one strand and under the next. Do the same with the remaining strands of that rope, taking two

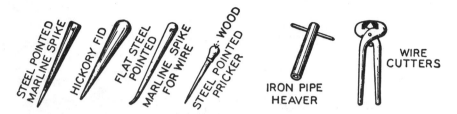

Fig. A2.10 Tools for splicing both fiber and wire rope.

SHORT SPLICE (1)   SHORT SPLICE (2)   SHORT SPLICE (3)

Fig. A2.11 Making a short splice.

or more tucks with each strand. Turn the line, and take one or two tucks with each strand of the other rope. Be sure to pull the strands up taut, and do not let the twist out of the strands.

Long Splice The long splice is used in running rigging because it does not appreciably enlarge the line and will pass through blocks and other small openings.

The long splice is begun just like the short splice, except that each end is unlaid for 15 turns, and if the strands are seized together, one strand must be left out (strand 1, line 1). This strand is unlaid, and the corresponding strand of the second line (strand 1, line 2) is laid in its place, making sure to twist it while laying it in, in order to retain the set of the line. When all but about 6 inches of strand 1, line 2 is laid in, an overhand knot is tied with the two number 1 strands, as shown in Fig. A2.12(A). If tied properly, this overhand knot will lie snugly in the groove; otherwise, it will bunch up.

After knotting the first pair of strands, cut the seizing and start unlaying a strand of line 2 (strand 2, line 1), laying in all but about 6 inches of it and knotting the two number 2 strands. One of the number 3 strands is then unlaid from 6 to 12 inches from the marriage point, the other number 3 strand laid in, and the two knotted. Then each strand is split. Half is passed over one strand and under the next in one direction (B). The other half of

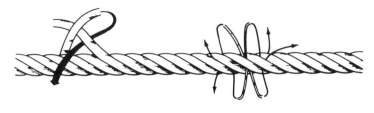

(A) (B)
TIE AN OVERHAND KNOT SPLIT STRANDS AND TUCK

Fig. A2.12 Long splice.

that strand goes over and under in the opposite direction. Thus, four tucks are taken at each knot.

A2.9 Splicing Braided Line The method of splicing a braided line depends upon its construction; indeed, braided line with a solid core cannot be spliced.

Halyard Splice The halyard splice is used on braided line with a hollow core. To make the splice (Fig. A2.13), unlay about 2 inches of the end and taper it. In a piece of wire several inches long, make an eye large enough to take the tapered end of the halyard. Thread the end into this eye. Insert a marline spike, pricker, or other tapered instrument in the side of the halyard, about 1½ inches up from the start of the taper. Work the spike up the center of the halyard about 2 inches and back out the side again. Pull the spike out, but hold the halyard so that the wire and the end of the halyard can be threaded through the holes made by the spike. Slip the halyard snap or ring over the end, and thread the wire through the bottom hole and out the top hole. Pull the end through. Discard the wire, and pull on the eye and standing part, working the bitter end back inside the halyard. With sail twine and needle, put a whipping around the splice, starting where the end enters the standing part.

Halyard Splice for Double-Braided Nylon Line When splicing double-braided nylon line, the end must be worked into the center. For line that is 3 inches in circumference or less, both a fid and a pusher are used. For line that is larger than 3 inches in circumference, only a wire fid is used. Steps 1, 2, and 3 of Fig. A2.14 show how to secure the fid to the line. Stamped on each fid is a number indicating the size of line for which the fid was made. Table A2.1 gives line fid size comparisons should the need arise to make a fid of your own. Fids also serve as rules for measuring while splicing,

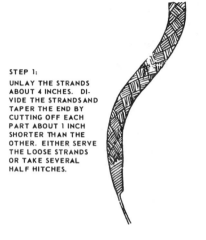

STEP 1:
UNLAY THE STRANDS
ABOUT 4 INCHES. DI-
VIDE THE STRANDS AND
TAPER THE END BY
CUTTING OFF EACH
PART ABOUT 1 INCH
SHORTER THAN THE
OTHER. EITHER SERVE
THE LOOSE STRANDS
OR TAKE SEVERAL
HALF HITCHES.

STEP 2:
INSERT MARLIN SPIKE
AS ILLUSTRATED, TO
MAKE A SMALL HOLE
IN THE HALYARD.

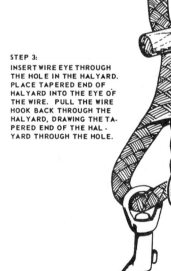

STEP 3:
INSERT WIRE EYE THROUGH
THE HOLE IN THE HALYARD.
PLACE TAPERED END OF
HALYARD INTO THE EYE OF
THE WIRE. PULL THE WIRE
HOOK BACK THROUGH THE
HALYARD, DRAWING THE TA-
PERED END OF THE HAL-
YARD THROUGH THE HOLE.

STEP 4:
THE SPLICE IS NOW MADE.
TO MAKE CERTAIN THAT
THE SPLICE WILL NOT PULL
OUT, YOU CAN, WITH NEE-
DLE AND SAIL TWINE, TAKE
A COUPLE OF TUCKS THROUGH
THE SPLICE.

Fig. A2.13 Halyard splice.

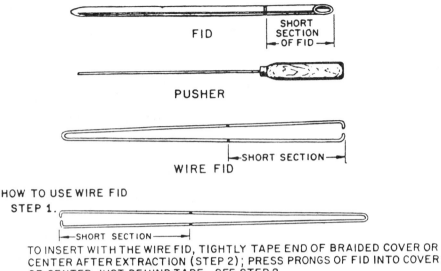

FID

SHORT
SECTION
—OF FID—

PUSHER

|—SHORT SECTION—|
WIRE FID

HOW TO USE WIRE FID
STEP 1.

|—SHORT SECTION—|

TO INSERT WITH THE WIRE FID, TIGHTLY TAPE END OF BRAIDED COVER OR
CENTER AFTER EXTRACTION (STEP 2); PRESS PRONGS OF FID INTO COVER
OR CENTER JUST BEHIND TAPE. SEE STEP 2.

TAPE
STEP 2.

COVER OR CENTER

TAPE WIRE FID TO BRAID BY WRAPPING TAPE IN A TIGHT, SMOOTH, SPIRAL,
STARTING ON THE BRAID AND WRAPPING IN THE DIRECTION OF THE ROUND
TIP OF THE FID. KEEP TAPE SMOOTH AND AVOID BUNCHING AS IT WILL BE
EASIER TO PASS FID THROUGH BRAID. SEE STEP 3.
STEP 3.

COVER OR CENTER

THE ROUND END OF THE FID CAN THEN BE INSERTED AND PUSHED
THROUGH WITHOUT A PUSHER.

Fig. A2.14 Fid used for splicing double-braided line.

as will be explained. In Fig. A2.15, which shows how to splice double-braided line, the wire fid lengths shown are one-half and one-third scale. Friction or masking tape and a soft lead pencil, crayon, or preferably, a wax marking pencil, are needed. Sharp pointed shears are also handy.

Both the splices described here, and the line on which they are used, were developed by the Sampson Cordage Works of Boston, Mass.

Standard Eye Splice in New Double-Braided Line   The standard eye splice can be performed on new line only. It retains up to 90 percent of the average new line strength. Until one has become familiar with splicing

Table A2.1 Braided-line Fid Specifications

SPECIFICATIONS FOR LINE SIZES 3" AND UNDER.

SHORT SECTION OF FID

TUBULAR FID

FID SIZE AND ROPE CIRCUMFERENCE	2-IN-1 BRAID ROPE DIAMETER	FID SHORT SECTION LENGTH	TOTAL FID LENGTH
3/4"	1/4"	2-1/16"	5-1/2"
1"	5/16"	2-1/2"	6-3/4"
1-1/8"	3/8"	2-7/8"	7-3/4"
1-1/4"	7/16"	3-9/16"	9-1/2"
1-1/2"	1/2"	4-1/8"	11"
1-3/4"	9/16"	3-5/8"	12-1/4"
2"	5/8"	4-1/8"	14"
2-1/4"	3/4"	4-3/4"	16"
2-3/4"	7/8"	4-3/4"	19"
3"	1"	5-1/4"	21"

SPECIFICATIONS FOR LINE SIZES 3" AND ABOVE.

WIRE FID

SHORT SECTION C

ROPE DIAMETER	ROPE CIRCUMFERENCE	WIRE DIAMETER t	TOTAL WIDTH W	FID LENGTH L	SHORT SECTION C	FID SCALE
1"	3"	3/16"	3/4"	10-1/2"	2-5/8"	1/2
1-1/8"	3-1/2"	3/16"	3/4"	12-1/4"	3"	1/2
1-1/4"	3-3/4"	3/16"	3/4"	13-1/4"	3-1/4"	1/2
1-5/16"	4"	3/16"	3/4"	14"	3-1/2"	1/2
1-1/2"	4-1/2"	3/16"	3/4"	16"	4"	1/2
1-5/8"	5"	3/16"	3/4"	17-1/2"	4-1/2"	1/2
1-3/4"	5-1/2"	1/4"	1-1/4"	19"	4-3/4"	1/2
2"	6"	1/4"	1-1/4"	21"	5-1/4"	1/2
2-1/8"	6-1/2"	1/4"	1-1/4"	23"	5-3/4"	1/2
2-1/4"	7"	1/4"	1-1/4"	25"	6"	1/2
2-1/2"	7-1/2"	1/4"	1-1/4"	26"	6-1/2"	1/2
2-5/8"	8"	1/4"	1-1/4"	28"	7"	1/2
2-7/8"	8-1/2"	1/4"	1-1/4"	30"	7-1/2"	1/2
3"	9"	5/16"	1-7/8"	32"	8"	1/2
3-1/4"	10"	5/16"	1-7/8"	35"	8-3/4"	1/2
3-1/2"	11"	5/16"	1-7/8"	39"	9-1/2"	1/2
4"	12"	5/16"	1-7/8"	42"	10-1/2"	1/2
4-1/4"	13"	5/16"	1-7/8"	46"	11-1/2"	1/2
4-5/8"	14"	3/8"	4-1/2"	33"	8-1/4"	1/3
5"	15"	3/8"	4-1/2"	35"	8-3/4"	1/3
5-1/4"	16"	3/8"	4-1/2"	37"	9-1/2"	1/3
5-1/2"	17"	3/8"	4-1/2"	40"	10"	1/3
6"	18"	3/8"	4-1/2"	42"	10-1/2"	1/3
6-1/4"	19"	3/8"	4-1/2"	44"	11"	1/3
6-1/2"	20"	3/8"	4-1/2"	47"	11-1/2"	1/3
7"	21"	3/8"	4-1/2"	49"	12-1/4"	1/3

NOTE: WIRE FID SIZES 3" CIRC. TO 13" CIRC. ARE 1/2 SCALE – OVER 13" CIRC. ARE 1/3 SCALE. THIS IS NECESSARY IN ORDER TO KEEP WIRE FIDS TO A PRACTICAL LENGTH.

STEP 1. FORMING THE LOOP

CORE MUST BE EXTRACTED FROM COVER
AT THIS POINT

X

1 LAYER OF TAPE

MARK

MARK R

FORM LOOP
DESIRED
SIZE

1 FID LENGTH

OR
2 WIRE FIDS

TIE A SLIP KNOT
ABOUT 5 FID LENGTHS FROM "X"

STEP 2. EXTRACTING THE CORE

PRYING OUT
THE CORE

R

COVER

1 LAYER OF TAPE

X

MARK 1

CORE

CORE

STEP 3. MEASURING

R

2 SHORT SECTIONS
WITH WIRE FID

MARK ON FID

COVER

MARK 3

CORE

MARK 2 MARK 1

ONE FID LENGTH PLUS ANOTHER
SHORT SECTION

SHORT
SECTION OF FID

STEP 4. MARKING THE COVER
FOR TAPERING

R T

MARKING
COVER STRANDS
R   T

READ INSTRUC-
TIONS CARE-
FULLY

X

COVER

CORE

MARK 3

MARK 2 MARK 1

STEP 5. TAPERING

R T

TAPERED COVER

CUTTING
PAIRS

REMOVING
CUT PAIRS

COVER

CORE

MARK 3

MARK 2

MARK 1

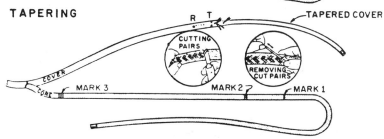

Fig. A2.15   Splicing double-braided line.

673

this material, each of the following steps (see Fig. A2.16) should be followed in precise detail, with reference to Figs. A2.14 and A2.15.

1. Tape the end to be spliced with one thin layer of tape, then measure one tubular fid length (two wire fid lengths because wire fid is one-half size) from the end of the line and mark—this is point R (reference), step 1. From R, form a loop the size of the eye desired and mark—this is point X, where you extract the core from inside the cover.

2. Tie a tight slipknot approximately five fid lengths from X in order to keep the core and cover from becoming uneven. Bend the line sharply at X. With the pusher or any sharp tool such as an ice pick, awl, or marlinespike, spread the cover strands to expose the core (step 2). First pry and then pull the core completely out of the cover from X to the taped end of the line. Put only one layer of tape on the end of the core. *Do not* pull cover strands away from the line when spreading the cover as doing so will distort the line unnecessarily. To assure the correct positioning of mark 1, do the following: Holding the exposed core, slide the cover as far back toward the tightly tied slipknot as you can. Then, firmly smooth the cover back from the slipknot toward the taped end. Smooth it again until all cover slack is removed. Then mark the core where it comes out of the cover (this is mark 1).

3. Again slide the cover toward the slipknot to expose more core. From mark 1, measure along the core toward X a distance equal to the short section of tubular fid (two short sections with wire fid), and make two heavy marks (this is mark 2). From mark 2, measure in the same direction one fid length plus another short section of the fid (with wire fid, use double measurements) and make three heavy marks (this is mark 3, step 3).

4. Note the nature of the cover braid: It is made up of strands, either one or two (pair). Notice that half the pairs revolve to the right around the rope and half revolve to the left. Beginning at R and working toward the taped end of the cover, count eight consecutive strands (single or pairs) which revolve to the right (or left). Mark the eighth strand (this is mark T, step 4). Make mark T go completely around the cover. Starting at T and working around the taped cover end, count and mark every fifth right and left strand (single or paired) until you have progressed down to the end of the taped cover.

5. Insert the fid into the core at mark 2, and slide it through and out at mark 3 (step 5). Add extra tape to the tapered cover end; then jam it tightly into the hollow end of the fid (see insert). Hold the

STEP 1.

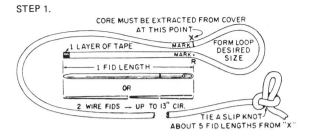

CORE MUST BE EXTRACTED FROM COVER
AT THIS POINT

1 LAYER OF TAPE

MARK 1

FORM LOOP
DESIRED
SIZE

MARK

R

1 FID LENGTH

OR

2 WIRE FIDS — UP TO 13" CIR.

TIE A SLIP KNOT
ABOUT 5 FID LENGTHS FROM "X"

ON ROPE OVER 1" DIAMETER, IT IS OFTEN EASIER TO PASS A SPIKE
OR SIMILAR OBJECT THROUGH THE ROPE INSTEAD OF TYING A SLIPKNOT.

STEP 2.

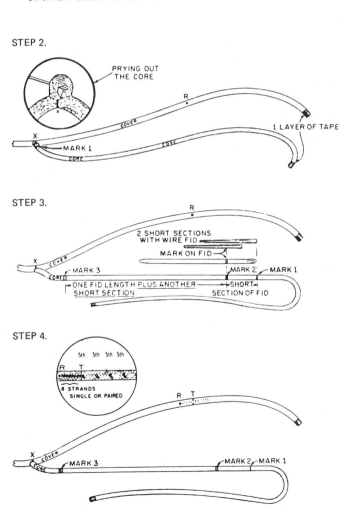

PRYING OUT
THE CORE

R

COVER

1 LAYER OF TAPE

CORE

X

MARK 1

CORE

STEP 3.

R

COVER

2 SHORT SECTIONS
WITH WIRE FID

MARK ON FID

X

MARK 3

CORE

MARK 2

MARK 1

ONE FID LENGTH PLUS ANOTHER
SHORT SECTION

SHORT
SECTION OF FID

STEP 4.

5th 5th 5th 5th

R T

8 STRANDS
SINGLE OR PAIRED

R T

X

COVER

MARK 3

CORE

MARK 2 MARK 1

Fig. A2.16 Completing the double-braided eye splice.

STEP 5.

STEP 6.

STEP 7.

STEP 8.

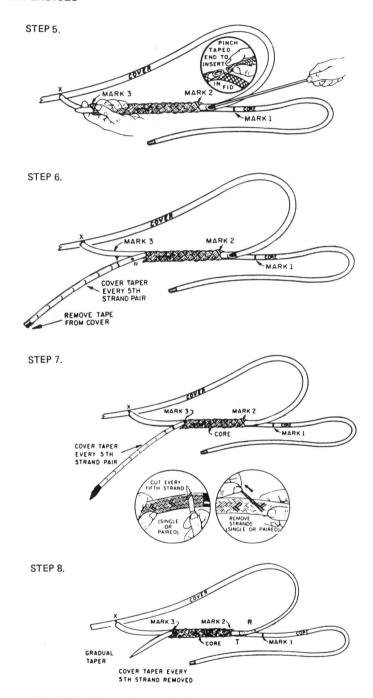

Fig. A2.16 Completing the double-braided eye splice (cont'd).

STEP 9.

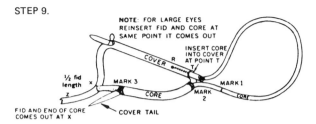

STEP 10.

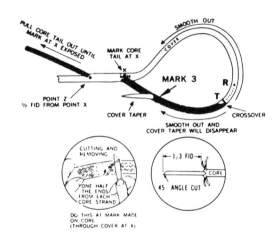

STEP 11.

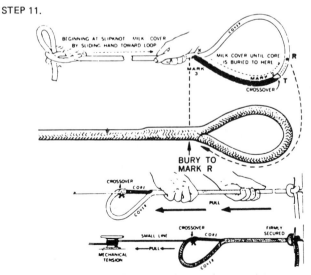

Fig. A2.16 Completing the double-braided eye splice (cont'd).

core lightly at mark 3; place the pusher point into the taped end; and push the fid and cover through from mark 2 and out at mark 3. With the wire fid, first press prongs into the cover and then tape over. Then, after the fid is on, milk the braid over the fid while pulling the fid through from mark 2 to mark 3. Take the fid off the cover. Continue pulling the cover tail through the core until mark R on the cover emerges from mark 3. Then remove the tape from the end of the taped cover (step 6).

6. Make sure that the tape is removed from the cover end. Start with the last marked pair of cover strands toward the end, and cut and pull them out completely (step 7). Cut and remove the next marked strands, and continue with each right and left marked strands until you reach point T (*Do not* cut beyond this point). The results should be a gradual taper ending in a point. Very carefully pull the cover back through the core until point T emerges from mark 2 of the core (step 8). From point X on the cover, measure approximately one-half fid length toward the slipknot on the line and mark this as point Z (step 9).

7. You are now ready to put the core back into the cover from T to Z. Insert your fid at T, and jam the taped core end tightly into the end of the fid. With the pusher, push the fid and core through the cover "tunnel" past point X to, and through, the cover at point Z. When using the wire fid, attach the fid to the taped core. After the fid is on, milk the braid over the fid while pulling through from T to Z. When pushing the fid past X to Z, make sure the fid does not catch any internal core strands. *Note:* Depending on eye size, the fid may not be long enough to reach from T to Z in one pass. If not, bring the fid out through the cover, pull the core through, and reinsert the fid into the exact hole it came out of, doing this as many times as needed to reach point Z.

8. Alternately pull on the core tail at Z and on the tapered cover at mark 3. The crossover must now be tightened until the crossover is equal to the diameter of the line. Remove all the slack from the eye area by smoothing the cover from point T toward X. Mark the core tail through the cover at point X. Pull the core tail out until the mark just made on the core is exposed at Z. The diameter of the core must now be reduced by cutting and removing one strand at each group around the complete circumference (step 10). Measure one-third fid length from the first reduction cut toward the end, and mark. Cut off the remaining tail at this point. Make the cut on a 45-deg angle to prevent a blunt end. With one hand, hold the crossover (mark T). Smooth the cover section of the eye out firmly and completely from the crossover toward mark X. The reduced-volume

core tail should disappear into the cover at Z. Smooth out the core section from the crossover toward mark 3, and the cover taper will disappear into the core. Hold the rope at the slipknot, and, with the other hand, milk the cover toward the splice, gently at first, then more firmly. The cover will slide over mark 3, mark 2, the crossover, T, and R (step 11). (It may be occasionally necessary to smooth out the eye during milking to prevent the reduced-volume tail from catching in the throat of the splice.)

If bunching occurs at the crossover, preventing full burying, smooth the cover from T to X. Grasp crossover at T with one hand, and then firmly smooth the cover slack (female side of eye) with the other hand towards the throat (X). Repeat as necessary until bunching disappears. Continue milking until all cover slack between the knot and the throat of the eye has been removed.

Note: Before burying the cover under the crossover, do the following:

(a) Anchor the loop of the slipknot to a stationary object before you start to bury. You can then use both hands and the weight of your body to more easily bury the cover over the core and crossover.

(b) Holding the crossover tightly, milk all excess cover from R to X. Flex and loosen the line at the crossover point during the final burying process. Hammering the cover at point X will help loosen the strands.

With larger ropes it is helpful to anchor the slipknot securely, attach a small line to the braided core at the crossover, and mechanically apply tension with either a block and tackle, capstan, come-a-long, or power winch. Tension will reduce the diameter of core and crossover for easier burying.

9. Prior to whipping, it is to your advantage to stitch-lock the splice to prevent no-load opening. You will need approximately one fid length of nylon or polyester whipping twine. The twine should be about the same size as the strands of line you are stitching. Strands cut from the line may be used. To begin the lock stitch, pass the twine (A) through the line as shown in step 1 of Fig. A2.17. Reinsert the twine as in step 2. (Ensure that all stitching is just snug. *Do not tighten.*) Continue until you have four complete stitches. After you have four stitches, turn the line 90 degrees, and pass the remaining end (B) through the line perpendicular to the original stitches in order to make four more stitches. The line should now look as it does in step 4. Now take ends A and B, tie a square knot, and bury it in between the cover and the core. You may now whip the line or leave it as it is.

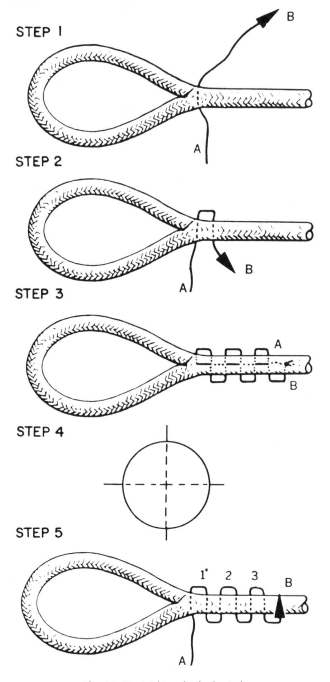

STEP 1

STEP 2

STEP 3

STEP 4

STEP 5

Fig. A2.17 Making the lock stitch.

Standard End-for-End Splice in Double-Braided Line The standard end-for-end splice can be performed on both new and used line. This is an all-purpose splice technique designed for people who generally splice used line as frequently as new line. It retains up to 85 percent of the average new line strength and up to 85 percent of the remaining used line strength. The steps are as follows:

1. Tape the end of each line with one thin layer of tape. Lay the two lines to be spliced side by side, measure one tubular fid length (two wire fid lengths because wire fid is one-half size) from the end of each line, and make a mark—this is point R, shown in step 1 of Fig. A2.18. From R, measure one short fid section length as scribed on the fid and then mark again—this is point X where you should extract the core from inside the cover. Be sure both ropes are identically marked. Then tie a tight slipknot approximately five fid lengths from X.

2. Bend the rope sharply at X. With the pusher or any sharp tool such as an ice pick, awl, or marlinespike, spread the cover strands to expose the core. First pry and then pull the core completely out of the cover from X to the end of the line. Put one layer of tape on the end of the core. (See step 2.) To assure correct positioning of mark 1, do the following: Holding the exposed core, slide the cover as far back toward the tightly tied slipknot as you can. Then, firmly smooth the cover back from the slipknot toward the taped end. Smooth again until all cover slack is removed. Then mark the core where it comes out of the cover—this is mark 1. Do the same thing to both lines.

3. Hold one core at mark 1, and slide the cover back to expose more core. From mark 1, measure along the core toward X a distance equal to the short section of fid, and make two heavy marks—this is mark 2. From mark 2, measure in the same direction one fid length plus another short section, and make three heavy marks (mark 3 in step 3). Mark the second core by laying it alongside the first and using it as an exact guide.

4. Note the nature of the cover braid; it is made up of strand pairs. Notice that half the pairs revolve to the right around the rope and half revolve to the left (step 4). Beginning at R and working toward the taped end of the cover, count seven consecutive pairs of cover strands that revolve to the right (or left). Mark the seventh pair. This is point T (see insert). Make point T go completely around the cover. Starting at T and working toward the taped cover end, count and mark every second right pair of strands for a total of six. Again, starting at T, count and mark every second left pair of strands for a total of six (see insert). Make both lines identical.

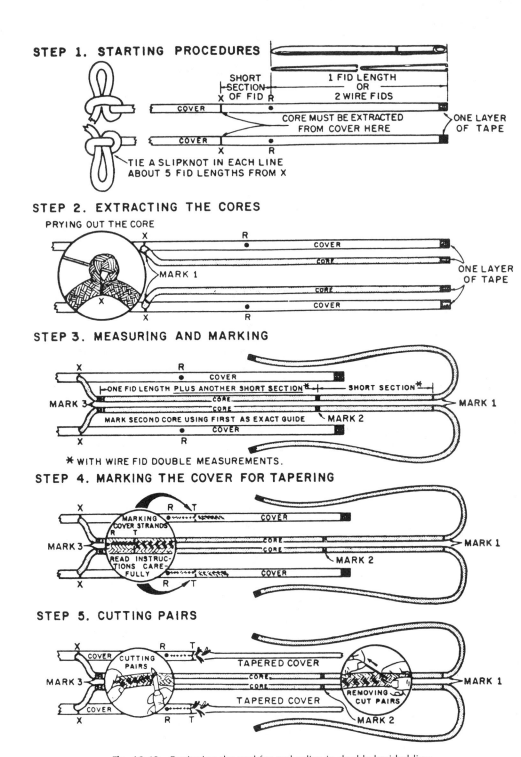

Fig. A2.18 Beginning the end-for-end splice in double-braided line.

5. First remove the tape form the cover end. Starting with the last marked pair of cover strands toward the end, cut and pull them completely out (see insert, step 5). Cut and remove the next marked strands and continue with each right and left marked strand until you reach point T. Do not cut beyond this point (see insert). Retape the tapered end. Cut and remove the marked strands on the other marked cover, again stopping at T. Retape the tapered end.

6. Reposition the lines for splicing according to the diagram in step 1, Fig. A2.19. Note how the cover on one line has been paired off with the core of the opposite line. Avoid twisting.

7. Insert the fid into one core at mark 2, and bring it out at mark 3. Add extra tape to the tapered cover end; then jam it tightly into the hollow end of the fid (see insert, step 2). Hold the core lightly at mark 3, and place the pusher point into the tapered end, pushing the fid end with the cover in it from mark 2 out at mark 3. When using a wire fid, attach the fid to the cover, then pull the fid through from mark 2 to mark 3. Pull the cover tail through the core until point T on the cover meets mark 2 on the core. Insert the other cover into the core in the same manner.

8. Now put the core back into the cover from T to X. Insert the fid at T, and jam the taped core tightly into the end of the fid. With the pusher, push the fid and core through the cover, bringing them out at point X. When using a wire fid, attach the fid to the taped core; then pull the fid to the taped core; then pull the fid and braid through from T to X. Do this to both cores (see step 3). Remove the tape from the end of the cover. Bring the crossover up tight by pulling on the core tail and on the tapered covered tail. Hold the crossover tightly and smooth out all excess braid, away from the crossover in each direction. The tapered cover tail will disappear at mark 3. Cut the core tail off close to point X.

9. Hold the rope at the slipknot, and, with the other hand, milk the cover toward the splice, gently at first and then more firmly. The cover will slide over mark 3, mark 2, the crossover, and R. Repeat the procedure with the other side of the splice. (See step 4.) Continue burying until all cover slack between the knot and the splice has been removed.

10. The splice is completed when all cover slack has been removed, and there is an opening in the splice approximately equal in length to the diameter of the rope. (See step 5.) If, at the opening, one side of the splice is noticeably longer than the other side, something is wrong. Check all steps, and remake the splice if necessary. Now untie the slipknots.

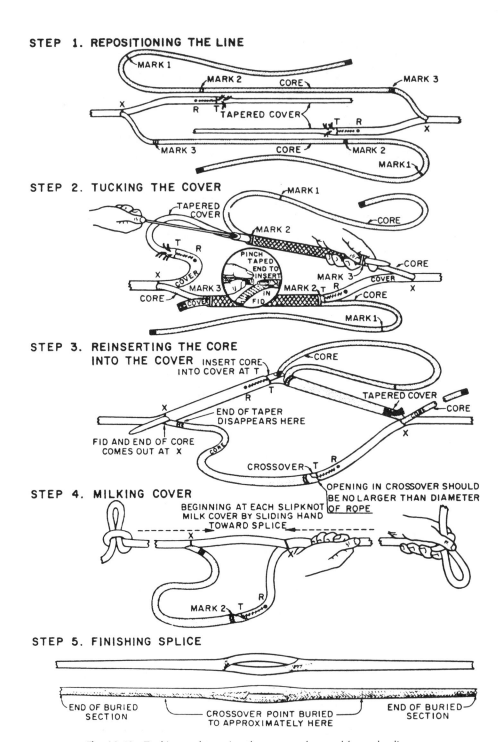

Fig. A2.19 Tucking and tapering the covers of an end-for-end splice.

684

Back Splice in Double-Braided Line   The double-braided back splice is a neat, permanent way to terminate the end of a line. It is flexible and can be tapered to reduce bulk. To make a back splice half as long as described, you use half measurements. When starting the back splice, follow steps 1, 2, and 3 of Fig. A2.15. Then start with Fig. A2.20, step 1 as follows:

1. Insert the fid into the core at mark 2. Slide the fid through and out at mark 3. Pinch the taped end of the cover, and jam it tightly into the hollow end of the fid (see insert). Hold the core tightly at mark 3, place the pusher point into the taped end, and push the fid and cover through from mark 2 and out at mark 3. When using wire fids for larger size lines, attach the fid to the taped cover. After the fid is on, milk the braid over the fid while pulling the fid through from mark 2 to mark 3.
2. Remove the tape from the cover end. Smooth the core from mark 2 toward mark 3 until the cover ends just disappear inside. (See step 3). Next, holding the core at mark 3, smooth the core from mark 3 to mark 2. Do so until all excess is eliminated.
3. Hold the rope at the slipknot, and, with the other hand, milk the cover toward the splice, gently at first and then more firmly. The cover will slide over mark 3, mark 2, and finally X. Be sure that all excess cover is milked out so that X (a bump) is well inside the cover. (See step 3.)
4. If final burying is difficult, flex to loosen the strands; then continue burying. Cut the protruding core off close at the cover. Once again, milk the cover toward the end so that it covers the cut-off core. (See step 4.)

A2.10   Splicing Plaited Line   Since plaited line is tightly braided, even small sizes cannot be spliced without using a fid. In fact, it may be necessary to make a fid to use with the smaller sizes of line if the fids obtained through the supply system prove too large. Should such be the case, a suitable fid can be fashioned from a 12- or 14-inch length of hardwood cut from a swab or broom handle by whittling a long tapering point at one end and sanding it smooth.

Other items needed to splice plaited line are a sharp knife, a length of twine, a marking pen or colored chalk, and a roll of masking or vinyl tape of narrow width. Ordinary electrical (friction) tape that is sticky on both sides should be avoided because the tape will be used on the ends of the working strands, and ends wrapped with sticky tape may be impossible to force under the strands of the standing part of the line.

Before attempting the splices described here, read the general instructions for each, fixing the basic procedure well in your mind. Then follow the instructions step by step.

STEP 1. TUCKING THE COVER

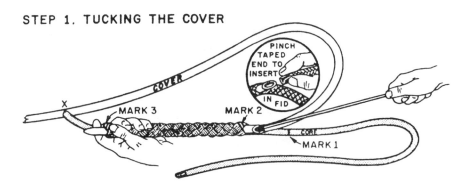

STEP 2. ADJUSTING THE CORE OVER COVER

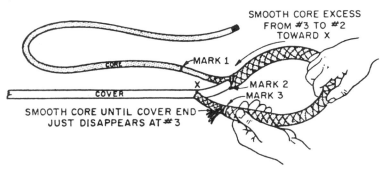

STEP 3. MILKING COVER

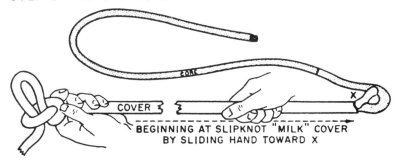

STEP 4. COMPLETED SPLICE

Fig. A2.20 Tucking the back splice in double-braided line.

Eye Splice Count from the end of the line nine pics or crowns. [A pic is the distance from the topmost point (crown) of one pair of strands to the crown of the next pair of strands of the same color (Fig. A2.21).] Tie a piece of twine securely around the line at this point, positioning it over the white crowns. Unlay the line a couple of turns. Cut one strand of each pair shorter than the other, and cut both ends at an angle. Then tape the ends, working from the standing part to the ends. (Take care not to mix the strands.) Unlay the rest of the line back to the twine.

As mentioned previously, this type of line is composed of two pairs of right-laid strands and two pairs of left-laid strands. In all illustrations shown here, the left-laid strands are white; the right-laid strands, black. If your line is all one color, use the pen to mark the right-laid strands from the end of the rope through the distance to be worked in making the splice (about five or six pics past the twine). From this point on, we shall refer only to black and white strands. Now proceed with the following steps:

1. Form the size of eye desired, and place the black strands on one side and the white strands on the other side of the standing part. Using the fid to open the line, tuck the two pairs of white strands under two successive black strands, as shown in Fig. A2.21. Take care not to drive the fid *through* a strand, rather than *under* it. (Contrary to usual practice, the writer found it more convenient to insert the fid in the direction the strand is to be tucked.) In all cases, tuck the pair of strands nearest the eye first.
2. Turn the eye over, and tuck the two pairs of black strands under the nearest white strands. Pull all four strands taut, completing the first

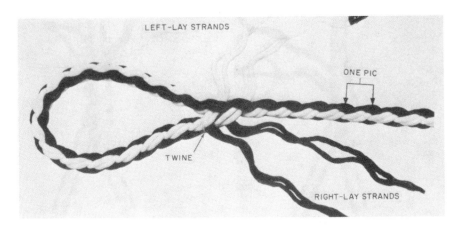

Fig. A2.21 Eye splice in plaited rope.

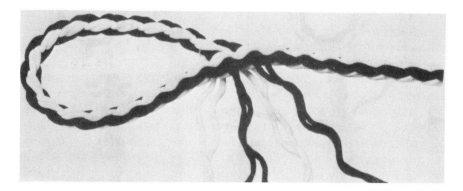

Fig. A2.22 Eye splice in plaited rope.

round of tucks. Your splice should now look like the one in Fig. A2.22.

3. Turn the eye over again, and position the two pairs of white strands so that they are lying on the adjacent white strands of the standing part. Tuck the white strands under the next pair of black strands, as shown in Fig. A2.23. Do not pull these strands taut as yet, but note that they are now doubling up.

4. Turn the eye over again, and position the two pairs of black strands so that they are lying over the adjacent black strands. Tuck them under the next pairs of white strands. (Notice that the first pair go under double-up white strands.) Pull taut all four pairs of strands. At this point your splice should look like that in Fig. A2.24.

5. Take at least one more tuck with each pair of strands.

6. Take an additional tuck with the pair of white strands and the pair of black strands nearest the eye. Your splice should now look like that in Fig. A2.25.

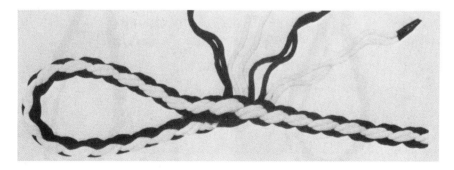

Fig. A2.23 Eye splice in plaited rope.

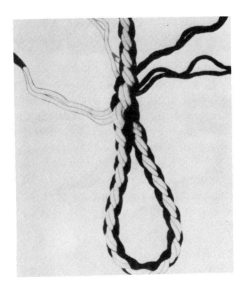

Fig. A2.24 Eye splice in plaited rope.

Fig. A2.25 Eye splice in plaited rope.

7. At this point, split the pairs of strands. Select the strand of each pair that is nearest the eye, tape it close to the rope, and cut off the portion that is above the tape, as shown in Fig. A2.26.

8. Take the remaining strands one by one. Instead of tucking them under a pair of strands of the opposite color, however, tuck each strand under only a single strand, as shown in Fig. A2.27. Then, tape and cut off the ends. In lieu of taping, heat and fuse all ends, but take care not to damage the rope while doing so. Achieve a better appearance by cutting the ends off flush with the splice and serving the entire splice.

Short Splice   Before starting the short splice, read the general instructions preceding the eye splice.

1. Lay the two pieces of line side by side, and if the strands are all one color, mark all the right-laid strands for a distance of 15 or 16 pics from the ends.

2. Count back from the ends a distance of 10 pics or crowns, and run marks completely around the lines at these points. Tie a piece of twine around each line at these marks. Position the twine over the black crowns on one line and over the white crowns on the other.

Fig. A2.26   Eye splice in plaited rope.

Fig. A2.27 Eye splice in plaited rope.

3. Unlay the pairs of strands back to the twine. Taper and tape the ends, as explained for the eye splice.
4. Lay out the lines as shown in Fig. A2.28, with the black strands at top and bottom. Make sure that the pairs run parallel to, rather than twist around, one another.
5. Bend back the top pairs of black strands, and then marry the ends, as follows: Pass the bottom pair of black strands from the right between the bottom pair of strands from the left, as shown in Fig. A2.29. Pass one pair of white strands from the right between the corresponding pair from the left, and pass the other pair of strands from the left between the opposite pair from the right. Finally, pass the top pair of black strands from the left between those from the right. Your lines should now look like those in Fig. A2.30.
6. Cut both twines. Grasp the four pairs of strands on the right in your right hand and those strands on the left in your left hand. Pull all strands up snug, and tie a piece of twine tightly around the entire marriage, as shown in Fig. A2.31. (Cut this piece of twine only if it gets hopelessly in the way during the next step.)
7. Using a fid to open the line, tuck the white pairs of strands from the left under the black strands on the right. (White strands tuck from left to right.) Next, tuck the white pairs from the right under

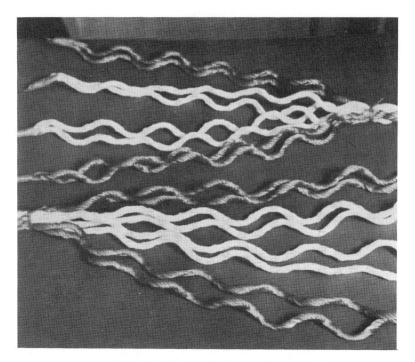

Fig. A2.28 Short splice in plaited rope.

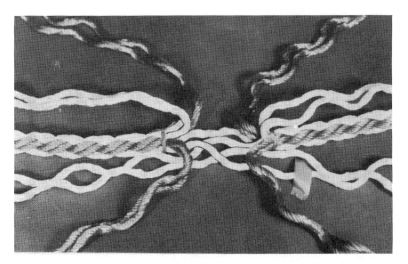

Fig. A2.29 Short splice in plaited rope.

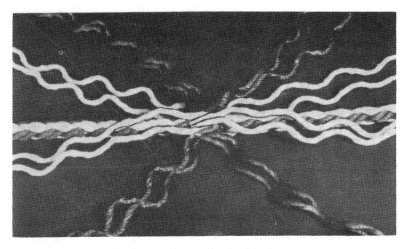

Fig. A2.30 Short splice in plaited rope.

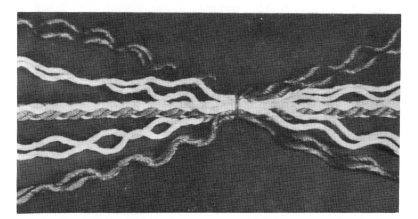

Fig. A2.31 Short splice in plaited rope.

the black strands on the left. Complete the first round of tucks by tucking the black strands under the white strands in the same fashion. (Black strands tuck from right to left.) Make sure that your splice now looks like that shown in Fig. A2.32.

8. Make two more rounds of tucks on each side of the marriage, as shown in Fig. A2.33.

9. Split the pairs, and using only one strand from each pair, make two additional rounds of tucks in each line, as shown in Fig. A2.34. (You can cut the tape from each pair of strands and retape the

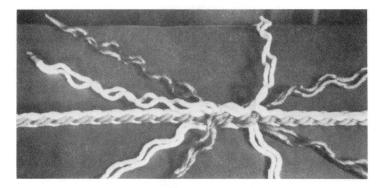

Fig. A2.32 Short splice in plaited rope.

Fig. A2.33 Short splice in plaited rope.

Fig. A2.34 Short splice in plaited rope.

Fig. A2.35 Short splice in plaited rope.

strand to be used, but it is faster just to cut the one strand at the end of the tape and leave the original tape in place.)

10. Tape adjacent ends together (black to white) and cut them off, leaving a length of about two pics. Your finished splice should look like that shown in Fig. A2.35, but even if it does not look this professional, it probably will be about 80 percent as strong as uncut line.

Long Splice Long splicing plaited line is similar to long splicing twisted rope in that strands from one line are laid in place of strands from the other line. The procedures are as follows:

1. On one line, line A of Fig. A2.36, count back from the end a distance of 30 pics, mark the point, and tie a piece of twine around the line. Call this point the center. Locate and mark the center point on line B in the same fashion, but tie the twine half a pic

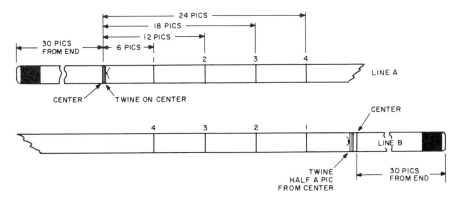

Fig. A2.36 Marking the lines for a long splice in plaited rope.

beyond it. Thus, the twine is positioned over the black crowns of one line and over the white crowns of the other. If your lines are all one color, mark the right-laid pairs from the center to the end of the line.

2. Lay each rope so that a pair of black strands runs along the top. Starting at center and working away from the ends, count off 5, 12, 18, and 24 pics. Mark these points around the entire circumference of the lines, and call the points 1, 2, 3, and 4, respectively, as shown in Fig. A2.36.

3. Unlay the strands a short distance, taper the ends, and tape them as explained for the eye splice. Unlay the lines back to the lashings, and position them as shown in Fig. A2.37.

4. Marry the bottom black strands by passing the pair from the left between the pair from the right, as shown in Fig. A2.38. Next marry the two pairs of white strands on the side away from you by passing the pair from the right through the pair from the left. Marry the top pairs of strands by passing the pair from the right through the pair from the left. Marry the remaining pairs by passing those from the left through those from the right. Thus, starting with the top pairs and working around the line away from you, the pairs will be left through right, right through left, right through left, and left through right.

5. Cut and remove lashings at both centers. Taking four pairs of strands in each hand, pull the marriages up tight so that the center markings coincide. Seize each of the four marriages individually,

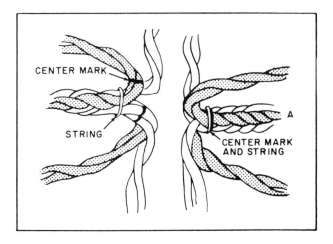

Fig. A2.37 Long splice in plaited rope.

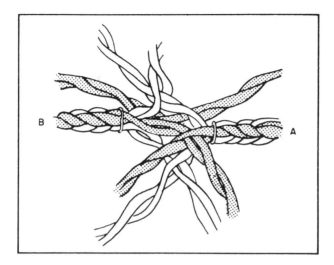

Fig. A2.38   Long splice in plaited rope.

taking care not to loosen them. (One method of achieving taut marriages is to place a piece of twine under each set of pairs before pulling the marriages tight.) Then, have an assistant pull on the four pairs of strands while you tie each marriage in turn. The lines should now look like those in Fig. A2.39.

6. Start splicing with the top black pair of strands, working from left to right. First cut off the outside pair (that pair coming from the right) at the marriage, as shown in Fig. A2.40. Cut the twine and pull the cut ends from under the first white pair of strands, as

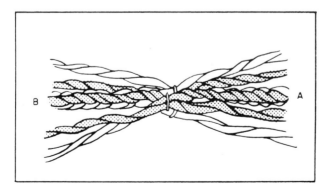

Fig. A2.39   Long splice in plaited rope.

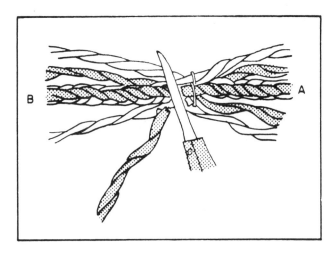

Fig. A2.40   Long splice in plaited rope.

shown in Fig. A2.41. Insert the black pair of strands coming from the left in place of those withdrawn. Now, and throughout the remainder of the splicing operation, make certain that the inserted strands are laid in parallel and not twisted over each other. If the strands become twisted, back them out an inch or so. Then, if you can, correct the situation by pulling tight first one strand and then the other. Otherwise, untwist the pair and then pull them taut.

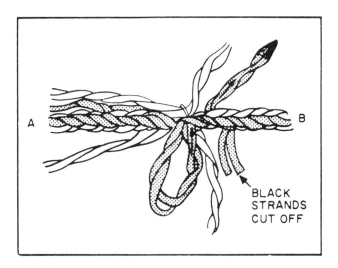

Fig. A2.41   Long splice in plaited rope.

Continue removing the cut pair one tuck at a time and immediately inserting the opposite pair, until the pair reaches point 3 (Fig. A2.36).

7. Having reached point 3, cut the tape holding the working pair and split the pair. Drop one strand at this point, and tuck the other individually until it reaches point 4. Choose the working strand and retape its end. Withdraw the directly opposite strand from under the two white strands, and tuck the working strand into its place. Continue this process until the strand reaches point 4.

8. Next, tuck the pair of white strands opposite you, working from right to left. Cut the cord securing the marriage, and cut the (outer) pair of strands coming from the left. Pull out the cut strands and tuck the other pair, as described in steps 6 and 7.

9. Repeat the procedure in steps 6 and 7 with the remaining white strands. Work to the right with the pair of strands coming from the left until point 1 is reached. At point 1, split the pair and continue tucking with a single strand until point 2 is reached.

10. Follow step 9 with the remaining black strands, but work to the left with the strands coming from the right. Your splice now should look like that in Fig. A2.42.

11. Now, cut off the ends of the strands, leaving them at least 4 pics long. Taper and tape the ends, as described. Work these ends into the center of the line for a distance of 3 pics, each strand in the direction in which it was tucked. Cut off flush the lenghts of strands remaining after this step, making the finished splice appear like that shown in Fig. A2.43.

A2.11 Seizings At times, eyes must be made in the bight of lines where they cannot be spliced. In such circumstances, seizings are used. There are many types of seizings, but the most common are the *flat, round, racking,* and *throat.*

Flat Seizing The flat seizing, shown in Fig. A2.44 (A) and (B), is light; it is used where the strain is not too great. To make one, a single layer of turns is taken around the two parts of the line. The seizing is secured with a clove hitch over the turns and between the two parts of the line.

Round Seizing The round seizing (C,D,E), which consists of two layers of turns, is secured in the same way as the flat seizing.

Racking Seizing The racking seizing (F,G) is used when the strain on each of the two parts of the line is different. It consists of figure-eight turns around the two, which are secured with a clove hitch in the usual manner.

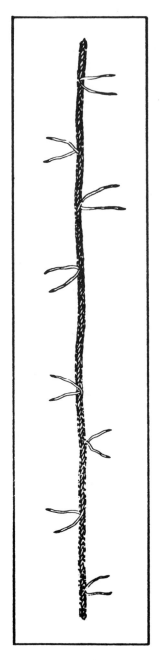

Fig. A2.42 Long splice in plaited rope.

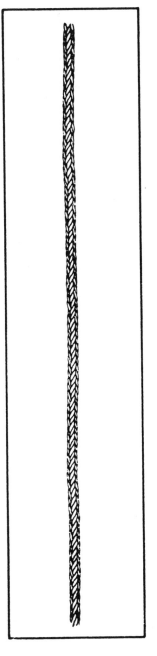

Fig. A2.43 Long splice in plaited rope.

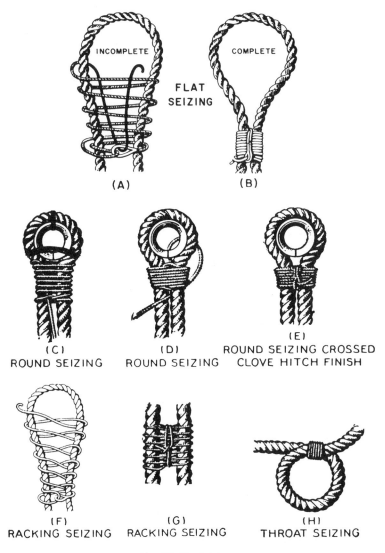

Fig. A2.44 Seizings.

Throat Seizing The throat seizing is used where a permanent eye is needed in the bight of a line. It consists of a round seizing applied as shown in Fig. A2.44(H). It is also secured with a clove hitch, but the hitch goes around both parts of the line instead of between them.

A2.12 Worming, Parceling, and Serving Worming, parceling, and serving are methods of preserving both wire and fiber rope, although they are

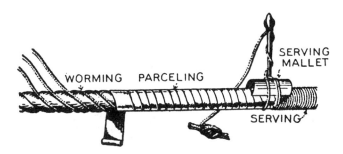

Fig. A2.45 Worming, parceling, and serving.

more commonly used on wire. *Worming* (Fig. A2.45) is marline or ratline (depending on the size of the rope—marline for the smaller, ratline for the larger), wound along in the grooves of the rope. *Parceling* consists of narrow strips of light canvas or cotton cloth spiral·wrapped along the rope. *Serving* is marline tightly wound on the rope by means of a serving mallet or board. For worming, parceling, and serving, the saying goes: "Worm and parcel with the lay; turn and serve the other way."

A2.13 Seizing Wire Rope Great care is exercised in the manufacture of wire rope to lay each wire in the strand and each strand in the rope under uniform tension. If the ends of the rope are not secured properly, the original balance of tension will be disturbed and maximum service will not be obtained, because some strands will carry a greater portion of the load than others. Before cutting steel wire rope, it is necessary to place at least three sets of seizings on each side of the intended cut. Each seizing should consist of eight turns of annealed-iron seizing wire. The distance between seizings should equal the rope's diameter.

To make a temporary wire rope seizing, wind on the seizing wire uniformly, using strong tension on the wire. After taking the required number of turns (step 1, Fig. A2.46), twist the ends of the wires counterclockwise (step 2). Grasp the ends with end-cutting nippers, and twist up the slack as shown in step 3. Do not try to tighten the seizing by twisting; rather, draw up on it as shown in step 4. Twist up the slack (step 5). Repeat steps 4 and 5 if necessary. Cut the ends and pound them down on the rope. If the final seizing (step 6), is to be permanent, or the rope is 1⅝ inches or more in diameter, use a serving bar or iron to increase tension on the seizing wire when putting on the turns.

A2.14 Splicing Wire Rope Wire rope is usually six-stranded with a hemp core. Normally, one works the strands separately, but in some splices, pairs may be worked. The work calls for special appliances and for a degree of skill such as can be acquired only by long practice under expert instruction.

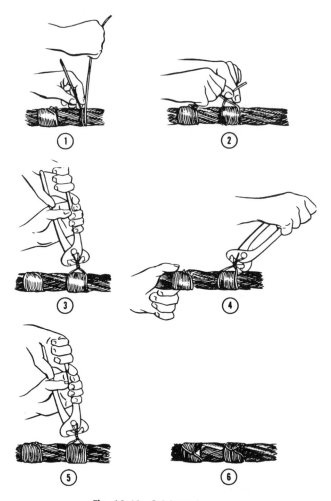

Fig. A2.46 Seizing wire rope.

Something may be learned from careful description, and much more from an occasional visit to a rigging loft, but the facilities available on shipboard do not permit doing the kind of work that can be accomplished with a rigger's bench, a turning-in machine, etc. Where a heavy rope is to be bent around a thimble or the parts otherwise brought together for splicing or seizing, a rigger's screw is needed. In the absence of this, a vise may be used, but less conveniently.

When splicing wire, always insert the marlinspike against the lay, but make sure that you do not shove it through the core. In tucking the strands of a splice, open out the lay of the rope and leave the spike in, holding the strands apart until the tuck has been made. With large wire, it is necessary to haul the strands through with a jigger. After a tuck is taken, the rope is hammered down with a wooden mallet. After the splice is completed, the strands are cut off with a pair of wire cutters.

Liverpool Eye Splice   The Liverpool splice is one of the most common and the easiest of the eye splices to put in. *Never use it, however, in a wire that, when loaded, is free to spin, because it is likely to pull out.*

To find the distance to which the strands should be unlaid, multiply the diameter of the wire by 36 inches. Find and measure off that distance, and put a seizing at that point. Another seizing should be put on just below the point where the first tuck is to be made. Next, cut the end seizings, carefully unlay the strand, and whip the ends of each strand tightly with several turns of sail twine or friction tape. Cut out the core, from the eye, and put it in the rigger's screw or a vise, with the unlaid strands on your left. Stretch out the standing part of the wire, lash it, and you are ready to go to work.

The first strand of the Liverpool goes under three strands, the second under two, and the third under one. They all enter at the same point but come out at different places, as shown in Fig. A2.47.

Strands 4, 5, and 6 are tucked as shown in Fig. A2.48(A). The succeeding tucks are made by wrapping each strand back around and under the strand it is already under, as shown in Fig. A2.48(B). To avoid kinking the strands on the last tucks, insert the spike and run it up the wire, as shown in steps 1 and 2 of Fig. A2.49. Follow the spike up with the strand, shove it under the spike, and pull taut. Keeping a strain on the strand, work the spike and strand back around and down together (steps 3 and 4 of Fig.

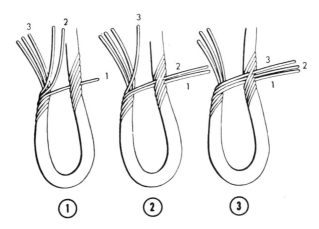

Fig. A2.47   Tucking the first three strands in a Liverpool splice.

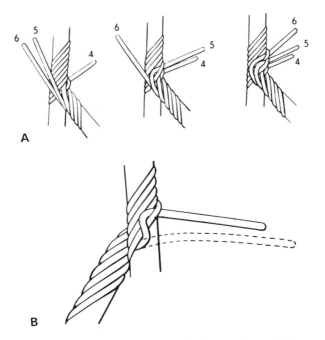

Fig. A2.48 Start of second round of tucks in a Liverpool splice.

A2.49). Hold the strand there, and work the spike back up the wire. Follow up with the strand, and take the last tuck. Work that strand back down and hold it there. Before pulling out the spike, run it back up until the strands of the standing wire bind the working strand in place. Make the second and third tucks with the remaining strands in the same way.

A locking tuck may be taken after completing the third round of tucks to decrease the possibility of the splice working out. For this tuck, take every other strand (2, 4, and 6, for example), pass each of thse with the lay over two strands, and tuck under the next strand. Each of these strands, therfore, goes over the adjacent working strand (as well as the two strands of the standing part) and locks the splice in place.

Short Splice To make a short splice, you need to unlay 2 or 3 feet of each rope, depending on its size. To determine the proper length, use the same formula as for the eye splice. Prepare each rope by seizing before unlaying and whipping each strand. Interlace the strands as is done with fiber rope, and then seize them. Remove one of the temporary seizings and commence tucking. Tucks go against the lay, over one and under two. Take four rounds of tucks, and then split each strand and bend half of it back out of the way. The halves bent back are dropped at this point. Take two

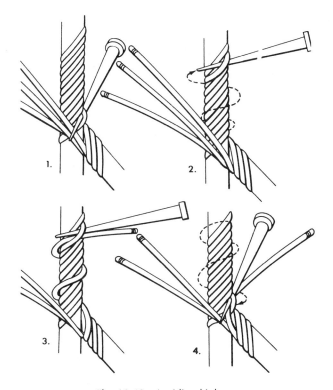

Fig. A2.49 Avoiding kinks.

more tucks with the other halves. Next, turn the wire and repeat the foregoing steps in the opposite direction. Beat out the splice with a wooden mallet, working from the center to the ends and turning the splice as you beat. To complete the work, cut off the strands and beat down the ends.

Long Splice   The recommended number of feet for a long splice in wire is 40 times the diameter of the wire. In other words, a long splice in ¾-in. wire would be 30 ft long, ½-inch wire would be 20 ft long, etc. For purposes of the following description, ¾-in. wire, or a splice of 30 ft, will be used. The steps for making a long splice (Fig. A2.50) are as follows:

1. Measure 15 feet from the ends of each wire and put on temporary seizings.
2. Cut the end seizings, unlay, and whip the strands. Cut out the core, interlace the strands, butt the ends of the rope together solidly, and seize in place.

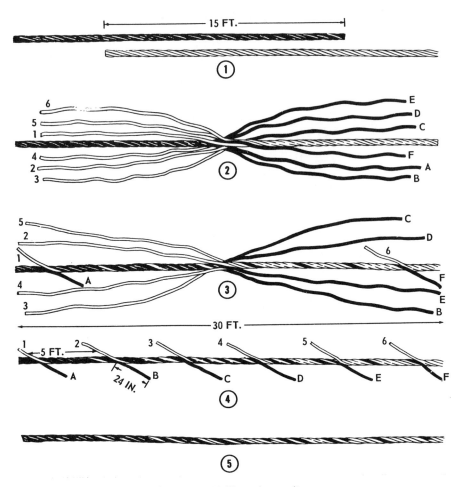

Fig. A2.50 Making a long splice.

3. Cut off the temporary seizing on one rope and start unlaying any one of the strands, laying the opposite strand from the other rope in the groove as you go. Lay in all but 2 feet of this strand, and cut off all but 2 feet of the unlaid strand.

4. Repeat step 3, unlaying the strand next to the strand laid in step 3, and the result will be a strand laid in each direction as shown in step 4.

5. Repeat step 3 with the next strand of the first rope, stopping 5 feet short of the meeting point of the first pair. Continue unlaying and laying in successive strands, working first one way and then the other, leaving 5-ft intervals between the meeting points. When all

strands are laid in, your splice should look like the one shown in step 5.

One method of securing the ends of a long splice is the same for wire rope as for fiber rope. Tie an overhand knot, and pull it taut. Then divide the ends in three parts, and tuck them separately, as shown in Fig. A2.51. The preferred method of securing the ends is illustrated in Fig. A2.51. Tuck the ends of the strands into the rope, replacing the core. Seize the strands at their meeting point, and cut off the end whippings. Untwist the strands so that the "form" or "set" is taken out. Next, build up the strands to be the same size as the core. It is possible to do so with successive seizings of seizing wire if the rope has a wire core. If the rope has a hemp core, service the strands with marline or wrap them with friction tape.

Secure a Spanish windlass on each side of the meeting point, as shown in step 1 of Fig. A2.52. Twist in opposite directions, opening the lay of the rope. Cut the core and pull out the ends a few inches. Shove a marline-spike under two adjacent strands, as in step 2. Now take off the Spanish windlasses, and work the spike along the rope, pulling out the core and laying in the strand until all the strand is in. Then cut off the core at that point, shove the end back in place, and pull out the spike. Repeat the process on all the other strand ends. Notice that the strands do not cross before tucking. After securing the ends, beat out the splice, as shown in step 3. A long splice with the ends secured in this manner does not alter the size of the rope and will almost defy detection after the rope has been in use a short time.

A2.15 Wire Rope Clips A temporary eye splice may be put in wire by using wire rope clips. The correct and incorrect ways of using these clips are shown in Fig. A2.53. The U-bolt always goes over the bitter end and the roddle on the standing part. Space the clips at a distance equal to six times the diameter of the wire. After the rope is under strain, tighten the clips again. On operating ropes, tighten the clips every few hours, and inspect the rope carefully at points where they occur. Pay particular attention to the wire at the clip farthest from the eye, because vibration and whipping are dampened there, and fatigue breaks are likely to occur.

Fig. A2.51 One method of securing ends of a long splice.

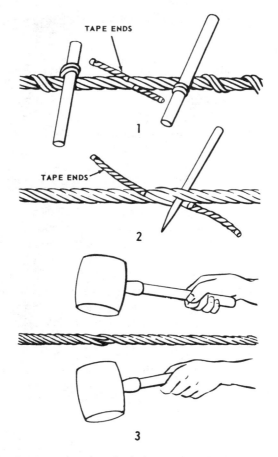

Fig. A2.52 Preferred method of securing ends in a long splice.

Fig. A2.53 Correct and incorrect use of wire rope clips.

Table A2.2 Number of Clips for Various Wire Ropes

Size of Rope (inches)	Number of Clips
$1/2$	2
$5/8$	3
$3/4$	3
$1/8$	4
1	4
$1\ 1/8$	5
$1\ 1/4$	5
$1\ 1/2$	6

To obtain maximum strength in the temporary eye splice, use the correct size and number of wire clips. Size is stamped on the roddle between the two holes. The correct number of clips to use for various sizes of wire ropes is shown in Table A2.2.

The improved type of wire rope clip shown in Fig. A2.54 has a few advantages over that of the U-bolt type. Both halves are identical and provide a bearing surface for both parts of the rope. Thus it cannot be put on wrong and it does not distort the wire. It also allows a full swing with a wrench.

A2.16 Wire Rope Clamped Splices In recent years, a method of fabricating wire-rope eye splices using steel clamps applied under great pressure has been developed. (See Fig. A2.55.) The resulting splices are 100 percent efficient and have the full strength of the rope itself. They are made at a much lower cost in man hours, and much less wire is used because no excess wire is needed for tucking. Splices of this type are widely used for cargo slings and other applications in the marine industry. Many naval amphibious and replenishment ships have the equipment on board to produce them. Clamps are available at present to splice wire ropes up to 1½ inches in diameter. In the clamping process, the metal clamp is squeezed into the wires and the wires forced together.

A2.17 End Connectors Various end connectors are used with wire rope to attach ropes to each other, to the ship, and to different assemblies. In the Navy, poured wire rope sockets are required for boat lifting slings, running rigging, and the life whenever the connection must equal 100 percent of the rope's breaking strength. Fiege connectors can usually be substituted for other applications.

Sockets Sockets are classed as open or closed, depending on whether they are the jaw and pin or loop types. They are connected to rope as

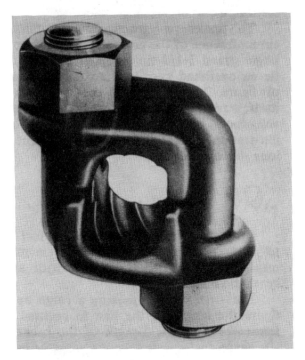

Fig. A2.54 Improved type of wire rope clip.

shown in Fig. A2.56. The rope end should be whipped (seized) near the end. Put on an additional seizing at a distance from the end of the rope equal to the length of the basket of the socket. It is very important that the seizings be secure to prevent untwisting of the wires and strands and the resultant unequal tension between the several wires after the socket is attached. Place the rope end upright in a vise. Remove the seizing at the bitter end. If the heart is hemp, cut it down to the remaining seizing. If the heart is wire, allow it to remain. Untwist the strands, and broom out the wire. The wires should be separated from one another but not straightened. Clean them carefully with methyl chloroform from the ends to as near the first seizing as possible; wipe dry. Dip them into muriatic acid diluted with an equal amount of water. (Carefully pour the acid into the water; *do not pour the water into the acid.*) Use no stronger solution, and take extra care that the acid does not touch any other part of the rope. To remove the acid, dip the wires into boiling water containing a small amount of soda. Heat the socket to about 300°F. Draw the wires together again with a piece of seizing wire, and foce the socket down over them until it reaches the seizing. Free the wires within the socket basket, and allow them

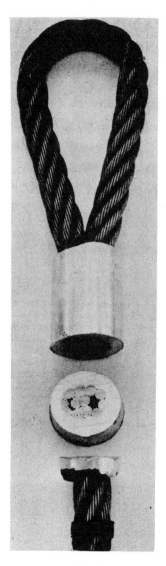

Fig. A2.55   Example of clamped 100-percent efficient eye splice.

to spread evenly and naturally. The ends of the wires should be level with the large end of the socket basket. Care should be taken to see that the centerline of the basket is lined up exactly with that of the rope (that is, that the socket is in a true straight line with the rope) so that each element under load will sustain its due share. Seal the small end of the socket

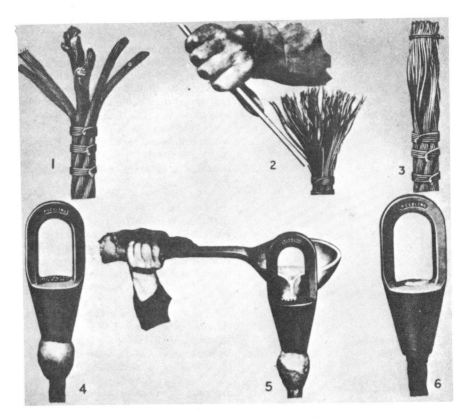

Fig. A2.56 Attaching a poured socket.

around the rope with putty, fire clay, or a similar substance. Fill the socket basket with molten zinc. The zinc must not be too hot, particularly on small ropes. The correct temperature is from 800 to 850°F. Allow the connector to cool in air or plunge it into cool, fresh water. Remove all seizing except that nearest the socket.

Installing Fiege-Type (Threaded, Compression) Connectors

Fiege-type wire rope connectors are equal in strength to 85 percent of the minimum breaking strength of 6 × 19, uncoated, high-grade, plow-steel wire rope of the size for which the connector was made. Typical examples of approved applications for Fiege-type wire rope connectors, wherein the design has provided an adequate safety factor, are:

1. Ships standing rigging
2. Boat booms

3. Life lines
4. Tiller ropes
5. Towed devices involving use of armored electrical cable
6. Wire rope antennas

Fiege-type wire rope connectors are made of three parts. They include a sleeve which slips over the end of the wire rope, a plug which is inserted to separate and hold the strands of the wire in the sleeve, and a covering socket. This combination locks onto the cable to make a strong flexible connection. Different types of plugs, as shown in Fig. A2.57, are provided for use with different types of wire rope. If the fitting is to be used on a wire center rope or on a strand, the order for the fitting should indicate the type of plug to be furnished.

The following procedure should be followed for installing Fiege-type wire rope connectors. Figure A2.58 illustrates the wire rope extension dimensions referred to in the following instructions.

1. Grooved plug on fiber core
   a. Apply seizing and cut rope at desired point of attachment. Apply a second seizing at dimension A (Fig. A2.58)
   b. Place rope in vise vertically and drive sleeve (and top seizing) on rope far enough to prevent fanning out, then remove top seizing.
   c. Insert screwdriver blade between rope stands to unlay, pry out fiber core, and cut off a length equal to dimension E (Fig. A2.58). Push stub back into center of rope.
   d. Push sleeve down over rope far enough to insert plug between strands. This prevents individual wires from fanning out.
   e. By alternately tapping sleeve and plug, drive them on rope the required distance, dimension C or D (Fig. A2.58), as applicable.
   f. Drive plug to a solid seat. This is very important.
   g. Compress extended strands to permit attaching socket portion of the fitting. Grip sleeve in vise and attach socket to sleeve, then tighten securely (Fig. A2.59).
2. Solid plug on wire-center rope 1/16 inch through 9/16 inch (Fig. A2.60).
   a. Apply seizing and cut rope at desired point of attachment. Apply a second seizing at dimension A (Fig. A2.58).
   b. Place rope in vise vertically and drive sleeve (and top seizing) on rope far enough to prevent fanning out, then remove top seizing.
   c. Drive sleeve down on rope the required distance, dimension B (Fig. A2.58).
   d. Fan out individual wires uniformly.
   e. Insert wire plug in as near center of fanned wires as possible.

Fiber Core Plug, Eight-Groove

For all fiber core wire ropes with eight strands. Sizes 3/8 inch and smaller and for all industrial-type fittings. Drawn brass or bronze — 1/2 inch and smaller. Steel-9/16 inch and larger.

Fiber Core Plug, Six-Groove

For all fiber core wire ropes (except 6 x 42 rope), with six strands. Sizes 5/16 inch and smaller, have no grooves. Cast bronze.

Wire-Center Plug (Solid)

For all wire-center wire ropes. 6 x 42 hemp-center rope 1/2 inch and smaller and for all industrial-type fittings. Drawn brass or bronze — 1/2 inch and smaller. Steel-9/16 inch and larger.

Wire-Center Plug (Two-Pieces)

For all wire-center wire rope sizes 9/16 inch and larger. Cast bronze.

Strand Plug (Hollow)

For all strands of seven or 19 wires 1/4 inch and larger. (Cannot be used interchangeably — 1 x 7 requires larger hole than 1 x 19.) Drawn bronze or steel.

Fig. A2.57 Fiege-type connector plugs.

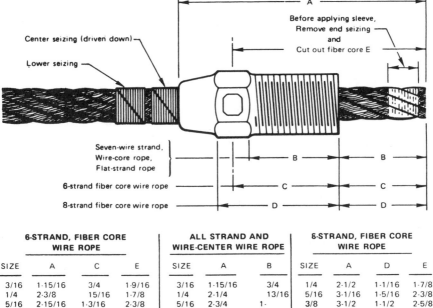

6-STRAND, FIBER CORE WIRE ROPE			
SIZE	A	C	E
3/16	1-15/16	3/4	1-9/16
1/4	2-3/8	15/16	1-7/8
5/16	2-15/16	1-3/16	2-3/8
3/8	3-5/16	1-5/16	2-5/8
7/16	3-7/8	1-9/16	3-1/8
1/2	4-3/8	1-3/4	3-1/2
9/16	5-1/16	1-15/16	3-7/8
5/8	5-1/16	1-15/16	3-7/8
3/4	5-7/8	2-1/4	4-1/2
7/8	6-15/16	2-11/16	5-3/8
1-	8-3/8	3-1/4	6-1/2
1-1/8	10-	3-3/4	7-1/2
1-1/4	11-7/8	4-3/8	8-3/4
1-3/8	14-1/4	5-1/4	10-1/2
1-1/2	16-1/8	6-1/8	12-1/4
1-5/8	18-3/16	7-1/16	14-1/8

ALL STRAND AND WIRE-CENTER WIRE ROPE		
SIZE	A	B
3/16	1-15/16	3/4
1/4	2-1/4	13/16
5/16	2-3/4	1-
3/8	3-1/8	1-1/8
7/16	3-5/8	1-5/16
1/2	4-1/8	1-1/2
9/16	4-3/4	1-5/8
5/8	4-3/4	1-5/8
3/4	5-1/2	1-7/8
7/8	6-1/2	2-1/4
1-	7-7/8	2-3/4
1-1/8	9-3/8	3-1/8
1-1/4	11-1/8	3-5/8
1-3/8	13-5/16	4-5/16
1-1/2	15-1/8	5-1/8
1-5/8	17-1/8	6-

6-STRAND, FIBER CORE WIRE ROPE			
SIZE	A	D	E
1/4	2-1/2	1-1/16	1-7/8
5/16	3-1/16	1-5/16	2-3/8
3/8	3-1/2	1-1/2	2-5/8
7/16	4-1/16	1-3/4	3-1/8
1/2	4-5/8	2-	3-1/2
9/16	5-3/8	2-1/4	3-7/8
5/8	5-3/8	2-1/4	3-7/8
3/4	6-1/4	2-5/8	4-1/2
7/8	7-3/8	3-1/8	5-3/8
1-	8-7/8	3-3/4	6-1/2
1-1/8	10-5/8	4-3/8	8-3/4
1-1/4	12-5/8	5-1/8	10-1/4
1-3/8	15-3/16	6-3/16	12-3/8
1-1/2	17-1/8	7-1/8	14-1/4
1-5/8	19-1/4	8-1/8	16-1/4

Fig. A2.58 Wire rope extension diameters.

  f. Drive plug to a solid seat. This is very important.
  g. Compress extended strands to permit attaching socket portion of the fitting. Grip sleeve in vice and attach socket to sleeve, then tighten securely. Remove seizing.
 3. Two-piece grooved plug on wire-center rope 9/16 inch and larger (Fig. A2.61).
  a. Apply seizing and cut rope at desired point of attachment. Apply a second seizing at dimension A (Fig. A2.58).
  b. Drive sleeve down on rope the required distance, dimension B (Fig. A2.58).
  c. Fan out strands preparatory to inserting split plug.

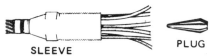

SLEEVE   PLUG

Wire rope passed through sleeve and strands fanned out
for insertion of fluted plug

SLEEVE   PLUG   SOCKET

Plug driven in and strands closed to apply socket

▼ INSPECTION HOLE

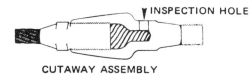

CUTAWAY ASSEMBLY

Socket applied showing twisted strands and completed
assembly

Fig. A2.59   Grooved plug on fiber core wire rope.

Wire rope passed through sleeve.

Wires broomed-out for insertion of solid plug.

Plug driven in and wires closed to apply socket.

INSPECTION HOLE

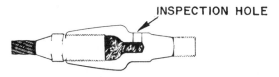

CUTAWAY ASSEMBLY

Socket applied showing twisted wires and completed
assembly.

Fig. A2.60   Solid plug on wire-center rope.

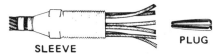

SLEEVE   PLUG

Wire rope passed through sleeve and strands fanned out
for insertion of two-piece fluted plug

SLEEVE   PLUG   SOCKET

Plug driven in and strands closed to apply socket

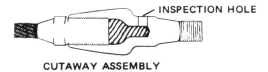

INSPECTION HOLE

CUTAWAY ASSEMBLY
Socket applied showing twisted strands and completed
assembly

Fig. A2.61   Two-pieced grooved plug on wire-center rope.

SLEEVE

Strand passed through sleeve.

SLEEVE   PLUG

Wires fanned out for insertion of hollow plug.

SLEEVE   PLUG   SOCKET

Plug driven in and wires closed to apply socket.

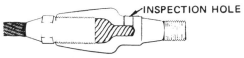

INSPECTION HOLE

CUTAWAY ASSEMBLY
Socket applied showing twisted wires and completed
assembly.

Fig. A2.62   Hollow plug on wire-center strand.

    d. Insert plug halves around center strand taking care that each outside strand lies in its proper groove.

    e. Using a hollow punch, drive plug to a solid seat.

    f. Compress extended strands to permit attaching socket portion of the fitting. Grip sleeve in vise and attach socket to sleeve, then tighten securely. Remove seizing.

4. Hollow plug on a wire-center strand (Fig. A2.62).

    a. Apply seizing and cut strand at desired point of attachment. Apply a second seizing at dimension A (Fig. A2.58).

    b. Place strand in vise vertically and drive sleeve (and top seizing) on strand far enough to prevent fanning out, then remove top seizing.

    c. Drive sleeve on strand the required distance, dimension B. (Fig. A2.58).

    d. Fan outside wires and insert drilled plug over center wire.

    e. Using a hollow punch, drive plug to solid seat.

    f. Compress extended wires to permit attaching socket portion of the fitting. Grip sleeve in vise and attach socket to sleeve, then tighten securely. Remove seizing.

NOTE: If the twist does not show across the inspection hole after carefully following the foregoing assembly instructions and extension dimensions, it indicates that not enough rope has been allowed to project beyond the sleeve mouth. In succeeding assemblies, allow more rope to project beyond the sleeve until the twist shows up satisfactorily.

Appendix 3

Mechanical Weight-Lifting Appliances

The advent of marine nuclear power has not relieved seamen of the necessity of having the same fundamental knowledge of ropes, tackles, and other weight-handling equipment that was required of their predecessors. True, the weights are heavier and are moved greater distances, and wire rope is often used now instead of fiber, but the same principles of mechanical advantage and friction still apply.

Tasks requiring the use of booms, tackles, topping lifts, and other mechanical appliances are the daily lot of seamen. Merchant vessels and naval cargo ships require the rigging of many different purchases for positioning and steadying cargo booms and for handling the weights after the booms have been rigged.

Anyone who is concerned with rigging or operating cargo booms should be thoroughly familiar with the forces set up in both. To this end, he should consult the manufacturer's tables to determine the strength of the wire or rope used in the standing and running rigging, and he should never exceed these loads. He should inspect all the rigging periodically, replacing worn parts and performing such preventive maintenance as may be specified by the manufacturer. Finally, he should be familiar with the fundamentals of applied mechanics and the effects of acceleration and deceleration on the rigging.

The weight-lifting appliances to be discussed here include blocks, tackle, shackles, swivels, and hooks. Line and wire characteristics are discussed in Appendix 1.

A3.1 Shackles Shackles are used to connect objects together: one wire eye to another, or a sling to a load, or a hook to a block, or a hook to a wire-rope eye. The uses of shackles in weight handling and other shipboard applications are too numerous to mention.

The most common shackle is the *anchor screw pin* type. Other types used on shipboard include *round pin* and *safety shackles.* (See Fig. A3.1.)

The following formula may be used to estimate the safe working load of a shackle (expressed in tons):

$$\text{Safe working load} = 3\ D^2$$

where D is the wire diameter of the shackle at the sides. Thus, for a 1-in. shackle, the safe working load is $3 \times (1),^2$ or 3 tons.

This formula is valid for older shackles. There is now, however, a requirement that newly manufactured shackles be properly marked (by raised or indented lettering) with the manufacturer's name, the size of the shackle, and the safe working load (1/4T, 1/2T, 1T, etc.).

A3.2   Hooks   The hook is customarily the point in weight-handling appliances where the load is attached. Because of its open construction, the hook is usually the weakest part of the appliance or cargo rig. Figure A3.2 shows various types of hooks. The latch across the opening of the safety hook is installed to prevent the load or sling ring from coming out of the hook if the strain is abruptly eased. Mousing a hook with marline or other small stuff accomplishes the same thing. It should be pointed out that mous-

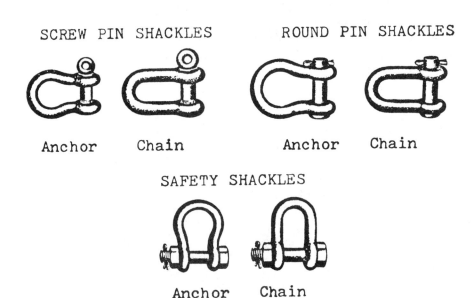

SCREW PIN SHACKLES   ROUND PIN SHACKLES

Anchor   Chain   Anchor   Chain

SAFETY SHACKLES

Anchor   Chain

Fig. A3.1   Types of shackles.

Safety Eye
Hook

Plain Eye
Hook

Portland   **New York**   **Seattle**

Common Types of Cargo Hooks

Fig. A3.2   Various types of hooks.

ing of a hook with line will do nothing to prevent it from opening out under excessive strain. A formula for estimating the safe working load of a hook, in tons, is as follows:

$$\text{Safe working load} = 2/3\ D^2$$

where D is the wire diameter of the hook at the back of the hook below the eye. As in the case of shackles, the formula is valid for older hooks. The newer hooks are stamped with the manufacturer's name, the size, and the safe working load.

The substitution of shackles for hooks is desirable for many heavy lifts because a shackle is about five times stronger than a hook of the same wire diameter.

A3.3   Swivels   Swivels are used together with shackles, blocks, and hooks in weight-lifting appliances. A swivel should be inserted in the makeup of a rig or load whenever a twist is possible. Two types of swivels (the most common types in shipboard use) are illustrated in Fig. A3.3. Swivels are somewhat stronger than shackles of the same size.

A3.4   Blocks   A *block,* in the nautical sense, consists of a frame of wood or steel within which one or more sheaves (pulleys) is fitted. Blocks take

Fig. A3.3 Types of swivels.

their names from the pupose for which they are used, the places they occupy, or from some peculiarity in their shape or construction. They are designated further as *single, double,* or *triple blocks* according to the number of sheaves they have. (See Fig. A3.4.)

The size of the block is determined by the circumference of the rope to be used with it. The size of the block, measured as the length of the cheek in inches, should be three times the circumference of the rope. The diameter of the sheave should be twice the circumference of the rope. Thus, a block for use with a 3-in. rope would be a 9-in. block, and its sheave diameter would be 6 in.

Because of their own greater strength, artificial fiber ropes require blocks of greater strength; therefore, ropes of artificial fiber must not be substituted for manila or other natural fiber ropes until it has been determined that the blocks are strong enough to handle them.

Blocks for use with wire rope are not so well standardized. Wire rope can be made to conform to widely varying specifications. When specifications for blocks are made, the advice of the manufacturer should be fol-

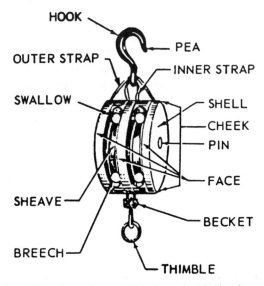

Fig. A3.4 Parts of a wood block used with fiber lines.

lowed as to the diameter of sheave or drum over which the wire is to be rove and to the speed of operation (linear speed of the wire). If such advice is not followed, the life of the rope will be materially shortened as a result of alternating bending and straightening as the wire passes over the sheave (drum).

A good rule of thumb to follow in regard to the proper size of a wire rope block is to use a sheave diameter that is twenty times the diameter of the rope. The diamond-type wire-rope block and the roller-bearing wire-rope block are illustrated in Figs. A3.5 and A3.6, respectively. In cargo-handling rigs, the diamond block is customarily used in the makeup of topping lifts, and the roller-bearing or "speed" block is used as the head-and-heel block of the boom through which the cargo whip is reeved.

A3.5 Moving Weights Most heavy weight handling on cargo vessels is done by means of one or more cargo booms. If only one boom is used, the weight is lifted from its initial position, the boom is swung until the weight is over its intended position, and the weight is then lowered. This method is satisfactory only for moving light loads because the boom guys must be readjusted as the boom swings.

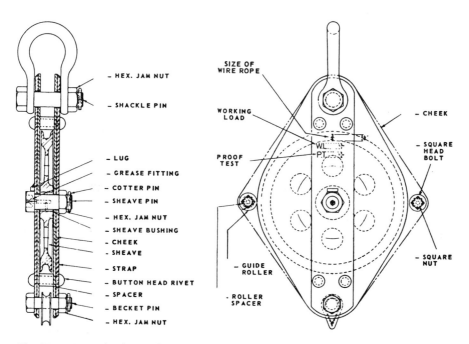

Fig. A3.5 Parts of a diamond-type block commonly used with wire rope having a low line speed.

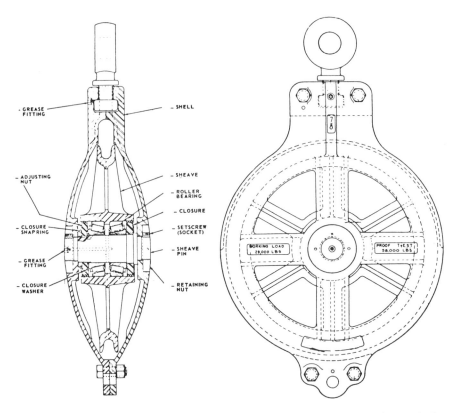

Fig. A3.6 Parts of a roller-bearing wire-rope block commonly used for cargo whips and other applications with high line speed.

A more common arrangement is the *yard-and-stay rig,* in which two booms are used. One boom, called the *hatch boom,* is rigged to plumb (over) the cargo hatch being worked, while the other, or *outboard boom* is rigged over the side to plumb a lighter or the dock. Two winches and two cargo runners or whips are necessary, one on each boom. Each runner is attached to a common hook that engages the load. For loading, the winch of the outboard boom hoists the load, or draft, high enough to clear the ship's side or other obstruction. The draft is then "racked" inboard, with the hatch boom winch heaving in and the other winch slacking off slowly until the load is entirely supported by the hatch boom. Finally, the hatch boom winch lowers the draft into the hold, with the outboard cargo runner being kept slack. For unloading, the cycle is reversed. (See Fig. A3.7.)

In any weight-handling operation, speed should be subordinated to

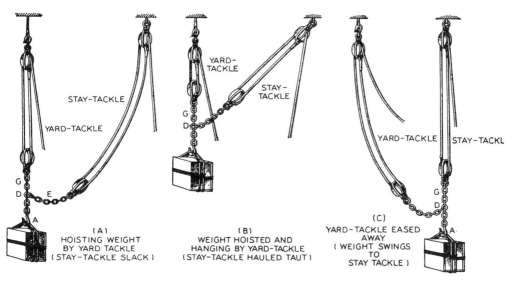

Fig. A3.7 Yard-and-stay tackles.

safety and smoothness of operation. Jerky movements caused by too rapid acceleration and deceleration put enormous strains on the standing and running rigging, which could result in the parting of one or more lines and the collapse of the entire rig, potentially damaging the load, the ship, and the operating personnel.

The greatest force must be applied at the time of starting a load, because it is necessary to overcome inertia. This force must be applied gradually lest the strain exceed the safe working load. Speed may be increased once the load is moving.

A3.6 Tackles An assemblage of ropes (falls) and blocks for the purpose of multiplying force is a *tackle* (See Fig. A3.8.)

The seaman speaks of *reeving* when he passes ropes around the sheaves of the blocks. These ropes are called *falls*. The *standing part* is that part of the fall made fast to one of the blocks. The *hauling part* is the end of the falls to which force is applied to handle the weight. To *overhaul* the falls is to separate the blocks. To *round in* is to bring the blocks together. The blocks are said to be *chock-a-block* or *two-blocked* when they are tight together.

Tackles are designated either according to the number of sheaves in the blocks that are used to make the tackle—for example, single, two-fold,

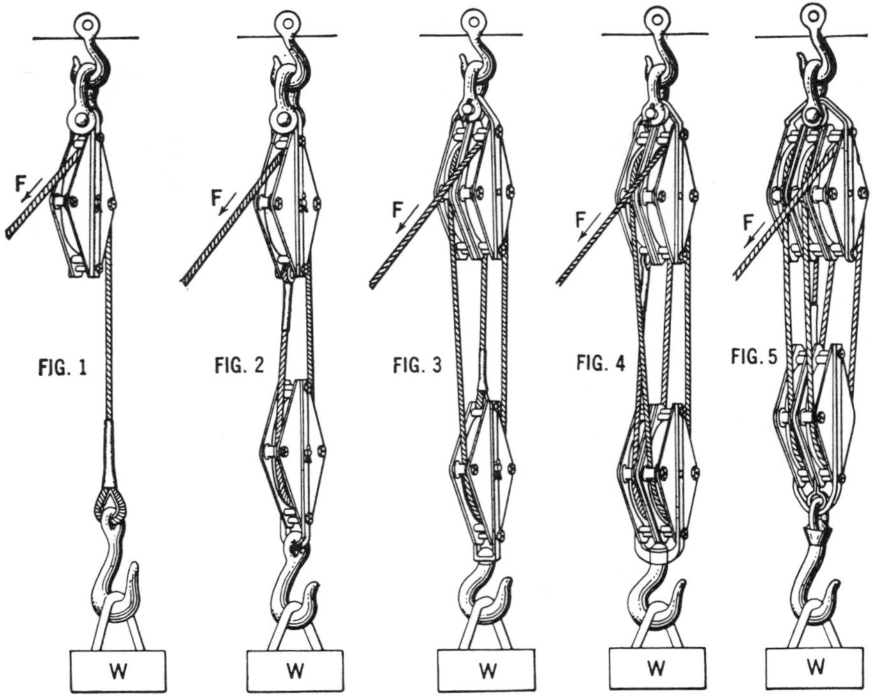

Ratio of Weight W to force F Necessary to Raise Weight

	Disregarding Friction	Allowing for Friction
Fig. 1	$F = W$	$\dfrac{F}{W} = \dfrac{11}{10}$
Fig. 2	$\dfrac{F}{W} = \dfrac{10}{20}$	$\dfrac{F}{W} = \dfrac{12}{20}$
Fig. 3	$\dfrac{F}{W} = \dfrac{10}{30}$	$\dfrac{F}{W} = \dfrac{13}{30}$
Fig. 4	$\dfrac{F}{W} = \dfrac{10}{40}$	$\dfrac{F}{W} = \dfrac{14}{40}$
Fig. 5	$\dfrac{F}{W} = \dfrac{10}{50}$	$\dfrac{F}{W} = \dfrac{15}{50}$
In a three-fold purchase	$\dfrac{P}{W} = \dfrac{10}{60}$	$\dfrac{F}{W} = \dfrac{16}{60}$
Luff on luff	$\dfrac{P}{W} = \dfrac{10}{120}$	$\dfrac{F}{W} = \dfrac{16}{120}$

F

FIG. 5

W

F

FIG. 4

W

FIG. 3

W

F

FIG. 2

W

F

FIG. 1

W

Fig. A3.8 Types of tackles.

Note: In this illustration the hauling part leads from the fixed block. The mechanical efficiency can always be increased if the hauling part is led from the movable block.

or three-fold purchase—or according to the purpose for which the tackle is used—for example, *yard tackles, stay tackles,* and *fore-and-aft tackles.* Other designations handed down from the past still persist—*luff tackles, gun tackles, Spanish burtons.* Common varieties include the following:

Single whips use a single fixed block, as shown in Fig. A3.9(A).

Runners use a single movable block, as shown in Fig. A3.9(B).

Whip and runners use a whip hooking to the hauling part of a runner.

Gun tackle purchases use a single fixed and a single movable block, as shown in Fig. A3.9(C).

Luff tackles use a single and a double block, as shown in Fig. A3.9(D). They are also called *jiggers* in the Navy.

Luff upon luffs use the double block of one luff tackle hooked to the hauling part of another, thus multiplying the power.

Two-fold purchases use two double blocks, as shown in Fig. A3.8(4).

Double luffs use a double and treble block, as shown in Fig. A3.8(5).

Three-fold purchases use two treble blocks. They are the heaviest purchase commonly used (Fig. A3.10).

Thwartship tackles are used on the heads of boat davits for rigging in. In a more general sense, the term is applied to any tackle leading across the deck. Similarly, a tackle for hauling out the backbone of an awning or for any other purpose where it has a fore-and-aft lead is known as a *fore-and-aft tackle.*

Hatch tackles are used at hatches for hoisting, lowering stores, etc.

Jiggers are small light tackles used for miscellaneous work about the ship. In the Navy, this term is usually reserved for the luff tackle.

Deck tacklers, which are heavy purchase, usually two-fold, are used in handling ground tackle, mooring ship, and generally for heavy work of any kind about the deck.

Yard-and-stay tackles take their names from their application with masts and yards, wehre they are used together for transferring stores from a boat alongside to the deck or hatch of a ship. The general principle involved in the yard-and-stay is of wide application on merchant ships where weights must be lifted from a dock and lowered through a hatch.

When working with tackles, it is sometimes necessary to know the mechanical advantage (MA), that is, the "multiplying force of the tackle." The basic formula for work applies here:

$$fD = Wd$$

This formula may be expressed as force times the distance through which it moves equals weight times the distance through which it moves. In any tackle with a movable block, the force is multiplied, and the hauling part moves a greater distance than the weight. In our formula, *d* represents the smaller distance.

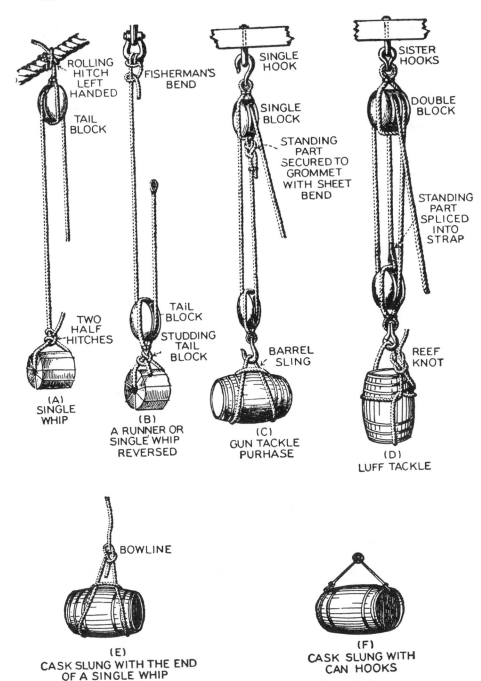

ROLLING HITCH LEFT HANDED

FISHERMAN'S BEND

SINGLE HOOK

SISTER HOOKS

TAIL BLOCK

SINGLE BLOCK

DOUBLE BLOCK

STANDING PART SECURED TO GROMMET WITH SHEET BEND

STANDING PART SPLICED INTO STRAP

TWO HALF HITCHES

TAIL BLOCK

STUDDING TAIL BLOCK

BARREL SLING

REEF KNOT

(A) SINGLE WHIP

(B) A RUNNER OR SINGLE WHIP REVERSED

(C) GUN TACKLE PURHASE

(D) LUFF TACKLE

BOWLINE

(E) CASK SLUNG WITH THE END OF A SINGLE WHIP

(F) CASK SLUNG WITH CAN HOOKS

Fig. A3.9 Tackles in use.

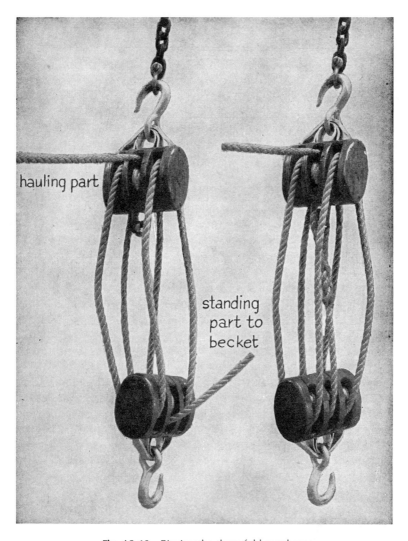

Fig. A3.10   Rigging the three-fold purchase.

In a two-fold purchase, for example, if *f* acting through 4 feet (*D*) moves the weight (*W*) 1 foot (*d*), we can write the fundamental equation as follows:

$$f \times D = W \times d$$
$$f \times 4 = W \times 1$$
$$f = \frac{W}{4}$$

The force has been multiplied four times. If the weight were, say, 100 lb, the force required to lift it would be:

$$\frac{W}{4} \text{ or } \frac{100 \text{ lb}}{4} = 25 \text{ lb}$$

Thus, to find the mechanical advantage of a tackle, one could experiment, making the necessary measurements and calculations. A simpler method would be to count the parts of the fall at the movable block.

Both of the foregoing methods of finding the MA ignore any friction in the tackle. Ordinarily, seamen can do the same, but if the power-to-weight ratio is so critical that friction must be considered, add 10 percent of the load for every sheave in the tackle (including fairlead blocks). For example, in a rig with a two-fold purchase and one fairlead block, add 50 percent to the load. Thus, with a 100-lb weight, the total load would be 150 lb. The force needed to lift this load would be:

$$\frac{150}{4} = 37.5 \text{ lb}$$

A3.7   Chain Hoists   Chain hoists, or *chain falls* as they are often called, provide a convenient and efficient method for hoisting loads by hand. Chief advantages of chain hoists are that one man can raise a load of several tons and the load can remain stationary without being secured. The slow lifting travel of a chain hoist permits small movements, accurate adjustments of height, and gentle handling of loads. For these reasons they are particularly useful in machinery spaces, but many times they come in handy on deck, too. There are four general types of chain hoists: *differential, spur gear, worm gear,* and *level* (*ratchet*). The differential and spur types (Fig. A3.11) are the most common.

The mechanical advantages of chain hoists vary from 5 to 250, depending on their rated capacities, which range from ½ to 40 tons. Although the most expensive, the spur gear is the most efficient chain hoist—losing only some 15 percent of its power through friction and other factors. The level type is suitable only for light tasks.

Ordinarily, chain hoists are constructed with their lower hook as the weakest part of the assembly. This is a precaution, so that the lower hook will start to spread open before the chain hoist itself is overloaded. Under ordinary circumstances, the pull exerted on a chain hoist by one or two men will not overload the hoist.

Chain hoists should be inspected at frequent intervals. Any evidence of spreading or excessive wear on the hook is sufficient cause to require its

Fig. A3.11 Chain hoists: Differential chain hoist at left; spur gear at right.

replacement. If the links of the chain are distorted, this is an indication that the chain hoist has been heavily overloaded and is probably unsafe for further use. Under such circumstances, the chain hoist should be surveyed (discarded).

A3.8 General Precautions In preparing for any lift with weight-handling appliances, in addition to ensuring that all components are of adequate size to accomplish the desired task, each part should be inspected to determine its condition. Fiber lines should be inspected for signs of excessive wear: fraying, rot, and dryness. The line should be twisted open to expose the interior of the strands. If the interior is grey, dried out, and powdery, the line is unsafe for use. Wire ropes should be examined for fish hooks, badly worn areas, and kinks. A badly worn wire rope should not be used. (Refer to wire rope wear criteria in Appendix 1.) Wooden blocks should be examined to ensure there are no cracked or rotted cheeks, worn pins, or cracked or badly worn metal parts. All metal fittings such as shackles, metal blocks, swivels, and hooks should be carefully examined for any signs of cracks, distortion, excessive wear, or metal fatigue. Remember that specifications are given for *new* components; the actual safe working load of the equipment you plan to use may be far less if it is worn or old.

Some excellent general precautions to take when using weight-handling gear are as follows:

1. Remember that the giving way of one part breaks and destroys other parts, frequently to an extent not readily repaired, and, furthermore, it endangers the men.
2. Heavy weights must never be allowed to drop, even for the shortest distances, but must be lowered to rest with a gentle motion and at the same time chocked to prevent rolling or sliding.
3. In raising or lowering heavy weights, closely follow up with blocks or chocks, whenever possible, to guard against any giving way of jacks or tackle.
4. All motions with heavy weights must be slow so as not to generate momentum.
5. Supports must have a firm base and cribbing, a level foundation, and be built up vertically.
6. All fittings or appliances used for securing lines must be strong and secure beyond any possibility of carrying away.
7. Be careful at all times to avoid any sudden shocks or strains.
8. Every operation should be done with spirit but without bustle or confusion.
9. Vigilance on the part of the person in charge should be unceasing to see all gear is rigged, handled, and operated correctly.
10. Do not permit men to step on a taut fall or get in dangerous positions, such as under weights, in the bight of a running rope, or at the end of a taut rope or cable that might give way.
11. Special precautions must be taken in wet weather when surfaces are slippery.
12. Overhaul tackle as frequently as necessary, keeping it free from rust, corrosion, and dirt as well as well oiled and operating freely.
13. Always ensure that decks are adequately shored to withstand the additional stresses of handling heavy weights.
14. Overloading decreases the strength of rope materially. Rope should never be loaded beyond one-third of its breaking load.
15. Keep wire rope well coated with a preservative lubricant and free of kinks or sharp bends.

Appendix 4

Inland Navigational Rules
Act of 1980

PUBLIC LAW 96–591—DEC. 24, 1980

Public Law 96–591
96th Congress

An Act

To unify the rules for preventing collisions on the inland waters of the United States, and for other purposes.

Be it enacted by the Senate and House of Representatives of the United States of America in Congress assembled, That this Act may be cited as the "Inland Navigational Rules Act of 1980".

SEC. 2. Inland Navigational Rules:

PART A—GENERAL

RULE 1

Application

(a) These Rules apply to all vessels upon the inland waters of the United States, and to vessels of the United States on the Canadian waters of the Great Lakes to the extent that there is no conflict with Canadian law.

(b)(i) These Rules constitute special rules made by an appropriate authority within the meaning of Rule 1(b) of the International Regulations.

(ii) All vessels complying with the construction and equipment requirements of the International Regulations are considered to be in compliance with these Rules.

(c) Nothing in these Rules shall interfere with the operation of any special rules made by the Secretary of the Navy with respect to additional station or signal lights and shapes or whistle signals for ships of war and vessels proceeding under convoy, or by the Secretary with respect to additional station or signal lights and shapes for fishing vessels engaged in fishing as a fleet. These additional station or signal lights and shapes or whistle signals shall, so far as possible, be such that they cannot be mistaken for any light, shape, or signal authorized elsewhere under these Rules. Notice of such special rules shall be published in the Federal Register and, after the effective date specified in such notice, they shall have effect as if they were a part of these Rules.

(d) Vessel traffic service regulations may be in effect in certain areas.

(e) Whenever the Secretary determines that a vessel or class of vessels of special construction or purpose cannot comply fully with the provisions of any of these Rules with respect to the number, position, range, or arc of visibility of lights or shapes, as well as to the disposition and characteristics of sound-signaling appliances, without interfering with the special function of the vessel, the vessel shall comply with such other provisions in regard to the number, position, range, or arc of visibility of lights or shapes, as well as to the disposition and characteristics of sound-signaling appliances, as the Secretary shall have determined to be the closest possible compliance with these Rules. The Secretary may issue a certificate of alternative compliance for a vessel or class of vessels specifying the closest possible compliance with these Rules. The Secretary of the Navy shall make these determinations and issue certificates of alternative compliance for vessels of the Navy.

(f) The Secretary may accept a certificate of alternative compliance issued by a contracting party to the International Regulations if he determines that the alternative compliance standards of the contracting party are substantially the same as those of the United States.

RULE 2

Responsibility

(a) Nothing in these Rules shall exonerate any vessel, or the owner, master, or crew thereof, from the consequences of any neglect to comply with these Rules or of the neglect of any precaution which may be required by the ordinary practice of seamen, or by the special circumstances of the case.

(b) In construing and complying with these Rules due regard shall be had to all dangers of navigation and collision and to any special circumstances, including the limitations of the vessels involved, which may make a departure from these Rules necessary to avoid immediate danger.

RULE 3

General Definitions

For the purpose of these Rules and this Act, except where the context otherwise requires:

(a) The word "vessel" includes every description of water craft, including nondisplacement craft and seaplanes, used or capable of being used as a means of transportation on water;

(b) The term "power-driven vessel" means any vessel propelled by machinery;

(c) The term "sailing vessel" means any vessel under sail provided that propelling machinery, if fitted, is not being used;

(d) The term "vessel engaged in fishing" means any vessel fishing with nets, lines, trawls, or other fishing apparatus which restricts maneuverability, but does not include a vessel fishing with trolling lines or other fishing apparatus which do not restrict maneuverability;

(e) The word "seaplane" includes any aircraft designed to maneuver on the water;

(f) The term "vessel not under command" means a vessel which through some exceptional circumstance is unable to maneuver as required by these Rules and is therefore unable to keep out of the way of another vessel;

(g) The term "vessel restricted in her ability to maneuver" means a vessel which from the nature of her work is restricted in her ability to maneuver as required by these Rules and is therefore unable to keep out of the way of another vessel; vessels restricted in their ability to maneuver include, but are not limited to:

(i) a vessel engaged in laying, servicing, or picking up a navigation mark, submarine cable, or pipeline;
(ii) a vessel engaged in dredging, surveying, or underwater operations;
(iii) a vessel engaged in replenishment or transferring persons, provisions, or cargo while underway;
(iv) a vessel engaged in the launching or recovery of aircraft;
(v) a vessel engaged in mine clearance operations; and
(vi) a vessel engaged in a towing operation such as severely restricts the towing vessel and her tow in their ability to deviate from their course.

(h) The word "underway" means that a vessel is not at anchor, or made fast to the shore, or aground;

(i) The words "length" and "breadth" of a vessel mean her length overall and greatest breadth;

(j) Vessels shall be deemed to be in sight of one another only when one can be observed visually from the other;

(k) The term "restricted visibility" means any condition in which visibility is restricted by fog, mist, falling snow, heavy rainstorms, sandstorms, or any other similar causes;

(l) "Western Rivers" means the Mississippi River, its tributaries, South Pass, and Southwest Pass, to the navigational demarcation lines dividing the high seas from harbors, rivers, and other inland waters of the United States, and the Port Allen-Morgan City Alternate Route, and that part of the Atchafalaya River above its junction with the Port Allen-Morgan City Alternate Route including the Old River and the Red River;

(m) "Great Lakes" means the Great Lakes and their connecting and tributary waters including the Calumet River as far as the Thomas J. O'Brien Lock and Controlling Works (between mile 326 and 327), the Chicago River as far as the east side of the Ashland Avenue Bridge (between mile 321 and 322), and the Saint Lawrence River as far east as the lower exit of Saint Lambert Lock;

(n) "Secretary" means the Secretary of the department in which the Coast Guard is operating;

(o) "Inland Waters" means the navigable waters of the United States shoreward of the navigational demarcation lines dividing the high seas from harbors, rivers, and other inland waters of the United States and the waters of the Great Lakes on the United States side of the International Boundary;

(p) "Inland Rules" or "Rules" mean the Inland Navigational Rules and the annexes thereto, which govern the conduct of vessels and specify the lights, shapes, and sound signals that apply on inland waters; and

(q) "International Regulations" means the International Regulations for Preventing Collisions at Sea, 1972, including annexes currently in force for the United States.

PART B—STEERING AND SAILING RULES

Subpart I—Conduct of Vessels in Any Condition of Visibility

RULE 4

Application

Rules in this subpart apply in any condition of visibility.

RULE 5

Look-out

Every vessel shall at all times maintain a proper look-out by sight and hearing as well as by all available means appropriate in the prevailing circumstances and conditions so as to make a full appraisal of the situation and of the risk of collision.

RULE 6

Safe Speed

Every vessel shall at all times proceed at a safe speed so that she can take proper and effective action to avoid collision and be stopped within a distance appropriate to the prevailing circumstances and conditions.

In determining a safe speed the following factors shall be among those taken into account:

(a) By all vessels:
(i) the state of visibility;
(ii) the traffic density including concentration of fishing vessels or any other vessels;
(iii) the maneuverability of the vessel with special reference to stopping distance and turning ability in the prevailing conditions;
(iv) at night the presence of background light such as from shores lights or from back scatter of her own lights;
(v) the state of wind, sea, and current, and the proximity of navigational hazards;
(vi) the draft in relation to the available depth of water.

(b) Additionally, by vessels with operational radar:
(i) the characteristics, efficiency and limitations of the radar equipment;
(ii) any constraints imposed by the radar range scale in use;
(iii) the effect on radar detection of the sea state, weather, and other sources of interference;

(iv) the possibility that small vessels, ice and other floating objects may not be detected by radar at an adequate range;

(v) the number, location, and movement of vessels detected by radar; and

(vi) the more exact assessment of the visibility that may be possible when radar is used to determine the range of vessels or other objects in the vicinity.

RULE 7

Risk of Collision

(a) Every vessel shall use all available means appropriate to the prevailing circumstances and conditions to determine if risk of collision exists. If there is any doubt such risk shall be deemed to exist.

(b) Proper use shall be made of radar equipment if fitted and operational, including long-range scanning to obtain early warning of risk of collision and radar plotting or equivalent systematic observation of detected objects.

(c) Assumptions shall not be made on the basis of scanty information, especially scanty radar information.

(d) In determining if risk of collision exists the following considerations shall be among those taken into account:

(i) such risk shall be deemed to exist if the compass bearing of an approaching vessel does not appreciably change; and

(ii) such risk may sometimes exist even when an appreciable bearing change is evident, particularly when approaching a very large vessel or a tow or when approaching a vessel at close range.

RULE 8

Action To Avoid Collision

(a) Any action taken to avoid collision shall, if the circumstances of the case admit, be positive, made in ample time and with due regard to the observance of good seamanship.

(b) Any alteration of course or speed to avoid collision shall, if the circumstances of the case admit, be large enough to be readily apparent to another vessel observing visually or by radar; a succession of small alterations of course or speed should be avoided.

(c) If there is sufficient sea room, alteration of course alone may be the most effective action to avoid a close-quarters situation provided that it is made in good time, is substantial and does not result in another close-quarters situation.

(d) Action taken to avoid collision with another vessel shall be such as to result in passing at a safe distance. The effectiveness of the action shall be carefully checked until the other vessel is finally past and clear.

(e) If necessary to avoid collision or allow more time to assess the situation, a vessel shall slacken her speed or take all way off by stopping or reversing her means of propulsion.

RULE 9

Narrow Channels

(a)(i) A vessel proceeding along the course of a narrow channel or fairway shall keep as near to the outer limit of the channel or fairway which lies on her starboard side as is safe and practicable.

(ii) Notwithstanding paragraph (a)(i) and Rule 14(a), a power-driven vessel operating in narrow channels or fairways on the Great Lakes, Western Rivers, or waters specified by the Secretary, and proceeding downbound with a following current shall have the right-of-way over an upbound vessel, shall purpose the manner and place of passage, and shall initiate the maneuvering signals prescribed by Rule 34(a)(i), as appropriate. The vessel proceeding upbound against the current shall hold as necessary to permit safe passing.

(b) A vessel of less than 20 meters in length or a sailing vessel shall not impede the passage of a vessel that can safely navigate only within a narrow channel or fairway.

(c) A vessel engaged in fishing shall not impede the passage of any other vessel navigating within a narrow channel or fairway.

(d) A vessel shall not cross a narrow channel or fairway if such crossing impedes the passage of a vessel which can safely navigate only within that channel or fairway. The latter vessel shall use the danger signal prescribed in Rule 34(d) if in doubt as to the intention of the crossing vessel.

(e)(i) In a narrow channel or fairway when overtaking, the vessel intending to overtake shall indicate her intention by sounding the appropriate signal prescribed in Rule 34(c) and take steps to permit safe passing. The overtaken vessel, if in agreement, shall sound the same signal. If in doubt she shall sound the danger signal prescribed in Rule 34(d).

(ii) This Rule does not relieve the overtaking vessel of her obligation under Rule 13.

(f) A vessel nearing a bend or an area of a narrow channel or fairway where other vessels may be obscured by an intervening obstruction shall navigate with particular alertness and caution and shall sound the appropriate signal prescribed in Rule 34(e).

(g) Every vessel shall, if the circumstances of the case admit, avoid anchoring in a narrow channel.

RULE 10

Vessel Traffic Services

Each vessel required by regulation to participate in a vessel traffic service shall comply with the applicable regulations.

SUBPART II—CONDUCT OF VESSELS IN SIGHT OF ONE ANOTHER

RULE 11

Application

Rules in this subpart apply to vessels in sight of one another.

RULE 12

Sailing Vessels

(a) When two sailing vessels are approaching one another, so as to involve risk of collision, one of them shall keep out of the way of the other as follows:

(i) when each has the wind on a different side, the vessel which has the wind on the port side shall keep out of the way of the other;

(ii) when both have the wind on the same side, the vessel which is to windward shall keep out of the way of the vessel which is to leeward; and

(iii) if a vessel with the wind on the port side sees a vessel to windward and cannot determine with certainty whether the other vessel has the wind on the port or on the starboard side, she shall keep out of the way of the other.

(b) For the purpose of the Rule the windward side shall be deemed to be the side opposite to that on which the mainsail is carried or, in the case of a square-rigged vessel, the side opposite to that on which the largest fore-and-aft sail is carried.

RULE 13

Overtaking

(a) Notwithstanding anything contained in Rules 4 through 18, any vessel overtaking any other shall keep out of the way of the vessel being overtaken.

(b) A vessel shall be deemed to be overtaking when coming up with another vessel from a direction more than 22.5 degrees abaft her beam; that is, in such a position with reference to the vessel she is overtaking, that at night she would be able to see only the sternlight of that vessel but neither of her sidelights.

(c) When a vessel is in any doubt as to whether she is overtaking another, she shall assume that this is the case and act accordingly.

(d) Any subsequent alteration of the bearing between the two vessels shall not make the overtaking vessel a crossing vessel within the meaning of these Rules or relieve her of the duty of keeping clear of the overtaken vessel until she is finally past and clear.

RULE 14

(a) Unless otherwise agreed, when two power-driven vessels are meeting on reciprocal or nearly reciprocal courses so as to involve risk of collision, each shall alter her course to starboard so that each shall pass on the port side of the other.

(b) Such a situation shall be deemed to exist when a vessel sees the other ahead or nearly ahead and by night she could see the masthead lights of the other in a line or nearly in a line or both sidelights and by day she observes the corresponding aspect of the other vessel.

(c) When a vessel is in any doubt as to whether such a situation exists she shall assume that it does exist and act accordingly.

(d) Notwithstanding paragraph (a) of this rule, a power-driven vessel operating on the Great Lakes, Western Rivers, or waters specified by the Secretary, and proceeding downbound with a following current shall have the right-of-way over an upbound vessel, shall propose the manner of passage, and shall initiate the maneuvering signals prescribed by Rule 34(a)(i), as appropriate.

RULE 15

Crossing Situation

(a) When two power-driven vessels are crossing so as to involve risk of collision, the vessel which has the other on her starboard side shall keep out of the way and shall, if the circumstances of the case admit, avoid crossing ahead of the other vessel.

(b) Notwithstanding paragraph (a), on the Great Lakes, Western Rivers, or water specified by the Secretary, a vessel crossing a river shall keep out of the way of a power-driven vessel ascending or descending the river.

RULE 16

Action by Give-Way Vessel

Every vessel which is directed to keep out of the way of another vessel shall, so far as possible, take early and substantial action to keep well clear.

RULE 17

Action by Stand-on Vessel

(a)(i) Where one of two vessels is to keep out of the way, the other shall keep her course and speed.

(ii) The latter vessel may, however, take action to avoid collision by her maneuver alone, as soon as it becomes apparent to her that the vessel required to keep out of the way is not taking appropriate action in compliance with these Rules.

(b) When, from any cause, the vessel required to keep her course and speed finds herself so close that collision cannot be avoided by the action of the give-way vessel alone, she shall take such action as will best aid to avoid collision.

(c) A power-driven vessel which takes action in a crossing situation in accordance with subparagraph (a)(ii) of this Rule to avoid collision with another power-driven vessel shall, if the circumstances of the case admit, not alter course to port for a vessel on her own port side.

(d) This Rule does not relieve the give-way vessel of her obligation to keep out of the way.

RULE 18

Responsibilities Between Vessels

Except where Rules 9, 10, and 13 otherwise require:

(a) A power-driven vessel underway shall keep out of the way of:
    (i) a vessel not under command;
    (ii) a vessel restricted in her ability to maneuver;
    (iii) a vessel engaged in fishing; and
    (iv) a sailing vessel.

(b) A sailing vessel underway shall keep out of the way of:
>(i) a vessel not under command;
>(ii) a vessel restricted in her ability to maneuver; and
>(iii) a vessel engaged in fishing.

(c) A vessel engaged in fishing when underway shall, so far as possible, keep out of the way of:
>(i) a vessel not under command; and
>(ii) a vessel restricted in her ability to maneuver.

(d) A seaplane on the water shall, in general, keep well clear of all vessels and avoid impeding their navigation. In circumstances, however, where risk of collision exists, she shall comply with the Rules of this Part.

SUBPART III—CONDUCT OF VESSELS IN RESTRICTED VISIBILITY

RULE 19

Conduct of Vessels in Restricted Visibility

(a) This Rule applies to vessels not in sight of one another when navigating in or near an area of restricted visibility.

(b) Every vessel shall proceed at a safe speed adapted to the prevailing circumstances and conditions of restricted visibility. A power-driven vessel shall have her engines ready for immediate maneuver.

(c) Every vessel shall have due regard to the prevailing circumstances and conditions of restricted visibility when complying with Rules 4 through 10.

(d) A vessel which detects by radar alone the presence of another vessel shall determine if a close-quarters situation is developing or risk of collision exists. If so, she shall take avoiding action in ample time, provided that when such action consists of an alteration of course, so far as possible the following shall be avoided:
>(i) an alteration of course to port for a vessel forward of the beam, other than for a vessel being overtaken; and
>(ii) an alteration of course toward a vessel abeam or abaft the beam.

(e) Except where it has been determined that a risk of collision does not exist, every vessel which hears apparently forward of her beam the fog signal of another vessel, or which cannot avoid a close-quarters situation with another vessel forward of her beam, shall reduce her speed to the minimum at which she can be kept on course. She shall if necessary take all her way off and, in any event, navigate with extreme caution until danger of collision is over.

PART C—LIGHTS AND SHAPES

RULE 20

Application

(a) Rules in this Part shall be complied with in all weathers.

(b) The Rules concerning lights shall be complied with from sunset to sunrise, and during such times no other lights shall be exhibited, except such lights as cannot be mistaken for the lights specified in these Rules or do not impair their visibility or distinctive character, or interfere with the keeping of a proper lookout.

(c) The lights prescribed by these Rules shall, if caried, also be exhibited from sunrise to sunset in restricted visibility and may be exhibited in all other circumstances when it is deemed necessary.

(d) The Rules concerning shapes shall be complied with by day.

(e) The lights and shapes specified in these Rules shall comply with the provisions of Annex I of these Rules.

RULE 21

Definitions

(a) "Masthead light" means a white light placed over the fore and aft centerline of the vessel showing an unbroken light over an arc of the horizon of 225 degrees and so fixed as to show the light from right ahead to 22.5 degrees abaft the beam on either side of the vessel, except that on a vessel of less than 12 meters in length the masthead light shall be placed as nearly as practicable to the fore and aft centerline of the vessel.

(b) "Sidelights" mean a green light on the starboard side and a red light on the port side each showing an unbroken light over an arc of the horizon of 112.5 degrees and so fixed as to show the light from right ahead to 22.5 degrees abaft the beam on its respective side. On a vessel of less than 20 meters in length the side lights may be combined in one lantern carried on the fore and aft centerline of the vessel, except that on a vessel of less than 12 meters in length the sidelights when combined in one lantern shall be placed as nearly as practicable to the fore and aft centerline of the vessel.

(c) "Sternlight" means a white light placed as nearly as practicable at the stern showing an unbroken light over an arc of the horizon of 135 degrees and so fixed as to show the light 67.5 degrees from right aft on each side of the vessel.

(d) "Towing light" means a yellow light having the same characteristics as the "sternlight" defined in paragraph (c) of this Rule.

(e) "All-round light" means a light showing an unbroken light over an arc of the horizon of 360 degrees.

(f) "Flashing light" means a light flashing at regular intervals at a frequency of 120 flashes or more per minute.

(g) "Special flashing light" means a yellow light flashing at regular intervals at a frequency of 50 to 70 flashes per minute, placed as far forward and as nearly as practicable on the fore and aft centerline of the tow and showing an unbroken light over an arc of the horizon of not less than 180 degrees nor more than 225 degrees and so fixed as to show the light from right ahead to abeam and no more than 22.5 degrees abaft the beam on either side of the vessel.

RULE 22

Visibility of Lights

The lights prescribed in these Rules shall have an intensity as specified in Annex I to these Rules, so as to be visible at the following minimum ranges:

(a) In a vessel of 50 meters or more in length:
    a masthead light, 6 miles;
    a sidelight, 3 miles;
    a sternlight, 3 miles;
    a towing light, 3 miles;
    a white, red, green or yellow all-round light, 3 miles; and
    a special flashing light, 2 miles.

(b) In a vessel of 12 meters or more in length but less than 50 meters in length:
    a masthead light, 5 miles; except that where the length of the vessel is less than 20 meters, 3 miles;
    a sidelight, 2 miles;
    a sternlight, 2 miles;
    a towing light, 2 miles;
    a white, red, green or yellow all-round light, 2 miles; and
    a special flashing light, 2 miles.

(c) In a vessel of less than 12 meters in length:
    a masthead light, 2 miles;
    a sidelight, 1 mile;
    a sternlight, 2 miles;
    a towing light, 2 miles;
    a white, red, green or yellow all-round light, 2 miles; and
    a special flashing light, 2 miles.

(d) In an inconspicuous, partly submerged vessel or object being towed:
    a white all-round light, 3 miles.

RULE 23

Power-Driven Vessels Underway

(a) A power-driven vessel underway shall exhibit:

(i) a masthead light forward; except that a vessel of less than 20 meters in length need not exhibit this light forward of amidships but shall exhibit it as far forward as is practicable;

(ii) a second masthead light abaft of and higher than the forward one; except that a vessel of less than 50 meters in length shall not be obliged to exhibit such light but may do so:

(iii) sidelights; and

(iv) a sternlight.

(b) An air-cushion vessel when operating in the nondisplacement mode shall, in addition to the lights prescribed in paragraph (a) of this Rule, exhibit an all-round flashing yellow light where it can best be seen.

(c) A power-driven vessel of less than 12 meters in length may, in lieu of the lights prescribed in paragraph (a) of this Rule, exhibit an all-round white light and sidelights.

(d) A power-driven vessel when operating on the Great Lakes may carry an all-round white light in lieu of the second masthead light and sternlight prescribed in paragraph (a) of this Rule. The light shall be carried in the position of the second masthead light and be visible at the same minimum range.

RULE 24

Towing and Pushing

(a) A power-driven vessel when towing astern shall exhibit:

(i) instead of the light prescribed either in Rule 23 (a)(i) or 23(a)(ii), two masthead lights in a vertical line. When the length of the tow, measuring from the stern of the towing vessel to the after end of the tow exceeds 200 meters, three such lights in a vertical line;

(ii) sidelights;

(iii) a sternlight;

(iv) a towing light in a vertical line above the sternlight; and

(v) when the length of the tow exceeds 200 meters, a diamond shape where it can best be seen.

(b) When a pushing vessel and a vessel being pushed ahead are rigidly connected in a composite unit they shall be regarded as a power-driven vessel and exhibit the lights prescribed in Rule 23.

(c) A power-driven vessel when pushing ahead or towing alongside, except as required by paragraphs (b) and (i) of this Rule, shall exhibit:

(i) instead of the light prescribed either in Rule 23(a)(i) or 23(a)(ii), two masthead lights in a vertical line;

(ii) sidelights; and

(iii) two towing lights in a vertical line.

(d) A power-driven vessel to which paragraphs (a) or (c) of this Rule apply shall also comply with Rule 23(a)(i) and 23(a)(ii).

(e) A vessel or object other than those referred to in paragraph (g) of this Rule being towed shall exhibit:

(i) sidelights;

(ii) a sternlight; and

(iii) when the length of the tow exceeds 200 meters, a diamond shape where it can best be seen.

(f) Provided that any number of vessels being towed alongside or pushed in a group shall be lighted as one vessel:

(i) a vessel being pushed ahead, not being part of a composite unit, shall exhibit at the forward end sidelights, and a special flashing light; and

(ii) a vessel being towed alongside shall exhibit a sternlight and at the forward end sidelights.

(g) An inconspicuous, partly submerged vessel or object being towed shall exhibit:

(i) if it is less than 25 meters in breadth, one all-round white light at or near each end;

(ii) if it is 25 meters or more in breadth, four all-round white lights to mark its length and breadth;

(iii) if it exceeds 100 meters in length, additional all-round white lights between the lights prescribed in subparagraphs (i) and (ii) so that the distance between the lights shall not exceed 100 meters: *Provided,* That any vessels or objects being towed alongside each other shall be lighted as one vessel or object;

(iv) a diamond shape at or near the aftermost extremity of the last vessel or object being towed; and

(v) the towing vessel may direct a searchlight in the direction of the tow to indicate its presence to an approaching vessel.

(h) Where from any sufficient cause it is impracticable for a vessel or object being towed to exhibit the lights prescribed in paragraph (e) or (g) of this Rule, all possible measures shall be taken to light the vessel or object towed or at least to indicate the presence of the unlighted vessel or object.

(i) Notwithstanding paragraph (c), on the Western Rivers (except below the Huey P. Long Bridge on the Mississippi River) and on waters specified by the Secretary, a power-driven vessel, when pushing ahead or towing alongside, except as paragraph (b) applies, shall exhibit:

      (i) sidelights; and

      (ii) two towing lights in a vertical line.

(j) Where from any sufficient cause it is impracticable for a vessel not normally engaged in towing operations to display the lights prescribed by paragraph (a), (c) or (i) of this Rule, such vessel shall not be required to exhibit those lights when engaged in towing another vessel in distress or otherwise in need of assistance. All possible measures shall be taken to indicate the nature of the relationship between the towing vessel and the vessel being assisted. The searchlight authorized by Rule 36 may be used to illuminate the tow.

RULE 25

Sailing Vessels Underway and Vessels Under Oars

(a) A sailing vessel underway shall exhibit:

      (i) sidelights; and

      (ii) a sternlight.

(b) In a sailing vessel of less than 20 meters in length the lights prescribed in paragraph (a) of this Rule may be combined in one lantern carried at or near the top of the mast where it can best be seen.

(c) A sailing vessel underway may, in addition to the lights prescribed in paragraph (a) of this Rule, exhibit at or near the top of the mast, where they can best be seen, two all-round lights in a vertical line, the upper being red and the lower green, but these lights shall not be exhibited in conjunction with the combined lantern permitted by paragraph (b) of this Rule.

(d)(i) A sailing vessel of less than 7 meters in length shall, if practicable, exhibit the lights prescribed in paragraph (a) or (b) of this Rule, but if she does not, she shall have ready at hand an electric torch or lighted lantern showing a white light which shall be exhibited in sufficient time to prevent collision.

(ii) A vessel under oars may exhibit the lights prescribed in this Rule for sailing vessels, but if she does not, she shall have ready at hand an electric torch or lighted lantern showing a white light which shall be exhibited in sufficient time to prevent collision.

(e) A vessel proceeding under sail when also being propelled by machinery shall exhibit forward where it can best be seen a conical shape, apex downward. A vessel of less than 12 meters in length is not required to exhibit this shape, but may do so.

RULE 26

Fishing Vessels

(a) A vessel engaged in fishing, whether underway or at anchor, shall exhibit only the lights and shapes prescribed in this Rule.

(b) A vessel when engaged in trawling, by which is meant the dragging through the water of a dredge net or other apparatus used as a fishing appliance, shall exhibit:

(i) two all-round lights in a vertical line, the upper being green and the lower white, or a shape consisting of two cones with their apexes together in a vertical line one above the other; a vessel of less than 20 meters in length may instead of this shape exhibit a basket;

(ii) a masthead light abaft of and higher than the all-round green light; a vessel of less than 50 meters in length shall not be obliged to exhibit such a light but may do so; and

(iii) when making way through the water, in addition to the lights prescribed in this paragraph, sidelights and a sternlight.

(c) A vessel engaged in fishing, other than trawling, shall exhibit:

(i) two all-round lights in a vertical line, the upper being red and the lower white, or a shape consisting of two cones with apexes together in a vertical line one above the other; a vessel of less than 20 meters in length may instead of this shape exhibit a basket;

(ii) when there is outlying gear extending more than 150 meters horizontally from the vessel, an all-round white light or a cone apex upward in the direction of the gear; and

(iii) when making way through the water, in addition to the lights prescribed in this paragraph, sidelights and a sternlight.

(d) A vessel engaged in fishing in close proximity to other vessels engaged in fishing may exhibit the additional signals described in Annex II to these Rules.

(e) A vessel when not engaged in fishing shall not exhibit the lights or shapes prescribed in this Rule, but only those prescribed for a vessel of her length.

RULE 27

Vessels Not Under Command or Restricted in Their Ability To Maneuver

(a) A vessel not under command shall exhibit:

(i) two all-round red lights in a vertical line where they can best be seen;

(ii) two balls or similar shapes in a vertical line where they can best be seen; and

(iii) when making way through the water, in addition to the lights prescribed in this paragraph, sidelights and a sternlight.

(b) A vessel restricted in her ability to maneuver, except a vessel engaged in mineclearance operations, shall exhibit:

(i) three all-round lights in a vertical line where they can best be seen. The highest and lowest of these lights shall be red and the middle light shall be white;

(ii) three shapes in a vertical line where they can best be seen. The highest and lowest of these shapes shall be balls and the middle one a diamond;

(iii) when making way through the water, masthead lights, sidelights and a sternlight, in addition to the lights prescribed in subparagraph (b)(i); and

(iv) when at anchor, in addition to the lights or shapes prescribed in subparagraphs (b) (i) and (ii), the light, lights or shapes prescribed in Rule 30.

(c) A vessel engaged in a towing operation which severely restricts the towing vessel and her tow in their ability to deviate from their course shall, in addition to the lights or shapes prescribed in subparagraphs (b) (i) and (ii) of this Rule, exhibit the lights or shape prescribed in Rule 24.

(d) A vessel engaged in dredging or underwater operations, when restricted in her ability to maneuver, shall exhibit the lights and shapes prescribed in subparagraphs (b) (i), (ii), and (iii) of this Rule and shall in addition, when an obstruction exists, exhibit:

(i) two all-round red lights or two balls in a vertical line to indicate the side on which the obstruction exists;

(ii) two all-round green lights or two diamonds in a vertical line to indicate the side on which another vessel may pass; and

(iii) when at anchor, the lights or shape prescribed by this paragraph, instead of the lights or shapes prescribed in Rule 30 for anchored vessels.

(e) Whenever the size of a vessel engaged in diving operations makes it impracticable to exhibit all lights and shapes prescribed in paragraph (d) of this Rule, the following shall instead be exhibited:

(i) Three all-round lights in a vertical line where they can best be seen. The highest and lowest of these lights shall be red and the middle light shall be white.

(ii) A rigid replica of the international Code flag "A" not less than 1 meter in height. Measures shall be taken to insure its all-round visibility.

(f) A vessel engaged in mineclearance operations shall in addition to the lights prescribed for a power-driven vessel in Rule 23, or to the lights or shapes prescribed for a vessel at anchor in Rule 30 as appropriate, exhibit three all-round green lights or three balls. One of these lights or shapes shall be exhibited near the foremast head and one at each end of the fore yard. These lights or shapes indicate that it is dangerous for another vessel to approach within 1000 meters of the mineclearance vessel.

(g) A vessel of less than 12 meters in length, except when engaged in diving operations, is not required to exhibit the lights or shapes prescribed in this Rule.

(h) The signals prescribed in this Rule are not signals of vessels in distress and requiring assistance. Such signals are contained in Annex IV to these Rules.

RULE 28

[Reserved]

RULE 29

Pilot Vessels

(a) A vessel engaged on pilotage duty shall exhibit:
   (i) at or near the masthead, two all-round lights in a vertical line, the upper being white and the lower red;
   (ii) when underway, in addition, sidelights and a sternlight; and
   (iii) when at anchor, in addition to the lights prescribed in subparagraph (i), the anchor light, lights, or shape prescribed in Rule 30 for anchored vessels.

(b) A pilot vessel when not engaged on pilotage duty shall exhibit the lights or shapes prescribed for a vessel of her length.

RULE 30

Anchored Vessels and Vessels Aground

(a) A vessel at anchor shall exhibit where it can best be seen:
   (i) in the fore part, an all-round white light or one ball; and
   (ii) at or near the stern and at a lower level than the light prescribed in subparagraph (i), an all-round white light.

(b) A vessel of less than 50 meters in length may exhibit an all-round white light where it can best be seen instead of the lights prescribed in paragraph (a) of this Rule.

(c) A vessel at anchor may, and a vessel of 100 meters or more in length shall, also use the available working or equivalent lights to illuminate her decks.

(d) A vessel aground shall exhibit the lights prescribed in paragraph (a) or (b) of this Rule and in addition, if practicable, where they can best be seen:
   (i) two all-round red lights in a vertical line; and
   (ii) three balls in a vertical line.

(e) A vessel of less than 7 meters in length, when at anchor, not in or near a narrow channel, fairway, anchorage, or where other vessels normally navigate, shall not be required to exhibit the lights or shape prescribed in paragraphs (a) and (b) of this Rule.

(f) A vessel of less than 12 meters in length when aground shall not be required to exhibit the lights or shapes prescribed in subparagraphs (d) (i) and (ii) of this Rule.

(g) A vessel of less than 20 meters in length, when at anchor in a special anchorage area designated by the Secretary, shall not be required to exhibit the anchor lights and shapes required by this Rule.

RULE 31

Seaplanes

Where it is impracticable for a seaplane to exhibit lights and shapes of the characteristics or in the positions prescribed in the Rules of this Part she shall exhibit lights and shapes as closely similar in characteristics and position as is possible.

PART D—SOUND AND LIGHT SIGNALS

RULE 32

Definitions

(a) The word "whistle" means any sound signaling appliance capable of producing the prescribed blasts and which complies with specifications in Annex III to these Rules.

(b) The term "short blast" means a blast of about 1 second's duration.

(c) The term "prolonged blast" means a blast of from 4 to 6 seconds' duration.

RULE 33

Equipment for Sound Signals

(a) A vessel of 12 meters or more in length shall be provided with a whistle and a bell and a vessel of 100 meters or more in length shall, in addition, be provided with a gong, the tone and sound of which cannot be confused with that of the bell. The whistle, bell and gong shall comply with the specifications in Annex III to these Rules. The bell or gong or both may be replaced by other equipment having the same respective sound characteristics, provided that manual sounding of the prescribed signals shall always be possible.

(b) A vessel of less than 12 meters in length shall not be obliged to carry the sound signaling appliances prescribed in paragraph (a) of this Rule but if she does not, she shall be provided with some other means of making an efficient sound signal.

RULE 34

Maneuvering and Warning Signals

(a) When power-driven vessels are in sight of one another and meeting or crossing at a distance within half a mile of each other, each vessel underway, when maneuvering as authorized or required by these Rules:

(i) shall indicate that maneuver by the following signals on her whistle: one short blast to mean "I intend to leave you on my port side"; two short blasts to mean "I intend to leave you on my starboard side"; and three short blasts to mean "I am operating astern propulsion."

(ii) upon hearing the one or two blast signal of the other shall, if in agreement, sound the same whistle signal and take the steps necessary to effect a safe passing. If, however, from any cause, the vessel doubts the safety of the proposed maneuver, she shall sound the danger signal specified in paragraph (d) of this Rule and each vessel shall take appropriate precautionary action until a safe passing agreement is made.

(b) A vessel may supplement the whistle signals prescribed in paragraph (a) of this Rule by light signals:

(i) These signals shall have the following significance: one flash to mean "I intend to leave you on my port side"; two flashes to mean "I intend to leave you on my starboard side"; three flashes to mean "I am operating astern propulsion";

(ii) The duration of each flash shall be about 1 second; and

(iii) The light used for this signal shall, if fitted, be one all-round white or yellow light, visible at a minimum range of 2 miles, synchronized with the whistle, and shall comply with the provisions of Annex I to these Rules.

(c) When in sight of one another:

(i) a power-driven vessel intending to overtake another power-driven vessel shall indicate her intention by the following signals on her whistle: one short blast to mean "I intend to overtake you on your starboard side"; two short blasts to mean "I intend to overtake you on your port side"; and

(ii) the power-driven vessel about to be overtaken shall, if in agreement, sound a similar sound signal. If in doubt she shall sound the danger signal prescribed in paragraph (d).

(d) When vessels in sight of one another are approaching each other and from any cause either vessel fails to understand the intentions or actions of the other, or is in doubt whether sufficient action is being taken by the other to avoid collision, the vessel in doubt shall immediately indicate such doubt by giving at least five short and rapid blasts on the whistle. This signal may be supplemented by a light signal of at least five short and rapid flashes.

(e) A vessel nearing a bend or an area of a channel or fairway where other vessels may be obscured by an intervening obstruction shall sound one prolonged blast. This signal shall be answered with a prolonged blast by any approaching vessel that may be within hearing around the bend or behind the intervening obstruction.

(f) If whistles are fitted on a vessel at a distance apart of more than 100 meters, one whistle only shall be used for giving maneuvering and warning signals.

(g) When a power-driven vessel is leaving a dock or berth, she shall sound one prolonged blast.

(h) A vessel that reaches agreement with another vessel in a meeting, crossing, or overtaking situation by using the radiotelephone as prescribed by the Bridge-to-Bridge Radiotelephone Act (85 Stat. 165; 33 U.S.C. 1207), is not obliged to sound the whistle signals prescribed by this Rule, but may do so. If agreement is not reached, then whistle signals shall be exchanged in a timely manner and shall prevail.

RULE 35

Sound Signals in Restricted Visibility

In or near an area of restricted visibility, whether by day or night, the signals prescribed in this Rule shall be used as follows:

(a) A power-driven vessel making way through the water shall sound at intervals of not more than 2 minutes one prolonged blast.

(b) A power-driven vessel underway but stopped and making no way through the water shall sound at intervals of not more than 2 minutes two prolonged blasts in succession with an interval of about 2 seconds between them.

(c) A vessel not under command; a vessel restricted in her ability to maneuver, whether underway or at anchor; a sailing vessel; a vessel engaged in fishing, whether underway or at anchor; and a vessel engaged in towing or pushing another vessel shall, instead of the signals prescribed in paragraphs (a) or (b) of this Rule, sound at intervals of not more than 2 minutes, three blasts in succession; namely, one prolonged followed by two short blasts.

(d) A vessel towed or if more than one vessel is towed the last vessel of the tow, if manned, shall at intervals of not more than 2 minutes sound four blasts in succession; namely, one prolonged followed by three short blasts. When practicable, this signal shall be made immediately after the signal made by the towing vessel.

(e) When a pushing vessel and a vessel being pushed ahead are rigidly connected in a composite unit they shall be regarded as a power-driven vessel and shall give the signals prescribed in paragraphs (a) or (b) of this Rule.

(f) A vessel at anchor shall at intervals of not more than 1 minute ring the bell rapidly for about 5 seconds. In a vessel of 100 meters or more in length the bell shall be sounded in the forepart of the vessel and immediately after the ringing of the bell the gong shall be sounded rapidly for about 5 seconds in the after part of the vessel. A vessel at anchor may in addition sound three blasts in succession; namely, one short, one prolonged and one short blast, to give warning of her position and of the possibility of collision to an approaching vessel.

(g) A vessel aground shall give the bell signal and if required the gong signal prescribed in paragraph (f) of this Rule and shall, in addition, give three separate and distinct strokes on the bell immediately before and after the rapid ringing of the bell. A vessel aground may in addition sound an appropriate whistle signal.

(h) A vessel of less than 12 meters in length shall not be obliged to give the above-mentioned signals but, if she does not, shall make some other efficient sound signal at intervals of not more than 2 minutes.

(i) A pilot vessel when engaged on pilotage duty may in addition to the signals prescribed in paragraphs (a), (b) or (f) of this Rule sound an identity signal consisting of four short blasts.

(j) The following vessels shall not be required to sound signals as prescribed in paragraph (f) of this Rule when anchored in a special anchorage area designated by the Secretary:
> (i) a vessel of less than 20 meters in length; and
> (ii) a barge, canal boat, scow, or other nondescript craft.

RULE 36

Signals To Attract Attention

If necessary to attract the attention of another vessel, any vessel may make light or sound signals that cannot be mistaken for any signal authorized elsewhere in these Rules, or may direct the beam of her searchlight in the direction of the danger, in such a way as not to embarrass any vessel.

RULE 37

Distress Signals

When a vessel is in distress and requires assistance she shall use or exhibit the signals described in Annex IV to these Rules.

PART E—EXEMPTIONS

RULE 38

Exemptions

Any vessel or class of vessels, the keel of which is laid or which is at a corresponding stage of construction before the date of enactment of this Act, provided that she complies with the requirements of—

(a) The Act of June 7, 1897 (30 Stat. 96), as amended (33 U.S.C. 154–232) for vessels navigating the waters subject to that statue;

(b) Section 4233 of the Revised Statutes (33 U.S.C. 301–356) for vessels navigating the waters subject to that statute;

(c) The Act of February 8, 1895 (28 Stat. 645), as amended (33 U.S.C. 241–295) for vessels navigating the waters subject to that statute; or

(d) Sections 3, 4, and 5 of the Act of April 25, 1940 (54 Stat. 163), as amended (46 U.S.C. 526 b, c, and d) for motorboats navigating the waters subject to that statute; shall be exempted from compliance with the technical Annexes to these Rules as follows:

(i) the installation of lights with ranges prescribed in Rule 22, until 4 years after the effective date of these Rules, except that vessels of less than 20 meters in length are permanently exempt;

(ii) the installation of lights with color specifications as prescribed in Annex I to these Rules, until 4 years after the effective date of these Rules, except that vessels of less than 20 meters in length are permanently exempt;

(iii) the repositioning of lights as a result of conversion to metric units and rounding off measurement figures, are permanently exempt; and

(iv) the horizontal repositioning of masthead lights prescribed by Annex I to these Rules:

(1) on vessels of less than 150 meters in length, permanent exemption.

(2) on vessels of 150 meters or more in length, until 9 years after the effective date of these Rules.

(v) the restructuring or repositioning of all lights to meet the prescriptions of Annex I to these Rules, until 9 years after the effective date of these Rules;

(vi) power-driven vessels of 12 meters or more but less than 20 meters in length are permanently exempt from the provisions of Rule 23(a)(i) and 23(a)(iv) provided that, in place of these lights, the vessel exhibits a white light aft visible all round the horizon; and

(vii) the requirements for sound signal appliances prescribed in Annex III to these Rules, until 9 years after the effective date of these Rules.

SEC. 3. The Secretary may issue regulations necessary to implement and interpret this Act. The Secretary shall establish the following technical annexes to these Rules: Annex I, Positioning and Technical Details of Lights and Shapes; Annex II, Additional Signals for Fishing Vessels Fishing in Close Proximity; Annex III, Technical Details of Sound Appliances; and Annex IV, Distress Signals. These annexes shall be as consistent as possible with the respective annexes to the International Regulations. The Secretary may establish other technical annexes, including local pilot rules.

SEC. 4. (a) Whoever operates a vessel in violation of this Act, or of any regulation issued thereunder, or in violation of a certificate of alternative compliance issued under Rule 1 is liable to a civil penalty of not more than $5,000 for each violation.

(b) Every vessel subject to this Act, other than a public vessel being used for noncommercial purposes, that is operated in violation of this Act, or of any regulation issued thereunder, or in violation of a certificate of alternative compliance issued under Rule 1 is liable to a civil penalty of not more than $5,000 for each violation, for which penalty the vessel may be seized and proceeded against in the district court of the United States of any district within which the vessel may be found.

(c) The Secretary may assess any civil penalty authorized by this section. No such penalty may be assessed until the person charged, or the owner of the vessel charged, as appropriate, shall have been given notice of the violation involved and an opportunity for a hearing. For good cause shown, the Secretary may remit, mitigate, or compromise any penalty assessed. Upon the failure of the person charged, or the owner of the vessel charged, to pay an assessed penalty, as it may have been mitigated or compromised, the Secretary may request the Attorney General to commence an action in the appropriate district court of the United States for collection of the penalty as assessed, without regard to the amount involved, together with such other relief as may be appropriate.

(d) The Secretary of the Treasury shall withhold or revoke, at the request of the Secretary, the clearance, required by section 4197 of the Revised Statutes of the United States (46 U.S.C. 91) of any vessel, the owner or operator of which is subject to any of the penalties in this section. Clearance may be granted in such cases upon the filing of a bond or other surety satisfactory to the Secretary.

SEC. 5. (a) The Secretary shall establish a Rules of the Road Advisory Council (hereinafter referred to as the Council) not exceeding 21 members. To assure balanced representation, members shall be chosen, insofar as practical, from the following groups: (1) recognized experts and leaders in organizations having an active interest in the Rules of the Road and vessel and port safety, (2) representatives of owners and operators of vessels, professional mariners, recreational boaters, and the recreational boating industry, (3) individuals with an interest in maritime law, and (4) Federal and State officials with responsibility for vessel and port safety. Additional persons may be appointed to panels of the Council in the performance of its functions.

(b) The Council shall advise, consult with, and make recommendations to the Secretary on matters relating to any major proposals for changes to the Inland Rules. The Council may recommend changes to the Inland Rules. The Council may recommend changes to the Inland Rules and International Regulations to the Secretary. Any advice or recommendation made by the Council to the Secretary shall reflect the independent judgment of the Council on the matter concerned. The Council shall meet at the call of the Secretary, but in any event not less than once during each calendar year. All proceedings of the Council shall be public, and a record of the proceedings shall be made available for public inspection.

(c) The Secretary shall furnish to the Council an executive secretary and such secretarial, clerical, and other services as are deemed necessary for the conduct of its business. Members of the Council who are not officers or employees of the United States shall, while attending meetings of the Council or while otherwise engaged in the business of the Council, be entitled to receive compensation at a rate fixed by the Secretary, not exceeding the daily equivalent of the current rate of basic pay in effect for GS–18 of the General Schedule under section 5332 of title 5, United States Code, including travel-time; and while away from their home or regular place of business, they may be allowed travel expenses, including per diem in lieu of subsistence, as authorized by section 5703 of title 5, United States Code. Payments under this section shall not render members of the Council officers or employees of the United States for any purpose.

(d) Unless extended by subsequent Act of Congress, the Council shall terminate 5 years from the date of enactment of this Act.

SEC. 6. The International Navigational Rules Act of 1977 (91 Stat. 308; 33 U.S.C. 1601), is amended as follows:
(1) in section 5 by amending subsection (a) to read as follows:
"The International Regulations do not apply to vessels while in the waters of the United States shoreward of the navigational

demarcation lines dividing the high seas from harbors, rivers, and other inland waters of the United States.'';

(2) in section 6, by adding a new subsection (d) as follows:

"(d) A certification authorized by this section may be issued for a class of vessels.'';

(3) in subsection (a) of section 9 by striking ''$500'' and inserting in lieu thereof ''$5,000''.

(4) in subsection (b) of section 9 by striking ''$500'' and inserting in lieu thereof ''not more than $5,000''.

SEC. 7. Sections 2, 4, 6(1), and 8(a) are effective 12 months after the date of enactment of this Act, except that on the Great Lakes, the effective date of sections 2 and 4 will be established by the Secretary. Section 5 is effective October 1, 1981.

SEC. 8. (a) The laws specified in the following schedules are repealed. Any prior rights or liabilities existing under these laws are not affected by their repeal.

ANNEXES

U.S. Code Title 33—Parts 84–88

ANNEX I

PART 84—ANNEX I: POSITIONING AND TECHNICAL DETAILS OF LIGHTS AND SHAPES

§ 84.01 Definitions.

(a) The term "height above the hull" means height above the uppermost continuous deck. This height shall be measured from the position vertically beneath the location of the light.

(b) The term "practical cut-off" means, for vessels 20 meters or more in length, 12.5 percent of the minimum luminous intensity (Table 84.15(b)) corresponding to the greatest range of visibility for which the requirements of Annex I are met.

(c) The term "Rule" or "Rules" means the Inland Navigation Rules contained in sec. 2 of the Inland Navigational Rules Act of 1980 (Pub. L. 96–591, 94 Stat. 3415, 33 U.S.C. 2001, December 24, 1980) as amended.

§ 84.03 Vertical positioning and spacing of lights.

(a) On a power-driven vessel of 20 meters or more in length the masthead lights shall be placed as follows:

(1) The forward masthead light, or if only one masthead light is carried, then that light, at a height above the hull of not less than 5 meters, and, if the breadth of the vessel exceeds 5 meters, then at a height above the hull not less than such breadth, so however that the light need not be placed at a greater height above the hull than 8 meters;

(2) When two masthead lights are carried the after one shall be at least 2 meters vertically higher than the forward one.

(b) The vertical separation of the masthead lights of power-driven vessels shall be such that in all normal conditions of trim the after light will be seen over and separate from the forward light at a distance of 1000 meters from the stem when viewed from water level.

(c) The masthead light of a power-driven vessel of 12 meters but less than 20 meters in length shall be placed at a height above the gunwale of not less than 2.5 meters.

(d) The masthead light, or the all-round light described in rule 23(c), of a power-driven vessel of less than 12 meters in length shall be carried at least one meter higher than the sidelights.

(e) One of the two or three masthead lights prescribed for a power-driven vessel when engaged in towing or pushing another vessel shall be placed in the same position as either the forward masthead light or the after masthead light, provided that the lowest after masthead light shall be at least 2 meters vertically higher than the highest forward masthead light.

(f)(1) The masthead light or lights prescribed in Rule 28(a) shall be so placed as to be above and clear of all other lights and obstructions except as described in paragraph (f)(2) of this section.

(2) When it is impracticable to carry the all-round lights prescribed in rule 27(b)(i) below the masthead lights, they may be carried above the after masthead light(s) or vertically in between the forward masthead light(s) and after masthead light(s), provided that in the latter case the requirement of § 84.05(d) shall be complied with.

(g) The sidelights of a power-driven vessel shall be placed at least one meter lower than the forward masthead light. They shall not be so low as to be interfered with by deck lights.

(h) [Reserved]

(i) When the Rules prescribe two or three lights to be carried in a vertical line, they shall be spaced as follows:

(1) On a vessel of 20 meters in length or more such lights shall be spaced not less than 1 meter apart, and the lowest

of these lights shall, except where a towing light is required, be placed at a height of not less than 4 meters above the hull;

(2) On a vessel of less than 20 meters in length such lights shall be spaced not less than 1 meter apart and the lowest of these lights shall, except where a towing light is required, be placed at a height of not less than 2 meters above the hull;

(3) When three lights are carried they shall be equally spaced.

(j) The lower of the two all-round lights prescribed for a vessel when engaged in fishing shall be a height above the sidelights not less than twice the distance between the two vertical lights.

(k) The forward anchor light prescribed in rule 30(a)(i), when two are carried, shall not be less than 4.5 meters above the after one. On a vessel of 50 meters or more in length this forward anchor light shall be placed at a height or not less than 6 meters above the hull.

§ 84.05 Horizontal positioning and spacing of lights.

(a) Except as specified in paragraph (b) of this section, when two masthead lights are prescribed for a power-driven vessel, the horizontal distance between them shall not be less than one quarter of the length of the vessel but need not be more than 50 meters. The forward light shall be placed not more than one half of the length of the vessel from the stem.

(b) On power-driven vessels 50 meters but less than 60 meters in length operated on the Western Rivers, the horizontal distance between masthead lights shall not be less than 10 meters.

(c) On a power-driven vessel of 20 meters or more in length the sidelights shall not be placed in front of the forward masthead lights. They shall be placed at or near the side of the vessel.

(d) When the lights prescribed in rule 27(b)(i) are placed vertically between the forward masthead light(s) and the after masthead light(s) these all-round lights shall be placed at a horizontal distance of not less than 2 meters from the fore and aft centerline of the vessel in the athwartship direction.

§ 84.07 Details of location of direction-indicating lights for fishing vessels, dredgers and vessels engaged in underwater operations.

(a) The light indicating the direction of the outlying gear from a vessel engaged in fishing as prescribed in rule 26(c)(ii) shall be placed at a horizontal distance of not less than 2 meters and not more than 6 meters away from the two all-round red and white lights. This light shall be placed not higher than the all-round white light prescribed in rule 26(c)(i) and not lower than the sidelights.

(b) The lights and shapes on a vessel engaged in dredging or underwater operations to indicate the obstructed side and/or the side on which it is safe to pass, as prescribed in rule 27(d)(i) and (ii), shall be placed at the maximum practical horizontal distance, but in no case less than 2 meters, from the lights or shapes prescribed in rule 27(b)(i) and (ii). In no case shall the upper of these lights or shapes be at a greater height than the lower of the three lights or shapes prescribed in rule 27(b)(i) and (ii).

§ 84.09 Screens.

(a) The sidelights of vessels of 20 meters or more in length shall be fitted with mat black inboard screens and meet the requirements of § 84.17. On vessels of less than 20 meters in length, the sidelights, if necessary to meet the requirements of § 84.17, shall be fitted with mat black inboard screens. With a combined lantern, using a single vertical filament and a very narrow division between the green and red sections, external screens need not be fitted.

(b) On power-driven vessels less than 12 meters in length constructed after July 31, 1983, the masthead light, or the all-round light described in rule 23(c) shall be screened to prevent direct illumination of the vessel forward of the operator's position.

§ 84.11 Shapes.

(a) Shapes shall be black and of the following sizes:

(1) A ball shall have a diameter of not less than 0.6 meter;

(2) A cone shall have a base diameter of not less than 0.6 meter and a height equal to its diameter;

(3) A diamond shape shall consist of two cones (as defined in paragraph (a)(2) of this section) having a common base.

(b) The vertical distance between shapes shall be at least 1.5 meter.

(c) In a vessel of less than 20 meters in length shapes of lesser dimensions but commensurate with the size of the vessel may be used and the distance apart may be correspondingly reduced.

§ 84.13 Color specification of lights.

(a) The chromaticity of all navigation lights shall conform to the following standards, which lie within the boundaries of the area of the diagram specified for each color by the International Commission on Illumination (CIE), in the "Colors of Light Signals," which is incorporated by reference. It is Publication CIE No. 2.2. (TC–1.6), 1975, and is available from the Illumination Engineering Society, 345 East 47th Street, New York, NY 10017. It is also available for inspection at the Office of the Federal

Register, Room 8401, 1100 L Street N.W., Washington, DC 20408. This incorporation by reference was approved by the Director of the Federal Register.

(b) The boundaries of the area for each color are given by indicating the corner co-ordinates, which are as follows:

(1) *White:*

x 0.525 0.525 0.452 0.31.0 0.310 0.443 y 0.382
  0.440 0.440 0.348 0.283 0.382

(2) *Green:*

| x 0.028 | 0.009 | 0.300 | 0.203 |
| y 0.385 | 0.723 | 0.511 | 0.356 |

(3) *Red:*

| x 0.680 | 0.660 | 0.735 | 0.721 |
| y 0.320 | 0.320 | 0.265 | 0.259 |

(4) *Yellow:*

| x 0.612 | 0.618 | 0.575 | 0.575 |
| y 0.382 | 0.382 | 0.425 | 0.406 |

§ 84.15   Intensity of lights.

(a) The minimum luminous intensity of lights shall be calculated by using the formula:

$$I = 3.43 \times 10^6 \times T \times tsD^2 \times K^{-D}$$

where I is luminous intensity in candelas under service conditions,

T is threshold factor 2×10^{-7} lux,

D is range of visibility (luminous range) of the light in nautical mines,

K is atmospheric transmissivity. For pre-

Table 84.15(b)

Range of visibility (luminous range) of light in nautical miles D	Minimum luminous intensity of light in candelas for K = 0.8 I
1	0.9
2	4.3
3	12
4	27
5	52
6	94

scribed lights the value of K shall be 0.8, corresponding to a meteorological visibility of approximately 13 nautical miles.

(b) A selection of figures derived from the formula is given in Table 84.15(b)

§ 84.17   Horizontal sectors.

(a)(1) In the forward direction, sidelights as fitted on the vessel shall show the minimum required intensities. The intensities shall decrease to reach practical cut-off between 1 and 3 degrees outside the prescribed sectors.

(2) For sternlights and masthead lights and at 22.5 degrees abaft the beam for sidelights, the minimum required intensities shall be maintained over the arc of the horizon up to 5 degrees within the limits of the sectors prescribed in rule 21. From 5 degrees within the prescribed sectors the intensity may decrease by 50 percent up to the prescribed limits; it shall decrease steadily to reach practical cut-off at not more than 5 degrees outside the prescribed sectors.

(b) All-round lights shall be so located as not to be obscured by masts, topmasts or structures within angular sectors of more than 6 degrees, except anchor lights prescribed in rule 30, which need not be placed at an impracticable height above the hull, and the all-round white light described in rule 23(d), which may not be obscured at all.

§ 84.19   Vertical sectors.

(a) The vertical sectors of electric lights as fitted, with the exception of lights on sailing vessels and on unmanned barges, shall ensure that:

(1) At least the required minimum intensity is maintained at all angles from 5 degrees above to 5 degrees below the horizontal;

(2) At least 60 percent of the

required minimum intensity is maintained from 7.5 degrees above to 7.5 degrees below the horizontal.

(b) In the case of sailing vessels the vertical sectors of electric lights as fitted shall ensure that:

(1) At least the required minimum intensity is maintained at all angles from 5 degrees above to 5 degrees below the horizontal;

(2) At least 50 percent of the required minimum intensity is maintained from 25 degrees above to 25 degrees below the horizontal.

(c) In the case of unmanned barges the minimum required intensity of electric lights as fitted shall be maintained on the horizontal.

(d) In the case of lights other than electric lights these specifications shall be met as closely as possible

§ 84.21   Intensity of non-electric lights.

Non-electric lights shall so far as practicable comply with the minimum intensities, as specified in the Table given in § 84.15.

§ 84.23   Maneuvering light.

Notwithstanding the provisions of § 84.03(f), the maneuvering light described in rule 34(b) shall be placed approximately in the same fore and aft vertical plane as the masthead light or lights and, where practicable, at a minimum height of one-half meter vertically above the forward masthead light, provided that it shall be carried not less than one-half meter vertically above or below the after masthead light. On a vessel where only one masthead light is carried the maneuvering light, if fitted, shall be carried where it can best be seen, not less than one-half meter vertically apart from the masthead light.

§ 84.25   Approval. [Reserved]

ANNEX II

PART 85—ANNEX II, ADDITIONAL SIGNALS FOR FISHING VESSELS FISHING IN CLOSE PROXIMITY

Sec.
85.1   General.
85.3   Signals for trawlers.
85.5   Signals for purse seiners.
       Authority: Sec. 3, Pub. L. 96–591; 49 CFR 1.46(n)(14).

§ 85.1   General.

The lights mentioned herein shall, if exhibited in pursuance of Rule 26(d), be placed where they can best be seen. They shall be at least 0.9 meter apart but at a lower level than lights prescribed in Rule 26(b)(i) and (c)(i) contained in the Navigational Rules Act of 1980. The lights shall be visible all around the horizon at a distance of at least 1 mile but at a lesser distance from the lights prescribed by these Rules for fishing vessels.

§ 85.3   Signals for trawlers.

(a) Vessels when engaged in trawling, whether using demersal or pelagio gear, may exhibit:

(1) When shooting their nets: two white lights in a vertical line;

(2) When hauling their nets: one

white light over one red light in a vertical line;

(3) When the net has come fast upon an obstruction: two red lights in a vertical line.

(b) Each vessel engaged in pair trawling may exhibit:

(1) By night, a search light directed forward and in the direction of the other vessel of the pair;

(2) When shooting or hauling their nets or when their nets have come fast upon an obstruction, the lights prescribed in paragraph (a) above.

§ 85.5 Signals for purse seiners.

Vessels engaged in fishing with purse scine gear may exhibit two yellow lights in a vertical line. These lights shall flash alternately every second and with equal light and occultation duration. These lights may be exhibited only when the vessel is hampered by its fishing gear.

ANNEX III

PART 86—ANNEX III: TECHNICAL DETAILS OF SOUND SIGNAL APPLIANCES

Subpart A—Whistles

§ 86.01 Frequencies and range of audibility.

The fundamental frequency of the signal shall lie within the range 70–525 Hz. The range of audibility of the signal from a whistle shall be determined by those frequencies, which may include the fundamental and/or one or more higher frequencies, which lie within the frequency ranges and provide the sound pressure levels specified in § 86.05.

§ 86.03 Limits of fundamental frequencies.

To ensure a wide variety of whistle characteristics, the fundamental frequency of a whistle shall be between the following limits:

(a) 70–200 Hz, for a vessel 200 meters or more in length;

(b) 130–350 Hz, for a vessel 75 meters but less than 200 meters in length;

(c) 250–525 Hz, for a vessel less than 75 meters in length.

Table 86.05

Length of vessel in meters	Fundamental frequency range (Hz)	For measured frequencies (Hz)	46 octave band level at 1 meter in Db referred to 2 × 10	Audibility range in nautical miles
200 or more	70–200	130–180	145	2
		180–250	143	
		250–1200	140	
75 but less than 200	130–350	130–180	140	
		180–250	136	1.5
		250–1200	134	
20 but less than 75	250–625	250–450	130	
		450–800	125	1.0
		800–1800	121	
12 but less than 20	250–525	250–450	120	
		450–800	115	0.5
		800–2100	111	

NOTE: The range of audibility in the table above is for information and is approximately the range at which a whistle may usually be heard on its forward axis in conditions of still air on board a vessel having average background noise level at the listening posts (taken to be 58 dB in the octave band centered on 250 Hz and 63 dB in the octave band centered on 500 Hz).

§ 86.05 Sound signal intensity and range of audibility.

A whistle on a vessel shall provide, in the direction of the forward axis of the whistle and at a distance of 1 meter from it, a sound pressure level in at least one ⅓-octave band of not less than the appropriate figure given in Table 86.05 within the following frequency ranges (±1 percent):

(a) 130–1200 Hz, for a vessel 75 meters of more in length;

(b) 250–1600 Hz, for a vessel 20 meters but less than 75 meters in length;

(c) 250–2100 Hz, for a vessel 12 meters but less than 20 meters in length.

In practice the range at which a whistle may be heard is extremely variable and depends critically on weather conditions; the values given can be regarded as typical but under conditions of strong wind or high ambient noise level at the listening post the range may be much reduced.

§ 86.07 Directional properties.

The sound pressure level of a directional whistle shall be not more than 4 dB below the sound pressure level specified in § 86.05 in any direction in the horizontal plane within ±45 degrees of the forward axis. The sound pressure level of the whistle in any other direction in the horizontal plane shall not be more than 10 dB less than the sound pressure level specified for the forward axis, so that the range of audibility in any direction will be at least half the range required on the forward axis. The sound pressure level shall be measured in that one-third octave band which determines the audibility range.

§ 86.09 Positioning of whistles.

(a) When a directional whistle is to be used as the only whistle on the vessel and is permanently installed, it shall be installed with its forward axis directed forward.

(b) A whistle shall be placed as high as practicable on a vessel, in order to reduce interception of the emitted sound by obstructions and also to minimize hearing damage risk to personnel. The sound pressure level of the vessel's own signal at listening posts shall not exceed 110 dB(A) and so far as practicable should not exceed 100 dB(A).

§ 86.11 Fitting of more than one whistle.

If whistles are fitted at a distance apart of more than 100 meters, they shall not be sounded simultaneously.

§ 86.13 Combined whistle systems.

(a) A combined whistle system is a number of whistles (sound emitting sources) operated together. For the purposes of the Rules a combined whistle system is to be regarded as a single whistle.

(b) The whistles of a combined system shall—

(1) Be located at a distance apart of not more than 100 meters,

(2) Be sounded simultaneously,

(3) Each have a fundamental frequency different from those of the others by at least 10 Hz, and

(4) Have a tonal characteristic appropriate for the length of vessel which shall be evidenced by at least two-thirds of the whistles in the combined system having fundamental frequencies falling within the limits prescribed in § 86.03, or if there are only two whistles in the combined system, by the higher fundamental frequency falling within the limits prescribed in § 86.03.

Note.—If due to the presence of obstructions the sound field of a single whistle or of one of the whistles referred to in § 86.11 is likely to have a zone of greatly reduced signal level, a combined whistle system should be fitted so as to overcome this reduction.

§ 86.15 Towing vessel whistles.

A power-driven vessel normally engaged in pushing ahead or towing alongside may, at all times, use a whistle whose characteristic falls within the limits perscribed by § 86.03 for the longest customary composite length of the vessel and its tow.

Subpart B—Bell or Gong

§ 86.21 Intensity of signal.

A bell or gong, or other device having similar sound characteristics shall produce a sound pressure level of not less than 110 dB at 1 meter.

§ 86.23 Construction.

Bells and gongs shall be made of corrosion-resistant material and designed to give a clear tone. The diameter of the mouth of the bell shall be not less than 300 mm for vessels of more than 20 meters in length, and shall be not less than 200 mm for vessels of 12 to 20 meters in length. The mass of the striker shall be not less than 3 percent of the mass of the bell. The striker shall be capable of manual operation. Note: When practicable, a power-driven bell striker is recommended to ensure constant force.

Subpart C—Approval

§ 86.31 Approval. [Reserved]

ANNEX IV

PART 87—ANNEX IV, DISTRESS SIGNALS

Sec
87.1 Need of assistance
87.3 Exclusive use
87.5 Supplemental signals
(Sec. 3, Pub. L. 96.591, 33
U.S.C. 2071; 49 CFR 1.46(n)(14))

§ 87.1 Need of assistance.

The following signals, used or exhibited either together or separately, indicate distress and need of assistance:

(a) A gun or other explosive signal fired at intervals of about a minute.

(b) A continuous sounding with any fog-signaling apparatus;

(c) Rockets or shells, throwing red stars fired one at a time at short intervals;

(d) A signal made by radiotelegraphy or by any other signaling method consisting of the group . . . — — — . . . (SOS) in the Morse Code,

(e) A signal sent by radiotelephony consisting of the spoken word "Mayday";

(f) The International Code Signal of distress indicated by N.C.

(g) A signal consisting of a square flag having above or below it a ball or anything resembling a ball;

(h) Flames on the vessel (as from a burning tar barrel, oil barrel, etc.);

(i) A rocket parachute flare or a hand flare showing a red light;

(j) A smoke signal giving off orange-colored smoke;

(k) Slowly and repeatedly raising and lowering arms outstretched to each side;

(l) The radiotelegraph alarm signal;

(m) The radiotelephone alarm signal;

(n) Signals transmitted by emergency position-indicating radio beacons;

(o) A high intensity white light flashing at regular intervals from 50 to 70 times per minute.

§ 87.3 Exclusive use.

The use or exhibition of any of the foregoing signals except for the purpose of indicating distress and need of assistance and the use of other signals which may be confused with any of the above signals is prohibited.

§ 87.5 Supplemental signals.

Attention is drawn to the relevant sections of the International Code of Signals, the Merchant Ship Search and Rescue Manual and the following signals:

(a) A piece of orange-colored canvas with either a black square and circle or other appropriate symbol (for identification from the air);

(b) A dye marker.

ANNEX V

PART 88—ANNEX V, PILOT RULES

Sec.
88.01 Purpose and applicability.
88.03 Definitions.
88.05 Copy of rules.
88.09 Temporary exemption from light

and shape requirements when operating under bridges.
88.11 Law enforcement vessels.
88.13 Lights on barges at bank or dock.
88.15 Lights on dredge pipelines.

Authority: Sec. 3, Pub. L. 96–591, 33 U.S.C. 2071; 49 CFR 1.46(n)(14).

§ 88.01 Purpose and applicability.

This part applies to all vessels operating on United States inland waters and to United States vessels operating on the Canadian waters of the Great Lakes to the extent there is no conflict with Canadian law.

§ 88.03 Definitions.

The terms used in this part have the same meaning as defined in the Inland Navigational Rules Act of 1980.

§ 88.05 Copy of rules.

After January 1, 1983, the operator of each self-propelled vessel 12 meters or more in length shall carry on board and maintain for ready reference a copy of the Inland Navigation Rules.

§ 88.09 Temporary exemption from light and shape requirements when operating under bridges.

A vessel's navigation lights and shapes may be lowered if necessary to pass under a bridge.

§ 88.11 Law enforcement vessels.

(a) Law enforcement vessels may display a flashing blue light when engaged in direct law enforcement activities. This light shall be located so that it does not interfere with the visibility of the vessel's navigation lights.

(b) The blue light described in this section may be displayed by law enforcement vessels of the United States and the States and their political subdivisions.

§ 88.13 Lights on barges at bank or dock.

(a) The following barges shall display at night and if practicable in periods of restricted visibility the lights described in paragraph (b) of this section—

(1) Every barge projecting into a buoyed or restricted channel.

(2) Every barge so moored that it reduces the available navigable width of any channel to less than 80 meters.

(3) Barges moored in groups more than two barges wide or to a maximum width of over 25 meters.

(4) Every barge not moored parallel to the bank or dock.

(b) Barges described in paragraph (a) of this section shall carry two unobstructed white lights of an intensity to be visible for at least one mile on a clear dark night, and arranged as follows:

(1) On a single moored barge, lights shall be placed on the two corners farthest from the bank or dock.

(2) On barges moored in group formation, a light shall be placed on each of the upstream and downstream ends of the group, on the corners farthest from the bank or dock.

(3) Any barge in a group, projecting from the main body of the group toward the channel, shall be lighted as a single barge.

(c) Barges moored in any slip or slough which is used primarily for mooring purposes are exempt from the lighting requirements of this section.

(d) Barges moored in well-illuminated areas are exempt from the lighting requirements of this section. These areas are as follows:

Chicago Sanitary Ship Canal
(1) Mile 293.2 to 293.9
(3) Mile 295.2 to 296.1
(5) Mile 297.5 to 297.8
(7) Mile 298 to 298.2
(9) Mile 298.6 to 298.8
(11) Mile 299.3 to 299.4
(13) Mile 299.8 to 300.5
(15) Mile 303 to 303.2

(17) Mile 303.7 to 303.9
(19) Mile 305.7 to 305.8
(21) Mile 310.7 to 310.9
(23) Mile 311 to 311.2
(25) Mile 312.5 to 312.6
(27) Mile 313.8 to 314.2
(29) Mile 314.6
(31) Mile 314.8 to 315.3
(33) Mile 315.7 to 316
(35) Mile 316.8
(37) Mile 316.85 to 317.05
(39) Mile 317.5
(41) Mile 318.4 to 318.9
(43) Mile 318.7 to 318.8
(45) Mile 320 to 320.3
(47) Mile 320.6
(49) Mile 322.3 to 322.4
(51) Mile 322.8
(53) Mile 322.9 to 327.2

Calumet Sag Channel
(61) Mile 316.5

Little Calumet River
(71) Mile 321.2
(73) Mile 322.3

Calumet River
(81) Mile 328.5 to 328.7
(83) Mile 329.2 to 329.4
(85) Mile 330 west bank to 330.2
(87) Mile 331.4 to 331.6
(89) Mile 332.2 to 332.4
(91) Mile 332.6 to 332.8

Cumberland River
(101) Mile 126.8
(103) Mile 191

§ 88.15 Lights on dredge pipelines.

Dredge pipelines that are floating or supported on trestles shall display the following lights at night and in periods of restricted visibility.

(a) One row of yellow lights. The lights must be—

(1) Flashing 50 to 70 times per minute,

(2) Visible all around the horizon,

(3) Visible for at least 2 miles on a clear dark night,

(4) Not less than 1 and not more than 3.5 meters above the water,

(5) Approximately equally spaced, and

(6) Not more than 10 meters apart where the pipeline crosses a navigable channel. Where the pipeline does not cross a navigable channel the lights must be sufficient in number to clearly show the pipeline's length and course.

(b) Two red lights at each end of the pipeline, including the ends in a channel where the pipeline is separated to allow vessels to pass (whether open or closed). The lights must be—

(1) Visible all around the horizon, and

(2) Visible for at least 2 miles on a clear dark night, and

(3) One meter apart in a vertical line with the lower light at the same height above the water as the flashing yellow light.

Index

773